# Vital Records

## of

# Farmington
# New Hampshire

# 1887-1938

Richard P. Roberts

HERITAGE BOOKS
2024

**HERITAGE BOOKS**
*AN IMPRINT OF HERITAGE BOOKS, INC.*

Books, CDs, and more—Worldwide

For our listing of thousands of titles see our website
at
www.HeritageBooks.com

Published 2024 by
HERITAGE BOOKS, INC.
Publishing Division
5810 Ruatan Street
Berwyn Heights, MD 20740

Copyright © 2001 Richard P. Roberts

All rights reserved. No part of this book may be reproduced or transmitted in any form or by any means, electronic or mechanical, including photocopying, recording or by any information storage and retrieval system without written permission from the author, except for the inclusion of brief quotations in a review.

International Standard Book Number
Paperbound: 978-0-7884-1860-0

## CONTENTS

Introduction ................................................................. 1
Births ........................................................................... 4
Marriages ................................................................ 138
Brides' Names ........................................................ 350
Deaths .................................................................... 384

# INTRODUCTION

Early vital records of many New Hampshire towns can be located either through the State's Vital Records Department or on microfilms made available through LDS Family History Centers. Some, however, have been lost or are inaccessible for various reasons. A valuable, but time-consuming, source of information for events occurring after 1886 is the vital statistics which are provided in a section of the Annual Town Reports of many New Hampshire towns. Many of these town reports have been collected at the New Hampshire State Library in Concord, as well as more local repositories.

Farmington stopped including the vital statistics in their reports in 1938. Fortunately, the information that was published prior to that date provides much more detail and is of greater use to genealogists. Other towns have continued to provide their vital statistics to the present day, but the information given is less detailed.

While the information provided is often very helpful, one must remember that it is not fool-proof or universally accurate, nor is it the primary source or the actual vital record itself. The fact that much of the data is self-reported suggests that it is reliable. However, errors in transcription, spelling (particularly with respect to French-Canadian and European families), and printing often are obvious. In addition, there may be, for example, two children listed as the third child of a particular couple, or the mother's maiden name, age or place of birth differs or is inconsistent from one entry to another. It is also important to note that a birth, marriage or death may have been reported in another town although the subject resided in Farmington, or the entry may not have been made in the first place.

Despite these shortcomings, the information contained in the Annual Town Reports can be a valuable tool for the genealogist. Marriage and death records from the late 1800's often identify parents who were married nearly a century before. Finally, those families that have remained in Farmington for several generations can be traced and connected to the present.

Births - To the extent the information is available, the entries in the list of births are given as follows: child's name; date of birth; place of birth (Farmington, unless otherwise indicated, either by the name of the town or by an asterisk); the number of children in the family; father's name, place of birth, age and occupation; and the mother's maiden name, age and place of birth. The residence of the parents is sometimes given when it is shown as other than Farmington.

At times, the given names of many children are missing from the early reports. In this case, the sex of the child is given and they are listed chronologically at the beginning of the surname heading. On occasion, the child's name can be determined from marriage or death records, as well as secondary sources. These names are shown in brackets where available.

Marriages - To the extent the information is available, the entries in the list of marriages follow this format: groom's name; groom's residence; bride's name; brides residence; date of marriage; place of marriage (Farmington, unless otherwise indicated, although no place of marriage is given in recent years); H, signifying husband's information, and W, signifying wife's information, each in the following order - age, occupation, number of the marriage (if other than first), father's name, father's place of birth, father's occupation, mother's name, mother's place of birth, and mother's occupation. The name of the official conducting the marriage has been omitted but is generally provided in the original document.

There is also a separate alphabetical listing of marriages by bride's name. Note that, where available, the maiden or father's name of a bride is given when it is a second or subsequent marriage.

Deaths - To the extent available, the entries in the list of deaths contain the following information: name of decedent; place of death; date of death; age at death; cause of death; marital status; birthplace; father's name; father's place of birth; mother's name; and mother's place of birth. Most of the entries listing a cause of death are self-explanatory.

There are additional resources which are certain to be useful in conjunction with the material contained in this book. There was a history of Farmington published in connection with the U.S. Bicentennial in 1976. There is also a Town Register from 1907 which includes a good deal of historical information, a listing of town officers from the incorporation of the town, as well as a comprehensive "census" of the town in that year listing family groups by surname. Finally, there are some compilations of cemetery inscriptions which are available at the major historical and genealogical libraries in Dover and Concord, among others.

In addition, because Farmington was a regional commercial and manufacturing center, many of the families listed in this volume may also be included in the prior works covering neighboring towns, particularly Alton, Wakefield, New Durham, Middleton and Milton.

# BIRTHS

**ABBOTT,**
- son, b. 5/31/1889; second; Frank F. Abbott (painter, 26, Wolfeboro) and Estella R. Abbott (27, Milton)
- son, b. 10/1/1912; first; Ernest R. Abbott (shoe operative, Concord) and Mabel Cotton (Wakefield)
- son [George], b. 4/11/1923; fifth; Ernest R. Abbott (shoeworker, Concord) and Mabel Ham (NH)
- Eleanor Myrtle, b. 9/16/1918; third; Ernest R. Abbott (shoeworker, Concord) and Mabel Ham (Milton)
- Judith Dand, b. 3/9/1934; first; Walter Abbott (clerk, Worcester, MA) and Marion Bradley (Montpelier, VT)
- Leslie Eugene, b. 11/12/1921; fourth; Ernest Abbott (shoemaker, Concord) and Mabel Ham (Milton)
- Mildred Irene, b. 9/9/1913; second; Ernest Abbott (shoemaker) and Mabel Cotton (Milton)

**ADAMS,**
- son, b. 3/20/1901; second; John G. Adams (upholstering, 37, Dover) and Leila B. Davis (32, Farmington)
- Altice M., b. 10/10/1914; third; Frank A. Adams (shoemaker, West Newbury, MA) and Rachael K. Leighton (Marblehead, MA)
- Bernice L., b. 6/30/1901; first; Frank A. Adams (shoemaker, 41, West Newbury, MA) and Rachel K. Leighton (32, Marblehead, MA)
- Doris Lillian, b. 8/18/1913; first; Eugene I. Adams (electrician, Farmington) and Carrie D. Walton (Seabrook)
- Floyd Atwood, b. 11/24/1911; second; Frank E. Adams (shoe operative, 51, West Madbury, MA) and Rachel Leighton (42, Marblehead, MA)
- Gladys Lucille, b. 4/18/1915; second; Eugene I. Adams (electrician, Farmington) and Carrie D. Walton (Seabrook)
- Jane Priscilla, b. 8/10/1928; fourth; Clarence W. Adams (plumber & carp., Ogunquit, ME) and Maude Bradshaw (Dorchester, MA)
- John T., b. 7/28/1896; first; John G. Adams (shoe laster, 31, Dover) and Leila B. Davis (27, Farmington)
- Joseph P., b. 1/28/1938; first; Walter W. Adams (shoeworker, PEI) and Mary A. Perrino (Concord)

**AIKEN,**
- son, b. 10/11/1910; first; Percy G. Aiken (shoemaker, Barnstead) and Edith Mason (Quincy, MA)

Oscar S., b. 12/16/1907; first; Edward J. Aiken (shoe cutter, 33, Barnstead) and Mary A. McKeneley (35, NB)

Robert Guy, b. 7/28/1929; first; George E. Aiken (laborer, Farmington) and Jeanette Coulombe (Westville)

William Robert, b. 1/13/1931; second; George Aiken (laborer, Farmington) and Jeanette Coulombe (Westville)

## ALLARD,

Edmond Arthur, b. 1/8/1937; seventh; Ovide Allard (storekeeper, Laconia) and Mary Croteau (Canada)

Robert Francis, b. 2/12/1935; sixth; Ovide Allard (store keeper, Laconia) and Mary Croteau (Canada)

## ALLEN,

George, b. 1/8/1912; second; Peter Allen (shoe operative, Greece) and Rose Garrett (Riviere de Loup, PQ)

Peter, Jr., b. 1/8/1912; first; Peter Allen (shoe operative, Greece) and Rose Garrett (Riviere de Loup, PQ)

Ruth B., b. 10/26/1898; first; W. Dean Allen (tailor, -4, Farmington) and Nellie A. Cloutman (24, Farmington)

## ALVEY,

stillborn son, b. 2/9/1922; first; Walter N. Alvey (train conductor, Appomattox, VA) and Maude E. Burrows (Milton); residence - Portsmouth

## AMAZEEN,

daughter [Nellie K.], b. 5/16/1887; first; R. A. Amazeen (tinsmith, 33, Farmington) and Nellie Knox (Milton)

Clarence A., b. 5/4/1888; second; George E. Amazeen (shoe cutter, 44, Farmington) and Clara A. Merrow (40, Alton)

Richard F., b. 7/23/1912; first; Clarence A. Amazeen (electrician, Farmington) and Gladys F. Wentworth (Baldwin, ME)

Vernon Edward, b. 3/4/1915; second; Clarence A. Amazeen (electrician, Farmington) and Gladys F. Wentworth (Baldwin, ME)

## AMES,

Gertrude E., b. 11/28/1930; second; Herbert B. Ames (shoeworker, Plymouth) and Josephine G. Cronin (Quincy, MA)

Phyllis Marjorie, b. 2/16/1928; first; Herbert B. Ames (shoemaker, Plymouth) and Josephine G. Cronin (Quincy, MA)

**ANDERSON,**
Ernest, b. 2/13/1916; seventh; Walter F. Anderson (shoe worker, Stoneham, MA) and Evelyn E. Hicks (Robinston, ME)

**ANDREASSON,**
Ramona Elaine, b. 8/10/1935; first; Nils Andreasson (farmer, Sweden) and Gertrude Tufts (Alton)

**ANDREWS,**
Agnes, b. 1/28/1899; fourth; Indian; Joseph Andrews (basket maker, 38, Calais, ME) and Esther Froses (29, NS)

**ARMSTRONG,**
son, b. 12/4/1904; first; Roy Armstrong (shoemaker, 19, Farmington) and Florence Montee (17, Farmington)
Elma Vivian, b. 3/18/1896; first; Winthrop C. Armstrong (shoemaker, 23, Farmington) and Lizzie Leighton (21, Farmington)

**ARNOLD,**
son, b. 3/21/1913; eighth; Samuel V. Arnold (shoe operative, Brockton, MA) and Sarah M. Godfrey (PEI)
daughter [Dorothy M.], b. 11/20/1915; ninth; Samuel V. Arnold (shoecutter, Brockton, MA) and Sarah M. Godfrey (PEI)
daughter, b. 2/27/1924; twelfth; Samuel V. Arnold (shoemaker, Brockton, MA) and Sarah M. Godfrey (PEI)
Ralph W., b. 3/8/1933; first; Ralph W. Arnold (shoemaker, Braintree, MA) and Mildred Hulse (England)
Robert W., b. 6/20/1921; eleventh; Samuel V. Arnold (shoe worker Brockton, MA) and Sarah M. Godfrey (PEI)
Samuel V., 3$^{rd}$, b. 1/26/1926; second; Samuel V. Arnold, Jr. (shoemaker, Brockton, MA) and Leona B. Crause (MA)
Wilfred Godfrey, b. 2/14/1919; tenth; Samuel V. Arnold (shoeworker, Brockton, MA) and Sarah M. Godfrey (PEI)

**AUCLAIR,**
Donald C., b. 4/8/1924; second; Dorilla W. Auclair (mechanic, NH) and Elsie A. Camm (England)

**AVERILL,**
Elsie M., b. 2/4/1909; first; John W. Averill (shoemaker, 36, Farmington) and Maude A. Rhines (26, New Durham)
Ernest N., b. 8/12/1888; sixth; Trask W. Averill (farmer, 46, Farmington) and Augusta A. Wallace (37, New Durham)
Mary B., b. 12/11/1889; seventh; Trask W. Averill (farmer, Farmington) and Augusta A. Runnals (New Durham)

**AVERY,**
daughter, b. 12/21/1890; eighth; Frank L. Avery (shoemaker, 50, Barnstead) and Sarah S. Berry (Strafford)
daughter, b. 11/30/1903; first; John E. Avery (lumberman, 21, Strafford) and Clara French (22, Pittsfield)
daughter, b. 6/3/1909; first; Frank Avery (shoemaker, Farmington) and Crissie Brooks (19, Farmington)

**BABB,**
son [Fred O.], b. 9/22/1895; third; John Babb (shoe fitter, 34, Farmington) and Edith M. Gray (21, Gonic)
daughter [Hazel M.], b. 10/30/1898; fourth; John Babb (shoemaker, 36, Farmington) and Edith Gray (25, Gonic)
daughter, b. 8/19/1901; fifth; John K. Babb (shoemaker, 41, Farmington) and Edith B. Gray (27, Gonic)
Grace, b. 6/7/1894; second; John K. Babb (shoemaker, 23, Farmington) and Edith Gray (20, Gonic)
John, b. 1/26/1892; first; John H. Babb (shoemaker, 30, Farmington) and Edith B. Gray (housewife, 18, Gonic)
Pauline M., b. 7/29/1900; first; Horatio N. Babb (undertaker, 25, Alton) and Jennie A. Small (26, Ossipee); residence - Roxbury, MA

**BACHELDER,**
daughter [Bernice], b. 7/7/1889; sixth; Edward K. Bachelder (shoemaker, Berwick, ME) and Inez A. Hussey (Rochester)

**BAGLEY,**
son, b. 12/12/1935; ninth; Victor C. Bagley (meat cutter, Whiting, ME) and Elizabeth Bryant (Princeton, ME)
Beverly E., b. 7/18/1927; eighth; Victor Bagley (meat cutter, Whiting, ME) and Eliza Bryant (Princeton, ME)

Victor, b. 4/29/1925; seventh; Victor Bagley (grocery clerk, Farmington) and Eliza L. Bryant (NH)

**BAILEY,**
son, b. 3/11/1889; third; George W. Bailey (merchant, 33, Manchester) and Martha L. Lang (34, Candia)
George William, b. 11/14/1937; first; George Bailey (laborer, Orleans, MA) and Doris LeRoy (Lee, MA)
Paul Edward, b. 8/21/1933; first; George E. Bailey (shoe shop employee, Farmington) and Doris Edgerly (Farmington)

**BANFILL,**
William S. L., b. 6/6/1906; fifth; William S. L. Banfill (sewing mac dlr., 36, Ossipee) and Rose A. Laforge (26, Richmond, Canada)

**BANISTER,**
Rolfe G., b. 12/24/1922; first; Rolfe G. Banister (school teacher, Colebrook) and Ellen F. Cunningham (Troy, MA)

**BANKS,**
daughter, b. 5/8/1891; first; Frank Banks (store keeper, 21, Saco, ME) and Dela Tanner (16, Farmington)
daughter, b. 12/–/1891; first; Edward Banks (farmer, 23, York, ME and Abbie D. Laurens (22, Farmington)

**BARBER,**
Marcia A., b. 3/2/1927; eighth; Maurice A. Barber (farmer, Malden VT) and Violet Ingall (Malden, VT)

**BARCOMB,**
Jean Anne, b. 11/8/1934; second; Albert E. Barcomb (physician, Malone, NY) and Lucille Beaupre (Burlington, VT)
Juanita Lucille, b. 10/11/1931*; first; Albert E. Barcomb (physician Malone, NY) and Lucille L. Beaupre (Burlington, VT)

**BARKER,**
Eda F., b. 3/5/1890; seventh; Hiram H. Barker (manufacturer, 38, Farmington) and Ella M. Peavey (Farmington)
Hiram L., b. 10/26/1912; second; Will T. Barker (Farmington) and Alta F. Leighton (Farmington)

Philip K., b. 1/20/1905; second; William D. Barker (boxmaker, 26, Portland) and Bernice C. Randall (28, Wollaston Heights, MA)

Shirley, b. 4/4/1911; first; Will T. Barker (laborer, 33, Farmington) and Alta F. Leighton (33, Farmington)

## BARNES,

stillborn son, b. 3/11/1908; second; Arland Barnes (shoemaker, 33, New Salem, MA) and Rosa Delange (24, Lowell, MA)

Ernest E., b. 9/1/1906; third; Arland Barnes (shoe worker, 32, New Salem, MA) and Permelia DeLodge (29, Nashua)

Ethel C., b. 8/31/1904; second; Arland S. Barnes (shoemaker, 29, New Salem, MA) and Permelia R. Delange (23, Lowell, MA)

Flossie M., b. 9/1/1911; sixth; Arland S. Barnes (shoemaker, 34, New Salem, MA) and Rosie Delodge (35, Nashua)

## BARTLETT,

son, b. 1/4/1923; second; Willis C. Bartlett (laborer, ME) and Maude R. Smart (NH); residence - Lawrence, MA

Calvin Coolidge, b. 1/7/1925; first; Mathew Bartlett (engineer, NH) and Doris L. Green (ME)

Florence Theresa Marie, b. 8/22/1928; second; Matthew Bartlett (laborer, Lancaster) and Doris L. Green (Skowhegan, ME)

Patricia Ann, b. 7/1/1938; third; William Bartlett (plumber, Lancaster) and Annie Garion (Bradford, VT)

## BASTON,

Burton W., Jr., b. 4/19/1928; second; Burton W. Baston (marble dealer, No. Berwick, ME) and Alfreda M. Currier (Farmington)

Elmira M., b. 1/30/1925; first; Burton W. Baston (marble cutter, ME) and Elfrieda M. Currier (Farmington)

Mary Currier, b. 7/10/1929; third; Burton W. Baston (stone mason, No. Berwick, ME) and Alfreda M. Currier (Farmington)

Mary E., b. 3/30/1932; fourth; Burton W. Baston (marbleworker, No. Berwick, ME) and Alfreda M. Currier (Farmington)

## BATCHELDER,

R[alph]. M., b. 10/28/1905; first; Albert M. Batchelder (shoe laster, 46, New Durham) and Laura Harrington (32, Canada)

Ralph M., Jr., b. 8/4/1929; first; Ralph M. Batchelder (shoe cutter, Farmington) and Izola G. Augustine (Brockton, MA)

**BAXTER,**
    stillborn son, b. 8/23/1914; fourth; D. Forest Baxter (shoemaker, Brockton, MA) and Fannie B. Clough (Alton)
    Clarence M., b. 4/13/1919; second; D. Forest Baxter (shoeworker, Brockton, MA) and Fannie E. Clough (Alton)

**BEAN,**
    stillborn son, b. 3/10/1900; first; Ivory U. Bean (farmer, 31, Farmington) and Ida M. Wyatt (29, Farmington)
    son, b. 2/23/1910; third; Frank L. Bean (jeweler, Embden, ME) and Agnes G. Horne (Farmington)
    daughter, b. 8/19/1911; fourth; Frank L. Bean (jeweler, 39, Concord, ME) and Agnes G. Horne (39, Farmington)
    Elmira, b. 12/21/1905; first; Frank L. Bean (farmer, 32, Concord) and Agnes G. Horne (33, Farmington)
    Joseph D., b. 4/21/1904; second; Ivory U. Bean (farmer, 36, Farmington) and Ida M. Wyatt (33, Farmington)

**BEAUCHEMIN,**
    daughter, b. 2/24/1906; third; Nelson H. Beauchemin (blacksmith, 25, Haverhill, MA) and Mary J. Tremblay (Chicotimi)
    daughter, b. 2/18/1909; fifth; Nelson H. Beauchemin (blacksmith, 28, Haverhill, MA) and Mary J. Tremblay (28, Canada)

**BELANGER,**
    daughter, b. 8/24/1910; fifth; William Belanger (shoemaker, Canada) and Della Lepine (Farmington)
    Lorraine C., b. 10/23/1933; first; Eugene Belanger (shoe shop emp, Rochester) and Marie Huppe (Quebec, Canada)
    Mabel, b. 11/30/1908; fourth; William Belanger (shoemaker, 31, Canada) and Della Lapine (21, Farmington)
    May, b. 5/10/1907; third; William W. Belanger (shoemaker, 27, Northam, Canada) and Delia Lepine (19, Farmington)
    Wilfred J., b. 2/2/1906; second; William W. Belanger (shoemaker, 26, Nordham, Canada) and Della C. Lepine (18, Farmington)

**BELEN,**
    son, b. 5/16/1889; ninth; Michael Belen (farmer, 40, Canada) and Caroline Belen (32, Canada)

**BELLAVANCE,**
daughter, b. 1/23/1914; tenth; Joseph Bellavance (shoemaker, St. Fabien, Canada) and Marianne Thibeault (Sandy Bay, Canada)

**BENNETT,**
daughter [Mabelle E.], b. 10/1/1909; first; Parker D. Bennett (farmer, 32, Farmington) and Grace M. Leighton (35, Dover)
daughter, b. 9/5/1912; second; Parker D. Bennett (farmer, Farmington) and Grace M. Leighton (Dover)

**BENSON,**
Lillian, b. 1/26/1908; first; Perley H. Benson (shoemaker, 30, Haverhill, MA) and Winnifred M. Avery (21, Farmington)

**BERRY,**
son, b. 7/31/1892; first; George H. Berry (shoemaker, 27, Strafford) and Emma L. Works (lady, 24, Farmington)
daughter, b. 12/7/1894; first; Irving N. Berry (farmer, 22, Farmington) and Lizzie A. Jones (18, Farmington)
daughter, b. 3/19/1908; seventh; Irving N. Berry (farmer, 36, Farmington) and Lizzie A. Jones (32, Farmington)
son [Winfield], b. 10/21/1909; eighth; Irving N. Berry (farmer, 38, Farmington) and Lizzie A. Jones (33, Farmington)
daughter, b. 2/16/1912; first; William Freeman Berry (laborer) and Lydia May Perkins (Bartlett)
stillborn son [Arthur, Jr.], b. 9/30/1927; first; Arthur Berry (shoemaker, New Durham) and Gladys Patch (Rochester)
Georgie Isabelle, b. 4/2/1898; third; Irving N. Berry (farmer, 26, Farmington) and Lizzie A. Jones (22, Farmington)
Hazel, b. 6/23/1902; fifth; Irving N. Berry (farmer, 31, Farmington) and Lizzie A. Jones (26, Farmington)
Helen K., b. 5/4/1894; first; George H. Berry (shoe cutter, 28, Strafford) and Grace F. Kennard (20, Epping)
Henry Franklin, b. 4/26/1896; second; Irving N. Berry (farmer, 24, Farmington) and Lizzie A. Jones (20, Farmington)
Horace P., b. 1/20/1906; sixth; Irving N. Berry (farmer, 24, Farmington) and Lizzie A. Jones (31, Farmington)
Lucinda M., b. 9/29/1899; fourth; Irving N. Berry (farmer, 28, Farmington) and Lizzie A. Jones (23, Farmington)

Pauline Edith, b. 9/29/1914; ninth; Irving N. Berry (farmer, Farmington) and Lizzie A. Jones (Farmington)
Robert M., b. 9/6/1911; first; James A. Berry (shoemaker, 28, S. Berwick, ME) and Jessie S. Morgan (27, Hebron, ME)

**BICKFORD,**
daughter [Stella P.], b. 2/29/1896; first; Walter H. Bickford (laborer 36, Gonic) and Mary Varney (35, Farmington)
stillborn son, b. 3/31/1901; second; Walter H. Bickford (farmer, 41 Rochester) and Mary A. Varney (40, Farmington)
son [Norman], b. 8/16/1906; first; Harry G. Bickford (farmer, 25, Farmington) and Annie M. Kimball (25, Farmington)
Bertha, b. 4/29/1934; fourth; Charles L. Bickford (Somersworth) ar Florence Connors (Farmington)
Charles L., Jr., b. 5/22/1928; first; Charles L. Bickford (shoemaker Somersworth) and Florence F. Conner (Farmington)
Charlotte E., b. 10/26/1930; third; Charles L. Bickford (laborer, Somersworth) and Florence F. Connor (Farmington)
Helen Ruth, b. 10/3/1926; fifth; Irving E. Bickford (lumberman, Albany, NY) and Winnie C. Sanborn (Rumney)
Lewis Richard, b. 6/30/1929; second; Charles L. Bickford (laborer, Somersworth) and Florence F. Connor (Farmington)

**BLAISDELL,**
son [Ernest O.], b. 4/17/1892; third; Orin M. Blaisdell (shoemaker, 42, Lebanon, ME) and Ada E. Jones (housewife, 31, Abington MA)
daughter [Eleanor F.], b. 12/14/1894; first; Clarence L. Blaisdell (shoemaker, 22, Lebanon, ME) and Ella F. Swinerton (18, Farmington)
son, b. 8/24/1896; fourth; Orin P. Blaisdell (shoemaker, 47, Lebanon, ME) and Ada E. Jones (36, W. Abington, MA)
son [R. H.], b. 3/19/1900; third; Clarence L. Blaisdell (shoemaker, 27, Lebanon, ME) and Ella F. Swinerton (22, Somersworth)
daughter [Bernice G.], b. 1/14/1901; sixth; Oren M. Blaisdell (shoemaker, 51, Lebanon, ME) and Ada E. Jones (39, Abington, MA)
daughter [Ruth L.], b. 1/10/1907; fourth; Clarence L. Blaisdell (shoemaker, 34, Farmington) and Ella T. Swinerton (29, Milton)

daughter, b. 12/22/1916; third; Ernest O. Blaisdell (shoeworker, Farmington) and Mary Bickford (Waterboro, ME)

Clarence L., b. 4/12/1897; second; Clarence L. Blaisdell (shoemaker, 24, Lebanon, ME) and Eller F. Swinerton (19, Somersworth)

Ernest, b. 11/21/1912; first; Ernest O. Blaisdell (shoemaker, Farmington) and Mary B. Bickford (Waterboro, ME)

Joan Betty, b. 1/14/1937; first; Fred Blaisdell (shoeworker, Farmington) and Effie Boles (Derry)

Lewis F., b. 11/12/1897; fifth; Orrin M. Blaisdell (shoemaker, 48, Lebanon, ME) and Ada E. Jones (37, Abington, MA)

Marjorie E., b. 7/8/1914; second; Ernest O. Blaisdell (shoemaker, Farmington) and Mary P. Bickford (Waterboro, ME)

Orin Elmer, b. 8/25/1921; first; Ernest O. Blaisdell (shoemaker, Farmington) and Bernice L. Glidden (Farmington)

**BLAKE,**

Frances Mary, b. 11/22/1926; first; George D. Blake (Dorchester) and Thelma V. Greene (Farmington)

**BLOUIN,**

Beatrice F., b. 7/26/1928; first; Ernest Blouin (shoemaker, Milton) and Jennie Connolly (Berwick, ME)

**BODWELL,**

son [Elmore], b. 6/26/1913; third; Albion W. Bodwell (Goodyear welter, Lincoln, NE) and Ethel L. Foss (Garland, ME)

Donald Chester, b. 10/10/1913; second; Chester A. Bodwell (shoemaker, Sanford, ME) and Ruth H. Prescott (Milton)

Ethel L., b. 9/11/1927; second; William S. Bodwell (shoe cutter, Lebanon, ME) and Annie M. Towle (Wakefield)

Frances L., b. 1/14/1910; first; Chester A. Bodwell (Goodyear stitcher, Springvale, ME) and Ruth H. Prescott (Milton Mills)

Raymond S., b. 12/7/1929; third; William S. Bodwell (shoeworker, Lebanon, ME) and Annie M. Towle (Wakefield)

Walter Calvin, b. 8/1/1926; first; William S. Bodwell (woodturner, Lebanon, ME) and Annie M. Towle (Wakefield)

**BOGART,**

Raymond E., Jr., b. 5/10/1933; third; Raymond V. Bogart (farmer, Northampton, MA) and Emma Bowen (Kennebunk, ME)

**BOLDUC,**
>daughter, b. 5/11/1914; Alfred Bolduc (pugilist, Rochester) and Agnes M. Churchill (Brookfield)

**BONNEY,**
>Wilfred, Jr., b. 11/27/1929; first; Wilfred Bonney (shoeworker, Marshville, MA) and Gladys Adams (Boston, MA)

**BONO,**
>stillborn daughter, b. 9/23/1889; second; Charles Bono (shoemak Canada) and Rosa Stone (Morey, ME)
>Robie B., b. 3/25/1887; first; Charles Bono (shoemaker, 49, Canada) and Rosie Stone (16, Stork, ME) (1888)

**BOUDREAU,**
>Gladys M., b. 6/24/1906; fourth; Lafayette C. Boudreau (laborer, 2 Wheelock, VT) and Eva M. Drew (22, Holderness)
>Leon, b. 7/3/1907; fifth; Lafayette Boudreau (laborer, 28, Wheeloc VT) and Eva Drew (23, Holderness)

**BOULDUC,**
>daughter, b. 2/2/1911; fourth; George Boulduc (laborer, 26, Rochester) and Delia Houle (24, Rochester)

**BOWDEN,**
>son [Fred], b. 8/24/1909; second; Frederick L. Bowden (shoemake 29, Kittery, ME) and Francis Strout (26, Montreal, Canada)
>son [George], b. 12/10/1910; third; Fred C. Bowden (shoemaker, Kittery) and Frances Stroude (Montreal, Canada)

**BOWLEY,**
>Winnifred E., b. 6/14/1914; second; Fred E. Bowley (chief of polic Newburyport) and Edith M. Swinerton (West Milton)

**BOYER,**
>son, b. 1/8/1909; second; Alfred Boyer (48) and Mary E. Cole (24, Madbury)

**BOYLE,**
>daughter, b. 6/25/1897; first; John T. Boyle (editor, 26, Montreal, PQ) and Annie A. Moriarty (26, Montpelier, VT)

**BRACKETT,**
Lorraine, b. 8/9/1930*; first; Erwin Brackett (paper hanger, Farmington) and Blanche Butler (NS)

**BRALEY,**
Betty Ann, b. 2/29/1928; fifth; Claude C. Braley (foreman shoe shop, Bristol) and Margaret E. Prang (Portland, ME)

**BRETT,**
Nicholas W., b. 11/17/1938; first; Wesley F. Brett (teacher, Keene) and Helen M. Pratt (Keene)

**BRIDGES,**
Marie J., b. 5/27/1927; first; Lawrence C. Bridges (shoeworker, MA) and Irene C. Auclair (Conway, MA); residence - Plaistow

**BROOKS,**
daughter, b. 9/8/1887; second; Pierce J. Brooks (shoemaker, 31, Alton) and Edith Tibbetts (Farmington)
daughter [Helen S.], b. 1/5/1889; second; Percy J. Brooks (shoemaker, Alton) and Edith Tibbetts (Farmington)
daughter [Lila I.], b. 5/21/1891; Pierce Brooks (shoemaker, Alton) and Edith Tebbetts (Farmington)
stillborn son, b. 7/24/1893; Percy Brooks (shoemaker, 37, Alton) and Edith Tibbetts (27, Farmington)
child [Hildred], b. 10/15/1894; fifth; Percey J. Brooks (shoemaker, 39, Alton) and Edith Tibbetts (29, Farmington)
daughter [Evelyn B.], b. 6/1/1898; seventh; Percy Brooks (shoemaker, 42, Alton) and Edith Tebbetts (33, Farmington)
son, b. 11/21/1925; third; William Brooks (shoeworker, England) and Annie G. Harriman (England)
Crissie, b. 5/7/1890; fourth; Perce J. Brooks (shoemaker, 34, Alton) and Edith Tibbetts (Farmington)
Faith E., b. 12/4/1933; first; Frank W. Brooks (shoeworker, Blythe, England) and Olive L. Harding (New Durham)

**BROUGH,**
Shirley A., b. 7/22/1938; second; Marshall Brough (shoeworker, Laconia) and Mary Hughes (Rochester)
Viola June, b. 1/11/1937; first; Marshall K. Brough (shoeworker, Lakeport) and Mary E. Hughes (Rochester)

**BROUILLARD,**
Patricia Anne, b. 10/28/1935; first; Henry Brouillard (laborer, Sanbornville) and Grace King (E. Weymouth, MA)

**BROWN,**
son, b. 2/3/1889; second; Horace O. Brown (lumberman, 25, Chelsea, MA) and Lilla E. Gray (Barrington)
daughter, b. 6/11/1890; second; John F. Brown (laborer, 36, Farmington) and Emma F. Jones (Rochester)
stillborn son, b. 2/26/1893; first; Joseph W. Brown (painter, 26, Newark, NJ) and Agnes Paterson (30, Windsor, PQ)
daughter, b. 10/4/1902; first; John A. Brown (teamster, 26, Alton) and Alice Tibbetts (18, Berwick, ME)
daughter, b. 4/4/1904; second; John A. Brown (teamster, 26, Farmington) and Alice Tibbetts (20, Berwick, ME)
daughter, b. 2/21/1905; third; John A. Brown (teamster, 27, Alton) and Alice M. Tibbets (20, Berwick, ME)
Edith E., b. 5/18/1912; first; Louis B. Brown (farmer, Strafford) and Bessie E. Judkins (Reading)
Lawrence K., b. 9/29/1921; first; Ira S. Brown (Oxford, ME) and Mildred Knox (Farmington)
Marshall L., b. 2/8/1924; second; Ira S. Brown (Oxford, ME) and Mildred Knox (Farmington)
Norma, b. 7/23/1907; first; Fred W. Browne (sic) (brush mfg'r, 28, New Durham) and Jennie B. Hayes (27, New Durham)
Rena C., b. 6/19/1907; third; Arthur C. Brown (knife maker, 32, Waltham, MA) and Nellie Mitchell (36, New Durham)

**BUBIER,**
Martha G., b. 10/19/1926; second; Victor J. Bubier (shoemaker, Lowell, MA) and Blanche Colbath (Wolfeboro)

**BUCKMAN,**
Richard M., Jr., b. 5/17/1929; fifth; Richard M. Buckman (laborer, Medford, MA) and Helen A. Buzzell (Lowell, MA)

**BUKER,**
son, b. 12/10/1916; second; W. H. Buker (school principal, ME) and Alice A. Foss (NH)

**BUNKER,**
daughter [Merle E.], b. 12/29/1912; first; Forrest W. Bunker (shoemaker, Farmington) and Grace M. Glidden (New Durham)
Leon Edmund, b. 4/22/1919; second; Forrest W. Bunker (shoeworker, Farmington) and Grace M. Glidden (New Durham)
Willie E., b. 6/9/1888; first; Cyrus Bunker (laborer, 20, Farmington) and Sadie Whitehouse (16, New Durham)

**BURBANK,**
Paul Hartfiel, b. 9/27/1936; first; Edmond Burbank (mill worker, E. Monmouth, ME) and Paula Hartfiel (Farmington)

**BURLEIGH,**
son [Dean], b. 2/7/1893; sixth; Harry A. Burleigh (shoemaker, 26, Portsmouth) and Estella M. Tuttle (34, Middleton)
stillborn daughter, b. 7/22/1895; tenth; Harry E. Burleigh (shoemaker, 29, Farmington) and Estella M. Tuttle (36, Middleton)
son, b. 4/7/1917; first; Ray C. Burleigh (shoeworker, Farmington) and Hazel F. Wentworth (Milton)
Henry, b. 2/13/1891; sixth; Harry A. Burleigh (shoe finisher, 24, Portsmouth) and Estella M. Tuttle (30, Middleton)
Lucy, b. 9/23/1889; sixth; Harry A. Burleigh (shoemaker, Portsmouth) and Estella M. Tuttle (Middleton)
Thelma W., b. 1/17/1912; first; Harry Alden Burleigh (shoe operative, Farmington) and Elda A. Kittredge (Vinalhaven, ME)

**BURNHAM,**
Lindon Place, b. 6/23/1915; first; Leroy L. Burnham (shoeworker, Farmington) and Eva M. Place (Middleton)
Orland Neal, b. 6/15/1922; third; Leroy L. Burnham (shoeworker, Farmington) and Eva M. Place (Middleton)
Robert Roy, b. 1/13/1927; first; Ralph H. Burnham (shoeworker, Salem, MA) and Mabel M. Clough (Wolfeboro)
Velma Eva, b. 7/9/1919; second; Leroy L. Burnham (shoeworker, Farmington) and Eva M. Place (Middleton)

**BURROWS,**
Willie H., b. 5/30/1890; first; William H. Burrows (shoemaker, 31, Natick, MA) and Mattie A. Kearney (Grand Falls, NB)

**BUSS,**
Edward A., b. 10/19/1892; second; George E. Buss (farmer, 34, West Boylston, MA) and Harriet M. Tucker (housewife, 23, Lester, MA)

**BUTLER,**
daughter, b. 12/27/1912; first; Leland K. Butler (machinist, S. Thomaston, ME) and Leila F. Young (S. Lebanon, ME)
Corinne, b. 10/21/1920; second; Cleveland Butler (shoemaker, S. Thomaston, ME) and Jeanette Napis (Woodsville, NY)

**BYRON,**
Marjorie, b. 10/23/1912; first; Raymond F. Byron (shoe operative, Weeden, Canada) and Alta L. Dodge (Barrington)

**CAHILL,**
daughter, b. 2/22/1915; seventh; John Joseph Cahill (shoeworker, New York City) and Ellen Teresa Mealey (Providence, RI)

**CALLAHAN,**
son, b. 2/14/1916; second; Thomas H. Callahan (factory manager, OH) and Alma M. Becker (PA); residence - New Durham

**CAMPBELL,**
child, b. 10/20/1924; Arthur B. Campbell (shoe operative, PEI) and Rosina L. Bailey (MA)

**CANNEY,**
son, b. 2/7/1889; first; Eugene Canney (laborer, 20, Farmington) and Hattie Maxfield (18, Gilmanton)
stillborn son, b. 12/18/1894; first; Isaac A. Canney (laborer, 38, Farmington) and Annie M. Colbath (23, Farmington)
daughter [Marjorie], b. 7/5/1922; first; Ralph W. Canney (farmer, New Durham) and Ethel M. Hayes (Milton)
son, b. 11/18/1932; fourth; Ralph W. Canney (poultryman, New Durham) and Ethel M. Hayes (Milton)

Benjamin Lorenzo, b. 10/11/1937; second; Raleigh Canney (wood heeler, Rochester) and Margaret Grant (Rockport, ME)
Betty Lou, b. 5/16/1936; third; Archie B. Canney (optometrist, Rochester) and Dora N. Hall (NB)
David Gadd, b. 10/12/1933; Merlin H. Canney (salesman, Gilmanton) and Marcia Gadd (W. Newbury, MA)
Ella May, b. 10/8/1937; fourth; Archie Canney (optometrist, Rochester) and Dora Hall (Penobsquist, NB)
Janiece May, b. 5/9/1938; eighth; Clifton C. Canney (shoeworker, Rochester) and Lulu J. Ballau (Bristol)
Lois Elaine, b. 7/2/1926; third; Ralph Canney (farmer, New Durham) and Ethel Hayes (Milton)
Lucille Grace, b. 7/10/1928; first; Carl B. Canney (journalist, Milton) and Alice L. Swinerton (Portsmouth)
Nervale B., b. 7/30/1934; first; Nervale B. Canney (laborer, Rochester) and Marjorie Blaisdell (Farmington)
Priscilla Joyce, b. 4/1/1938; fifth; Ralph Canney (poultry dealer, New Durham) and Ethel Hayes (Milton)
Ronald David, b. 4/18/1938; second; Mervale Canney (shoeworker, Rochester) and Marjorie Blaisdell (Farmington)
Ursula, b. 3/26/1923; first; Merlin H. Canney (shoeworker, Gilmanton) and Doris Leighton (Farmington)

**CARD,**
son [William L.], b. 2/26/1895; second; Ollan H. Card (shoemaker, 24, Farmington) and Mary E. Yeaton (18, Springvale, ME)
daughter, b. 4/16/1906; first; Alvin W. Card (section hand, 35, Farmington) and Flora E. Miller (32, New Durham)
Faith, b. 12/30/1887; eighth; George V. Card (shoemaker, 45, Newcastle) and Nancy Sampson (Dexter, ME)

**CARDINAL,**
son, b. 8/5/1914; seventh; John B. Cardinal (farmer, Canada) and Rose M. Rock (Epping)
son [Leo H.], b. 12/11/1915; eighth; John B. Cardinal (teamster, Canada) and Rose Rock (Epping)
son, b. 3/6/1923; first; John Cardinal, Jr. (shoemaker, Epping) and Helen Burrows (Middleton)
Betty Lucille, b. 3/14/1934; second; Carroll Cardinal (laborer, New Durham) and Ruth Wilkins (Farmington)

Carol Dean, b. 1/6/1933; first; Carol Cardinal (shoeworker, New Durham) and Ruth C. Wilkins (Farmington)
Harold Leo, b. 2/4/1935; first; Leo Cardinal (shoeworker, Farmington) and Catherine Caman (Boston, MA)
Joan, b. 1/9/1937; first; Raymond Cardinal (shoeworker, Epping) and Rita Coulombe (Westville)
John Curtis, b. 9/23/1935; third; Carroll Cardinal (carpenter, Farmington) and Ruth Wilkins (Farmington)
Rosana, b. 3/1/1920; ninth; John B. Cardinal (farmer, Montreal, Canada) and Rosana Rock (Epping)
Samuel, b. 10/19/1922; ninth; John B. Cardinal (lumberman, Canada) and Rosanna Rock (Epping)

**CARLETON,**
Will, b. 10/10/1887; first; Ed. E. Carlton (merchant tailor, 27, Farmington) and Gertrude Smith (Farmington)

**CARON,**
son, b. 1/8/1922; fourth; Robert Caron (shoeworker, Boston, MA) and Elizabeth D. Place (Farmington)

**CARPENTER,**
stillborn son, b. 4/25/1934; second; Phyllis Carpenter (East Rochester)

**CARTER,**
son, b. 8/5/1908; third; William Carter (stone mason, 53, Newport, VT) and Lula Davis (39, Farmington)
Charles, b. 2/11/1911; first; Charles William Carter (shoe operative 22, Sanbornville) and Mildred May Nichols (21, Ossipee)
Elizabeth Wood, b. 4/30/1904; first; Albert E. Carter (merchant, 53 Wilton, ME) and Lizzie M. Wood (38, Farmington)
Helen Winnifred, b. 5/29/1892; third; Albert E. Carter (furniture dealer, 41, Wilton, ME) and Catherine Dame (housewife, 32, Farmington)
Mattie O., b. 6/17/1887; second; Albert E. Carter (furniture dealer, 36, Milton, ME) and Kate A. Dame (Farmington)

**CARTIER,**
Marie Aurore, b. 11/23/1894; first; John Cartier (shoemaker, 25, St Almer, PQ) and Mary Lourse (23, St. Marcel, PQ)

**CASEY,**
Gordon W., Jr., b. 5/30/1929; first; Gordon W. Casey (shoe cutter, Derry) and Katherine H. Trafton (Union)

**CATE,**
Rita June, b. 5/11/1936; fifth; Harry Cate (magician) and Laura Page (Exeter)

**CATES,**
son, b. 2/28/1903; third; Alfred A. Cates (laborer, 30, Harrison, ME) and Florence G. Richardson (25, Sulloway)

**CATHCART,**
daughter [Kathryn], b. 3/3/1908; first; Fred F. Cathcart (laborer, 20, East Rochester) and A. Bernice Haddock (21, Farmington)
son [Herbert R.], b. 7/13/1912; third; Fred Cathcart (laborer, East Rochester) and Bernice Haddock (Farmington)
son, b. 9/2/1915; fifth; Fred F. Cathcart (shoeworker, Rochester) and Bernice Haddock (Farmington)
stillborn daughter, b. 2/19/1917; sixth; Fred F. Cathcart (shoemaker, East Rochester) and Bernice Haddock (Farmington)
daughter, b. 8/3/1918; seventh; Fred Cathcart (Rochester) and Bernice Haddock (Farmington)
son [Robert], b. 1/28/1920; eighth; Fred Cathcart (shoemaker, East Rochester) and Bernice Haddock (Farmington)
daughter, b. 3/16/1927; seventh; Fred Cathcart (shoeworker, NH) and Bernice Haddock (Farmington)
Madeline Murle, b. 4/7/1914; fourth; Fred T. Cathcart (shoemaker, Rochester) and Bernice Haddock (Farmington)
Ruth E., b. 3/15/1910; second; Fred F. Cathcart (shoe finisher, 22, E. Rochester) and Bernice Haddock (23, Farmington)

**CAULSTONE,**
Frances Delda, b. 2/11/1926; first; Emile A. Caulstone (shoe foreman, Cape Breton) and Delda L. Ferland (NH)

**CHABOT,**
Mary Elline, b. 1/14/1916; second; Fred Chabot (lumberman, Canada) and Elizabeth Richardson (Northwood Narrows)

**CHAGNON,**
son [Richard], b. 4/19/1926; second; Raymond N. Chagnon (shoemaker, So. Berwick, ME) and Aida F. Letourneau (Rochester)
Raymond M., b. 8/25/1924; first; Raymond Chagnon (shoecutter, ME) and Altea D. Letourneau (NH)
Robert Donald, b. 8/1/1938; fourth; Raymond Chagnon (shoeworker, S. Berwick, ME) and Alden Diana (Rochester)
Roland Charles, b. 5/16/1929; third; Raymond N. Chagnon (shoemaker, S. Berwick, ME) and Alvea D. Letourneau (Rochester)

**CHAMBERLIN,**
Harold S., b. 12/19/1888; first; George W. Chamberlin (school teacher, 29, Lebanon, ME) and Hattie Sherman (29, Lebanon, ME)

**CHAMPAGNE,**
Francois Conrad, b. 4/10/1935; third; Francis Champagne (shoeworker, Suncook) and Gladys Moore (Lynn, MA)
Germaine F., b. 11/25/1932; first; Francois J. Champagne (shoe operator, Suncook) and Gladys M. Moore (Lynn, MA)
Rene Theodore, b. 10/17/1933; second; Francois Champagne (shoeworker, Suncook) and Gladys Moore (Lynn, MA)

**CHASE,**
daughter, b. 1/5/1902; first; Fred C. Chase (shoemaker, 56, Rochester) and Cora E. Hurd (17, Rochester)
daughter, b. 5/10/1911; second; Frank M. Chase (expressman, 27, Auburn, ME) and Kate Kinch (28, PEI)
Carolyn Priscilla, b. 2/8/1935; third; Fred Chase (shoeworker, Dover) and Priscilla Curtis (Farmington)
Dolores Jean, b. 12/23/1933; second; Fred M. Chase (shoeworker, Dover) and Priscilla Curtis (Farmington)
Joamie Carline, b. 3/5/1932; first; Fred Chase (woodworker, Dover) and Priscilla Curtis (Farmington)
Melvin Robert, Jr., b. 10/27/1937; first; Melvin Chase (shoeworker, New Durham Ridge) and Albina Parent (Salmon Falls)

**CHENEY,**
Robert Arnold, b. 1/6/1927; first; Arnold J. Cheney (shoecutter, Lynn, MA) and Bernice P. Towle (New Durham)

**CHESLEY,**
daughter, b. 3/24/1898; third; Herbert J. Chesley (shoemaker, 33, So. Wolfeboro) and Annie M. Kimball (21, So. Wolfeboro)
son [G. E.], b. 4/3/1899; fourth; Herbert J. Chesley (shoemaker, 35, New Durham) and Annie M. Kimball (22, Wolfeboro)
son [Fred], b. 1/1/1902; fifth; Herbert J. Chesley (shoemaker, 38, New Durham) and Annie M. Kimball (25, Wolfeboro)
stillborn daughter, b. 5/23/1922; second; Harold J. Chesley (shoeworker, Farmington) and Ruby A. Burnham (Boston, MA)
Addie L., b. 3/14/1890; first; Frank B. Chesley (farmer, 33, Farmington) and Sadie Foss (Rochester)
Bessie M., b. 10/30/1888; second; Irving Chesley (clerk, 32, New Durham) and Emma Berry (34, New Durham)
Donald B., b. 4/27/1917; first; Harold J. Chesley (shoemaker, Farmington) and Ruby A. Burnham (Boston, MA)
Harold L., b. 2/3/1890; fourth; Irving J. Chesley (clerk, 33, New Durham) and Emma J. Berry (New Durham)
Harry M., b. 2/3/1890; third; Irving J. Chesley (clerk, 33, New Durham) and Emma J. Berry (New Durham)
J. Ralph, b. 3/3/1895; third; Frank B. Chesley (farmer, 38, Farmington) and Sadie B. Foss (25, Rochester)
Louise May, b. 7/18/1922; first; Ralph J. Chesley (farmer, Farmington) and Ethel M. Thompson (Barrington)
Mabel F., b. 4/5/1893; second; Frank B. Chesley (farmer, 36, Farmington) and Sadie B. Foss (22, Rochester)
Marian L., b. 3/16/1890; second; George L. Chesley (engineer, 36, Brookfield) and Annie J. Stevens (Thomasville, GA)
Norman, b. 11/29/1907; seventh; Herbert Chesley (clerk, 43, New Durham) and Annie Kimball (30, Wolfeboro)
Norman, b. 4/26/1932*; first; Norman Chesley (shoe treer, Farmington) and Irene Blatchford (Andover, MA)
Pauline, b. 2/26/1927; second; Ralph J. Chesley (farmer, Farmington) and Ethel M. Thompson (Barrington)

**CHILD,**
daughter, b. 6/28/1910; second; Charles E. Child (machinist, Farmington) and N. Susie Fletcher (Hollis, ME)

daughter [Ethel], b. 4/29/1916; fifth; Charles E. Child (machinist, Farmington) and Nellie Susie Fletcher (Hollis, ME)
son [James], b. 12/31/1920; sixth; Charles E. Child (machinist, Farmington) and N. Susie Fletcher (Hollis, ME)
Donald, b. 1/9/1915; fourth; Charles E. Child (machinist, Farmington) and N. Susie Fletcher (Hollis, ME)
Dora, b. 1/9/1915; third; Charles E. Child (machinist, Farmington) and N. Susie Fletcher (Hollis, ME)

**CHUBBUCK,**
son, b. 7/16/1902; first; Walter H. Chubbuck (painter, 26, Somerville, MA) and Grace M. Cleveland (20, Hubbardston, MA)
daughter, b. 8/23/1904; second; Walter H. Chubbuck (office work, 28, Dorchester, MA) and Grace M. Cleveland (22, Hubbardston, MA)

**CLANCY,**
Frank Barker, b. 2/22/1913; first; Frank W. Clancy (mfg., Santa Fe NM) and Eda F. Barker (Farmington)

**CLAPP,**
Austin R., b. 11/8/1910; first; Lawrence R. Clapp (physician, Cambridge, MA) and Helen W. Rhone (Wilkes-Barre, PA)
Rosamond W., b. 10/30/1911; second; Lawrence R. Clapp (physician, 30, Cambridge, MA) and Helen W. Rhone (26, Wilkes-Barre, PA)

**CLARK,**
son, b. 12/7/1919; fourth; Florence Clark (Alton)

**CLEMENT,**
Ralph George, b. 8/1/1919; second; Ralph W. Clement (meatcutter, Moultonboro) and Catherine A. Hannagan (Lawrence, MA)

**CLEMENTS,**
Nancy Elaine, b. 10/24/1937; first; Gordon Clements (shoeworker, Lowell, MA) and Rita Prescott (Farmington)

**CLOFLIN,**
Mary Alice, b. 12/6/1933; fifth; Clyde Cloflin (truckman, Fairfield, VT) and Alice Colby (Lunenburg, VT)

**CLOUGH,**
son, b. 11/15/1938; first; Eli L. Clough (baker, York, ME) and Melva G. Kehoe (Melrose, MA)
Blanche M., b. 10/2/1890; fifth; Daniel B. Clough (shoemaker, 44, Alton) and Lydia F. Young (Alton)

**CLOUTMAN,**
daughter, b. 1/6/1887; first; Edwin F. Cloutman (lawyer, 35, Alton) and Ellen F. Cloutman (Mt. Vernon)
daughter, b. 10/2/1892; fourth; Herman J. Cloutman (shoemaker, 32, Farmington) and Ava B. Runnells (housewife, 29, New Durham)
son, b. 11/18/1892; third; James A. Cloutman (shoe trimmer, 53, New Durham) and Myra L. Rollins (housewife, 33, Rollinsford)
daughter, b. 9/8/1898; fourth; Herman J. Cloutman (shoemaker, 38, Farmington) and Ara B. Runnells (35, New Durham)
daughter [Ellen E.], b. 1/29/1905; second; John F. Cloutman, Jr. (shoe mfgr., 27, Farmington) and Bessie E. Wentworth (23, Middleton)
son [Richard F.], b. 1/14/1907; third; John F. Cloutman (shoe mf'g'r, 29, Farmington) and Bessie E. Wentworth (25, Middleton)
Hattie M., b. 4/25/1888; second; Herman J. Cloutman (stock fitter, 28, Farmington) and A. Bertha Runnals (25, New Durham)
John, b. 9/7/1903; first; John F. Cloutman, Jr. (shoe m'f'r, 26, Farmington) and Bessie E. Wentworth (22, Middleton)
Orris E., b. 7/2/1890; third; Herman J. Cloutman (shoe cutter, Farmington) and ----- Runnals (New Durham)
Thomas B. R., b. 8/7/1896; fifth; Herman J. Cloutman (shoemaker, 36, Alton) and Ava B. Runnells (33, New Durham)

**COBB,**
daughter, b. 10/31/1904; second; Willis Cobb (sawyer, 31, Wilmington, VT) and Mary Hostler (21, East Dorset, VT)

**COGHLAN,**
George W., b. 2/7/1897; fifth; Frances Coghlan (38, Boston, MA) and Annie Moran (37, Boston, MA)

**COLBATH,**
daughter, b. 4/13/1889; first; William L. Colbath (shoemaker, 26, Middleton) and Prue A. Morris (20, Greville, NS)
daughter [Bessie M.], b. 7/24/1889; first; Clarence Colbath (shoemaker, Middleton) and Lizzie L. Morris (NS)
son [Guy], b. 8/11/1890; second; William L. Colbath (shoemaker, 28, Middleton) and Prue A. Morris (23, Greville, NS)
Arthur L., b. 7/7/1917; second; Lauren G. Colbath (shoeworker, Farmington) and Grace S. Thurston (N. Berwick, ME)
Catherine, b. 7/20/1912; first; Guy S. Colbath (laborer, Farmington) and Lulu Harrison (Tenant's Harbor)
Floyd Nelson, b. 7/8/1931*; sixth; Lauren Colbath (shoeworker, Farmington) and Grace Thurston (No. Berwick, ME)
Harrison D., b. 8/8/1917; second; Guy Colbath (shoe cutter, Farmington) and Lulu Harrison (Tenant's Harbor, ME)
Harry G., b. 1/19/1920; third; Lauren G. Colbath (heel burnisher, Farmington) and Grace G. Thurston (N. Berwick)
Lawrence W., b. 2/11/1925; fourth; Lauren G. Colbath (shoecutter, Farmington) and Grace E. Thurston (No. Berwick, ME)
Robert George, b. 10/6/1926; fifth; Loren G. Colbath (shoemaker, Farmington) and Grace G. Thurston (New Durham)

**COLE,**
Leon, b. 6/7/1888; second; Frank Cole (28, Dover) and Nellie Cole (24, Wolfeboro)

**COL[E]MAN,**
Charles D., Jr., b. 12/11/1904; first; Charles D. Coleman (real est. dealer, 38, Royalston, MA) and Helen C. Kingsbury (35, Dover)
David Bessey, b. 1/16/1932; third; Charles D. Colman (real estate, Farmington) and Lela Alberta Bessey (Dover)

**COLEY** [see Coly],
daughter [Marian], b. 3/13/1892; seventh; Frank Coley (laborer, 36, Fox River, Canada) and Amelia Preston (housewife, 36, Fox River, Canada)

**COLLINS,**
daughter [Eva M.], b. 1/7/1903; second; Steven Collins (lumberman, 39, NS) and Mary E. Tufts (35, Alton)

**COLOMY,**
daughter, b. 9/5/1887; second; Oscar L. Colomy (shoe stitcher, 35, New Durham) and Ella Clough (Dover)
son [Ralph], b. 11/–/1891; sixth; George A. Colomy (farmer, 36, Farmington) and Bell Jones (35, Great Falls)
daughter, b. 2/27/1894; seventh; George A. Colomy (shoemaker, 38, Farmington) and Eliza Bell Jones (37, Great Falls)
son, b. 1/15/1895; first; Horatio S. Colomy (shoemaker, 25, Farmington) and Florence F. Tibbetts (17, Wolfeboro)
daughter, b. 2/19/1895; ninth; George A. Colomy (farmer, 39, Farmington) and Eliza B. Jones (36, Somersworth)

**COLY** [see Coley],
son, b. 2/8/1891; sixth; Frank A. Coly (laborer, 34, Canada) and Mary Preston (34, Canada)

**COMEE,**
Herman O., b. 2/4/1912; second; Arthur E. Comea (sic) (shoe operative, No. Dana, MA) and Emma Blake (Templeton, MA)

**COMMISKY** [see Cummisky],
Catherine L., b. 10/1/1888; third; Thomas Commisky (blacksmith, 27, PEI) and Della Fitzgerald (14, Ireland)

**CONANT,**
daughter, b. 6/12/1909; first; Charles Conant (moving picture op., 29, Providence, RI) and Eva B. Carron (23, Manchester)

**CONNOR,**
daughter [Lillian M.], b. 4/–/1891; third; Charles E. Connor (shoe cutter, 32, Gilmanton) and Florence A. Miller (29, New Durham)
stillborn daughter, b. 9/13/1899; sixth; Michael Connor (laborer, 53) and Abbie M. Richardson (40, Farmington)
son [Charles E.], b. 8/4/1909; first; Charles E. Connor (shoemaker, 25, Farmington) and Florence E. Chick (20, Alton)
daughter [listed as Cannon], b. 10/9/1911; second; George W. Connor (shoemaker, 25, Milton) and Bertha E. Clark (20, Alton)
daughter [Marion E.], b. 5/13/1912; second; Charles Edward Connor (shoe operative, Farmington) and Florence E. Clarke (Alton)

son, b. 8/28/1914; third; Charles E. Connor (shoemaker, Farmington) and Florence E. Clark (Alton)
daughter [Ellen], b. 12/10/1916; fourth; Charles Ed Connor (shoeworker, Farmington) and Florence E. Clarke (Alton)
Florence F., b. 4/22/1908; first; George W. Connor (shoemaker, 2C Milton) and Bertha Clarke (16, Alton)

COOK,
daughter [Gladys], b. 2/19/1894; third; Charles A. Cook (shoemaker, 28, Brockton, MA) and Addie Burnham (28, Farmington)
Rosie May, b. 2/15/1922; fifth; Herbert Cook (farmer, Barnstead) and Anna R. Dolby (New York City); residence - Barnstead

CORSON,
daughter, b. 7/25/1890; second; John F. Corson (clerk, 27, Rochester) and Minnie A. Dow (Moultonboro)
son, b. 9/9/1901; first; Walter Corson (shoemaker, 21, Farmington) and Sadie Rand (18, Portland, ME)
stillborn son, b. 2/23/1918; first; Walter N. Corson (chauffeur, Farmington) and Nancy B. Currier (Amesbury, MA); residence - Haverhill, MA
Ida May, b. 1/14/1912; first; George A. Corson (farmer, New Durham) and Olive D. Richardson (Farmington)

COTCHA,
Ralph E., b. 3/4/1899; second; Louis Cotcha (laborer, 36, Canada) and Kildia Anies (29, Canada)

COTTON,
son [Arthur I.], b. 2/26/1889; third; Charles H. Cotton (shoemaker, 37, Wolfeboro) and Viola A. Edgerly (33, New Durham)
son [Harry E.], b. 9/5/1900; seventh; Benjamin Cotton (fireman, 49, Milton) and Phoeba Tibbetts (30, Rochester)

COTY,
Edwin E., b. 8/22/1889; second; Edwin E. Coty (laborer, Candia) and Emma J. Ham (Farmington)

**COULSEN,**
son, b. 7/22/1888; Stearns E. Coulsen (shoemaker, 28, Dover) and Rosa B. Hilton (24, Wells, ME); residence - Great Falls

**COURNAYER,**
William James, b. 11/19/1936; sixth; Druilla Cournayer (shoeworker, Manchester) and Alice E. Pinkham (Derry)

**CROSBY,**
Gloria Louise, b. 4/20/1928; fifth; Lloyd J. Crosby (shoecutter, NS) and Edith M. Feeney (Lynn, MA)
Lloyd Loronzo, b. 12/25/1933; second; Lloyd I. Crosby (laborer, NS) and Ruth E. Horne (Rochester)
Marjorie Ruth, b. 2/13/1932; second; Lloyd I. Crosby (shoeworker, NS) and Ruth Horne (Rochester)

**CROSS,**
Hazel Louise, b. 3/9/1934; sixth; Frank Cross (lumberman, Meredith Ctr.) and Doris Dennis (Lyme)
Norma Louise, b. 10/2/1932; fourth; Frank G. Cross (lumberman, Meredith) and Doris Dennis (Lyme)

**CUMMINGS,**
daughter, b. 8/6/1925; third; Earle H. Cummings (foreman, box fac., Stoughton, ME) and Frances S. Fownes (Rochester)

**CUMMISKY** [see Commisky],
stillborn daughter, b. 5/21/1890; fourth; Thomas Cummisky (blacksmith, 29, PEI) and Della Fitzgerald (25, Ireland)
James E., d. 8/17/1887; second; Thomas Cummisky (blacksmith, 27, Ft. Augustine, PEI) and Della Fitzgerald (Co. Waterford, Ireland)

**CURRIER,**
son [Ray B.], b. 5/7/1889; second; A. Burns Currier (shoemaker, 29, Farmington) and Sadie A. Leary (22, Great Falls)
daughter [Mary C.], b. 2/18/1897; first; Charles V. Currier (meat carver, 31, Farmington) and Mary E. Ring (26, Farmington)
son [Perry N.], b. 12/20/1899; first; Fred E. Currier (shoemaker, 26, Farmington) and Lizzie A. Willey (20, New Durham)

stillborn son, b. 6/2/1902; second; Charles V. Currier (farmer, 36, Farmington) and Mary Ring (31, Farmington)
child [Elfreda M.], b. 12/–/1902; Fred E. Currier and Abbie E. Wille
daughter [Mary C.], b. 6/19/1904; third; Charles V. Currier (meat cutter, 37, Farmington) and Mary E. Ring (33, Farmington)
son, b. 10/6/1904; third; Fred E. Currier (shoemaker, 31, Farmington) and Abbie Willey (24, New Durham)
son [Charles F.], b. 12/13/1907; third; Charles V. Currier (farmer, 41, Farmington) and Mary E. Ring (37, Farmington)
Albert, b. 1/12/1911; fourth; Fred E. Currier (farmer, 37, Farmington) and Abbie L. Willey (31, New Durham)
Alberta Lorene, b. 4/15/1933; first; Charles Currier (carpenter, Farmington) and Merle Bunker (Farmington)
Beverly G., b. 1/6/1933; first; Herbert H. Currier (laborer, Lee) and Ruth L. Rhines (New Durham)
Corrine F., b. 8/26/1926; first; Ray B. Currier (shoemaker, Farmington) and Lillian M. Connors (Farmington)
Everett B. E., b. 8/16/1917; fifth; Fred E. Currier (farmer, Farmington) and Abbie L. Willey (New Durham)
Fred E., b. 2/28/1909; fifth; Fred E. Currier (farmer, 36, Farmington) and Abbie L. Willey (29, New Durham)
Fred E., b. 7/9/1935; first; Fred E. Currier (garage mechanic, Farmington) and Eleanor W. Babb (Rochester)
George R., b. 3/26/1892; third; Burns A. Currier (shoe cutter, 32, East Farmington) and Sadie A. Lary (housewife, 20, Great Falls)
Margaret Lillian, b. 7/3/1913; first; Richard Currier (shoe operative) and Lillian Dunn
Marion W., b. 8/10/1914; sixth; Fred E. Currier (farmer, Farmington) and Abbie L. Willey (New Durham)

**CURTIS,**
stillborn daughter, b. 6/26/1889; first; Edwin Curtis (farmer, Farmington) and Jennie O. Rollins (Farmington)
daughter, b. 5/22/1897; second; Everett E. Curtis (shoemaker, 21, Milton) and Annie E. Wentworth (17, Acton, ME)
son [Chester F.], b. 7/31/1904; first; Fred Curtis (shoemaker, 23, Farmington) and Carrie E. Howard (26, Farmington)
son [Norman W.], b. 3/27/1906; second; Fred Curtis (shoemaker, 25, Farmington) and Carrie E. Howard (28, Farmington)

son [Reginald W.], b. 10/4/1906; second; Willie B. Curtis (farmer, 34, Farmington) and Bessie Gilman (26, Hallowell, ME)

daughter [Evelyn J.], b. 5/21/1908; third; Fred Curtis (shoemaker, 27, Farmington) and Carrie Howard (30, Farmington)

daughter, b. 6/14/1908; first; Eric P. Curtis (shoemaker, 21, Farmington) and Minerva Hanscom (16, Union)

Doris Bessie, b. 5/11/1904; first; William B. Curtis (farmer, 32, Farmington) and Bessie J. Gilman (23, Hallowell, ME)

Eloris B., b. 9/24/1927; first; Norman W. Curtis (shoemaker, New Durham) and Bernice T. Hurd (Rochester)

Jessie B., b. 6/27/1893; ninth; James C. Curtis (dead, 44, Newcastle) and Lizzie N. Leighton (40, Farmington)

Perley C., b. 7/2/1890; second; Edward Curtis (farmer, 33, Farmington) and Jennie Rollins (Farmington)

Priscilla L., b. 11/30/1912; third; William B. Curtis (electrician, Farmington) and Bessie J. Gilman (Hallowell, ME)

**CYR,**

Firmen G. E., b. 2/26/1926; first; Edward N. Cyr (contractor, builder, Canada) and Bella M. Perry (Berlin)

James Conrad, b. 5/20/1927; fourth; Elzear G. Cyr (carpenter, PQ) and Hedwidge Therault (Canada)

**DAME,**

son [Erving W.], b. 3/25/1912; third; Walter S. Dame (shoemaker, Farmington) and Ethel M. Young (Alton)

daughter, b. 3/20/1914; first; William H. Dame (farmer, Rochester) and Mabel F. Chesley (Farmington)

Frank C., b. 12/2/1905; second; Walter S. Dame (shoemaker, 31, Farmington) and Ethel M. Young (25, Alton)

Nettie Elfrieda, b. 7/3/1902; first; Walter S. Dame (shoemaker, 28, Farmington) and Ethel M. Young (21, Alton)

Norman Frank, b. 12/9/1920; third; Walter H. Dame (boxmaker, Rochester) and Mabel T. Chesley (Farmington)

**DAMON,**

Richard David, b. 4/12/1937; third; Sheldon Damon (mgr., A&P, Revere, MA) and Beatrice Chase (Meredith)

**DAUDELIN,**
    Wanda Fay, b. 5/7/1934; eighth; Alfred Daudelin (shoeworker, Chicago, IL) and Bessie Brown (Manchester)

**DAVIDSON,**
    Karleen B., b. 8/23/1933; fourth; Walter Davidson (weaver, Belfast Ireland) and Corinne Thurston (Farmington)
    Kathleen B., b. 8/23/1933; third; Walter Davidson (weaver, Belfast Ireland) and Corinne Thurston (Farmington)

**DAVIS,**
    son [Forrest], b. 6/20/1892; first; Arthur N. Davis (heel maker, 21, Farmington) and Edith A. Ricker (lady, 20, Farmington)
    daughter [Hazel], b. 7/16/1892; first; George A. Davis (farmer, 21, Farmington) and Eliza Davis (housewife, 20, Farmington)
    son [Harry W.], b. 7/4/1894; second; Charles E. Davis (laborer, 35, Wolfeboro) and Ella A. Bunker (28, Farmington)
    daughter, b. 8/5/1895; Samuel Y. Davis (shoe cutter, 36, Farmington) and Nellie Berry (27, New Durham)
    son [Fred M.], b. 1/29/1897; fourth; Charles E. Davis (stove dealer 39, Wolfeboro) and Eller A. Bunker (31, Farmington)
    daughter [Sadie G.], b. 8/21/1899; fifth; Charles E. Davis (laborer, 41, Wolfeboro) and Ella A. Bunker (33, Farmington)
    daughter [Elizabeth G.], b. 10/8/1900; first; Alonzo I. Davis (grocer clerk, 44, New Durham) and Effie C. Goodwin (32, West Lebanon, ME)
    stillborn son, b. 7/28/1901; sixth; Charles E. Davis (laborer, 45, Wolfeboro) and Ella A. Bunker (35, Farmington)
    son [Norman G.], b. 5/3/1903; seventh; Charles E. Davis (laborer, 47, Wolfeboro) and Ella A. Bunker (36, Farmington)
    son [Albert M.], b. 10/22/1903; second; Alonzo I. Davis (shoe worker, 48, New Durham) and Effie C. Goodwin (35, Lebanon, ME)
    daughter [Anne P.], b. 10/13/1904; fourth; George A. Davis (farmer 33, Farmington) and Eliza Davis (32, Farmington)
    daughter [Hazel], b. 10/15/1906; first; Earle R. Davis (shoemaker, 22, Dover) and Bessie M. Haddock (18, Farmington)
    daughter [Dorothy], b. 10/16/1907; second; Earl Davis (shoemaker 24, Dover) and Bessie Haddock (18, Farmington)
    daughter, b. 1/22/1909; third; Earle R. Davis (shoemaker, 25, Dover) and Bessie Haddock (19, Farmington)

daughter, b. 7/7/1910; fifth; George A. Davis (farmer, Farmington)
and Eliza Davis (Farmington)
son [Edgar R.], b. 10/3/1910; fourth; Earle R. Davis (shoemaker,
Dover) and Bessie Haddock (Farmington)
daughter, b. 5/23/1912; fifth; Earle R. Davis (shoemaker, Dover)
and Bessie Haddock (Farmington)
son [Louis], b. 4/15/1921; first; Harry Davis (shoeworker, Armenia)
and Clara E. Hurd (Farmington)
Albert H., b. 10/3/1902; third; George A. Davis (farmer, 31,
Farmington) and Eliza Davis (30, Farmington)
Donald, b. 8/2/1922; second; Harry Davis (shoemaker, Armenia)
and Clara Hurd (Farmington)
Eric Neal, b. 9/14/1892; second; Samuel G. Davis (shoe cutter, 33,
Farmington) and Eliza E. Davis (housewife, 24, New Durham)
Ethel M., b. 5/21/1888; first; Charles E. Davis (teamster, 30,
Wolfeboro) and Ella A. Bunker (22)
Eva M., b. 1/18/1895; first; George W. Davis (teleg. operator, 25,
Lyme) and Ruby M. Harding (23, Strafford)
George Edward, b. 6/4/1933; third; Charles S. Davis (shoemaker,
Wolfeboro) and Effie Willey (New Durham)
Irene, b. 8/20/1928; first; Hazel Evelyn Davis (Farmington)
Robert, b. 9/5/1931*; first; Harry Davis (shoeworker, Haverhill, MA)
and Margaret Hogan (Cambridge, MA)
Robert C., b. 3/6/1920; second; Harry W. Davis (shoemaker,
Farmington) and Alice D. Chamberlin (New Durham)
Russell Archie, Jr., b. 11/2/1937; first; Russell Davis (shoeworker,
Lakeport) and Violetta Rogers (Farmington)
Ruth E., b. 7/31/1901; second; George A. Davis (farmer, 30,
Farmington) and Eliza E. Davis (29, Farmington)

**DEIMER,**
Agnes Pearl, b. 2/27/1935; first; George Deimer (shoeworker,
Albania) and Pearl H. Crane (Newfoundland)

**DERBY,**
Hervie William, b. 4/28/1932; eighth; Charles Derby (laborer,
Montpelier, VT) and Sylvia V. Cook (Barnstead)
Leona Barbara, b. 8/3/1926; seventh; Charles L. Derby (carpenter,
Montpelier, VT) and Sylvia Cook (Barnstead)
Leslie Paul, b. 11/17/1937; ninth; Charles Derby (VT) and ----- Cook
(Barnstead)

Mildred M., b. 1/2/1924; sixth; Charles L. Derby (carpenter, Montpelier, VT) and Sylvia V. Cook (Barnstead)

**DEXTER,**
son [Fred], b. 12/29/1916; first; Ernest F. Dexter (shoeworker, Barrington) and Ruth E. Remick (Westboro, MA)
son [Robert], b. 3/23/1924; third; Ernest Dexter (shoecutter, NH) and Ruth E. Remick (MA)
daughter, b. 9/11/1933; fourth; Ernest F. Dexter (shoe shop emp., Barrington) and Ruth Remick (Westboro, MA)
Earline Ruth, b. 1/18/1921; second; Ernest Dexter (shoe worker, Barrington) and Ruth Remick (Westboro, MA)
Frederick, b. 12/9/1907; first; James R. Dexter (shoe cutter, 20, Alton) and Cora E. Nutter (22, Alton)
Patricia Myrtle, b. 8/9/1937; first; Fred Dexter (shoeworker, Farmington) and Florence Otis (Springfield, MA)

**DICEY,**
Harold, b. 2/25/1888; first; George R. Dicey (button hole optr., 30, Alton) and Nellie F. Prescott (26, Alton)

**DICKEY/DICKIE,**
son [Ralph], b. 6/17/1907; first; Howard A. Dickey (laborer, 26, NB) and Bessie W. Chesley (18, Farmington)
son [Charles], b. 11/16/1908; second; Howard Dickey (laborer, 28, NB) and Bessie M. Chesley (20, Farmington)
son [Kenneth W.], b. 9/21/1910; third; Howard A. Dickie (shoemaker, NB) and Bessie M. Chesley (Farmington)
son, b. 8/18/1912; fourth; Howard A. Dickie (shoe operative, NB) and Bessie M. Chesley (Farmington)
Anna, b. 11/24/1935; second; Kenneth W. Dickey (laborer, Farmington) and Phyllis Carpenter (East Rochester)
Deidre, b. 10/4/1936; stillborn; first; Ralph Dickie (truckman, Farmington) and Shirley Pinkham (Milton)
Kenneth H., b. 9/29/1938; third; Kenneth Dickie (laborer, Farmington) and Phyllis Carpenter (E. Rochester)

**DODGE,**
John Herbert, b. 4/21/1925; first; Harry I. Dodge (shoemaker, NH) and Mabel I. Smith (NH)

**DOLBY,**
daughter [Agnes M.], b. 8/18/1892; first; Arthur P. Dolby
    (shoemaker, 21, Alton) and Mary A. Hoye (lady, 26, Dover)
son, b. 4/1/1900; fourth; Arthur P. Dolby (shoe-worker, 30, Alton)
    and Mary A. Hoy (31, Dover)
Arthur J., b. 6/10/1897; third; Arthur C. Dolby (shoemaker, 28,
    Alton) and Mary Hoy (32, Dover)
Herbert K., b. 8/16/1893; second; Arthur P. Dolby (shoemaker, 23,
    Alton) and Mary A. Hoye (27, Dover)

**DOLLIVER,**
son [Stanley], b. 3/24/1889; first; Fred B. Dolliver (carpenter, 35,
    Port Medway, NS) and Mary A. Ring (30, Dover)
Harvey Richard, b. 2/11/1926; first; Stanley Dolliver (shoemaker,
    Farmington) and Kathleen E. Hendry (Groton, VT)
Mary Kathleen, b. 5/29/1932; second; Stanley M. Dolliver
    (shoeworker, Farmington) and Kathleen Hendry (Groton, VT)

**DORE,**
son, b. 2/22/1888; second; Herbert W. Dore (shoemaker, 28,
    Wakefield) and Flora Burnham (25, Farmington)
son [Frank], b. 9/4/1902; third; Eugene Dore (teamster, 50, Alton)
    and Etta E. Davis (41, New Durham)
daughter [Eunice], b. 6/9/1907; second; Ernest Dore (photographer,
    31, Farmington) and Inez Clough (26, Wolfeboro)
son [Kenneth], b. 9/11/1915; second; Fred L. Dore (sawyer, New
    Durham) and Liana Blanche Durkee (Newport, VT); residence -
    New Durham
Alice M., b. 8/13/1889; fifth; Herbert W. Dore (shoemaker,
    Wakefield) and Flora E. Burnham (Farmington)
Esther B., b. 2/13/1909; third; Ernest Dore (photographer, 32,
    Farmington) and Inez Bell Clough (27, Rochester)
Eva I., b. 6/1/1892; sixth; Herbert W. Dore (shoe finisher, 32,
    Wakefield) and Flora E. Burnham (housewife, 29, Farmington)
Herbert B., b. 2/22/1888; third; Herbert W. Dore (shoemaker, 28,
    Wakefield) and Flora Burnham (25, Farmington)
John Robert, b. 7/15/1920; first; Clarence M. Dore (box mill, Alton)
    and Christie M. Nutter (Alton)

**DOUGLAS[S],**
daughter, b. 4/17/1916; second; Robert R. Douglas (shoeworker, Winston-Salem, NC) and Rena M. Abbott (Concord)
Robert R., b. 3/1/1927; fourth; Robert R. Douglas (shoeworker, NC and Rena M. Abbott (Concord)
Virginia B., b. 6/18/1914; first; Robert R. Douglass (shoemaker, Winston-Salem, NC) and Rena M. Abbott (Concord)

**DOW,**
daughter, b. 7/17/1913; first; William Dow (shoe operative, NH) ar Edith May Stanley (ME)
Lawrence R., b. 10/18/1917; third; William Dow (shoeworker, Bethlehem) and Edith M. Stanley (Parsonsfield, ME)
Phillis, b. 4/6/1916; second; William Dow (laborer, Bethlehem) and Edith M. Stanley (Parsonsfield, ME)
Vivian, b. 12/3/1904; first; W. M. Dow (21, Canada) and M. Bernhardt (21, Manchester)

**DOWNING,**
stillborn child, b. 6/–/1891; second; Woodbury Downing (farmer, 2( Farmington) and Winnie Wormwood (19, Rochester)
stillborn son, b. 4/16/1897; first; Edward J. Downing (farmer, 21, Farmington) and Kittie C. Miller (18, LaGrange, MO)
daughter, b. 6/14/1898; first; Edward J. Downing (farmer, 23, Farmington) and Katie Miller (19)
son, b. 2/27/1901; third; Edward J. Downing (farmer, 25, Farmington) and Kattie C. Miller (22, Legrange, ME)

**DRAPEAU [see Dropean],**
son, b. 1/5/1893; fifth; Cleophos Drapeau (laborer, 38, PQ) and Rosa Duclos (34, PQ)
Paul Donald, b. 6/17/1937; third; Edward G. Drapeau (shoeworker, Sanbornville) and Dorothy Sibley (Wakefield)
Philip David, b. 7/28/1938; first; Henry Drapeau (shoeworker, Wolfeboro) and Barbara R. Tufts (Farmington)
Ramona, b. 1/3/1935; first; Ida Drapeau (Sanbornville)
Robert Bruce, b. 5/21/1935; second; Edward Drapeau (shoeworker Sanbornville) and Dorothy K. Sibley (Sanbornville)
Roger William, b. 4/14/1934; first; Edward G. Drapeau (shoeworke Sanbornville) and Dorothy Sibley (Sanbornville)

**DRAWN,**
son, b. 2/22/1897; third; Stephen Drawn (teamster, 25, Ossipee) and Carrie Peavey (26, Farmington)

**DREW,**
son, b. 2/10/1887; second; Charles E. Drew (shoemaker, 34, Farmington) and Lizzie Childs (Milton)
daughter [Ethel M.], b. 5/17/1889; third; Charles E. Drew (shoemaker, 37, Farmington) and Mary E. Child (37, Milton)
stillborn son, b. 2/4/1894; eighth; Frank J. Drew (shoemaker, 36, Gilmanton) and Lizzie H. Young (36, Dover)
son [Frank W.], b. 6/30/1895; ninth; Frank E. Drew (shoemaker, 38, Gilmanton) and Lizzie H. Young (38, Dover)
daughter, b. 11/9/1903; first; Charles E. Drew (box maker, 28, Alton) and Lizzie M. Whittier (26, Barrington)
stillborn son, b. 1/27/1936; fourth; Robert Drew (police officer, Middleton) and Grace Lord (Lebanon, ME)
Alice, b. 11/27/1889; sixth; Frank J. Drew (shoemaker, Gilmanton) and Lizzie H. Young (Dover)
Allan Elbert, b. 8/1/1915; first; John J. Drew (shoe worker, Middleton) and Catherine T. Finnegan (Ireland)
Earnest, b. 4/1/1898; first; Earnest Drew and Fanny Hayes
Grace Marion, b. 8/9/1934; third; Robert B. Drew (police officer, Middleton) and Grace M. Drew (West Lebanon, ME)
Helen Joanne, b. 9/16/1933; first; Elmer Drew (shoeworker, Middleton) and Helen Pike (Farmington)
John James, Jr., b. 1/24/1918; second; John James Drew (ship workman, Middleton) and Catherine T. Finnegan (Ireland)
Margaret Ellen, b. 3/10/1926; third; John J. Drew (mill fireman, Middleton) and Catherine Finnegan (Ireland)
Roberta May, b. 10/19/1931; second; Robert B. Drew (salesman, Middleton) and Grace M. Lord (W. Lebanon, ME)

**DROPEAN** [see Drapeau],
stillborn child, b. 4/3/1890; fourth; Cleophas P. Dropean (laborer, 36, Canada) and Rosie Dropean (Canada)

**DUFRESNE,**
stillborn son, b. 3/26/1908; sixth; William Dufresne (laborer, 48, NH) and Helen Cota (44, Canada)

**DUNTLEY,**
Lura Maud, b. 5/14/1888; Charles A. Duntley (shoe finisher, 27, Alton) and Charlotte Wingate (29, Farmington)

**DUQUETTE,**
Leon Raymond, b. 5/27/1916; eighth; Henry Duquette (boxmaker, Canada) and Albertina LaPlante (Canada)

**DURKEE,**
Donald Porter, b. 1/18/1929; second; Porter Durkee (brushmaker, Danvers, MA) and Stella H. Swinerton (Farmington)

**DUSTIN,**
stillborn son, b. 12/27/1891; first; Fred R. Dustin (conductor, 24) and Abbie E. Lucas (17, Farmington)

**EASON,**
Martin Regw'd, b. 3/20/1934; fourth; Walter R. Eason (laborer, Springfield, MA) and Mary A. Shapleigh (ME)

**EASTMAN,**
Angelina, b. 2/16/1927; first; Everett Eastman (junk dealer, North Conway) and Rosa B. York (Pittsfield)
Everett Edward, Jr., b. 12/7/1928; second; Everett E. Eastman (junk dealer, Ossipee) and Rosa B. York (Pittsfield)

**EDGERLY,**
son [Earle M.], b. 6/9/1887; third; Ervill M. Edgerly (laborer, 24, Farmington) and Carrie M. Quint (Farmington)
daughter [Helen P.], b. 8/–/1891; first; Willie H. Edgerly (stock fitter, 23, Farmington) and Mattie A. Corson (22, Barrington)
son [George H.], b. 8/29/1892; second; Willie H. Edgerly (shoemaker, 24, Farmington) and Mattie A. Corson (housewife, 23, Barrington)
daughter, b. 10/18/1902; fifth; Willie H. Edgerly (teamster, 34, Farmington) and Mattie A. Corson (33, Barrington)
daughter, b. 10/17/1904; seventh; Will H. Edgerly (laborer, 36, Farmington) and Mattie A. Corson (36, Barrington)
daughter [Earline], b. 10/14/1908; first; Earl M. Edgerly (shoemaker, 21, Farmington) and Ethel M. Drew (19, Farmington)

daughter, b. 12/24/1910; second; Earl Edgerly (shoe cutter, Farmington) and Ethel M. Drew (Farmington)

daughter [Doris E.], b. 4/23/1913; third; Earle M. Edgerly (shoemaker, Farmington) and Ethel M. Drew (Farmington)

Alta M., b. 2/18/1894; third; Will H. Edgerly (shoemaker, 25, Farmington) and Mattie H. Corson (25, Barrington)

Aurelie Maude, b. 4/8/1915; second; Clyde H. Edgerly (clerk, Farmington) and Mary V. Anderson (North Conway)

Beatrice J., b. 3/3/1892; first; Frank E. Edgerly (shoe manufacturer, 30, Farmington) and Janet A. Ricker (housewife, 28, New Durham)

Brenda Mae, b. 4/4/1927; fourth; Clyde H. Edgerly (shoeworker, Farmington) and Mary V. Anderson (North Conway)

Fred L., b. 7/25/1910; eighth; Willie H. Edgerly (laborer, Farmington) and Mattie Corson (Barrington)

Glena M., b. 6/5/1921; third; Clyde H. Edgerly (shoe worker, Farmington) and Mary V. Anderson (N. Conway)

John D., b. 8/2/1907; seventh; William H. Edgerly (teamster, 38, Farmington) and Mattie Corson (38, Barrington)

Robert M., b. 3/19/1923; first; Earle M. Edgerly (shoecutter, NH) and Bessie M. MacKenzie (MA)

Velda M., b. 12/1/1917; third; Clyde H. Edgerly (shoeworker, Farmington) and Mary V. Anderson (N. Conway)

## EDWARDS,

Stanley R., b. 12/8/1892; first; Charles M. Edwards (shoe finisher, 25, Otisfield, ME) and Cora E. Aspinwall (housewife, 21, Middleton)

## ELDRIDGE,

Dorothy Jane, b. 8/13/1932*; second; Lester Eldridge (shoeworker, Wolfeboro) and Ruth Webster (Farmington)

Lee, b. 12/22/1929; first; Lester Eldridge (shoeworker, Wolfeboro) and Ruth M. Webster (Farmington)

## ELKINS,

daughter, b. 1/2/1892; first; Cyrus Elkins (teamster, 47, Farmington) and Clara E. Joy (housewife, No. Berwick, ME)

daughter, b. 10/8/1914; third; Hazel Elkins (Farmington)

**ELLIOTT,**
son [William], b. 5/24/1897; fourth; George S. Elliott (farmer, 45, Concord) and Ida Nealey (25, Lowell, MA)
son [Norman A.], b. 1/7/1905; first; William A. Elliott (merchant, 34 Farmington) and Florence E. Holmes (15, Brentwood, MA)
son [William J.], b. 2/6/1906; second; William A. Elliott (mechanic, 36, Farmington) and Florence E. Holmes (16)
daughter [Florence E.], b. 4/7/1907; third; William A. Elliott (merchant, 38, Farmington) and Florence E. Golmes (19, Brentwood)
son [Jesse], b. 10/16/1913; first; W. A. Elliott (mechanic, Farmington) and Annie Goodwin (Ogunquit, ME)
daughter, b. 11/10/1914; second; Arthur W. Elliott (mechanic, Farmington) and Annie B. Dunnells (Wells, ME)
stillborn son, b. 11/25/1932; first; Jesse Elliott (New Durham) and Leona F. Molsan (Farmington)
Eddie, b. 5/13/1896; third; George S. Elliott (horse dealer, 42, Concord) and Ida Nealy (24, Lowell, MA)
Frank G., b. 1/9/1899; fifth; George S. Elliott (farmer, 47, Concord) and Ida Nealey (26, Lowell, MA)
Lillian, b. 2/21/1917; third; William A. Elliott (mechanic, Farmington) and Annie B. Goodwin (Wells, ME)
Norman Theodore, b. 4/30/1936; second; Theodore Elliott (motion pic. op., Bow) and Mabel C. Swaine (Rochester)
Ruth E., b. 4/21/1907; tenth; Frank Elliott (teamster, 30, MA) and Minnie Graton (32, NH)

**ELLIS,**
son [Leon], b. 12/22/1910; first; James Ellis (farmer, Farmington) and Etta G. Varney (Farmington)
son [Arthur W.], b. 12/10/1911; second; James Ellis (22, Farmington) and Etta J. Varney (23, Farmington)
son [Kenneth], b. 8/26/1932; fifth; Leon Ellis (laborer) and Jeanette O. Ward (Rochester)
Carroll Neal, b. 10/20/1938; sixth; Leon Ellis (shoeworker, Farmington) and Jeannette Ward (Rochester)
James, b. 7/30/1889; second; Dana F. Ellis (shoemaker, Alton) and Emma M. Dickinson (Biddeford, ME)

**EMERSON,**
child, b. 10/17/1888; first; Charles A. Emerson (laborer, 24, New Durham) and Dora O'Gray (21, Rochester)
daughter, b. 8/30/1900; second; Augustus F. Emerson (teamster, 35, Rollinsford) and Flora B. Hurd (21, Farmington)
Bessie, b. 1/30/1911; ninth; Burton E. Emerson (sawyer, 38, Raymond) and Mary E. Kenney (33, NB)
Clifford Allen, b. 7/29/1938; seventh; Clifford Emerson (plumber, Pittsfield) and Lucy Tuttle (Athens, ME)
Esther Mabel, b. 12/2/1932; fifth; Clifton Emerson (plumber, Pittsfield) and Lucy Tuttle (Athens, ME)
Gerald M., b. 12/23/1909; eighth; Bert E. Emerson (sawyer, 37, Raymond) and Mary E. Kenney (31, NB)
Robert William, b. 11/20/1938; first; Alfred S. Emerson (shoeworker, Derry) and Mildred Fossett (E. Boston, MA)
Verna M. B., b. 2/1/1934; sixth; Clifton Emerson (plumber, Pittsfield) and Lucy Jane Tuttle (Athens, ME)

**EMERY,**
daughter [Ida Estella], b. 9/–/1891; first; Clifton E. Emery (shoemaker, 20, Milton) and Mary J. Hurd (19, Farmington)
daughter, b. 12/12/1897; fourth; Edward A. Emery (farmer, 50, Middleton) and Viola A. Edgerly (42, New Durham)
son [George], b. 2/5/1899; fifth; Edwin A. Emery (farmer, 52, Middleton) and Viola A. Edgerly (43, New Durham)
Evelyn F., b. 7/10/1917; second; Walter C. Emery, Jr. (laundry man, Portsmouth) and Mary E. Mercer (Portsmouth)
John Mercer, b. 6/6/1914; first; Walter C. Emery, Jr. (laundryman, Portsmouth) and Mary E. Mercer (Portsmouth)

**ENGLISH,**
Theas Madene, b. 12/1/1918; second; W. J. English (schoolteacher, Ireland) and Ruth E. Johnson (Lebanon)

**EVANS,**
Florence Ella, b. 3/21/1923; sixth; Samuel Evans (farmer, MA) and Rachael H. Parker (MA)
Florence M., b. 11/13/1888; George H. Evans (printer, 23, Great Falls) and Ida O. Corson (24, Barrington)
Robert C., b. 6/29/1924; second; Robert C. Evans (shoemaker, Middleton) and Marion S. Whitehouse (Berwick, ME)

**FALL,**
stillborn daughter, b. 2/13/1891; first; William E. Fall (painter, 21, Farmington) and Nellie White (18, Rochester)
son [Otis], b. 3/30/1896; third; W. E. Fall (mechanic, 26, Farmington) and Nellie A. White (26, Farmington)
daughter, b. 3/26/1899; fourth; William E. Fall (painter, 28, Farmington) and Nellie A. White (29, Gonic)
son, b. 4/16/1917; second; Virgil Fall (carpenter, Ossipee) and Let N. Piper (Effingham)
Fannie C., b. 10/12/1887; Charles F. Fall (shoecutter, 32, Farmington) and Gertrude Smith (Farmington)
Lawrence R., b. 1/14/1916; first; Henry S. Fall (shoeworker, Somersworth) and Rosie B. Varney (Farmington)
Richard W., b. 12/31/1917; second; Henry S. Fall (machinist, Somersworth) and Rosie E. Varney (Farmington)
Theresa, b. 12/12/1923; first; Louise Fall (Tuftonboro)

**FARRINGTON,**
James Boag, b. 5/14/1936; first; J. T. Farrington (shoeworker, ME) and Edith M. Roark (ME)

**FEENEY,**
son, b. 4/9/1924; second; Raymond O. Feeney (shoecutter, MA) and Edna M. Whitehouse (Alton)

**FERLAND,**
Beverly Frances, b. 6/22/1936; first; Emile Ferland (shoeworker, Farmington) and Frances Clough (Acton, ME)
Elna Alice, b. 4/3/1915; eleventh; Thomas G. Ferland (shoemaker, Canada) and Mary D. Marcoux (Rochester)
Joseph, b. 4/3/1915; stillborn; twelfth; Thomas G. Ferland (shoemaker, Canada) and Mary D. Marcoux (Rochester)
Joseph E[mile]. A., b. 5/7/1912; seventh; Thomas J. Ferland (shoe operative, PQ, Canada) and Mary D. Marcou (Rochester)
Robert Armand, b. 8/5/1937; second; Emile Ferland (shoeworker, Farmington) and Frances Clough (Acton, ME)

**FERRETTI,**
son [Fred G.], b. 12/27/1894; second; Ralph Ferretti (merchant, 29, Italy) and Fannie Casassa (28, Italy)

son [Johnnie R.], b. 1/18/1896; third; Ralph A. Ferretti (fruit dealer, 30, Genoa, Italy) and Fannie Casassa (28, Genoa, Italy)

son, b. 2/25/1905; fourth; Ralph A. Ferretti (merchant, 41, Priosa, Italy) and Fannie L. Casassa (38, Tarcilia, Italy)

daughter [Louise E.], b. 4/14/1906; fifth; Ralph A. Ferretti (merchant, 42, Preiosa, Italy) and Fannie Cassassa (39, Genoa, Italy)

**FIELD,**
son [Vernon B.], b. 4/8/1907; first; George Field (shoemaker, 21) and Ethel Bodwell (21, Somersworth)

Vivian A., b. 9/16/1909; second; George V. Field (shoemaker, 23, Caribou, ME) and Ethel Bodwell (23, Somersworth)

**FIFIELD,**
Albert D., b. 3/21/1888; Albert F. Fifield (machinist, 33, Biddeford, ME) and Jennie Kelley (24, Farmington)

**FISHER,**
Everett C., b. 8/23/1917; third; Shirley Fisher (shoemaker, Easton, MA) and Maizie Thomas (Attleboro, MA)

**FLANDERS,**
stillborn son, b. 4/20/1889; first; Herman S. Flanders (shoe cutter, 27, Danbury) and Augusta J. Berry (21, New Durham)

**FLETCHER,**
son, b. 9/24/1890; first; Henry A. Fletcher (shoemaker, 24, New Durham) and Clara Brown (17, Rochester)

daughter, b. 11/6/1891; first; Fred P. Fletcher (merchant, 29, New Durham) and Ella R. Jones (27, Barnstead)

**FLOYD,**
Caroline Eloise, b. 12/18/1919; fourth; Charles W. Floyd (merchant, Springfield, ME) and Jennie L. Claydon (Fredericton, NB)

**FOLSOM,**
Ethel Miriam, b. 5/19/1918; first; Earle M. Folsom (shoeworker, Rochester) and Abigail B. Hinkley (Gloucester, MA)

**FOSS,**
- son [Harold J.], b. 11/–/1891; second; James W. Foss (farmer, 31, Rochester) and Katie M. Hobbs (21, Farmington)
- son [Henry T.], b. 1/9/1895; fourth; James E. Foss (farm, 36, Rochester) and Katie M. Hobbs (25, Farmington)
- Barbara Louise, b. 2/20/1923; first; Andrew J. Foss (merchant, NH) and Iona M. Hale (NH)
- Calvin James, b. 3/16/1922; second; Harold J. Foss (farmer, Farmington) and Alice M. Foss (Center Strafford)
- Donald Clyde, b. 2/20/1936; first; Woodrow Foss (truck driver, Strafford) and Erelene Terrill (Middleton)
- Henry Irving, b. 9/25/1888; second; Henry I. Foss (laborer, 24, Farmington) and Mattie Jones (20, Medway, MA)
- Mildred J., b. 9/4/1911; first; Henry E. Foss (Sailor, USN, 22, Farmington) and Margaret E. Conway (19, Providence, RI); residence - Portsmouth
- Sumner Henry, b. 8/1/1913; first; Harold G. Foss (farmer, Farmington) and Alice Foss (Strafford)

**FOSTER,**
- son, b. 9/24/1908; second; Augustus Foster (shoemaker, 41, FL) and Emma J. Dufresne (20, Laconia)
- son [Louis], b. 10/6/1908; second; Charles W. Foster (shoemaker, 33, Nashua) and Bessie M. Walsh (29, Berwick, ME)
- son, b. 2/5/1910; third; Charles W. Foster (shoemaker, Nashua) and Bessie M. Welch (Berwick, ME)
- son [Charles A.], b. 12/6/1912; fourth; Charles W. Foster (shoemaker, Nashua) and Bessie M. Welch (Berwick, ME)
- stillborn son, b. 1/22/1933; first; Kenneth R. Foster (postal mail clerk, Berwick, ME) and Gladys McAllister (Rochester)
- Doris Jean, b. 9/28/1930; fifth; Frank E. Foster (woodheeler, E. Pepperell, MA) and Ethel Buzzell (Limerick, ME)
- Louis Wilbur, b. 6/9/1938; first; Louis W. Foster (shoeworker, Farmington) and Glendora Lashon (Skowhegan, ME)

**FOWLER,**
- Frank Clarence, b. 7/31/1915; first; Clarence D. Fowler (plumber, Strafford) and Marion Parshley (Strafford)

**FREEMAN,**
Gloria June, b. 2/26/1936; eighth; Maynard Freeman (shoeworker, Rockland, ME) and Sarah Belle Wilson (Rochester)

**FREETHY,**
Robert Preston, b. 2/21/1926; first; Wilbert Freethy (shoemaker, Chocorua) and Laura Scruton (Farmington)

**FRENCH,**
son, b. 6/11/1903; third; Alden C. French (teamster, 24, Middleton) and Laurentine E. Runnells (21, New Durham)
son, b. 6/14/1908; fourth; Alden C. French (teamster, 28, Milton) and Laurentina E. Runnells (25, New Durham)

**FULLER,**
Andrew A., b. 2/6/1918; first; Harry F. Fuller (clergyman, New York City) and Julia C. Mettberg (Brooklyn, NY)

**FULTON,**
Albert Edward, b. 1/9/1935; third; George Fulton (shoeworker, South Franklin) and Eleanor Howard (Farmington)
Arthur George, b. 9/18/1932; second; George A. Fulton (shoeworker, Franklin, MA) and Eleanor Howard (Farmington)

**FURBER,**
son, b. 10/3/1912; second; Walter Furber (shoe operative, Manchester) and Nellie J. Benway (Port Henry, NY)
son, b. 6/16/1914; third; Walter Furber (shoemaker, Manchester) and Nellie Benway (Ripton, NY)
son, b. 2/23/1916; fourth; Walter Furber (laster, NH) and Nellie Benway (NY)
Donald J., b. 8/24/1936; first; Otto J. Furber (clerk, Alton) and Evelyn A. Tanner (Farmington)
Janet Gertrude, b. 7/23/1923; second; John C. Furber (shoemaker, Alton) and Lucina M. Bird (St. Albans)
Richard F., b. 8/13/1938; first; Myron Furber (merchant, Rochester) and Margaret Stevens (Farmington)

**FURBUSH,**
　Kenneth W., b. 4/15/1933; second; Ralph Furbush (hotel worker, Old Orchard Beach, ME) and Irene H. Wentworth (Old Orchard, ME)

**GAGNON,**
　Lucien Ernest, b. 12/6/1938; third; Lucien Gagne (shoeworker, Salem, MA) and Ruth Southwick (Beverly, MA)

**GAMBLIN,**
　Jean Marion, b. 7/20/1932; third; John S. Gamblin (filling station oper., NB) and Lottie M. Sharp (NB)

**GARDNER,**
　Patricia, b. 8/24/1936; second; Uel Gardner (owner, battery sta., Durham, ME) and Dorothy H. Gray (Farmington)
　Uel Francis, b. 1/2/1933; Uel A. Gardner (mechanic, Durham, ME) and Dorothy H. Gray (Farmington)

**GARLAND,**
　son, b. 3/13/1887; second; Edgar E. Garland (shoemaker, Middleton) and Josephene Peabody (Strafford)
　stillborn daughter, b. 4/4/1897; first; J. Orris Garland (shoemaker, 36, Rye) and Emma R. French (33, Stratham)
　stillborn son, b. 7/31/1904; second; William P. Garland (sawyer, 31, Farmington) and Lona Gray (19, Farmington)
　son [Carlton H.], b. 7/20/1906; seventh; Eli Garland (shoemaker, 38, Alton) and Fannie A. Kimball (33, Wolfeboro)
　daughter, b. 3/12/1908; eighth; Eli Garland, Jr. (shoemaker, 40, Alton) and Fannie A. Kimball (34, Wolfeboro)
　daughter, b. 7/14/1927; first; Wilfred E. Garland (laborer, Farmington) and Lillian E. Gray (Portsmouth)
　son, b. 7/11/1933; second; Robert Garland (shoeworker, Rochester) and Annie Tarbox (Rochester)
　stillborn daughter, b. 7/25/1934; third; Robert Garland (shoeworker, Rochester) and Annie Tarbox (Rochester)
　Carl Franklin, b. 5/22/1931; fourth; Charles H. Garland (farmer, Farmington) and Marion L. ----- (Gorham, ME)
　Doris Marie, b. 9/21/1921; first; Wilfred E. Garland (farmer, Rochester) and Norma M. Smith (Mars Hill, ME)

Goldie Louise, b. 1/14/1933; sixth; Charles H. Garland (farmer, Farmington) and Marion Whitten (Gorham, ME)

Kenneth Robert, b. 7/11/1935; first; Robert E. Garland (shoe worker, Rochester) and Annie Tarbox (Rochester)

Norman C., b. 2/28/1898; second; J. Weston Garland (clerk, 27, Rye) and Edna M. Chesley (27, Wolfeboro)

Wilford E., Jr., b. 6/3/1928; second; Wilford E. Garland (laborer, Farmington) and Lillian M. Gray (Portsmouth)

**GEARY,**

Barbara Rolene, b. 8/18/1932; first; Paul Geary (shoeworker, Wolfeboro) and Barbara Remick (Dover)

Beverly Eunice, b. 1/6/1936; third; Paul Geary (aviator, Wolfeboro) and Barbara Remick (Dover)

**GELINAS,**

Albert Louis, b. 5/5/1931; third; Ernest Gelinas (storekeeper, Newmarket) and Yvonne Messier (Rochester)

Gloria Rita, b. 8/28/1928; second; Ernest J. Gelinas (merchant, Newmarket) and Evonne Messur (Rochester)

Pauline Jayne, b. 3/25/1933; second; William E. Gelinas (clerk, Rochester) and Florence Leighton (Farmington)

Robert Eugene, b. 11/2/1932; fourth; Ernest Gelinas (storekeeper, Newmarket) and Yvonne Messer (Rochester)

Roger Paul, b. 3/20/1930; second; Ernest Gelinas (prop. market, Newmarket) and Yvonne Messier (Rochester)

Theresa Anita, b. 3/2/1935; fifth; Ernest Gelinas (grocer, Newmarket) and Yvonne Messier (Rochester)

**GIBBS,**

son [Marshall P.], b. 11/10/1901; first; Ralph P. Gibbs (shoe laster, 25, E. Bridgewater, MA) and Grace Emery (21, Farmington)

daughter [Arlene F.], b. 8/15/1904; second; Ralph P. Gibbs (shoeworker, 27, Bridgewater, MA) and Grace B. Emery (24, Farmington)

Beverly Jane, b. 9/21/1927; second; Marshall F. Gibbs (shoeworker, Farmington) and Betha A. Littlefield (Farmington)

Marcia F., b. 11/15/1925; first; Marshall F. Gibbs (shoeworker, Farmington) and Bertha A. Littlefield (Farmington)

Marshall F., Jr., b. 6/9/1933; fourth; Marshall F. Gibbs (shoemaker, Farmington) and Bertha A. Littlefield (Farmington)

Roberta Anne, b. 10/16/1929; third; Marshall F. Gibbs (shoemake Farmington) and Bertha Littlefield (Farmington)

**GILBERT,**
Lawrence R., b. 4/13/1921; second; Wilfred Gilbert (garage man, Milton) and Vera M. Remick (Westboro)
Phyllis Arlene, b. 12/20/1918; first; Wilfred Gilbert (US Army, Milton) and Vera Remick (Westboro, MA)

**GILES,**
daughter [Pearle N.], b. 7/9/1892; second; Fred A. Giles (box maker, 34, Epsom) and Amanda Kimball (housewife, 37, Alton)
daughter [Evelyn M.], b. 2/6/1895; third; Fred A. Giles (laborer, 37 Epsom) and Amanda Kimball (40, Alton)
Dorothy H., b. 5/13/1923; fourth; LeRoy S. Giles (teamster, Rochester) and Ellen Goutier (Hampton Falls); residence - Rochester

**GILLIS,**
Mildred V., b. 9/14/1920; first; George H. Gillis (shoe mfg., Lynn, MA) and Eloise Elinor Roger (Frederick City, MD)

**GILMAN,**
son [Erman F.], b. 6/13/1890; third; Warren L. Gilman (shoemaker 39, Alton) and Annie B. Avery (Farmington)
daughter [Gladys L.], b. 12/–/1891; first; Frank I. Gilman (painter, 23, Farmington) and Melissa E. Moore (24, Milton)
son [Lloyd M.], b. 9/1/1893; second; Frank F. Gilman (painter, 25, Farmington) and Melissa Moore (25, Milton)
son [Vertal P.], b. 1/15/1896; fourth; Warren L. Gilman (mechanic, 45, Alton) and Annie B. Avery (35, Farmington)
son, b. 3/4/1901; first; Leon E. Gilman (shoemaker, 23, Farmingto and Carrie M. Montee (19, Farmington)
son, b. 4/3/1912; first; Leo D. Gilman (decorator, Farmington) and Caroline E. Goodrich (Cornish, ME)
son, b. 8/31/1914; first; Lloyd M. Gilman (clerk, Farmington) and Helen W. Carter (Farmington)
son, b. 11/5/1916; second; Lloyd M. Gilman (clerk, Farmington) an Helen W. Carter (Farmington)

son [Donald], b. 10/20/1926; third; Erman F. Gilman (shoemaker, Farmington) and Martha E. Lougee (Farmington)
Etta M., b. 1/3/1897; first; stillborn; Warren E. Gilman (shoemaker, 26, Kingston) and Maud A. Clark (26, St. Johns, NB)
Glendon Lloyd, b. 2/23/1918; third; Lloyd M. Gilman (clerk, Farmington) and Helen W. Carter (Farmington)
Norris Vernon, b. 9/6/1921; second; Erman F. Gilman (shoemaker, Farmington) and Martha E. Lougee (Farmington)
Wallace E., b. 9/8/1916; first; Erman F. Gilman (shoeworker, Farmington) and Martha E. Lougee (Farmington)

**GILMORE,**
daughter, b. 1/10/1889; first; Frank S. Gilmore (shoemaker, 23, Milton) and Mary A. Robinson (17, Farmington)

**GLASS,**
Eleanor Louise, b. 5/16/1918; second; Eugene Glass (shoeworker, Greensboro, SC) and Eleanor F. Blaisdell (Farmington)

**GLIDDEN,**
daughter [Hazel M.], b. 3/4/1891; first; Ira W. Glidden (shoemaker, 28, Parsonsfield, ME) and Nellie A. Watson (22, Wakefield)
son, b. 2/5/1892; third; Martin V. B. Glidden (farmer, 36, Alton) and Frances A. Tibbetts (housewife, 29, Farmington)
daughter [Bernice L.], b. 4/5/1899; fourth; Martin V. B. Glidden (farmer, 43, Alton) and Frances A. Tibbetts (35, Farmington)
stillborn son, b. 8/2/1937; fifth; Ormand Glidden (shoeworker, Alton) and Elsie M. Fifield (Conway)
stillborn son, b. 8/2/1937; sixth; Ormand Glidden (shoeworker, Alton) and Elsie M. Fifield (Conway)
daughter, b. 4/25/1938; second; Elmer F. Glidden (laborer, Milton) and Rose Patenaude (Lowell, MA)
Arlene, b. 6/13/1933; third; Armand Glidden (shoemaker, Alton) and Elsie Fifield (Conway)
Clyde, Jr., b. 8/21/1930; second; Clyde Glidden (mechanic, New Durham) and Reta Rollins (Farmington)
Corine Audrey, b. 9/22/1921; fourth; Sidney M. Glidden (woodworker, Farmington) and Alice P. Glidden (New Durham)
David Ormand, b. 4/9/1936; fourth; Ormand Glidden (shoeworker, Alton) and Elsie Mae Fifield (Conway)

Delma Lorraine, b. 6/10/1933; first; Lauriston W. Glidden (shoemaker, New Durham) and Alberta I. Spinney (Kittery Point, ME)

Emma, b. 12/13/1893; second; Ira W. Glidden (shoemaker, 31, Parsonsfield, ME) and Nellie A. Watson (25, Wakefield)

George W., b. 3/23/1894; first; Herbert S. Glidden (laborer, 17, Rochester) and Alma L. Wyatt (18, Farmington); residence - Rochester and Farmington

Helen E., b. 2/10/1925; fifth; Maud A. Glidden (Hooksett)

James Earl, b. 9/23/1930; second; Ormond Glidden (shoeworker, Alton) and Elsie Fifield (Conway)

Lynda Belle, b. 5/4/1922; fourth; George Glidden (farmer, Farmington) and Maud Nickless (Hooksett, MA)

Natalie Meserve, b. 11/1/1935; first; Ernest Glidden (shoeworker, Alton) and Evelyn Otis (Farmington)

Norma Otis, b. 6/16/1938; second; Ernest Glidden (shoeworker, Alton) and Evelyn Otis (Farmington)

Norma Rosalie, b. 8/28/1922; first; Clyde Glidden (woodturner, New Durham) and Reta Rawlins (Farmington)

**GOODRICH,**
daughter, b. 12/1/1887; second; Hiram H. Goodrich (laster, 34, Saco, ME) and Ella Goodrich (Gloucester, MA)

Arthur W., b. 10/10/1895; third; Hiram M. Goodrich (farmer, 43, Biddeford) and Ella Wilson (38, New Gloucester)

**GOODSON,**
Gertrude Ethel, b. 7/15/1914; second; Francis Goodson (chauffeur Rochester) and Ethel M. Birch (ME)

**GOODWIN,**
son [John], b. 8/21/1910; third; John F. Goodwin (shoemaker, York ME) and Inez Ham (Alton)

son [Eugene T.], b. 9/10/1911; fourth; John F. Goodwin (shoe laster, 42, York, ME) and Inez J. Ham (33, Alton)

son, b. 12/26/1916; fifth; John F. Goodwin (shoecutter, ME) and Inez Ham (NH)

Derald Henry, b. 5/17/1934; second; John F. Goodwin (laborer, Farmington) and Otabelle M. Willey (Middleton)

Eugene T., Jr., b. 3/21/1938; first; Eugene Goodwin (shoeworker, Farmington) and Bernice Stevens (Middleton)

Iona Mae, b. 2/12/1936; first; Alice Goodwin (Alton)
John F., b. 2/11/1933; first; John F. Goodwin (laborer, Farmington) and Odabelle M. Willey (Middleton)

**GORDON,**
son, b. 11/6/1926; fourth; Frank Gordon (shoemaker, Dover) and Nellie F. Young (Farmington)
Barbara Ola, b. 9/20/1930; fifth; Frank Gordon (shoeworker, Dover) and Nellie F. Young (Farmington)
Edward Albert, b. 7/6/1934; seventh; Frank Gordon (shoeworker, Dover) and Nellie F. Young (Farmington)
Lloyd Fred, b. 4/19/1933; sixth; Frank Gordon (shoeworker, Dover) and Nellie Young (Farmington)
Mary Florence, b. 9/20/1925; third; Frank Gordon (shoemaker, Farmington) and Nellie F. Young (Farmington)
Morris Everett, b. 7/14/1923; second; Frank Gordon (shoemaker, Dover) and Nellie F. Young (Farmington)
Norman F., b. 11/4/1921; first; Frank Gordon (shoemaker, Dover) and Nellie Young (Farmington)

**GOUIN,**
daughter, b. 1/3/1934; first; Walter J. Gouin (laborer, Westfield) and Agnes Clare (Laconia)

**GOULET,**
Louise Josephine, b. 4/8/1929; fifth; Emile R. Goulet (jeweler, Canada) and Josephine Chretien (Canada)

**GRANT,**
Gail Patricia, b. 3/20/1938; third; Frank Grant (mechanic, East Rochester) and Francis Hughes (Barrington)

**GRAY,**
son [Fred C.], b. 5/27/1894; second; John I. Gray (farmer, 32, Farmington) and Ellen F. Varney (31, Farmington)
daughter, b. 12/17/1896; second; William E. Gray (farmer, 32, Farmington) and Emma E. Varney (28, Farmington)
daughter [Marion E.], b. 12/15/1898; first; Francis E. Gray (mechanic, 26, New Durham) and Adeliza Dickey (21, NB)

daughter [Dorothy H.], b. 4/24/1904; second; Frances E. Gray (laborer, 31, New Durham) and Adeliza Dickie (26, Chipman, NB)

son [Alfred R.], b. 3/12/1906; first; Ellis S. Gray (shoe foreman, 42, Warren, ME) and Edith G. Butler (36, Warren, ME)

son [Roland G.], b. 7/20/1922; first; George R. Gray (shoemaker, Grafton) and Elsie M. H. Berry (Farmington)

son, b. 12/20/1924; third; Everett Gray (shoeworker, NH) and Sadie Duesh (NH)

daughter, b. 5/26/1928; sixth; Everett S. Gray (shoemaker, Grafton) and Sadie G. Dewhurst (Newport)

Aileen L., b. 1/30/1924; second; George R. Gray (shoemaker, NH) and Elsie M. Berry (NH)

Alice M., b. 9/4/1889; first; John I. Gray (farmer, Farmington) and E. F. Varney (Farmington)

Chester Elwin, b. 10/11/1930; seventh; Samuel J. Gray (shoeworker, Gilmanton) and Mildred Marshall (Cambridge, MA)

Donald Frederick, b. 9/5/1936; fifth; George Gray (petroleum dealer, Grafton) and Elsie Berry (Farmington)

Edwin Leroy, b. 4/2/1922; first; Everett S. Gray (shoemaker, Grafton) and Sadie E. Dewhurst (Newport)

Ernest Everett, b. 3/3/1935; third; John I. Gray (farmer, Farmington) and Emiline Green (Alton)

Ethel May, b. 1/31/1921; first; Arthur L. Gray (farmer, Farmington) and Lillian M. Gray (Alton)

Everett Delma, b. 8/6/1923; second; Everett L. Gray (shoemaker, Farmington) and Sadie G. Dewhurst (NH)

George Chester, b. 3/3/1926; fourth; Everett L. Gray (shoemaker, NH) and Sadie G. Dewhurst (Newport)

Harland Leroy, b. 2/9/1928; fourth; George R. Gray (shoemaker, Grafton) and Elsie M. Berry (Farmington)

Irving, b. 12/15/1927; seventh; Samuel J. Gray (laborer, Gilmanton) and Mildred Marshall (Cambridge, MA)

Louise May, b. 5/22/1927; fifth; Everett L. Gray (shoeworker, NH) and Sadie Galater (Newport)

Norman Lewis, b. 11/21/1932; seventh; Samuel Gray (shoeworker, Gilmanton) and Mildred Marshall (Cambridge, MA)

Robert Albert, b. 1/20/1931; eighth; Everett Gray (shoeworker, Grafton) and Sadie Dewhurst (Newport)

Roger Lewis, b. 11/17/1929; seventh; Everett Gray (shoeworker, Grafton) and Sadie G. Dewhurst (Newport)

Virginia June, b. 5/2/1926; third; George R. Gray (shoemaker, Grafton) and Elsie M. Berry (Farmington)

Wilbur, b. 9/9/1934; tenth; Sam Gray (shoeworker, Gilmanton I.W.) and Mildred Marshall (Cambridge, MA)

William Edmond, b. 7/30/1928; second; John I. Gray (farmer, Farmington) and Evelyn M. Green (Alton)

Zelma, b. 9/24/1922; fifth; Samuel J. Gray (laborer, Gilmanton) and Mildred Marshall (Cambridge, MA)

**GREELEY,**

Arthur, b. 6/20/1903; second; Philip H. Greeley (physician, 32, Swanville, ME) and Nina G. Vose (30, Waterville, ME)

Henry P., b. 8/24/1901; first; Philip H. Greeley (physician, 31, Swanville, ME) and Nina G. Vose (28, Skowhegan, ME)

**GREENWOOD,**

Loraine Joan, b. 1/10/1933; first; Arthur Greenwood (shoeworker, Somersworth) and Beatrice Hamilton (Milton Mills); residence - Rochester

Ralph Neil, b. 6/30/1935; second; Arthur Greenwood (shoeworker, Somersworth) and Beatrice Hamilton (Milton Mills)

**GRENIER,**

son, b. 6/18/1916; second; Alfred Grenier (shoeworker, Springvale, ME) and Maud C. Horn (Farmington); residence - Rochester

Carlene, b. 7/2/1922; first; Wilfred Grenier (woodworker, New Durham) and Nettie E. Chesley (Farmington)

Gloria June, b. 5/1/1927; second; Wilfred Grenier (machinist, Rochester) and Nettie E. Chesley (Farmington); residence - New Durham

**GRIFFIN,**

son, b. 1/31/1910; first; Jesse D. Griffin (laborer, Concord) and Catherine Dickson (Laconia)

**GUILMET,**

daughter, b. 11/3/1912; fifth; Joseph J. Guilmet (shoemaker, Dover) and Blanche A. Fall (Farmington); residence - Haverhill, MA

Louis A., b. 3/27/1906; first; Joseph E. Guilmet (shoemaker, 22, Somersworth) and Blanche A. Fall (20, Farmington)
Patricia Anne, b. 12/1/1937; first; Rudolph Guilmet (lumberman, Lawrence, MA) and Mary Ring (Farmington)

**GUISTINA,**
Daniel Della, b. 2/8/1922; first; Daniel Della Guistina (garage, Italy) and Pierina Pinbeni (Italy)

**GURNEY,**
Fred Francis, b. 9/13/1918; second; Fred Gurney (lumberman, Waterville, ME) and Evelyn M. McDonald (Ireland); residence Alton Bay

**HACKETT,**
son [Ira E.], b. 11/30/1906; fourth; Wesley Hackett (section hand, 31, Danvers, MA) and Gertrude M. Evans (32, Alton)
son [Henry], b. 4/29/1910; sixth; Wesley Hackett (RR section hand Pittsfield) and Gertrude M. Evans (Alton)
son, b. 2/6/1917; seventh; Wesley Hackett (RR section foreman, Danvers, MA) and Gertrude Evans (Alton)
Barry James, b. 10/16/1935; third; George L. Hackett (shoeworker, Farmington) and Velma Gooch (Alton)
Betty Jean, b. 9/4/1933; second; George Hackett (shoeworker, Farmington) and Velma Gooch (Alton)
Frances E., b. 1/9/1930; third; William Hackett (section RR, Danvers, MA) and Sarah E. Hayward (Fairfield, ME)
Fred, b. 5/5/1904; fourth; Westley Hackett (section hand, 29, Danvers) and Gertrude M. Evans (30, Farmington)
George E., b. 8/17/1901; third; Wesley Hackett (section hand, 26, Danvers, MA) and Gertrude May Evans (27, Alton)
George Edward, Jr., b. 3/20/1931*; first; George E. Hackett (shipper in shoe shop, Farmington) and Velma Gooch (Alton)
Richard Clayton, b. 5/29/1928; eighth; William Hackett (RR section, Danvers, MA) and Sadie Etta (Fairfield, ME)
Selina, b. 1/6/1900; second; Wesley Hackett (laborer, 23, Danvers, MA) and Gertrude N. Evans (25, Alton)

**HADDOCK,**
son [Herbert R.], b. 8/30/1898; fourth; Howard R. Haddock (shoemaker, 39, Haverhill) and Luella B. Tibbetts (35, Farmington)
Bessie S., b. 4/9/1889; third; Howard R. Haddock (shoemaker, 30, Haverhill, MA) and Luella B. Tibbetts (25, Middleton)

**HAINES,**
son, b. 4/2/1908; first; Roland Haines (shoemaker, 19, Rochester) and Nellie M. Place (18, Farmington)

**HALE,**
Clayton B., b. 5/10/1920; first; Merton H. Hale (shoe worker, New Durham) and Lila I. Brooks (Farmington)
Corie Edgar, Jr., b. 11/15/1930*; first; Corie Edgar Hale (shoecutter, Farmington) and Flora Johnson (Machias, ME)

**HAM,**
son [John], b. 9/11/1889; sixth; Clarence M. Ham (laborer, Farmington) and Mary E. Peavey (Tuftonboro)
son [Benjamin], b. 5/11/1890; first; Herman Ham (shoemaker, 26, Dover) and Ida B. Stevens (17, Alton)
daughter, b. 2/19/1892; second; Herman Ham (shoemaker, 27, Dover) and Ida B. Stevens (housewife, 18, Alton)
daughter, b. 5/26/1893; third; Irving L. Ham (shoemaker, 26, Farmington) and Carrie E. Wentworth (23, Farmington)
daughter [Emma F.], b. 4/4/1895; seventh; Clarence M. Ham (laborer, 37, Farmington) and Mary E. Peavey (36, Tuftonboro)
daughter, b. 1/24/1898; ninth; Clarence M. Ham (laborer, 46, Farmington) and Mary E. Peavey (39, Tuftonboro)
daughter, b. 5/24/1898; fourth; Irving L. Ham (shoemaker, 31, Farmington) and Carrie E. Wentworth (29, Farmington)
son, b. 12/16/1899; tenth; Clarence C. Ham (laborer, 42, Farmington) and Mary E. Peavey (41, Tuftonboro)
daughter, b. 6/26/1900; fifth; Irving L. Ham (shoemaker, 33, Farmington) and Carrie E. Wentworth (30, Farmington)
daughter [Beth Lydia], b. 5/8/1913; second; John H. Ham (shoecutter, Farmington) and Alfreda J. Staples (Peabody, MA)
Blanche, b. 9/9/1888; second; Irving I. Ham (shoemaker, 21, Farmington) and Carrie Wentworth (18, Farmington)

Eric, b. 9/4/1893; first; Elwin Ham (shoemaker, 29, Farmington) a
  Addie B. Burrows (21, Farmington)
Forrest E., b. 6/24/1911; first; Fred E. Ham (machinist, 24,
  Haverhill, MA) and Bessie M. Colbath (21, Farmington)
George Wesley, Jr., b. 1/4/1936; first; George W. Ham
  (shoeworker, Milton) and Lucille Horne (Rochester)
James, b. 8/13/1893; eighth; Clarence M. Ham (shoemaker, 37,
  Farmington) and Mary E. Ham (35, Tuftonboro)
John H., b. 6/22/1924; third; John H. Ham (shoecutter, NH) and
  Alfreda J. Staples (MA)
Mildred Eileen, b. 10/27/1911; first; John H. Ham (shoe cutter, 22,
  Farmington) and Alfreda Jennie Staples (21, Peabody, MA)

**HAMBLIN,**
son, b. 7/4/1901; second; Caleb E. Hamblin (carpenter, 37,
  Falmouth, MA) and F. Mabel Wilson (25, Harwich, MA)

**HAMMOND,**
Charles D., b. 2/4/1889; fourth; Frank M. Hammond (supt. gas
  works, 27, North Easton, MA) and Lisa Skinner (31, Dana, MA

**HANCOCK,**
Ellison, b. 7/23/1925; fifth; Frank E. Hancock (shoeworker, Salem,
  MA) and Hazel M. Babb (Farmington)
Ellsworth F., b. 9/2/1917; first; Frank E. Hancock (shoemaker,
  Salem, MA) and Hazel M. Babb (Farmington)
Frank E., b. 4/2/1924; fourth; Frank E. Hancock (shoemaker,
  Salem, MA) and Hazel M. Babb (Farmington)
Georgia Edith, b. 2/20/1920; second; Frank E. Hancock
  (shoemaker, Salem, MA) and Hazel M. Babb (Farmington)
Mildred G., b. 4/30/1922; third; Frank Hancock (shoeworker, Salem
  MA) and Hazel M. Babb (Farmington)

**HANNAH,**
Helena Leona, b. 10/5/1931; first; Leon Hannah (farmer, Canada)
  and Eva Perrault (Canada)

**HANSCOM,**
daughter [Ellen E.], b. 1/30/1905; fifth; Frank Hanscom (laborer, 34
  Middleton) and Julia Reed (32, Wakefield)

**HANSON,**
stillborn son, b. 4/28/1893; first; Alvin G. Hanson (blacksmith, 22, Barnstead) and Mary E. Clough (17, Boston, MA)
son [Herbert W.], b. 6/3/1895; second; Alvin G. Hanson (blacksmith, 26, So. Barnstead) and Mary E. Clough (21, Boston)
son, b. 2/7/1898; second; Chester Hanson (laborer, 24, St. Stephen, NB) and Emma A. Tasker (21, Pittsfield)
daughter, b. 11/6/1902; third; Chester H. Hanson (blacksmith, 28, St. Stephens, NB) and Emma H. Tasker (25, Loudon)
Chester P., b. 5/22/1896; first; Chester Hanson (blacksmith, 23, St. Stephens, NB) and Emma Tasker (20, Loudon)
Robert Willis, b. 5/27/1920; first; Willis C. Hanson (RR engineer, Somersworth) and Helen H. Roberts (Farmington)
Roline F., b. 10/22/1904; fourth; Chester H. Hanson (blacksmith, 31, St. Stephens, NB) and Emma A. Tasker (28, Loudon)

**HARDING,**
Dorothy E., b. 7/9/1929; fifth; Joseph H. Harding (foreman mechanic, New Durham) and Merle H. Bennett (Dover)

**HARRIMAN,**
daughter, b. 4/4/1911; first; Charles I. Harriman (laborer, 25, Somersworth) and Alice M. Ham (19, Farmington)
Herbert Carl, b. 6/11/1934; first; Cyrus Harriman (shoeworker, Alton Bay) and Doris Depatra (New Haven, CT)
Nancy Anne, b. 11/17/1934; first; Frederick Harriman (truckman, Alton) and Jane Swift (Lynn, MA)
Rhea Louise, b. 9/29/1937; second; Cyrus L. Harriman (shoeworker, Alton) and Doris E. LaPatra (New Haven, CT)

**HARRISON,**
Hazel Marie, b. 10/13/1915; first; William J. Harrison (Goodyear operator, Clark Island, ME) and Marie M. Regis (Derry)

**HART,**
daughter [Altha M.], b. 7/24/1901; third; Dana B. Hart (shoemaker, 34, Milton) and Nettie J. Stevens (33, Middleton)
daughter, b. 9/4/1924; second; Walter H. Hart (trainman, RR, NH) and Hazel R. Ham (NH)

Dana Richard, b. 3/29/1936; fourth; Donald B. Hart (shoeworker, Farmington) and Alice B. Dupre (Epping)

Donald Bryan, b. 12/21/1906; fourth; Dana B. Hart (farmer, 39, Milton) and Mattie J. Stevens (39, Middleton)

Donald Byron, Jr., b. 12/21/1928; first; Donald B. Hart (farmer, Farmington) and Alice Dupere (Epping)

Gloria May, b. 10/11/1931; third; Donald Hart (farmer, Farmington) and Alice Dupere (Epping)

Mildred Beulah, b. 1/8/1930; second; Donald B. Hart (farmer, Farmington) and Alice B. Dupere (Epping)

**HARTFIEL,**

son [Norman R.], b. 7/8/1905; first; Ray Hartfiel (shoemaker, 27, Dayton, KY) and Ruth Tufts (19, Middleton)

daughter [Ellen], b. 2/7/1907; second; Ray Hartfiel (shoemaker, 29, Dayton, KY) and Ruth Tufts (21, Middleton)

Beatrice M., b. 5/1/1910; fourth; Ray Hartfiel (shoemaker, Dayton, KY) and Ruth C. Tufts (Middleton)

Ruth E., b. 2/21/1908; third; Ray Hartfiel (shoemaker, 30, Dayton, KY) and Ruth Tufts (22, Middleton)

**HARTFORD,**

daughter, b. 9/4/1889; first; Edwin L. Hartford (shoe cutter, Dover) and Etta Merrow (Milton)

son [Leroy L.], b. 12/19/1894; first; Edwin L. Hartford (heel maker, 27, Dover) and Carrie S. Gray (17, Rochester)

daughter, b. 11/22/1903; fifth; John C. Hartford (shoemaker, 25, Denmark, ME) and Grace M. Hurd (30, Oxford, ME)

Annie Mae, b. 9/20/1933; first; Harold Hartford (shoemaker, East Rochester) and Eva Hughes (Barrington)

Beverly Ann, b. 3/8/1937; fifth; Harold G. Hartford (laborer, East Rochester) and Eva Hughes (Barrington)

Gertrude E., b. 9/20/1933; second; Harold Hartford (shoemaker, East Rochester) and Eva Hughes (Barrington)

Joyce E., b. 10/11/1934; second; Harold Hartford (laborer, East Rochester) and Eva Mae Hughes (Barrington)

Robert William, b. 1/8/1936; fourth; Harold Hartford (shoeworker, East Rochester) and Eva Mae Hughes (Barrington)

Ronald Richard, b. 12/31/1934; third; Louis M. Hartford (laborer, East Rochester) and Eleanor L. Hughes (Rochester)

**HAYES,**
son, b. 3/4/1887; fourth; George I. Hayes (shoemaker, 31, New Durham) and Eva E. Hayes (Belgrade, ME)
son [Maurice W.], b. 7/–/1891; third; Edward W. Hayes (shoe manufacturer, 43, Farmington) and Georgie A. Howe (37, Farmington)
son, b. 7/21/1894; third; Frank C. Hayes (bookkeeper, 38, Farmington) and Ida E. Connor (29, Farmington)
daughter, b. 3/13/1899; fifth; Charles E. Hayes (machine agent, 34, New Durham) and Georgia A. Hurd (22, South Berwick, ME)
son [Ralph], b. 8/7/1900; first; Alfonzo C. Hayes (shoe cutter, 24, New Durham) and Eva Caswell (22, Barnstead)
daughter [Laura E.], b. 12/14/1901; second; Alfonzo C. Hayes (shoe cutter, 27, New Durham) and Eva V. Caswell (23, Barnstead)
daughter, b. 8/1/1904; third; Alfonzo C. Hayes (hostler, 30, New Durham) and Eva B. Caswell (26, Barnstead)
daughter, b. 10/23/1909; third; Arthur G. Hayes (shoemaker, 28, New Durham) and Ethel M. Brooks (22, Farmington)
daughter [Theora], b. 10/23/1910; second; John P. Hayes (machinist, Farmington) and Lura S. Johnson (Farmington)
daughter [Iris Ella], b. 3/16/1911; fourth; Arthur G. Hayes (shoemaker, 28, New Durham) and Ethel M. Brooks (23, Farmington)
son [Maurice], b. 7/13/1916; second; Maurice W. Hayes (Goodyear welter, Alton) and Addie S. MacDonald (Lawrence, MA); residence - Alton
daughter, b. 3/13/1922; fourth; Arthur G. Hayes (shoeworker, New Durham) and Ethyl Brooks (Farmington)
A. Fred, b. 5/12/1907; second; Arthur G. Hayes (printer, 25, New Durham) and Ethel M. Brooks (19, Farmington)
Annie M., b. 12/27/1888; Frank C. Hayes (shoe manufacturer, 32, Farmington) and Ida E. Connor (23, Farmington)
Benjamin, b. 10/3/1925; fifth; Harry I. Hayes (shoemaker, NH) and Addie M. Hill (Strafford)
E. Pauline, b. 12/16/1908; second; William T. Hayes (clerk, 42, Farmington) and Inez Roberts (26, Rochester)
Frank P., Jr., b. 7/9/1923; second; Frank P. Hayes (shoemaker, Farmington) and Doris B. Curtis (Farmington)
Franklin B., b. 12/1/1902; first; Guy G. Hayes (shoemaker) and Clara M. Horne

Fred Raymond, b. 11/18/1900; first; Thomas T. Hayes (lumberman, 29, New Durham) and Eva Bessie Corson (18, Middleton)
Helen F., b. 3/–/1891; second; Frank C. Hayes (bookkeeper, 34, Farmington) and Ida E. Connor (26, Gilmanton)
Leon R., b. 5/2/1905; first; John R. Hayes (lumber mfgr., 24, Farmington) and Lura S. Johnson (21, Farmington)
Margy, b. 2/29/1904; first; Nehemiah B. Hayes (shoemaker, 61, New Durham) and Kate A. Sullivan (26, Cork County, Ireland)
Marion E., b. 4/28/1906; first; Arthur G. Hayes (printer, 24, New Durham) and Ethel M. Brooks (18, Farmington)
Robert, b. 11/2/1914; first; Maurice W. Hayes (shoemaker, Farmington) and Addie S. MacDonald (Farmington)
Ruhama, b. 8/20/1907; first; William T. Hayes (clerk, 41, Farmington) and Inez Roberts (25, Rochester)
Una Bessie, b. 1/8/1926; third; Frank P. Hayes (shoemaker, NH) and Doris B. Curtis (Farmington)
Virginia F., b. 1/30/1922; first; Frank P. Hayes (foreman, Farmington) and Doris B. Curtis (Farmington); residence - New Durham
William Tarlton, b. 11/30/1911; third; William T. Hayes (clerk, 45, Farmington) and Inez Roberts (29, Rochester)

**HAYNES,**
M. A. [daughter], b. 8/8/1905; first; John L. Haynes (shoemaker, 34, Farmington) and Nellie M. Leighton (27, Farmington)

**HAZEL,**
stillborn daughter, b. 2/1/1904; first; Walter T. Hazel (hostler, 37, Gloucester, MA) and Jennie P. Tarr (35, Gloucester, MA)

**HENDERSON,**
daughter, b. 3/15/1898; first; Herbert Henderson (farmer, 25, Farmington) and Flora Hurd (23, Farmington)
Franklin, b. 2/19/1911; second; William D. Henderson (clerk, 30, Farmington) and Mable D. Nickerson (29, Dedham, MA)
Lewis, b. 7/29/1899; eighth; George F. Henderson (farmer, 43, Farmington) and Lewancha M. Davis (31, Farmington)
Ruth G., b. 8/7/1895; first; Sylvanus B. Henderson (shoe operator, 20, Gloucester) and Winnifred Davis (22, Lee)

**HERSOM,**
Evelyn Grace, b. 2/18/1923; first; Fred A. Hersom (farmer, Lebanon, ME) and Grace Bunnell (Colebrook); residence - Lebanon, ME

**HIGGINS,**
Leslie Almon, b. 9/12/1913; second; Almon Elmer Higgins (shoemaker, Portland, ME) and Hala French (Los Angeles, CA)

**HILL,**
daughter, b. 9/10/1894; second; Albert L. Hill (clergyman, 27, Goodwin Mills, ME) and Florence B. Hamilton (25, Cape Elizabeth)
daughter, b. 6/28/1908; first; John S. Hill (laborer, 53, Strafford) and Hattie M. Kimball (23, Farmington)
son, b. 4/25/1917; fourth; Carroll C. Hill (shoemaker, Rockland, ME) and Ruth E. Libbey (W. Newfield, ME)
Arlene, b. 2/19/1927; second; Earle A. Hill (mill worker, New Durham) and Effie M. Thurston (Berwick, ME); residence - New Durham
Charles S., b. 6/6/1910; second; John S. Hill (laborer, Strafford) and Hattie M. Kimball (Farmington)
Earline, b. 2/19/1927; first; Earle A. Hill (mill worker, New Durham) and Effie M. Thurston (Berwick, ME); residence - New Durham
Katherine E., b. 5/19/1926; first; Arthur Hill (shoemaker, Rochester) and Elna B. Tirrell (Farmington); residence - Rochester

**HILTON,**
George William, b. 9/17/1934; first; George Hilton (laborer, Wells, ME) and Martha Adams (Ogunquit, ME)

**HITCHCOCK,**
son, b. 10/5/1921; fourth; Fred Hitchcock (farmer, England) and Matilda E. Labeus (Germany)
daughter, b. 1/31/1923; fifth; Fred Hitchcock (farmer, England) and Matilda Laben (Germany)

**HOAGE,**
son, b. 5/15/1924; fifth; James H. Hoage (clerk, Portland, ME) and Lucilla F. Hatch (Portland, ME)

son, b. 6/28/1925; sixth; James Hoage (grocery clerk, Portland, ME) and Lucille Hatch (NH)
daughter, b. 5/6/1928; seventh; James H. Hoage (clerk, Portland, ME) and Lucille Hatch (Farmington)
Betty Lou, b. 8/28/1930; eighth; James H. Hoage (storekeeper, Portland, ME) and Lucille F. Hatch (Portland, ME)
Donald Carl, b. 9/26/1932; ninth; James Hoage (store manager, Portland, ME) and Lucille Hatch (Portland, ME)
Donna Jean, b. 4/26/1935; tenth; James Hoage (store keeper, Portland, ME) and Lucille F. Hatch (Portland, ME)
Robert Clark, b. 5/29/1921; third; William A. Hoage (shoe worker, Portland, ME) and Mary E. Vincent (Fredericton, NB)

**HOGAN,**
son [Edward], b. 7/21/1909; first; Edward Hogan (shoemaker, 23, Lowell, MA) and Florence Campbell (21, Alton)
son [Kenneth], b. 2/12/1913; second; Edward F. Hogan (shoemaker, Lowell, MA) and Florence Tufts (Alton)
daughter [Margaret A.], b. 8/15/1914; third; Edward Hogan (shoemaker, Lowell, MA) and Florence Tufts (Alton)
daughter, b. 2/1/1918; fourth; Edward F. Hogan (shoeworker, Lowell, MA) and Florence M. Tufts (Alton)
son [Robert], b. 3/7/1920; fifth; Edward F. Hogan (shoemaker, Lowell, MA) and Florence M. Tufts (Alton)
daughter, b. 3/1/1923; sixth; Edward Hogan (shoemaker, Lowell, MA) and Florence Tufts (Alton)
daughter, b. 7/15/1924; seventh; Edward F. Hogan (shoemaker, Lowell, MA) and Florence Kimball (Alton)
son [John], b. 8/18/1925; fifth; Edwin Hogan (shoelaster, NH) and Florence M. Kimball (Farmington)
son [Richard], b. 12/22/1928; ninth; Edward F. Hogan (shoeworker, Lowell, MA) and Florence M. Kimball (Farmington)
Anna Alice, b. 3/17/1935; sixth; Joseph Hogan (shoeworker, New York City) and Pauline Terrill (Springvale, ME)
Patricia, b. 9/3/1930; tenth; Edward F. Hogan (shoeworker, Lowell, MA) and Florence M. Kimball (Alton)
Pauline Hazel, b. 2/10/1938; sixth; Joseph I. Hogan (shoeworker, New York City) and Pauline H. Tirrell (Springvale, ME)

**HOLDEN,**
son, b. 2/24/1916; second; H. Gerald Holden (shoeworker, ME) and Mabel J. Holden (NH)

**HOLMES,**
son, b. 10/–/1891; first; Charles W. Holmes (shoemaker, 23, Strafford) and Georgie Chesley (22, Farmington)
Charles L., b. 10/19/1892; first; Fred W. Holmes (shoemaker, 24, New Durham) and Minnie L. Pitman (housewife, 18, Farmington)
Gladdis M., b. 1/11/1897; first; Wilber F. Holmes (trav. salesman, 36, Tuftonboro) and Mamie G. Woodman (33, So. Tamworth)
Ralph, b. 12/28/1893; second; Charles W. Holmes (shoemaker, 25, Strafford) and Georgie M. Chesley (25, Farmington)

**HOPPER,**
Arthur Jeffrey, b. 4/4/1930*; second; Stanley R. Hopper (theological student, Fresno, CA) and Eva H. Bagley (Fresno, CA)

**HORNE,**
son [Charles A.], b. 6/20/1887; second; William H. Horne (shoemaker, 32, Farmington) and Mary E. Colbath (Wakefield)
daughter, b. 3/–/1891; second; Arista E. Horne (restaurateur, 33, Middleton) and Clara I. Parker (25, Middleton)
daughter [Edna M.], b. 6/23/1892; third; Clarence E. Horne (stable keeper, 41, Farmington) and Agnes L. Moore (housewife, 35, Natick, MA)
son [Earle E.], b. 11/12/1903; first; Irving E. Horne (clerk, 33, Farmington) and Lena G. Lucas (23, Farmington)
son [Blanchard R.], b. 9/4/1906; second; Irving E. Horne (clerk, 36, Farmington) and Lemar G. Lucas (26, Farmington)
stillborn son, b. 9/23/1906; first; Lorenzo A. Horne (reporter, 30, Rochester) and Elsie M. Pinkham (20, Farmington)
daughter, b. 7/18/1907; second; William W. Horne (shoemaker, 37, NH) and Bertha I. Jones (29, NH)
daughter, b. 3/23/1908; fourth; Frank O. Horne (shoemaker, 24, NH) and Elsie Varney (22, NH)
daughter, b. 7/12/1909; third; William H. Horne (shoemaker, 38, Whitefield) and Bertha I. Jones (36, Canaan)
son [George H.], b. 11/6/1915; first; William A. Horne (shoemaker, Farmington) and Mildred Perkins (Newfield, ME)

Barbara H., b. 5/1/1929; first; Harold E. Horne (shoemaker, Rochester) and Florence E. Burrell (E. Rochester)

Charles F., b. 4/28/1906; third; Fred I. Horne (shoemaker, 28, Farmington) and Marion Grimes (27, Dover)

Clarence W., b. 11/10/1917; second; William H. Horne (shoeworker, Farmington) and Mildred N. Perkins (Hampton)

Eva May, b. 12/7/1911; third; Irving E. Horn (sic) (clerk, 41, Farmington) and Lennar G. Lucas (31, Farmington)

Harry Burton, b. 4/25/1923; seventh; Lorenzo A. Horne (lumber mill operator, Rochester) and Elsie M. Pinkham (Farmington)

Margaret Irene, b. 8/2/1929; first; Hollis E. Horne (laborer, Belmont) and Elma M. Hart (Groton)

Oscar R., b. 3/29/1903; second; Fred I. Horne (shoemaker, 24, Farmington) and Mary Grimes (25, Dover)

Pearl, b. 10/19/1904; second; Fred I. Horne (shoemaker, 25, Farmington) and Mary N. Savage (27, Dover)

**HOWARD,**

daughter [Eva M.], b. 12/2/1887; ninth; Emery Howard (laborer, 39, Barrington) and Emma Canney (Madbury)

stillborn daughter, b. 10/17/1891; first; John W. Howard (laborer, 34, Barrington) and Annie Ferrell (27, Boston, MA)

son [Everett A.], b. 5/30/1905; tenth; Herbert Howard (shoemaker, 35, Rochester) and Lizzie Miller (35, Dover)

daughter, b. 5/3/1907; eleventh; Herbert Howard (shoemaker, 37, Gonic) and Elizabeth Miller (36, Dover)

stillborn son, b. 11/29/1908; eighth; Herbert O. Howard (shoemaker, 39, Gonic) and Elizabeth Nutter (37, Dover)

daughter, b. 7/9/1910; seventh; Herbert Howard (shoemaker, Gonic) and Lizzie Miller (Dover)

daughter, b. 10/23/1911; eighth; Herbert O. Howard (shoemaker, 42, Gonic) and Lizzie T. Miller (40, Dover)

Betty Louise, b. 1/27/1937; third; Herbert F. Howard (shoeworker, Dover) and Celinda H. Myers (Shelburne, VT)

Clayton E., b. 12/14/1929; first; Everett A. Howard (laborer, Farmington) and Annette Joy (Union)

Donald Leslie, b. 12/7/1934; second; Emery Howard (shoeworker, Northwood) and Jeanette Adams (Hampstead)

John Franklin, b. 7/14/1922; second; Herbert F. Howard (shoeworker, Dover) and Celinda Myers (Shelburne, VT)

Lawrence F., b. 7/20/1917; second; Herbert F. Howard (shoemaker, Dover) and Mary Patch (Alton)
Mabel, b. 7/30/1903; ninth; Herbert Howard (shoemaker, 33, Rochester) and Lizzie Miller (33, Dover)
Madeline P., b. 5/3/1916; first; Fred W. Howard (shoeworker, Haverhill, MA) and Madeline R. Ames (Rochester)
Myrtie May, b. 7/4/1920; third; Herbert F. Howard (shoemaker, Farmington) and Mary M. Patch (Alton)
Richard Harry, b. 12/6/1933; first; Emery Howard (shoeworker, Northwood Narrows) and Jeanette Adams (Barnstead)
Ronald J., b. 11/15/1938; first; Everett A. Howard (shoeworker, Farmington) and Marion Fossett (Everett, MA)

**HOWE,**
Lena R., b. 2/16/1907; first; Frank R. Howe (merchant, 23, Farmington) and Lena Duquette (17, Canada)

**HUCKINS,**
daughter [Laura E.], b. 7/5/1888; second; John A. Huckins (farmer, 22) and Ethel M. Huckins (19, Strafford)
son [Alden D.], b. 2/20/1891; fourth; John Huckins (farmer, 25, Farmington) and Ethel M. Scruton (21, Strafford)
son [J. Leslie], b. 9/7/1901; fifth; John A. Huckins (farmer, 35, Farmington) and Ethel M. Scruton (32, Strafford)
son, b. 3/17/1906; sixth; John A. Huckins (farmer, 40, Farmington) and Ethel M. Scruton (37, Strafford)
Alice Elizabeth, b. 5/23/1918; second; E. Guy Huckins (farmer, Farmington) and Ruth Brock (Rochester)
Everett G., d. 6/17/1887; first; John Huckings (sic) (farmer, 22, Farmington) and Ethel Huckings (Strafford)
John Herbert, b. 6/12/1934; second; Leslie Huckins (farmer, Farmington) and Annabelle Eton (Webster)
Mary Ethel, b. 12/24/1916; first; E. Guy Huckins (farmer, Farmington) and Ruth A. Brock (Rochester)
Robert Morris, b. 11/3/1925; third; E. Guy Huckins (farmer, Farmington) and Ruth A. Brock (Rochester)

**HULL,**
Doris M., b. 10/23/1907; second; Arthur Hull (shoemaker, 29, Rochester) and Lillian Parshley (23, Strafford)

Marjorie Arlene, b. 8/6/1913; second; Walter F. Hull (shoe operative, Dover) and Eleanor F. Blaisdell (Farmington)

**HUNT,**
son [Robert], b. 12/9/1915; fifth; Loren D. Hunt (Goodyear operator Epping) and Alice G. Connor (Haverhill, MA)
Alice E., b. 11/3/1919; seventh; Loren Hunt (machinist, Epping) an Alice G. Connor (Haverhill)
Barbara L., b. 10/24/1922; eighth; Loren D. Hunt (shoeworker, Epping) and Alice G. O'Connor (Haverhill, MA)
Edith M., b. 11/19/1924; Loren D. Hunt (shoestitcher, Epping) and Alice G. O'Connor (MA)
Irving Westley, b. 4/22/1918; sixth; Loren D. Hunt (shoeworker, Epping) and Alice G. Connor (Haverhill, MA)
Loren D., b. 9/19/1912; third; Loren D. Hunt (shoe operative, NH) and Ellis Gertrude Connor (MA)
Margaret Antoinette, b. 6/25/1914; fourth; Loring David Hunt (Goodyear operator, Epping) and Alice G. Connor (Haverhill, MA)
Mary E., b. 6/4/1911; second; Loren D. Hunt (shoemaker, 32, Epping) and Alice G. Connor (25, Haverhill, MA)
Wilfred, b. 1/28/1929*; third; William Hunt (farmer, New Baltimore, NY) and Marguerite Bonney (Kingston, MA)

**HUNTRESS,**
Nellie, b. 12/4/1890; first; Edwin M. Huntress (shoe finisher, 37, Boston, MA) and Eldora L. Leach (Lebanon, ME)

**HURD,**
son [Henry B.], b. 9/11/1896; first; Willie G. Hurd (laborer, 29, Milton) and Nellie A. Varney (27, Farmington)
daughter, b. 3/11/1898; second; Willie G. Hurd (laborer, 31, Milton) and Nellie Varney (29, Milton)
son [J. G.], b. 8/16/1899; third; Willie G. Hurd (laborer, 32, Milton) and Nellie A. Varney (30, Farmington)
daughter [Bernice T.], b. 8/23/1901; fourth; Will G. Hurd (teamster, 33, Milton) and Nellie A. Varney (32, Farmington)
child, b. 12/5/1902; Harry W. Hurd and Cora P. Canney
stillborn daughter, b. 2/1/1903; fifth; Willie G. Hurd (teamster, 36, Milton) and Nellie A. Varney (34, Farmington)

daughter, b. 1/23/1905; sixth; William G. Hurd (teamster, 38, Milton) and Nellie A. Varney (36, Farmington)

stillborn son, b. 5/16/1907; seventh; Will G. Hurd (farmer, 38, Milton) and Nellie A. Varney (37, Farmington)

daughter, b. 6/20/1907; first; Thomas Hurd (shoemaker, 26, Berwick, ME) and Cassie M. Tebbetts (26, Farmington)

daughter, b. 6/27/1909; second; Thomas Hurd (mfg. shoe findings, 29, Berwick, ME) and Cassie M. Tibbetts (29, Farmington)

son, b. 7/21/1910; third; Thomas Hurd (shoemaker, Berwick, ME) and Cassie Tibbetts (Farmington)

daughter, b. 9/10/1911; Thomas Hurd (shoemaker, 32, Berwick, ME) and Cassie M. Tibbetts (32, Farmington)

daughter, b. 4/18/1913; fifth; Thomas Hurd (shoemaker, Berwick, ME) and Cassie M. Tibbetts (Farmington)

**HUSSEY,**

son, b. 8/18/1912; first; Leland M. Hussey (shoe operative, Berwick, ME) and M. Delia Dunn (Southville, MA)

**HUTCHINS,**

stillborn son, b. 9/–/1891; first; Charles E. Hutchins (barber, 30, Madison) and Annie D. Coffin (32, Berwick)

son, b. 9/3/1895; Frank J. Hutchins (painter, 33, Madison) and Alice M. Wiggin (25, Farmington)

William R., b. 4/30/1924; first; William R. Hutchins (weaver, Springvale, ME) and Floretta L. C. Arnold (NH)

**IRISH,**

son, b. 3/7/1925; second; Earle W. Irish (shoeworker, NH) and Gladys E. Littlefield (Farmington)

Neal Alvard, b. 6/1/1920; first; Earle W. Irish (shoe worker, Conway) and Gladys E. Littlefield (Farmington)

**JACKSON,**

Betty Jeanne, b. 8/22/1933; second; William Jackson (shoeworker, Orford) and Gladys Vickers (Middlebury, VT)

William H., b. 1/24/1932*; first; William H. Jackson (shoe shop emp., Orford) and Gladys Vickers (Middlebury, VT)

**JACOBS,**
son [Albert], b. 7/20/1887; first; John L. Jacobs (laborer, 33, Rochester) and Amanda Currier (Canada)

**JAMIESON,**
Gilbert Edward, b. 10/21/1933; second; Rev. Paul Jamieson (minister, Rockland, ME) and Hannah Fall (Fall River, MA)

**JEFFERSON,**
son [Donald], b. 12/4/1912; third; Chester D. Jefferson (expressman, Boston, MA) and Stella M. Stackpole (Lebanon, ME)

**JENKINS,**
son [Harold], b. 2/27/1889; first; James K. Jenkins (shoemaker, 24, Lebanon, ME) and Laura Bell Hall (20, Dover)

**JEWELL,**
Leora A., b. 5/23/1922; second; Arthur Jewell (shoeworker, Joliet, IL) and Edna M. Horne (Farmington)

**JOHNSON,**
daughter [Jennie Bell], b. 3/20/1892; first; John Johnson (farmer, 26, Farmington) and Ida S. Meserve (housewife, 21, Madbury)
stillborn daughter, b. 1/10/1938; first; William Johnson (restaurant, Dover) and Grace Merrill (MA)
Paul, b. 9/–/1891; first; John D. Johnson (physician, 31, Port Byron, NY) and M. Adeline Barnes (Port Byron, NY)
Stella Constance, b. 1/21/1926; first; Andrew D. Johnson (boxmaker, Epping) and Constance I. Martin (New Bedford, MA)

**JONDREY,**
Evelyn Mae, b. 3/14/1929; second; Arnold Jondrey (laborer, Elmore, VT) and Emelyn Kimball (New York City)

**JONES,**
son, b. 6/7/1892; second; Onslow B. Jones (shoemaker, 21, Alton) and Amy L. Marston (housewife, 19, Alton)
son, b. 2/21/1896; fourth; D. W. Jones (mill superintendent, 33, Clifton Park, NY) and Iva Y. Beers (33, Lyons Plains, CT)

daughter, b. 8/19/1897; third; Everett J. Jones (shoemaker, 29, Candia) and Mattie C. Healey (29, Boston, MA)
daughter, b. 3/17/1898; first; David W. Jones (supt. of mill, 34) and Jessie G. Leighton (28, Farmington)
Earl M., b. 1/3/1893; third; Onslow B. Jones (shoemaker, 22, Farmington) and Amy L. Marston (20, Alton)
Evelyn M., b. 7/31/1906; first; Arthur R. Jones (clerk, 24, New Durham) and Lucy A. Worster (29, Somersworth)
Frances, b. 5/10/1911; first; Wilbur C. Jones (freight clerk, 32, New Durham) and Violet Stanley (23, Springfield, MA)

**JOSLIN,**
Ronald Sidney, b. 6/29/1938; first; Victor Joslin (shoeworker, Ashland, ME) and Goldie I. White (Ashland, ME)

**JOY,**
child, b. 2/14/1888; fifth; Cynthia Joy
stillborn son, b. 1/11/1928; first; Samuel Joy (mechanic, New Durham) and Hedwidge Cyr (Canada)

**KATAVALOS,**
Dorothy Loraine, b. 6/20/1935; second; Philip Katavalos (laborer, Lowell, MA) and Dorothy Cox (Edmunds, ME)

**KELLEY,**
son [Charles], b. 10/15/1887; first; Everett B. Kelley (laborer, 19, Farmington) and Emma F. Kelley (Portsmouth)
son, b. 7/28/1890; second; Everett B. Kelley (shoemaker, 22, Farmington) and Emma F. Kelley (Portsmouth)
son [Harry A.], b. 7/30/1890; James R. Kelley (clerk, 40, Derby, VT) and Ella Nason (NB)
Albert A., b. 4/23/1927; stillborn; first; Albert A. Kelley (shoeworker, Farmington) and Delma E. Dame (Wakefield)

**KENNEY,**
Richard Herbert, b. 10/26/1929; first; Raleigh D. Kenney (chauffeur, Rochester) and Florence Leighton (Farmington)

**KENNISTON,**
daughter, b. 9/27/1889; second; Samuel E. Kenniston (shoemaker, Dover) and Carrie E. Emery (Milton)

**KENT,**
Doris, b. 7/31/1912; third; Frank M. Kent (shoemaker, Eliot, ME) and Ethel M. Frothingham (Portsmouth)

**KEYES,**
Grace Ella, b. 2/10/1916; second; Lynn P. Keyes (farmer, VT) and Vera M. Robins (MA); residence - W. Townsend, MA

**KIMBALL,**
son [John], b. 11/3/1887; Samuel W. Kimball (shoemaker, 27, Middleton) and Addie R. Young (Farmington)
daughter [Edith B.], b. 1/22/1889; fourth; Samuel W. Kimball (shoemaker, 28, Middleton) and Addie R. Young (23, Farmington)
son [Herbert], b. 11/21/1889; eighth; David S. Kimball (shoemaker, Middleton) and Nellie M. Hanscomb (Dover)
daughter, b. 11/11/1890; second; Frank A. Kimball (expressman, 24, Middleton) and Kate S. Gray (21, Kingston)
daughter, b. 9/4/1891; first; Seth Kimball (farmer, 32, Alton) and Mamie Shaw (21, Farmington)
daughter, b. 4/6/1892; tenth; David S. Kimball (shoemaker, 40, Middleton) and Nellie Howard (housekeeper, 39, Dover)
son, b. 12/21/1892; third; Frank A. Kimball (laborer, 25, Middleton) and Katie S. Gray (housewife, 22, Kingston)
son, b. 5/3/1893; eleventh; David S. Kimball (shoemaker, 41, Middleton) and Nellie M. Hanscom (40, Dover)
daughter [Florence], b. 12/17/1893; fifth; Samuel W. Kimball (shoemaker, 33, Middleton) and Addie A. Young (28, Farmington)
son [Ernest], b. 3/30/1895; first; Clara Kimball (20, Middleton)
daughter, b. 7/17/1901; third; Martin L. H. Kimball (lumberman, 31, Alton) and Alice Hurd (23, Alton)
daughter, b. 7/19/1903; first; Alphonzo E. Kimball (laborer, 23, Middleton) and Myrtle Glidden (18, New Durham)
daughter, b. 6/16/1907; fourth; Alphonzo E. Kimball (laborer, 27, Middleton) and Myrtie E. Glidden (22, New Durham)
son [Oris S.], b. 6/16/1907; fifth; Alphonzo E. Kimball (laborer, 27, Middleton) and Myrtie E. Glidden (22, New Durham)
daughter, b. 2/22/1909; sixth; Alphonso Kimball (laborer, 29, Middleton) and Myrtie Glidden (23, New Durham)

daughter, b. 11/12/1911; second; Raymond H. Kimball (shoe
operative, 23, ME) and Louise Pippen (23, NH)
Chester A., b. 8/11/1914; first; John V. Kimball (shoemaker,
Farmington) and Sayde L. Gerrish (Haverhill, MA)
Doris Louise, b. 6/9/1915; third; Raymond Kimball (shoeworker,
Newfield, ME) and Louise Pippin (Union)
Edna Mary, b. 12/25/1897; second; Harry B. Kimball (teamster, 26,
Middleton) and Mabel M. Dixon (26, Farmington)
Gene Melvin, b. 6/17/1934; second; David Kimball, Jr. (shoeworker,
Hampstead) and Alice Ward (Portsmouth)
Harold L., b. 6/7/1902; third; Harry B. Kimball (laborer, 30,
Middleton) and Mabel M. Dixon (30, Farmington)
Helen Blanch, b. 8/23/1904; fourth; Harry B. Kimball (teamster, 32,
Middleton) and Mabel Dixon (32, Farmington)
Norman L., b. 7/5/1895; first; Harry B. Kimball (engineer, 23,
Middleton) and Mabel M. Dixon (23, Farmington)

**KING,**
daughter, b. 1/1/1913; fourth; Henry B. King (shoemaker, Calais,
ME) and Clara M. Stevens (Westfield, NB)
son, b. 8/19/1927; first; Charles A. King (salesman, Calais, ME) and
Bernice Wiggin (Bangor, ME)
Arlene Irene, b. 3/29/1931; fourth; Harry A. King (boxmaker, Alton)
and Irene M. Woodman (Alton)
Barbara May, b. 6/24/1934; first; Wendall King (shoeworker, Perry,
ME) and Sadie Chase (Meredith)
Carol June, b. 11/14/1937; third; Wendel King (shoeworker, Perry,
ME) and Sadie Chase (Meredith)
Eleanor Marie, b. 10/16/1935; second; Wendell King (shoeworker,
Perry, ME) and Sadie Chase (Meredith)
Elizabeth A., b. 10/29/1933; fifth; Harry A. King (box maker, Alton)
and Irene Woodman (Alton)
Gloria Maude, b. 9/21/1935; seventh; Harry E. King (highway
worker, Alton) and Irene M. Woodman (Alton)
James Earle, b. 8/17/1937; third; Frank King (laborer, Grand Pre,
NS) and Lucille Colbath (Milton Mills)
Robert Bruce, b. 2/27/1938; first; Samuel J. King (physician,
Ridgley, MD) and Francis Shelley (Williamsburg, PA)
Virginia, b. 12/22/1929; seventh; Stephen R. King (shoeworker,
Calais, ME) and Harriet D. Brooks (Leominster, MA)

**KINGSBURY,**
James Carlton, b. 7/22/1933; sixth; Sandy Kingsbury (farmer, Blaine, ME) and Ada Howard (Londonderry, NS)

**KINSMAN,**
son [Richard], b. 3/18/1930; first; Frank Kinsman (storekeeper, Wolfeboro) and Anne Towle (Farmington); residence - Somersworth

**KITCHEN,**
daughter [Norma L.], b. 3/25/1913; first; Paul L. Kitchen (shoe operative, Williamsport, PA) and Abbie L. Hanscam (Portsmouth)

**KNAPP,**
son [Arthur], b. 7/28/1920; second; Arthur C. Knapp (farmer, KS) and Delsie V. Van Metter (KS)

**KNOX,**
daughter [Mildred], b. 5/5/1897; third; Ulysses S. Knox (carpenter, 32, Stowe, ME) and Addie E. Whitehouse (30, Middleton)
son, b. 6/18/1912; first; Fred L. Knox (drug clerk, Farmington) and Millie B. Leighton (Farmington)
Arline E., b. 12/4/1917; second; Fred L. Knox (clerk, Farmington) and Mildred B. Leighton (Farmington)
Daniel D., b. 10/7/1938; second; Earl L. Knox (carpenter, Ossipee) and Lillian Campbell (Rowley, MA)
Fred, b. 3/16/1894; second; Ulysses S. Knox (carpenter, 30, Chatham) and Addie E. Whitehouse (28, Middleton)
Harry Wendell, b. 10/21/1923; first; Harry Knox and Blanche Rowe
Jacqueline Ann, b. 4/28/1935; second; Earl L. Knox (carpenter, W. Ossipee) and Lillian A. Campbell (Rowley, MA)
John Wesley, b. 4/18/1927; sixth; Earle L. Knox (carpenter, NH) and Eva Bickford (NH)
Muriel E., b. 2/21/1925; second; Harry Knox (carpenter, Farmington) and Blanche Rowe (Gilmanton)
Phyllis May, b. 12/4/1926; third; Harry Knox (carpenter, Farmington) and Blanche Rowe (Farmington)

**LACHANCE,**
Roberta Lee, b. 8/13/1936; first; P. LaChance (mgr., grocery store, Canada) and Venita O'Neil (Dover)

**LAJOIE,**
Florence M., b. 9/22/1927; first; Wilbrod Lajoie (mechanic, Lawrence, MA) and Exilia M. Willett (Rochester)
Richard A., b. 1/3/1932*; second; Wilbrod Lajoie (garage mgr., Lawrence, MA) and Exilia Willette (Rochester)

**LAMPER,**
Elizabeth M., b. 6/17/1923; second; Harland Lamper (laborer, Alton) and Annie I. Leighton (Middleton)

**LANCE,**
Ernest, b. 7/18/1927; seventh; Tony Lance (mason, Italy) and Ethel Berry (Rochester)

**LANGLEY,**
Edith R., b. 4/20/1935; first; Edith R. Langley (Moultonboro)

**LAPENE** [see Lepene, Lepine],
daughter, b. 2/20/1887; third; Peter Lapene (laborer, 28, Canada) and Ellen Fitzgerald (Canada)

**LAROCHE,**
Donald J., b. 1/25/1938; first; Lionel J. LaRoche (shoeworker, Canada) and Ethel May Lord (Porter, ME)

**LASALLE,**
daughter, b. 10/1/1902; third; Joseph I. LaSalle (barber, 21, Carthage, NY) and Clara M. Hudson (20, Hermon, NY)
Abd'a Z., b. 5/8/1908; sixth; Joseph I. Laselle (sic) (barber, 31, Carthage, NY) and Clara Hudson (26, Herman, NY)
Darold J., b. 7/24/1904; fourth; Joseph I. LaSalle (barber, 27, Carthage, NY) and Clara Hudson (23, Hermon, NY)
Lucy S., b. 6/6/1905; fifth; Joseph I. LaSalle (barber, 28, Carthage, NY) and Clara M. LaSalle (23, Herman, NY)

**LAWRENCE,**
son, b. 8/17/1927; first; Abbott Lawrence (shoeworker, Boston, MA and Arlene Place (Milton)
son, b. 5/10/1929; second; Abbott W. Lawrence (shoemaker, Boston, MA) and Arlene C. Place (Union)
James Oliver, b. 12/27/1936; fifth; A. W. Lawrence (shoeworker, Boston, MA) and Arlene C. Place (Farmington)
John W., b. 1/22/1938; first; John W. Lawrence (shoeworker, E. Bridgewater, MA) and Altice M. Adams (Farmington)
Richard Abbott, b. 11/27/1931; third; Abbott W. Lawrence (shoeworker, Boston, MA) and Arlene C. Place (Union)
Roger Arthur, b. 9/20/1933; fourth; Abbott W. Lawrence (shoemaker, Boston, MA) and Arlene C. Place (Farmington)

**LAWTON,**
Barbara Flora, b. 11/29/1938; second; James B. Lawton (shoeworker, Gloucester, MA) and Ida Cournoyer (Canada)

**LEAHY,**
James F., b. 10/24/1902; first; Joseph P. Leahy (shoemaker, 34, Farmington) and Alice J. Teague (32, Rochester)
James F., Jr., b. 4/29/1926; first; James F. Leahy (supply clerk, Farmington) and Margery Remick (Springvale, ME)

**LEAVITT,**
daughter, b. 7/5/1887; first; Charles J. Leavitt (lawyer, 27, Effingham) and Alice M. Tibbetts (Wolfeboro)
Roland G., b. 8/23/1898; first; Sidney A. Leavitt (merchant, -5, Farmington) and Isabella L. Giles (23, Northwood)

**LEBEL[L],**
stillborn child, b. 2/17/1930; second; Alfred LeBell (shoe cutter, Haverhill, MA) and Blanche Marcotte (Salmon Falls)
Corrine Doris, b. 1/2/1928; first; Alfred Lebel (shoemaker, Haverhill, MA) and Blanche Marcotte (Canada)

**LEE,**
Amelia Francis, b. 10/28/1901; first; Edward M. Lee (farmer, 59, Moultonboro) and Nellie L. Barry (35, Moultonboro)

**LEFAVOUR,**
Betty Jean, b. 12/2/1929; third; Ernest E. Lefavour (B&M station agent, Marblehead, MA) and Harriett Thayer (Farmington)
Robert Ernest, b. 3/3/1926; second; Ernest Lefavour (RR station agent, Marblehead, MA) and Harriet Thayer (Farmington)

**LEGRO,**
son [James], b. 8/30/1889; first; Edwin Legro (orange grower, Farmington) and Alice A. McClelland (Indianapolis, IN); residence - Astabula, FL

**LEIGHTON,**
daughter [Hazel M.], b. 5/7/1898; second; John H. Leighton (shoemaker, 24, Farmington) and Annie L. Perkins (22, Farmington)
daughter [Dorris], b. 12/22/1899; third; John H. Leighton (shoemaker, 25, Farmington) and Annie M. Perkins (23, Farmington)
daughter [Doris L.], b. 3/1/1903; fourth; John H. Leighton (shoemaker, 28, Farmington) and Annie Perkins (26, Farmington)
son [George], b. 1/6/1904; fourth; Harry I. Leighton (shoe cutter, 34, Farmington) and Maggie Troy (41, Danvers, MA)
Blanch E., b. 2/28/1896; first; John H. Leighton (shoemaker, 21, Farmington) and Annie Perkins (20, Farmington)
Millie B., b. 10/21/1888; A. F. Leighton (shoe finisher, 32, Farmington) and Emma Bennett (30, Farmington)
Robert Frank, b. 6/1/1933; first; Frank Leighton (laborer, Milton) and Cora B. Tufts (Middleton)
Roger W., b. 7/9/1917; first; Walter E. Leighton (shoeworker, Milton) and Georgia F. Lamper (Alton)

**LEONARD,**
Richard Lester, b. 12/11/1929; second; Lester S. Leonard (shoe cutter, NE) and Ruth E. Davis (Farmington)
Robert M., b. 3/1/1925; first; Lester S. Leonard (shoecutter, NE) and Ruth E. Davis (NH)

**LEPENE** [see Lapene, Lepine],
Donald M., b. 1/11/1938; second; Lawrence Lepene (elect. contractor, Farmington) and Nellie L. Miles (Farmington)

Richard L., b. 10/5/1932*; first; Lawrence A. Lepene (electrician, Farmington) and Nellie Miles (Farmington)

**LEPINE** [see Lapene, Lepene],
daughter, b. 10/22/1889; fourth; Joseph Lepine (laborer, Canada) and Georgie Veno (Canada)
son [John E.], b. 8/–/1891; fifth; Peter Lepine (shoe cutter, 38, Montreal, Canada) and Ellen Fitzgerald (42, Montreal, Canada)
son, b. 8/6/1920; third; John Lepine (shoe cutter, Farmington) and Hattie Maude Gray (Alton)
Delia, b. 11/26/1888; fourth; Peter Lepine (shoe cutter, 34, Montreal, Canada) and Ellen Lepine (39, Canada)
Lorance O., b. 12/24/1909; first; John E. Lepine (shoemaker, 18, Farmington) and Hattie M. Gray (20, Alton)

**LESPERANCE**,
Alvin Lewis, Jr., b. 5/4/1929; second; Alvin L. Lesperance (shoemaker, Lancaster) and Pauline H. Tirrell (Springvale, ME)
Barbara, b. 12/10/1927; first; Edwin Lesperance (shoeworker, Lancaster) and Pauline Tirrell (Springvale, ME)
Beverly P., b. 12/26/1930; third; Alvin Lesperance (laborer, Lancaster) and Pauline Tirrell (Springvale, ME)
Richard Keith, b. 6/26/1933; fifth; Alwyn Lesperance (shoeworker, Lancaster) and Pauline Terrill (Springvale, ME)

**LETOURNEAU**,
Annette, b. 1/8/1920; sixth; Louis Letourneau (farmer, Brocton, PQ) and Odenca Marcoux (Rochester)
Mary A. C., b. 4/8/1917; fifth; Louis Letourneau (shoeworker, Canada) and Audiana Marcoux (Rochester)

**LEVEILLEE** [see Leveiller],
Annette Deana, b. 5/17/1937; first; Walter Leveillee (shoeworker, Woonsocket, RI) and Marie Letourneau (Rochester)

**LEVEILLER** [see Leveillee],
Simon Louise, b. 10/19/1938; second; Walter Leveiller (shoeworker, Farmington) and Marie Letourneau (Rochester)

**LEVERILL,**
Estelle Yvette, b. 1/15/1927; first; Camille Leverill (laborer, Canada) and Alice Roy (Canada)

**LEVERTUE,**
Ralph Robert, b. 4/15/1927; first; Ralph R. Levertue (laborer, Rochester) and Alice K. Cathcart (Farmington)

**LEVESQUE,**
son [Joseph], b. 3/8/1924; first; Joseph A. Levesque (soldier, Lowell, MA) and Aurel S. Scott (NH)
Robert Albion, b. 5/23/1936; first; Alfred Levesque, Jr. (shoeworker, Sanford, ME) and Geraldine E. Bodwell (Springvale, ME)

**LEWIS,**
Benjamin F., b. 11/27/1927; first; Benjamin F. Lewis (shoeworker, Conway) and Addie E. Lougee (Farmington)

**LIBBEY,**
son, b. 7/22/1923; first; Joshua T. Libbey (laborer, Evansham) and Mabel Stanley (Evansham)
Charles F., b. 3/22/1897; first; Charles E. Libbey (locomotive fireman, 26, Concord) and Emma Dame (26, Farmington); residence - Amesbury, MA
Ida Jennie, b. 4/2/1925; second; Joshua Libbey (laborer, Effingham) and Mabel Stanley (Effingham)

**LIBERTY,**
Frank Philip, b. 1/10/1897; third; Joseph S. Liberty (shoemaker, 44, Senora, Canada) and Katy Fitch (40, New Haven, CT)
Fredrick P., 3$^{rd}$, b. 1/17/1937; first; Fredrick P. Liberty (shoeworker, Haverhill, MA) and Margaret Follansbee (Haverhill, MA)
Gail Norma, b. 2/18/1938; second; Fredrick Liberty (foreman, Haverhill, MA) and Margaret Follansbee (Haverhill, MA)
Sara Penfield, b. 5/31/1933; first; Normand P. Liberty (shoe salesman, Haverhill, MA) and Evelyn Howard (Cambridge, MA)

**LIGHT,**
Lloyd Paul, b. 9/2/1938; third; Peter P. Light (shoeworker, ME) and Ruth Garnier (Skowhegan, ME)

**LITTLEFIELD,**
daughter [Gladys E.], b. 5/1/1896; second; Fred A. Littlefield (blacksmith, 27, Fitchburg, MA) and Alma F. Kimball (23, Middleton)
daughter [Alte F.], b. 7/21/1897; third; Fred A. Littlefield (blacksmith, 28, Fitchburg, MA) and Alma F. Kimball (24, Middleton)
Bertha, b. 7/3/1903; fourth; Fred A. Littlefield (mechanic, 34, Fitchburg, MA) and Alma F. Kimball (30, Middleton)
Donald Albert, b. 6/26/1938; first; Donald Littlefield (truck driver, Berwick, ME) and Hilda M. Senter (S. Kingston)
Ethel Blanche, b. 6/5/1895; first; Fred A. Littlefield (blacksmith, 22, Fitchburg) and Alma F. Kimball (22, Middleton)

**LOCKE,**
daughter [Luella A.], b. 4/24/1890; second; Henry P. Locke (carriage painter, 22, Gilmanton) and Jennie M. Locke (Nottingham)
son, b. 7/15/1897; third; Henry P. Locke (painter, 29, Gilmanton) and Jennie M. Foss (29, Nottingham)

**LORD,**
son, b. 11/8/1921; third; William C. Lord (ice dealer, Rochester) and Elsie Pope (Wells, ME)
stillborn daughter, b. 12/17/1926; fourth; William Lord (fuel & ice dealer, Rochester) and Elsie Pope (Wells, ME)
Frank W., b. 9/24/1917; first; William C. Lord (shoemaker, Rochester) and Elsie J. Pope (Wells Beach, ME)
Lois Pearl, b. 10/31/1930; fifth; William S. Lord (wood & coal dealer, Rochester) and Elsie J. Pope (Wells, ME)
Robert Edward, b. 2/23/1920; second; William C. Lord (shipbuilder, Rochester) and Elsie J. Pope (Wells, ME)

**LOUGEE,**
son [Herbert C.], b. 7/4/1900; seventh; Nehemiah Lougee (shoemaker, 45, Farmington) and Julia Place (42, Sandwich)
stillborn daughter, b. 12/25/1904; second; Jacob Lougee (shoemaker, 26, Farmington) and Hattie Dyer (29, Sanbornville)
Addie E., b. 1/1/1910; fourth; Jacob A. Lougee (shoemaker, Farmington) and Hattie M. Dyer (Wakefield)

Edna E., b. 2/8/1889; first; William Lougee (shoemaker, 28, Alton) and A. Jennie Berry (30, New Durham)

Effie M., b. 7/19/1903; first; Jacob Lougee (shoemaker, 25, Farmington) and Hattie M. Dyer (28, Sanbornville)

Florence D., b. 7/2/1891; first; Chester N. Lougee (barber, 50, VT) and Catherine Foye (36, Milton)

Jean Annette, b. 6/21/1930*; first; Walter J. Lougee (shoecutter, Farmington) and Clarice A. Carpenter (Warren)

Joan Anita, b. 9/22/1931*; second; Walter Jacob Lougee (shoe cutter, Farmington) and Clarice Carpenter (Warren)

June Carmen, b. 6/24/1918; first; Herbert C. Lougee (shoeworker, Farmington) and Yvonne Labassiere (Marlboro, MA)

Martha E., b. 6/11/1892; sixth; Nehemiah Lougee (shoemaker, 37, Farmington) and Julia E. Place (housewife, 34, Farmington)

Mildred P., b. 11/13/1911; third; John S. Lougee (shoe operative, 30, PA) and Jessie M. Kimball (20, NH)

Walter, b. 4/15/1907; third; Jacob A. Lougee (shoemaker, 28, Farmington) and Hattie M. Dyer (31, Sanbornville)

**LOVEJOY,**

son, b. 3/6/1915; first; Willis A. Lovejoy (elec. RR foreman, Blanchard, ME) and Lura S. Johnson (Farmington); residence - Dover

**LOVERING,**

daughter [Marguerite], b. 12/13/1905; first; George A. Lovering (merchant, 24, Farmington) and Irma L. Davis (19, Farmington)

daughter [Madaline], b. 6/24/1909; second; Albert G. Lovering (clerk, 27, Farmington) and Irma L. Davis (23, Farmington)

Frank E., b. 3/25/1912; third; George Albert Lovering (clerk, Wakefield) and Irma L. Davis (Farmington)

**LOWELL,**

child, b. 11/5/1888; third; Stillman R. Lowell (shoe stitcher, 24, So. Hiram, ME) and Cora E. Lowell (21)

Norma Joan, b. 3/11/1926; seventh; Llewellyn Lowell (lumberman, NH) and Annie D. Woods (Somersworth)

Orson James, b. 8/11/1920; fifth; Lewellyn W. Lowell (lumber, New Durham) and Anna Woods (Somersworth)

**LUCIER,**
Roland G., b. 11/14/1915; fourth; Joseph Lucier (shoemaker, Canada) and Alma Phaneuf (Marlboro, MA)

**LUMB,**
son, b. 10/11/1900; fifth; Thomas S. Lumb (shoemaker, 32, England) and Lottie Marie Cutty (27, W. Brookfield, MA)

**LUND,**
son, b. 9/26/1907; first; Carol Lund (shoemaker, 19, Deerfield) an Delia Dunn (19, Southville, MA)

**MACK,**
son, b. 6/26/1889; first; James W. Mack (box maker, NS) and Winifred L. Cave (Alburgh, VT); residence - Nashua

**MAGEE,**
Charles A., b. 10/2/1924; first; Charles A. Magee (shoecutter, NH) and Cecelia B. Lawrence (MA)
George Wyman, b. 4/4/1926; second; Charles Magee (shoemaker Manchester) and Cecelia B. Lawrence (Jamaica Plain, MA)

**MANSFIELD,**
son, b. 8/25/1913; second; Ralph L. Mansfield (shoemaker, Dover and Grace Nutter (Farmington)

**MANSON,**
daughter, b. 7/5/1887; fifth; George H. Manson (laster, 40, Limeric ME) and Lizzie M. Longfellow (Boston, MA)

**MANSUR,**
Theresa Antoinette, b. 8/11/1935; seventh; Ernest Mansur (disable veteran, South Wakefield) and Mary Tetreau (Rutland, VT)

**MARCHAND,**
Leona F., b. 3/24/1924; first; Goodyear H. Marchand (barber, Rochester) and Florence H. Reynolds (Lynn, MA)

**MARCHANT,**
Virginia Louise, b. 8/9/1929; first; Frank A. Marchant (steamfitter, Gloucester, MA) and Estella M. Card (Brockton, MA); residence - Gloucester, MA

**MARCOU,**
William A., b. 6/8/1918; ninth; Fred Marcou (sawyer, Sheffield, VT) and Lila A. Ainsworth (E. Montpelier, VT)

**MARCOUX,**
Beatrice V., b. 2/21/1909; third; Joseph E. Marcoux (shoemaker, 29, Canada) and Annie Woods (25, Somersworth)
Gideon, b. 10/21/1917; eighth; Gideon J. Marcoux (shoeworker, Rochester) and Estella M. Lemire (Uxbridge, MA)
Joseph C., b. 3/18/1910; fourth; Joseph E. Marcoux (shoemaker, Canada) and Annie D. Woods (Somersworth)

**MARR,**
Clayton Remick, b. 7/22/1930; second; Charles O. Marr (shoeworker, Freeport, ME) and Pauline E. Remick (Farmington)
Jacqueline D., b. 3/17/1929; first; Charles O. Marr (shoeworker, Freeport, ME) and Pauline E. Remick (Farmington)

**MARSH,**
Fred Erskine, b. 12/21/1929; third; Fred E. Marsh (plumber, Gilmanton I.W.) and Gladys M. Dore (Alton)
Jennie Arlene, b. 8/22/1922; second; Fred E. Marsh (plumber's helper, Gilmanton) and Gladys M. Dore (Alton)

**MARSHALL,**
son, b. 12/21/1918; first; Lauriston B. Marshall (US Navy, Malden, MA) and Georgia A. Towle (Farmington); residence - Revere, MA
George Fredrick, b. 3/1/1935; first; George Marshall (store clerk, Medford, MA) and Elizabeth Hunt (Farmington)

**MARSTON,**
daughter, b. 7/9/1910; first; William H. Marston (shoemaker, Hopkinton, MA) and Sarah Dervire (Rogersville, NB)

daughter, b. 4/14/1912; second; William H. Marston (heelmaker, Hopkinton, MA) and Sarah Derwin (Rodgerville, NB)

**MARTIN,**
daughter, b. 9/3/1911; second; Jonathan A. Martin (stone cutter, 3?, Scotland) and Lillian C. Mason (25, Quincy, MA)
son, b. 2/23/1938; first; Theodore Martin (int. decorator, Cambridge, MA) and Beatrice Maly (Cambridge, MA)
Wesley G., b. 4/20/1912; first; William A. Martin (farmer, Taunton, MA) and Edith M. Gray (Farmington)

**MATTHEWS,**
son, b. 5/27/1898; first; Nelson H. Matthews (shoemaker, 24, Rochester) and Alice Pinkham (23, Farmington)
daughter, b. 8/30/1900; second; Nelson H. Matthews (shoemaker, 27, Rochester) and Alice Pinkham (26, Farmington)
daughter, b. 7/25/1904; third; Nelson H. Mathews (shoemaker, 30, Rochester) and Alice Pinkham (29, Farmington)

**MAYER,**
Leo, b. 1/15/1893; first; Max Mayer (merchant, 33, Griesheim, Germany) and Bertha Huz (21, Thingstadt, Germany)

**MAYOTTE,**
son [Harry C.], b. 12/25/1915; first; Fred Mayotte (Niggerhead [sic] op'tor, Nashua) and Lizzie Howard (Dover)

**McCOLLOUGH,**
child, b. 11/--/1924; Robert J. McCollough (shoeworker, Springvale, ME) and Sylvia Foss (Machias, ME)

**McCORMICK,**
daughter, b. 9/23/1889; fourth; Thomas J. McCormick (shoemaker, Malden, MA) and Helen L. Tanner (Farmington)
Medora, b. 2/11/1888; third; T. J. McCormick (32, Cambridge, MA) and Helen L. Tanner (21, Farmington)

**McCRILLIS,**
Robert Harold, b. 2/17/1929; first; Wilford H. McCrillis (shoeworker, Stoneham, MA) and Effie M. Howard (Farmington)

**McDONALD,**
daughter [Addie S.], b. 10/21/1891; first; Daniel McDonald (carpenter, 27, PEI) and Nellie M. Whitehouse (21, Middleton)
daughter [Florence E.], b. 12/14/1892; second; Daniel McDonald (carpenter, 28, PEI) and Nellie M. Whitehouse (housewife, 23, Middleton)

**McGIBBON,**
daughter, b. 7/15/1904; third; Andrew McGibbon (machinist, 40, Milton Mills) and Florence D. Willis (30, Brockton, MA)
Edward W., b. 5/25/1909; fourth; Andrew J. McGibbon (master mechanic, 46, East Saugus, MA) and Florence Willis (35, Brockton, MA)

**McKEAN,**
Robert James, b. 10/9/1937; second; Gerald McKean (shoeworker) and Margaret Taylor (Worcester, MA)

**McKENNEY,**
Norman, b. 11/29/1912; first; Alfred R. McKenney (mill, Scarboro, ME) and Ethel Gray (Rochester); residence - Rochester

**MERCIER,**
son, b. 10/24/1912; ninth; Anselme Mercier (clerk, Canada) and Kilda Grenier (Canada)

**MERRILL,**
Arlene Betty, b. 3/16/1929; second; Wilbur Merrill (shoeworker) and Catherine Roark (Boston, MA)
Arthur Harcott, b. 10/22/1933; first; Arthur H. Merrill (shoe shop emp., Farmington) and Alice Stevens (Attleboro, MA)
Everett Leroy, b. 12/20/1935; first; Leroy Merrill (shoeworker, Springfield, MA) and Esther Hedges (Springfield, MA)
Irene Beth, b. 3/16/1929; first; Wilbur Merrill (shoeworker) and Catherine Roark (Boston, MA)
Ralph Edward, b. 3/25/1937; second; Arthur Merrill (shoeworker, Hamilton, MA) and Alice Stevens (Attleboro, MA)

**MESERVE,**
daughter [Florence A.], b. 3/6/1891; third; Samuel Y. Meserve (McKay stitcher, 68, Rochester) and Julia S. Gilman (33, Danvers, MA)
son, b. 8/19/1908; first; Karl Meserve (shoe cutter, 20, Farmington) and Hildred C. Peterson (18, Lockport, NS)
son, b. 3/9/1910; second; Karl G. Meserve (shoe cutter, Farmington) and Hildred C. Peterson (Lockport, NS)
son, b. 10/28/1915; third; Karl G. Meserve (shoecutter, Farmington) and Hildred C. Peterson (NS)
Carl G., b. 9/11/1888; Samuel Y. Meserve (McK' stitcher, 63, Rochester) and Julia S. Gilman (29, Danvers, MA)

**MILES,**
daughter, b. 1/14/1914; first; John F. Miles (shoemaker, Portsmouth) and Sarah A. Barsantee (Portsmouth)

**MILLER,**
son [Ray], b. 6/27/1909; second; William G. Millar (sic) (laborer, 2 Dover) and Faith Card (21, Farmington); residence - Dover
Beverly Ann, b, b. 1/24/1937; first; Ray S. Miller (shoeworker, Lowell, MA) and Flora B. Reynolds (Lynn, MA)
Dorothy M., b. 3/2/1910; fourth; Harry T. Miller (shoemaker, Salem MA) and Hattie West (NS)
Edward, b. 6/9/1929; second; Ray S. Miller (laborer, Farmington) and Elsie M. Young (Farmington)
Herman, b. 4/3/1911; first; Joseph Miller (shoemaker, 21, Boston, MA) and Gertrude Montgomery (18, Dover)
Richard, b. 9/20/1928; eighth; John H. Miller (cook, Farmington) and Lois G. Hatch (Lyman, ME)
Roy S., Jr., b. 7/6/1928; first; Roy S. Miller (laborer, Farmington) and Elsie M. Young (Farmington)

**MILLINER** [see Milner],
son [Robert], b. 6/10/1918; second; James W. Milliner (teamster, NS) and Ardena B. French (New Durham)
son [Elmor], b. 7/22/1919; third; James W. Milliner (teamster, NB) and Ardena E. French (New Durham)

**MILNER** [see Milliner],
Vinton, b. 7/24/1920; fourth; James W. Milner (woodsman, NB) and Ardena French (New Durham)

**MILTON,**
Mabel Alice, b. 8/3/1937; second; George Milton (lumberman, Wells, ME) and Martha Adams (Ogunquit, ME)

**MONTEE,**
daughter [Florence M.], b. 9/3/1887; third; John Montee (laborer, 35, Canada) and Lucy Montee (Graham, ME)

**MONTGOMERY,**
Claire Elaine, b. 7/20/1935; first; Melvin Montgomery (shoe worker, Farmington) and Ruth E. Wentworth (Lebanon, ME)
Marion Clara, b. 9/4/1913; first; William P. Montgomery (shoemaker, Lynn, MA) and Lillie M. Pitts (New Bedford, MA)
Mary M., b. 10/31/1895; third; William W. Montgomery (hotel keeper, 34, Fairfield, VT) and Mary Margarette (31, Penacook)
Melvin A., b. 12/29/1914; second; William P. Montgomery (shoemaker, Lynn, MA) and Lillian Pitts (New Bedford, MA)
Ralph Sherman, b. 1/28/1922; first; William Montgomery (shoeworker, Lynn, MA) and Ida Chase (Dover)
Ruth Lillian, b. 11/29/1937; second; Melvin Montgomery (shoeworker, Farmington) and Ruth Wentworth (Lebanon, ME)

**MOONEY,**
Elizabeth Mary, b. 11/25/1925; fourth; Francis Mooney (manufacturer, MA) and Geneva Perry (VT)
George W., b. 9/21/1924; third; Francis J. Mooney (manufacturer, MA) and Geneva Perry (VT)

**MORRISON,**
son, b. 8/3/1890; first; John R. Morrison (shoemaker, 28, CA) and Ellen A. Morrill (27, Wilmot)
daughter, b. 10/17/1932*; fourth; Roger H. Morrison (dentist, Boston, MA) and Mary Corson (Milton)
Barbara Jean, b. 11/9/1929; second; Roger H. Morrison (dentist, Boston, MA) and Mary L. Corson (Milton)
Edward Hamlin, b. 1/20/1931*; third; Roger Morrison (dentist, Boston, MA) and Mary L. Corson (Milton)

Mary Louise, b. 8/14/1935; fifth; Roger Morrison (dentist, Boston, MA) and Mary Corson (Milton)

**MOTT,**
Clarence M., Jr., b. 4/21/1926; first; Clarence Mott (shoemaker, East Rochester) and Alma Randall (Greenville)
Constance J., b. 4/27/1927; second; Clarence M. Mott (shoeworke East Rochester) and Alma E. Randall (ME)

**MOULTON,**
daughter [Arabell], b. 1/15/1887; seventh; George E. Moulton (watchman, 32, Moultonboro) and Janette Hill (New Durham)
daughter, b. 6/24/1890; ninth; George E. Moulton (edge setter, 36 Tamworth) and Jeanette C. Hill (New Durham)
stillborn son, b. 10/23/1899; first; Justin C. Moulton (shoemaker, 2 Farmington) and Minnie M. Ham (19, Farmington)
son [Harold], b. 9/26/1900; second; Chester A. Moulton (shoemaker, 21, Farmington) and Edith M. Ham (20, Farmington)
son, b. 9/12/1902; fourth; Chester A. Moulton (farmer, 22, Farmington) and Edith M. Ham (23, Farmington); residence - New Durham
daughter, b. 3/30/1904; fifth; Chester Moulton (laborer, 25, Farmington) and Edith Ham (24, Farmington); residence - Ne Durham
son [Herbert J.], b. 5/23/1906; second; John P. Moulton (farmer, 3 Farmington) and Martha A. Babb (25, New Durham)
daughter [Doris I.], b. 8/9/1927; third; Chester E. Moulton (laborer, Farmington) and Teresa M. Carpenter (Sanford, ME)
Addie J., b. 5/4/1888; eighth; George E. Moulton (heel burner, 33, Tamworth) and Jeanette C. Hill (30)
Chester A., b. 7/12/1925; second; Chester Moulton (laborer, Farmington) and Tresa Carpenter (Sanford, ME)
Chester E., b. 6/24/1933; fifth; Chester W. Moulton (laborer, Farmington) and Teresa M. Carpenter (Sanford, ME)
Doris J., b. 5/17/1900; first; John P. Moulton (farmer, 24, Farmington) and Martha A. Babb (20, New Durham)
Evelyn Arlene, b. 7/18/1928; first; Herbert F. Moulton (laborer, NH and Elizabeth A. Lane (East Rochester)
John Herbert, b. 12/27/1929; second; Herbert P. Moulton (laborer, Milton Mills) and Elizabeth A. Carpenter (E. Rochester)

Robert Edwin, b. 10/19/1929; fourth; Chester E. Moulton (laborer, Farmington) and Theresa M. Carpenter (Sanford, ME)

Shirley Arlene, b. 3/17/1935; sixth; Chester E. Moulton (shoeworker, Farmington) and Theresa Carpenter (Sanford, ME)

**MUDGETT,**
Stanley Robert, b. 2/25/1938; first; Robert Mudgett (shoeworker, C. Sandwich) and Elizabeth Carter (Farmington)

**MURPHY,**
daughter [Estella], b. 12/25/1894; eighth; William S. Murphy (laborer, 51, Dover, NS) and Mary M. Harding (33)

Bertha A., b. 1/24/1893; seventh; William Murphy (laborer, 52, NS) and Margaret Harding (31, NS)

**MYERS,**
Eugene Francis, b. 11/11/1937; second; William Myers (shoeworker, Manchester) and Irene Coulombe (Weare, MA)

**NASON,**
son [Leslie I.], b. 4/22/1890; second; Laureston M. Nason (shoe stitcher, 30, Eaton) and Abbie M. Ayers (Wakefield)

Ethel B., b. 8/20/1888; Laureston M. Nason (stitcher, 27, Eaton) and Abbie M. Ayers (20, Wakefield)

**NEDEAU,**
son [Ralph I.], b. 6/29/1894; second; Walter S. Nedeau (shoemaker, 21, Farmington) and Bina C. Labonte (24, Farmington)

son, b. 3/4/1916; second; Ralph I. Nedeau (shoeworker, Farmington) and Alda A. Marcoux (Rochester)

Dorothy A., b. 6/5/1915; first; Ralph I. Nedeau (shoeworker, Farmington) and Alda A. Marcoux (Rochester)

Harold G., b. 5/8/1893; first; Walter S. Nedeau (shoemaker, 20, Farmington) and C. Bina Labonte (23, Farmington)

**NENNDORF,**
Joan, b. 10/27/1921; third; Otto C. Nenndorf (steamfitter, Boston, MA) and Marjorie E. Hurney (Boston, MA)

**NEWMAN,**
Aleane, b. 3/3/1893; third; Frank C. Newman (shoemaker, 27, Portsmouth) and Jennie E. Tucker (24, Penacook)
Harold D., b. 6/22/1887; first; Frank Newman (shoemaker, 21, Portsmouth) and Eva J. Tucker (Penacook)
Merle F., b. 7/26/1889; second; Frank C. Newman (shoemaker, Portsmouth) and Eva J. Tucker (Penacook)

**NICHOLS,**
son [Ivan], b. 2/13/1899; second; Archie B. Nichols (shoe cutter, 28, W. Concord) and Mary Osborne (31, Gilmanton)
Inette Marie, b. 1/13/1927; third; Fred Nichols (shoeworker, Amesbury, MA) and Eva E. Roy (St. Charles, PQ)
Lilah E., b. 7/13/1890; first; Joseph E. Nichols (dentist, 39, Ashbury, MA) and Ella C. Smith (Boston, MA)
Lionel F., b. 8/3/1924; first; Fred J. Nichols (shoemaker, Amesbury MA) and Eva E. Roy (Sherbrook, Canada)
Ruth E., b. 9/10/1924; second; Joseph Nichols (laborer, NH) and Mary Peavey (NH)
Vivian F., b. 10/17/1895; first; Archie B. Nichols (shoe cutter, 24, Concord) and May C. Osborn (28, Gilmanton)
William Eddy, b. 2/3/1928; fourth; Fred Nichols (shoemaker, Amesbury, MA) and Eva Roy (Canada)

**NOUSE,**
stillborn daughter, b. 1/31/1908; first; Ernest Nouse (RR, 20, Medway, MA) and Grace O'Connell (19, Medway, MA); residence - Medway, MA

**NOYES,**
Herbert L., b. 10/5/1910; first; Everett N. Noyes (shoemaker, Farmington) and Henrietta Johnson (New Hampton)
Herbert Neil, b. 1/27/1887; first; Chester S. Noyes (shoemaker, 32, Oakham, MA) and Inez Whitehouse (Middleton)
Russell D., b. 11/18/1898; first; William B. Noyes (school teacher, 27, Farmington) and Susie E. Dowe (22, Farmington)

**NUTE,**
son, b. 10/15/1889; first; Frank E. Nute (shoemaker, Farmington) and Eva M. Gilman (Hallowell, ME)

son, b. 12/24/1916; seventh; Raymond E. Nute (shoeworker, Farmington) and Florence Beesley (ME)

Harry, b. 3/–/1891; third; Eugene P. Nute (shoe manufacturer, 39, Farmington) and Nellie S. Parker (34, Wolfeboro)

Mollie E., b. 4/7/1893; fourth; Eugene P. Nute (shoe manufacturer, 41, Farmington) and Nellie S. Parker (36, Wolfeboro)

Rhoda W., b. 1/11/1924; second; Harry A. Nute (mail carrier, Farmington) and Helen Wadleigh (Wakefield)

**NUTTER,**

son, b. 6/13/1887; second; Charles E. Nutter (saloon keeper, 35, Barnstead) and Iva Cloutman (Alton)

son, b. 2/28/1889; first; John M. Nutter (shoemaker, 29, Milton) and Edith M. Brown (21, Farmington)

daughter, b. 8/22/1889; third; Charles E. Nutter (restauranteur, Barnstead) and Iva I. Cloutman (Alton)

son, b. 2/7/1890; third; George M. Nutter (shoemaker, 30, Pittsfield) and Leah K. Hayes (Farmington)

daughter [Zelma], b. 7/28/1901; second; Joseph F. Nutter (shoe heeler, 44, Gilmanton) and Lilla E. Babb (29, Riverphillip, NS)

son [Ralph A.], b. 11/11/1903; third; Joseph F. Nutter (shoemaker, 46, Gilmanton) and Lilla E. Babb (31, River Philip, NS)

daughter, b. 9/17/1908; second; Harry F. Nutter (clerk, 26, Farmington) and Lucy B. Bennett (24, Farmington)

son, b. 12/25/1908; first; John C. Nutter (agt. & shoemaker, 21, Alton) and Julia Dufresne (21, Laconia)

son, b. 7/9/1927; fifth; Arthur J. Nutter (shoeworker, Alton) and Ethel E. Brown (Alton)

Harry W., b. 4/20/1911; first; Charles Watson (wood carver, 20) and Hazel Nutter (18, Dover); residence - Alton

Hazel Irene, b. 10/10/1899; first; J. Freeman Nutter (shoemaker, 41, Gilmanton) and Lilla E. Babb (27, NS)

Pauline, b. 1/26/1926; fourth; Arthur Nutter (shoemaker, NH) and Ethel E. Brown (NH)

Robert Dana, b. 6/23/1930; sixth; Arthur John Nutter (shoe cutter, Alton) and Ethel E. Brown (Laconia)

Rogers Alfred, b. 4/15/1913; fifth; Joseph F. Nutter (shoemaker, Gilmanton) and Lilla E. Babb (River Philip, NS)

Winnie B., b. 3/21/1888; George M. Nutter (shoemaker, 28, Pittsfield) and Lettie Hayes (23)

**OIKLE,**
Aubrey M., b. 8/10/1929; fifth; Vernon Oikle (laborer, NS) and Hazel E. Mason (Halifax, NS)
Earle Allen, b. 2/16/1931; sixth; Vernon A. Oikle (shoeworker, Shelburne, NS) and Hazel E. Mason (Halifax)

**OTIS,**
son, b. 3/13/1889; second; John D. Otis (wheelwright, 39, Farmington) and Susie B. Pitman (35, Barnstead)
son, b. 7/27/1892; third; John D. Otis (carriage builder, 42, Farmington) and Susan B. Pitman (housewife, 42, Barnstead)
son [Clarence], b. 5/6/1909; second; George E. Otis (farmer, 37, Farmington) and Naomia Babb (28, Strafford)
Esther E., b. 9/25/1907; first; Norman L. Otis (undertaker, 23, Farmington) and Susie M. Meserve (24, Danvers, MA)
Evelyn N., b. 12/23/1909; second; Norman L. Otis (undertaker, 26 Farmington) and Susie Meserve (26, Danvers, MA)
Gerald Edwin, b. 9/11/1908; first; Albert J. Otis (teamster, 32, Farmington) and Leora F. Horne (24, Alton)
Hazel S., b. 12/30/1909; first; Harry L. Otis (clerk, 20, Farmington) and Josephine Sullivan (22, Newton, MA)

**PACKER,**
child, b. 10/16/1924; Leroy H. Packer (shoeworker, Haverhill, MA) and Dorothy A. Rhodes (Portsmouth)
Elaine June, b. 6/25/1926; second; Leroy H. Packer (shoemaker, Haverhill, MA) and Dorothy A. Rhodes (Portsmouth)

**PAGE,**
son [Ernest], b. 1/16/1902; fourth; Walter E. Page (shoemaker, 27, Manchester) and Bertha M. Healey (22, Danbury)
Joseph, b. 4/9/1929; first; Harold Page (laborer, Farmington) and Lydia Ferland (Farmington)
Raymond Charles, b. 8/1/1937; first; Raymond Page (shoeworker, Rochester) and Ona Gray (Grafton)

**PAIGE,**
June Louise, b. 8/8/1935; second; Della Paige (Loudon)
Kenneth H., b. 12/8/1938; second; Della H. Paige (Loudon)

**PARE,**
son, b. 10/16/1930*; Conrad Pare (woodheeler, Norwich, PQ) and Alma Dupre (Hudson, MA)

**PARENT,**
daughter, b. 8/26/1925; ninth; Edward Parent (teamster, Canada) and Celam Carron (Canada)
Albert Edward, b. 5/16/1920; tenth; Edward Parent (wood chopper, Canada) and Celina Caron (Canada)
Alice M., b. 12/10/1918; ninth; Edward Parent (woodcutter, Canada) and Salina Caron (Canada)
Evelyn, b. 11/11/1917; stillborn; eighth; Edward Parent (woodsman, Canada) and Celavaire Carron (Canada); residence - Rollinsford
Gaudias, b. 9/9/1926; thirteenth; Edward Parent (wood dealer, Canada) and Celinde Caron (Canada)
Lena, b. 3/5/1923; eleventh; Edward Parent (laborer, Canada) and Selina Coran (Canada)

**PARKER,**
son, b. 1/5/1914; third; James H. Parker (laborer, Portland, ME) and Elizabeth S. Grimes (Dover)
Rachel M., b. 9/29/1899; second; John C. Parker (physician, 35, Lebanon, ME) and Jennie E. Mirrless (26, Providence, RI)
Sewall C., b. 12/16/1910; first; Frank S. Parker (shoemaker, Wolfeboro) and Catherine M. Carroll (Ireland)

**PARKINSON,**
Everton Harry, Jr., b. 9/20/1936; second; Everton Parkinson (head master, Lawrence, MA) and Edna Hoffman (Manchester)

**PARROCK,**
son, b. 9/2/1910; first; William R. Parrock (shoemaker, Cambridge, MA) and Maude Furber (Alton)

**PARSHLEY,**
Ardys Laurel, b. 9/1/1925; first; Richmond H. Parshley (clerk, Strafford) and Bernice A. Adams (Farmington)
Floyd Atwood, b. 9/5/1935; fifth; Richmond Parshley (store mgr., Strafford) and Bernice Adams (Farmington)

Frank Charles, b. 11/21/1927; third; Richmond H. Parshley (merchant, Strafford) and Bernice A. Adams (Farmington)
Lois Adams, b. 1/9/1931; fourth; Richmond Parshley (mgr. of stor Strafford) and Bernice Adams (Farmington)
Richmond H., b. 11/19/1926; second; Richmond Parshley (prop. candy store, Strafford) and Bernice Adams (Farmington)

**PARTICELLI,**
Celestine, b. 7/3/1905; fifth; Giovanni Particelli (clerk, 38, Lucca, Italy) and Amelia Bansanti (38, Lucca, Italy)

**PATCH,**
son, b. 2/9/1908; fifth; John Patch (laborer, 39, Milton) and Gertrude Clarke (29, Gilmanton); residence - Milton

**PAULIOT,**
daughter, b. 3/15/1911; second; Edward J. Pauliot (shoemaker, 3( Sanbornville) and Excelia Sturgeon (28, Milton Mills)

**PAULSON,**
daughter, b. 8/3/1914; first; John A. Paulson (farmer, Sweden) an( Alice M. Huckins (Strafford)
Charles Ufford, b. 1/24/1918; third; John A. Paulson (farmer, Sweden) and Alice M. Huckins (Strafford)
Robert A., b. 9/17/1916; second; John A. Paulson (farmer, Swede and Alice M. Huckins (Strafford)

**PEARL,**
son [Preston L.], b., 4/13/1895; second; Preston A. Pearl (coal dealer, 37, Farmington) and Mattie Carney (30, NS)
son [Harold H.], b. 8/29/1902; first; Hervey Pearl (painter, 39, Farmington) and Ina B. Canney (33, Alton)
Florence M., b. 11/13/1898; third; Preston A. Pearl (coal dealer, 4( Farmington) and Mattie Keanney (33, NS)
Millie, b. 7/13/1893; first; Preston A. Pearl (wood & coal dealer, 35 Farmington) and Mattie A. Came (28, NB)

**PEARSON,**
son, b. 7/7/1899; first; Frank P. Pearson (clergyman, 34, Newburyport, MA) and Rose Sanborn (31, Holderness)

son [Haydn], b. 4/2/1901; second; Frank Pearson (clergyman, 36, Newburyport, MA) and Rose R. Sanborn (33, Holderness)
daughter, b. 4/5/1902; third; Frank P. Pearson (clergyman, 37, Newburyport, MA) and Rose R. Sanborn (34, Holderness)

## PEAVEY,
son [Merton L.], b. 7/–/1891; first; Will L. Peavey (pharmacist, 26, Farmington) and Alice E. Leavitt (22, Farmington)
Carrol W., b. 10/31/1904; second; Ernest F. Peavey (shoe cutter, 47, Farmington) and Edna P. Wallace (21, Farmington)
Cyril W., b. 5/9/1903; first; Ernest F. Peavey (shoe cutter, 45, Farmington) and Pansy Wallace (20, Farmington)
Edna J., b. 4/13/1890; second; Henry K. Peavey (shoe cutter, 31, Farmington) and Josephine A. Jenkins (New Durham)

## PELLERIN,
John Lewis, b. 1/25/1932*; first; Jesse L. Pellerin (headmaster, Hanover) and Cora Stacey (Manchester)
Mary Ann, b. 11/23/1934; second; Jesse Pellerin (headmaster, Hanover) and Cora Stacy (Manchester)

## PELLETIER,
Carol Louise, b. 8/31/1936; first; Louis P. Pelletier (shoeworker, Farmington) and Marion L. Blaisdell (Derry)
Cynthia Anne, b. 9/8/1938; second; Louis Pelletier (shoeworker, Sanford, ME) and Marion Blaisdell (Derry)
Joseph R. L., b. 8/12/1912; third; George J. Pelletier (grocer, Springvale, ME) and M. Delia Dunn (Fraserville, PQ)
Lawrence, b. 9/8/1914; first; David L. Pelletier (grocery clerk, ME) and Marion Jones (Farmington)

## PENCE,
Arthur Leland, b. 8/13/1921; fifth; Horace C. Pence (shoe cutter, Cutler, ME) and Cecil Bertha Stanley (Parsonsfield, ME)
Edward L., b. 6/12/1912; second; Horace C. Pence (shoemaker, Cutler, ME) and Cecil Bertha Stanley (Parsonsfield, ME)
Elizabeth Ida, b. 4/4/1915; third; Horace C. Pence (shoemaker, Cutler, ME) and Cecil Bertha Stanley (Parsonsfield, ME)
Horace Stanley, b. 4/22/1920; fourth; Horace C. Pence (shoe cutter, Cutler, ME) and Cecil B. Stanley (Parsonsfield, ME)

Lester C., b. 6/5/1911; first; Horace C. Pence (shoemaker, 22, Cutler, ME) and Cecil Bertha Stanley (20, Parsonsfield, ME)

**PENNOCK,**
son, b. 4/17/1926; second; Eddie Pennock (shoemaker) and Sarah E. Emery (Fairfield, ME); residence - Lowell, MA

**PERION,**
Joseph, b. 8/16/1911; eighth; Joseph P. Perion (laborer, 42, Saint Mary, Canada) and Delphine Boulouger (34, Canada)

**PERKINS,**
son [Malcolm R.], b. 9/19/1889; second; Luther H. Perkins (carpenter, Milton) and Teresa McDonald (PEI)
stillborn son, b. 6/8/1891; third; B. Frank Perkins (carriage manufacturer, 35, Strafford) and Lucy A. Stiles (35, Strafford)
son, b. 7/20/1901; first; Lewellyn C. Perkins (shoemaker, 24, No. Berwick, ME) and Mary A. Turigan (22, Ireland)
daughter, b. 2/11/1902; first; John H. Perkins (clerk, 26, Strafford) and Winifred B. Hill (23, Strafford)
son [Ralph L.], b. 8/21/1902; second; Llewellyn C. Perkins (shoemaker, 26, Berwick, ME) and Mary A. Flunigan (24, Kileouly, Ireland)
daughter, b. 3/24/1908; fourth; Llewellyn C. Perkins (laborer, 31, Berwick, ME) and Mary A. Finnegan (29, Ireland)
Abbie G., b. 4/22/1912; fifth; Everett C. Perkins (physician, Berwick, ME) and Louise M. Todd (Rowley, MA)
Alice M., b. 10/11/1906; third; Everett C. Perkins (physician, 36, Berwick, ME) and Louise M. Todd (33, Rowley, MA)
Charles Lugene, b. 11/4/1933; first; Charles L. Perkins (laborer, Meredith) and Mary Carolyn Austin (West Canaan)
Constance J., b. 5/13/1923; second; Herbert S. Perkins (shoemaker, New Durham) and Rosana Pouliot (Rochester)
Daniel N., b. 10/22/1909; fourth; Everett C. Perkins (physician, 39, Berwick, ME) and Louise M. Todd (35, Rowley, MA)
Edith G., b. 2/3/1938; third; Otis J. Perkins (laborer, Wolfeboro) and Hattie E. Twombly (Wolfeboro)
Ernest Ray, b. 3/13/1936; third; Charles Perkins (laborer, Meredith) and Mary Austin (West Canaan)
Herbert, Jr., b. 12/15/1917; first; Herbert Perkins (shoemaker, New Durham) and Rosanna Pouliot (Rochester)

Leon C., b. 1/5/1901; second; James N. Perkins (shoeworker, 29, Middleton) and Eolie E. Cater (24, Strafford)

Luther E., b. 4/2/1895; third; Luther H. Perkins (mechanic, 45, Farmington) and Teresa McDonald (34)

Lyndall, b. 1/5/1901; first; James N. Perkins (shoeworker, 29, Middleton) and Eolie E. Cater (24, Strafford)

Marion E., b. 10/26/1902; first; Alton M. Perkins (shoemaker, 21, Brookfield) and Mertie M. Lucas (17, Farmington)

Maurice Lloyd, b. 11/9/1936; second; Lloyd Perkins (filling station, Milton) and Dora Hayes (Dover)

**PERRAULT,**

Ronald T., b. 5/21/1930; second; Eldros Perrault (laborer, Sanford, ME) and Beatrice Morin (Springvale, ME)

**PETERSON,**

daughter, b. 3/9/1897; sixth; Enos L. Peterson (picture framer, 31, Lockeport, NS) and Sarah M. McDonald (26, PEI)

son [Dallas], b. 2/3/1899; seventh; Enoch L. Peterson (picture framer, 33, NS) and Sarah M. McDonald (28, PEI)

son, b. 5/5/1901; sixth; Enos L. Peterson (prac. machinist, 35, Lockport, NS) and Sarah McDonald (31, Souris, PEI)

son [Lester], b. 4/27/1904; ninth; Enos L. Peterson (machinist, 39, NS) and Sarah Burnham (35, PEI)

son [Lindsay V.], b. 8/15/1907; tenth; Enos L. Peterson (machinist, 41, NS) and Sarah McDonald (37, PEI)

son, b. 4/29/1909; eleventh; Enos L. Peterson (machinist, 43, NS) and Sarah M. McDonald (39, PEI)

Hazel, b. 5/9/1895; fifth; Enos L. Peterson (picture framer, 29, Lockeport, NS) and Sarah M. McDonald (25, PEI)

**PHILBRICK,**

Wesley John, b. 3/17/1934; first; Wesley Philbrick (laborer, Wolfeboro) and Louise Clough (Wolfeboro)

**PICAR,**

daughter, b. 11/6/1887; second; Louis Picar (laborer, Canada) and Dena Picar (Canada)

**PIKE,**
daughter, b. 7/16/1889; second; John C. Pike (shoemaker, Middleton) and Alice M. Arnold (Wells, ME)
daughter [Mary Alice], b. 2/24/1891; second; Harris Pike (watchman, 28, Canada) and Adell Bishop (24, Canada)
son [Harry], b. 2/6/1894; third; Harris Pike (mechanic, 31, St. Stevens, NB) and Hattie Bishop (27, Mt. Calmet, BQ)
daughter [Viola M.], b. 12/14/1896; fourth; John C. Pike (shoemaker, 31, Middleton) and Alice Arnold (26, Wells, ME)
daughter, b. 7/9/1901; third; Ernest E. Pike (hotel clerk, 27, St. Stephens, NB) and Maud E. Kenney (21, Lebanon, ME)
daughter [Josephine R.], b. 11/24/1901; fifth; John C. Pike (shoe laster, 36, Middleton) and Alice M. Arnold (31, Wells, ME)
daughter [Alice E.], b. 5/18/1906; sixth; John C. Pike (shoemaker, 40, Middleton) and Alice M. Arnold (36, Wells, ME)
son, b. 9/17/1906; fourth; Edgar E. Pike (heel fitter, 34, Farmington) and Maude Kenney (25, Lebanon)
daughter, b. 8/4/1910; seventh; John C. Pike (shoemaker, Middleton) and Alice Arnold (Wells, ME)
daughter, b. 2/13/1911; first; J. Elver Pike (shoe operative, 27, Farmington) and E. Ellen Cloutman (30, Farmington)
Audrey Una, b. 1/12/1927; second; Sumner Pike (shoeworker, Rochester) and Edith C. Cameron (Hoboken, NJ)
Bertha C., b. 10/28/1890; third; John C. Pike (shoemaker, 25, Middleton) and Alice M. Arnold (20, Wells, ME)
Ellen Pearl, b. 4/20/1912; second; John Elver Pike (shoemaker, Farmington) and Elizabeth E. Cloutman (Farmington)
Etta H., b. 7/26/1924; first; Sumner E. Pike (shoemaker, Rochester) and Edith C. Cameron (W. Hoboken, NJ)
Harry R., b. 3/27/1925; first; Harry Pike (shoeworker, Farmington) and Florence G. Dodge (Farmington)
John C., b. 3/11/1888; John L. Pike (laster, 22, Middleton) and Alice Arnold (18, Wells, ME)
John E., Jr., b. 7/8/1921; third; John E. Pike (poultry merchant, Farmington) and Ellen E. Cloutman (Farmington)
Royden Harold, b. 11/7/1930*; second; Harry Pike (shoemaker, Farmington) and Florence G. Dodge (Farmington)

**PILLSBURY,**
Betty Lou, b. 12/8/1933; fourth; Chester Pillsbury (shoeworker, Andover, MA) and Marie David (Puerto Rico)

Chester, Jr., b. 8/9/1928; second; Chester Pillsbury (gardener, Andover, MA) and Maria David (Puerto Rico)
Marie, b. 10/19/1935; fifth; Chester Pillsbury (shoeworker, Andover, MA) and Marie E. David (Puerto Rico)

**PINKHAM,**
daughter [Vellie J.], b. 3/25/1887; second; Frank Pinkham (grocery clerk, 29, New Durham) and Sophronia C. Pinkham (Farmington)
daughter, b. 4/4/1887; second; James Y. Pinkham (shoe finisher, 36, Wolfeboro) and Hester E. Davis (Farmington)
daughter, b. 3/10/1892; second; Seth Pinkham (shoemaker, 27, Alton) and Nellie M. Davis (housewife, 21, Farmington)
son, b. 10/11/1892; first; David T. Pinkham (peddler, 21, Farmington) and Hattie F. Goodwin (lady, 19, Milton Mills)
stillborn son, b. 9/26/1895; third; Alphonzo R. Pinkham (shoemaker, 45, Hollis, ME) and Georgie E. Wigglesworth (38, Farmington)
stillborn son, b. 6/1/1909; second; Clifton S. Pinkham (shoe cutter, 22, Pittsfield) and Mary Anderson (23, No. Conway)
Clifton S., b. 7/16/1908; first; Clifton S. Pinkham (shoemaker, 27, Pittsfield) and Mary Anderson (29, Conway)
Clinton C., b. 6/2/1888; Seth H. Pinkham (shoemaker, 24, Alton) and Nellie Davis (17, Northwood)
John A., b. 9/13/1895; second; James Y. Pinkham (shoe fitter, 41, Wolfeboro) and Hester A. Davis (32, Farmington)

**PIPER,**
son, b. 10/20/1902; fifth; Edwin L. Piper (shoemaker, 48, Wolfeboro) and Bertha Tripp (34, Sanford, ME)
stillborn son, b. 6/29/1925; fourth; Leba Piper (Effingham Falls)
Dorothy A., b. 12/8/1921; fourth; Leba Piper (Effingham)
Vernon Fall, b. 8/8/1920; third; Leba M. Piper (Effingham Falls)

**PLACE,**
daughter, b. 8/6/1887; third; Albert J. Place (carpenter, 23, Farmington) and Mary J. Place (Dover)
daughter [Nellie], b. 1/19/1890; fourth; James A. Place, Jr. (carpenter, 23, Farmington) and Mary J. Austin (Dover)
daughter, b. 7/20/1906; seventh; James A. Place (carpenter, 42, Farmington) and Mary Austin (38, Dover)

son [Clyde], b. 7/16/1915; fourth; Percy Place (shoeworker, Farmington) and Freena M. Lover (Wakefield)
son, b. 4/18/1918; fourth; Percy Place (shoemaker, Farmington) and Freena ----- (Wakefield)
Frank Arthur, b. 3/27/1937; second; Norman W. Place (shoework( Wakefield) and Alma Parsons (Northwood)
Lawrence E., b. 1/11/1932; first; Percy Place (shoeworker, Middleton) and Esther Belle Dore (Farmington)
Roger, b. 11/14/1919; sixth; Percy Place (shoemaker, Farmington and Freena ----- (Union)
Stanley L., b. 9/19/1912; third; Percy Place (shoe operative, Farmington) and Freena Lover (Milton)

**PLUMMER,**
daughter, b. 1/18/1890; eleventh; Lorenzo C. Plummer (shoemak( 43, Farmington) and Ella J. Osborne (Gilmanton)

**POLLARD,**
Richard, Jr., b. 4/21/1923; second; Richard Pollard (shoeworker, Millis, MA) and Belle Bickford (NH)
Virginia F., b. 6/29/1922; first; Richard Pollard (shoeworker, Millis, MA) and Mary B. Bickford (Waterboro)

**POND,**
stillborn son, b. 4/21/1902; first; William Pond (shoemaker, 26, West Medbury, MA) and Cassie Tebbetts (22, Farmington)

**POULIOT,**
Gloria Ruth, b. 9/1/1937; second; Edward Pouliot (shoeworker, Milton Mills) and Flora Rollins (S. Berwick, ME)

**PRESCOTT,**
daughter [Rita M.], b. 9/29/1914; first; G. Almon Prescott (electrician, Strafford) and Florence E. MacDonald (Farmington)
daughter, b. 9/16/1916; second; George A. Prescott (electrician, Strafford) and Florence E. MacDonald (Farmington)
son [Leonard], b. 5/27/1918; third; George A. Prescott (electrician, Strafford) and Florence E. McDonald (Farmington)

**PRESTON,**
daughter, b. 12/3/1889; seventh; James F. Preston (lumberman, Fox River) and Elizabeth Dupresne (Fox River)
daughter, b. 11/–/1891; eighth; James F. Preston (laborer, 38, Canada) and Elizabeth Ash (38, Canada)
daughter, b. 2/16/1897; tenth; James S. Preston (mechanic, 45, Fox River, Canada) and Elizabeth Ash (45, Fox River, Canada)
Arthur Walter, b. 6/29/1932; first; Russell W. Preston (laborer, East Rochester) and Marie C. Raab (Des Moines, IA)
Effie A., b. 3/11/1888; sixth; James F. Preston (36, Canada) and Elizabeth Dupresne (36, Canada)
Jerry, b. 7/11/1893; ninth; James F. Preston (laborer, 39, Canada) and Elizabeth Nosh (39, Canada)

**PRIDE,**
Ernest T., b. 27/1896; first; Henry W. Pride (stone cutter, 36, Portland, ME) and Rosalie Henaff (19, Sidney, Cape Breton)

**PRIME,**
William Merrill, b. 11/29/1915; first; William I. Prime (dentist, VT) and Blanche C. Heath (NH)
Winona D., b. 6/16/1917; second; William I. Prime (dentist, VT) and Blanche C. Kelley (NH)

**PULSIFER,**
stillborn son, b. 8/24/1907; first; Walter H. Pulsifer (merchant, Madbury) and Helen Lovering (Farmington)
Charles Henry, b. 5/13/1936; fourth; John Pulsifer (shoeworker, Milton) and Rachel Stanhope (Dennisville, ME)
John Lincoln, b. 7/20/1932; third; John L. Pulsifer (shoe operative, Milton) and Rachel Stanhope (Densmore, ME)
Norma Madelyn, b. 8/6/1928; second; John L. Pulsifer (shoemaker, Milton) and Rachael H. Stanhope (Dennysville, ME)
Patricia I., b. 8/29/1926; first; John L. Pulsifer (shoemaker, Milton) and Rachael H. Stanhope (Edmunds, ME)
Winnifred A., b. 1/14/1910; first; John L. Pulsifer (shoemaker, Milton) and Ruth A. Avery (Farmington)

**RAAB,**
    daughter, b. 3/14/1929; tenth; Adolph G. Raab (carpenter, Germany) and Marion Kopp (Homestead, IA)

**RAND,**
    child, b. 12/28/1906; third; George M. Rand (carpenter, 30, Randolph) and Rosie E. Perkins (23, Bartlett)
    Louise E., b. 4/22/1923; second; Ernest Rand (shoeworker, Milton) and Grace Ham (Farmington)
    Melvin Clifford, b. 3/14/1921; first; Ernest Wilotte Rand (shoe worker, Milton) and Grace G. Ham (Farmington)

**RANDALL,**
    Evelyn May, b. 10/10/1928; first; Roland E. Randall (laborer, Nottingham) and Hazel S. Smith (Nottingham)
    Roswell J., b. 3/29/1918; first; John F. Randall (shoeworker, New Durham) and Ina Glidden (Farmington)

**RANSIER,**
    stillborn son, b. 12/15/1890; first; A. J. Ransier (harness maker, 26, Charleston, SC) and Francis Witsell (19, St. Augustine, FL)

**REED,**
    son, b. 4/22/1916; second; Dana C. Reed (shoeworker, Boston, MA) and Rosie L. Bruce (Boston, MA)
    Ella A., b. 5/10/1917; first; Charles S. Reed (shoemaker, Natick, MA) and Edna E. Barrett (Francestown)

**REEVES,**
    Beulah May, b. 11/15/1922; stillborn; second; Howard V. Reeves (foreman, Freetown, PEI) and Eva G. Dodge (Barrington)
    Pearl Helen, b. 3/21/1913; first; Howard V. Reeves (shoe operative, PEI) and Eva Dodge (Barrington)

**REGIS,**
    daughter, b. 7/13/1915; second; John Regis (shoeworker, Nashua) and Bessie Haddock (Farmington)
    son, b. 9/28/1916; third; John D. Regis (shoeworker, Nashua) and Bessie S. Haddock (Farmington)
    Elda, b. 2/23/1919; fourth; John D. Regis (shoeworker, Nashua) and Bessie S. Haddock (Farmington)

John Darrell, b. 5/1/1914; first; John Regis (operator, Derry) and Bessie Haddock (Farmington)
Regina Pearl, b. 5/26/1927; eleventh; John D. Regis (shoeworker, Nashua) and Bessie Haddock (Farmington)

**REID,**
Doris W., b. 1/8/1917; first; Frederick W. Reid (shoemaker, NS) and Cassie M. Skillins (ME)
Virginia Mabel, b. 11/23/1916; first; Philip F. Reid (shoeworker, NB) and Mabel Stanley (NH)

**REMICK,**
daughter [Pauline], b. 1/14/1908; ninth; Nathaniel P. Remick (shoemaker, 45, Sutton, MA) and Mary Sprague (35, Grafton, MA)
son [Everett], b. 12/11/1911; tenth; Nathaniel P. Remick (shoemaker, 48, Sutton, MA) and Mary Sprague (38, Grafton, MA)
son, b. 12/19/1913; first; Joseph F. Remick (shoemaker, Worcester, MA) and Vianna F. Varney (Farmington)
stillborn child, b. 4/19/1927; first; Clayton S. Remick (shoeworker, ME) and Elva P. Holland (ME)
Elwood C., b. 9/3/1918; second; Charles E. Remick (shoeworker, Milton) and Hattie M. Kimball (Farmington)
Florence L., b. 9/17/1917; first; Charles E. Remick (shoemaker, Milton) and Hattie M. Kimball (Farmington)
George P., b. 5/18/1916; second; Joseph F. Remick (shoeworker, Worcester, MA) and Vianna F. Varney (Farmington)
Robert Wallace, b. 1/28/1923; third; Edgar Remick (shoemaker, Milton) and Carrie Grace (Albany)

**REYNOLDS,**
George Carlton, b. 6/29/1923; first; George Reynolds (shoemaker, MA) and Frances N. Perkins (NH)
George W., b. 2/24/1921; thirteenth; Elmer S. Reynolds (lumberman, New Durham) and Gertrude Clark (Gilmanton)

**RHODES,**
daughter, b. 2/16/1913; fourth; Nicholas Rhodes (shoemaker, Oswego) and Ada Rackham (New Glasgow, NF)

**RICE,**
daughter, b. 8/26/1912; first; Clarence Rice (laborer, MA) and Add Garland (Rochester); residence - Haverhill, MA

**RICHARDS,**
Floyd Frederick, b. 3/5/1920; first; Fred L. Richards (restaurant keeper, Canada) and Amelia Belanger (Littleton)

**RICHARDSON,**
son, b. 8/16/1887; Charles O. Richardson (paper maker, 36, Fayette, ME) and Gertie E. Card (Farmington); residence - Bridgewater, MA

daughter, b. 10/3/1889; second; James W. Richardson (shoemaker, Upton, ME) and Agnes L. Richards (Cambridge)

son [Alfred J. L.], b. 12/7/1895; fourth; Ai J. Richardson (laborer, 3, Upton, ME) and Lydia A. Holden (36, Stewartstown)

daughter [Annie M.], b. 9/24/1897; fifth; Ai J. Richardson (mason, 40, Upton, ME) and Lydia Holden (39, Stewartstown)

daughter, b. 10/2/1900; first; Joel A. Richardson (laborer, 40, Rinsey, PQ) and Katie P. L. Richardson (18, Magalloway)

stillborn son, b. 4/23/1935; ninth; Alfred Richardson (laborer, Farmington) and Blanche Daniels (Yarmouth, ME)

Alfred J. L., Jr., b. 11/7/1923; fourth; Alfred J. L. Richardson (laborer, Farmington) and Blanche Daniels (Yarmouth, ME)

Arline Jessie, b. 8/21/1915; first; Ernest A. Richardson (farmer, Northwood) and Marion W. Thompson (New Durham)

Beatrice M., b. 11/12/1921; second; Ernest A. Richardson (farmer, Northwood) and M. Richardson (New Durham)

Carleton David, b. 6/2/1937; tenth; Alfred Richardson (railroad emp., Farmington) and Blanche Daniels (Yarmouth, ME)

Catherine A., b. 3/1/1921; third; Alfred J. L. Richardson (RR laborer, Farmington) and Blanche Daniel (Yarmouth, ME)

Edson E., b. 6/24/1930; seventh; Alfred J. S. Richardson (B & M RR, Farmington) and Blanche Daniels (Yarmouth, ME)

Eleanor Lydia, b. 9/16/1928; sixth; Alfred J. L. Richardson (track laborer, Farmington) and Blanche R. Daniels (Yarmouth, ME)

John Edwin, b. 8/1/1919; second; Alfred J. L. Richardson (shoemaker, Farmington) and Blanche R. Daniels (Yarmouth, ME)

Olive D., b. 8/3/1892; third; A. J. Richardson (farmer, 33, Upton, ME) and Lydia A. Holden (housewife, 32, Stewartstown)

Oliver Arthur, b. 1/29/1933; eighth; Alfred J. L. Richardson (RR employee, Farmington) and Blanche R. Daniels (Yarmouth, ME)

Oman Philip, b. 9/6/1925; fifth; Alfred J. L. Richardson (RR section hand, Farmington) and Blanche R. Daniels (Yarmouth, ME)

**RICKER,**
stillborn daughter, b. 4/8/1893; first; Charles H. Ricker (laborer, 37, Wolfeboro) and Mary A. Cloutman (23, Farmington)

daughter, b. 7/15/1903; fourth; Bertred E. Ricker (shoemaker, 29, Farmington) and Mattie Kearney (38, St. John, NB)

daughter, b. 8/8/1903; sixth; Charles H. Ricker (laborer, 48, Wolfeboro) and Mary A. Cloutman (33, Farmington)

stillborn son, b. 6/22/1906; second; B. E. Ricker (shoemaker, 32, Farmington) and Mattie Kearney (40, Fredericton, NB)

stillborn son, b. 4/11/1911; first; Irving J. Ricker (musician, 25, Farmington) and Mable G. Ross (25, Acton, ME)

son [Robert], b. 2/4/1919; third; Fred Ricker (shoeworker, S. Berwick, ME) and Alta M. Edgerly (Farmington)

Arlene Matty, b. 9/5/1923; fifth; Peter Ricker (shoemaker, So. Berwick, ME) and Alta M. Edgerly (Farmington)

George, b. 9/24/1895; third; Charles H. Ricker (laborer, 40, Wolfeboro) and Mary Cloutman (25, Farmington)

Harriet S., b. 12/4/1913; second; Harry W. Ricker (clerk, Wolfeboro) and Adelaide M. Quint (Milton)

John, b. 4/7/1898; fourth; stillborn; Charles H. Ricker (laborer, 43, Wolfeboro) and Mary A. Cloutman (28, Farmington)

Mabel, b. 5/23/1899; fifth; Charles H. Ricker (laborer, 44, Wolfeboro) and Mary A. Cloutman (30, Farmington)

Ralph Albert, b. 8/29/1920; fourth; Peter Ricker (shoemaker, S. Berwick, ME) and Alta May Edgerly (Farmington)

Randall, b. 1/24/1906; first; Harry Ricker (clerk, 32, Wolfeboro) and Addie Quint (30, Farmington)

**RIEF,**
Leslie Jean, b. 3/18/1936; first; Leslie Rief (shoeworker, Canada) and Marjorie Roberts (Rochester)

**RILEY,**
James Clyde, b. 4/4/1937; first; James A. Riley (laborer, Methuen, MA) and Glenna M. Edgerly (Farmington)

**RING,**
- Annie Ellen, b. 11/18/1918; second; Terrence F. Ring (shoeworker, Farmington) and Mary E. Flynn (Rockport, MA)
- Mary Catherine, b. 9/25/1916; first; Terrence F. Ring (shoeworker, Farmington) and Mary E. Flynn (Rockport, MA)

**RIOUX,**
- Ronald Joseph, b. 7/28/1913; thirteenth; Alfred J. Rioux (brickmaker, Canada) and Emily M. Morin (Canada)

**ROBERTS,**
- stillborn son, b. 9/26/1889; first; Charles W. Roberts (shoe cutter, Farmington) and Carrie E. Cloutman (Alton)
- daughter [Helen], b. 12/21/1890; second; Will W. Roberts (pharmacist, 40, Farmington) and Eloise A. Flanders (33, Danbury)
- son [Perley James], b. 6/7/1891; second; Herbert H. Roberts (farmer, 37, Farmington) and Mary E. Noyes (36, IL)
- daughter [Gertrude Lurleen Estelle], b. 9/30/1897; first; Frank H. Roberts (shoemaker, 30, Farmington) and Gertrude E. Lund (25, Warren)
- daughter [Winona], b. 6/3/1898; first; Elmer D. Roberts (merchant 0, Gorham, ME) and Lizzie H. Hand (30, Burlington, VT)
- son [Charles Connor], b. 6/14/1906; first; Harry F. Roberts (shoe cutter, 20, Farmington) and Edith F. Connor (19, Farmington)
- David Charles, b. 11/9/1935; second; Charles C. Roberts (shoeworker, Farmington) and Amelia King (Dover)
- Eloise, b. 4/5/1911; first; George C. Roberts (druggist, 24, Farmington) and Florence I. Lougee (22, Farmington)
- Janet Mae, b. 11/18/1934; third; Albert Roberts (painter, Laconia) and Mae Alcock (Newfoundland)
- Shirley, b. 10/11/1911; fourth; Harry Roberts (fireman, 25, Rochester) and Edith F. Connor (24, Farmington)

**ROBINSON,**
- son, b. 6/2/1887; second; Willie Robinson (laborer, 18, Rochester) and Sadie Robinson (Rochester)

**ROGERS,**
son [George], b. 3/22/1913; second; George J. Rogers (shoe operative, Boston, MA) and Irenia P. Davis (San Francisco, CA)
Eldon R., b. 1/23/1911; first; Charles C. Rogers (physician, 33, Windham, ME) and Alice I. Roberts (28, Rochester)
Harold Floyd, b. 2/12/1926; sixth; George I. Rogers (shoemaker, Haverhill, MA) and Irene P. Jones (San Francisco, CA)
John C., b. 6/2/1921; fourth; George J. Rogers (shoe worker, Haverhill, MA) and Irene P. Jones (San Francisco, CA)
Roy, b. 8/15/1923; fifth; George J. Rogers (shoemaker, Haverhill, MA) and Irene P. Jones (San Francisco)
Violetta P., b. 9/11/1916; third; George P. Rogers (shoeworker, Haverhill, MA) and Irene P. Jones (San Francisco, CA)

**ROLLINS,**
daughter [Lillian M.], b. 10/10/1887; first; John A. Rollins (29, Rochester) and Ruth L. Towle (Wolfeboro)
daughter [Elsie F.], b. 11/28/1889; second; John A. Rollins (shoemaker, Rochester) and Ruth L. Towle (New Durham)
stillborn son, b. 7/23/1890; second; Irving Rollins (shoemaker) and Annie Hubbard
son [Harold C.], b. 6/–/1891; third; John A. Rollins (shoe packer, 33, Rochester) and Ruth L. Towle (28, New Durham)
daughter [Abbie J.], b. 3/22/1892; fourth; Irving H. Rollins (shoemaker, 36, Alton) and Annie M. Hubbard (housewife, 38, Farmington)
daughter, b. 9/29/1892; first; Edwin F. Rollins (teamster, 24, New Durham) and Vinnie E. Burnham (housewife, 18, Farmington)
daughter [Abbie E.], b. 7/17/1902; first; Irving H. Rollins (laborer, 41, Alton) and Hattie F. Clark (17, Alton)
son [Roland], b. 5/18/1904; second; Erving H. Rollins (laborer, 41, Alton) and Hattie F. Clark (19, Alton)
daughter, b. 9/14/1905; third; Irving H. Rollins (laborer, 47, Alton) and Hattie F. Clark (20, Alton)
daughter [Venna M.], b. 4/30/1911; fifth; Irving H. Rollins (laborer, 53, Farmington) and Addie F. Clark (24, Alton)
daughter, b. 12/29/1913; first; Cyrus Rollins, Jr. (shoemaker, Somersworth) and Nellie Chandler (Hampton Beach)
daughter [Flora E.], b. 12/7/1915; sixth; Irving H. Rollins (shoeworker, Alton) and Mattie F. Clark (Alton)

son, b. 3/29/1920; first; Harold C. Rollins (woodturner, Farmington) and Ella C. Winn (Farmington)

child, b. 11/–/1924; Ernest E. Rollins (woodworker, Alton) and Julia M. Burroughs (Union)

Albert Henry, b. 9/3/1930; second; Winslow Rollins (caretaker, Caratunk, ME) and Beatrice Coffin (Berwick, ME)

Echia A., b. 3/6/1896; first; H. S. Rollins (shoemaker, 24, New Durham) and Alice B. Gilman (20, Hallowell, ME)

Evelyn M., b. 10/14/1910; first; Cyrus Rollins, Jr. (shoemaker, Somersworth) and Maggie E. Burke (Wolfeboro)

George H., b. 1/31/1909; fourth; Irving H. Rollins (laborer, 51, Alton) and Addie F. Clarke (23, Alton)

Gertrude L., b. 7/22/1916; third; Harry M. Rollins (farmer, MA) and Dorothy S. Sellers (Farmington)

Grover T., b. 10/11/1888; second; Irving H. Rollins (shoemaker, 34, Alton) and Hannah M. Hubbard (35, Farmington)

June, b. 2/10/1923; first; Ernest Rollins (woodturner, Alton) and Julia Burrows (Union)

Leone, b. 3/16/1907; first; Louie R. Rollins (music teacher, 18, Bennington) and Bessie F. Innis (20, Lawrence, MA)

Lois Swain, b. 12/7/1918; second; Rupert L. Rollins (shoemaker, Alton) and Marion Swain (Rochester)

Louise F., b. 6/30/1921; second; Harold C. Rollins (wood turner, Farmington) and Ella C. Winn (Farmington)

Pauline Alice, b. 4/7/1933; third; Winslow Rollins (laborer, Corretunk, ME) and Beatrice Coffin (Berwick, ME)

Raymond Joseph, b. 2/19/1927; first; Venna W. Rollins (Farmington)

**ROSS,**
Marie Isabelle, b. 7/28/1928; stillborn; first; Napoleon Ross (musician, Canada) and Marie Ange (Canada)

**ROUCKEY,**
son, b. 7/3/1929; second; George A. Rouckey (shoemaker, Lebanon, ME) and Gertrude E. Ricker (New Durham)

Frances P., b. 7/26/1924; first; George H. Rouckey (shoemaker, NH) and Gertrude Ricker (NH)

**ROUSSEAU,**
daughter, b. 12/25/1913; first; Frank N. Rousseau (shoemaker, Canada) and Hattie Dwyer (Canada)

**ROY,**
son [Charles], b. 9/21/1909; third; Romeo Roy (shoemaker, 30, Canada) and Lea Jerves (34, Canada)
Blanche A., b. 3/9/1911; fourth; Romnald O. Roy (shoemaker, 32, Canada) and Lea Jarvais (35, Canada)

**ROYER,**
Gaynell Ann, b. 9/30/1933; fourth; Leo E. Royer (shoemaker, Dover) and Esther A. Houle (Rochester)

**RUNNALS** [see Runnels],
son, b. 3/28/1889; first; Forrest L. Runnals (shoemaker, 31, New Durham) and Ida M. Champion (21, Wakefield)

**RUNNELLS,**
daughter, b. 5/4/1905; second; Paul M. Runnells (laborer, 29, New Durham) and Blanche B. White (19, New Durham)
son, b. 4/26/1907; third; P. M. Runnells (laborer, 31, New Durham) and Blanche B. White (23, New Durham)

**RUNNELS** [see Runnals],
stillborn daughter, b. 6/13/1892; third; Forrest L. Runnels (shoemaker, 35, New Durham) and Ida M. Champion (housewife, 25, Wakefield)

**RUSSELL,**
daughter [Annie], b. 8/27/1889; first; George F. Russell (shoe cutter, Deerfield, NY) and Lotta A. Chamberlin (Alton)
daughter [Theresa], b. 8/–/1891; second; George F. Russell (clerk, 51, Utica, NY) and Lottie A. Colomy (27, Alton)
David Verdrum, b. 3/12/1923; second; Verdrum Russell (shoemaker, Lynn, MA) and Evelyn Rhodes (Portsmouth)
Dorothy Arline, b. 3/19/1933; L. Richard Russell (Danvers, MA) and Etta I. Wentworth (Danvers, MA)
Lee Calvin, b. 1/4/1926; third; Verdrum W. Russell (shoemaker, Lynn, MA) and Evelyn M. Rhodes (Portsmouth)

Muriel Joy, b. 6/4/1921; first; Verdrum W. Russell (shoe worker, Lynn, MA) and Evelyn M. Rhodes (Portsmouth)
Virginia Louise, b. 4/26/1930; third; Luther Richard Russell (farmer Danvers, MA) and Etta I. Wentworth (Danvers, MA)

## ST. CYR,
Ethelyn May, b. 10/11/1927; second; Clarence R. St. Cyr (laborer, Lebanon, ME) and M. Pauline Davis (Farmington); residence Springvale, ME

## ST. PIERRE,
James W., b. 7/24/1912; first; Frank St. Pierre (shoemaker, Wolfeboro) and Nellie M. Tyler (Boston, MA)

## SABOURIN,
Claire Elaine, b. 10/10/1932*; fourth; Arthur J. Sabourin (wood hee mfg., Lowell, MA) and Gladys Gondreault (Haverhill, MA)

## SALISBURY,
Lindel Clifford, b. 2/4/1915; second; Clifford K. Salisbury (shoeworker, ME) and Nina Richardson (MA)

## SANBORN,
daughter, b. 8/17/1890; first; Almon C. Sanborn (shoemaker, 28, Gilmanton) and Emma A. Richardson (24, Farmington)
son, b. 5/19/1898; second; Will G. Sanborn (laborer, –7, Wolfebor and Maud M. Kenney (19, Rochester)
son [William], b. 5/6/1915; second; Roland R. Sanborn (farmer, Rochester) and Alice M. Gray (Farmington)
Beatrice May, b. 2/28/1923; fifth; Roland R. Sanborn (farmer, Rochester) and Alice M. Gray (Farmington)
Carleton Ira, b. 4/11/1914; first; Roland R. Sanborn (farmer, Rochester) and Alice M. Gray (Farmington)
Ivory Maurice, b. 4/17/1918; third; Roland R. Sanborn (farmer, Rochester) and Alice M. Gray (Farmington)
Marjorie Alice, b. 4/11/1919; fourth; Roland R. Sanborn (carpenter, Rochester) and Alice M. Gray (Farmington)
Nellie Winn, b. 11/8/1931*; stillborn; seventh; Roland Sanborn (shoe shop emp., Rochester) and Grace Haddock (Ossipee)

**SANSOUCIE,**
son, b. 10/11/1900; second; William Sansoucie (grocer, 33, Haverhill, MA) and Mary Wentworth (23, Farmington); residence - Haverhill, MA
Gladys Manila, b. 6/7/1898; first; William L. Sansoucie (shoemaker, 31, Plaistow) and Mary L. Wentworth (20, Farmington)
Joseph L., b. 7/13/1897; first; Joseph Sansoucie (shoemaker, 27, Worcester, MA) and Elizabeth E. Drapeau (14, Strafford)

**SAUNDERS,**
Mabel R., b. 11/7/1894; second; Herbert C. Saunders (mechanic, 30, Lowell) and Eliza R. Walker (23, Boston)

**SAVOY,**
Philip A., b. 9/21/1924; fourth; Jennie Savoy (Dover)

**SAWYER,**
Mabel Auria, b. 9/25/1913; first; Eva Pearl Sawyer (LaGrange, ME)
Roscoe I., b. 3/16/1910; first; Horatio M. Sawyer (laborer, Milbridge, ME) and Mary Drew (Brookfield)

**SCHLENKER,**
Nellie, b. 4/19/1888; first; John Schlenker (baker, 36, Germany) and Lizzie M. Pike (26, Middleton)

**SCHOCH,**
son, b. 4/23/1914; first; Edgar J. Schock (sic) (shoemaker, Reading, PA) and Mary Agnes Nixon (Gonic)
stillborn daughter, b. 7/28/1915; second; Edgar J. Schoch (shoeworker, Reading, PA) and Mary A. Nixon (Rochester)
son, b. 6/20/1916; third; Edgar J. Schoch (shoeworker, Reading, PA) and Mary Agnes Nixon (Rochester)

**SCOFIELD,**
Irene Sonia, b. 9/30/1927; fourth; Ernest Scofield (surveyor, Newark, NJ) and Yoome Cyr (Canada)

**SCOTT,**
son, b. 11/20/1889; third; Edward J. Scott (telegraph operator, NB) and Argie E. Yeaton (Alfred, ME)

stillborn daughter, b. 7/4/1891; fourth; Edward J. Scott (telegraphe 26, NB) and Angie Yeaton (22, Alfred, ME)
Joseph A., b. 9/6/1907; Joseph W. Scott (shoemaker, 30, Feemin Hill, ME) and Adeline Downs (27, Quincy, MA)

SCRUTON,
son [Gilbert P.], b. 2/14/1902; second; Irving J. Scruton (farmer, 2 Farmington) and Lizzie F. Preston (23, Fox River, Canada)
daughter [Laura], b. 6/12/1903; third; Irving J. Scruton (farmer, 28 Farmington) and Lizzie Preston (25, Fox River, Canada)
son, b. 11/8/1905; fourth; Irving J. Scruton (farmer, 31, Farmingto and Lizzie F. Preston (27, Canada)
Frank I., b. 2/13/1922; first; Arthur Scruton (farmer, Farmington) and Mabel G. Kendall (Ossipee)
Jerold F., b. 7/19/1900; first; Irving J. Scruton (laborer, 26, Farmington) and Lizzie F. Preston (22, Fox River, Canada)
Joan Marie, b. 6/7/1934; first; Gilbert Scruton (woodturner, Farmington) and Esther Whitehouse (Somersworth)
Sarah E., b. 8/8/1908; fourth; Irving Scruton (laborer, 34, Farmington) and Lizzie Preston (30, Fox River, Canada)

SEAVEY,
daughter, b. 4/12/1889; first; Edwin A. Seavey (shoemaker, 37, Boston, MA) and Susie Tibbetts (21, Wakefield)
Claude E., b. 7/17/1893; second; Edwin A. Seavey (shoemaker, 4 Boston, MA) and Susie Tibbetts (26, Wakefield)
Marion, b. 1/26/1894; second; Joseph E. Seavey (farmer, 42, Alexandria) and Nellie S. Jones (42, Gilmanton)

SECORD,
Gloria Ann, b. 11/5/1930; fourth; Harold B. Secord (shoeworker, Jamaica Plain, MA) and Gertrude M. McNary (Beverly, MA)

SENTER,
Norman Web'r, b. 12/31/1929; second; Lawrence Senter (chef, Lynn, MA) and Eunice E. Sellers (Andover, MA)

SEWELL,
Sally Jeanne, b. 4/8/1938; second; Samuel Sewell (shoeworker, Exeter) and Ellen A. Prescott (Farmington)

**SHANNON,**
son, b. 3/31/1910; first; Leander Shannon (machinist, Alton) and Gladys Kimball (Wolfeboro)

**SHAW,**
son, b. 5/26/1901; eighth; Malcom Shaw (blacksmith, 40, PEI) and Alice M. Connors (32, New York City)
Albert Charles, b. 2/15/1929; fourth; William H. Shaw (shoemaker, Farmington) and Mabel Ricker (Farmington)
Barbara L., b. 12/3/1924; first; William H. Shaw (shoeworker, NH) and Mabel Ricker (NH)
Ethel May, b. 7/28/1926; second; W. H. Shaw (shoemaker, Farmington) and Mabel Ricker (Farmington)
Virginia A., b. 11/22/1927; third; William H. Shaw (shoemaker, Farmington) and Mabel Ricker (Farmington)

**SHEVENELL,**
son [Edward], b. 1/27/1903; second; Charles E. Shevenell (keeper bdg. house, 34, Biddeford, ME) and Trixie Brodrick (22, Cleveland, OH)

**SILVER,**
daughter, b. 2/18/1904; first; Joseph Silver (laborer, 26, Canada) and Ethel Glidden (14, Alton)
Betty Louise, b. 4/24/1937; second; John J. Silver (shoeworker, CA) and Alice Pinkham (Alton)

**SILVIA,**
Carol Jean, b. 2/10/1925; second; John J. Silvia (shoecutter) and Gladys L. Wilkes (NH)
Irene Janet, b. 10/24/1923; first; John J. Silvia (shoecutter, Oakland, CA) and Gladys T. Wilkes (Barnstead)
Priscilla, b. 3/17/1927; third; John Silvia (shoeworker, Oakland, CA) and Gladys Wilkes (Barnstead)

**SIMONDS,**
Frank E., b. 9/16/1908; first; Eugene F. Simonds (merchant, 39, Sharon, VT) and Cynthia Davis (28, Alton)

**SINCLAIR,**
Eno Joseph, b. 12/16/1935; first; Eno L. Sinclair (stock clerk, Webster, MA) and Doris S. Hamilton (Manchester)

**SMALL,**
daughter, b. 4/30/1912; fifth; Leslie F. Small (machinist, Brighton, MA) and Lena E. Flint (New Durham)

**SMART,**
child, b. 11/25/1888; sixth; Joel Smart (farmer, 43, Howland, ME) and Mary A. Smart (34, Dover)
daughter, b. 8/19/1893; seventh; Joel Smart (farmer, 48, Whitney Bridge, ME) and Mary A. Smith (39, Dover)
son [Jerry E.], b. 3/9/1896; eighth; Joel Smart (farmer, 51, Whitney Ridge, ME) and Mary A. Smith (41, Dover)
stillborn son, b. 1/4/1930*; third; Jeremiah Smart (shoemaker, Farmington) and Ada Barsantee (Portsmouth)
stillborn daughter, b. 6/9/1937; fourth; Jeremiah Smart (shoeworker Farmington) and Ada Barsantee (Portsmouth)
David Neal, b. 12/9/1926; first; Jeremiah E. Smart (shoemaker, Farmington) and Ada F. Barsantee (Portsmouth)

**SMITH,**
son, b. 5/–/1891; second; Eugene A. Smith (barber, 31, Montpelier, VT) and Myrtle Hutchins (28, Montpelier, VT)
son [Albert Melvin], b. 1/20/1905; first; William A. Smith (laborer, 21, Gilmanton) and Iona B. Richardson (16, Norton Mills, VT)
son [Walter], b. 9/1/1907; third; James W. Smith (shoemaker, 33, Lowell, MA) and Abbie S. Smith (30, Barrington, NS)
son [Warren], b. 10/7/1912; sixth; William Albert Smith (laborer, Alton) and Iona B. Knights
son [Earl L.], b. 7/5/1914; seventh; William A. Smith (laborer, Alton) and Iona B. Knight (Norton Mills, VT)
stillborn son, b. 2/24/1923; fourth; Irving Smith (laborer, NH) and Beatrice Glidden (NH)
Alfred J., b. 12/4/1909; fourth; William A. Smith (laborer, 26, Alton) and Iona B. Knight (21, VT)
Clarence L., b. 5/13/1920; third; Leland C. Smith (shoe worker, Moultonboro) and A. Maude Jones (Farmington)
Edmond, b. 8/29/1907; third; William A. Smith (laborer, 24, Alton) and Iona B. Richardson (18, Norton Mills, VT)

George H., b. 11/5/1917; eighth; William A. Smith (boxmaker, Alton) and Iona B. Knight (Norton Mills, VT)

James Davis, b. 7/12/1922; first; John H. Smith (farmer, North Conway) and Hazel Davis (Farmington)

Melvina G., b. 6/24/1924; fifth; Irving S. Smith (laborer, Alton) and Beatrice I. Glidden (New Durham)

Olive Etta, b. 1/12/1916; seventh; William Albert Smith (teamster, Alton) and Iona B. Knight (Norton Mills, VT)

**SOMERS,**

Kathryn Edith, b. 9/12/1920; fourth; George W. Somers (fruit, Athens, Greece) and Margaret K. Young (Perth, Scotland); residence - Provincetown, MA

**SONGER,**

Annie E., b. 10/12/1909; second; John S. Songer (shoemaker, 28, PA) and Jessie M. Kimball (18, Farmington)

Morris Joseph, b. 2/10/1916; fifth; John Songer (shoe operative, PA) and Jessie Kimball (NH)

Teresa Clara, b. 10/14/1914; fourth; John S. Songer (shoemaker, PA) and Jessie May Kimball (Union)

**SOUCEY,**

son, b. 1/20/1925; first; Alma Soucey (Salmon Falls)

**SOUTER,**

Virginia Elizabeth, b. 4/30/1935; first; William Souter (shoeworker, Somerville, MA) and Eileen Mathews

**SPEAR,**

daughter [Dorothy], b. 3/12/1913; first; Fred Robert Spear (shoe cutter, East Boston, MA) and Ruth Talpey Gordon (Manchester)

Charles E., b. 6/30/1917; second; Howard M. Spear (shoeworker, MA) and Ruth Varney (Acton, ME)

Dorothea June, b. 12/19/1920; second; Howard M. Spear (shoemaker, East Boston, MA) and Ruth M. Varney (Acton, ME)

Gloria Myrtle, b. 5/16/1925; third; Howard M. Spear (shoeworker, South Boston, MA) and Ruth M. Varney (Acton, ME)

Harold Roberts, b. 7/11/1914; first; John D. Spear (foreman stitche room, Anson, ME) and Florence B. Stackpole (Lebanon, ME)
John Edwin, b. 8/21/1930*; second; Fred Spear (shoe cutter, Boston, MA) and Viola Pike (Farmington)
Robert Frederick, b. 3/6/1929; first; Fred R. Spear (shoe cutter, Boston, MA) and Viola Pike (Farmington)
Wayne Lloyd, b. 5/6/1928; fourth; Howard M. Spear (shoemaker, So. Boston, MA) and Ruth M. Varney (Acton, ME)

**SPENCER,**
son, b. 2/22/1889; fifth; Frank P. Spencer (laborer, 37, Berwick, ME) and Fannie Cooper (37, Berwick, ME)

**STANLEY,**
daughter, b. 9/1/1907; first; Leonard Y. Stanley (shoemaker, 18, Trenton, ME) and Elizabeth St. Peter (18, Wolfeboro)
Harold L., b. 12/31/1917; second; Ernest Stanley (laborer, Hollis, ME) and Clara Downing (Middleton)
Orrin D., b. 5/24/1920; fourth; Ernest Stanley (laborer, Hollis, ME) and Clara J. Downing (Middleton)
Percy A., b. 5/20/1910; third; Leonard Stanley (shoemaker, Bangor ME) and Mary St. Peter (Wolfeboro)
Rose M., b. 12/3/1916; third; Ernest Stanley (farmer, Hollis, ME) and Clara Downing (Middleton)
Stella May, b. 4/21/1919; fourth; Ernest Stanley (laborer, Hollis, ME) and Clara Downing (Middleton)

**STANTON,**
daughter, b. 2/27/1898; first; James Stanton (laborer, 28) and Mary E. Elliott (19, Farmington)

**STAPLES,**
son, b. 11/9/1901; fourth; Will M. Staples (clerk, 33, Danvers, MA) and Eliza Acorn (32, PEI)
son, b. 6/8/1903; fifth; William M. Staples (teamster, Danvers, MA) and Eliza Acorn (35, PEI)
Alberta E., b. 6/3/1934; fourth; Charles Staples (farmer, Wolfeboro) and Doris Willard (Alton)
Charles F., Jr., b. 1/8/1936; fourth; Charles F. Staples (laborer, Wolfeboro) and Doris V. Willard (Alton)

**STEBBINS,**
daughter, b. 1/21/1919; second; Richard E. Stebbins (sawyer, Newbury, VT) and Sarah E. Dapheny (New Durham)

**STEVENS,**
son [Percy E.], b. 1/29/1887; first; Eugene Stevens (laster, 28, Middleton) and Etta E. Everett (Plympton, NS)
son, b. 7/25/1889; second; James E. Stevens (shoemaker, Middleton) and Etta E. Everett (NS)
son [Dean L.], b. 5/–/1891; first; Rockwell J. Stevens (shoemaker, 35, Middleton) and Abbie Leeds (37, Alton)
daughter, b. 4/9/1910; second; Percy E. Stevens (shoemaker, Farmington) and Phoebe E. Youyng (Bowdenville, ME)
son [Sylvester], b. 2/8/1911; third; Mrs. Nellie Stevens (Farmington)
daughter, b. 3/27/1911; first; Carroll C. Stevens (clerk, 22, Farmington) and Nellie M. Swiniton (20, Milton)
daughter [Marguerite F.], b. 7/22/1911; first; Philemon E. Stevens (shoemaker, 24, Biddeford, ME) and Helen S. Brooks (22, Farmington)
son [James], b. 11/6/1912; second; Philemon E. Stevens (shoemaker, Biddeford, ME) and Helen S. Brooks (Farmington)
son, b. 12/12/1914; third; Philemon E. Stevens (shoemaker, Biddeford, ME) and Helen S. Brooks (Farmington)
son [Lawrence], b. 5/5/1916; fourth; Philemon E. Stevens (shoemaker, Biddeford, ME) and Helen S. Brooks (Farmington)
Elwin P., b. 9/26/1908; first; Percy E. Stevens (shoemaker, 21, Farmington) and Phoebe Young (18, Baldwinsville, MA)
Gerald Erwin, b. 7/29/1937; third; James P. Stevens (farmer, NH) and Frances Manley (ME)
James Philemon, b. 12/19/1933; first; James P. Stevens (laborer, Farmington) and Francis Manley (Barnardsville, ME)
Lillian May, b. 10/24/1923; first; William C. Stevens (shoemaker, Thomaston, ME) and Lillian Arnold (Farmington)
Linnie, b. 8/24/1909; second; Ronella S. Stevens (dead, 23, Farmington) and Nellie Abbott (21, Farmington)
Mertie L., b. 7/7/1908; first; Ronello L. Stevens (farmer, 23, Farmington) and Nellie F. Abbott (20, Farmington)
Ronald Eugene, b. 11/25/1935; second; James Stevens (laborer, Farmington) and Francis J. Manley (Barnard Siding, ME)

Waneta P., b. 9/6/1938; fourth; James I. Stevens (farmer, Farmington) and Frances Manley (ME)

**STONE,**
daughter, b. 7/–/1891; second; Nelson E. Stone (shoemaker, 24, Franklin Falls) and Hattie M. Chamberlin (18, Alton)

**STROUT,**
son, b. 4/6/1911; fourth; Wilmot F. Strout (shoemaker, 38, Steuben ME) and May Cole (35, Sackville)

**STURTEVANT,**
Flora Arlene, b. 7/4/1927; fourth; Leon H. Sturtevant (farmer, MA) and Jessie F. MacIntosh (Boston, MA)

**SULLIVAN,**
son, b. 9/4/1908; third; John E. Sullivan (shoe foreman, 35, Nashua) and Catherine J. Delorey (29, NS)
Cornelius H., Jr., b. 5/24/1926; second; Cornelius H. Sullivan (shoemaker, Manchester) and Maxine G. Long (Snowville)
Eileen E., b. 2/2/1925; first; Cornelius Sullivan (shoecutter, Manchester) and Maxine Long (Snowville)
Marie Martha, b. 3/31/1938; second; Mortimer Sullivan (shoeworker, Manchester) and Mary Kimball (Auburn, ME)
Mary Anna, b. 2/20/1938; seventh; Thomas Sullivan (shoeworker, Manchester) and Gladys Wilkes (Barnstead)
Maureen Lois, b. 5/17/1936; sixth; Thomas Sullivan (shoeworker, Manchester) and Gladys Wilkes (Barnstead)
Mortimer F., b. 3/4/1932; first; Mortimer F. Sullivan (shoemaker, Manchester) and Mary F. Kimball (Auburn, ME)
Roberta June, b. 12/29/1927; third; Cornelius Sullivan (shoecutter, Manchester) and Maxine Long (Snowville)
Wayne Carlton, b. 2/27/1933; fourth; Cornelius H. Sullivan (shoe shop employee, Manchester) and Maxine Long (Snowville)

**SWINERTON,**
Estelle, b. 4/19/1905; second; Herbert B. Swinerton (shoemaker, 25, Somersworth) and Estella M. Blaisdell (24, Farmington)
Evelyn Blanch, b. 11/9/1900; first; Herbert E. Swinerton (shoemaker, 21, Somersworth) and Esther M. Blaisdell (19, Farmington)

Oren Herbert, b. 3/28/1913; third; Herbert B. Swinerton (shoe operative, Somersworth) and Esther M. Blaisdell (Farmington)

**TANNER,**
son, b. 9/18/1889; second; Edwin H. Tanner (carpenter, Farmington) and Mary O'Hara (Belfast, Ireland)
daughter, b. 3/2/1891; third; Hervey E. Tanner (carpenter, 27, Farmington) and Mary A. O'Hara (25, Ireland)
son [Stanley], b. 10/30/1892; fourth; Edwin H. Tanner (carpenter, 28, Farmington) and Mary A. Chase (housewife, 39, Belfast, Ireland)
son, b. 12/10/1896 in Rochester; first; Ralph G. Tanner (farmer, 19, Chicago, IL) and Alice B. Sanborn (19, Boston, MA)
son, b. 5/2/1906; first; Lincoln G. Tanner (fireman, 24, Chicago, IL) and Delia M. Downing (27, Farmington); residence - Somerville, MA
son [Austin D.], b. 9/10/1909; third; Herbert Tanner (farmer, Farmington) and Marie A. Devaney (Ireland)
daughter [Leona A.], b. 4/8/1911; first; George Irving Tanner (shoemaker, 32, Farmington) and Gertrude May Smart (18, Farmington)
daughter [Evelyn], b. 8/19/1912; second; George Irving Tanner (shoe operative, Farmington) and Gertrude M. Smart (Farmington)
son, b. 6/25/1914; third; George I. Tanner (shoemaker, Farmington) and Gertrude M. Smart (Farmington)
Eva M., b. 7/11/1888; first; Edwin H. Tanner (25) and Mary A. O'Hara (22, Belfast, Ireland)
Herbert, b. 2/17/1908; second; Herbert Tanner (farmer, 31, Farmington) and Mary E. Devaney (24, Ireland)

**TARNEY,**
Lloyd Walter, b. 3/19/1929; fifth; Martin Tarney (salesman, Dover) and Grace Whitehouse (Strafford)
Philip M., b. 9/13/1924; second; Martin Tarney (laborer, Dover) and Grace Whitehouse (Strafford)

**TAYLOR,**
Priscilla Ann, b. 9/18/1938; third; Harold M. Taylor (shoeworker, MT) and Ethel Boles (Derry)

**TEAGUE,**
Marjorie, b. 7/23/1907; second; Edward O. Teague (shoe mfg'r, 35 Warren, ME) and Nellie Douglas (31, Silver City, ID)
Ralph E., Jr., b. 10/8/1917; first; Ralph E. Teague (B&M RR, Beverly, MA) and Helen Merrow (Milton); residence - Beverly, MA

**TEBBETTS** [see Tibbetts],
son, b. 8/27/1889; first; Frank G. Tebbetts (merchant, Gilmanton) and Mary A. Cloutman (Farmington)
Henry M., b. 9/12/1922; third; Fred O. Tebbetts (shoemaker, Epping) and Elna B. Armstrong (Farmington)
Thelma Marion, b. 8/12/1919; third; Grace May Tebbetts (Milton)

**TERRELL** [see Terrill, Tirrell],
daughter, b. 10/29/1913; first; Melvin S. Terrell (shoemaker, Lebanon, ME) and Mardell Howard (Dover)
Carl Delmont, b. 11/4/1914; third; Charles M. Terrell (shoemaker, Marlboro, MA) and Goldie H. Stanley (Otis, ME)
Elnor B., b. 7/6/1909; first; Kate Preston (24, MI)
Helen Louise, b. 12/12/1911; second; Charles M. Terrell (shoemaker, 25, Wakefield, MA) and Goldie H. Stanley (19, Otis, ME)

**TERRILL** [see Terrell, Tirrell],
Irene Elizabeth, b. 7/10/1919; Melvin S. Terrill (shoeworker, Lebanon, ME) and Mardel E. Howard (Dover)

**TERRINE,**
son, b. 12/11/1898; second; John Terrine (laborer, 34, Canada) and Clara Lessane (24, Canada)

**THAYER,**
Hattie A., b. 9/22/1890; second; Walter H. Thayer (carriage dealer, Sebago, ME) and Susan A. Lord (Great Falls)
James, b. 3/1/1907; first; Elmer F. Thayer (shoe mf'g'r, 45, South Weymouth, MA) and Annie M. Edgerly (36, Farmington)
James Edgerly, b. 9/13/1938; second; James E. Thayer (cashier, Farmington) and Beulah Perkins (Alton)
Sylvia Louise, b. 6/25/1936; first; James Thayer (bank cashier, Farmington) and Beulah Perkins (Alton)

**THEROUX,**
son, b. 2/15/1895; fifth; Joseph Theroux (shoemaker, 28, Canada) and Rose Cartier (28, Canada)

**THERRIEN,**
Alfred, b. 12/21/1929; second; Edward N. Therrien (shoeworker, Farmington) and Edith E. Armstrong (Manchester)
Edward N., Jr., b. 11/19/1928; first; Edward N. Therrien (shoecutter, Farmington) and Edith E. Armstrong (Manchester)
Mary E., b. 10/14/1932; fourth; Edward N. Therrien (shoe laster, Farmington) and Edith E. Armstrong (Manchester)
Paul Armstrong, b. 5/29/1931; third; Edward Therrien (shoecutter, Farmington) and Edith E. Armstrong (Manchester)

**THOMAS,**
Bette Mae, b. 12/27/1937; fourth; Joseph Thomas (shoeworker, Rochester) and Elizabeth Zimmer (Okarche, OK)
Blanche R., b. 1/10/1927; first; Walker Thomas (salesman, Falmouth, ME) and Ethel M. Daniels (Yarmouth, ME); residence - Falmouth, ME
Joseph T., Jr., b. 7/19/1934; third; Joseph Thomas (shoeworker, Rochester) and Elizabeth Zimmer (OK)

**THOMPSON,**
son [Raymond C.], b. 6/16/1889; first; James H. Thompson (shoemaker, 30, Farmington) and Hattie Dow (28, Barnstead)
daughter [Agnes M.], b. 2/19/1894; first; Charles W. Thompson (shoemaker, 38, Farmington) and Jennie L. Emmons (36, Kennebunk)
Charles H., b. 2/12/1908; fourth; Hervey J. Thompson (farmer, 41, Farmington) and Florence Foss (32, Rochester)
Julia Eleanor, b. 7/28/1926; first; Elmer E. Thompson (farmer, New Durham) and Marion C. Tuttle (Barrington)
Lloyd G., b. 9/17/1919; second; John C. Thompson (farmer, Concord) and Julia Emerson (Farmington)

**THROUX,**
daughter, b. 6/26/1911; sixth; George Throux (laborer, 30, Suncook) and Matilda Duckworth (30, Readville, MA); residence - Hooksett

**THURBER,**
son, b. 1/16/1910; third; Frank W. Thurber (insurance, Cornish, VT) and Gertrude E. Pinkham (Milton)

**THURSTON,**
daughter, b. 8/30/1909; third; Herbert H. Thurston (barber, 28, Milton) and Ethel R. Higgin (20, Gorham, ME)
son [Richard], b. 9/29/1926; first; Milton Thurston (barber, NH) and Beatrice M. Hartford (E. Rochester)
daughter, b. 6/13/1929; second; Milton H. Thurston (barber, Plymouth) and Beatrice M. Hartford (E. Rochester)
Alma Louise, b. 6/12/1929; first; Hanis Thurston (teamster, Plymouth) and Alta Littlefield (Farmington)
Bernice M., b. 3/29/1906; first; Willie F. Thurston (sawyer, 26, Newton) and Grace Ham (18, Milton)
Juanita Louise, b. 5/10/1926; first; Percy L. Thurston (shoemaker, NH) and Grace E. Hayden (NH)
Kathleen, b. 4/11/1913; fourth; Herbert H. Thurston (barber, Milton) and Ethel R. Higgins (Gorham)

**TIBBETTS** [see Tebbetts],
daughter, b. 7/4/1887; fourth; Jared P. Tibbetts (undertaker, 51, Farmington) and Mary E. Tibbetts (Dover)
son, b. 3/7/1889; second; George F. Tibbetts, 2$^{nd}$ (saloon keeper, 30, Farmington) and Etta M. Chesley (31, Farmington)
stillborn daughter, b. 7/8/1898; first; Frank M. Tibbetts (fireman, -7, Rochester) and Linnie V. Williams (22, PEI)
daughter, b. 12/12/1901; first; Harris C. Tibbetts (engineer, 34, Farmington) and Inez Harris (24, Alton)
daughter, b. 9/28/1904; second; Harris C. Tibbetts (teamster, 37, Farmington) and Inez Ham (26, Gilmanton)
daughter, b. 12/21/1909; fourth; John Tibbetts (shoemaker, 29, Portsmouth) and Jennie B. Sanborn (20, Acton, ME)
daughter, b. 12/15/1920; fourth; Grace Tibbetts (Milton)
Barbara Arlene, b. 7/5/1933; second; Fred Tibbetts (laborer, Epping) and Elna Armstrong (Farmington)
Flora Jeanette, b. 6/20/1926; third; Grace M. Tibbetts (Milton)
Jean Elna, b. 5/3/1931; fifth; Fred Tibbetts (laborer, Epping) and Elna Armstrong (Farmington)

**TILTON,**
son, b. 12/9/1913; first; Sumner A. Tilton (shoemaker, East Rochester) and Hilda Brooks (Farmington)
Barbara, b. 1/23/1920; third; Charles A. Tilton (shoe cutter, Deerfield) and Ruby B. Davis (Pittsfield)
Donna Muriel, b. 10/21/1921; fourth; Charles Adams Tilton (shoeworker, Deerfield) and Ruby Blanche Davis (Pittsfield)
Floyd D., b. 4/25/1924; fifth; Charles A. Tilton (shoecutter, Deerfield) and Ruby B. Davis (Pittsfield)
Jeanette D., b. 8/23/1927; sixth; Charles A. Tilton (shoe cutter, Deerfield) and Ruby D. Davis (Pittsfield)
Robert, b. 10/16/1928; seventh; Charles A. Tilton (shoecutter, Deerfield) and Ruby B. Davis (Pittsfield)
Ruth Elizabeth, b. 8/8/1918; second; Charles A. Tilton (shoeworker, Deerfield) and Ruby B. Davis (Pittsfield)

**TIRRELL** [see Terrell, Terrill],
Harold Alvin, Jr., b. 1/11/1930*; first; Harold Alvin Tirrell (shoe laster, Springvale, ME) and Helen Earle (Alton)
Howard H., b. 11/3/1926; seventh; Melvin S. Tirrell (shoemaker, Lebanon, ME) and Mardel Howard (Dover)
Louise Ethel, b. 11/25/1928; third; Clarence P. Tirrell (shoeworker, Springvale, ME) and Sadie E. King (Bath, ME)
Mardell C., b. 9/10/1921; fifth; Melvin S. Tirrell (shoemaker, Lisbon, ME) and Mardell Howard (Dover)
Mildred E., b. 10/12/1917; third; Melvin S. Tirrell (shoeworker, Lebanon, ME) and Mardel E. Howard (Dover)
Stanley W., b. 12/28/1917; fourth; Charles M. Tirrell (shoemaker, Salem, MA) and Goldie Stanley (Otis, ME)

**TNEEY,**
son [Joseph], b. 8/17/1906; fourth; George Tneey (laborer, 43, Exeter) and Edith M. Ricker (24, Strafford)
daughter [Mildred E.], b. 11/22/1907; fifth; George Tneey (laborer, 45, Exeter) and Edith Ricker (26, NH)

**TOWLE,**
daughter, b. 4/9/1890; second; Tristam F. Towle (painter, 22, New Durham) and Annie B. Trafton (Great Falls)
son [Fred A.], b. 6/1/1891; third; Tristum F. Towle (painter, 24, New Durham) and Annie B. Trafton (25, Great Falls)

daughter, b. 8/6/1902; third; Tristram F. Towle (painter, 34, New
    Durham) and Katie E. Erner (28, Ireland)
daughter, b. 4/20/1911; sixth; Tristram F. Towle (painter, 41, New
    Durham) and Kate Earner (38, Ireland)
Annie, b. 5/14/1909; fifth; Tristum F. Towle (shoemaker, 41, New
    Durham) and Kate Earner (36, Ireland)
Barbara Louise, b. 6/6/1937; first; Tris Towle (shoeworker, Dover)
    and Adrian Langevin (Rochester)
Floyd Stanley, b. 9/1/1937; third; Floyd Towle (mill worker, New
    Durham) and Marion Holder (Millis, MA)
Hazel Irene, b. 2/10/1889; first; Tristram F. Towle (painter, 20, New
    Durham) and Annie B. Trafton (22, Great Falls)
Jean Caroline, b. 10/17/1928; second; Floyd R. Towle and Marion
    Holder
Nancy E., b. 1/10/1932*; third; Harold J. Towle (bookkeeper,
    Bristol) and Agnes O'Connor (Cambridge, MA)
Phyllis June, b. 6/17/1925; first; Floyd R. Towle (shoecutter, NH)
    and Marion Holder (MA)
Ruth B., b. 5/27/1894; first; Tristam F. Towle (painter, 26, New
    Durham) and Katie Evans (19, Ireland)

**TOZIER,**
Carl Albert, b. 2/17/1914; second; Granville E. Tozier (shoemaker,
    Danvers, MA) and Annie M. Wiggin (Milton Mills)

**TRASK,**
son [Ralph C.], b. 10/–/1891; second; Lyman W. Trask (shoemaker,
    32, Strafford) and Ida E. Whitehouse (31, New Durham)
daughter, b. 7/31/1924; second; Ralph C. Trask (shoecutter,
    Farmington) and Helen D. Yeaton (Wakefield)
Evelyn Louise, b. 1/26/1933; fourth; Ralph C. Trask (shoeworker,
    Farmington) and Helen D. Yeaton (Sanbornville)
Patricia, b. 12/25/1929; third; Ralph C. Trask (shoe cutter,
    Farmington) and Helen D. Yeaton (Wakefield)

**TRIPP,**
son [John], b. 7/18/1897; first; Charles H. Tripp (farmer, 30,
    Sanford, ME) and Ella Bickford (28, Farmington)
Edwin Webster, b. 3/24/1938; first; Fauntleroy Tripp (shoeworker,
    Milton) and Laura Webster (Farmington)

**TSIVOGION,**
Jordan C., b. 8/24/1915; second; Constantine Tsivogion (merchant, Constantinople) and Lucinda Stern (Boston, MA); residence - Boston, MA

**TUFTS,**
daughter, b. 4/29/1912; first; William D. Tufts (shoe operative, Middleton) and Dolly M. Wallace (Milton)
Barbara, b. 6/13/1920; second; William Tufts (lumberman, Middleton) and Dolly Wallace (Milton)
Carlton W., b. 11/24/1921; third; Frank I. Tufts (laborer, Middleton) and Lucy E. Huckins (Alton)
Earl, b. 10/28/1888; fifth; David H. Tufts (miller, 35, Strafford) and M. Corinne Tufts (32, Strafford)
Joanna Louise, b. 4/20/1937; first; Myron Tufts (shoeworker, Middleton) and Louise Kinney (Westville, ME)
Lauriston S., b. 11/4/1933; first; Evelyn Tufts (Alton)
Merton Eugene, b. 1/3/1928; fourth; Isaac F. Tufts (laborer, Middleton) and Lucy E. Goodwin (Alton)
William W., b. 10/2/1924; third; William D. Tufts (lumberman, NH) and Dollie Wallace (NH)

**TURMELL[E],**
daughter [Lauretta M.], b. 4/15/1909; ninth; Thomas R. Turmell (shoemaker, 39, Canada) and Marie O. Ducbois (37, Canada)
Floyd L., b. 2/9/1915; first; Ernest J. Turmelle (shoeworker, Rochester) and Elna V. Armstrong (Farmington)
Raymond J., b. 7/11/1910; tenth; Thomas R. Turmelle (shoemaker, Canada) and Marie O. Durboie (Canada)

**TURNER,**
Evelyn Louise, b. 10/24/1921; fifth; Charles B. Turner (farmer, Washington, ME) and Louisa D. Fricke

**TUTTLE,**
son [Stanley R.], b. 12/31/1907; fourth; Levi W. Tuttle (lumberman, 41, Middleton) and Joan L. Lowell (29, New Durham)
stillborn son, b. 5/25/1924; fourth; Earle Tuttle (electrician, NH) and Margaret Clowney (SC)
daughter [Barbara], b. 10/11/1925; second; Archie Tuttle (laborer, Boston, MA) and Lena R. Lesperance (NH)

Anna Margaret, b. 4/11/1921; second; Earle M. Tuttle (electrician, Cambridge, MA) and Margaret Clowney (Fairfield, SC)

Blanche E., b. 1/16/1906; third; Levi Tuttle (laborer, 41, New Durham) and Johan L. Lowell (26, New Durham)

Earle Montel, Jr., b. 12/30/1919; first; Earl Montel Tuttle (shoe operator, Cambridge, MA) and Margaret R. Cloning (SC)

Eugene Albert, b. 8/24/1926; fifth; Eugene A. Tuttle (shoemaker, Alton) and Maude R. Smart (Farmington)

Fred R., b. 11/11/1915; second; Lester G. Tuttle (teamster, Epping) and Fannie Drew (Wakefield)

Gladys M., b. 11/12/1896; second; Will Tuttle (laborer, 26, Rochester) and Ida M. Kent (25, Wolfeboro)

Joan Faith, b. 6/14/1934; first; Fred Tuttle (shoeworker, Farmington) and Marion Marsh (Laconia)

Robert Shirley, b. 2/27/1923; third; Earle M. Tuttle (laborer, MA) and Margaret Clowney (SC)

**VACHON,**

Barbara Louise, b. 2/7/1935; fifth; Joseph Vachon (woodsman, Lancaster) and Inez Elliott (Gilmanton I.W.)

William Dennis, b. 9/19/1933; fifth; Joseph Vachon (laborer, Lancaster) and Inez Elliott (Gilmanton I.W.)

**VAN VLECK,**

Donald F., b. 3/20/1925; first; John F. Van Vleck (shoecutter, MD) and Helen P. Colbath (Portsmouth)

**VANASSI,**

Robert Leo, b. 2/4/1935; first; Armand L. Vanassi (shoeworker, Canada) and Doris Trace (Ipswich, MA)

**VARNEY,**

daughter [Belle], b. 3/4/1891; second; Owen N. Varney (farmer, 38, Farmington) and Lillian B. Downing (25, Farmington)

daughter, b. 9/11/1892; third; Alfred C. Varney (shoemaker, 37, Alfred, ME) and Eva A. Blake (housewife, 33, Milton)

daughter [Flossie], b. 5/19/1895; first; Fred S. Varney (shoemaker, 21, Tuftonboro) and Angeline H. Corson (22, Barrington)

daughter [Rosetta], b. 1/27/1897; second; Fred Varney (shoemaker, 23, Farmington) and Angie Corson (24, Barrington)

daughter, b. 4/3/1899; fourth; Alfred C. Varney (shoemaker, 44, Alfred, ME) and Eva A. Blake (39, Milton)

son [Walter E.], b. 6/19/1899; fourth; Fred Varney (laborer, 22, Farmington) and Angeline Corson (21, Barrington)

son [Linnie V.], b. 1/4/1902; first; Elvin V. Varney (shoemaker, 28, Farmington) and Eldora B. Brown (28, Alton)

son [Ralph George], b. 4/26/1902; first; Lewis N. Varney (shoemaker, 24, Farmington) and Grace F. Pinkham (20, Middleton)

son, b. 7/8/1903; second; Lewis N. Varney (shoemaker, 26, Farmington) and Grace F. Pinkham (20, Middleton)

son, b. 1/10/1905; fourth; Elvin V. Varney (shoemaker, 33, Farmington) and Dora N. Brown (33, Alton)

daughter, b. 2/22/1924; fourth; Harold C. Varney (shoe manufacturer, Swampscott, MA) and Dora B. Morrill (Berwick, ME)

Albert Raymond, b. 7/21/1919; second; Benjamin E. W. Varney (rivetter, Alton) and Esther E. Thompson (New Durham); residence - Rochester

Bertie, b. 3/4/1889; second; Alfred C. Varney (shoemaker, 34, Alfred, ME) and Eva A. Blake (30, Milton)

Betty Louise, b. 3/24/1938; third; Lloyd I. Varney (shoeworker, Bath, ME) and Laura Bernard (Gonic)

Eda, b. 10/20/1925; third; Martin Varney (laborer, Dover) and Grace A. Whitehouse (Strafford)

Etta, b. 2/28/1888; first; Owen M. Varney (farmer, 34, Farmington) and Lillie B. Varney (21, Farmington)

Gene William, b. 6/10/1938; second; George W. Varney (shoeworker, Lynn, MA) and Evelyn Tufts (Alton)

John Almont, b. 9/17/1926; fourth; Martin Varney (laborer, Dover) and Grace Whitehouse (Strafford)

Kenneth H., b. 12/12/1917; first; Benjamin E. W. Varney (farmer, Farmington) and Esther E. Thompson (New Durham); residence - New Durham

Marjorie May, b. 2/27/1923; first; Martin Varney (laborer, Dover) and Grace Whitehouse (Strafford)

Ralph Everett, b. 10/10/1925; first; Linnie V. Varney (laborer, Farmington) and Ruth E. Nourse (MA)

Robert H., b. 9/29/1927; second; Linnie V. Varney (mechanic, Farmington) and Ruth E. Nourse (Fitchburg, MA)

Viana F., b. 4/7/1898; third; Fred Varney (laborer, 23, Farmington) and Angie E. Corson (23)

Vivian Doris, b. 8/21/1916; first; Albert L. Varney (shoeworker, Farmington) and Doris J. Moulton (Farmington)

William Hanis, b. 5/12/1937; first; Ralph G. Varney (shoeworker) and Kathleen Thurston (Farmington)

**VENO,**

Florence, b. 7/25/1910; second; George Veno (shoemaker, Ossipee) and Minerva Hanscom (Union)

**VICKERS,**

son, b. 10/8/1924; first; William J. Vickers (electrician, England) and Della F. Glidden (New Durham)

Ruth Ann, b. 12/24/1934; first; Charles Vickers (electrician, England) and Delia Beaulieu (Limestone, ME)

Wallace Robert, b. 5/30/1928; second; William T. Vickers (electrician, England) and Della F. Glidden (New Durham)

**WADSWORTH,**

daughter, b. 9/22/1915; seventh; Herbert Wadsworth (baker, Bradford, England) and Stella B. Gillis (Sanford, ME)

Frank, b. 11/10/1912; sixth; Herbert Wadsworth (baker, Bradford, England) and Stella Gillis (Sanford, ME)

**WALDRON,**

stillborn daughter, b. 12/18/1890; first; Harry C. Waldron (lumber manufacturer, 32, Farmington) and Nellie M. Broughey (Milford, MA)

son [Robert], b. 3/8/1912; first; Donald H. Waldron (millman, Farmington) and Gladys A. Prescott (Alton)

Philip H., b. 7/20/1893; third; Harry C. Waldron (box manufacturer, 35, Farmington) and Nellie Broughey (30, Milford, MA)

Phyllis, b. 2/24/1919; second; Donald H. Waldron (lumber worker, Farmington) and Gladys A. Prescott (Alton)

Richard K., b. 2/22/1895; Harry C. Waldron (lumber mfg., 36, Farmington) and Nellie M. Bronghey (32, Milford, MA)

Shirley Barbara, b. 4/28/1937; third; Robert Waldron (shoeworker, Farmington) and Evelyn Pinkham (North Lebanon, ME)

**WALKER,**
daughter, b. 5/30/1909; first; William B. Walker (carpenter, 24, Farmington) and Reta M. B. Meserve (23, Charlestown, MA)

**WALLACE,**
Fred C., b. 8/20/1888; first; Edgar F. Wallace (provisioner, 28, New Durham) and Clara E. Littlefield (26, Westford, MA)

**WALSH,**
Corinne, b. 3/13/1921; first; Leroy F. Walsh (shoe worker, Bridgewater, MA) and Arline F. Gibbs (Farmington)
Frank Robert, b. 4/16/1925; third; Leroy Walsh (shoewelter, Bridgewater, MA) and Arline F. Gibbs (Farmington)
Robert N., b. 6/17/1922; second; Leroy Walsh (shoeworker, Bridgewater, MA) and Arlene Gibbs (Farmington)

**WARE,**
George Leighton, b. 10/28/1908; third; Arthur A. Ware (shoemaker, 31, Waterville, ME) and Nellie Leighton (31, Lynn, MA)
Iris Elmira, b. 12/26/1911; fourth; Arthur A. Ware (shoemaker, 34, Waterville, ME) and Nellie M. Leighton (34, Lynn, MA)
Lucille, b. 1/31/1914; fourth; Arthur Ware (shoemaker, Waterville) and Nellie Leighton (Lynn, MA)
Thelma E., b. 11/12/1906; second; Arthur A. Ware (shoe stock fitter, 30, Waterville, ME) and Nellie M. Leighton (29, Farmington)

**WATSON,**
stillborn son, b. 5/19/1921; first; Elmer Watson (farmer, Alton) and Mariana Duquette (Rochester)
Lyle N., b. 8/20/1889; second; Charles F. Watson (shoemaker, Gilmanton) and Ada A. Dore (Alton)
Richard Edward, b. 11/18/1928; second; William M. Watson (shoeworker, Alton) and Dorothy E. Page (Dover)
William M., b. 12/20/1927; first; William M. Watson (shoeworker, Alton) and Dorothy E. Paige (Dover)

**WATTON,**
Dorothy Alice, b. 5/2/1918; first; Wilbur E. Watton (farmer, Thomaston, ME) and Fannie O. Wyatt (Farmington)

**WAUGH,**
daughter, b. 8/7/1900; third; Charles M. Waugh (trav'g salesman, 33, Cambridge, MA) and Mary E. Proctor (22, Farmington); residence - Cambridge, MA

**WEBBER,**
daughter, b. 10/6/1901; first; Parker G. Webber, Jr. (laborer, 21, No. Shapleigh, ME) and Iva A. Weeks (20, Gilmanton)
Charles E., b. 12/17/1914; first; Horace E. Webber (shoemaker, Brockton, MA) and Annie M. Richardson (Farmington)
Georgia Anna, b. 5/2/1916; second; Horace E. Webber (shoeworker, Brockton, MA) and Annie M. Richardson (Farmington); residence - Hudson

**WEBSTER,**
son [Charles W.], b. 8/25/1904; third; Charles L. Webster (shoemaker, 38, East Kingston) and Annie M. Gray (34, Merrimack, MA)
daughter [Ruth], b. 8/28/1908; fourth; Charles L. Webster (shoe foreman, 42, East Kingston) and Annie M. Gray (38, Merrima MA)
daughter, b. 8/25/1910; fifth; Charles L. Webster (shoe foreman, East Kingston) and Annie M. Gray (Merrimac, MA)
daughter [Laura J.], b. 2/9/1915; sixth; Charles L. Webster (foreman, East Kingston) and Annie M. Gray (Merrimac, MA)
Elizabeth, b. 4/3/1920; second; William R. Webster (knife maker, Lee) and Effie A. Willey (New Durham)

**WEDGEWOOD,**
daughter, b. 11/18/1900; first; Irving S. Wedgewood (shoemaker, 22, Farmington) and Fannie E. Kenniston (18, Farmington)
son, b. 4/23/1902; second; Irving S. Wedgewood (shoemaker, 23, Farmington) and Fannie E. Kenniston (19, Farmington)

**WELCH,**
son, b. 10/5/1907; first; Harry H. Welsh (sic) (laborer, 32, Berwick, ME) and Ethel G. Pryor (23, Portsmouth)
son, b. 9/15/1909; second; Harold Welch (shoemaker, 32, No. Berwick, ME) and Ethel Pryor (25, Portsmouth)

**WENTWORTH,**
son [Herbert], b. 9/19/1887; first; Martin G. Wentworth (shoemaker, 24, Milton) and Georgie Gerrish (Lebanon, ME)
daughter, b. 4/3/1889; fifth; Austin N. Wentworth (shoemaker, Barnstead) and Abbie D. Wentworth (Farmington)
son [Joseph D.], b. 10/31/1889; second; Joseph T. Wentworth (shoemaker) and Martha A. Wentworth (Middleton)
son, b. 8/4/1895; third; Martin G. Wentworth (shoe laster, 32, Milton) and Georgie A. Gerrish (29, Lebanon)
son, b. 4/20/1900; first; David W. Wentworth (shoemaker, 45, Milton) and Mary L. Colbath (41, Middleton)
daughter, b. 11/8/1900; first; Alvin S. Wentworth (shoemaker, 27, Farmington) and Mary H. Evans (23, New Durham)
Arline Barbara, b. 6/29/1919; third; Joseph Dean Wentworth (shoeworker, Farmington) and Jennie M. Savoie (Dover)
Charles Albert, b. 10/2/1920; second; Alvin Wentworth (shoemaker, Farmington) and Catherine Tirrell (Fruitport, MI)
Harry E., b. 6/9/1924; second; Alice Wentworth (Farmington)
Janette Frances, b. 8/22/1923; fourth; Dean J. Wentworth (shoemaker, Farmington) and Jennie M. Savoy (Dover)
Jonathan H., b. 10/16/1904; second; Samuel W. Wentworth (teamster, 29, Plaistow) and Georgia M. Proctor (23, Bradford, MA)
Loren Everett, b. 1/8/1921; second; Reginald Wentworth (laborer, New Durham) and Mary E. Ham (Farmington)
Miriam L., b. 3/24/1906; third; Samuel W. Wentworth (teamster, 30, Plaistow) and Georgia Proctor (25, Bradford, MA)
Richard, b. 2/6/1922; third; Reginald R. Wentworth (teamster, New Durham) and Mary Ham (Farmington)
Ruth, b. 11/12/1919; first; Reginald R. Wentworth (shoemaker, New Durham) and Mary Ham (Farmington)

**WESSELL,**
son, b. 3/5/1889; first; George W. Wessel (sic) (shoemaker, 23, Danvers, MA) and Eugenia M. Flanders (18, Farmington)
daughter, b. 2/22/1892; second; George Wessell (shoemaker, 26, Salem, MA) and Genie Flanders (housewife, 21, Farmington)

**WEYMOUTH,**
son [Carl H.], b. 12/5/1908; first; Harold E. Weymouth (foreman, 31, Roxbury, MA) and Winnie B. Nutter (21, Farmington)

son, b. 12/15/1913; second; Harold E. Weymouth (boxmaker, Boston, MA) and Winnie B. Nutter (Farmington)
daughter, b. 2/28/1923; second; Harold Weymouth (laundryman, Roxbury, MA) and Vera Cate (Brookfield)
son [Philip], b. 6/21/1925; third; Harold E. Weymouth (laundryman Roxbury) and Vera C. Cate (Brookfield)
Carl Hayes, Jr., b. 10/16/1931*; second; Carl Hayes Weymouth (prop. bowling alley, Farmington) and Theora Hayes (Farmington)
Janet, b. 8/5/1933; third; Carl H. Weymouth (truck driver, Farmington) and Theora Hayes (Farmington)
Joan, b. 4/28/1930*; first; Carl H. Weymouth (Farmington) and Theora Hayes (Farmington)
Maurice Cate, b. 4/6/1922; first; Harold Weymouth (laundryman, Roxbury, MA) and Vera W. Cate (Brookfield)

**WHEELER,**
daughter, b. 3/24/1887; first; Edward Wheeler (laundryman, 30, VT and Mattie M. Wheeler (Alburgh, VT)
daughter, b. 9/3/1899; fourth; Curtland Wheeler (shoemaker, 37, NS) and Olive A. Swinerton (24)
Preston F., b. 8/27/1896; third; Curtland Wheeler (shoemaker, 33, Isle La Motte, VT) and Olive Annie Swinerton (22, Somersworth)

**WHITE,**
son [William], b. 1/8/1930; third; Sterling M. White (auto mechanic, Fort Fairfield, ME) and Julia A. Clough (Dover)
stillborn daughter, b. 1/13/1933; fifth; Sterling White (mechanic, Fort Fairfield, ME) and Julia Clough (Dover)
Donna Jean, b. 4/18/1937; fifth; Sterling White (auto mechanic, Fort Fairfield, ME) and Julia A. Clough (Dover)
Hattie, b. 9/16/1888; fourth; Harley C. White (farmer, 40, Wenham, MA) and Mary E. Johnson (34, Farmington)
Helen, b. 6/12/1889; fourth; George L. White (clergyman, 35, New Gloucester, ME) and Sarah G. Ganniver (34, Brunswick, ME)
Jennie A., b. 11/4/1896; first; George A. White (fireman, 21, Beverly, MA) and Josie E. Averill (18, Farmington)
Mary G., b. 1/3/1925; first; Jennie White (Farmington)
Richard Lee, b. 7/14/1931; fourth; Sterling White (trucking, Fairfield, ME) and Julia Clough (Dover)

**WHITEHOUSE,**
son [Perley E.], b. 8/7/1887; fourth; Daniel P. Whitehouse (shoemaker, 34, Middleton) and Marilla J. Howard (New Durham)
daughter [Sylvia S.], b. 10/13/1898; fourth; Winslow Whitehouse (laborer, 26, Middleton) and Maggie Cassidy (25, Boston)
daughter [Matilda], b. 10/29/1901; fourth; Nicholas W. Whitehouse (laborer, 28, Middleton) and Maggie Cassidy (27, Boston, MA)
daughter [Edna M.], b. 12/2/1901; third; Albert Whitehouse (shoemaker, 29, Middleton) and Alice Jones (24, Alton)
daughter [Elizabeth F.], b. 6/15/1911; second; Frank I. Whitehouse (clerk, 25, Farmington) and Fannie C. Fall (23, Farmington)
Dorothy L., b. 2/21/1909; first; Frank I. Whitehouse (clerk, 23, Farmington) and Fannie C. Fall (21, Farmington)
Iva Bell, b. 2/6/1892; first; Charles W. Whitehouse (farmer, 27, Middleton) and Addie M. Canney (housewife, 31, Farmington)
John, b. 5/12/1891; sixth; Daniel P. Whitehouse (shoemaker, 37, Middleton) and Marilla J. Howard (36, New Durham)
Ruth Evelyn, b. 5/31/1915; third; Frank I. Whitehouse (merchant, Farmington) and Fannie C. Fall (Farmington)
Thelma Ruth, b. 9/10/1918; first; Ralph H. Whitehouse (shoeworker, Wolfeboro) and Bonnibel I. Demerritt (Milton)
William, b. 8/13/1903; sixth; Nicholas W. Whitehouse (laborer, 30, Middleton) and Maggie Cassidy (32, Boston, MA)

**WIGGIN,**
stillborn son, b. 10/3/1895; first; Oscar E. Wiggin (heel fitter, 20, Dover) and Winnie M. Fall (19, Farmington)
son, b. 2/21/1914; third; Harry F. Wiggin (mechanic, Brookfield) and Alice R. Woodward (York, ME)
Bernice, b. 10/8/1896; first; Uriah S. Wiggin (heel manufacturer, 27, Dover) and Bertha M. Ricker (20, Wolfeboro)
Helen, b. 1/22/1911; second; Archie C. Wiggin (laborer, 34, Farmington) and Maude R. Smart (24, Farmington)
Henry C., b. 3/17/1910; first; Archie C. Wiggin (laborer, Farmington) and Maude R. Smart (Farmington)
Lewis R., b. 2/5/1912; third; Archie C. Wiggin (laborer, Farmington) and Maud R. Smart (Farmington)

**WIKE,**
son, b. 7/6/1911; third; Benjamin Wike (shoe operator, 33, England and Marion G. Lord (21, Kittery, ME)
Frederick L., b. 10/22/1909; second; Benjamin Wike (shoemaker, 31, Barnsley, England) and Marion Lord (20, Kittery, ME); residence - Manchester

**WILBUR,**
Marion E., b. 1/15/1925; first; John Wilbur (barber, Canada) and Ethel May Brown (MA); residence - Boston, MA

**WILKES,**
Lona Jean, b. 1/25/1934; fourth; Gladys Wilkes (Barnstead)

**WILKINS,**
son [Robert R.], b. 4/30/1913; first; Solon C. Wilkins (laborer, Wolfeboro) and Grace L. Haddock (Ossipee)
daughter [Ruth], b. 11/19/1914; second; Solon C. Wilkins (shoemaker, Wolfeboro) and Grace L. Haddock (Ossipee)
son, b. 9/26/1916; third; Solon C. Wilkins (fireman, NH) and Grace Haddock (NH)
son [Richard], b. 5/16/1918; fourth; Solon C. Wilkins (laborer, Wolfeboro) and Grace Haddock (Ossipee)
Altana, b. 5/19/1929; ninth; Arthur W. Wilkins (carpenter, Acton, ME) and Violet M. Devoll (Skowhegan, ME)
Artana, b. 5/19/1929; seventh; Arthur W. Wilkins (carpenter, Acton ME) and Violet M. Devoll (Skowhegan, ME)
Arthur, b. 5/19/1929; eighth; Arthur W. Wilkins (carpenter, Acton, ME) and Violet M. Devoll (Skowhegan, ME)
Joyce Ernestine, b. 3/5/1933; first; Robert Wilkins (shoe shop employee, Farmington) and Arline Richardson (Farmington)
Leslie M., b. 10/16/1928; second; Leslie O. Wilkins (barber, Wolfeboro) and Geraldine Abbott (Centre Ossipee)
Lyford H., b. 11/27/1927; first; Leslie O. Wilkins (barber, Wolfeboro and Geraldine Abbott (Ossipee)
Richard L., b. 12/24/1935; first; Robert R. Wilkins (laborer, Farmington) and Irma L. Place (Springvale, ME)
Robert Romaine, b. 7/4/1937; second; Robert Wilkins (electrician, NH) and Erma Place (ME)

**WILLARD,**
son [Rodney], b. 9/14/1927; second; Frank Willard (shoemaker, Alton) and Ettola G. Bubier (Newport, ME)
Joan Maria, b. 7/11/1937; first; Maurice Willard (shoeworker, Alton) and Irene Mosher (Chicopee Falls, MA)
Joyce C., b. 10/16/1938; second; Maurice Willard (shoeworker, Alton) and Irene Mosher (Chicopee Falls, MA)
Lester Justin, b. 2/1/1920; first; Smith Willard (shoemaker, Alton) and Gertrude Bishop (RI)
Madeline B., b. 12/27/1925; first; Frank N. Willard (shoeworker, Alton) and Ettola G. Bubier (Newport, ME)
Norma, b. 9/5/1925; fifth; Raymond Willard (shoemaker, Alton) and Annie Elliott (Ogunquit, ME)
Sterlin Frank, b. 7/4/1928; third; Frank U. Willard (shoeworker, Alton) and Ettola G. Bubier (Newport, ME)
Thelma A., b. 8/27/1924; fourth; Raymond C. Willard (shoeworker, Alton) and Annie B. Elliott (Ogunquit, ME)

**WILLET,**
stillborn son, b. 3/17/1889; third; George Willet (laborer, 50, Oldtown, ME) and Annie Hagan (32, Ireland)

**WILLEY,**
stillborn daughter, b. 7/3/1889; first; Charles Willey (shoemaker, New Durham) and Etta Aspinwall (New Durham)
son, b. 3/4/1903; first; Almon E. Willey (shoemaker, 45, New Durham) and Esther C. Cilley (19, Colerain, MA)
son [George E.], b. 12/15/1910; second; J. Dana Willey (peddler, Middleton) and Celia R. Lougee (Gilmanton)
Charles D., b. 9/19/1921; first; John D. Willey (laborer, Farmington) and Celia R. Lougee (Gilmanton)
Kendall Lee, b. 11/2/1932*; first; Charles D. Willey (mill employee, Farmington) and Pauline Worster (Farmington)

**WILLSON,**
son [Paul J.], b. 12/1/1913; third; Charles W. T. Willson (clerk, Farmington) and Nellie M. Joy (Fridley, MN)
son, b. 4/10/1917; fourth; Charles W. T. Willson (clerk, Farmington) and Nellie Joy (New Durham)
Allen T., b. 7/28/1908; first; Charles W. T. Willson (grocer, 24, Farmington) and Nellie M. Joy (20, Fredley, MN)

Emma M., b. 3/20/1912; second; Charles W. T. Willson (clerk, Farmington) and Nellie M. Joy (Fridley, MN)
John Carlyle, b. 9/8/1918; fifth; Charles W. T. Willson (grocer, Farmington) and Nellie M. Joy (Minneapolis, MN)
Paul Emery, b. 4/7/1937; second; Paul Wilson (sic) (ins. collector, Farmington) and Dorothea Demeritt (Milton)
Thelma Joy, b. 10/14/1935; first; Paul J. Willson (shoeworker, Farmington) and Dorothea Demeritt (Milton)

### WINN,
son, b. 3/13/1898; first; George E. Winn (farmer, 23, W. Lebanon, ME) and Helen Barker (23, Farmington)
daughter, b. 8/27/1899; second; George E. Winn (farmer, 34, Wes Lebanon, ME) and Helen Barker (24, Farmington)

### WINSLOW,
daughter, b. 1/6/1903; fifth; Anson J. Winslow (teamster, 45, Casco ME) and Nellie Edwards (36, Poland, ME)

### WITHAM,
Harry C., b. 3/19/1910; first; Walter Goodwin (shoe operative, 25, Dover) and Carrie Bell Witham (25, Dover)

### WOOD,
daughter, b. 6/–/1891; fifth; John A. Wood (blacksmith, 31, NS) and Katie McCloud (30, NS)

### WOODMAN,
Mary Ellen, b. 8/5/1935; second; Jesse Woodman (shoe worker, Middleton) and Evelyn Curtis (Farmington)
Melvin George, b. 2/17/1937; first; Walter Woodman (laborer, Alton) and Doris L. Tufts (Middleton)
Norma Evelyn, b. 10/25/1932; first; Jessie Woodman (shoeworker, Middleton) and Evelyn Curtis (Farmington)

### WORKS,
Jennie M., b. 11/9/1890; third; James A. Works (blacksmith, 24, Lebanon) and Mary E. Ham (20, Berwick, ME)
Walter S., b. 8/7/1888; second; James A. Works (blacksmith, 22, Berwick, ME) and Mary E. Ham (18, Berwick, ME)

**WORSTER,**
daughter [Pauline J.], b. 6/3/1909; first; Henry Worster (laborer, 26, Berwick, ME) and Clara Laclair (22, Danville)
son, b. 7/12/1922; sixth; Henry Worster (salesman, Somersworth) and Clara Leclair (Farmington)
son [George], b. 10/19/1925; seventh; Henry H. Worster (shoemaker, NH) and Clara F. LeClair (Danville)
Arvard C., b. 8/21/1911; first; Moses J. Worster and Hazel M. -----
Irene May, b. 9/1/1934; first; Wilfred H. Worster (shoeworker, Farmington) and Laura Hussey (Sanford, ME)
Richard Clayton, b. 6/18/1915; fourth; Henry Worster (painter, Berwick, ME) and Clara Leclair (Danville)
Robert Arthur, b. 5/24/1913; third; Henry H. Worster (painter, Somersworth) and Clara Leclair (Danville)
Wilfred H., b. 8/19/1911; second; Henry H. Worster (shoemaker, 28, Somersworth) and Clara LeClair (24, Danville)

**WRIGHT,**
Glenn Chessely, b. 11/25/1916; second; Frank C. Wright (farmer, Crescent City, CA) and Anna Downing (Farmington)
Glynn Chesley, b. 11/6/1915; first; Frank C. Wright (farmer, Crescent City, CA) and Anna A. Downing (Farmington); residence - New Durham

**WYATT,**
daughter, b. 2/28/1888; sixth; Asa Wyatt (laborer) and Arabella C. Wyatt
daughter [Fannie], b. 5/8/1894; third; George H. Wyatt (farmer, 28, Farmington) and Alice L. True (30, Yarmouth)
stillborn son, b. 3/7/1909; first; Charles Wyatt (farmer, 32, Farmington) and Louise Chesley (19, Farmington)
Marion Alice, b. 10/19/1919; second; Ralph F. Wyatt (farmer, Farmington) and Ellen E. Thompson (Barrington)
Natalie L., b. 2/25/1923; fourth; Ralph T. Wyatt (farmer, Farmington) and Ellen E. Thompson (Barrington)
Virginia Lee, b. 1/25/1925; fifth; Ralph F. Wyatt (farmer, Farmington) and Ellen E. Thompson (Barrington)

**YATES,**
son, b. 9/11/1937; second; Frederick G. Yates (shoeworker, Littleton) and Albina L. Pagean (Canada)

**YORK,**
daughter, b. 1/20/1889; fifth; Fred A. York (laborer, 25, Gilmanton) and Annie Jones (28, Chichester)
daughter [Fannie], b. 8/23/1890; first; Charles F. York (teamster, Middleton) and Lizzie Bickford (Dover)
son [Frank], b. 3/21/1908; sixth; William York (laborer, 44, NH) and Mary Kimball (30, NH)
Grace Marie, b. 11/23/1927; first; Moses York (shoemaker, ME) and Eleanor M. Carly (ME)
Isabel, b. 2/10/1903; second; Wells York (laborer, 40, Pittsfield) and Caroline Sims (25, Canada)
Marion E., b. 7/14/1933; fourth; Rosa E. York (Pittsfield)

**YOUNG,**
son [Raymond], b. 10/26/1888; eighth; Frank V. Young (farmer, 36) and Mary Varney (32)
daughter [Elsie M.], b. 9/2/1909; third; Charles T. Young (farmer, 51, Farmington) and Daisy Drew (26, NH)
daughter, b. 9/29/1911; first; Fred Young (shoemaker, 22, Farmington) and Maude M. Young (22, Haverhill, MA)
daughter, b. 1/20/1916; fourth; Charles T. Young (farmer, Farmington) and Daisy Drew (Wakefield)
son [Willard], b. 1/28/1919; fifth; Fred R. Young (farmer, Middleton) and Alice E. Heath (Union); residence - Middleton
stillborn daughter, b. 6/3/1928; first; Malcolm J. Young (shoemaker, Farmington) and Ethel McCullough (Rochester)
Alvah H., b. 3/1/1887; first; Herbert S. Young (box maker, 21, Alton) and Susie Pettigrew (Farmington)
Arlene Eleanor, b. 4/3/1915; third; Fred R. Young (farmer, Middleton) and Alice E. Heath (Wakefield)
Charles Samuel, b. 1/15/1920; fifth; Charles T. Young (shoemaker, Farmington) and Daisy Drew (Sanbornville)
Elizabeth E., b. 9/14/1930; second; Malcolm J. Young (shoemaker, Farmington) and Ethel E. McCullough (Rochester)
Elton V., b. 10/18/1908; first; Perley E. Young (laborer, 21, Dover) and Nina V. Richardson (18, Middleboro, MA)
Florence, b. 5/1/1905; second; Charles G. Young (farmer, Farmington) and Daisy D. Drew (Wakefield)
John Malcolm, b. 2/13/1932; second; Malcolm J. Young (shoemaker, Farmington) and Ethel E. McCullough (Farmington)

Josie A., b. 5/15/1903; first; Charles T. Young (farmer, 46, Farmington) and Daisy Drew (20, Wakefield)
Lillian Augusta, b. 6/26/1933; fourth; Malcolm Young (salesman, Farmington) and Ethel McCullough (Rochester)
Malcolm J., b. 10/21/1901; first; Eugene C. Young (hotel clerk, 34, Newark, NJ) and Mina A. Brackett (29, New Durham)
Stanley R., b. 2/9/1895; seventh; Herbert S. Young (box maker, 28, Alton) and Susie E. Pettigrew (31, Farmington)
Walter H., b. 10/4/1920; second; Walter Young (motion picture, Rochester) and Edna Olsen (Rochester)

**YUDOVITZ,**
stillborn daughter, b. 3/25/1925; second; George Yudovitz (shoecutter, Brockton, MA) and Mildred E. Metcalf (Brockton)

# MARRIAGES

**ABBOTT,**

Edward P. of Farmington m. Goldie M. **Dean** of Laconia 3/25/1922; H - 39, painter, b. Bethlehem, s/o Charles S. Abbott and Belle Nourse (Bethlehem, housewife); W - 28, teacher, b. Laconia, d/o Eugene F. Dean (Madison, ME, carpenter) and Ida M. Blake (Groton, MA, housekeeper)

Ernest R. of Farmington m. Mabel **Ham** of Farmington 5/11/1912; - 21, laborer, b. Concord, s/o Charles Abbott (NY, brakeman) and Belle Nurse (Bethlehem, housekeeper); W - 19, housekeeper, b. Milton, d/o Charles Ham (Farmington, laborer) and Phebe Tibbetts (Rochester, housekeeper)

Walter D. of Farmington m. Marion J. **Bradley** of Farmington 8/4/1931; H - 21, chauffeur, b. Worcester, MA, s/o Daniel H. Abbott and Hannah Daud; W - 22, teacher, b. Montpelier, VT, d/o James E. Bradley (Prescott, ON, mechanic) and Alice Cullen (Randolph, VT, housewife)

**ADAMS,**

Edgar N. of Farmington m. Verna **Willey** of New Durham 6/30/1923; H - 21, shoeworker, b. Dover, ME, s/o Alvah A. Adams (MN, carpenter) and Emma Forbus (Solon, ME, housekeeper); W - 18, shoeworker, b. Alton, d/o Edward Willey (New Durham, knifemaker) and Mary Randall (New Durham, housekeeper)

Eugene I. of Farmington m. Carrie D. **Walton** of Farmington 5/23/1913; H - 16, electrician, b. Farmington, s/o John G. Adams (shoemaker) and Leila Davis (Farmington, housekeeper); W - 22, at home, b. Seabrook, d/o Arthur E. Walton (Seabrook, minister) and Susie J. Eaton (Seabrook, housekeeper)

Frank A. of Farmington m. Rachel **Leighton** of Farmington 7/4/1899; H - 39, shoemaker, 2nd, b. West Newbury, s/o Jerry M. Adams (West Newbury, farmer) and Mary N. Adams (West Newbury, housewife); W - 30, shoe stitcher, b. Marblehead, d/o George Leighton and Margaret Leighton (NS, housewife)

John G. of Farmington m. Leiler B. **Davis** of Farmington 10/26/1895; H - 31, shoemaker, 2nd, b. Dover. s/o John T. Adams (Dover, official) and Mary A. Adams (Middleton); W - 26, housework, b. Farmington, d/o George N. Davis (Alexandria, farmer) and Angelia Davis (Farmington, housewife)

Walter W. of Farmington m. Mary A. **Perrino** of Farmington 6/6/1937 in Concord; H - 37, shoeworker, 2$^{nd}$, b. PEI, s/o Thomas Adams (PEI, landscape gdr.) and Mary Jerome (PEI, at home); W - 27, shoeworker, b. Concord, d/o Raphael Perrino (Italy, contractor) and Louise DelVisco (Italy, at home)

## AICHLER,

Alonzo of Gonic m. Dorothea **Tufts** of Farmington 12/4/1937; H - 25, millworker, b. Plainville, CT, s/o Herbert Aichler (Plainville, CT, deceased) and Jenefer Wheeler (Orange, MA, housewife); W - 19, housework, b. Alton, d/o Moses Tufts (Middleton, farmer) and Evelyn Jones (Alton, housewife)

## AIKEN[S],

George of Farmington m. Jeanette **Coulombe** of Rochester 1/21/1929; H - 22, laborer, b. Farmington, s/o Percy Aiken (Farmington, merchant) and Edith Mason (Quincy, MA, housewife); W - 19, shoe operative, b. Westville, d/o Eugene Coulombe (Westville, shoe operator) and Emilda Labonte (Westville, housewife)

Percy G. of Farmington m. Ethel **Mason** of Farmington 1/29/1910; H - 19, shoe cutter, b. Barnstead, s/o David Aikens (Barnstead, farmer) and Annie Shaw (Barnstead, housewife); W - 23, housekeeping, b. Quincy, MA, d/o John Mason (Quincy, MA, stone pol.) and Isabelle McDonald

Percy G. of Farmington m. Marion R. R. **Hillman** of Farmington 8/27/1921; H - 30, teamster, 2$^{nd}$, b. Barnstead, s/o David Aiken (Barnstead, farmer) and Annie Shaw (Concord, housewife); W - 29, housekeeper, b. Jackman, ME, d/o Allen J. Hillman (NB) and Mary McDonald (PEI)

Vaughn N. of Farmington m. Georgia F. **Cheney** of Farmington 8/29/1934 in Gonic; H - 40, shoeworker, 2$^{nd}$, b. Barnstead, s/o David Aiken (Barnstead, carpenter) and Annie F. Shaw (Concord, at home); W - 41, shoeworker, 2$^{nd}$, b. Farmington, d/o George W. Hurd (Farmington, farmer) and Sophia J. Foss (Strafford, housewife)

## ALLEN,

C. R. of Rochester m. Grace L. **Tanner** of Rochester 8/23/1899; H - 25, C. R. Allen, b. Rochester, s/o Charles A. Allen (Barrington, farmer) and Mary A. Allen (Durham, housewife); W - 33, shoe stitcher, b. Farmington, d/o Henry W. Tanner (Farmington, farmer) and Martha Tanner (ME, housewife)

Charles L. of Rochester m. Mildred I. **Abbott** of Farmington 6/29/1932 in Rochester; H - 51, mill operative, 2nd, b. Gonic, s/o Edrick Allen (Barrington, deceased) and Sarah Dayton (Barrington, deceased); W - 21, housework, b. Farmington, d/o Ernest Abbott (Farmington, shoe operative) and Mabel Ham (Farmington, housewife)

W. Dean of Farmington m. Nellie A. **Cloutman** of Farmington 11/8/1897; H - 23, mer. tailor, b. Farmington, s/o Lester H. Allen (Chelsea, VT) and Myra G. Allen (Limerick, ME, housekeeper); W - 23, housekeeper, b. Farmington, d/o John F. Cloutman (New Durham, shoe mfr.) and Ellen E. Cloutman (Bradford, MA)

**ALVEY,**

Walter M. of Portsmouth m. Maude E. **Dufrane** of Farmington 10/16/1921; H - 41, RR conductor, 2nd, b. VA, s/o William Alvey and Harriett Jenkins; W - 28, shoeworker, 2nd, b. Milton, d/o Will S. Burrows (Milton, teamster) and Emma Knowles

**AMAZEEN,**

Clarence A. of Farmington m. Gladys I. **Wentworth** of Farmington 8/5/1911; H - 23, electrician, b. Farmington, s/o George E. Amazeen (Farmington, shoe cutter) and Clara A. Merrill (Alton, housekeeper); W - 19, typist, b. Farmington, d/o William T. Wentworth (Sebago, ME, mechanic) and Blanche Small (Nashua, shoe lacer)

R. Alden of Farmington m. Myra F. **Trefethen** of Farmington 7/28/1889; H - 34, tinsmith, b. Portsmouth, s/o Rufus Amazeen (New Castle, farmer) and Caroline Amazeen (Portsmouth); W - 29, stitcher, b. New Castle, d/o Llewellyn Trefethen (dead) and Dorothy S. Trefethen

R. Alden of Farmington m. Martha A. **Lydecker** of Farmington 9/16/1902; H - 47, tinsmith, 3rd, widower, b. Portsmouth, s/o Rufus Amazeen (New Castle, farmer) and Caroline P. Sherman (Portsmouth, dead); W - 38, dressmaker, b. Nyack, NY, d/o Abraham B. Lydecker (Nyack, NY, dead) and Martha Lougee (Alton, dead)

Walter of Farmington m. Lillian F. **Parkhurst** of Milton 5/11/1920; H - 39, shoeworker, 2nd, b. Milton, s/o Charles Amazeen

(Farmington, farmer) and Emma Rollins (Standish, ME, housewife); W - 27, shoeworker, b. Lynn, MA, d/o Frank Parkhurst (machinist) and Isabelle Dunn (housewife)

Walter M. of Milton m. Helen A. **Brock** of Farmington 6/13/1936; H - 24, shoeworker, b. Lynn, MA, s/o Walter Amazeen (Milton, shoeworker) and Emily J. Morton (Cheshire, MA, deceased); W - 18, maid, b. Beverly, MA, d/o George A. Brock (No. Berwick, janitor) and Mary Stickney (Boston, MA, deceased)

## ANDERSON,

John F. of Farmington m. Annie **Bickford** of Dover 5/9/1891; H - 32, spinner, b. Portland, ME, s/o John Anderson (dead); W - 25, weaver, b. Lisbon, ME, d/o Charles Bickford (farmer)

Leslie W. of Farmington m. Hazel A. **Perkins** of Milton 2/3/1917 in Milton; H - 21, shoeworker, b. Stoneham, MA, s/o Walter F. Anderson (Stoneham, MA, shoeworker) and Evelyn Hicks (Robbinston, ME, housewife); W - 18, housekeeper, b. Middleton, d/o Harry O. Perkins (Dover, sawyer) and Lena Labonte (Middleton, housewife)

## ANDREWS,

Fred A. of Brockton, MA m. Annie W. **Richardson** of Farmington 9/9/1896; H - 23, shoe cutter, b. Portland, ME, s/o Henry O. Andrews (Camden, ME) and Alice A. Andrews (Lubec, ME); W - 26, shoe stitcher, b. Farmington, d/o Charles B. Richardson (Meredith) and Charlotte J. Richardson (Alton, housekeeper)

## ARMSTRONG,

Harry W. of Farmington m. Nellie F. **Leonard** of Farmington 6/23/1921; H - 52, shoeworker, b. Somersworth, s/o Charles W. Armstrong and Alice E. Martin (Somersworth, housekeeper); W - 48, shoeworker, $2^{nd}$, b. Sanford, ME, d/o George Steen and Margaret Goodall

John M. of Boston, MA m. Anna A. **Russell** of Boston, MA 8/6/1918; H - 36, auditor, b. Farmington, s/o Charles M. Armstrong (Scotland, shoemaker) and Alice E. Martin (Somersworth); W - 36, clerk, $2^{nd}$, b. Malone, NY, d/o Edward Hardin (England, farmer) and Katherine Smith (Malone, NY, housekeeper)

Roy of Farmington m. Florence M. **Montee** of Farmington 12/3/1904; H - 18, shoemaker, b. Farmington, s/o Charles M.

Armstrong (Glasgow, Scotland, shoe operator) and Alice E. Martin (Somersworth, housewife); W - 17, housekeeper, b. Farmington, d/o John Montee (Canada, shoemaker) and Lucy E. Winter (Gorham, ME, shoe stitcher)

Roy L. of Farmington m. Nellie M. **Dunn** of Farmington 12/11/1909 in Rochester; H - 23, shoeworker, divorced, b. Farmington, s/o Charles M. Armstrong (Glasgow, Scotland, shoemaker) and Alice E. Martin (Somersworth, housewife); W - 19, shoeworker, d/o Jerry Dunn (Brookford, shoemaker) and Nellie Cocorain (Cork, Ireland, housewife)

Winthrop C. of Farmington m. Lizzie **Leighton** of Farmington 7/31/1894 in Alton; H - 21, shoemaker, b. Farmington, s/o Charles M. Armstrong (Scotland, shoemaker) and Alice E. Armstrong (Somersworth, housewife); W - 20, b. Farmington, d/o George F. Leighton (Farmington) and Margaret Leighton (NS, housekeeping)

Winthrop C. of Farmington m. Charlotte G. **Spear** of Farmington 12/15/1923 in Rochester; H - 53, shoeworker, 2$^{nd}$, b. Farmington, s/o Charles Armstrong and Alice Martin; W - 33, shoeworker, b. Brockton, MA, d/o Edward J. Spear and Lucy P. -----

**ARNOLD,**

Ralph of Farmington m. Mildred **Hawkes** of Milton 8/26/1931 in Rochester; H - 25, shoe cutter, b. S. Braintree, MA, s/o Samuel V. Arnold (Brockton, MA, shoe cutter) and Sarah Godfrey (PEI, housewife); W - 27, at home, 2$^{nd}$, b. England, d/o William Hulse (England, mill hand) and Frances Darlington (England, at home)

Samuel V., Jr. of Farmington m. Leona B. **Crouse** of South Lee 6/23/1922; H - 21, shoeworker, b. Brockton, MA, s/o Samuel V. Arnold (Brockton, shoeworker) and Sarah M. Godfrey (PEI, housewife); W - 18, shoeworker, b. Roxbury, d/o Archie Crouse (PEI, blacksmith) and Belle Jackson (South Lee, housewife)

**ASHLAND,**

George of Farmington m. Marion E. **Trainor** of Farmington 11/14/1932; H - 36, cook, 2$^{nd}$, b. Aintap Arm, s/o John Ashland (deceased) and Dudu Ashland (deceased); W - 25, at home, b.

Wakefield, d/o James Trainor (deceased) and Lulu Trainor (Wakefield, nurse)

**ASPINWALL,**
Cyrus G. of Farmington m. Ida J. **Brown** of Wolfeboro 3/25/1891; H - 23, hostler, b. New Durham, s/o John G. Aspinwall (Rollinsford, shoemaker); W - 18, weaver, b. Alton, d/o McKensie W. Brown (dead)

**AUBIN,**
Edwin S. of Lewiston, ME m. Ada A. **Golder** of Lewiston, ME 7/31/1907 in Dover; H - 35, ex. auditor, b. Fayette, ME, s/o Frank B. Aubin (St. Jarvis, Mon't., machinist) and Evangeline Randall (E. Deersfield, ME, housekeeper); W - 40, b. Lewiston, ME, d/o Orrin S. Golder (Phippsburg, ME, farmer) and Maria E. Golder (Lewiston, ME, housekeeper)

**AUCLAIR,**
Albany of Farmington m. Ethel B. **Moulton** of Farmington 12/5/1926; H - 25, shoeworker, b. Suncook, s/o Existe Auclair and Clarina Champaigne; W - 21, shoeworker, b. New Durham, d/o Chester Moulton (Farmington, laborer) and Flora D. Howard (Farmington, housekeeper)

Dorilla of Farmington m. Elsie **Camm** of Montreal, Canada 9/28/1922; H - 22, mechanic, b. Suncook, s/o Existe Auclair and Clarina Champagne (Canada, housekeeper); W - 22, stenographer, b. England, d/o Arthur Camm (England) and Caroline ----- (England, housekeeper)

**AVERILL,**
John W. of Farmington m. Ada M. **Rhines** of Farmington 10/13/1906; H - 33, shoe worker, b. Farmington, s/o Trask W. Averill (Farmington, farmer) and Augusta A. Wallace (New Durham); W - 23, shoe worker, b. New Durham, d/o Irving C. Rhines (New Durham, shoemaker) and Angie Brown (Limerick, ME)

**AVERY,**
James F. of Farmington m. Lizzie N. **Leighton** of Farmington 12/2/1890; H - 26, shoemaker, b. Rochester, s/o Azariah Avery (Strafford, farmer) and Susan E.; W - 18, stitcher, b.

Farmington, d/o Henry C. Leighton (Farmington, shoe cutter) and Georgie

**BABB,**
Charles H. of Farmington m. Lizzie **Grover** of Farmington 8/26/1893; H - 38, stone cutter, 2$^{nd}$, b. Conway, s/o Alberton Babb (dead) and Mary E. Babb (dead); W - 28, lady, b. Portland, ME, d/o Fred Grover (dead) and Laura Grover (dea

Fred O. of Farmington m. Teresa A. **Pratt** of Lawrence, MA 5/3/1919; H - 23, shoeworker, b. Farmington, s/o John K. Bab (Farmington, shoemaker) and Edith Gray; W - 19, shoeworke b. Epping, d/o Samuel Pratt (farmer) and Addie M. Tyler (boarding house)

Horatio N. of Farmington m. Jennie A. **Small** of Farmington 12/31/1898; H - 23, undertaker, b. Alton, s/o Solomon Babb (Northwood, laborer) and Emily Babb; W - 24, b. Ossipee, d/c Isaac H. Small and Jennie W. Young (Scotland, housewife)

John K. of Farmington m. Edith B. **Gray** of Farmington 3/12/1891; H - 29, shoemaker, b. Farmington, s/o Leonard Babb (dead); W - 18, housekeeper, b. Rochester, d/o Orin Gray (Concord, sawyer)

**BABBITT,**
Will Crane of Farmington m. Ruth Elizabeth **Allen** of Farmington 9/9/1925 in Alton Bay; H - 29, asst. mgr. fact., b. Katonah, NY s/o William A. Babbitt (Keeseville, NY, sec. mfg. assn.) and Margaret J. Crane (Burlington, VT, housewife); W - 26, at home, b. Farmington, d/o W. Dean Allen (Farmington, manufacturer) and Nellie A. Cloutman (Farmington, housewife

**BAGLEY,**
Newman V. of Farmington m. Charlotte F. **Felker** of Farmington 8/19/1934 in Ctr. Ossipee; H - 20, clerk, b. Woodland, ME, s/c Victor Bagley (Whiting, ME, clerk) and Elizabeth Bryant (Princeton, ME, at home); W - 20, shoeworker, b. Dover, d/o George E. Felker (Somersworth) and Ethel M. Hurd (Dover, a home)

**BAILEY,**
George E. of Farmington m. Doris E. **Edgerly** of Farmington 4/15/1933; H - 25, shoeworker, b. Orleans, MA, s/o George W

Bailey (Middleboro, MA) and Jessie McDavid (Glasgow, Scotland, shoeworker); W - 19, shoeworker, b. Farmington, d/o Earle M. Edgerly (Milton, shoeworker) and Ethel Drew (Farmington, deceased)

Nelson of Dover m. Fannie **Tuttle** of Farmington 11/26/1921; H - 40, shoeworker, b. Fremont, s/o Nelson Bailey (Canada) and Mary Bailey (Canada); W - 27, shoeworker, 3$^{rd}$, b. Union, d/o James A. Drew (Brookfield, retired) and Clara A. Glidden (New Durham, housewife)

Rufus of Farmington m. Ellen M. **Brown** of Laconia 11/9/1905; H - 80, retired, 2$^{nd}$, b. Alexandria, s/o John Bailey (Salisbury, farmer) and Rachel Haynes (Alexandria); W - 66, housekeeper, 2$^{nd}$, b. Sanbornton, d/o Noah Smith (Sanbornton, farmer) and Mary J. Daniels (Sanbornton)

**BALDWIN,**

Frank L. of Farmington m. Rebecca E. **Harriman** of Farmington 5/6/1908 in Conway; H - 27, shoemaker, b. Newark, NJ, s/o John Baldwin (NY, printer) and Mary Dyer (Ireland); W - 21, shoemaker, b. Berlin Falls, d/o Allen O. Harriman (Albany, farmer) and Jennie M. Blakeley (Tamworth)

**BANKS,**

Edward D. of York, ME m. Abbie D. **Willey** of Farmington 6/16/1891; H - 22, farmer, b. York, ME, s/o Charles Banks (York, ME, mason); W - 21, shoe fitter, 2$^{nd}$, b. Farmington, d/o Isaac Laurens (dead)

Frank E. of Biddeford, ME m. Adella G. **Tanner** of Farmington 6/26/1889; H - 21, clerk, b. Biddeford, ME, s/o Cyrus K. Banks (Buxton, ME, lumber dealer) and Abigail S. Banks; W - 18, lady, b. Farmington, d/o George W. Tanner (Exeter, edge setter) and Ellen F. Tanner (Sanford, ME)

**BANNON,**

John P. of Saugus, MA m. Anne P. **Davis** of Farmington 1/21/1937 in Brattleboro, VT; H - 45, chauffeur, b. Lowell, MA, s/o John C. Bannon (Groveland, MA) and Julia A. Murphy (Lowell, MA); W - 32, b. Farmington, d/o George A. Davis (Farmington) and Eliza Davis (Farmington)

**BARBOUR,**
George J. of Avon, MA m. Catherine M. **Churchill** of Farmington 7/15/1915; H - 23, shoecutter, b. Webster, MA, s/o Oliver C. Barbour (Webster, MA, shoecutter) and Mary E. Labonte (Webster, MA, housekeeper); W - 18, b. Sanbornville, d/o Charles Churchill (farmer) and Amanda Place (Middleton, shoeworker)

**BARDIS,**
Peter M. of Farmington m. Lydia **Quile** of M'gan'e, MI 2/8/1924 in Winchendon, MA; H - 22, clerk, b. Lowell, MA, s/o Michael Bardis and Anna -----; W - 22, housekeeper, b. Finland, d/o Victor Quile

**BARKER,**
Charles B. of Farmington m. Minnie P. **Davis** of Farmington 4/8/1901; H - 27, clerk, b. Farmington, s/o Hiram H. Barker (Farmington) and Ella M. Peavey (Milton); W - 28, teacher, b. Lawrence, MA, d/o George E. Davis (manufacturer) and Arianna P. Davis (Farmington, artist)

Hiram L. of Farmington m. Eleanor D. **Secord** of Farmington 3/20/1937; H - 23, shoeworker, b. Farmington, s/o Will T. Barker (Farmington, deceased) and Alta Leighton (Farmington, at home); W - 18, clerk, b. Gilmanton, d/o Harold Secord (Jamaica Plain, MA, shoeworker) and Gertrude McNary (Beverly, MA, shoeworker)

Will T. of Worcester, MA m. Alta F. **Leighton** of Farmington 9/23/1907; H - 29, b. Farmington, s/o Hiram H. Barker (Farmington) and Ella M. Peavey (Farmington); W - 29, d/o John W. Leighton (Farmington, shoeworker) and Jennie Tibbetts (Farmington)

**BARRETT,**
James O. of Farmington m. Carrie E. **Lucas** of Farmington 9/15/1924; H - 61, merchant, 2nd, b. Hinsdale, s/o Ira Barrett and Eliza Barrett; W - 61, housekeeper, 2nd, b. Quincy, MA, d/o Henry Sawyer (Quincy, MA) and Caroline E. Sawyer (Bangor, ME)

**BARTLE,**

Carl Raymond of Milton Mills m. Dora Evelyn **Austin** of Farmington 9/25/1928; H - 26, minister, b. Preston, NY, s/o Chester W. Bartle (Oxford, NY, farmer) and Julia E. Ells (Guilford, NY, housewife); W - 32, at home, b. Somerset, MA, d/o Ulyss E. Austin (Belgrade, ME, farmer) and Mary L. Fogg (Randolph, MA, housewife)

**BARTLETT,**

Matthew J. of Farmington m. Doris L. **Greene** of Farmington 4/19/1920; H - 23, engineer, b. Lancaster, s/o Joseph Bartlett (Rumford Falls, ME, jobber) and Clara Loson (Lancaster, housewife); W - 19, shoeworker, b. Skowhegan, ME, d/o Lexis Greene (Fairfield, ME, painter) and Annie Nichols (Skowhegan, ME, housewife)

**BASTON,**

Burton W. of Farmington m. Elfreda M. **Currier** of Farmington 3/17/1923 in Alton; H - 48, marble cutter, $2^{nd}$, b. N. Berwick, ME, s/o William B. Baston (York, ME, salesman) and Elmira Morton (York, ME, housekeeper); W - 20, teacher, b. Farmington, d/o Fred E. Currier (Farmington, farmer) and Abbie Willey (New Durham, housekeeper)

**BATCHELDER,**

Albert M. of Farmington m. Laura M. **Harrington** of Farmington 11/15/1904; H - 45, shoemaker, b. New Durham, s/o M. C. Batchelder (shoemaker) and Angeline Gilman (Alton, housewife); W - 31, boxmaker, b. Norfolk Co., ON, d/o John S. Harrington (East Zona, ON, clergyman) and Elizabeth Harrington (East Zona, ON, housewife)

Ralph M. of Farmington m. Isola G. **Augustine** of Brockton, MA 7/14/1928 in Rochester; H - 22, shoecutter, b. Farmington, s/o Albert Batchelder (New Durham, shoeworker) and Laura Harrington (Canada, housewife); W - 23, school teacher, b. Brockton, MA, d/o John A. Augustine (Sweden, shoeworker) and Hulda Hallstream (Sweden, housewife)

**BAXTER,**

Daniel Forest of Brockton, MA m. Fannie B. **Berry** of Farmington 4/11/1914; H - 42, shoeworker, b. Brockton, MA, s/o Daniel F.

Baxter and Elizabeth Porter; W - 31, shoeworker, 2nd, b. Alton d/o Daniel B. Clough (Alton, farmer) and Lydia F. Young (Alton, housekeeper)

**BEAN,**
Frank L. of Farmington m. Agnes G. **Horne** of Farmington 10/9/1896; H - 23, clerk, b. Brookfield, s/o Amos J. Bean (Caritunk, ME) and Angie M. Bean (Concord, ME, housekeeper); W - 24, housekeeper, b. Farmington, d/o John W. Horne (Farmington, farmer) and M. Elizabeth Horne (Somersworth, housekeeper)

Ivan A. of Farmington m. Ida M. **Wyatt** of Farmington 1/17/1893; H - 24, stone mason, b. Farmington, s/o Ivan Bean (Alfred, ME, farmer) and Roxana Nutter (Farmington, housekeeper); W - 22, lady, b. Farmington, d/o Lyman Wyatt (Farmington, farmer) and Mary Wyatt (dead)

**BEAULIEU,**
Joseph C. of Farmington m. Eugenie L. **Berry** of Somersworth 9/2/1923 in Somersworth; H - 48, section hand, b. Canada, s/o Louis Beaulieu (Canada, farmer) and Cleophe Tardif; W - 38, mill worker, 2nd, b. Canada, d/o Ferdinand Landry and Elzire Emond

**BECK,**
Charles W. of Farmington m. Reta M. **White** of Farmington 8/27/1933; H - 54, shoeworker, 3rd, b. Gilmanton, s/o J. Horace Beck (Gilmanton, farmer) and Marie Sanderson (Gilmanton, deceased); W - 50, shoeworker, b. Farmington, d/o Harley White (Gilmanton, deceased) and Mary Johnson (Farmington, deceased)

**BECKWITH,**
Frederick M. of Farmington m. Doris **Arnold** of Farmington 6/30/1929; H - 20, shoeworker, b. Randolph, ME, s/o Wayman Beckwith (Kingman, ME, shoeworker) and Sylvia Records (Madison, housewife); W - 18, clerk, b. Nottingham, d/o Samuel V. Arnold (Nottingham, shoeworker) and Sarah Crouse (NB, housewife)

**BEERS,**

Alfred W. of Farmington m. Ardella L. **Clancy** of Farmington 7/10/1915; H - 24, electrician, b. Lynn, MA, s/o Frederick Beers (CT, clerk) and Hattie I. Whitney (Lynn, MA); W - 23, teacher, b. NM, d/o Harry S. Clancy (New York, NY, lawyer) and Susie Harrison (VA)

**BELANGER,**

William of Farmington m. Della **Lapine** of Farmington 5/17/1904; H - 23, shoemaker, b. Northam, Canada, s/o George Belanger (Northam, Canada, farmer) and Delia Pratt (Northam, Canada, housewife); W - 15, b. Farmington, d/o Peter Lapine (Montreal, Canada, farmer) and Ellen Fitzgerald (Brumpton Falls, Canada, housewife)

William Eugene of Farmington m. Marie Leda **Huppe** of Rochester 6/15/1931 in Rochester; H - 26, shoeworker, b. Rochester, s/o William Belanger (Canada, shoeworker) and Delia Lepine (Farmington, housewife); W - 29, shoeworker, b. Quebec, Canada, d/o Henri Huppe (Canada) and Celamire Grenier (Canada)

**BELLEVILLE,**

Ernest L. of N. Rochester m. Juliet L. **Letourneau** of Farmington 6/16/1930; H - 28, iceman, b. Milton, s/o Fred Belleville (Canada, RR foreman) and Mary Seymour (Canada, housework); W - 22, shoe operative, b. Rochester, d/o Louis Letourneau (Canada, truckman) and Odianna Marcoux (Rochester, housework)

**BENNETT,**

Orville D. of Farmington m. Rena **Hamilton** of Farmington 1/13/1928; H - 21, chef, b. Haverhill, MA, s/o Orville F. Bennett (Providence, CT, plumber); W - 23, housekeeper, b. Milton Mills, d/o Harry Hamilton (E. Rochester, shoeworker) and Minnie G. Remick (Milton Mills, housewife)

Parker D. of Farmington m. Grace M. **Leighton** of Farmington 10/28/1905; H - 28, farmer, b. Farmington, s/o Stephen W. Bennett (Farmington, farmer) and Emily M. Leighton (Farmington); W - 31, housekeeper, b. Dover, d/o Samuel R. Leighton (Farmington, shoemaker) and Ellen L. Colbath (Farmington)

Roland F. of Springfield m. Katherine E. **Lawton** of Farmington 11/8/1936; H - 23, traffic dept., b. Gloucester, MA, s/o Fred S Bennett (Alton, supervisor) and Eldora Pinkham (West Milton housewife); W - 22, bookkeeper, b. Rockport, MA, d/o Edmor Lawton (Lewiston, ME, baker) and L. MacEachen (Glouceste MA, housewife)

**BENSON,**

Perley H. of Brooklyn, NY m. Winnifred M. **Avery** of Brooklyn, NY 12/31/1906; H - 29, shoe cutter, b. Biddeford, ME, s/o Frank Benson (Biddeford, ME) and Nettie B. Welch (Biddeford, ME) W - 20, shoe stitcher, b. Farmington, d/o Frank L. Avery (Barnstead, janitor) and ----- (Strafford)

Warren of Farmington m. Mamie E. **Marston** of West Paris, ME 1/8/1910; H - 25, shoemaker, b. Grey, ME, s/o George E. Benson (at sea, 2$^{nd}$ mate) and Francis E. Thurlew (Litchfield, ME, housekeeper); W - 25, shoemaker, divorced, b. West Paris, ME, d/o Charles W. Swan (Bryants Pond, ME, railroading) and Mary W. Aldrich (West Paris, ME, housekeeping)

**BERGSTROM,**

Leroy of Boston, MA m. Flora **McKennay** of Boston, MA 6/11/1914 H - 21, meat cutter, b. S. Boston, MA, s/o Oscar Bergstrom (Sweden, sea captain) and Annie Young (Cape Breton, lady); W - 24, shoe inspector, b. NS, d/o Charles McKennay (NS, watchman) and Mary Rapp (NS, housekeeper)

**BERRY,**

Arthur L. of Farmington m. Gladys L. **Patch** of Farmington 6/4/192 in Alton; H - 27, shoeworker, b. New Durham, s/o John L. Berr and Fannie B. Clough (Alton, housekeeper); W - 15, shoeworker, b. Rochester, d/o John Patch and Gertrude M. Clark (Gilmanton I.W., housekeeper)

Arthur R. of Farmington m. Cora E. **Lane** of Farmington 1/29/1891 H - 24, shoe manufacturer, b. Bangor, ME, s/o Benjamin Berry (Moultonboro, sail maker); W - 27, dressmaker, b. Farmington d/o William H. Lane (Lowell, MA, shoe cutter)

Charles H. of Farmington m. Clara **Barker** of Farmington 4/11/189 in Rochester; H - 35, merchant, b. Barnstead, s/o Plummer O.

Berry (dead) and Abbie E. Berry (Barnstead, housekeeper); W - 53, lady, b. Farmington, d/o Hiram Barker (Farmington, dead)

Charles M. of Farmington m. Gertrude F. **Senter** of Farmington 9/1/1938 in Alton; H - 62, woodworker, 3$^{rd}$, b. Farmington, s/o Stephen Berry (Bangor, ME, deceased) and Hannah Edgerly (Middleton, deceased); W - 63, housekeeper, 3$^{rd}$, b. Wakefield, MA, d/o Austin Stevens (Parsonsfield, ME, deceased) and Evelyn Fisher (Malden, MA, deceased)

Elverton C. of Farmington m. Jessie L. **Morgan** of Hebron 4/27/1906; H - 22, shoemaker, b. So. Berwick, ME, s/o Frank P. Berry (Portland, ME, shoemaker) and Emma E. Davis (New Durham, housewife); W - 22, school teacher, b. Hebron, d/o Andrew Morgan (Hebron, farmer) and Annie L. Putney (housewife)

Elverton C. of Farmington m. Persis A. **Hill** of Berlin 6/23/1920 in Berlin; H - 36, game warden, 2$^{nd}$, b. S. Berwick, s/o Frank P. Berry (Portland, ME, shoeworker) and Emma I. Davis (Alton, housewife); W - 24, teacher, b. Berlin, d/o Eugene Hill and Rose Leighton (Randolph, seamstress)

Frank H. of Farmington m. Manetta E. **Flanders** of Laconia 1/19/1925 in Tilton; H - 27, salesman, b. Gilmanton, s/o Lyman E. Berry (New Durham, farmer) and Ella Page; W - 30, mill operative, b. Alton, d/o Calvin H. Flanders (Alton) and Luella Sawyer

George H. of Farmington m. Emma L. **Works** of Farmington 11/23/1888; H - 23, shoe cutter, b. Strafford, s/o Samuel, Jr. (Bangor, ME, shoemaker) and Vienna (Barnstead, shoe stitcher); W - 20, shoe stitcher, b. Farmington, d/o George T. (Farmington, blacksmith) and Eunice (Farmington, housekeeper)

Irving N. of Farmington m. Lizzie A. **Jones** of Farmington 6/23/1894 in New Durham; H - 22, farmer, b. Farmington, s/o John M. Berry, 2$^{nd}$ (Barnstead) and Mary C. Berry (Farmington, housekeeping); W - 18, b. Farmington, d/o Edward F. Jones (Boston, MA, shoe cutter) and Lucinda Jones (Farmington)

Joseph of Farmington m. Callie J. **Corpening** of Chelesburg, VA 5/8/1919 in Richmond, VA; H - 50, farmer, 2$^{nd}$, b. New Durham, s/o Joseph Berry (New Durham, farmer) and Betsey Scruton (Farmington, housekeeper); W - 40, housekeeper, 2$^{nd}$, b. Lenore, NC, d/o Nichols Jenkins (Lenore, farmer) and Rebecca Poplin (Caldwell Co., housekeeper)

Joseph E. of New Durham m. Gertrude M. **Berry** of Alton 6/30/1934 in Alton; H - 64, farmer, 3rd, b. New Durham, s/o Joseph G. Berry (deceased) and Betsey Scruton (Farmington, deceased) W - 51, at home, b. Alton, d/o William H. Berry (Alton, blacksmith) and Martha Garland (Barnstead, deceased)

Zanello D. of New Durham m. Magean E. **Hale** of Farmington 12/31/1889 in Manchester; H - 32, farmer, b. New Durham, s/o Ichabod P. Berry (New Durham, farmer) and Almira F. Berry (Alton); W - 23, housekeeper, b. Bridgton, ME, d/o John R. Hale (Waterford, ME, farmer) and Eleanor R. Hale (Livermore ME)

**BICKFORD,**

Charles L. of Farmington m. Florence F. **Connor** of Farmington 5/30/1927; H - 20, shoeworker, b. Somersworth, s/o Harry L. Bickford (Dover) and Clara M. Corson (Somersworth); W - 19, at home, b. Farmington

Edward H. of Rochester m. Nellie **Gray** of Farmington 11/27/1923 in Rochester; H - 46, farmer, b. Rochester, s/o George F. Bickford (Farmington, farmer) and Georgianna George (Pittsfield, housekeeper); W - 28, housekeeper, b. Rochester, d/o William Gray (Farmington, retired) and Emma Varney (Farmington, housekeeper)

George F. of Farmington m. Mattie C. **Hartford** of Farmington 7/31/1912 in New Durham; H - 29, teamster, b. New Durham, s/o Charles D. Bickford (New Durham, farmer) and Mary L. Downs (Wakefield, housekeeper); W - 36, teacher, b. Middleton, d/o Nelson P. Hartford (No. Conway, laborer) and --- Downing (Middleton, housekeeper)

Harry G. of Farmington m. Annie M. **Kimball** of Rochester 7/22/1903; H - 21, farmer, b. Farmington, s/o Isaac Bickford (Rochester, farmer) and Julia Hatch (Lincoln, housewife); W - 22, school teacher, b. Gonic, d/o John Kimball (Middleton, farmer) and Ida M. Jones (Gilmanton, housewife)

Moses R. of Stowe, ME m. Arolin A. **Roberts** of Farmington 5/12/1890; H - 40, farmer, b. Porter, ME, s/o Horatio Bickford (dead) and Lucy; W - 38, stitcher, d/o Samuel B. Roberts (laborer)

Robert G. of Farmington m. Beatrice M. **Hartfiel** of Farmington 4/14/1934; H - 23, chauffeur, b. Rochester, s/o Albert R. Bickford (Dover, railroad) and Florence L. Grant

(Somersworth, deceased); W - 23, bookkeeper, b. Farmington, d/o Ray Hartfiel (Dayton, KY, deceased) and Ruth Tufts (Middleton, at home)

Sylvester R. of Dresden, ME m. Lucia H. **Goodwin** of Dresden, ME 12/1/1917; H - 29, laborer, b. Dresden, ME, s/o Leonard Bickford (Dresden, ME, farmer) and Ida P. Robinson (Chesterville, ME, housewife); W - 21, shoeworker, b. Dresden, ME, d/o George Goodwin (Dresden, ME, farmer) and Alice Ham (Dresden, ME, housewife)

Walter H. of Farmington m. Mary A. **Varney** of Farmington 9/9/1895; H - 35, farmer, b. Rochester, s/o John T. Bickford (Rochester, farmer) and Phebe H. Bickford (Strafford, housewife); W - 35, housekeeper, b. Farmington, d/o Ivory Varney (Farmington) and Elma Varney (Gilmanton)

**BISHOP,**

Everett J. of Farmington m. Ella M. **Young** of Farmington 9/30/1924; H - 46, woodworker, $2^{nd}$, b. Scituate, RI, s/o Robert C. Bishop (Johnson, RI, carpenter) and Hannah F. Kimball (Scituate, RI, housewife); W - 36, shoeworker, b. Farmington, d/o Frank V. Young (farmer) and Mary E. Varney (Farmington, housewife)

**BLAISDELL,**

Archie M. of Farmington m. Emma M. **Weeks** of Milton 12/2/1910; H - 27, shoe cutter, b. Alton, s/o Benjamin A. Blaisdell (Wolfeboro, butcher) and Abbie Horne (Alton, housekeeper); W - 18, bookkeeper, b. Wakefield, d/o B. M. Weeks (Wakefield, farmer) and ----- (Blue Hill, ME, housekeeper)

Clarence L. of Farmington m. Ella F. **Swinerton** of Milton 9/9/1894 in Milton; H - 22, shoemaker, b. Lebanon, ME, s/o Orin M. Blaisdell (Lebanon, ME, shoemaker) and Jennie Blaisdell (Lebanon, ME); W - 18, b. Somersworth, d/o Richard Swinerton (farmer) and Augusta Swinerton (housewife)

Ernest O. of Farmington m. Mary B. **Bickford** of Farmington 2/24/1911; H - 18, shoemaker, b. Farmington, s/o Orrin M. Blaisdell (E. Lebanon, ME, shoemaker) and Ada E. Jones (Farmington, housekeeper); W - 17, shoe operator, b. Parsonsfield, ME, d/o Fred Bickford (Parsonsville, ME, farmer) and Marie Smith (Limington, ME, housekeeper)

Ernest O of Farmington m. Bernice L. **Glidden** of Farmington 5/27/1920; H - 28, shoeworker, 2$^{nd}$, b. Farmington, s/o Orrin N Blaisdell (Lebanon, ME, shoeworker) and Ada E. Jones (Alton housewife); W - 20, shoeworker, b. Farmington, d/o Martin V. B. Glidden (Alton, woodturner)

Frank D. of Rochester m. Annie **Remick** of Farmington 5/26/1928 in Rochester; H - 30, lea. bd. mill, b. E. Lebanon, ME, s/o Adelbert Blaisdell (Lebanon, ME, farmer) and Jennie Randall (Alton, housewife); W - 34, shoe operative, b. CT, d/o Nathaniel Remick (Sutton, MA, shoe operative) and Katherine Scollard (Kingston, MA, housewife)

### BLAKE,

George O. of E. Milton, MA m. Thelma V. **Greene** of Farmington 8/9/1926 in Dover; H - 22, b. Boston, MA, s/o George W. Blake (druggist) and Mary J. Mahoney; W - 18, b. Skowhegan, ME, d/o Clarence Greene (Skowhegan, ME, painter) and Macil M. Burke (Wolfeboro, housewife)

### BLANCHARD,

Carl C. of Farmington m. Eva M. **Collins** of Farmington 6/21/1923 in Alton; H - 28, shoeworker, b. Bellows Falls, VT, s/o E. J. Blanchard (Keene, retired) and Sarah E. Chase (Ludlow, VT, housekeeper); W - 20, bookkeeper, b. Farmington, d/o Stephen Collins (NS, lumberman) and Mary E. Tufts (Alton, housekeeper)

### BOBINEAU,

William of Farmington m. Virginia I. **Billings** of Farmington 11/5/1938; H - 22, mechanic, b. NS, s/o A. Bobineau (Canada painter) and Mabel Theal (Canada, housekeeper); W - 20, clerk, b. Newton U. F., MA, d/o Tresk Billings (Needham, MA, deceased) and Frances Harvey (Amesbury, MA, housewife)

### BODWELL,

William S. of Farmington m. Annie M. **Towle** of Farmington 7/3/1925; H - 41, woodturner, 2$^{nd}$, b. W. Lebanon, ME, s/o Sumner Bodwell and Susan F. Murray; W - 26, shoeworker, b. Wakefield, d/o Charles E. Towle and Bertha Staples (Middleton, MA)

**BOISVERT,**
Arthur of Rochester m. Beatrice **Hamilton** of Farmington 6/25/1932 in Rochester; H - 23, shoe operative, b. Somersworth, s/o Albert Boisvert (Somersworth, shoe operative) and Severine Lacasse (Canada, housewife); W - 21, at home, b. Milton, d/o Harry Hamilton (Rochester, shoe operative) and Minnie Remick (Milton, shoe operative)

**BOUCHER,**
Lucian of Alton m. Althea M. **Hart** of Farmington 10/30/1922; H - 23, farmer, b. Canada, s/o Leon Boucher (Canada, carpenter) and Vianna Lemestair (Canada, housewife); W - 21, housekeeper, b. Farmington, d/o Dana Hart (Milton, farmer) and Mattie J. Stevens

**BOUVIER,**
William of Woonsocket, RI m. Freda **Cooper** of Farmington 1/1/1931; H - 33, salesman, b. Southbridge, MA, s/o Alexander Bouvier (Union, CT, farmer) and Mary S. Gentis (Canada, housewife); W - 30, housework, 2$^{nd}$, b. Hinesburg, VT, d/o Fred Dwyer (Starksboro, VT, truckman) and Bertha Place (Hinesburg, VT, housewife)

**BOWDEN,**
Winslow of Farmington m. Barbara **Geary** of Farmington 3/27/1937; H - 20, shoeworker, b. Penobscot, ME, s/o Roscoe Bowden (Penobscot, ME, leatherboard) and Clydia Richardson (Worcester, MA, housewife); W - 21, shoeworker, 2$^{nd}$, b. Dover, d/o Fred Remick (Farmington, shoeworker) and Ruth Towle (Dover, shoeworker)

**BOWERS,**
Charles A. of Farmington m. Edith M. **Cook** of Farmington 6/24/1924; H - 59, retired police, 3$^{rd}$, b. Clinton, MA, s/o Frank Bowers and Mary Smith; W - 59, dressmaker, 3$^{rd}$, b. Lynn, MA, d/o Carey F. Carleton and Mary E. Downey (Farmington)

Charles A. of Farmington m. Ida May **Hale** of Farmington 7/28/1932; H - 68, retired, 4$^{th}$, b. Clinton, MA, s/o Francis Bowers (deceased) and Mary Smith (deceased); W - 64, housekeeper, 2$^{nd}$, b. Rochester, d/o Alvah C. Rhines (deceased) and Lydia F. French (deceased)

**BOWLEY,**

Fred E. of Farmington m. Edith **Swinerton** of Milton 12/13/1904 i Milton; H - 24, shoemaker, 2nd, divorced, b. Newburyport, MA s/o Charles E. Bowley (Kingston, mill hand) and Abbie E. Winkley (Newburyport, MA, housewife)

**BOYD,**

Charles M. of Farmington m. Grace L. **Avery** of Farmington 9/7/1895; H - 24, mill operative, b. NS, s/o James A. Boyd (NS, farmer) and Annie Boyd (NS, housewife); W - 20, shoe stitcher, b. Farmington, d/o Frank L. Avery (Barnstead, shoemaker) and Sarah S. Avery (Strafford, housewife)

John A. of Farmington m. Esther E. **Varney** of Farmington 6/2/19: in Gonic; H - 51, barber, 2nd, b. E. Boothbay, ME, s/o Abijah F Boyd (China, ME, ship carpenter) and Helen I. Boyd (E. Boothbay, ME, housewife); W - 27, shoeworker, 2nd, b. New Durham, d/o Hervey J. Thompson (Strafford, farmer) and Florence J. Foss (Rochester, housewife)

**BRACKETT,**

Erwin H. of Farmington m. Kate M. **Perkins** of Farmington 7/29/1903; H - 24, photographer, b. New Durham, s/o Hiram Brackett (Ossipee, farmer) and Augusta A. French (Farmington, housewife); W - 26, shoe stitcher, b. Farmington d/o Robert R. Perkins (Farmington, farmer) and Mary J. Wiggin (Farmington, housewife)

**BRADSHAW,**

Frank H. of Farmington m. Emma F. **Jenkins** of Farmington 12/20/1913 in Rochester; H - 48, carpenter, b. Charlestown, MA, s/o Isaac Bradshaw (NB, shipbuilder) and Delia Harding (NB); W - 47, shoeworker, 2nd, b. Milton, d/o George H. Smith and Ruth H. Smith

**BRAGDON,**

Harold I. of Farmington m. Evelyn L. **Gooch** of Alton 8/9/1924 in Alton; H - 23, painter, b. Plymouth, ME, s/o Gordon Bragdon and Emma Buckman; W - 18, at home, b. Alton, d/o Wilbur Gooch (Alton, foreman) and Bertha Elkins (Melrose, MA, housewife)

**BRANDIS,**

Arthur E. of Rochester m. Lennar G. **Flanders** of Farmington 9/21/1938 in Rochester; H - 51, leatherboard mill, 2$^{nd}$, b. Rochester, s/o Walter Brandis (NS, deceased) and M. Whitehouse (Barrington, deceased); W - 58, housekeeper, 3$^{rd}$, b. Farmington, d/o Freeman Lucas (New Durham, deceased) and E. Whitehouse (Gonic, deceased)

**BRAWN,**

Fred L. of Farmington m. Edith M. **Nute** of Milton 12/24/1891 in Milton; H - 24, box maker, b. Milton, s/o Frank Brawn (dead); W - 17, shoe worker, b. Milton, d/o George E. Nute (Milton, shoemaker)

**BREADY,**

Frank A. of Calais, ME m. Annie **Russell** of Farmington 6/3/1928; H - 58, quality man, 2$^{nd}$, b. Westfield, MA, s/o James B. Bready and Esther Miller; W - 38, at home, b. Farmington, d/o George F. Russell (Deerfield, NY, retired) and Lottie Chamberlin (Alton, housewife)

**BREEN,**

Timothy E. of Farmington m. Ardena **Berry** of Farmington 2/15/1896; H - 33, stable keeper, b. Vernon, CT, s/o John Breen (So. Windsor, CT, farmer) and Johanna Breen (Vernon, CT); W - 30, shoe stitcher, b. Barnstead, d/o Plummer O. Berry (Barnstead) and Abbie E. Berry (Barnstead, housekeeper)

**BRIDGES,**

Henry L. of Farmington m. Gretchen **Greene** of Farmington 12/31/1926; H - 23, shoeworker, b. Newburyport, s/o Henry W. Bridges (Newburyport, MA, farmer) and Mabel L. Grant (NS, housewife); W - 22, at home, b. Cornville, ME, s/o Alexis Greene (Skowhegan, ME, watchman) and Annie Nichols (Starks, ME, housewife)

Lawrence of Farmington m. Irene Celia **Auclair** of Farmington 7/1/1926; H - 24, shoeworker, b. Newburyport, s/o Henry W. Bridges (Newburyport, MA, farmer) and Mabel L. Graham (Centerville, NS, housewife); W - 20, shoeworker, b. Conway,

MA, d/o Felix Auclair (Canada, shoeworker) and Emma
Lamache (Cohoes, housewife)

**BRIGGS,**
Allen S. of Sanford, ME m. Beth Lydia **Ham** of Farmington
6/20/1936 in Keene; H - 28, garage worker, b. Sanford, ME,
s/o William Briggs (England, mill worker) and Sarah Schofield
(England, mill worker); W - 23, dental work, b. Farmington, d/o
John Ham (Farmington, shoeworker) and A. Jennie Staples
(Peabody, MA, housewife)

**BROOKS,**
Frank W. of Farmington m. Olive L. **Harding** of Farmington
6/17/1932 in Lebanon, ME; H - 22, shoeworker, b. England, s/o
William Brooks (England, shoeworker) and Jennie Harrison
(England, housewife); W - 17, at home, b. New Durham, d/o
Joseph Harding (New Durham, wood worker) and Merle
Bennett (Dover, housewife)
Pierce J. of Farmington m. Edith E. **Stillings** of Farmington
6/5/1887 in New Durham; H - 31, shoemaker, b. Alton, s/o
David F. Brooks (Augusta, ME, shoemaker) and Sophia S.
Brooks; W - 22, stitcher, 2$^{nd}$, b. Farmington, d/o Alvin C.
Tibbetts (Farmington, carpenter)
Vincent Y. of Rochester m. Alice E. **Parent** of Farmington
3/15/1938; H - 20, millworker, b. Rochester, s/o Edward Brooks
(Dover, millworker) and Gladys York (Rochester, housewife);
W - 19, shoeworker, b. Farmington, d/o Edward Parent
(Canada, deceased) and Celanise Caron (Canada, housewife)

**BROUGH,**
Marshall of Farmington m. Mary E. **Hughs** of Farmington 8/8/1936
in W. Milton; H - 21, carpenter, b. Lakeport, s/o Nathan Brough
(W. Randolph, blacksmith) and Alice Danforth (Belmont,
housewife); W - 18, shoeworker, b. Rochester, d/o Henry
Hughs (Dover) and Gertrude Ross (Barrington, housewife)

**BROUILLARD,**
Henry of Sanbornville m. Grace **King** of Farmington 5/24/1935 in
Berwick, ME; H - 21, truck driver, b. Sanbornville, s/o Simon
Brouillard (Canada, laborer) and Ida Martin (Canada,
deceased); W - 21, shoeworker, b. E. Weymouth, MA, d/o

Stephen King (Calais, ME, shoeworker) and Harriet Brooks (Worcester, MA, shoeworker)

**BROWN,**
Albert J. of Roxbury, MA m. Violet T. **Rowohlt** of Farmington 12/14/1933; H - 23, mechanic, b. Lindenville, VT, s/o Albert Brown (deceased) and Anna Johnson (Rawleigh, MA, shoeworker); W - 22, at home, b. Jersey City, NJ, d/o George Rowohlt (Germany, produce broker) and Anna Gieseke (Germany, housewife)

Ira S. of Farmington m. Mildred **Knox** of Farmington 10/5/1918 in Rochester; H - 18, shoeworker, b. Oxford, ME, s/o L. D. Brown (Bethlehem, carpenter) and Alice Hackett; W - 21, at home, b. Farmington, d/o Ulysses S. Knox (Chatham, carpenter) and Addie Whitehouse (Middleton, housekeeper)

John A. of Farmington m. Alice M. **Tibbetts** of Berwick, ME 2/26/1902; H - 24, farmer, $2^{nd}$, divorced, b. Alton, s/o Charles Brown (VT, dead) and Angeline Brown (Alton, dead); W - 18, housekeeper, b. Berwick, ME, d/o John H. Tibbetts (Cincinnati, OH, farmer) and Elisa J. Hadley (Dunbarton, housekeeper)

John W. of Farmington m. Augustia D. **Dore** of Milton 7/3/1892 in Milton; H - 33, shoemaker, b. Milton, s/o Joseph E. Brown (Wolfeboro, 61, farmer) of Farmington and Lizzie M. Brown (dead); W - 25, shoe stitcher, b. Milton, d/o Stephen D. Dore (Milton, 61, farmer) and Maloina F. Dore (Milton, 58, housekeeper) of Milton

Leander F. of Farmington m. Jennie M. F. **Richards** of Farmington 7/11/1904 in Rochester; H - 48, farmer, $2^{nd}$, divorced, b. W. Newbury, MA, s/o Osgood Brown (W. Bethel, ME, horse trainer) and Ann M. Chase (W. Newbury, MA, housewife); W - 38, housekeeper, $2^{nd}$, widow, b. Effingham, d/o Andrew J. Ford (Buxton, ME, sailor) and M. Ellen Abbott (Ossipee, housewife)

Listan M. of Fryeburg, ME m. Eleanor **Lord** of Fryeburg, ME 6/5/1934; H - 29, clerk, b. Bridgton, ME, s/o Lewis S. Brown (Stoneham, ME, deceased) and Clare E. Pike (Waterford, ME, housewife); W - 19, tel. operator, b. Fryeburg, ME, d/o Walter Lord (Fryeburg, ME, laborer) and Ida Ela (Fryeburg, ME, housewife)

Vinal H. of White Rock m. Arazona M. **Davis** of Farmington 9/30/1912 in Dover; H - 52, blacksmith, $2^{nd}$, b. Pembroke, ME, s/o Levi G. Brown and Jonnah C. (Pembroke, ME); W - 47, lady, b. Framingham, MA, d/o William S. Davis and Lizzie M. Davis (Framingham, MA)

**BROWNE,**
Fred W. of Farmington m. Jennie B. **Hayes** of Farmington 2/24/1903; H - 23, clerk, b. New Durham, s/o John B. Brown (Augusta, ME, shoe cutter) and Lydia F. Davis (New Durham, housewife); W - 22, housekeeper, b. New Durham, d/o Nehemiah B. Hayes (New Durham, shoe maker) and Martha A. Durgin (New Durham)

Henry A. of Farmington m. Ethel V. **Card** of Farmington 10/2/1898 H - 24, clerk, b. New Durham, s/o John B. Browne (Augusta, ME, shoe cutter) and Lydia F. Browne (New Durham, housewife); W - 22, lady, b. Farmington, d/o William W. Card (New Castle, shoe cutter) and Caroline Card (New Castle, housewife)

Lindley R. of Farmington m. Lillian M. **Wingate** of Farmington 10/12/1887; H - 20, shoemaker, b. Farmington, s/o Charles H. Browne (New Durham, shoemaker) and Almedia S. Browne; W - 22, b. Farmington, d/o William Wingate (Farmington, farmer) and Eliza Wingate

**BUBIER,**
Victor J. of Alton m. Blanche A. **Colbath** of Farmington 3/7/1925; H - 20, shoeworker, b. Lowell, MA, s/o Scott Bubier (Hudson, ME, laborer) and Belle A. Paige (Alton, housewife); W - 18, housekeeper, b. Wolfeboro, d/o Frank Colbath (Gilmanton, farmer) and Gertrude Otis

**BUNKER,**
Charles T. of Farmington m. Clara **Colomy** of Farmington 5/1/1911; H - 36, shoe cutter, $2^{nd}$, b. Loudon, s/o Charles S. Bunker (Gilmanton, carpenter) and Mary Jacobs (Gilmanton, housekeeper); W - 36, shoe stitcher, $2^{nd}$, b. Middleton, d/o David Kimball (Middleton, farmer) and Nellie Hanscom (Dover housekeeper)

Cyrus S. of Farmington m. Sadie E. **Whitehouse** of Farmington 6/29/1888 in Middleton; H - 19, shoemaker, b. Farmington, s/o Sherburn (Farmington, farmer) and Relief (housekeeper); W - 16, housekeeper, b. Wolfeboro, d/o Thomas (Middleton, farmer) and Ellen (VT, deceased)

Forest W. of Farmington m. Grace M. **Glidden** of Farmington
5/28/1909 in Rochester; H - 20, shoeworker, b. Farmington, s/o
Cyrus Bunker (Farmington, shoeworker) and Sadie E.
Whitehouse (Middleton, shoeworker); W - 21, shoeworker, b.
New Durham, d/o John F. Glidden (New Durham, farmer) and
Dora B. Brown (Middleton, housewife)

Sidney P. of Farmington m. Nellie M. **Wood** of Buckfield, ME
1/1/1896 in New Durham; H - 49, carpenter, $2^{nd}$, b. Gilmanton,
s/o Charles Bunker (Barnstead) and Mary Bunker (Gilmanton);
W - 49, shoe stitcher, $2^{nd}$, b. Buckfield, ME, d/o Elbridge
Tucker (Buckfield, ME) and Lois Tucker (Sumner, ME,
housewife)

**BURBANK,**

Lindley A. of Farmington m. Nellie G. **Hodgdon** of Farmington
4/22/1893; H - 25, tinsmith, b. Parsonsfield, ME, s/o William S.
Burbank (dead) and Harriet N. Burbank (dead); W - 23, lady, b.
Farmington, d/o Westbury Hodgdon (shoemaker) and Ellen A.
Hodgdon (Farmington, housewife)

**BURKE,**

Dana L. of Farmington m. Gertrude **Montgomery** of Farmington
12/25/1916; H - 22, shoeworker, b. Milton, s/o Ed Burke
(Milton) and Ethel Rollins (Wolfeboro, housewife); W - 22,
shoeworker, $2^{nd}$, b. Dover, d/o Fred Montgomery (Danvers,
MA, shoeworker) and Emma Hackett (housewife)

Edmund A. of Dover m. Anna **Goodwin** of Farmington 7/1/1936 in
Dover; H - 23, clerk, b. Dover, s/o Alfred Burke (Somersworth,
lineman) and Y. Morrissette (Dover, housewife); W - 21,
shoeworker, b. Lynn, MA, d/o Lawrence Goodwin (Dover,
shoeworker) and Agnes Mulligan (Lynn, MA, housewife)

Stephen of Farmington m. Lizzie D. **Hutchinson** of Brunswick, ME
1/4/1892 in South Alton; H - 26, merchant, b. Wolfeboro, s/o
Samuel Burke (dead) and Mary J. Burke (Poland, ME, 55,
housekeeper) of Farmington; W - 26, dressmaker, b.
Brunswick, ME, d/o Daniel Hutchinson (dead) and Harriete
Fickett (Brunswick, ME, 60, housekeeper) of Brunswick, ME

**BURLEIGH,**

Charles P. of Farmington m. Violet E. **Scott** of Farmington
11/28/1928; H - 21, shoeworker, b. Rochester, s/o Henry W.

Burleigh (Providence, RI, painter) and Flora MacDonald (Rochester, housewife); W - 27, shoeworker, 2$^{nd}$, b. Dalton, MA, d/o Joseph Scott (CT, shoeworker) and Adelaide Shepar (Windsor, MA, housewife)

Harry A., Jr. of Farmington m. Eldie **Kittridge** of Northfield, VT 2/25/1911; H - 20, shoeworker, b. Farmington, s/o Harry A. Burleigh (Portsmouth, shoemaker) and Estella Tuttle (Middleton, housewife); W - 20, shoeworker, b. Vinalhaven, ME, d/o Frank W. Kittridge (Northfield, VT, stone mfg.) and Eldie A. Thomas (N. Haven, ME, housewife)

Harry A., Jr. of Farmington m. Mildred A. **Tuttle** of Farmington 12/10/1921; H - 31, shoeworker, 2$^{nd}$, b. Farmington, s/o Harry A. Burleigh (Portsmouth, shoeworker) and Estella Tuttle (New Durham, housewife); W - 21, bookkeeper, b. Hyde Park, MA, d/o Roy Tuttle (Livermore Falls, ME, conductor) and Sadie M Young (Boston, shoeworker)

Henry of Farmington m. Caroline S. **Rogers** of Farmington 4/18/1889 in Rochester; H - 55, carpenter, 2$^{nd}$, b. Boston, MA s/o Henry Burleigh (Newmarket, dead) and Susan A. Burleigh (Boston, MA); W - 51, housekeeper, 2$^{nd}$, b. Bartlett, d/o Ira Place (Bartlett, dead) and Nancy J. Place (Farmington)

Henry A. of Farmington m. Estella M. **Corson** of Farmington 1/26/1889; H - 21, shoemaker, b. Portsmouth, s/o Henry Burleigh (Stratham, carpenter) and Lucy Burleigh (Portsmouth); W - 29, housekeeper, 3$^{rd}$, b. Middleton, d/o Stephen Tuttle (farmer) and Mary A. Tuttle (New Durham)

Ray C. of Farmington m. Hazel F. **Wentworth** of Farmington 3/29/1917; H - 19, shoeworker, b. Middleton, s/o Harry A. Burleigh (Natick, MA, shoeworker) and Estella Corson (Exeter housewife); W - 19, stenographer, b. Milton, d/o George E. Wentworth and Lillian Wentworth (housewife)

**BURNHAM,**

Charles T. of Farmington m. Clara M. **Chesley** of Farmington 6/29/1910 in Rochester; H - 34, shoemaker, widower, b. Farmington, s/o Charles S. Burnham (Wakefield, shoemaker) and Alen H. Pinkham (Farmington, housewife); W - 30, shoe stitcher, divorced, b. New Durham, d/o Charles F. Towle (Wolfeboro, shoemaker) and Emma F. Witham (New Durham housewife)

Charlie T. of Farmington m. Nellie M. **Perkins** of Farmington 5/11/1901; H - 23, shoemaker, b. Farmington, s/o Charles S. Burnham (Farmington, shoemaker) and Ellen H. Pinkham (Farmington, housewife); W - 25, b. Farmington, d/o James H. Perkins (Dover, shoemaker) and Mary F. Dixon (Lebanon, ME, housewife)

Frank of Farmington m. Grace C. **Smart** of Farmington 2/21/1897 in Milton; H - 26, shoe worker, b. Farmington, s/o Robert T. Burnham (Wakefield, s. leather cutter) and Nancy Burnham (Farmington); W - 18, shoe fitter, b. Dover, d/o Joel Smart (Whitney Ridge, farmer) and Mary A. Smart (Dover, housekeeper)

George H. of Farmington m. Addie L. **Scruton** of Farmington 3/28/1896 in Rochester; H - 28, shoemaker, b. Farmington, s/o Robert T. Burnham (New Durham, shoemaker) and Nancy Burnham (Farmington, housewife); W - 25, school teacher, b. Farmington, d/o John F. Scruton (Strafford, farmer) and Sarah E. Scruton (Strafford)

Leroy L. of Farmington m. Eva May **Place** of Farmington 12/28/1912; H - 31, shoeworker, b. Farmington, s/o Charles S. Burnham (Middleton, shoemaker) and Ellen Pinkham (Farmington, housekeeper); W - 23, shoeworker, b. Middleton, d/o William Place (Farmington, shoemaker) and Lydia A. Whitehouse (Middleton)

Ralph H. of Farmington m. Doris **Corson** of Farmington 2/11/1935; H - 35, bowling prop., $2^{nd}$, b. Salem, MA, s/o George H. Burnham (Farmington, shoeworker) and Addie Scruton (Farmington, housewife); W - 28, shoeworker, $2^{nd}$, b. Berwick, ME, d/o George Rouckey (New Zealand, laborer) and Myrtle Downes (So. Lebanon, ME, housewife)

Robert T. of Farmington m. Alice L. **Hurlburt** of Farmington 5/26/1900; H - 64, stock fitter, $3^{rd}$, b. New Durham, s/o Thomas Burnham (dead) and Eliza Burnham (dead); W - 37, housekeeper, $2^{nd}$, b. Plymouth, d/o William Kelley (dead) and Ann Kelley (Plymouth, housekeeper)

**BURROWS,**

Alverton of Farmington m. Carrie **Farrington** of Farmington 8/30/1899; H - 28, shoemaker, b. Farmington, s/o Daniel Burrows (Middleton, laborer) and Belle Burrows (Farmington, lady); W - 20, lady

**BURTON,**
Henry A. of Yarmouth, ME m. Madaline A. **Day** of Freeport, ME 5/1/1929; H - 26, mechanic, b. Lynn, MA, s/o Charles Burton (NF, moulder) and Bessie Cole (NF, housewife); W - 25, at home, 2$^{nd}$, b. Bath, ME, d/o Jackson Day and Annie Moore (W Southport, ME, housewife)

**BUTLER,**
Cleveland of Farmington m. Mary E. **Nutter** of Farmington 6/29/1906; H - 21, shoe worker, b. Rockland, ME, s/o Leland Butler (Rockland, ME, farmer) and Irene Copeland (Warren, ME); W - 21, school teacher, b. Farmington, d/o Frank O. Nutter (Farmington, teamster) and Sarah Pike (Middleton)

George F. of Farmington m. Irene **Furber** of Farmington 11/11/1928; H - 22, clerk, b. Derry, s/o Thomas E. Butler (Farmington, shoeworker) and Ada L. Witt (Hudson, MA); W - 20, stenographer, b. Alton, d/o Frank Leon Furber (Alton, grocer) and Flora A. Jones (Middleton, shoeworker)

George F. of Farmington m. Margaret A. **Hunt** of Farmington 8/12/1935 in Lakeport; H - 28, store clerk, 2$^{nd}$, b. Derry, s/o Thomas E. Butler (Farmington, deceased) and Ada L. Witt (Hudson, MA, deceased); W - 21, shoeworker, b. Farmington, d/o Loren D. Hunt (Epping, shoeworker) and Alice O'Connor (Haverhill, MA, shoeworker)

Thomas E. of Farmington m. Ada L. **Witt** of Pepperell, MA 7/29/1896 in So. Framingham, MA; H - 36, shoemaker, b. Farmington, s/o John N. Butler (Ireland, laborer) and Annie Butler (Ireland); W - 31, dressmaker, 2$^{nd}$, b. Hudson, MA, d/o William T. Witt (Marlboro, MA, shoemaker) and Susan M. Witt (Stowe, MA)

**CALL,**
Louis of Farmington m. Sadie L. **Dore** of Farmington 8/2/1924; H - 59, carpenter, 2$^{nd}$, b. Concord, s/o Horace Call and Emma Smart; W - 53, shoeworker, 3$^{rd}$, b. Milton, d/o George Shortridge (Wolfeboro) and Carrie Mason (Newburyport)

**CALLENDER,**
Willard D. of Farmington m. Ruby J. **Hodgkins** of Newcastle, ME 8/4/1928 in Damariscotta, ME; H - 26, minister, b. Thompen, PA, s/o Stephen Callender (Laporte, PA, farmer) and Elizabeth

Rider (England, housewife); W - 28, teacher, b. Alna, ME, d/o
Roswell Hodgkins (Jefferson, ME, farmer) and Mary E. Jones
(Alna, ME, housewife)

**CAMERON,**
Allen of Auburn, ME m. Mamie **Coburn** of Auburn, ME 7/16/1916;
H - 22, shoecutter, b. Scotchtown, NB, s/o Stephen Cameron
(PEI, foreman) and Annie Pervis (Scotchtown, NB,
housekeeper); W - 22, d/o Morris Coburn (Harvey, NB, farmer)
and Marion ----- (Harvey, NB, housekeeper)

**CAMM,**
Stewart A. of Farmington m. Edna H. **Stevens** of Farmington
5/14/1923 in Rochester; H - 22, shoeworker, b. Lester,
England, s/o Arthur Camm (England) and Caroline Shipley
(England); W - 26, shoeworker, b. Beverly, MA, d/o Joseph A.
Stevens (Beverly, MA, farmer) and Louise A. ----- (Beverly,
MA, housekeeper)

**CANNEY,**
Carl B. of Farmington m. Alice L. **Swinerton** of Farmington
8/31/1927; H - 39, reporter, 2nd, b. Milton, s/o George D.
Canney and Addie B. Hatch (N. Berwick, ME, housekeeper);
W - 28, stenographer, b. Portsmouth, d/o William Swinerton
and Grace Durgin (Greenland, shoeworker)
Henry J. of New Durham m. Mary E. **Wilson** of Farmington
10/2/1895; H - 32, salesman, b. New Durham, s/o Thomas H.
Canney (New Durham, farmer) and Belle R. Canney
(Hopkinton, housewife); W - 30, school teacher, b. Farmington,
d/o Henry Wilson (Philadelphia, PA, farmer) and Lucy Wilson
(Rochester, housewife)
Isaac A. of Farmington m. Annie M. **Colbath** of Farmington
7/28/1894 in Rochester; H - 38, farmer, b. Farmington, s/o
Laban L. Canney (Farmington, farmer) and Rachel H. Canney
(Somersworth, housewife); W - 22, school teacher, b.
Farmington, d/o Francis W. Colbath (Farmington, farmer) and
Ellen A. Colbath (New Durham, housewife)
Merlin H. of Farmington m. Doris L. **Leighton** of Farmington
5/21/1922 in New Durham; H - 19, shoeworker, b. Gilmanton,
s/o Henry J. Canney (New Durham, cattle drover) and Helen
A. Nelson (Plymouth, housewife); W - 19, shoeworker, b.

Farmington, d/o John H. Leighton (shoeworker) and Annie Perkins (housewife)

Merlin H. of Farmington m. Marcia R. **Gadd** of Rochester 4/27/1932; H - 29, salesman, 2$^{nd}$, b. Gilmanton I.W., s/o Henry J. Canney (New Durham, retired) and Helen A. Nelson (No. Woodstock, housewife); W - 23, registered nurse, b. W. Newbury, MA, d/o Samuel Gadd (W. Newbury, MA, RR mail clerk) and Bertha R. Ross (Haverhill, MA, deceased)

Mervale of Rochester m. Marjorie **Blaisdell** of Farmington 9/10/1932; H - 20, shoeworker, b. Rochester, s/o Frank Canney (Rochester, shoeworker) and Edith Osborne (Yankton SD, housekeeper); W - 18, housekeeper, b. Farmington, d/o Ernest Blaisdell (Farmington, shoeworker) and Mary Bickford (Waterboro, ME, shoeworker)

Ralph W. of Farmington m. Ethel Maude **Hayes** of Milton 9/6/1921 in Milton; H - 25, farmer, b. New Durham, s/o Henry Canney (New Durham, drover) and Mary Wilson (Rochester, teacher); W - 18, teacher, b. Milton, d/o Guy L. Hayes (Milton, carpenter) and Myrta E. Clements (Lebanon, ME, housewife)

**CARD,**

Alvin W. of Farmington m. Florette P. **Miller** of New Durham 8/22/1903 in New Durham; H - 32, clerk, b. Farmington, s/o James W. Card (New Castle, shoe cutter) and Ellen M. Tibbetts (Farmington, shoe stitcher); W - 29, shoe stitcher, b. New Durham, d/o James A. Miller (Milton, farmer) and Ella Glidden (Ashland, housewife)

Alvin W. of Farmington m. Carrie M. **Howard** of Farmington 12/24/1924; H - 52, laborer, 2$^{nd}$, b. Farmington, s/o James W. Card (New Castle, shoeworker) and Mary E. Tibbetts (Farmington, housekeeper); W - 45, shoeworker, 2$^{nd}$, b. Alton, d/o Martin Stevens (Alton, shoeworker) and Melana Taylor (Concord, housekeeper)

Berton B. of Farmington m. Mamie A. **Haynes** of Farmington 10/17/1899; H - 29, merchant, b. Farmington, s/o Thomas F. Card (New Castle, shoe cutter) and Mary Card (New Durham, housewife); W - 25, lady, b. Farmington, d/o Charles H. Haynes and Lizzie Haynes (Farmington, housewife)

Edward F. of Farmington m. Prue A. **Colbath** of Farmington 10/13/1900 in Milton; H - 30, teamster, b. Farmington, s/o George V. Card (New Castle, shoemaker) and Nancy J.

Sampson (Dexter, ME, housekeeper); W - 30, housekeeper, 2$^{nd}$, b. Parrsboro, NS, d/o ---- Morris (Parrsboro, NS, dead) and Lizzie Norris (Parrsboro, NS, dead)

Oliver H. of Farmington m. Minnie E. **Yeaton** of Springvale, ME 5/31/1892 in Rochester; H - 21, shoemaker, b. Farmington, s/o William W. Card (New Castle, 56, shoemaker) and Caroline J. Card (Portland, ME, 51, housewife) of Farmington; W - 17, lady, b. Springvale, ME, d/o Joseph Yeaton (Springvale, ME, 51, tailor) and Nancy Yeaton (Springvale, ME, 46, housewife) of Springvale, ME

Ralph H. of Farmington m. Catherine **Guay** of Farmington 7/7/1929; H - 36, electrician, b. Farmington, s/o Olion H. Card (Farmington, teamster) and Mary E. Yeaton (Alfred, ME, housewife); W - 36, stenographer, b. OH, d/o George Guay and Elizabeth Camden

William L. of Farmington m. Bernice G. **Blaisdell** of Farmington 6/30/1924; H - 29, electrician, b. Farmington, s/o Olin H. Card (Farmington, laborer) and Mary E. Yeaton (Alfred, ME, housewife); W - 23, teacher, b. Farmington, d/o Orin Blaisdell (Lebanon, ME, shoeworker) and Ada E. Jones (Abington, MA, housewife)

**CARDINAL,**

Carroll C. of Farmington m. Ruth C. **Wilkins** of Farmington 4/2/1932; H - 20, farmer, b. New Durham, s/o John B. Cardinal (Canada, farmer) and Rosanna Rock (Epping, housewife); W - 18, shoeworker, b. Farmington, d/o Solon Wilkins (Ossipee, deceased) and Grace Haddock (Ossipee, housewife)

Ernest of Rochester m. Velda M. **Edgerly** of Farmington 12/1/1934 in Rochester; H - 21, shoeworker, b. Farmington, s/o John Cardinal (Canada, farmer) and Rose A. Rock (Epping, housewife); W - 18, shoeworker, b. Farmington, d/o Clyde H. Edgerly (Farmington, shoeworker) and Violet Anderson (North Conway, shoeworker)

Jonny B. of Farmington m. Helen R. **Burrows** of Middleton 5/6/1922; H - 21, teamster, b. Epping, s/o John Cardinal (Canada, millman) and Rosy Rock (Epping, housewife); W - 18, shoeworker, b. Middleton, d/o David Burrows (Milton, farmer) and Mina Pinkham (Milton, housewife)

Leo H. of Farmington m. Jeanette **Coulombe** of Farmington 5/14/1938; H - 22, shoeworker, 2$^{nd}$, b. Farmington, s/o John B.

Cardinal (Canada, farmer) and Rose Rock (Epping, housewife); W - 27, shoeworker, 2nd, b. Westville, d/o Eugene Coulombe (Haverhill, MA, farmer) and Imelda Guilmet (Canada, shoeworker)

Leon J. of Farmington m. Estella **Marcoux** of Farmington 3/1/1936 H - 28, truckman, b. Epping, s/o John Cardinal (Canada, lumberman) and Rosa Rock (Epping, housewife); W - 30, housekeeper, 2nd, b. Oxbridge, d/o Tim Lemire (Middlebury, MA, hotelkeeper) and Mamie Belmore (Canada, housewife)

Raymond of Farmington m. Rita B. **Coulombe** of Farmington 5/2/1936; H - 25, shoeworker, b. Epping, s/o John Cardinal (Canada, farmer) and Rosana Rock (Epping, housewife); W - 23, shoeworker, b. Westville, d/o Eugene Coulombe (Westville, farmer) and Imelda Guilmette (Canada, housewife)

## CAREY,

Marcus P. of Farmington m. Marion **Montgomery** of Farmington 9/4/1936; H - 24, shoeworker, b. Lawrence, MA, s/o Frank Carey (Lawrence, MA, deceased) and Mary Timmons (Lawrence, MA, housewife); W - 22, shoeworker, 2nd, b. Farmington, d/o W. Montgomery (Lynn, MA, shoeworker) and Lillian Pitts (Bedford, MA, deceased)

## CARR,

Ai of Berlin m. Eleanora E. D. **Lowell** of Farmington 9/3/1927; H - 21, lumberman, b. Carlisle, MA, s/o Alvah A. Carr (Carlisle, MA, lumberman) and Annie Colomy (NS, housewife); W - 25, lady, 2nd, b. Boston, MA, d/o Mayland E. Lowell (Canaan, road com.) and Nora A. Hopkins (Bristol, chiropodist)

## CARTER,

Albert E. of Farmington m. Lizzie May **Wood** of Farmington 7/2/1901; H - 50, upholsterer, b. Wilton, ME, s/o Hiram Carter (Concord, dead) and Hannah Mayhew (Martha's Vineyard, MA, dead); W - 35, school teacher, b. Farmington, d/o George W. Wood (Ossipee, station agent) and Lucy J. Jones (New Durham)

Joseph P. of Fryeburg, ME m. Gertrude E. **Steadman** of Farmington 9/12/1909; H - 27, stone mason, b. No. Conway, s/o William Carter (Newport, VT, stone mason) and Abbie J. Emery (Bartlett); W - 25, housekeeper, divorced, b. Scituate,

RI, d/o Robert C. Bishop (Johnston, RI, farmer) and Hannah F. Kimball (Scituate, RI)

Wilfred of Cambridge, MA m. Mary **O'Connor** of Farmington 7/18/1936; H - 43, truck driver, b. Cambridge, MA, s/o Lewis Carter (Cambridge, MA, retired) and Minnie Couchie (Canada, at home); W - 30, shoeworker, b. Cambridge, MA, d/o Eugene O'Connor (Ireland, retired) and Catherine Cotter (Ireland, at home)

William of Lebanon, ME m. Leila B. **Adams** of Farmington 8/4/1907 in Milton; H - 52, stone mason, $2^{nd}$, b. Newport, VT, s/o William C. Carter (England, hotel keeper) and Mary Whitcomb (England); W - 38, housekeeper, $2^{nd}$, b. Farmington, d/o George N. Davis (Barnstead, farmer) and Angelia A. Small (Durham)

William C. of Farmington m. Mildred **Nichols** of Farmington 7/17/1909; H - 21, laborer, b. Sanbornville, s/o Wiliam Carter (Newport, VT, stone mason) and Etta Valley (New Durham, shoeworker); W - 19, housekeeper, b. Ossipee, d/o Frank Nichols (farmer) and Liza Cotton

**CASEY,**

Gordon W. of Farmington m. Katherine H. **Trafton** of Farmington 1/5/1929; H - 18, counter man, b. Derry, s/o James E. Casey and Edith P. Reeves (Amherst, NS, clerk); W - 21, domestic, b. Union, d/o Reuben M. Trafton (Milton Mills, barber) and Iva M. Ham (Farmington, housewife)

**CATE,**

David W. of Farmington m. Mary A. **Huckins** of Farmington 11/15/1913 in Portsmouth; H - 49, engineer, $2^{nd}$, b. Rollinsford, s/o David O. Cate (Greenland) and Emily A. Gilman (Gilmanton); W - 44, housekeeper, b. Madbury, d/o John B. Huckins (Madbury) and Mary A. Morrison (Alton)

Frank O. of Farmington m. Nellie F. **Strainge** of Rochester 2/20/1892; H - 36, shoemaker, $3^{rd}$, divorced, b. Wolfeboro, s/o James M. Cate (Wolfeboro, 56, farmer) and Saraptie Cate (Rumford, ME, 54, housekeeper) of Wolfeboro; W - 19, housekeeper, b. Rochester, d/o Henry Strainge (England, 49, shoemaker) and Sarah Strainge (Rochester, 49, housekeeper) of Rochester

John H. of Farmington m. Ora E. **Cassidy** of Farmington 11/10/1893; H - 35, mill operative, b. Farmington, s/o John G. Cate (dead) and Mary A. Cate (dead); W - 18, mill operative, b. Rochester, d/o George E. Beacham (Rochester, mill operator) and Mary E. Beacham (Rochester, mill operator)

**CATES,**
Alfred A. of Farmington m. Florence **Simonds** of Farmington 6/28/1902; H - 29, teamster, 2$^{nd}$, widower, b. Harrison, ME, s/o Charles A. Cates (Oxford, ME, laborer) and Philena Libby (Naples, ME, housewife); W - 25, housekeeper, 2$^{nd}$, widow, b. Upton, ME, d/o Ai J. Richardson (Magalloway, ME, mason) and Myra Crosby (Ashland, housekeeper)

Charles E. of Farmington m. Amy E. **Moulton** of Farmington 1/31/1893; H - 24, laborer, b. Bridgton, ME, s/o Charles A. Cates (Alfred, ME, laborer) and Eleanor Cates (Bridgton, ME, housewife); W - 24, lady, b. Farmington, d/o Joseph P. J. Moulton (Milton, laborer) and Harriet Moulton (Tamworth, housewife)

**CATHCART,**
Fred F. of Farmington m. Lura B. **Haddock** of Farmington 12/5/1907; H - 20, b. East Rochester, s/o Fred J. Cathcart (Brookline, barber) and Alice M. Reddy (Portland, ME); W - 22, shoeworker, b. Farmington, d/o Howard Haddock (shoemaker) and Luella Tebbetts (Middleton)

Fred J. of Farmington m. Lucretta I. **Rhines** of Farmington 6/17/1906; H - 39, barber, 2$^{nd}$, widower, b. Brookline, s/o Allan Cathcart (Ireland) and Mary Lynch (Ireland); W - 31, shoe stitcher, b. New Durham, d/o Alvah Rhines (New Durham, farmer) and Lydia French (Alton)

Herbert R. of Farmington m. Pauline **Laney** of New Durham 11/20/1937 in Alton; H - 25, pipe fitter, b. Farmington, s/o Fred Cathcart (Farmington) and Bernice Haddock (Farmington, shoeworker); W - 21, shoeworker, b. Alton, d/o George Laney (Skowhegan, ME, laborer) and Hazel Nutter (Dover, shoeworker)

**CAULSTONE,**
Emile A. of Farmington m. Delda **Ferland** of Farmington 11/6/1923 in Rochester; H - 28, shoeworker, 2$^{nd}$, b. Poughkeepsie, NY,

s/o William A. Caulstone (Sweden, retired) and Elise M. Scopfer (Geneva, Switzerland, housekeeper); W - 20, shoeworker, b. Rochester, d/o Thomas Ferland (Canada, shoeworker) and Mary Marcoux (Rochester, housewife)

**CAVE,**
Clinton J. of Norwood, MA m. Agnes **Leithhead** of Walpole, MA 7/15/1925; H - 32, laborer, b. Rochester, s/o John Cave (North Hampton) and Georgianna Downing (Farmington); W - 36, gold layer, $2^{nd}$, b. Hyde Park, MA, d/o John Leithhead (Scotland) and Louisa Henderson (Scotland)

**CHABOT,**
Alfred of Farmington m. Elizabeth **Richardson** of Farmington 2/22/1913; H - 28, sawyer, b. Canada, s/o Peter M. Chabot and Orilie Bilodeau; W - 17, shoeworker, b. Northwood, d/o Bert Richardson (Northwood) and Alice Garland (Farmington, housekeeper)

**CHAMPAGNE,**
Francois of Farmington m. Gladys **Moore** of Farmington 4/18/1932; H - 24, shoeworker, b. Suncook, s/o David Champagne (Canada, lumberjack) and Victoria Lepetre (Canada, housewife); W - 24, shoeworker, b. Lynn, MA, d/o Fred Moore (deceased) and Mary E. Cole (Dover, housewife)

**CHANDLER,**
Willis C. of Farmington m. Ella J. **Browne** of Farmington 10/4/1904; H - 23, dentist, b. W. Minot, ME, s/o Frederick Chandler (No. Conway, physician) and Ann E. Millett (Minot, ME, housewife); W - 22, bookkeeper, b. Farmington, d/o John B. Browne (Augusta, ME, shoe cutter) and Lydia F. Davis (New Durham, housewife)

**CHASE,**
Fred M. of New Durham m. Priscilla L. **Curtis** of Farmington 7/5/1931; H - 25, b. Dover, s/o Fred H. Chase (Dover, woodworker) and Ella B. Davis (Wells, ME, housewife); W - 18, b. Farmington, d/o Willie B. Curtis (Farmington, farmer) and Bessie J. Gilman (Hallowell, ME, nurse)

Melvin M. of New Durham m. Albina O. **Parent** of Farmington 10/10/1931; H - 23, b. New Durham, s/o Fred H. Chase (Dover, woodworker) and Ella B. Davis (Wells, ME, housewife); W - 19, b. Salmon Falls, d/o Edward Parent (Canada, laborer) and Celina Caron (Canada, housewife)

**CHENEY,**

Arnold J. H. of Farmington m. Bernice P. **Towle** of Farmington 6/15/1918; H - 22, soldier, b. Lynn, MA, s/o Owen W. Cheney (Wells, ME) and Ida E. Hutchins (Lynn, MA, housewife); W - 24, shoeworker, b. New Durham, d/o George L. Towle and Phoebe E. Leighton

Morris Emery of Berwick, ME m. Marion Ruth **Tebbetts** of Berwick ME 8/9/1915; H - 21, clerk, b. Somersworth, s/o Arthur D. Cheney (Somersworth, baggagemaster) and Lucy G. Emery (Somersworth, housekeeper); W - 20, at home, b. Berwick, ME, d/o Walter R. Tebbetts (Somersworth, clothier) and Carrie E. Stillings (Berwick, ME, housewife)

Owen W. of Farmington m. Georgia M. **Hurd** of Farmington 8/14/1908; H - 37, engineer, $2^{nd}$, b. Wells, ME, s/o James H. Cheney (Wells, ME, farmer) and Silvina Morton (Gloucester, MA); W - 22, shoemaker, b. Farmington, d/o George H. Hurd (Farmington, farmer)

**CHESLEY,**

Benjamin P. of Farmington m. Adelaide E. **Hayes** of Farmington 1/14/1896; H - 73, farmer, b. Middleton, s/o Benjamin Chesley (Durham) and Abigail P. Chesley (Rochester); W - 55, housekeeper, $2^{nd}$, b. Danvers, MA, d/o Orin Putnam (Danvers, MA) and Sally P. N. Putnam (Danvers, MA)

Frank B. of Farmington m. Sadie **Foss** of Rochester 8/13/1889 in Strafford; H - 31, farmer, b. Farmington, s/o John F. Chesley (Farmington, farmer) and Hannah E. Chesley (Farmington); W - 19, housekeeper, b. Rochester, d/o Luther Foss (Rochester, shoemaker) and Abbie Foss (Rochester)

George L. of Farmington m. Lois I. **Morgan** of Farmington 4/27/1910; H - 55, engineer, widower, b. Brookfield, s/o James C. Chesley (Alton, junk dealer) and Sarah A. Lord (Exeter, housewife); W - 42, shoeworker, divorced, b. Conway, d/o Henry D. Durgin (Freedom, farmer) and Mehitable Allard (Albany, housewife)

Harry M. of Farmington m. Grace M. **Leighton** of Farmington 9/3/1924; H - 34, shoeworker, b. Farmington, s/o Irving J. Chesley (New Durham, clerk) and Emma J. Berry (New Durham); W - 33, shoeworker, b. Middleton, d/o Charles F. Leighton (Middleton, farmer) and Lucy A. Drew (Eaton, housewife)

Herbert J. of Farmington m. Annie M. **Kimball** of Wolfeboro 1/25/1892; H - 27, shoemaker, b. Wolfeboro, s/o John F. Chesley (dead) and Lydia F. Chesley (dead); W - 17, housekeeper, b. Wolfeboro, d/o George D. Kimball (Wolfeboro, 46, spinner) and Nancy J. Kimball (Alton, 46, housekeeper) of Wolfeboro

Norman of Farmington m. Clara I. **Blatchford** of Farmington 6/23/1931 in Winchester; H - 23, shoeworker, b. Farmington, s/o Herbert J. Chesley (Wolfeboro, merchant) and Annie Kimball (Wolfeboro, housewife); W - 21, school teacher, b. Andover, MA, d/o Archer Blatchford (Pigeon Cove, MA, express agent) and Rena Smith (Andover, MA, housewife)

Ralph J. of Farmington m. Ethel M. **Thompson** of Barrington 6/14/1921 in Rochester; H - 26, farmer, b. Farmington, s/o Frank B. Chesley (Farmington, farmer) and Sadie Foss; W - 24, clerical work, b. Barrington, d/o W. I. M. Thompson (Barrington, farmer) and Ida F. Raynes (Bangor, ME, housewife)

Walter L. of Farmington m. Nettie I. **Dow** of Farmington 3/31/1888 in Northwood; H - 22, shoemaker, b. Wolfeboro, s/o John F. (New Durham, farmer) and Lydia (Cochituate, MA, deceased); W - 21, bookkeeper, b. Northwood, d/o Samuel T. (Northwood, shoemaker) and Lucy V. (Epsom, deceased)

**CILLEY,**

Clifton H. of Rochester m. Margaret L. **Currier** of Farmington 8/20/1929 in Nottingham; H - 22, trucking, b. Nottingham, s/o George J. Cilley (trucking) and Alice M. Harvey (Nottingham, housewife); W - 16, at home, b. Farmington, d/o George R. Currier (Farmington, shoeworker) and Lillian Dunn

**CLAFLIN,**

Clyde P. of Alton m. Alice C. **Johnson** of Farmington 1/5/1924 in Alton; H - 19, woodchopper, b. Fairfield, ME, s/o Brad Paradee (Fairfield, VT, farmer) and Edna Oakes (housewife); W - 18, waitress, b. Lunenburg, VT, d/o Arthur Johnson (farmer) and Bertha Colby (housewife)

**CLARK,**
Albert H. of Farmington m. Marcia L. **Brough** of Farmington 11/23/1929; H - 20, laborer, b. Strafford, s/o Herbert Clark (Lebanon, ME, laborer); W - 18, at home, b. Lakeport, d/o Nate Brough and Alice Danforth (Farmington, housewife)

**CLARKE,**
Clarence B. of Farmington m. Florence M. **Larochelle** of Farmington 1/24/1910 in Dover; H - 33, painter, b. Gilmanton, s/o Frank Clarke (Manchester, laborer) and Fannie Smith (Alton, housekeeper); W - 29, housekeeping, widow, b. Orrington, ME, d/o Samuel Ranney (Canada, carpenter) and Angeline Murry (housekeeper)

**CLAY,**
Franklin B. of Farmington m. Lucy M. **Joy** of Farmington 9/6/1890 in Middleton; H - 37, farmer, 2$^{nd}$, b. Alton, s/o Abigail Pinkham W - 20, housekeeper, b. N. Berwick, ME, d/o Cynthia Joy

**CLEMENTS,**
Charles G. of Farmington m. Rita M. **Prescott** of Farmington 9/4/1936; H - 22, shoeworker, b. Lowell, MA, s/o Frederick Clements (Lowell, MA, clerical work) and Grace M. Gordon (Lowell, MA, at home); W - 21, shoeworker, b. Farmington, d/ George Prescott (Strafford, mechanic) and F. McDonald (Farmington, shoeworker)

Ralph W. of Farmington m. Catherine A. **Riley** of Farmington 4/30/1919 in Rochester; H - 32, meatcutter, 2$^{nd}$, b. Moultonboro, s/o George Clements (Moultonboro, blacksmith) and Lulu M. Nichols (Moultonboro); W - 24, housekeeper, 2$^{nd}$, b. Lawrence, MA, d/o John Hannagan (England, fireman) and Mary Gallagher (England, housekeeper)

**CLOUGH,**
Percy B. of Quincy, MA m. Bertha G. **Nunan** of Portland, ME 11/12/1933; H - 25, accountant, b. Kennebunkport, ME, s/o Walter Clough (Kennebunkport, ME, contractor) and Annie Bailey (Carltown, NS, housewife); W - 25, hairdresser, b.

Kennebunkport, ME, d/o Howard Nunan (Kennebunkport, ME, fishman) and ----- (Kennebunkport, ME, deceased)

**CLOUTMAN,**
John F., Jr. of Farmington m. Bessie E. **Wentworth** of Farmington 7/12/1902; H - 25, manufacturer, b. Farmington, s/o John F. Cloutman (New Durham, manufacturer) and Ellen E. Kimball (Groveland, dead); W - 20, shoe stitcher, b. Middleton, d/o Joel H. Wentworth (Farmington, shoemaker) and Martha A. Perkins (Middleton, shoe stitcher)

**COBB,**
Walter P. of Center Ossipee m. Ida M. **Colomy** of Farmington 12/23/1895; H - 21, station agent, b. Conway, s/o Joseph G. Cobb (Limington, ME, engineer) and Annie L. Cobb (Newfield, housekeeper); W - 20, school teacher, b. Farmington, d/o George A. Colomy (Farmington, farmer) and Eliza B. Colomy (Somersworth, housewife)

**COLBATH,**
Bert D. of Farmington m. Emma L. **Kelley** of Winthrop, MA 11/27/1918; H - 43, shoeworker, $2^{nd}$, b. Farmington, s/o Dudley J. Colbath and Sarah E. Colbath; W - 31, nurse, b. Boston, d/o John Kelley and Anna Sutherland

Clarence E. of Farmington m. Lizzie **Morris** of Farmington 3/17/1888; H - 28, shoemaker, b. Middleton, s/o Lauren A. (Middleton, shoemaker) and Almira (New Durham, housekeeper); W - 21, dressmaker, b. NS

Clarence E. of Farmington m. Georgia E. **Pinkham** of Farmington 1/9/1926; H - 65, shoeworker, $2^{nd}$, b. Middleton, s/o Laura Colbath and Elmira Willey; W - 68, housekeeper, $2^{nd}$, b. Farmington

Frank N. of Exeter m. Gertrude B. **Otis** of Farmington 4/19/1901 in New Durham; H - 37, carpenter, $2^{nd}$, b. Gilmanton I.W., s/o Frank D. Colbath (Gilmanton I.W., farmer) and Annetta J. Place (Gilmanton I.W.); W - 19, housekeeper, b. Farmington, d/o George Otis (farmer) and Clara Pinkham (Farmington)

Guy S. of Farmington m. Lulu I. **Harrison** of Farmington 2/11/1911; H - 19, shoemaker, b. Farmington, s/o William Colbath (Middleton, farmer) and Prue M. Morris (NS, housewife); W -

17, b. Tenants Harbor, d/o James Harrison (Scotland, paving cutter) and Mary A. Monahan (Scotland, housewife)

Irving E. of Farmington m. Viola **Dudley** of Farmington 4/14/1894; H - 27, shoe laster, b. Middleton, s/o Lauren A. Colbath (Middleton, lining cutter) and Almira Colbath (New Durham, housekeeper); W - 27, shoe stitcher, $2^{nd}$, divorced, b. Farmington, d/o Charles C. Dudley (Tamworth, laborer) and Lydia Dudley (Wolfeboro, housekeeping)

Lauren G. of Farmington m. Grace G. **Thurston** of New Durham 2/26/1913 in Alton; H - 27, shoeworker, b. Farmington, s/o William L. Colbath (Middleton, farmer) and Fannie G. Colbath (Newmarket); W - 19, shoeworker, b. North Berwick, d/o Josiah Thurston (Epping, sawyer) and Selvia Newark (York Beach, ME, housekeeper)

William L. of Farmington m. Prudence A. **Hagan** of Farmington 10/8/1888; H - 25, shoemaker, $2^{nd}$, b. Middleton, s/o Lauren A. (Middleton, shoe cutter) and Almira E. (New Durham, housekeeper); W - 20, stitcher, b. NS, d/o ----- (deceased)

Willie L. of Farmington m. Vonie **Colbath** of New Durham 5/30/1905 in New Durham; H - 42, laborer, $3^{rd}$, b. Middleton, s/o Lorin A. Colbath (Middleton, shoe cutter) and Annie E. Willey (New Durham); W - 46, shoe stitcher, $2^{nd}$, b. New Durham, d/o Marie Sumner

**COLEMAN,**

Harold L. of Farmington m. Ruth **Stanhope** of Farmington 2/3/1934 in Rochester; H - 26, chauffeur, b. Concord, s/o W. J. Coleman (Springfield, MA, painter) and Catherine Owen (Canada, deceased); W - 35, shoeworker, $2^{nd}$, b. Reading, VT, d/o Alex Peoples (deceased) and Eliza Jarvis (Canada, housewife)

Ira of Farmington m. Bessie L. **Scruton** of Farmington 7/19/1905; H - 26, mill hand, b. Wolfeboro, s/o Henry J. Colman (Wolfeboro, farmer) and Emma Whitten (Wolfeboro); W - 23, bookkeeper, b. Farmington, d/o Edward J. Scruton (Farmington, shoe cutter) and Lovey E. Otis (Farmington)

Joseph W. of Farmington m. Mary A. **Linscott** of Farmington 9/21/1901; H - 76, farmer, $2^{nd}$, b. Dover, s/o Calvin Coleman (Dover, dead) and Phoebe Coleman (Dover, dead); W - 54, b. Farmington, d/o Freeman P. Howe (Farmington, dead) and Adeline A. Roberts (Farmington, dead)

**COLLINS,**

Eugene F. of Farmington m. Clara V. **Creager** of Farmington 5/14/1911; H - 32, salesman, 2nd, b. Laconia, s/o James Collins (Goffstown, retired) and Lenora M. Hodge (Plymouth, housekeeper); W - 25, dentist's asst., 2nd, b. Derby, VT, d/o Arthur G. Creager (Canada, carpenter) and Lois S. Emery (Enosburg Falls, VT, housekeeper)

Stephen of Farmington m. Mary E. **Tufts** of Alton 9/24/1902; H - 36, contractor, b. Windsor, NS, s/o George Collins (Windsor, NS, dead) and Eliza Hutchinson (England, dead); W - 34, housekeeper, b. Alton, d/o Samuel Tufts (dead) and Susan Chamberlin (dead)

**COLOMY,**

Horatio S. of Farmington m. Florence F. **Tibbetts** of Milton 9/1/1894 in Wakefield; H - 24, shoemaker, b. Farmington, s/o John F. Colomy and Alice J. Colomy (New Castle, housekeeping); W - 17, b. Milton, d/o Walter Tibbetts (farmer) and Hattie Tibbetts (housewife)

Horatio S. of Farmington m. Clara B. **Kimball** of Farmington 12/24/1901; H - 31, stock fitter, 2nd, b. Farmington, s/o John F. Colomy (Farmington, dead) and Alice J. Curtis (New Castle); W - 26, shoe stitcher, b. Middleton, d/o David S. Kimball (Middleton, dead) and Nellie M. Hanscom (Dover, housekeeping)

Ralph S. of Farmington m. Harriet A. **Thayer** of Farmington 5/16/1913 in Rochester; H - 21, Am. Exp. D'r, b. Farmington, s/o George A. Colomy (Farmington, farmer) and Belle Jones (Farmington, housekeeper); W - 22, tel. operator, b. Farmington, d/o Walter H. Thayer (Gray, ME, salesman) and Susan A. Lord (Lebanon, ME, housekeeper)

**CONNOR,**

Charles E. of Farmington m. Florence E. **Clark** of Farmington 9/17/1904; H - 20, shoe finisher, b. Farmington, s/o Michael Connor (New Brunswick, ME, laborer) and Abbie Richardson (Barnstead, housewife); W - 16, housekeeper, b. Alton, d/o Frank Clark (Manchester, laborer) and Fannie Smith (Alton, housewife)

Charles F. of Farmington m. Emma L. **Downes** of Rochester 3/30/1928; H - 18, shoe operative, b. Farmington, s/o Charles

E. Connor (Farmington, shoe operative) and Florence Clark (Alton, shoe operative); W - 17, housework, b. Rochester, d/o George A. Downes (Northwood, mill operative) and Cora E. Hurd (Rochester, housewife)

George W. of Farmington m. Bertha **Clarke** of Farmington 2/17/1908; H - 20, shoemaker, b. Milton, s/o Michael Connor (Manchester, shoemaker) and Abbie Richardson (Alton); W - 16, housekeeper, b. Alton, d/o Frank Clark (laborer) and Fannie Smith (Alton)

**CONNORS,**

Joseph N., Jr. of Farmington m. Anna E. **Ludden** of Rochester 6/5/1937 in Rochester; H - 26, shoeworker, b. Roxbury, MA, s/o Joseph N. Connors (Roxbury, MA, shoeworker) and Mary E. Connors (Charlestown, MA, at home); W - 26, telephone op., b. Rochester, d/o Thomas Ludden (Ireland, boxmaker) and Mary Ludden (Ireland, at home)

**CONTOIS,**

Raymond of Farmington m. Emily **Ripley** of Methuen, MA 5/5/1928 in Salem; H - 21, carpenter, b. Lawrence, MA, s/o John E. Contois (Quebec, carpenter) and Beatrice P. Grass (NS, housewife); W - 19, millworker, b. Methuen, MA, d/o Charles Ripley (England, millworker) and Sarah Nillson (Olneyville, RI)

**COOK,**

Ansel P. of Conway m. Clara **Batchelder** of Gorham, ME 3/4/1901 H - 57, farmer, 2nd, b. Conway, s/o Nathaniel Cook (Conway, farmer) and Lovice Johnson (Conway, housewife); W - 57, housewife, 2nd, b. Kennebunk, ME, d/o William Eastman (Hollis, ME, shoemaker) and Rodia Greene (Hollis, ME, housewife)

Ernest P. of Farmington m. Enid **Hayes** of Rochester 1/19/1937 in Rochester; H - 21, shoeworker, b. No. Barnstead, s/o Herbert Cook (No. Barnstead, shoeworker) and Anna Dolby (Providence, RI, housewife); W - 18, shoeworker, b. Rochester, d/o Walter E. Hayes (Farmington, deceased) and Etta E. Roberts (Farmington, shoeworker)

Henry N. of Barnstead m. Edith M. **Sutton** of Farmington 9/21/1907; H - 49, mill hand, 2nd, b. Milton, s/o Moses W. Cook (Milton, farmer) and Freelove Downing (Holderness, housekeeper); W - 41, housekeeper, 2nd, b. Newton, MA, d/o Carey F. Carleton (Haverhill, MA, farmer) and Mary E. Downing (Farmington)

Nathaniel P. of Barnstead m. Cynthia **Caverly** of Barnstead 4/22/1893 in New Durham; H - 19, farmer, b. Barnstead, s/o Moses Cook (dead) and Frelove S. Cook (Milton, housekeeper); W - 18, lady, b. Barnstead, d/o ----- (dead) and ----- (dead)

## COOKE,

John H. of Farmington m. Liberty W. **Wentworth** of Farmington 5/2/1888; H - 43, farmer, 2nd, b. Milton, s/o Isaac (Somersworth, deceased) and Elizabeth (Milton, housekeeper); W - 46, housekeeper, 3rd, b. Farmington, d/o Samuel (Farmington, deceased) and Jane (Wolfeboro)

## COPP,

Arthur Leroy of Farmington m. Elizabeth A. **Wood** of Ossipee 4/12/1909; H - 19, teamster, b. Bangor, ME, s/o Daniel B. Copp (NB, teamster) and Lizzie McNorton (Milo Jct., ME, housekeeper); W - 17, housekeeper, b. No. Wolfeboro, d/o Frank J. Wood (Ossipee, lumberman) and E. Jane Speedy (NB, housekeeper)

## CORSON,

George A. of Farmington m. Oiive D. **Richardson** of Farmington 12/24/1910; H - 30, farmer, b. New Durham, s/o Henry Corson (New Durham, farmer) and May J. Gilbert (New Durham, housewife); W - 18, shoemaker, b. Farmington, d/o Ai J. Richardson (Upton, ME, mason) and Lydia A. Holden (Stewartstown, housewife)

Walter N. of Farmington m. Sadie **Rand** of Farmington 5/11/1901 in New Durham; H - 20, shoemaker, b. Farmington, s/o Charles Corson (Farmington, shoemaker) and Estella M. Tuttle (Middleton, housewife); W - 18, b. Portland, ME, d/o A. Oscar Rand (New Durham, mill hand) and Eliza McDonald (New Caster, NS, housewife)

Walter N. of Farmington m. Nancy B. **Currier** of Amesbury, MA 5/27/1917; H - 32, chauffeur, 2nd, b. Farmington, s/o Charles Corson (Farmington) and Estella M. Tuttle (Farmington, housewife); W - 21, at home, b. Amesbury, MA, d/o Leonard Currier and Annie S. Peterson (Amesbury, MA, housewife)

**COTTON,**
Harry E. of Farmington m. Ivadell M. **Nichols** of Farmington 12/21/1920; H - 20, fireman, b. Farmington, s/o Benjamin D. Cotton and Phoebe L. Tibbetts (Rochester, housekeeper); W 16, at home, b. Wolfeboro Falls, d/o Elbert J. Nichols (Ossipee, laborer) and Copelia Ash

**COULOMBE,**
Almanzor of Farmington m. Mary **Wyeik** of Farmington 9/3/1937 i Sanford, ME; H - 24, shoeworker, b. Haverhill, MA, s/o Edwa Coulombe (Canada, corner moulder) and Mary Pouliot (Canada, housewife); W - 22, at home, b. Haverhill, MA, d/o Kastanto Wyeik (Lithuania, retired) and Petrona Stanley (Lithuania, housewife)

**COX,**
Herbert M. of Melrose, MA m. Eva N. **Browne** of Farmington 12/21/1898; H - 26, clerk, b. Amherst, MA, s/o Enoch Cox an Caroline Cox; W - 24, b. Farmington, d/o Charles P. Browne (New Durham, shoemaker) and Almedia S. Browne (Acton, ME, shoe stitcher)

**CRAMER,**
William A. of Barnston, PQ m. Amanda **Tibbetts** of Farmington 9/9/1896; H - 69, blacksmith, 2nd, b. Melbourne, PQ, s/o Jeremiah Cramer (NY) and Betsey Wakefield (Stanstead, PQ W - 70, housekeeper, 2nd, b. Stanstead, PQ, d/o Erastus Lee (Stanstead, PQ) and Mary A. Cooley (Ossipee)

**CRANE,**
Donald P. of Quincy, MA m. Estelle C. **Nims** of Farmington 5/4/1918; H - 23, soldier, b. Quincy, MA, s/o Emery L. Crane (Quincy, MA, city clerk) and Ada Zeigler Crane (Bainbridge, GA, lady); W - 21, teacher, b. Keene, d/o Myron A. Nims (Harrisville, bookkeeper) and Ada Belle Nims (Surry, lady)

**CROCKETT,**
Willard E. of Farmington m. Lilla **Faulkner** of Rochester 10/27/1913; H - 27, clerk, b. Princeton, ME, s/o James H. Crockett (Princeton, ME, mechanic) and Stella Legacy (Princeton, ME); W - 21, at home, b. Rochester, d/o Charles A. Faulkner (druggist) and Nellie Faulkner (housekeeper)

**CROSBY,**
Charles M. of Farmington m. Marie V. **Plummer** of Farmington 4/25/1896; H - 27, shipping clerk, b. Barnstead, s/o John Q. Crosby (Barnstead, farmer) and Melissa A. Crosby (Farmington, housekeeper); W - 18, stitcher in mill, b. Farmington, d/o Lorenzo C. Plummer (Gilmanton, shoemaker) and Ellen O. Plummer (Alton, housekeeper)

George M. of Farmington m. Mary J. **Tanguay** of Dover 5/23/1925; H - 49, fireman, b. Sanford, ME, s/o Charles W. Crosby (Gilmanton, shoeworker) and Eliza A. Martin; W - 49, tailoress, b. Dover, d/o Alixe Tanguay and Mary Tanguay

**CROUSE,**
Henry A. of Farmington m. Annie B. **Jackson** of Farmington 8/2/1898; H - 26, laborer, b. NS, s/o Henry A. Crouse (NS, farmer) and Sophia Crouse (NS, housewife); W - 19, b. Nottingham, d/o Mary A. Jackson (Middleton, shoe stitcher)

**CROWELL,**
Saul J. of Farmington m. Laura D. **Constant** of Farmington 11/14/1894; H - 25, farmer, b. NS, s/o Charles H. Crowell (NS, farmer) and Catherine Crowell (NS, housekeeper); W - 19, b. Canada, d/o John H. Constant (Canada, lumberman) and Mrs. Constant (Canada, housekeeper)

**CROWTHER,**
Dyson of Boston, MA m. Rosa L. **Newcome** of Warren, ME 8/30/1918; H - 52, govt. insp., 2nd, b. England, s/o Henry Crowther and Hannah Dyson; W - 46, housekeeper, 2nd, b. Warren, ME, d/o Leland Butler (S. Thomaston, ME, farmer) and Irene Copeland (Warren, ME, housekeeper)

**CUMMISKY,**
Peter M. of Farmington m. Martha E. **McCarty** of PEI 9/1/1889 in Rochester; H - 24, hostler, b. PEI, s/o Michael Cummisky (Ireland, farmer) and Catherine Cummisky (Ireland); W - 21, housekeeper, b. PEI, d/o Charles McCarty (PEI, farmer) and Elizabeth McCarty (PEI)

**CURRIER,**
Albert E. of Farmington m. Eva M. **Howard** of Farmington 5/29/1935 in E. Rochester; H - 23, shoeworker, b. Farmington, s/o Fred E. Currier (Farmington, farmer) and Abbie Willey (New Durham, housewife); W - 22, shoeworker, $2^{nd}$, b. Van Buren, ME, d/o Dennis Burgoyne (Van Buren, ME, farmer) and Annie Albert (Van Buren, ME, housewife)

Charles F. of Farmington m. Merle E. **Bunker** of Farmington 12/17/1932 in Sanford, ME; H - 25, carpenter, b. Farmington, s/o Charles V. Currier (Farmington, farmer) and Mary Ring (Farmington, housewife); W - 20, at home, b. Farmington, d/o Forest Bunker (Farmington, foreman) and Grace Glidden (New Durham, housewife)

Charles V. of Farmington m. Mary A. **Ring** of Farmington 10/31/1891 in Pittsfield; H - 24, stock fitter, b. Farmington, s/o George E. Currier (Hopkinton, farmer); W - 21, school teacher, d/o Dennis Ring (Ireland, blacksmith)

Fred E. of Farmington m. Lizzie A. **Willey** of Farmington 9/16/1899 in Milton; H - 26, shoemaker, b. Farmington, s/o George E. Currier (Holliston, MA, farmer) and Mary C. Currier; W - 20, b. Farmington, d/o Almon Willey (Farmington, shoemaker) and Lizzie Willey

Fred E., Jr. of Farmington m. Eleanor W. **Babb** of Rochester 2/25/1934 in Portsmouth; H - 23, mechanic, b. Farmington, s/o Fred E. Currier (Farmington, farmer) and Abbie Willey (New Durham, housewife); W - 20, clerk, b. Rochester, d/o Guy Babb (Gonic, cook) and Florence L. Otis (Rochester, waitress)

George R. of Farmington m. Aurie P. **Lord** of Farmington 11/18/1922 in Seabrook; H - 30, bowling, pool, $2^{nd}$, b. Farmington, s/o Augustus B. Currier (Farmington, shoeworker) and Sarah A. Lary (Rochester, housewife); W - 24, shoeworker, $2^{nd}$, b. Rochester, d/o Frank C. Lord (Dover, farmer) and Emma L. Grant (Rochester, housewife)

George Richard of Farmington m. Lillian F. **Dunn** of Farmington 3/8/1913; H - 20, shoeworker, b. Farmington, s/o Burnes Currier (Farmington, shoeworker) and Sadie A. Lary (Somersworth, shoeworker); W - 18, shoeworker, b. Hudson, MA, d/o Jeremiah Dunn (Brookfield, MA, shoeworker) and Nellie B. Dunn (Ireland, housekeeper)

George W. of Farmington m. Idana **Horne** of Rochester 7/2/1892 in Rochester; H - 28, shoemaker, b. Farmington, s/o George C. Currier (Natick, ME, 56, farmer) and Mary E. Currier (57, housewife) of Farmington; W - 28, lady, $2^{nd}$, widow, b. Strafford, d/o ----- (dead) and ----- (dead)

Herbert H. of Lee m. Ruth L. **Rhines** of Farmington 5/29/1932 in Exeter; H - 20, farmer, b. Lee, s/o John H. Currier (Gonic, farmer) and Etta May Davis (Moultonboro, housewife); W - 18, at home, b. New Durham, d/o Herman A. Rhines (New Durham, woodturner) and Lucy Belle Dow (Bristol, housewife)

John T. of Farmington m. Ida B. **Burroughs** of Barnstead 3/10/1892 in Alton; H - 24, shoe cutter, b. Farmington, s/o George E. Currier (Holliston, MA, 57, farmer) and Mary Currier (Farmington, 55, housewife) of Farmington; W - 18, shoe stitcher, b. Barnstead, d/o George F. Burroughs (Barnstead, 42, shoemaker) and Delia A. Burroughs (Great Falls, 42, housewife) of Barnstead

Ray B. of Farmington m. Lillian M. **Conner** of Farmington 12/29/1909; H - 20, clerk, b. Farmington, s/o Augustus B. Currier (Farmington, shoecutter) and Sarah A. Leary (Somersworth, shoeworker); W - 18, shoeworker, b. Farmington, d/o Charles E. Conner (Farmington, shoecutter) and Florence A. Miller (New Durham, shoeworker)

**CURTIS,**

Asa A. of Farmington m. Ada Estella **Blaisdell** of Farmington 8/31/1901; H - 22, shoeworker, b. Milton, s/o Moses P. Curtis (Milton, shoemaker) and Juliette F. Cook (Milton); W - 17, shoe stitcher, b. Farmington, d/o Orin M. Blaisdell (Lebanon, ME, shoemaker) and Ada Jones (Farmington)

Chester F. of Milton m. Cora **Estes** of Farmington 2/14/1924; H - 20, US Army, b. Farmington, s/o Fred Curtis (Farmington, shoeworker) and Carrie Howard (Farmington, housewife); W - 30, shoeworker, $2^{nd}$, b. Belmont, ME, d/o Fidelphus Flagg

(Belmont, ME, farmer) and Hattie M. Jackson (Belmont, ME, housewife)

Clarence L., Jr. of Farmington m. Velma L. **Clough** of Farmington 9/22/1935; H - 25, salesman, b. Portland, ME, s/o Clarence L. Curtis (Harpswell, ME, retired) and Eva M. Curtis (Portland, at home); W - 23, clerk, b. Dover, d/o Eli F. Clough (Dover, farmer) and Addie M. Clough (Barrington, at home)

Everett I. of Farmington m. Annie J. **Wentworth** of Acton, ME 9/22/1894 in Milton Mills; H - 18, shoe finishing, b. Milton, s/o Moses P. Curtis (Farmington, shoemaker) and Juliet Curtis (Milton, housekeeper); W - 15, b. Acton, ME, d/o John Wentworth (Milton, farmer) and Augusta Wentworth (Milton, housekeeper)

Fred of Farmington m. Carrie E. **Howard** of Farmington 7/31/1901 in Milton; H - 20, shoemaker, b. Farmington, s/o Moses P. Curtis (Milton, shoemaker) and Juliette F. Cook (Milton); W - 23, housekeeper, b. Farmington, d/o Frank Howard (Barrington, dead) and Hannah M. Brown (Barrington)

Henry B. of Farmington m. Lizzie M. **Runnells** of New Durham 4/25/1901 in Wolfeboro; H - 23, shoecutter, b. Milton, s/o Moses P. Curtis (Milton, shoemaker) and Juliette F. Cook (Milton); W - 22, housekeeper, b. New Durham, d/o Paul M. Runnells (farmer) and Mary J. Colomy

Irving S. of Farmington m. Hattie B. **Amazeen** of Milton 7/1/1895 in Rochester; H - 39, farming, b. Farmington, s/o William A. Curtis (New Castle, farmer) and Melissa S. Curtis (Farmington, housewife); W - 16, housekeeper, b. Milton, d/o Charles S. Amazeen (Farmington, farmer) and Emma Amazeen (Standish, ME, housewife)

Norman W. of Farmington m. Bernice T. **Hurd** of Farmington 1/15/1927; H - 20, shoeworker, b. Farmington, s/o Fred Curtis (Milton, shoeworker) and Carrie E. Howard (Farmington, housewife); W - 25, shoeworker, b. Farmington, d/o W. G. Hurd (Milton, teamster) and Nellie A. Varney (Milton, housewife)

Reginald W. of Farmington m. Lillian R. **Dore** of Manchester 11/28/1926; H - 20, shoeworker, b. Farmington, s/o Willie B. Curtis (Farmington, farmer) and Bessie Gilman (Hallowell, ME housewife); W - 24, domestic, b. Milton, d/o Blanche E. Dore (Farmington, housekeeper)

Sylvester R. of Farmington m. Fannie E. **Webster** of Farmington
5/5/1907; H - 47, shoe laster, b. Farmington, s/o Rufus Curtis
(New Castle, farmer) and Sophia A. Place (Middleton); W - 40,
shoe stitcher, b. Farmington, d/o Joseph F. Webster
(Newmarket, shoeworker) and Sarah L. Avery (Epsom)

William B. of Farmington m. Bessie J. **Gilman** of Farmington
3/26/1903; H - 31, farmer, b. Farmington, s/o William A. Curtis
(New Castle, farmer) and Melissa S. Pinkham (housewife,
housewife); W - 22, lady, b. Hallowell, ME, d/o William H.
Gilman (Hallowell, ME, retired) and Emma M. Bowman
(Augusta, ME, housewife)

**CUTTING,**

Walter L. of Farmington m. Mary M. **Pelletier** of So. Berwick
6/5/1897 in Salmon Falls; H - 24, harness maker, b. W.
Gardiner, ME, s/o Samuel R. Cutting (Gardiner, ME,
mechanic) and Alice M. Cutting (Gardiner, ME, housekeeper);
W - 18, shoe stitcher, b. So. Berwick, d/o Joseph Pelletier
(Canada, mechanic) and Emily Pelletier (Canada,
housekeeper)

**DAILEY,**

Frank of Farmington m. Alice **Reynolds** of New Durham 1/1/1901
in Dexter; H - 40, farmer, $2^{nd}$, b. Newbury, VT, s/o Walter
Dailey (Whitefield, farmer) and Susan Cutting (Fairlee); W -
31, housekeeper, $2^{nd}$, b. Norwich, VT, d/o Ira Stowell (Thetford,
VT, farmer) and Bell Simonds (Norick, VT)

**DALLEN,**

Frank A. of Louisville, KY m. Georgie M. **Stott** of Portsmouth
8/2/1894; H - 22, veterinary dentist, b. Louisville, KY, s/o
Moses Dallen (Louisville, KY) and Mary J. Dallen (Louisville,
KY); W - 22, b. Portsmouth, d/o John W. Stott (Yorkshire,
England) and Athe M. Stott (ME)

**DAME,**

Frank H. of Farmington m. Annie M. **Knox** of Farmington
10/30/1893; H - 22, clerk, b. Farmington, s/o Albert W. Dame
(Farmington, shoemaker) and Amanda Dame (Farmington,
housewife); W - 20, lady, b. Farmington, d/o James R. Knox

(Farmington, shoemaker) and Annette Knox (Farmington, housekeeper)

Kenneth O. of Rochester m. Madaline **Lovering** of Farmington 6/28/1937 in Keene; H - 29, photographer, b. Rochester, s/o Harry Dame (Rochester, carpenter) and Sarah Varity (No. Andover, MA, deceased); W - 28, clerk, b. Farmington, d/o George Lovering (Union, deceased) and Irma Davis (Farmington, housewife)

Walter S. of Farmington m. Ethel M. **Young** of Alton 9/2/1899 in Alton; H - 25, shoemaker, b. Farmington, s/o Jonathan Dame and Lydia Dame; W - 19, b. Alton, d/o George Young and Hannah Young (Alton)

### DAVENPORT,

Hollis L. of Farmington m. Esther E. **Otis** of Farmington 9/10/1933 H - 23, undertaker assistant, b. Putney, VT, s/o Charles Davenport (Bartonville, VT, farmer) and Mary Wright (Grafton VT, housewife); W - 25, schoolteacher, b. Farmington, d/o Norman L. Otis (Farmington, undertaker) and Susie Otis (Danvers, MA, housewife)

### DAVIS,

Albert H. of Farmington m. Charlotte S. **Hurd** of Farmington 10/17/1936 in Chichester; H - 32, printer, b. Farmington, s/o George A. Davis (Farmington, farmer) and Eliza Davis (Lawrence, MA, housewife); W - 22, shoeworker, b. Syracuse, NY, d/o Arthur Hurd (Acton, ME, shoeworker) and Elizabeth Webber (Milton Mills, shoeworker)

Albert M. of Farmington m. Reta B. **Geddis** of Rochester 11/11/1933; H - 30, garage prop., b. Farmington, s/o Alonzo Davis (New Durham, garage attnd.) and Effie Goodwin (W. Lebanon, ME, deceased); W - 29, bank teller, b. Rochester, d/o John Geddis (Belfast, Ireland, shoeworker) and Altie Jordan (Dover, shoeworker)

Alonzo I. of Farmington m. Cora E. **Goodwin** of Lebanon, ME 5/16/1899; H - 44, clerk, $2^{nd}$, b. New Durham, s/o Thomas N. Davis and Elizabeth C. Davis (Farmington); W - 31, school teacher, b. W. Lebanon, ME, d/o George N. Goodwin (W. Lebanon, ME, farmer) and Hannah Goodwin (W. Lebanon, ME, housewife)

Arthur N. of Farmington m. Edith A. **Ricker** of Rochester 6/12/1890 in Rochester; H - 19, shoemaker, b. Farmington, s/o George N. Davis (Alexandria, farmer) and Angelia A. (Salmon Falls); W - 17, stitcher, b. Farmington, d/o William M. Ricker (farmer) and Clara

Carl T. of Farmington m. Grace **Batchelder** of Farmington 12/5/1909; H - 25, shoeworker, b. Farmington, s/o John F. Davis (Farmington, shoemaker) and Ida M. Place (Farmington, shoeworker); W - 23, housekeeper, b. Farmington, d/o Edward K. Batchelder (Somersworth, clerk) and Inez Hussey (Rochester)

Charles S. of Farmington m. Effie A. **Webster** of Farmington 8/13/1932 in East Rochester; H - 40, shoeworker, b. Wolfeboro, s/o Charles E. Davis (Wolfeboro, retired) and Ella A. Bunker (deceased); W - 39, housekeeper, $2^{nd}$, b. New Durham, d/o Edwin M. Willey (New Durham, farmer) and Mary A. Randall (deceased)

Earle R. of Farmington m. Bessie S. **Haddock** of Farmington 7/21/1906; H - 22, shoemaker, b. Dover, s/o Charles F. Davis (Biddeford, bookkeeper) and Clara B. Leighton (Farmington, dressmaker); W - 17, b. Farmington, d/o Howard Haddock (Haverhill, MA, shoemaker) and Lou Tibbetts (Farmington)

Frank M. of Farmington m. Etta L. **Brown** of Farmington 7/27/1888 in Middleton; H - 27, teamster, b. Norridge, VT, s/o Sewall (Alton, deceased) and Mary (Norridge, VT); W - 28, housekeeper, $2^{nd}$, b. Barrington, d/o John and Clarissa

George A. of Farmington m. Eliza **Davis** of Farmington 5/31/1891; H - 20, farmer, b. Farmington, s/o Samuel Davis (dead); W - 18, housekeeper, b. Farmington, d/o George E. Davis (dead)

George F. of Farmington m. Addie S. **Warren** of Farmington 1/28/1892 in Milford, MA; H - 24, shoemaker, b. Milton, s/o John F. Davis (Dover, 50, shoemaker) and Frances Davis (Barrington, 47, housekeeper) of Farmington; W - 32, shoe stitcher, $2^{nd}$, divorced, b. Alton, d/o Charles W. Dunlley (Sandwich, 57, carpenter) and Lovina Dunlley (Gilmanton, 55, housekeeper) of Farmington

George F. of Farmington m. Laura S. **Campbell** of Union 11/18/1917; H - 49, shoeworker, $2^{nd}$, b. Milton, s/o John F. Davis (Dover, shoeworker) and Francena M. Locke (Barrington, housekeeper); W - 49, housekeeper, b. Wakefield, d/o John F. Campbell (Wakefield, lumber dealer) and Hannah Waldron (Wakefield, housewife)

George H. of Farmington m. Emma **Smith** of Berwick, ME 9/2/1890; H - 30, shoe cutter, b. Farmington, s/o George N. Davis (Alexandria, farmer) and Abbie C.; W - 27, stitcher, b. Berwick, ME

George W. of Farmington m. Ruby M. **Harding** of Strafford, VT 4/24/1894 in Vershire, VT; H - 24, telegrapher, b. Lyme, s/o Alfred Davis (Londonderry) and Clarinda Davis (Lyme); W - 22, school teacher, b. Strafford, VT, d/o Jasper H. Harding (Pomfret, VT, clergyman) and Druscilla W. Harding (Pomfret, VT, housekeeper)

Harry F. of Farmington m. Margaret A. **Hogan** of Farmington 2/16/1931; H - 20, shoeworker, b. Haverhill, MA, s/o George J Rogers (Haverhill, MA, shoeworker) and Irene P. Jones (San Francisco, CA, shoeworker); W - 18, shoeworker, b. Farmington, d/o Joseph M. Hogan and Anna A. Hogan (New York, NY, housekeeper)

Harry W. of Farmington m. Alice D. **Chamberlin** of New Durham 4/15/1916 in New Durham; H - 21, shoeworker, b. Farmington, s/o Charles Davis (laborer) and Ella Bunker (Farmington, housewife); W - 20, shoeworker, b. New Durham, d/o Irving Chamberlin (New Durham, farmer) and Edith Thurrell (N. Berwick, ME, housewife)

Hiram A. of Laconia m. Mary A. **Horne** of Farmington 1/24/1898; H - 77, 4th, b. New Durham, s/o Timothy Davis (Wakefield, farmer) and Ann Davis (Milton, housekeeper); W - 49, 2nd, b. Barnstead, d/o Kingsbury G. Kanne (Barnstead, currier) and Abigail H. Kaine (Moultonboro, tailoress)

John of Portland, ME m. Carolina **Shipley** of Rochester 9/22/1921 in Alton; H - 50, laborer, b. Portland, ME, s/o Samuel Davis and Eliza Witham; W - 42, cook, 2nd, b. England

John B. of Farmington m. Martha E. H. **Akerley** of So. Berwick, ME 12/31/1903; H - 67, carpenter, 2nd, b. Barnstead, s/o Timothy Davis (Milton, farmer) and Ann Appleby (Milton); W - 51, housekeeper, 2nd, b. Kempt, NS, d/o Joseph S. Hazel (Parrsboro, NS, shipbuilder) and Margaret F. Rolfe (Kempt, NS)

John F. of Farmington m. Lizzie A. **Gray** of Farmington 9/16/1892; H - 28, shoemaker, b. Farmington, s/o Nathaniel Davis (dead) and Amanda F. Davis (Woburn, ME, 49, housekeeper) of

Farmington; W - 30, lady, 2nd, divorced, b. Pittsfield, d/o Wells York (teamster, 55) and ----- (Pittsfield, 50, housewife) of Pittsfield

John F. of Farmington m. Isabelle **Doughty** of Farmington 8/13/1912; H - 48, laborer, b. Farmington, s/o Nathaniel Davis (Barnstead, laborer) and Mandy Richardson (Woburn, MA, housekeeper); W - 37, housekeeper, 2nd, b. Birch Island, ME, d/o John Avis (Castine, ME, fisherman) and Mary Arm (England, housekeeper)

John F. of Farmington m. Daisy **Young** of Farmington 1/15/1929; H - 64, carpenter, 3rd, b. Farmington, s/o Nathaniel Davis and Amanda Richardson (Woburn, MA, housekeeper); W - 46, housekeeper, 2nd, b. Sanbornville, d/o James Drew (Brookfield, laborer) and Clara Glidden

John M. of Wells, ME m. Lucy H. **Sanborn** of Auburn, ME 2/14/1907; H - 51, farmer, 2nd, b. Wells, ME, s/o Owen M. Davis (Wells, ME, farmer) and Catherine Davis (London, England); W - 47, tailoress, 2nd, b. Wakefield, d/o Isaac D. Watson (Wolfeboro, carpenter) and Ester J. Teare (Ramsay, England)

Norman G. of Farmington m. Violet M. **Leighton** of Middleton 10/20/1928 in Union; H - 25, shoeworker, b. Farmington, s/o Charles F. Davis (Wolfeboro) and Ella Bunker; W - 23, shoeworker, b. Middleton, d/o Walter F. Leighton (Middleton, carpenter) and Elizabeth Drew (Middleton, housewife)

Ralph E. of Farmington m. Ella A. **Roberts** of Farmington 3/10/1897; H - 25, shoe cutter, b. Alton, s/o James Davis (Alton, farmer) and Martha E. Davis (New Durham); W - 31, milliner, b. Farmington, d/o Joseph A. Roberts (Farmington, shoe cutter) and Phoebe E. Roberts (New Durham)

Russell A. of Lakeport m. Violetta P. **Rogers** of Farmington 3/28/1937 in Alton; H - 22, shoeworker, b. Lakeport, s/o Archie F. Davis (Laconia, machinist) and Evelyn Winchester (Lakeport, at home); W - 20, shoeworker, b. Farmington, d/o George Rogers (Haverhill, MA, shoeworker) and Irene Jones (San Francisco, CA, shoeworker)

**DERBY**,

Charles L. of Farmington m. Selvia V. **Cook** of Barnstead 8/6/1909; H - 24, mill hand, b. Montpelier, s/o Clark Derby (Hartford, CT, farmer) and Nellie Reynolds (Brattleboro, VT); W - 16, housekeeper, b. Barnstead, d/o Nat P. Cook (Milton, farmer) and Cynthia Caverly (Strafford)

**DEXTER,**
Ernest F. of Farmington m. Ruth E. **Remick** of Farmington 6/11/1916 in Milton; H - 20, shoeworker, b. Barrington, s/o Lewis F. Dexter (Shelburne, teamster) and Jennie Crowell (Shelburne, shoeworker); W - 17, shoeworker, b. Westboro, MA, d/o Nathaniel P. Remick (Sutton, MA, shoeworker) and Mary Sprague (Grafton, MA, housekeeper)

Frank L. of Farmington m. Bertha **Pike** of Farmington 11/29/1906; H - 20, shoe worker, b. NS, s/o Lewis Dexter (NS, river driver) and Jane Crowle (NS); W - 16, shoe worker, b. Farmington, d/o John C. Pike (Middleton, shoemaker) and Alice Arnold (Wells, ME)

Fred of Rochester m. Florence **Otis** of Farmington 6/6/1936; H - 21, shoeworker, b. Farmington, s/o Ernest Dexter (New Durham, shoeworker) and Ruth Remick (Springvale, shoeworker); W - 21, clerk, b. Springfield, MA, d/o Leon Otis (Lyman, ME, carpenter) and Florence Whiting (Worcester, MA deceased)

James R. of Farmington m. Cora E. **Nutter** of Alton 1/17/1906; H - 19, shoe cutter, b. Alton, s/o Fred Dexter (shoemaker) and Margie A. Raitt (Eliot, ME); W - 20, shoe skiver, b. Alton, d/o John Nutter (shoe trimmer)

Owen S. of Farmington m. Hazel **Gault** of Farmington 8/25/1917; H - 22, shoeworker, b. New Durham, s/o Foster Dexter (NS, lumberman) and Jennie Crowel (NS, shoeworker); W - 17, housekeeper, 2nd, b. Northfield, d/o Charles W. Gault (storekeeper) and Ida B. Varney (Gonic, housekeeper)

Owen S. of Farmington m. Ella **Angevine** of Rochester 3/13/1920 in Rochester; H - 26, shoeworker, 2nd, b. New Durham, s/o Foster Dexter (Upper Clyde, NS, lumberman) and Jennie Crowell (Upper Clyde, NS, shoeworker); W - 29, waitress, 2nd, b. Richmond, PQ, d/o Frederick Robbins (Bar Mills, ME, janitor) and Luanda Pease (Richmond, PQ, housewife)

**DICKEY** [see Dickie],
Howard A. of Farmington m. Bessie M. **Chesley** of Farmington 10/30/1906; H - 24, teamster, b. NB, s/o Adam Dickey (NS, teamster) and Mary Watson (NB); W - 18, bookkeeper, b.

Farmington, d/o Irving J. Chesley (New Durham, clerk) and Emma Berry (New Durham)

**DICKIE** [see Dickey],

Kenneth W. of Farmington m. Phyllis **Welch** of Farmington 4/13/1935; H - 24, truck driver, b. Farmington, s/o Howard Dickie (N. Brunswick, ME, coal dealer) and Bessie M. Chesley (Farmington, housewife); W - 22, shoeworker, $2^{nd}$, b. East Rochester, d/o Harry Carpenter (So. Berwick, ME, mill worker) and Eliza E. Carpenter (Rochester, housewife)

Ralph of Farmington m. Shirley **Pinkham** of Farmington 3/5/1936; H - 28, truck driver, b. Farmington, s/o Howard Dickie (NB, coal dealer) and Bessie Chesley (Farmington, housewife); W - 24, shoeworker, b. Milton, d/o Harry Pinkham (Milton, farmer) and Fannie Hayes (Milton, housewife)

**DIEMER**,

Spero of Milton m. Pearl **Crane** of Farmington 10/11/1928 in Union; H - 38, shoeworker, b. Albania, s/o George Diemer and Catherine Rand; W - 18, domestic, b. NF, d/o Allen Crane and Ellen Earl

**DIERAUER**,

William of Farmington m. Maxine E. **Daudelin** of Farmington 3/27/1937 in Newton; H - 25, shoeworker, b. Haverhill, MA, s/o Harry Dierauer (Salamanca, NY, shoe foreman) and Velma Horne (Haverhill, MA, housewife); W - 19, shoeworker, b. Westbrook, ME, d/o Alfred Daudelin (Chicago, IL, shoeworker) and Bessie Brown (Manchester, shoeworker)

**DIXON**,

Elmore H. of Farmington m. Annie L. **Towle** of Farmington 12/24/1896; H - 29, clerk, b. Eliot, ME, s/o Alvin Dixon (Eliot, ME, carpenter) and Mary A. Dixon (Eliot, ME); W - 25, shoe stitcher, b. New Durham, d/o William A. Towle (Dover, farmer) and Mary J. Towle (Stanstead, PQ, housewife)

**DODGE**,

Kenneth W. of Farmington m. Emmeline M. **Farnam** of Farmington 4/15/1932 in Rochester; H - 20, shoeworker, b. Rochester, s/o Clifford Dodge (Rochester, farmer) and Edna M. Maxfield

(Rochester, housewife); W - 19, shoeworker, b. Rochester, d/o George Farnam and Mabel G. Kendal (Ossipee, housewife)

**DOLBY,**
Arthur P. of Farmington m. Mary A. **Hoye** of Dover 5/8/1892; H - 21, school teacher, b. Alton, s/o Henry I. Dolby (Hopkinton, 5, hotel keeper) and Ellen A. Dolby (Alton, 50, housewife) of Farmington; W - 25, lady, b. Dover, d/o James Hoye (dead) and Bridget Hoye (dead)

**DOLE,**
George E. of Farmington m. Irene F. **Butler** of Farmington 11/15/1931 in Rochester; H - 38, shoe mfgr., $2^{nd}$, b. Haverhill MA, s/o Charles E. Dole (Georgetown, MA, banker) and Eliza B. Noyes (Salem, MA, housewife); W - 23, bookkeeper, $2^{nd}$, b. Alton, d/o F. Leon Furber (Alton, merchant) and Flora A. Jone (Middleton, housewife)

**DORE,**
Clarence M. of Farmington m. Christa A. **Nutter** of Farmington 11/25/1917 in Alton; H - 28, shoeworker, b. Alton, s/o Loami Dore (Alton) and Hannah Waldron (Middleton, housekeeper); W - 24, clerk, b. Alton, d/o John J. Nutter (Alton, shoemaker) and Elmira F. Lamper (Alton)

Daniel C. of Farmington m. Sadie L. **Davis** of Farmington 5/22/1908 in Dover; H - 61, shoemaker, $2^{nd}$, b. Alton, s/o Hen Dore (Alton) and Susanna L. Rollins (Alton); W - 37, shoemaker, $2^{nd}$, b. Brookfield, d/o George F. Shortridge (Brookfield, farmer) and -----

Ernest of Farmington m. Inez B. **Clough** of Wolfeboro 9/17/1904 i Wolfeboro; H - 28, artist, b. Farmington, s/o Daniel C. Dore (Alton, shoemaker) and Emma A. Towne (Natick, MA, housewife); W - 23, housekeeper, b. Rochester, d/o George H Clough (Barnstead, physician) and Hattie A. Jones (Milton, housewife)

Leon of Alton m. Doris V. **Hale** of Farmington 9/18/1917 in Alton; H - 22, woodturner, b. Alton, s/o William H. Dore (Alton, farmer) and Grace L. Rollins (New Durham, housewife); W - 16, shoeworker, b. New Durham, d/o Corie Hale (Lee, ME, farmer and Ida M. Rhines (Rochester, housekeeper)

**DOTY,**

Benjamin of Farmington m. Fannie **York** of Farmington 8/21/1924; H - 60, shoeworker, 3rd, b. Warren, ME, s/o George R. Doty and Mary P. Linniken; W - 34, housekeeper, b. Farmington, d/o Charles F. York (laborer) and Lizzie Bickford

Benjamin F. of Farmington m. Nellie **York** of Farmington 7/28/1888 in Milton; H - 25, heel trimmer, b. Warren, ME, s/o George R. (Searsmont, ME) and Mary P. (Weld, ME, housekeeper); W - 17, box maker, b. Middleton, d/o Joseph (Middleton, saloon keeper) and Augusta (Concord, housekeeper)

Benjamin F. of Farmington m. Nellie M. **Morrill** of Farmington 11/29/1916; H - 53, shoeworker, 2nd, b. Warren, ME, s/o George R. Doty (Knox, ME, farmer) and Mary P. Limkin (Brook, ME, housewife); W - 46, shoeworker, 4th, b. Middleton, d/o Warren Whitehouse (Middleton, farmer) and ----- (Middleton, housewife)

**DOUCETTE,**

Alex of Farmington m. Florence **Marquise** of Ashland 5/18/1930; H - 27, laborer, 2nd, b. Lawrence, MA, s/o Alex Ducette and Mary Myotte (Canada, domestic); W - 38, domestic, 2nd, b. Methuen, MA, d/o William Clark (Ayer, MA, laborer) and Louise Snyder (England, housewife)

Alexander of Farmington m. Cora **Duval** of Farmington 8/9/1922; H - 21, shoeworker, b. Lawrence, MA, s/o Alexander Doucette and Mary Myotte (Taunton, MA, housekeeper); W - 18, housekeeper, b. Fitchburg, MA, d/o George Duval (Canada, weaver) and Sarah Duval (Canada, housewife)

**DOUGLASS,**

Donald R. of E. Rochester m. Irene M. **Auclair** of Farmington 6/19/1926 in Alton; H - 21, garage, b. E. Rochester, s/o George H. Douglass (Wells, ME, RR emp.) and Mary E. Magoon (Guilford, ME, mill); W - 18, hotel, b. Belmont, d/o Existe Auclair (Woonsocket, RI, lumberman) and Clarina Champaigne (Canada, housewife)

Robert R. of Farmington m. Rena M. **Abbott** of Farmington 11/28/1912; H - 20, shoeworker, b. NC, s/o J. C. Douglass (NC, stonecutter) and Barsheba Wilkinson (NC); W - 20, lady, b. Concord, d/o Charles S. Abbott (Boston, MA, engineer) and Belle Nourse (Bethlehem, housekeeper)

**DOWNING,**

Edward J. of Farmington m. Katie C. **Miller** of LaGrange, MO 1/27/1896; H - 20, farmer, b. Farmington, s/o James S. Downing (Farmington) and Addie S. Downing (Rochester); W - 16, b. Quincy, IL, d/o Lewis Miller (shoemaker) and Annie Miller (housewife)

Henry H. of Farmington m. Ella M. **Rodden** of Dover 1/2/1899; H - 19, shoemaker, b. Farmington, s/o Henry C. Downing (Farmington, merchant) and Ella M. Downing (New Durham, housewife); W - 19, lady, b. Dover, d/o Barney Rodden (Dover) and Lizzie Rodden (Dover)

Jeremiah W. of Farmington m. Elizabeth J. **Bowden** of Great Falls 7/9/1891 in New Durham; H - 71, farmer, $2^{nd}$, b. Middleton, s/o Samuel Downing (dead); W - 63, housekeeper, $3^{rd}$, b. Great Falls, d/o George W. Morrison (dead)

Woodbury H. of Farmington m. Julie E. **Nutter** of Rochester 4/1/1896 in Rochester; H - 31, farmer, $2^{nd}$, b. Farmington, s/o James H. Downing (Farmington, farmer) and Addie S. Downing (Rochester); W - 33, housekeeper, $2^{nd}$, b. NB, d/o James Greenlaw (NB, farmer) and Mary Greenlaw

**DRAKE,**

Raymond P. R. of Farmington m. Clara **Colomy** of Farmington 5/16/1914; H - 34, electrician, b. MI, s/o Edwin Drake (carpenter); W - 39, shoeworker, $3^{rd}$, b. Middleton, d/o David Kimball (Middleton, farmer) and Nellie Hanscom (Dover, housekeeper)

**DRAWBRIDGE,**

Robert W. of Middleton m. Charlotta R. **Davis** of Farmington 9/29/1897; H - 29, minister, b. Chelsea, MA, s/o George D. Drawbridge (Lewis, England, int. decorator) and Abigail Drawbridge (Kennebunk, housewife); W - 31, b. So. Alton, d/o James Davis (Alton, farmer) and Martha E. Davis (New Durham, housework)

**DREW,**

Clifford T. of Farmington m. Crissie C. **Brooks** of Farmington 4/19/1919 in Rochester; H - 28, shoeworker, b. Milton, s/o Horace Drew and Maggie Walker; W - 28, shoeworker, $2^{nd}$, b.

Farmington, d/o P. J. Brooks (Alton, shoemaker) and Edith Tibbetts (Farmington, housewife)

Clifton H. of Farmington m. Elizabeth T. **Ellis** of Alton 11/27/1917; H - 28, chauffeur, b. Milton, s/o Horace Drew (Conway, farmer) and Maggie Walker (England, housewife); W - 28, housekeeper, b. Alton, d/o Elbridge Ellis (Alton, carpenter) and Elizabeth Hayes (Alton, housewife)

George F. of Farmington m. Mary E. **Drew** of Farmington 2/10/1912; H - 56, foreman, $2^{nd}$, b. Farmington, s/o Alonzo E. Drew (engineer) and Mary E. Place (ME, housewife); W - 57, dressmaker, $2^{nd}$, b. Milton, d/o James S. Childs (Cambridge, MA, carpenter) and Mary J. Goodwin (Lebanon, ME, housewife)

John J. of Middleton m. Katherine T. **Finnegan** of Farmington 4/22/1914; H - 20, shoemaker, b. Middleton, s/o Horace Dew (Eden, farmer) and Maggie Walker (England, housewife); W - 23, housekeeper, b. Ireland, d/o James Finnegan (Ireland, farmer) and Ellen Rafferty (Ireland, housewife)

Philip L. of Farmington m. Helen A. **Ricker** of Alton 3/14/1903; H - 38, carpenter, $2^{nd}$, b. Dayton, ME, s/o Jeremiah Drew (Dayton, ME, farmer) and Mary E. Libby (Dayton, ME, housewife); W - 21, housekeeper, b. Alton, d/o Charles H. Ricker (Barrington, merchant) and Emma A. Stevens (New Durham, housewife)

William D. of Farmington m. Flossie **Elkins** of S. Berwick, ME 10/18/1919 in Rochester; H - 34, lumberman, $2^{nd}$, b. Middleton, s/o Horace Drew and Maggie Walker; W - 38, shoeworker, $2^{nd}$, b. Middletown, PA, d/o Christian Sinniger (Middletown, PA, farmer) and Caroline C. Lang (Boston, MA)

**DRUE,**
Joseph of Farmington m. Annie **McAskill** of Cochituate, MA 4/19/1887 in Chelsea, MA; H - 62, farmer, $2^{nd}$, b. Alton, s/o John Drue (Alton) and Charlotte Drue; W - --

**DUDLEY,**
Horace I. of Farmington m. Martha J. **Whitehouse** of Farmington 10/6/1887; H - 21, shoemaker, b. Farmington, s/o Charles C. Dudley (Tamworth, shoemaker) and Lydia A. Dudley; W - 20, b. Middleton, d/o Thomas L. Whitehouse (shoemaker) and Ellen E. Whitehouse

**DUFRESNE,**
Harry D. of Farmington m. Maude E. **Burrows** of Farmington 6/24/1911; H - 19, shoe cutter, b. Whitingham, VT, s/o N. F. Dufresne (Derby, VT, shoemaker) and Nellie Cota (Canaan, housekeeper); W - 18, shoeworker, b. Milton, d/o Will S. Burrows (Milton, shoemaker) and Emma S. Knowles (Middleton, housekeeper)

**DUPERRE,**
Raymond of Farmington m. Geraldine **St. Pierre** of Farmington 2/22/1936; H - 28, shoeworker, b. Rochester, s/o Alfred Duperre (shoeworker) and Adelaide Vachon (Rochester, deceased); W - 21, shoeworker, b. Springvale, d/o Henry St. Pierre (Somersworth, farmer) and Annie Duval (Manchester, deceased)

**DUQUETTE,**
Lewis J. of Farmington m. Bessie **Corson** of Farmington 10/23/1909; H - 23, farmer, b. Canada, s/o Joseph Duquette (Canada, farmer) and Caroline Cinavon (Canada, housewife); W - 20, housekeeper, b. Rochester, d/o John Corson (farmer)

**DURANT,**
Harry E. of Farmington m. Susan E. **Robinson** of Farmington 12/13/1936; H - 43, shoeworker, 2$^{nd}$, b. Haverhill, MA, s/o Bert Durant (Haverhill, MA, deceased) and Aura E. Parker (Newport, ME, at home); W - 51, shoeworker, 2$^{nd}$, b. Kennebunk, d/o James Robinson (deceased) and Esther J. Emery (deceased)

**DURGIN,**
Benjamin F. of East Rochester m. Nora **Donaldson** of Farmington 12/21/1901; H - 53, shoemaker, 2$^{nd}$, b. Cornish, ME, s/o Benjamin Durgin (Cornish, ME, farmer) and Dorcas Berry (Cornish, ME, dead); W - 35, housekeeper, 3$^{rd}$, b. Montreal, PQ, d/o Richard LaPrice (Paris, France, dead) and Artinice Antell (Paris, Frances)

**DURKEE,**
Porter J. of Farmington m. Estella A. **Swinerton** of Farmington 4/14/1923; H - 21, woodturner, b. Danvers, MA, s/o George F. Durkee (Port Maryland, NS, farmer) and Rose I. Gould (Middleton, MA, housekeeper); W - 18, shoeworker, b. Farmington, d/o Herbert Swinerton (Somersworth, shoeworker) and Esther Blaisdell (Farmington, housekeeper)

**DUSTIN,**
Fred A. of Manchester m. Abbie E. **Lucas** of Farmington 10/10/1891; H - 24, shoemaker, b. Concord, s/o Alvah Dustin (dead); W - 16, housekeeper, b. Farmington, d/o Freeman D. Lucas (New Durham, shoe cutter)

**EATON,**
Almon W. of Union m. Clara **Jones** of Union 12/30/1896; H - 27, shoe business, b. Brookfield, s/o Abial C. Eaton (Brookfield) and Sally A. Eaton (Wolfeboro); W - 28, b. Wolfeboro, d/o Henry Jones (Wolfeboro) and Martha Jones

Charles C. of Rochester m. Minnie F. **Smart** of Farmington 10/27/1918 in Rochester; H - 33, boxmaker, 2nd, b. Epping, s/o Charles Eaton (Nottingham, boxmaker) and Julia St. John (Manchester, housewife); W - 30, boxmaker, b. Farmington, d/o Joel Smart (Lowland, ME, farmer) and Mary A. Smith (Dover, housewife)

**EDGERLY,**
Clyde H. of Farmington m. Mary V. **Anderson** of Farmington 5/7/1912; H - 27, shoeworker, b. Farmington, s/o Erville M. Edgerly (Farmington, farmer) and Carrie M. Quint (Farmington, housekeeper); W - 26, shoeworker, 2nd, b. No. Conway, d/o George Anderson (No. Conway, lumberman) and Mary Miller (No. Conway, housekeeper)

Earle M. of Farmington m. Ethel M. **Drew** of Farmington 4/1/1908 in Rochester; H - 20, b. Farmington, s/o Erville M. Edgerly (Farmington, mill hand) and Carrie M. Quint (Farmington); W - 18, b. Farmington, d/o Charles E. Drew (Farmington, shoemaker) and Lizzie Childs (Farmington)

Frank E. of Farmington m. Nettie A. **Ricker** of New Durham 5/16/1889 in New Durham; H - 28, shoe manufacturer, b. Farmington, s/o Hosea B. Edgerly (Farmington, shoe manufacturer) and Maria Edgerly (Rochester); W - 26, school teacher, b. New Durham, d/o Ira S. Ricker (Dover, farmer) and Mary E. Ricker (Barrington)

Frank H. of New Durham m. Serena J. **Littlefield** of Farmington 11/24/1935; H - 43, woodturner, b. New Durham, s/o Charles Edgerly (Dover, deceased) and Minnie Comely (Milton, deceased); W - 63, housewife, 3$^{rd}$, b. PEI, d/o Charles Murrey (PEI, deceased) and Mary Frost (PEI, deceased)

George W. of Farmington m. Laura A. **Berry** of Alton 10/12/1895; - 42, carpenter, 2$^{nd}$, b. Strafford, s/o David L. Edgerly (New Durham) and Elmira B. Chamberlain (New Durham); W - 27, dressmaker, 2$^{nd}$, b. Barnstead, d/o Thomas S. Straw (Alton) and Louisa A. Straw (Barnstead, housework)

Walter C. of Farmington m. Maude F. **Parrock** of Farmington 1/7/1928; H - 50, brushmaker, 2$^{nd}$, b. Northwood, s/o Charles W. Edgerly and Anna Drew; W - 36, housekeeper, 2$^{nd}$, b. Alton, d/o George E. Furber (Alton, carpenter) and Ada A. Nutter (Barnstead, housekeeper)

Willie H. of Farmington m. Mattie A. **Corson** of Farmington 1/7/1891 in New Durham; H - 22, stock fitter, b. Farmington. s/o John H. Edgerly (New Durham, farmer); W - 21, housekeeper, b. Rochester, d/o Lorenzo Corson (dead)

**EDWARDS,**

Charles M. of Farmington m. Cora E. **Aspinwall** of Farmington 5/7/1889; H - 21, shoemaker, b. Otisfield, ME, s/o Alonzo Edwards (Otisfield, ME, shoemaker) and Judith Edwards (Raymond, ME); W - 17, housekeeper, b. Middleton, d/o John G. Aspinwall (Dover, shoemaker) and Frances P. Aspinwall (Middleton)

Glenn of Gilmanton I.W. m. Mildred E. **Hayes** of Farmington 6/12/1937; H - 23, trucking, b. Chandoken, NY, s/o Thomas Edwards (England, sales manager) and Sadie Rossman (NY, housewife); W - 19, shoeworker, b. New Durham, d/o Colo Hayes (New Durham, mechanic) and Bertha MacCarlie (Farmington, saleswoman)

**ELDRIDGE,**

Lester of Farmington m. Ruth **Webster** of Farmington 6/16/1928; H - 20, shoeworker, b. Wolfeboro, s/o Bert Eldridge (Ossipee, farmer) and Agnes Bodge (Wolfeboro, housewife); W - 19, bookkeeper, b. Farmington, d/o Charles Webster (shoeworker) and Annie Gray (housewife)

**ELKINS,**
Arthur A. of Farmington m. Olga I. **Langford** of Rochester 8/4/1934; H - 33, salesman, 2$^{nd}$, b. Boston, MA, s/o Fred G. Elkins (Trowbridge, England) and Florence Sinniger (Harrisburg, PA, shoeworker); W - 25, hairdresser, b. Raymond, d/o Calvin H. Langford (deceased) and Stella Nelson (Portsmouth, at home)

Bert H. of Farmington m. Mary A. **Cooley** of Farmington 5/26/1896 in Milton; H - 22, heel fitter, b. Farmington, s/o Ira Elkins (Farmington, shoemaker) and Caroline A. Elkins (Effingham, housewife); W - 16, housekeeper, b. Canada, d/o Frank Cooley (Canada, teamster) and Millian Cooley (Canada, housewife)

Bert H. of Farmington m. Anna R. **Cook** of Farmington 10/24/1931 in Chichester; H - 57, shoeworker, 2$^{nd}$, b. Farmington, s/o Ira Elkins (Farmington, shoeworker) and Caroline Lewis (Effingham, housewife); W - 40, housekeeper, 2$^{nd}$, b. Providence, RI

Charles of Farmington m. Etta M. **Hartsford** of Farmington 3/26/1892; H - 31, shoemaker, b. Farmington, s/o Ira Elkins (Farmington, 58, shoemaker) and Caroline Elkins (Ossipee, 55, housewife) of Farmington; W - 21, shoe fitter, 2$^{nd}$, divorced, b. Acton, ME, d/o Millett W. Merrow (Milton Mills, 47, mill worker) of Union Village and Annie E. Lewis (New York, 37, housewife) of Farmington

Cyrus of Farmington m. Carrie E. **Whitten** of Farmington 12/31/1890 in Rochester; H - 45, teamster, 3$^{rd}$, b. Farmington, s/o John C. Elkins (dead) and Axie; W - 24, box maker, 2$^{nd}$, b. Alton, d/o Horace Joy (dead) and Cynthia

Leroy T. of Farmington m. Maude A. **Littlefield** of Farmington 4/30/1906; H - 28, shoe cutter, b. Rochester, s/o George Elkins (Farmington, pattern maker) and Laura I. Hoyt (Rochester, dressmaker); W - 19, shoe stitcher, b. Kennebunk, ME, d/o George Littlefield (Kennebunk, ME, painter) and Mary Hughes (housewife)

**ELLIOTT,**

Ernest E. of Farmington m. Parmelia **Guilbault** of Gonic 2/21/1938 in Gonic; H - 23, shoeworker, b. Farmington, s/o William Elliot (Farmington, bicycle repairer) and Annie Dunnells (Wells Beach, ME, shoeworker); W - 19, shoeworker, b. Gonic, d/o Joseph Guilbault (Canada, brickmaker) and Mary Genereux (Canada, housewife)

Jesse of Farmington m. Leona F. **Moisan** of Farmington 3/18/1933 H - 19, shoeworker, b. Farmington, s/o Arthur Elliott (mechanic) and Annie Dunnel (Ogunquit, ME, shoeworker); W - 17, housewife, b. New Durham, d/o Fred Moisan (Canada, woodchopper) and Clara Boucher (New Durham, housekeeper

William A. of Farmington m. Lillian E. **Ryan** of Farmington 2/24/1888; H - 17, shoemaker, b. Farmington, s/o Jesse M. (Barnstead, carpenter) and Rosetta S. (Farmington, housekeeper); W - 20, housekeeper, b. Cambridge, MA, d/o ---- (policeman)

William A. of Farmington m. Florence E. **Holmes** of Farmington 8/31/1904; H - 34, merchant, $2^{nd}$, widower, b. Farmington, s/o Jesse M. Elliott (Barnstead, wheelwright) and Rosezette S. Otis (Farmington, housewife); W - 15, housekeeper, b. Brentwood, d/o Fred E. Holmes (Portsmouth) and Angie N. Holmes (housewife)

William A. of Farmington m. Annie B. **Goodwin** of Farmington 8/5/1913; H - 43, mechanic, $3^{rd}$, b. Farmington, s/o Jesse M. Elliott (Barnstead, wheelwright) and Rosette Otis (Farmington, housekeeper); W - 19, housekeeper, $2^{nd}$, b. Ogunquit, ME, d/o Aaron Dunnell (Ogunquit, fisherman) and Clara Fitzgerald (York, ME, housekeeper)

**ELLISON,**

William Henry of Springfield, MA m. Beatrice Janet **Edgerly** of Farmington 3/3/1915; H - 23, merchant, b. Brentwood, NY, s/o George W. Ellison (Brooklyn, NY, doctor) and Adah G. Withall (Rochester, NY, housewife); W - 22, b. Farmington, d/o Frank E. Edgerly (Farmington, shoe mfgr.) and Janet A. Ricker (New Durham, housewife)

**ELWELL,**

Charles F. of Kennebunk, ME m. Millie L. **Furbish** of Kennebunk, ME 7/15/1888; H - 22, wood worker, b. Kennebunk, ME, s/o

John (Buxton, ME, teamster) and Esther (Kennebunk, ME, housekeeper); W - 22, housekeeper, d/o Frank E. (farmer) and Elizabeth (Holderness, housekeeper)

George F. of Rochester m. Rose M. **Cook** of Farmington 3/19/1937 in Rochester; H - 24, shoeworker, b. Lynn, MA, s/o George Elwell (Gloucester, MA, painter) and Annie Lawrence (Providence, RI, housewife); W - 15, student, b. Farmington, d/o Herbert Cook (Barnstead, shoeworker) and Anna Elkins (Providence, RI)

**EMERSON,**

Augustus F. of Barnstead m. Flora B. **Hurd** of Farmington 6/2/1900; H - 34, teamster, b. Rollinsford, s/o George H. Emerson (Barnstead, farmer) and Mary E. Emerson (housekeeper); W - 20, housekeeper, b. Farmington, d/o George H. Hurd (farmer) and Sophine J. Hurd (housekeeper)

Everett W. of Farmington m. Edna M. **Kimball** of Farmington 7/30/1921; H - 26, salesman, b. Alton, s/o Charles W. Emerson (Alton, painter) and Mary E. Hunt (Boston, housewife); W - 23, stenographer, b. Farmington, d/o Harry B. Kimball (Middleton, clerk) and Mabel Dixon (Farmington, housewife)

Horten C. of Farmington m. Sadie E. **Hayes** of Farmington 4/1/1894; H - 20, shoemaker, b. Alton, s/o John A. Emerson (Bristol, shoemaker) and Abbie J. Emerson (Alton); W - 19, b. Alfred, ME, d/o John O. Hayes (dead) and Mrs. H. E. Wentworth (Barrington, housewife)

J. Ralph of Rochester m. Dorothy **Parkhurst** of Farmington 4/22/1929; H - 24, motor veh. ins., b. Brockton, s/o John N. Emerson (Stoughton, MA, shoe mfgr.) and Helen Brady (Canton, MA, housewife); W - 23, stenographer, b. Hallowell, ME, d/o Frank W. Parkhurst (Stoneham, MA, foreman) and Isabelle F. Dunn (Stoneham, MA, housewife)

William I. of Farmington m. Mary A. **Langley** of Durham 9/22/1922; H - 29, elec. contractor, b. Alton, s/o Charles Emerson (Alton, painter) and Mary E. Hunt (Epping, housewife); W - 27, school teacher, b. Durham, d/o E. J. Langley (Durham, farmer) and Edith A. ----- (NB, housewife)

**EMERY,**

Alden C. of Farmington m. Ethel E. **Rogers** of Farmington 8/20/1938 in Wolfeboro; H - 49, farmer, 2$^{nd}$, b. Chester, s/o Nathan Emery (Auburn, farmer) and Sarah Rich (Belvedere, VT, deceased); W - 46, housekeeper, 2$^{nd}$, b. MS, d/o Alonzo O'Neal (Henderson, TN, farmer) and Flora Melton (MS, housewife)

Clifton E. of Farmington m. Mary J. **Hurd** of Farmington 12/16/1890; H - 19, shoemaker, b. Milton, s/o Edward A. Emery (Middleton, shoemaker) and Fannie S. (Milton); W - 18 housekeeper, b. Farmington, d/o G. C. W. Hurd (Farmington, farmer) and Sophia J. (Strafford)

Edwin A. of Farmington m. Viola **Cotton** of Farmington 4/8/1897; H - 50, farmer, 2$^{nd}$, b. Middleton, s/o Daniel C. Emery (Dover, farmer) and Abigail Emery (Middleton); W - 42, laundress, 2$^{nd}$, b. New Durham, d/o David L. Edgerly (New Durham, clergyman) and Elmira B. Edgerly (New Durham)

George of Farmington m. Lillian **Hurd** of New Durham 4/4/1924 in New Durham; H - 25, lumberman, b. Farmington, s/o Augustus Emery and Viola Edgerly; W - 38, housekeeper, b. Lowell, MA, d/o Joseph Hurd and Martha Dyson

William of Farmington m. Florence **Power** of Farmington 6/24/1916 in Dover; H - 46, shoeworker, b. Newmarket, s/o William Emery (Canada, shoeworker) and Mary Richmond (Canada); W - 30, shoeworker, 2$^{nd}$, b. Haverhill, MA, d/o Clarence Pray (Haverhill, shoeworker)

**EMMOND,**

Henry B. of Ontonagan, MI m. Abbie E. **Lucas** of Farmington 5/8/1901; H - 34, lumberman, 2$^{nd}$, b. Rockland, MI, s/o Thomas Emmond (Canada, farmer) and Mary Powers (Ireland, housewife); W - 26, stitcher, 2$^{nd}$, b. Farmington, d/o Freeman D. Lucas (New Durham, farmer) and Emma Whitehouse (Strafford, shoe stitcher)

**EVANS,**

Charles W. of Farmington m. Alice M. **Tibbetts** of Milton 8/24/1892; H - 27, section hand, b. Alton, s/o Robert Evans (dead) and Mary Evans (New Durham, 64, housekeeper) of Alton; W - 16, lady, b. Milton, d/o Luke Tibbetts (Milton, 55, farmer) and Abbie Tibbetts (Milton, 57, housekeeper) of Milton

Elmer E. of Farmington m. Etta May **Currier** of Farmington
6/21/1931; H - 42, barber, 2nd, b. Standish, ME, s/o John W.
Evans (Raymond, ME, farmer) and Hattie B. Jones (Naples,
ME, housekeeper); W - 37, housekeeper, 2nd, b. Moultonboro,
d/o George W. Davis (Tuftonboro, farmer) and Aurilla A.
Jewett (Barnstead, housekeeper)

James E. of Farmington m. Cora E. **Cave** of Farmington
11/28/1891; H - 20, hostler, b. New Durham, s/o Ezra H. Evans
(New Durham, shoemaker); W - 20, housekeeper, b. Alburg,
VT, d/o Henry J. Cave (England, farmer)

Wilbur J. of Farmington m. Isabelle A. **Hall** of Auburn, ME
11/1/1890; H - 26, druggist, b. Alton, s/o Joseph B. Evans
(Alton, farmer) and Ann E. (Alton); W - 18, stitcher, b. Auburn,
ME, d/o Charles B. Hall (Portland, ME, farmer) and Adelaide
B. (Deering, ME)

**FALL,**

Henry S. of Farmington m. Rose E. **Varney** of Farmington
11/6/1915; H - 21, shoeworker, b. Berwick, ME, s/o Elmer S.
Fall (Chelsea, MA, shoemaker) and Lavonia Ricker (Lebanon,
ME, housekeeper); W - 18, shoeworker, b. Farmington, d/o
Fred Varney (Farmington, shoeworker) and Angie Corson
(Farmington, housekeeper)

Horace P. of Farmington m. Nellie B. **Burroughs** of Farmington
6/29/1893; H - 30, pharmacist, b. Farmington, s/o Otis Fall
(dead) and Rosalie Fall (dead); W - 27, lady, b. Middleton, d/o
William Burrows (Farmington, peddler) and Marcia Burrows
(Farmington, housewife)

William E. of Farmington m. Nellie A. **White** of Rochester
10/1/1890 in Rochester; H - 21, painter, b. Farmington, s/o
Otis W. Fall (Wolfeboro, shoemaker) and Mary A. (New
Durham); W - 20, housekeeper, 2nd, b. Chelsea, MA, d/o
George W. Rowe (Barnstead, farmer) and Lizzie M. (Chelsea,
MA)

**FANNING,**

John A. of Farmington m. Mary J. **Metcalf** of Farmington
8/24/1908; H - 33, shoemaker, b. Winsor, NS, d/o James E.
Fanning (Winsor, NS, engineer) and Mary J. Swinner (Winsor,
NS); W - 29, housekeeper, b. Middleboro, England, d/o James

Metcalf (Middleboro, England, police sergt.) and Mary J. Swe(Middleboro, England)

**FARWELL,**
Fred T. of Farmington m. Angie **Walker** of Farmington 1/11/1902; - 37, shoemaker, b. Wilmot Flats, s/o Thurston T. Farwell (Ne London Hill, dead) and Harriett E. Chase (Wilmot Flats, dead W - 34, shoe stitcher, b. Barnstead, d/o Mark Walker (Barnstead, dead) and Addie S. Perkins (Exeter, dead)

**FERGUSON,**
Arthur C. of Fryeburg, ME m. Florence V. **Putney** of Farmington 12/19/1898; H - 29, physician, b. Springvale, ME, s/o Charles F. Ferguson (Shapleigh, ME) and Martha O. Ferguson (Waterboro, ME); W - 25, school teacher, b. Boston, MA, d/o Alfred C. Putney and Susan Putney

**FERLAND,**
Emile A. of Farmington m. Francis **Pike** of Milton 12/14/1935 in Milton Mills; H - 23, shoeworker, b. Farmington, s/o Thomas Ferland (Canada, deceased) and Mary Marcoux (Rochester, a home); W - 23, shoeworker, 2$^{nd}$, b. Milton Mills, d/o Dennis Clough (Acton, ME, machinist) and Minnie Marsh (S. Berwick ME, at home)

Robert W. of Rochester m. Alberta L. **Osgood** of Farmington 6/4/1937 in Dover; H - 24, shoeworker, b. Rochester, s/o Wilfred Ferland (Canada, shoeworker) and Rose Martineau (Rochester, shoeworker); W - 22, office, b. Fremont, d/o George Osgood (Epping, shoeworker) and Mary Reeda (Fremont, shoeworker)

**FERNALD,**
Frank G. of Lynn, MA m. Nellie M. **Raitt** of Lynn, MA 4/24/1911; H 52, painter, 2$^{nd}$, b. Eliot, ME, s/o Augustus Fernald (Eliot, ME) and Octavia Green (Eliot, ME); W - 47, operative, b. Eliot, ME d/o Gilman Raitt and Mary Mason

Winfield G. of Rochester m. Abbie **Huckins** of Farmington 5/29/1933; H - 23, locksmith, b. Rochester, s/o Byron Fernald (Jackson, blacksmith) and Bertha Hawkins (Denmark, ME, housework); W - 27, nurse, b. Farmington, d/o John I. Huckins

(Farmington, deceased) and Ethel Scruton (Strafford, housework)

**FERRIS,**
Harry J. of Providence, RI m. Elizabeth **Hemingway** of Dorchester, MA 8/25/1917; H - 27, actor, b. Newport, RI, s/o Henry Ferris and Elizabeth Wilson (Hartford, CT, at home); W - 29, actress, 2nd, b. Cincinnati, OH, d/o James Gorman (London, England, salesman) and Leavy Bartlett

**FISHER,**
Ira of Farmington m. Ethel M. **Gault** of Farmington 10/21/1933; H - 54, laborer, 2nd, b. Lunenburg, VT, s/o Goodwell Fisher (Blackriver, NY, deceased) and Alfreda Smith (West Farley, VT, deceased); W - 47, housewife, 2nd, b. Meredith, d/o George Perkins (Meredith, deceased) and Annie Clark (Oak Hill, deceased)

John E. of Farmington m. Harriet E. **Manchester** of Providence, RI 11/7/1908 in Dover; H - 22, teamster, b. Canada, s/o Eugene Fisher (NS, farmer) and Sarah Johnson (Canada); W - 20, housekeeper, b. Providence, RI, d/o George Manchester (England, mill hand) and Jennie Rollins (Providence, RI)

**FLANDERS,**
Arthur L. of Farmington m. Cora E. **Gilman** of Alton 6/17/1887 in Alton; H - 30, manufacturer, b. Concord, s/o Langdon S. Flanders (Concord, manufacturer) and Eliza A. Flanders; W - 26, teacher, b. Alton, d/o S. E. B. Gilman (Alton, farmer) and Mary J. Gilman

Herman F. of Farmington m. Augusta J. **Berry** of Farmington 5/23/1887 in Franklin; H - 24, shoecutter, b. Farmington, s/o Samuel B. Flanders (Danbury) and Marcia A. Flanders; W - 19, b. New Durham, d/o Elwin E. Berry (New Durham, laborer) and Emma J. Berry

Herman F. of Farmington m. Lena G. **Horne** of Farmington 11/1/1924; H - 61, shoeworker, 3rd, b. Farmington, s/o Samuel Flanders and Marcia A. Brown; W - 44, housekeeper, 2nd, b. Farmington, d/o Freeman D. Lucas and Emma Whitehouse

Herman T. of Farmington m. Helen W. **Tripp** of New Bedford, MA 4/3/1890; H - 27, shoe cutter, 2nd, b. Farmington, s/o Samuel B. Flanders (dead) and Marcia A. (Danbury); W - 20, milliner,

b. New Bedford, MA, d/o Philip M. Tripp (New Bedford, MA, sea captain) and Catherine F. (Lowell, MA)

**FLETCHER,**
Fred P. of Farmington m. Augusta A. **Brainard** of Farmington 1/27/1896; H - 34, merchant, 3$^{rd}$, b. New Durham, s/o James A. Fletcher (Dracut, MA, sole leather cutter) and Elizabeth G. Fletcher (New Durham, housewife); W - 41, shoe fitter, 2$^{nd}$, b. Hanson, MA, d/o Henry L. Thayer and Mary H. Thayer

**FOLGER,**
Anton W. of Madbury m. June L. **Daudelin** of Farmington 6/21/1937; H - 24, meat cutter, b. Portland, ME, s/o Anton Folger (Germany, meat cutter) and Anna Spilliman (Switzerland, at home); W - 20, at home, b. Northwood, d/o Alfred Daudelin (Chicago, IL, shoeworker) and Bessie Brown (Manchester, shoeworker)

**FORSAITH,**
Samuel S. of Farmington m. Lizzie M. **Young** of Farmington 7/12/1890; H - 26, shoemaker, b. England, s/o Alexander Forsaith (England, gardener) and Margaret (England); W - 34, housekeeper, b. Farmington, d/o Jonathan Young (Strafford, laborer) and Hannah S. (Rochester)

**FOSS,**
Charles A. of Farmington m. Lizzie M. **Richardson** of Northwood 9/29/1895 in Strafford Center; H - 33, shoemaker, b. Farmington, s/o William H. Foss (Strafford) and Charlotte Foss (Northwood, housework); W - 17, housework, d/o Eben Richardson (shoemaker) and Lavonia Richardson (housewife)

Harold J. of Farmington m. Alice M. **Foss** of Ctr. Strafford 6/22/1913 in Rochester; H - 21, farmer, b. Farmington, s/o James Will Foss (Rochester, farmer) and Katie M. Hobbs (Farmington); W - 18, b. Ctr. Strafford, d/o Henry R. Foss (Strafford, farmer) and Addie Tripp (Barnstead)

James W. of Farmington m. Katie M. **Hobbs** of Farmington 2/1/1888 in Strafford; H - 28, farmer, b. Rochester, s/o Richard H. (Rochester, deceased) and Lydia (Freedom); W - 18, housekeeper, b. Farmington, d/o John F. (farmer) and Melinda (housekeeper)

Sumner H. of Farmington m. Evelyn M. **Brock** of Strafford 10/1/1938 in Rochester; H - 25, speartender, b. Farmington, s/o Harold Foss (Farmington, navy yard) and Alice Foss (Strafford, housewife); W - 23, r. nurse, b. Strafford, d/o Edgar Brock (Strafford, farmer) and Mildred Hall (Barnstead, housewife)

Wilbur E. of Farmington m. Minnie E. **Tuttle** of Strafford 8/22/1910 in Rochester; H - 21, RR fireman, b. Farmington, s/o James W. Foss (Rochester, farmer) and Hattie M. Hobbs (Farmington, housewife); W - 20, school teacher, b. Strafford, d/o James W. Tuttle (Strafford, farmer) and Elvina S. Kenniston (Sandwich, housewife)

**FOSTER,**

Charles A. of Farmington m. Josephine S. **Smith** of New London, CT 3/5/1932 in New London, CT; H - 19, shoeworker, b. Farmington, s/o Charles W. Foster and Bessie M. Welch; W - 16, none, b. Farmington, ME, d/o Walter Thurston and Florence Thurston

Kenneth R. of Farmington m. Marguerite A. **Barton** of Pittsfield 9/14/1925 in Dover; H - 21, RR mail clerk, b. Berwick, ME, s/o Charles W. Foster (Nashua, shoeworker) and Bessie M. Welch (Berwick, ME, housewife); W - 18, waitress, b. Pittsfield, d/o George A. Barton (Pittsfield, truckman) and Flora B. Roberts (housewife)

Kenneth R. of Farmington m. Lillian G. **McAllister** of Rochester 8/2/1932 in Rochester; H - 29, mail clerk, 2nd, b. Berwick, ME, s/o Charles W. Foster (Nashua, shoeworker) and Bessie M. Welch (Berwick, ME, housewife); W - 28, office assistant, b. Rochester, d/o James McAllister (Ireland, farmer) and Marguerite Lowe (Ireland, housewife)

William C. of Farmington m. Mabel G. **Head** of Farmington 1/30/1926; H - 42, shoeworker, 2nd, b. Gardiner, ME, s/o Alfred G. Foster (Bangor, ME, laborer) and Rebecca A. Strong (Gardiner, ME, housewife); W - 46, housekeeper, 2nd, b. Warren, d/o Francis I. Gerald and Lucy A. Gerald

**FOWLER,**

Clarence D. of Farmington m. Alice N. **Smith** of Farmington 5/14/1910; H - 21, knife maker, b. Strafford, s/o Arthur E. Fowler (England, sawyer) and Irene L. Harden (Wilmington,

MA, housewife); W - 20, housekeeper, b. Barnet, VT, d/o Norris Smith (Lyman, farmer) and Hattie B. Emery (Haverhill, housewife)

Clarence D. of Farmington m. Marion M. **Parshley** of Barrington 12/25/1914 in Strafford; H - 25, steamfitter, $2^{nd}$, b. Strafford, s/o Arthur Fowler (England, sawyer); W - 17, at home, b. Strafford, d/o Charles E. Parshley (laborer) and Mary E. Jewe (Strafford, housekeeper)

FREELOVE,

William B. of Farmington m. Myrtle **Marston** of Lynn, MA 1/29/1917; H - 19, cook, b. McClane, AR, s/o Theodore Freelove (Fall River, MA, cook) and Ida B. Holden (Freeville, NY, housewife); W - 18, lady, b. Northwood, d/o Carl Marston (Loudon, shoeworker) and Josephine Chaplin (Canterbury, housewife)

FREETHY,

Wilbert A. of Farmington m. Laura **Scruton** of Farmington 6/30/1923; H - 30, shoeworker, $2^{nd}$, b. Albany, s/o Stephen M. Freethy and Grace Harriman (Albany, housewife); W - 30, shoeworker, b. Farmington, d/o James I. Scruton (Farmington laborer) and Elizabeth Preston (Springvale, ME, housekeeper)

FRENCH,

Bert L. of Farmington m. Sarah **Clark** of Farmington 10/21/1917; H - 50, laborer, b. Farmington, s/o Charles H. French and Martha Wentworth; W - 48, housekeeper, $2^{nd}$, b. Ireland, d/o Patrick Riley and Bridget Finnegan

Leslie of Farmington m. Agnes **Pike** of Farmington 12/23/1916 in Rochester; H - 34, shoeworker, b. Bartlett, s/o John French (Whitefield, painter) and Etta Eastman (Bartlett, housewife); W - 26, shoeworker, $2^{nd}$, b. Acton, ME, d/o Mark E. Wiggin (Acton, ME, mill hand) and Susie Day (Shapleigh, ME, housewife)

FROST,

Wendell of Wareham, MA m. Olivine F. **Howland** of Wareham, MA 10/10/1936; H - 28, police officer, b. Wareham, MA, s/o Albert E. Frost (S. Middleboro, MA, deceased) and Mary Evans (Boston, MA, housewife); W - 25, teacher, b. So. Dartmouth, d/o William Howland (Acushnet, MA, farmer) and M. Fechtenmayer (Bedford, MA, housewife)

**FULLER,**
Perley of Auburn, ME m. Marion **Hanscom** of Lewiston, ME 7/31/1916; H - 26, shoeworker, b. Winthrop, ME, s/o John Fuller and Orrie Howard (Monmouth, ME, housekeeper); W - 32, bookkeeper, b. Lewiston, ME, d/o Charles Hanscom (Lewiston, ME, teamster) and Mary Lane (Wells, ME)

**FURBER,**
John C. of Farmington m. Addie F. **Brooks** of Farmington 6/12/1917 in Dover; H - 23, shoeworker, b. Alton, s/o George E. Furber (Alton, teamster) and Ada A. Nutter (Barnstead, housewife); W - 33, shoeworker, b. Alton, d/o Alonzo S. Brooks (Alton, supt. factory) and Abbie G. Hurd (Loudon, housewife)

John E. of Farmington m. Lucina M. **Bird** of Farmington 3/12/1921 in Rochester; H - 27, shoeworker, $2^{nd}$, b. Alton, s/o George E. Furber (Alton, millhand) and Ada A. Nutter (Barnstead, housewife); W - 25, shoeworker, $2^{nd}$, b. St. Albans, VT, d/o John Bird (St. Albans, VT, boilermaker) and Lucina Curtis (St. Albans, VT, housewife)

Myron of Farmington m. Marguerite F. **Stevens** of Farmington 3/9/1937; H - 31, clerk, b. Rochester, s/o F. Leon Furber (Alton, merchant) and Flora A. Jones (Middleton, shoeworker); W - 25, clerk, b. Farmington, d/o Philomen Stevens (Biddeford, ME, shoeworker) and Helen Brooks (Farmington, deceased)

Otto J. of Farmington m. Evelyn **Tanner** of Farmington 7/12/1933; H - 28, clerk, b. Alton, s/o Frank L. Furber (Alton, merchant) and Flora Jones (Middleton, shoeworker); W - 20, shoe clerk, b. Farmington, d/o George I. Tanner (Farmington, caretaker) and Gertrude Smart (Farmington, shoeworker)

Will E. of Middleton m. Sarah N. **Farnham** of Middleton 1/18/1912; H - 24, painter, b. Alton, s/o George E. Furber (Alton, teamster) and Ada Nutter (Barnstead, housekeeper); W - 28, weaver, $2^{nd}$, b. Middleton, d/o Daniel Jones (Middleton, farmer) and Emma H. Perkins (Middleton, housekeeper)

**FURNANS,**

John E. of New Bedford, MA m. Iris St. Helena **Dame** of Farmington 6/14/1905; H - 31, salesman, b. New Bedford, MA, s/o John Fernans (Island of Flores, sailor) and Mary S. Thomas (Island of Flores); W - 26, teacher, b. Farmington, d/o Albert W. Dame (Haverhill, MA, shoe cutter) and Adelaid A. Roberts (New Durham)

**GAGNON,**

Joseph A. E. of Malden, MA m. Leona M. **Bush** of Farmington 11/16/1929; H - 26, mechanic, b. Laconia, s/o Octave Gagnon (Canada, farmer) and Rosanna Blanchard (Canada); W - 22, nurse, 2$^{nd}$, b. Farmington, d/o Louie R. Rollins (Bennington, music teacher) and Bessie F. Innis (Lawrence, MA, housewife)

**GARDNER,**

Uel A. of Farmington m. Dorothy H. **Gray** of Farmington 6/29/1929; H - 21, painter, b. Durham, ME, s/o Charles A. Gardner (London, England, painter) and Edith L. Cole (NB, housewife); W - 25, school teacher, b. Farmington, d/o Francis E. Gray (New Durham, blacksmith) and Addie Dickey (NB, housewife)

**GAREY,**

Newman A. of Farmington m. Susan J. **Whitehouse** of Farmington 11/2/1892; H - 32, druggist, b. Milton, s/o Samuel Garey (Saco, ME, 62, farmer) of Limerick, ME; W - 34, shoe stitcher 2$^{nd}$, widow, b. Milton, d/o Henry C. Amazeen (New Castle, 65, farmer) and Abigail Amazeen (Milton, 60, housewife) of Milton

**GARLAND,**

Edgar E. of Farmington m. Mary Ann **Turcott** of Farmington 12/26/1895 in Strafford Blue Hill; H - 21, shoemaker, 2$^{nd}$, b. Middleton, s/o Alfred Garland (Rochester) and Harriet Garland (Farmington, housework); W - 25, mill operative, 2$^{nd}$, b. Portland, ME, d/o Frank Turcott and Ellen Turcott

J. Weston of Farmington m. Edna M. **Chesley** of Farmington 9/23/1893; H - 22, clerk, b. Rye, s/o Joseph W. Garland (Rye, road agent) and Annie D. Garland (Rye, housewife); W - 22, lady, b. Wolfeboro, d/o John Chesley (dead) and Lydia Chesley (dead)

James M. of Farmington m. Nellie M. **Henderson** of Madbury 6/4/1895 in Farmington Merrills; H - 21, farmer, b. Farmington, s/o Alfred Garland (Middleton) and Harriet Peavey (Farmington, housewife); W - 15, housewife, b. Farmington, d/o George F. Henderson (Farmington, farmer) and Axie Henderson (Farmington, housewife)

John of Farmington m. Gertrude **Ettinger** of Farmington 5/9/1908; H - 35, heel cutter, b. Alton, s/o Eli Garland (Alton, shoemaker) and Sarah J. Corson (New Durham); W - 31, housekeeper, b. NS, d/o John Ettinger (NS, shipbuilder) and Sarah Elliott (NS)

Wilfred E. of Farmington m. Lillian E. **Gray** of Farmington 12/20/1926 in E. Rochester; H - 37, laborer, 2nd, b. Farmington, s/o Charles L. Garland (Farmington, farmer) and Mary E. Sullivan (Deerfield, housekeeper); W - 16, at home, b. Portsmouth, d/o Herbert J. Gray (Strafford, junk dealer) and Daisy M. Emery (Kittery, ME, housekeeper)

## GEARY,

Richard A. of Farmington m. Lola E. **Greenier** of S. Lebanon, ME 4/30/1932 in East Rochester; H - 21, shoeworker, b. S. Wolfeboro, s/o Anthony W. Geary (Waterboro, ME, woodchopper) and Alice R. Perkins (Milton, housewife); W - 21, housekeeper, b. E. Rochester, d/o Pete Greenier (Three Rivers, Canada, laborer) and Bertha M. McCrillis

## GELINAS,

William E. of Rochester m. Florence E. **Canney** of Farmington 10/16/1932 in Wolfeboro; H - 27, clerk, b. Kennebunk, ME, s/o Louis E. A. Gelinas (Canada, retired) and Victoria Plourde (Canada, housewife); W - 21, shoe operative, 2nd, b. Farmington, d/o Guy F. Leighton (Farmington, shoecutter) and Matilda Theroux (Hooksett, housewife)

## GIBBS,

Marshall P. of Farmington m. Bertha A. **Littlefield** of Farmington 7/22/1922 in East Rochester; H - 20, shoeworker, b. Farmington, s/o Ralph P. Gibbs (Middleboro, MA, foreman) and Grace B. Emery (Milton, housewife); W - 19, at home, b. Farmington, d/o Fred Littlefield (Fitchburg, insurance) and Alma Kimball (housewife)

Ralph P. of Farmington m. Grace B. **Emery** of Farmington
1/24/1898; H - 21, shoemaker, b. Bridgewater, MA, s/o Andrew
B. Gibbs (Middleboro, MA, butcher) and Dora B. Gibbs
(Middleboro, MA, housewife); W - 17, shoe stitcher, b.
Farmington, d/o Edward A. Emery (Farmington, laborer) and
Fannie Emery (Milton, shoe stitcher)

**GILBERT,**
George of Bethlehem m. Lilla **Tuttle** of New Durham 12/17/1904; H
- 31, lumberman, b. Spain, s/o William Gilbert (Spain, sailor)
and Alice Brenette (France, housewife); W - 18, housekeeper,
b. New Durham, d/o William Tuttle (New Durham, farmer)
Wilfred of Farmington m. Vera M. **Remick** of Farmington
1/20/1917; H - 21, shoeworker, b. Milton, s/o Daniel Gilbert
(Farmington, laborer) and Ida M. Duntley (Farmington,
housewife); W - 20, at home, b. Westboro, MA, d/o Nathaniel
P. Remick (Sutton, MA, shoeworker) and Mary E. Sprague
(Grafton, MA, housewife)

**GILES,**
Fred A. of Farmington m. Emma I. **Davis** of Farmington 7/26/1919;
H - 61, millman, $2^{nd}$, b. Epsom, s/o Perley Giles and Clara S.
Grant (Epsom, housekeeper); W - 56, boxmaker, $2^{nd}$, b. Alton,
d/o Manoah G. H. Gilman and Mary A. Ford

**GILLIS,**
George A. of Manchester m. Bessie F. **Emerson** of Farmington
3/31/1929; H - 30, vulcanizer, b. Springvale, ME, s/o Alfred V.
Gillis and Mabel D. Ames (Lynn, MA, bookkeeper); W - 25,
stenographer, b. Barnstead, d/o Augustus F. Emerson (Dover,
lumberman) and Flora Hurd (Farmington, housewife)

**GILMAN,**
Erman F. of Farmington m. Martha E. **Lougee** of Farmington
12/19/1915; H - 25, shoeworker, b. Farmington, s/o Warren L.
Gilman (Alton, road agent) and Annie B. Avery (Farmington,
housekeeper); W - 23, shoeworker, b. Rochester, d/o
Nehemiah Lougee (Farmington) and Julia E. Place (Sandwich,
housekeeper)
Ernest F. of Farmington m. Althea V. **Rogers** of Manchester
4/27/1927 in Manchester; H - 54, electrician, $2^{nd}$, b. Hallowell,

ME, s/o William H. Gilman and Emma Bowman; W - 34, clerk, b. Dorchester, MA, d/o Timothy O. Rogers and Harriett Nickerson

Frank I. of Farmington m. Melissa E. **Moore** of Milton 6/14/1891; H - 22, painter, b. Farmington, s/o Winslow H. Gilman (Tamworth, shoe cutter); W - 23, housekeeper, b. Milton, d/o William E. Moore (Lowell, MA, farmer)

John S. of Farmington m. E. Maude **Garland** of Milton 7/7/1906 in Milton; H - 25, school teacher, b. Alton, s/o S. E. P. Gilman (Alton, farmer) and Nancy J. Cooper (Alton); W - 26, school teacher, b. Farmington, d/o Llewellyn Garland (Milton, shoemaker) and Cora B. Goodall (Middleton)

Leo D. of Farmington m. Caroline E. **Goodrich** of Farmington 8/19/1911; H - 33, painter, b. Farmington, s/o Byron C. Gilman (Farmington, painter) and Abbie B. Stevens (Alton, dressmaker); W - 22, shoeworker, $2^{nd}$, b. Cornish, ME, d/o George Goodrich (Saco, ME, blacksmith) and Sarah A. Bickford (S. Parsonsfield, ME, housekeeper)

Leon E. of Farmington m. Carrie M. **Montee** of Farmington 10/20/1900 in Milton; H - 22, shoemaker, b. Farmington, s/o Warren L. Gilman (Alton, shoemaker) and Anna Belle Avery (Farmington, housekeeper); W - 19, housekeeper, b. Farmington, d/o John Montee (St. Kanoz, Canada, shoemaker) and Lucy M. Winters (Gorham, ME, housekeeper)

Lloyd M. of Farmington m. Helen W. **Carter** of Farmington 1/31/1914; H - 20, clerk, b. Farmington, s/o Frank I. Gilman (Farmington, painter) and Melissa Moore (Milton, housekeeper); W - 21, nurse, b. Farmington, d/o Albert Carter (furniture dealer) and Katie Dame

Ruel P. of Farmington m. Melinda Frances **Davis** of Farmington 10/1/1892; H - 25, shoemaker, b. Danvers, MA, s/o Stephen F. Gilman (Alton, 69, shoemaker) and Amanda M. Gilman (Danvers, MA, 56, housewife) of Danvers, MA; W - 24, dressmaker, b. New Durham, d/o George F. Davis (New Durham, 45, merchant) of Washington, DC and Ruth Davis (New Durham, 45, housewife) of New Durham

**GILSON,**

Levi H. of Farmington m. S. Alice **Downing** of Farmington 5/20/1890 in Rochester; H - 40, box maker, b. Kittery, ME, s/o

Levi Gilson (dead) and Martha; W - 22, housekeeper, b. Farmington, d/o James H. Downing (farmer) and Addie S.

Lewis F. of Farmington m. Lillian M. **Chesley** of Farmington 2/4/1903 in Rochester; H - 23, telegraph operator, b. Farmington, s/o Franklin Gilson (Kittery, ME, railroading) and Clara A. Jones (Alton); W - 24, sales lady, b. Milton Mills, d/o George L. Chesley (engineer) and Mary A. Archibald

## GLASS,

Eugene of Farmington m. Eleanor F. **Blaisdell** of Farmington 4/25/1915; H - 29, shoeworker, b. NC, s/o Alfred Glass (NC, farmer) and Lucy Parker (NC, housewife); W - 20, shoeworke $2^{nd}$, b. Farmington, d/o Clarence Blaisdell (Farmington, shoeworker) and Ella Swinerton (Farmington, housekeeper)

## GLEASON,

Charles S. of Wareham, MA m. Eleanor **McCarthy** of E. Brewster, MA 2/9/1919; H - 53, physician, $2^{nd}$, b. Oakland, ME, s/o Benjamin Gleason (Canaan, ME, farmer) and Caroline McNilne (Bingham, ME, at home); W - 32, at home, $2^{nd}$, b. Germany, d/o Gustave Zacharias (Germany, mill owner) and Amelia V. Kushbaum (Germany, at home)

## GLIDDEN,

Augustus of Farmington m. Mary **Spence** of Farmington 5/29/1897 H - 40, shoemaker, $3^{rd}$, b. Alton, s/o Levi F. Glidden (Effingham, farmer) and Livonia Glidden (Alton, housekeeper) W - 24, shop work, b. NS, d/o David Spence and Elizabeth McDaniel (NS, housekeeper)

Bernard S. of Farmington m. Rosanna **Cardinal** of Farmington 5/20/1938; H - 20, shoeworker, b. New Durham, s/o Sidney Glidden (Farmington, shoeworker) and Alice Glidden (New Durham, housewife); W - 18, shoeworker, b. Farmington, d/o John Cardinal (Canada, farmer) and Rosanna Rock (Epping, housewife)

Clyde R. of New Durham m. Reta **Rollins** of Farmington 8/15/1920 H - 19, laborer, b. New Durham, s/o Ira Glidden (New Durham, laborer) and Lila Randall (New Durham, housewife); W - 16, at home, b. Farmington, d/o Irving Rollins (Farmington, laborer) and Bertha Clark

Ernest E. of Alton m. Evelyn **Otis** of Farmington 2/18/1934 in Alton; H - 22, shoeworker, b. Alton, s/o Earl Glidden (Alton, painter) and Flora Lamper (Alton, housewife); W - 24, teacher, b. Farmington, d/o Norman L. Otis (Farmington, undertaker) and Susie Meserve (Danvers, MA, housewife)

Frank E. of Farmington m. Marie R. **Patnande** of Somersworth 6/8/1935 in Somersworth; H - 18, farmer, b. Milton, s/o George W. Glidden (Farmington, deceased) and Maude Nickless (Hooksett, housewife); W - 24, shoeworker, b. Lowell, MA, d/o John B. Patnande (Ashburnham, MA, CWA) and Mary Channard (Canada, housewife)

Howard C. of Natick, MA m. Martha B. **Hayes** of Farmington 8/20/1900; H - 30, clerk, b. Natick, MA, s/o Phineas Glidden (New Durham, dead) and Hannah R. Kimball (Natick, MA, housekeeper); W - 26, housekeeper, b. New Durham, d/o Elihu Hayes (New Durham, dead) and Sarah E. Colbath (New Durham, dead)

Stanley of Farmington m. Addie **Goldsmith** of Wolfeboro 1/21/1912 in Alton; H - 19, shoemaker, b. Alton, s/o Woodbury Glidden (Alton, shoemaker) and Ella Young (Alton); W - 20, shoemaker, b. Water Village, d/o Lavitte Goldsmith (Water Village, jobber) and Susan Clough (Water Village)

**GOODELL,**

James H. of Alton m. Catherine M. **Currier** of Farmington 10/15/1927; H - 32, shoeworker, b. Alton, s/o James W. Goodell (Alton, farmer) and Annie T. Grimes (Ireland, housekeeper); W - 23, at home, b. Farmington, d/o Charles Currier (Farmington, farmer) and Mary Ring (Farmington, housewife)

**GOODROW,**

Middie of Farmington m. Louise **Chartier** of Alton 8/15/1927; H - 26, laborer, b. Somersworth, s/o James Goodrow (Canada, farmer) and Melvina Mater (Somersworth, housewife); W - 18, shoeworker, b. Boscawen, d/o Louis Chartier (laborer) and Hannah Wise (Groton, housewife)

**GOODRUM,**

William of Farmington m. Ida B. **Trask** of Farmington 6/1/1895; H - 20, shoemaker, b. Coaticook, Canada, s/o John A. Goodrum

(England, farmer) and Ann W. Goodrum (Ireland, housekeeping); W - 22, housekeeper, b. Rochester, d/o James A. Trask and Maria Trask (housewife)

**GOODSTONE,**
John of Farmington m. Arline **Wilkins** of Farmington 11/14/1936; - 22, shoeworker, 2nd, b. Liverpool, England, s/o Joseph Goodstone (Liverpool, England) and Elizabeth Ferrell (Liverpool, England, at home); W - 21, shoeworker, 2nd, b. Farmington, d/o E. Richardson (Northwood, state rd. work) ar Marion Thompson (Dexter, at home)

**GOODWIN,**
Charles E. of Farmington m. Mertie **Chesley** of Farmington 12/29/1910; H - 21, shoemaker, b. Rochester, s/o John F. Goodwin (York, ME, shoemaker) and Mary E. Foss (Gonic, housewife); W - 18, shoemaker, b. Wolfeboro, d/o Herbert J. Chesley (Farmington, shoemaker) and Annie E. Kimball (Wolfeboro, housewife)

Charles E. of Farmington m. Fannie J. **Bailey** of Farmington 11/3/1923 in Rochester; H - 31, shoeworker, 2nd, b. Rochester s/o John F. Goodwin (York, ME, shoeworker) and Mary E. Foss; W - 28, shoeworker, 4th, b. Union, d/o James A. Drew (Brookfield, laborer) and Clara A. Glidden

Eugene T. of Farmington m. Bernice L. **Stevens** of Farmington 6/25/1937 in West Milton; H - 25, shoeworker, b. Farmington, s/o John Goodwin (York, ME, deceased) and Inez Ham (Alton, deceased); W - 21, housework, b. Middleton, d/o Albert Stevens (Middleton, farmer) and Bernice Tufts (Middleton, deceased)

John F. of Farmington m. Helen A. **Hoyt** of Wolfeboro 12/12/1896 in Wolfeboro; H - 28, shoemaker, b. Berwick, ME, s/o John L. Goodwin (Berwick, ME, carpenter) and Jane Goodwin (Berwick, ME, housekeeper); W - 21, housekeeper, b. Moultonboro, d/o Charles Hoyt (Moultonboro, carpenter) and May Hoyt (Moultonboro, housekeeper)

Ralph L. of Gilmanton m. Roberta T. **Hayes** of Farmington 4/23/1938; H - 22, truck driver, b. Gilmanton, s/o Ernest Goodwin (Gilmanton, merchant) and Florence Watson (Pittsfield, postmistress); W - 18, shoeworker, b. New Durham d/o Colo E. Hayes (New Durham, mechanic) and Bertha MacCarlie (Farmington, ME)

Richard J. P. of Malden, MA m. Lucie M. **Davis** of Farmington 10/24/1906; H - 69, physician, 2$^{nd}$, widower, b. Boston, MA, s/o Richard Goodwin (Wakefield, blacksmith) and Mary A. Roberts (Rochester); W - 51, shoe stitcher, 2$^{nd}$, widow, b. Nottingham, d/o John B. Furber (Newmarket, farmer) and Lavina Bachelder (North Hampton)

## GORDON,

Frank of Farmington m. Nellie **Young** of Farmington 12/24/1919 in New Durham; H - 20, shoeworker, b. Dover, s/o Harry Vickery and Mary J. Gordon; W - 24, shoeworker, b. Farmington, d/o Frank V. Young (farmer) and Mary Varney (New Durham, housewife)

## GOUIN,

Walter J. of Farmington m. Agnes **Clare** of Laconia 8/15/1933 in Old Orchard, ME; H - 37, chef, b. Newton, s/o Joel Gouin (Canada, deceased) and Emily Martel (Canada, deceased); W - 37, laborer, b. Birchfield, Ireland, d/o Thomas Clare (Birchfield, Ireland, laborer) and Bridget Fitzpatrick (Sandfield, Ireland, deceased)

## GOWIN,

William L. of Farmington m. Ella E. **Ainsley** of Farmington 6/26/1918 in Sanbornville; H - 18, shoeworker, b. Laconia, s/o William T. Gowin (Canada, meatcutter) and Albina Joher (Canada, housewife); W - 20, shoeworker, b. Scituate, MA, d/o Albert Ainsley (Scituate, MA, farmer) and Mary J. Emerson (Scituate, MA, housewife)

## GRACE,

Irving S. of Farmington m. Allie A. **Horne** of Farmington 8/8/1891 in Rochester; H - 21, shoemaker, b. Farmington, s/o Benjamin Grace (New Durham, farmer); W - 24, shoe stitcher, b. Farmington, d/o John W. Horne (dead)

John A. of Farmington m. Flora M. **Grace** of Farmington 1/18/1912 in Milton; H - 18, farmer, b. VT, s/o Chandler Grace (Chatham, farmer) and Abbie E. (Conway, housewife); W - 18, lady, b.

Tamworth, d/o Frank L. Grace (Madison) and Lizzie B. (Conway)

**GRAVELLE,**
Arthur of Farmington m. Ruby **Pulsifer** of Farmington 11/28/1928; H - 58, shoeworker, 2$^{nd}$, b. Montreal, Canada, s/o Peter Gravelle and Joe Labelle (Canada); W - 40, shoeworker, 2$^{nd}$, b. Farmington, d/o Frank Avery and Sarah D. Burleigh (Strafford, housekeeper)

**GRAY,**
Arthur M. of Farmington m. Lillian M. **Greene** of Alton 6/4/1919 in Alton; H - 21, farmer, b. Farmington, s/o John I. Gray (Farmington, farmer) and Ellen F. Varney (Farmington, housewife); W - 20, housekeeper, b. Alton, s/o Walter Greene (Alton) and Rosa Estes

Clyde S. of Farmington m. Leola M. **Meader** of Rochester 4/16/1930 in Dover; H - 28, farmer, b. Rochester, s/o Willey E. Gray and Emma Varney (Farmington); W - 19, domestic, b. Rochester, d/o Albert E. Meader (Rochester, mail carrier) and Eunice Scruton (Farmington)

Ernest L. of Farmington m. Doris M. **Wormstead** of Farmington 1/1/1937; H - 23, shoeworker, b. New London, s/o Listan Gray (deceased) and Nettie Morse; W - 18, shoeworker, b. Saugus, MA, d/o Joseph Wormstead (Saugus, MA, farmer) and Mabel Spidell (Lynn, MA, shoeworker)

Frank P. of Farmington m. Erline M. **Foss** of Farmington 11/1/1937; H - 23, shoeworker, b. Grafton, s/o Samuel Gray (Gilmanton, truckman) and Mildred Marshall (Cambridge, MA, housewife); W - 19, at home, 2$^{nd}$, b. Middleton, d/o Charlie Terrill (Melrose, MA, shoeworker) and Goldie Stanley (Otis, ME, shoeworker)

George R. of Farmington m. Elsie M. H. **Berry** of Farmington 6/19/1921; H - 19, shoeworker, b. Grafton, s/o Leston E. Gray and Nettie A. Morse; W - 16, at home, b. Farmington, d/o Charles H. Berry (Barnstead) and Clara Barker (Farmington)

Irving A. of Farmington m. Thelma **Berry** of Farmington 12/24/1929; H - 25, farmer, b. Rochester, s/o Willie E. Gray (Farmington, farmer) and Emma Varney (Farmington); W - 25, shoeworker, b. New Durham, d/o John Berry and Fannie Baxter

John Ivory of Farmington m. Evelyn May **Greene** of Alton 10/17/1924 in Rochester; H - 20, farmer, b. Farmington, s/o John I. Gray (Farmington, farmer) and Ellen F. Varney (Farmington, housewife); W - 19, housekeeper, b. Alton, d/o Walter Greene (Alton) and Rosa Estes (Alton, housewife)

Joseph L. of Hall Co., NE m. Mary A. **Pinkham** of Farmington 6/7/1887; H - 48, farmer, b. Strafford, s/o Jethro I. Gray and Lucretia Gray; W - 36, 3$^{rd}$, d/o John Hussey

## GRENIER,

Alfred of Farmington m. Maud **Hayes** of Farmington 9/1/1917 in Exeter; H - 27, shoeworker, b. Canada, s/o Archie Grenier (Canada, boxmaker) and Mary Grenier (Canada, housekeeper); W - 33, housekeeper, b. Farmington, d/o Arista Horne (Middleton, bartender) and Clara Parker (Farmington, shoeworker)

Alfred J. of Farmington m. Marion **Hanson** of Alton 4/24/1926 in Rochester; H - 33, shoeworker, 2$^{nd}$, b. Canada, s/o Archie Grenier (Canada, boxmaker) and Mary Silvon; W - 23, music teacher, b. Alton, d/o Chester Hanson (Canada, blacksmith) and Emma Tasker (Loudon, housewife)

## GRISWOLD,

Horace D. of Farmington m. Emily B. **Eldridge** of Auburn, ME 10/29/1911; H - 50, shoeworker, 3$^{rd}$, b. Concord, VT, s/o George J. Griswold (St. Johnsbury, VT, painter) and Lucretia C. Moulton (Concord, VT, housekeeper); W - 35, shoe stitcher, b. Lancaster, d/o Walter S. Eldridge (Stockholden, NY, doctor) and Amelia Eldridge (Germany, shoe stitcher)

## GRONDIN,

Raymond P. of Rochester m. Gretchen L. **Glidden** of Farmington 9/3/1934 in Rochester; H - 29, printer, b. Rochester, s/o Honore Grondin (Canada, mail carrier) and Regina Pennell (St. Albans, VT, at home); W - 24, shoeworker, b. New Durham, d/o Harry Glidden (New Durham, sawyer) and Lilla Randall (New Durham, housewife)

## GUILMET,

Napoleon of Farmington m. Melina **Lajoie** of Farmington 2/10/1923 in Nashua; H - 59, lumber dealer, 3$^{rd}$, b. Canada, s/o Peter

Guilmet (Canada, farmer); W - 49, housekeeper, 2nd, b. Canada, d/o Baptiste Coutois (Canada, laborer) and Delvina Cote (Canada)

Rudolph of Farmington m. Mary C. **Ring** of Farmington 9/24/1935; H - 26, leather business, b. Lawrence, MA, s/o Napoleon Guilmet (Canada, deceased) and Anna Duchene (Canada, deceased); W - 19, maid, b. Farmington, d/o Terrence Ring (Farmington, shoeworker) and Mary Flynn (Rockport, MA, housewife)

## HACKETT,

George E. of Alton m. Velma I. **Gooch** of Farmington 8/16/1930; H - 29, shoeworker, b. Farmington, s/o Wesley Hackett (Danvers, MA, RR foreman) and Gertrude Evans (Alton, housewife); W - 18, shoeworker, b. Alton, d/o Harold C. Gooch (Alton, salesman) and Alice M. Britt (Northampton, MA, housewife)

William of Farmington m. Sadie **Emery** of Farmington 3/11/1928; H - 57, section hand, 2nd, b. Danvers, MA, s/o William R. Hacket and Olive J. Marston (Sandwich); W - 39, housework, 2nd, b. Fairfield, ME, d/o Henry W. Haywood and Etta Johnson

## HADDOCK,

Hector R. of Farmington m. Leanor M. **DuBois** of Farmington 7/7/1912; H - 27, shoemaker, b. Farmington, s/o Howard Haddock (Haverhill, MA, shoemaker) and Luella B. Tibbetts (Farmington, housekeeper); W - 22, shoemaker, 2nd, b. Farmington, d/o Henry DuBois (Canada, loom fixer) and Mary DuBois (Canada, housekeeper)

## HADLEY,

Eugene P. of Laconia m. Nettie A. **Randall** of Farmington 12/25/1920 in Laconia; H - 57, trainman, 2nd, b. Hill, s/o Stephen Hadley (Belmont, farmer) and Sarah E. Chase (Canterbury, housewife); W - 50, shoestitcher, b. Canada, d/o George W. Page (Sheffield, VT, shoemaker) and Elizabeth Young (Farmington, housewife)

## HALE,

C. Edgar of Farmington m. Flora B. **Johnson** of Farmington 1/28/1928 in Rochester; H - 20, shoeworker, b. New Durham, s/o Corie Hale (Lee, ME, shoeworker) and Ida M. Rhines (Rochester, housekeeper); W - 18, shoeworker, b. Machias, ME, d/o Joseph B. Johnson (Machias, ME, gardener) and Grace Berry (Marshfield, ME, housewife)

Corie E. of Farmington m. Ida M. **Rines** of New Durham 3/18/1890 in Alton; H - 34, shoe cutter, b. Lee, ME, s/o John R. Hale (Westford, ME, farmer) and Eleanor R.; W - 21, stitcher, b. Rochester, d/o Alvah Rines (New Durham, farmer) and Lydia

Merton H. of Farmington m. Lila I. **Brooks** of Farmington 5/30/1918 in Rochester; H - 21, shoeworker, b. New Durham, s/o Corie G. Hale and Ida M. Rhines (Farmington, housework); W - 20, shoeworker, b. Farmington, d/o Percy J. Brooks (Alton, shoeworker) and Edith Tibbetts (Farmington, housewife)

**HALL,**

Errol S. of Farmington m. Edith F. **Roberts** of Farmington 11/19/1913; H - 23, shoeworker, b. Farmington, s/o John E. S. Hall (Farmington, clerk) and Frances Davidson (New Castle); W - 26, shoeworker, 2$^{nd}$, b. Farmington, d/o Charles T. Connor (Farmington, shoemaker) and Florence Miller (New Durham, shoemaker)

Frank A. of Farmington m. Gertie M. **Drew** of Farmington 3/9/1906; H - 21, heel cutter, b. Rochester, s/o Andrew J. Hall (Dover, carrier) and Agnes M. Watson (Lebanon, housekeeper); W - 26, housekeeper, 2$^{nd}$, divorced, b. Rochester, d/o Frank J. Drew (Gilmanton, shoemaker) and Lizzie H. Young (Derry)

Fred W. of Barre, VT m. Grace R. **Canney** of Farmington 12/20/1919 in Laconia; H - 24, teacher, b. Barrington, s/o Minnie L. Hall (Barrington, housekeeper); W - 17, student, b. New Durham, d/o Isaac Canney (Farmington, teamster) and Annie M. Colbath (Farmington, housewife)

John E. S. of Farmington m. Fannie L. **Davidson** of Farmington 11/17/1888 in New Castle; H - 20, book-keeper, b. New Durham, s/o Asa A. (Strafford, carpenter) and Maria L. (New Durham, housekeeper); W - 22, housekeeper, b. New Castle, d/o Ralph (New Castle, boat builder) and Lucretia (New London, CT, housekeeper)

**HAM,**

Benjamin of Farmington m. Emma J. **Taber** of Haverhill, MA 10/19/1913 in Sanbornton; H - 23, shoemaker, b. Farmington, s/o Herman Ham (Dover, shoemaker) and Ida B. Stevens (Concord, housekeeper); W - 24, at home, b. Haverhill, MA, d/o Nathan B. Taber (Vassalboro, ME, shoemaker) and ----- (Exeter, housekeeper)

Charles E. of Farmington m. Phebe L. **Tibbetts** of Milton 6/3/1891 in Milton; H - 28, farmer, b. Farmington, s/o Moses Ham (Alton, farmer); W - 20, housekeeper, b. Rochester, d/o Luke Tibbitts (Rochester, farmer)

Charles E. of Farmington m. Lena M. **Roberts** of Farmington 6/12/1895 in Milton; H - 25, mechanic, 2nd, b. Farmington, s/o Moses Ham (Alton, farming) and Lizzie Ham (Barnstead); W 21, housekeeper, b. Pittsfield, d/o Bard P. Roberts (Milton) and Nettie M. Roberts (Portland, ME, housework)

Edwin of Farmington m. Addie **Burrows** of Farmington 7/24/1893 in Gilmanton; H - 29, shoemaker, b. Farmington, s/o William P. Ham (Middleton, dead) and Hannah P. Ham (Farmington, housekeeper); W - 21, lady, b. Farmington, d/o Daniel Burrows (Middleton, laborer) and Frances Burrows (Farmington, housewife)

Eric N. of Farmington m. Martha E. **Dexter** of Farmington 5/26/1917 in Dover; H - 24, shoeworker, b. Farmington, s/o Elwin Ham (Farmington, shoeworker) and Addie Burrows (Farmington); W - 28, shoeworker, b. Gilmanton, d/o Caleb Dexter and Hattie Gault (Gilmanton)

George W. of Farmington m. Addie May **Scott** of Farmington 10/17/1914; H - 23, shoeworker, b. Milton, s/o Charles Ham (New Durham, brickmaker) and Phoebe L. Tibbetts (Rochester, housekeeper); W - 29, shoeworker, 2nd, b. Nottingham, d/o Erastus Leathers (Nottingham) and Mary A. Jackson (New Durham, shoeworker)

Herman of Farmington m. Ida B. **Stevens** of Alton 12/1/1888 in Milton; H - 25, heel burnisher, b. Dover, s/o Benjamin (deceased) and Wealthy; W - 16, housekeeper, d/o Martin (Alton, farmer) and Melinda (Concord, housekeeper)

Irving C. of Farmington m. Pearl **Gray** of Farmington 7/23/1906 in Milton; H - 24, shoe cutter, b. Farmington, s/o Clarence M. Ham (Farmington, farmer) and Mary E. Peavey (Tuftonboro); W - 25, housekeeper, b. Milton, d/o George H. Gray (Alexandria, shoemaker) and Ina M. Downs (Milton, shoe stitcher)

Irving L. of Farmington m. Carrie E. **Wentworth** of Farmington 2/13/1887 in Milton; H - 19, shoemaker, b. Farmington, s/o William Ham (Alton, shoemaker) and Hannah Ham; W - 17, b. Farmington, d/o Alvin Wentworth (Farmington, shoemaker) and Henrietta Wentworth

John H. of Farmington m. Alfreda J. **Staples** of Farmington 2/25/1911; H - 21, shoecutter, b. Farmington, s/o Clarence M. Ham (Farmington, farmer) and Mary E. Peavey (Farmington, housewife); W - 20, housekeeper, b. Peabody, MA, d/o William M. Staples (Danvers, MA, canvasser) and Eliza Acone (PEI, housewife)

William M. of Farmington m. Celia E. **Moulton** of Farmington 2/14/1898; H - 21, shoemaker, b. Farmington, s/o Clarence M. Ham (Farmington, laborer) and Mary E. Ham (Tuftonboro, housewife); W - 18, shoe stitcher, b. Farmington, d/o George E. Moulton (Farmington, laborer) and J. Moulton (New Durham)

## HAMBLETT,

Charles H. of Derry m. Edith B. **Kimball** of Farmington 5/29/1915 in Nashua; H - 28, shoeworker, 2nd, b. Derry, s/o Eugene H. Hamblett (Auburn, carpenter) and Elvira E. Corliss (Hudson, housekeeper); W - 24, waitress, b. Farmington, d/o Samuel W. Kimball (Middleton, shoeworker) and Addie R. Young (Farmington)

## HAMEL,

Henry T. of Farmington m. Blanch G. **Ricker** of Farmington 10/3/1900 in New Durham; H - 24, shoe finisher, b. Alton, s/o Philip Hamel (Montreal, PQ, laborer) and Delia M. Bono (Montreal, PQ, housekeeper); W - 24, housekeeper, b. Alton, d/o Augustus Ricker (shoemaker) and Augusta Currier (Belmont, dead)

## HANCOCK,

Frank A. of Farmington m. Hazel M. **Babb** of Farmington 11/17/1916; H - 20, shoecutter, b. Salem, MA, s/o Jesse Hancock and Georgia Henderson (Salem, MA); W - 18, at home, b. Farmington, d/o John K. Babb (shoeworker) and Edith Gray

**HANNAFORD,**

Thomas H. of Farmington m. Mary J. **Melvin** of Farmington 7/24/1937; H - 43, contractor, b. Medford, MA, s/o William Hannaford (Medford, MA, deceased) and Mary Dean (St. Johns, NB, deceased); W - 41, nurse, b. Providence, RI, d/o Mitchell Melvin (Natick, MA, deceased) and Mary Bryan (St. Johns, NB, deceased)

**HANSON,**

Chester H. of Farmington m. Emma A. **Tasker** of Farmington 8/18/1895 in New Durham; H - 22, farmer, b. St. Stephens, NB, s/o Richard Hanson (Rocabac, NB, farmer) and Elmira Hanson (Rocabac, NB, housewife); W - 19, housewife, b. Pittsfield, d/o John Tasker (Loudon) and Elizabeth F. Tasker (New Durham)

Frederick J. of Farmington m. Louisa **Thompson** of Somersworth 9/12/1927 in Somersworth; H - 27, purchasing agent, b. Bangor, ME, s/o Frederick Hanson and Mary V. Connors; W - 19, packer, b. Somersworth, d/o James Thompson (Canada, millhand) and Florida Demers (Canada, housewife)

Julian R. of Farmington m. Maud R. **Smith** of Canaan 7/30/1902; H - 21, clerk, b. Farmington, s/o Charles B. Hanson (Rochester, dead) and Fannie Jones (Alton, housekeeper); W - 20, bookkeeper, b. Canaan, d/o Alden E. Smith (Orange, merchant) and Rozella Bullock (Grafton, housewife)

Julian R. of Farmington m. Harriett B. **Simonds** of Farmington 9/29/1923; H - 41, painter, 2nd, b. Farmington, s/o Charles B. Hanson and Fannie B. Jones; W - 44, shoeworker, 2nd, b. Swampscott, MA, d/o Joseph F. Simonds and Martha Littlefield

**HARMON,**

John H. of Farmington m. Lucinda R. **Granville** of Farmington 10/5/1892 in East Rochester; H - 34, shoemaker, b. Limerick, ME, s/o Joseph Harmon (Limerick, ME, 75, farmer) and Susan Harmon (Limerick, ME, 69, housewife) of Limerick, ME; W - 34, shoe stitcher, b. Effingham, d/o John R. Granville (dead) and Mary Granville (Effingham, 55, housekeeper) of Alton

**HARRIMAN,**

Cyrus of Farmington m. Doris **DePatra** of Farmington 7/13/1933; H - 23, shoeworker, b. Alton, s/o Cyrus L. Harriman (Stoneham,

ME, shoeworker) and Maude Kimball (Wolfeboro, housewife); W - 23, at home, b. New Haven, CT, d/o Frank DePatra (mill worker) and Nettie Ellis (housewife)

Stanley of Gardiner, ME m. Ruby R. **Cronk** of Farmington 9/8/1925; H - 29, druggist, b. Gardiner, ME, s/o Charles W. Harriman and Jennie E. Wilkins (Phillips, ME, housekeeper); W - 29, at home, b. Quincy, MA, d/o Nelson W. Cronk (Eastport, ME, baker) and Flora V. Brown (Campello, NB, housewife)

HARRISON,

William J. of Farmington m. Marie Malina **Regis** of Farmington 10/30/1914 in Rochester; H - 22, shoeworker, b. Clark Isl., ME, s/o James Harrison (Furness, Scotland, paving cutter) and Mary A. Monaghan (Dalbeattie, Scotland, housewife); W - 18, shoeworker, b. Derry, d/o Joseph Regis (Canada, shoemaker) and Josephine Gouget (Nashua, housewife)

HART,

Donald B. of Farmington m. Alice B. **Dupere** of Farmington 5/21/1928; H - 21, farmer, b. Farmington, s/o Dana Hart (Milton, farmer) and Mattie Stevens; W - 21, domestic, b. Epping, d/o Joseph Dupere (Canada, RR man) and Clara Rock

HARTFIEL,

Roy of Farmington m. Ruth **Tufts** of Middleton 9/7/1904; H - 26, stock fitter, b. Dayton, KY, s/o Paul Hartfiel (Dayton, KY, cabinet maker) and Mary Bernica (Dayton, KY, housewife); W - 18, housekeeper, b. Middleton, d/o George Tufts (Middleton, farmer) and Emma Whitehouse (Middleton, housewife)

HARTFORD,

Edwin L. of Farmington m. Mary E. **Merrow** of Farmington 6/21/1888; H - 20, heel fitter, b. Dover, s/o George (Rochester) and Julia A. (Dover, housekeeper); W - 17, shoe fitter, b. Acton, ME, d/o ----- (Acton, ME, teamster) and Annie (New York City, housekeeper)

Edwin L. of Farmington m. Carrie S. **Grey** of Farmington 3/22/1894 in Dover; H - 26, heel fitter, 2nd, divorced, b. Dover, s/o George Hartford (dead) and Julia A. Hartford (dead); W - 18, housekeeper, d/o Orin W. Gray (millman) and Carrie O. Gray (housekeeper)

**HATCH,**
Frank David of Wells Beach m. Elsie I. **McCullough** of Farmington 11/24/1927 in Ogunquit, ME; H - 21, fish dealer, b. Wells Beach, ME, s/o George William Hatch (Wells, ME, fish dealer and Charlotte Gammon (Boston, MA, housewife); W - 21, nurse, b. Rochester, d/o Andrew McCullough (Ireland, farmer) and Elizabeth Herron (Ireland)

**HAYDEN,**
Everett of Farmington m. Pauline **Whitehouse** of Alton 10/17/1925 in Somersworth; H - 24, laborer, b. Freedom, s/o Melvin Nelson (Beverly, ME, carpenter) and Gertrude Nelson (Ossipee, housekeeper); W - 18, housekeeper, b. Alton, d/o Albert Whitehouse (Farmington, watchman) and Alice Whitehouse (housewife)

**HAYES,**
A. Fred of Farmington m. Marion E. **Hall** of Farmington 9/15/1934 in Dover; H - 27, shoeworker, b. Farmington, s/o Arthur G. Hayes (New Durham, shoeworker) and Ethel Brooks (Farmington, housewife); W - 27, teacher, b. Weare, d/o Clarence C. Hall (Roxbury, MA, machinist) and Goldie M. Hall (Weare, housewife)

Alphonzo C. of Farmington m. Eva B. **Caswell** of Farmington 10/16/1897 in New Durham; H - 24, shoe cutter, b. New Durham, s/o Nemiah B. Hayes (New Durham, clerk) and Martha A. Hayes (New Durham); W - 19, lining maker, b. Barnstead, d/o Samuel D. Caswell (Barnstead, farmer) and Laura A. Caswell (Barnstead, housework)

Arthur G. of Farmington m. Ethel M. **Brooks** of Farmington 10/14/1905; H - 24, printer, b. New Durham, s/o Seth W. Hayes (Farmington, knife finisher) and Lucilla Tash (New Durham); W - 18, housekeeper, b. Farmington, d/o Percy J. Brooks (Alton, shoemaker) and Edith Tibbetts (Farmington)

Arthur J. of Sanford, ME m. Vivian M. **Shaw** of Sanford, ME 7/11/1938; H - 27, mechanic, $2^{nd}$, b. Sanford, ME, s/o John Hayes (Canada, deceased) and Emma Sanborn (Hollis Center, ME, housewife); W - 21, shoeworker, b. Springfield, MA, d/o

James Shaw (Portsmouth, millworker) and Frances Clayton (England, deceased)

Arthur S. of Rochester m. Gertrude **Reynolds** of Farmington 2/8/1936 in Rochester; H - 21, boxmaker, b. Rochester, s/o Sidney Hayes (Rochester, railroad) and Edith Foss (Rochester, housewife); W - 16, at home, b. Alton, d/o Elmer Rollins (New Durham, woodsman) and Gertrude Clark (Gilmanton I.W., housewife)

Charles L. of Farmington m. Fannie M. **White** of Lebanon, ME 12/3/1891 in Lawrence, MA; H - 23, school teacher, b. Farmington, s/o Levi Hayes (dead); W - 23, school teacher, b. Lebanon, ME, d/o Martin White (farmer)

Eugene B. of Farmington m. Maud A. **Lovejoy** of Dover 11/24/1895 in Dover; H - 21, heel mfg., b. Farmington, s/o James E. Hayes (Farmington, heel mfg.) and Emily P. Hayes (Farmington, housewife); W - 17, b. Dover, d/o George W. Lovejoy (Farmington, shoemaker) and Etta Lovejoy (Indianapolis, IN, housewife)

Forrest E. of Rochester m. Flora E. **Rollins** of Farmington 2/1/1935 in Rochester; H - 22, box shop, b. Rochester, s/o Sidney Hayes (Rochester, railroad emp.) and Edith Foss (Rochester, at home); W - 19, shoe worker, b. Farmington, d/o Irving Rollins (Alton) and Hattie Clark (Alton, deceased)

Frank C. of Farmington m. Ida E. **Connor** of Farmington 5/18/1887; H - 30, book keeper, b. Farmington, s/o Israel Hayes (Milton, manufacturer) and Anna F. Hayes; W - 21, book keeper, b. Farmington, d/o William A. Connor (Gilmanton, farmer) and Mary S. Connor

Guy Golden of Farmington m. Clara Maude **Horne** of Farmington 8/12/1902; H - 16, shoemaker, b. New Durham, s/o Frank P. Hayes (New Durham, dead) and Lena A. Young (NY, housewife); W - 19, waitress, b. Farmington, d/o Arista E. Horne (Salisbury, bar tender) and Clara I. Parker (Farmington, shoeworker)

Harry I. of Farmington m. Annie M. **Norman** of Madbury 6/9/1910 in Madbury; H - 32, shoemaker, b. New Durham, s/o Benjamin Randall (New Durham, farmer) and Fannie E. Hayes (New Durham, shoeworker); W - 22, housekeeper, b. Cambridgeport, d/o Charles J. Norman (So. Berwick, farmer) and Mary L. Nichols (Warnpaco, WI, housewife)

Harry I. of Farmington m. Addie M. **Huckins** of Farmington 10/14/1922; H - 42, shoeworker, 2nd, b. New Durham, s/o Benjamin Randall (New Durham, farmer) and Fannie E. Haye (New Durham, housekeeper); W - 36, housekeeper, 2nd, b. Strafford, d/o John S. Hill (Strafford, laborer) and Laura E. Kimball (Alton, housewife)

Ira C. of Farmington m. Mary D. **Everett** of Farmington 12/28/189; H - 24, shoemaker, b. New Durham, s/o Franklin Hayes (dead) and Ann Augusta Hayes (New Durham, 41, housekeeper) of Farmington; W - 22, shoe stitcher, b. Plimpton, NS, d/o Jeremiah Everett (Plimpton, NS, 63, farmer) and Matilda Everett (Plimpton, NS, 58, housewife) of Plimpton, NS

John R. of Farmington m. Lura S. **Johnson** of Farmington 5/16/1903; H - 22, mill operator, b. Farmington, s/o James E. Hayes (Farmington, farmer) and Mary E. Peavey (Farmington); W - 18, bookkeeper, b. Farmington, d/o Freeman Johnson (Wolfeboro, ice dealer) and Carrie Church (Madison)

Maurice W. of Farmington m. Addie S. **MacDonald** of Farmington 11/28/1913; H - 22, shoeworker, b. Farmington, s/o E. Winslo Hayes (Farmington, farmer) and Georgia A. Horne (Farmington, housekeeper); W - 22, school teacher, b. Farmington, d/o Nellie Whitehouse (Middleton, shoeworker)

Nehemiah B. of Farmington m. Katie **Sullivan** of Farmington 9/8/1902 in New Durham; H - 59, teamster, 2nd, widower, b. New Durham, s/o Samuel Hayes (New Durham, dead) and Mary Whitehouse (Middleton, dead); W - 26, lady, b. Skull, Cork, Ireland, d/o Jeremiah Sullivan (Skull, Cork, Ireland, farmer)

Seth W. of Farmington m. Lillian A. **Willey** of Farmington 4/23/1898; H - 40, shoemaker, 2nd, b. Farmington, s/o John F. Hayes (Farmington, farmer) and Ann Hayes (Farmington, housewife); W - 38, shoe stitcher, 2nd, b. Middleton, d/o Solomon Rollins (Alton, farmer) and Lucinda Rollins (Middleton, housewife)

Thomas T. of Farmington m. Eva B. **Corson** of Farmington 11/18/1899; H - 28, engineer, b. New Durham, s/o Frank P. Hayes (Alton, hotel keeper) and Abbie Hayes; W - 17, b. Natick, MA, d/o Charles Corson and Estella Corson (Middleton)

William T. of Farmington m. Ursula B. **Wedgewood** of Farmington 8/3/1887; H - 21, grocer, b. Farmington, s/o Ezekiel C. Hayes (Farmington, shoemaker) and Lydia H. Hayes; W - 20, b. Milton, d/o Elbridge L. Wedgewood (Milton, meat and provision dealer) and Sylvania B. Wedgewood

William T. of Farmington m. Inez A. **Roberts** of Farmington 2/21/1906; H - 39, clerk, 2nd, divorced, b. Farmington, s/o Ezekiel C. Hayes (Farmington, shoe cutter) and Lydia H. Tarleton (New Castle); W - 23, b. Rochester, d/o Henry K. Roberts (Rochester, carpenter) and Mabel R. Hill (Northwood)

Winfield A. of Farmington m. Mary I. **Garvis** of Lebanon, ME 8/30/1924 in Wolfeboro; H - 70, shoeworker, 2nd, b. Farmington, s/o Aaron Hayes and Mary E. Rand; W - 60, domestic, 2nd, b. Farmington, d/o John Hayes and Hannah E. Hayes

Winfield S. of Farmington m. Etta K. **Davis** of Farmington 11/3/1893; H - 39, shoemaker, b. Farmington, s/o Aaron Hayes (Farmington, dead) and Mary E. Hayes (housekeeper); W - 24, lady, b. Farmington, d/o Nathaniel Davis (dead) and Amanda Davis (Farmington, housekeeper)

Winfield S. of Farmington m. Mary I. **Hayes** of Farmington 12/17/1910; H - 56, shoemaker, divorced, b. Farmington, s/o Aaron Hayes (Farmington, blacksmith) and Mary E. Rand (Farmington, housewife); W - 45, shoemaker, divorced, b. Barrington, d/o John O. Hayes (Somersworth, sawyer) and Hannah E. Howard (Rochester, housewife)

**HAYNES,**

Frank H. of Farmington m. Flora M. **Averill** of Farmington 3/7/1895; H - 26, truckman, b. Parsonsfield, s/o Charles N. Haynes (Parsonsfield) and H. Lizzie Haynes (Springvale, ME, housekeeper); W - 20, b. Saco, ME, d/o Benjamin Averill (York, blacksmith) and Lizzie N. Averill (Farmington, ME, housewife)

John L. of Farmington m. Grace M. **Tibbetts** of New Durham 8/14/1905 in Rochester; H - 34, shoemaker, b. Parsonsfield, ME, s/o Charles M. Haynes (Parsonsfield, ME, mill hand) and H. Lizzie Lord (Springvale, ME); W - 20, school teacher, b. New Durham, d/o Albinus B. Tibbetts (New Durham, farmer) and Mary F. Amazeen (Milton)

John S. of Farmington m. Ellen E. **Varney** of Farmington 9/23/1893; H - 47, last maker, 2nd, b. Concord, s/o John Haynes (Farmington, last maker) and Sybal A. Haynes (dead); W - 40, housekeeper, b. Milton, d/o John W. Varney (dead) and Lydia W. Varney (Milton, housekeeper)

Roland of Farmington m. Nellie **Place** of Farmington 9/15/1907; H - 18, shoeworker, b. Rochester, d/o William Haines (London, painter) and Laura Abbott (Ossipee); W - 17, shoeworker, b. Farmington, d/o James A. Place (Farmington, carpenter) and Mary Austin (Dover)

**HEBERT,**

Placide of Rochester m. Edna **Raab** of Farmington 10/6/1930 in Rochester; H - 22, shoeworker, b. Canada, s/o Archie Hebert (Canada, RR section) and Odelie Sylvain (Canada, housewife); W - 22, shoeworker, b. IA, d/o Adolph Raab (Germany, carpenter) and Marie Kopp (IA, housewife)

**HELM,**

Harold of Farmington m. Helen **Collins** of Farmington 2/9/1918 in Dover; H - 21, engineer, b. Ossipee, s/o Charles W. Helm and Emma Ames; W - 22, waitress

**HENDERSON,**

Herbert J. of Farmington m. Grace J. **Marsh** of Acton, ME 8/9/1906 in Salem; H - 30, farmer, b. Farmington, s/o George Henderson (Farmington, farmer) and Lawaxa Downs (Farmington); W - 21, housekeeper, b. Acton, ME, d/o Stephen Marsh (Acton, ME, farmer) and Martha Marsh (Acton, ME)

Lewis F. of Farmington m. Eva M. **Horne** of Farmington 10/7/1938 in W. Milton; H - 37, painter, 2nd, b. Farmington, s/o G. Henderson (Farmington, deceased) and L'w'chia Downs (Farmington, deceased); W - 24, shoeworker, b. Farmington, d/o Irving Horne (Farmington, shoeworker) and Lennar Lucas (Farmington, shoeworker)

**HERRING,**

William M. of Farmington m. Edith E. **Pinkham** of Farmington 6/14/1893; H - 34, clerk, b. Farmington, s/o George M. Herring (dead) and Ellen M. Herring (Farmington, housekeeper); W -

23, lady, b. Farmington, d/o Levi L. Pinkham (New Durham, merchant) and Augusta Pinkham (Alton, housewife)

**HERRMAN,**
John of Philadelphia, PA m. Philura A. D. **Racine** of Farmington 11/9/1907; H - 66, gentleman, 3$^{rd}$, b. Philadelphia, s/o Ezekiel Herrman (Germany, foreman) and Mary Mack (Wind Gap, PA); W - 61, housekeeper, 3$^{rd}$, b. W. Danville, VT, d/o Cyrus Davidson (Keene, farmer) and Sally Sulham (Canada)

**HILL,**
Horace G. of Lee m. Mary W. **Canney** of Farmington 1/19/1907 in Rochester; H - 40, farmer, b. Lee, s/o John W. Hill (Lee, farmer) and Mary J. Caldwell (Barrington); W - 40, school teacher, 2$^{nd}$, b. Farmington, d/o Henry Wilson (Farmington, farmer) and Lucie Whitehouse (Rochester)

Ivan L. of Farmington m. Grace **Harriman** of Albany 2/16/1902; H - 24, shoemaker, b. New Durham, s/o Mark Hillard (Lewiston, ME, stone mason) and Jennette Hill (New Durham, dead); W - 28, shoe worker, b. Brownfield, ME, d/o Allen Harriman (Albany, farmer) and Jennie Harriman (Albany, housewife)

Jonathan S. of Farmington m. Hattie M. **Kimball** of Farmington 3/31/1906; H - 51, mill hand, 2$^{nd}$, widower, b. Strafford, s/o Stephen B. Hill (Strafford, farmer) and Lucy B. Holmes (Hiram, ME); W - 20, housekeeper, b. Farmington, d/o Samuel Kimball (Middleton, shoemaker) and Addie Young (Farmington)

Loren S. of Farmington m. Ada B. **Colbath** of Farmington 5/29/1906; H - 24, mill hand, b. Strafford, s/o John S. Hill (Strafford, mill hand) and Laura E. Kimball (Alton, housewife); W - 24, paper box maker, b. Middleton, d/o Frank Colbath (Middleton, shoemaker) and Hattie Crane (housewife)

**HOADLEY,**
J. Emery of Concord m. Virginia B. **Douglas** of Farmington 3/11/1934 in Brattleboro, VT; H - 26, clerk, 2$^{nd}$, b. Somerville, MA, s/o Chester A. Hoadley (Lynn, MA) and Marion F. Pratt (Waltham, MA); W - 19, b. Farmington, d/o Robert R. Douglas (Winston-Salem, NC) and Rena M. Abbott (Concord)

**HODGDON,**

Ellsworth A. of Farmington m. Cora **Dixon** of Farmington 10/29/1887 in Rochester; H - 26, coachman, b. Lebanon, ME, s/o Chandler Hodgdon (farmer) and Mary Hodgdon; W - 29, stitcher, 2$^{nd}$, d/o Warren Maine (farmer)

**HODGENS,**

James T. of Concord m. Gladys G. **Warburton** of Farmington 12/28/1931; H - 28, real estate, b. Butte, MT, s/o James Hodgens (PA, retired) and Harriett Crow; W - 30, furrier, 3$^{rd}$, b Millville, NB, d/o Mortimer Armstrong (Farmington, shoeworker) and Mildred D. Whitlock (Millville, NB, furrier)

**HOGAN,**

Edward F. of Farmington m. Florence M. **Kimball** of Farmington 7/19/1908 in Wolfeboro; H - 23, mill hand, b. Lowell, MA, s/o Edward Hogan (CA, moulder) and Mary Higgins (NY); W - 20, shoemaker, b. Alton, d/o Frank Kimball (Farmington, laborer) and Mary E. Tufts (Alton)

Francis J. of Farmington m. Marion E. **Connor** of Farmington 6/3/1933; H - 22, shoeworker, b. Cambridge, MA, s/o Joseph Hogan (NY, deceased) and Anna A. O'Rielly (Cambridge, MA, housewife); W - 21, shoeworker, b. Farmington, d/o Edward Connor (Farmington, deceased) and Florence Clark (Alton, deceased)

Joseph of Farmington m. Venna **Rollins** of Farmington 6/29/1929; H - 21, shoeworker, b. Bronx, NY, s/o Joseph Hogan and Anna O'Rielly (Cambridge, MA, housekeeper); W - 18, shoeworker, b. Farmington, d/o Irving Rollins (Alton, shoeworker) and Hattie Clark (Alton)

**HOLMES,**

Charles W. of Farmington m. Georgie M. **Chesley** of Farmington 5/29/1890; H - 21, shoemaker, b. Strafford, s/o William P. Holmes (Strafford, carpenter) and Sarah T. (Tamworth); W - 21, stitcher, b. Farmington, d/o George W. Chesley (Farmington, shoemaker) and Delphina E.

Fred W. of Farmington m. Minnie L. **Pitman** of Farmington 5/26/1892; H - 22, shoemaker, b. Farmington, s/o John R. Holmes (Farmington, 55, optician) and Fannie F. Holmes (Bristol, ME, 54, housekeeper) of Farmington; W - 19, lady, b.

Farmington, d/o Charles H. Pitman (Farmington, 45, printer) and Emma J. Garland (Farmington, 40, housewife) of Farmington

Ralph L. of Farmington m. Aurie P. **Lord** of Farmington 12/15/1915; H - 21, clerk, b. Farmington, s/o Charles W. Holmes (Farmington, foreman) and Georgia M. Chesley (Farmington, housekeeper); W - 19, shoeworker, b. Rochester, d/o Frank Lord (Dover, farmer) and Ella Grant (Rochester, housekeeper)

Ralph L. of Farmington m. Jean A. **St. Laurence** of Haverhill 7/1/1924; H - 30, shoeworker, $2^{nd}$, b. Farmington, s/o Charles W. Holmes (Strafford, shoeworker) and Georgia Chesley (Farmington, housewife); W - 22, shoeworker, b. Haverhill, MA, d/o J. B. St. Laurence (Canada, shoeworker) and Marie Dwyer (NY)

**HORNE,**

Everett E. of Farmington m. Emma E. **Berry** of New Durham 12/30/1893; H - 25, teamster, b. Middleton, s/o John W. Horne (dead) and Sarah E. Horne (Middleton, housewife); W - 18, lady, b. New Durham, d/o Stephen Berry (New Durham, farmer) and ----- (New Durham, housekeeper)

Fred I. of Farmington m. Marion **Savage** of Farmington 10/8/1902; H - 23, shoemaker, b. Farmington, s/o Clarence E. Horne (Farmington, farmer) and Fannie Lord (Lebanon, shoeworker); W - 25, shoeworker, $2^{nd}$, divorced, b. Dover, d/o John Grimes (NY, dead) and Marion Grimes (NJ, housekeeper)

Herbert F. of Dover m. Amy M. **Barker** of Farmington 6/16/1918; H - 42, salesman, $2^{nd}$, b. Milton, s/o Frank G. Horne (Milton, sales mgr.) and Mary C. Weeks (Wakefield, housewife); W - 41, lady, b. Farmington, d/o John H. Barker (Wolfeboro) and Luella T. Leighton (Farmington)

Irving E. of Farmington m. Lena G. **Lucas** of Farmington 7/12/1903 in Milton; H - 33, clerk, b. Farmington, s/o Stephen B. Horne (New Durham, farmer) and Clara Twombly (Farmington, housewife); W - 23, housekeeper, b. Farmington, d/o Freeman D. Lucas (New Durham, farmer) and Emma Whitehouse (Gonic, shoe stitcher)

Izah A. of Farmington m. Ida M. **Holmes** of Farmington 10/8/1894; H - 30, livery, b. Farmington, s/o Stephen F. Horne (Farmington, farmer) and Lucy A. Horne (Mexico, ME); W - 33,

b. Strafford, d/o William P. Holmes (Strafford, carpenter) and Sarah T. Holmes (Tamworth, housekeeper)

Izah A. of Farmington m. Jennie M. **Whitehouse** of Farmington 11/21/1925 in Milton; H - 61, liveryman, 2$^{nd}$, b. Farmington, s Stephen F. Horne and Lucy A. Whitman; W - 25, teacher, b. Boston, MA

William H. of Farmington m. Mildred **Perkins** of Newfields, ME 12/3/1914 in Rochester; H - 29, shoeworker, b. Farmington, s William H. Horne (Farmington, shoemaker) and Mary Colbath (Wakefield, shoemaker); W - 23, housekeeper, b. Newfield, ME, d/o Isaiah B. Perkins (farmer) and Rebecca H. Perkins

William H. of Farmington m. Mabel E. **Sherman** of Conway 4/1/1922 in Laconia; H - 37, shoeworker, 2$^{nd}$, b. Farmington, s/o Henry Horne (Farmington, farmer) and Mary E. Colbath (Wakefield, housewife); W - 37, shoeworker, 2$^{nd}$, b. Conway, d/o Frank Leavitt (Conway, carpenter) and Sadie E. Adams (Middleton, housekeeper)

## HOVEY,

Charles N. of Farmington m. Cora E. **Lufkins** of Salem, MA 5/17/1916; H - 52, bookkeeper, b. Charlestown, MA, s/o George H. Hovey (Cambridge, MA, currier) and Melissa F. Davis (New Durham, housewife); W - 50, nurse, 2$^{nd}$, b. Salem MA, d/o James C. Ballard (Salem, MA, captain) and Emmelin A. Jenks (Salem, MA, housewife)

## HOWARD,

Elroy C. of Farmington m. Mrs. Lizzie **Moore** of Farmington 2/6/1909; H - 24, shoemaker, b. Farmington, s/o Frank Howar (Rochester, laborer) and Hannah Brown (Barrington, housekeeper); W - 24, housekeeper, widow, b. Madbury, d/o Charles Woodis (Dover, shoemaker) and Lydia Cole (Madbury housekeeper)

Emery E. of Rochester m. Jeanette E. **Adams** of Farmington 4/15/1933; H - 21, shoeworker, b. Northwood, s/o Harry H. Howard (Dover, blacksmith) and Bertha L. Haynes (London, deceased); W - 19, shoeworker, b. Hampstead, d/o Horace Adams (Hampstead, sawyer) and Sarah Page (Atkinson, shoeworker)

Everett A. of Farmington m. Annette E. **Joy** of Union 5/4/1929 in Dover; H - 24, shoeworker, b. Farmington, s/o Herbert O.

Howard (Gonic) and Lizzie Miller (Dover, housewife); W - 18, shoeworker, b. Union, d/o Frank D. Joy (So. Berwick, ME, RR man) and Alice Kimball (Middleton, housewife)

Fred W. of Alton m. Madeline **Ames** of Farmington 1/6/1916; H - 19, shoeworker, b. Haverhill, MA, s/o Fred J. Howard (Gilmanton, farmer) and Grace Amazeen; W - 19, housekeeper, b. Rochester, d/o Will Ames (teamster)

Herbert, Jr. of Farmington m. Mamie **Patch** of Farmington 5/7/1915; H - 20, shoeworker, b. Dover, s/o Herbert Howard (Farmington, shoeworker) and Lizzie Miller (Dover, housewife); W - 21, shoeworker, b. Sanbornville, d/o John Patch (Union, laborer) and Gertrude Clark (Milton Mills, housekeeper)

## HOWE,

Frank R. of Farmington m. Lena **DuQuette** of Farmington 9/24/1913; H - 31, trav. salesman, 2$^{nd}$, b. Farmington, s/o Frank L. Howe (Barrington, salesman) and Ida M. Miller (Somersworth, housekeeper); W - 25, housekeeper, b. Canada, d/o Joseph DuQuette (Canada, farmer) and Caroline DuQuette (Canada, housekeeper)

## HOWES,

Leroy F. of S. Montville, ME m. Alice R. **Bishop** of LaGrange, ME 10/28/1931; H - 24, laborer, b. Liberty, ME, s/o Clarence Howes (Liberty, ME, farmer) and Hattie Davis (Freedom, ME, housewife); W - 26, teacher, b. LaGrange, ME, d/o Lewis Bishop (LaGrange, ME, farmer) and Sadie Paige

## HOYT,

Lindsay F. of Somersworth m. Maude D. **Tweedy** of Alton 9/2/1903 in Rochester; H - 28, shoe salesman, b. Somersworth, s/o Frank R. Hoyt (Barrington, shoe maker) and Jennie Thompson (New Brunswick, ME); W - 24, milliner, b. Taunton, MA, d/o George Tweedy (Taunton, MA, jeweler) and Mary E. Wilbur (Taunton, MA)

## HUBBARD,

Harry I. of Farmington m. Emma **Coaty** of Farmington 6/2/1902 in Milton; H - 28, laborer, b. Farmington, s/o ----- Evans and Anne Hubbard (Farmington, dead); W - 37, housekeeper, 2$^{nd}$, widow, b. Barnstead, d/o Moses Ham (dead)

**HUCKINS,**
J. Leslie of Farmington m. E. Annabelle **Eaton** of Webster 7/12/1930 in Rochester; H - 28, farmer, b. Farmington, s/o John A. Huckins (Farmington, farmer) and Ethel M. Scruton (Strafford, housekeeper); W - 21, teacher, b. Webster, d/o Herbert B. Eaton (No. Reading, MA, farmer) and Edith M. Gerrish (Webster, housewife)

Walter of Farmington m. Maybelle **Wentworth** of Farmington 4/2/1933 in East Rochester; H - 25, laborer, b. Strafford, s/o Edgar Huckins (deceased) and Addie Hill (deceased); W - 18, shoeworker, b. New Durham, d/o Edwin Wentworth (deceased and Alice Mooring (Ossipee, shoeworker)

**HULL,**
Walter F. of Farmington m. Eleanor F. **Blaisdell** of Farmington 4/7/1912; H - 18, shoemaker, b. Dover, s/o Tom Hull (Dover, shoemaker) and Eva Sloper (Dover, housekeeper); W - 17, shoemaker, b. Farmington, d/o Clarence L. Blaisdell (Farmington, shoemaker) and Ella S. Swinerton (Milton)

**HUNT,**
Loren D. of Farmington m. Elaine M. **Kimball** of Laconia 10/27/1934 in Laconia; H - 22, shoeworker, b. Farmington, s/o Loren D. Hunt (Epping, shoeworker) and Alice O'Connor (Haverhill, MA, at home); W - 23, needleworker, b. Meredith, d/o Herman Kimball (Meredith, carpenter) and Lillian Tuttle (Meredith, at home)

**HUNTINGTON,**
Harold of Dover m. Violet E. **Hawkes** of Farmington 5/22/1938; H - 23, baker, 2nd, b. Burlington, VT, s/o L. Huntington (Rutland, VT, electrician) and Mary E. Crane (Danville, VT, housewife); W - 25, shoeworker, 2nd, b. Berwick, ME, d/o James Clark (Berwick, ME, laborer) and Myrtle Downs (Lebanon, ME, housewife)

**HUNTRESS,**
Ralph of Farmington m. Grace P. **Hussey** of Farmington 2/21/1937; H - 23, WPA worker, b. Haverhill, MA, s/o Eugene Huntress (Farmington, shoeworker) and Florence Prisby (Franklin, deceased); W - 22, shoeworker, 2nd, b. Old Orchard

Beach, d/o David Plimpton (Spofford Lake, ME, carpenter) and Grace LaPointe (Limerick, ME, housewife)

**HURD,**

George of Farmington m. Cora E. **Brown** of Farmington 4/7/1887; H - 55, shoemaker, 2nd, widower, b. Farmington, s/o John Hurd (Farmington, farmer) and Abigail Hurd; W - 28, 2nd, b. Wolfeboro, d/o Henry A. Whitten (Wolfeboro, mason) and Lydia K. Whitten

Harry W. of Farmington m. Cora P. **Canney** of Farmington 8/11/1901; H - 30, farmer, b. Farmington, s/o Jeremiah P. Hurd (Farmington, farmer) and Sarah E. Place (Farmington); W - 29, housekeeper, b. Ayer, MA, d/o Charles H. Canney (Melvin Village, dead) and Julia A. Canney (dead)

J. G. of Farmington m. Minnie A. **LeTair** of Farmington 1/30/1938; H - 39, laborer, b. Farmington, s/o William Hurd (Milton, retired) and Nellie Varney (Farmington, housewife); W - 49, shoeworker, 2nd, b. Derring, ME, d/o Charles Humphrey (Machias, ME, deceased) and Susan Stevens (Gouldsboro, ME, deceased)

Thomas of Farmington m. Cassandra M. **Tibbetts** of Farmington 11/17/1906; H - 26, shoemaker, b. Berwick, ME, s/o George H. Hurd (Andover, MA, drummer) and Eva S. Plummer (Gilmanton); W - 26, shoe worker, b. Farmington, d/o William Tibbetts (Brockton) and Angie E. Pinkham (East Alton)

William R. of Rochester m. Eva **Downing** of Farmington 5/3/1935 in West Milton; H - 22, shoeworker, b. Conway, s/o Benjamin Hurd (Conway, carpenter) and Evelyn Rideout (Conway, shoeworker); W - 21, shoeworker, b. New Durham, d/o Frank Downing (Farmington, farmer) and Matilda Anderson (Sweden, housewife)

**HURLBURT,**

Charles W. of Farmington m. Emma **Tauwait** of Farmington 8/23/1911; H - 32, shoeworker, b. Manchester, s/o Willis Hurlburt (Plymouth, railroader) and Alice Kelley (Ellsworth, housekeeper); W - 26, shoeworker, 2nd, b. Monkton, NB, d/o ----- Renton (farmer)

**HUSSEY,**

Leland M. of Farmington m. M. Delia **Dunn** of Farmington 3/18/1912; H - 20, restaurant, b. Berwick, ME, s/o Herman Hussey (Berwick, ME, supt. shoe shop) and Vera Ellis (Milton); W - 22, lady, d/o Jeremiah Dunn (shoemaker)

**HUTCHINS,**

William R. of Springvale, ME m. Floretta L. C. **Arnold** of Farmington 6/2/1923 in Rochester; H - 19, weaver, b. Springvale, ME, d/o William J. Hutchins (Shapleigh, ME, laborer) and Mary E. Garvin (Acton, ME, housekeeper); W - 16, shoeworker, b. Braintree, MA, d/o Samuel V. Arnold (Brockton, MA, shoeworker) and Sarah Godfrey (PEI, housekeeper)

**INGERSON,**

Edgar A., Jr. of No. Conway m. Mildred F. **French** of Farmington 11/10/1928 in Rochester; H - 28, mechanic, b. Lancaster, s/o Edgar A. Ingerson (Lancaster, mail carrier) and Rosamond Hillier (Cookshire, PQ, teacher); W - 19, waitress, b. Rochester, d/o John L. French (Farmington, station agent) and Alice M. Beecher (Rochester, shoeworker)

**IRISH,**

Earle W. of Farmington m. Gladys E. **Littlefield** of Farmington 5/13/1916; H - 20, shoeworker, b. Conway, s/o Neal D. Irish (Lovell, ME, carpenter) and Carrie Perish (Albany); W - 20, shoeworker, b. Farmington, d/o Fred A. Littlefield (Fitchburg, MA, insurance agt.) and Alma Kimball (Middleton, housewife)

**IRVING,**

Charles J. of Roxbury, MA m. Ida **Smallman** of Roxbury, MA 7/29/1934 in Milton; H - 47, chauffeur, $2^{nd}$, b. Kent Co., NB, s/o William Irving (Kent Co., NB, farmer) and ----- (Mill Branch, NB, at home); W - 48, packer, $2^{nd}$, b. Roxbury, MA, d/o Robert G. Lutz (Germany, deceased) and Frances C. Lindner (Germany, deceased)

JACKSON,
Harry S. of Farmington m. Elenora **Beattie** of Manchester 4/3/1935 in Manchester; H - 30, D. Sec. of State, b. Astoria, LI, s/o Harry M. Jackson (Yonkers, NY, retired) and Flora Stewart (England, housewife); W - 32, at home, 2$^{nd}$, b. Manchester, d/o Aratas Carpenter (Manchester, paper mfg.) and Alice Burnham (Manchester, housewife)

William H. of Farmington m. Gladys **Vickers** of Farmington 12/6/1930; H - 20, shoeworker, b. Oxford, s/o Charles S. Jackson (Dudsville, PQ, carpenter) and Elizabeth Hearn (Cookshire, PQ, housewife); W - 18, shoeworker, b. Middleboro, VT, d/o Charles Vickers (Sheffield, England) and Lillian Stewart (England)

JENKINS,
Alfred T. of Farmington m. Mary **Eagan** of Farmington 3/13/1917; H - 22, shoeworker, b. Camden, NJ, s/o Kirk Jenkins and Frances King (housekeeper); W - 19, shoeworker, b. Peabody, MA, d/o John Eagan and Katherine Collen

Ralph C. of Farmington m. Bernice M. **Hart** of Farmington 10/13/1909 in New Durham; H - 24, bookkeeper, b. Milton, s/o Henry A. Jenkins (Lebanon, farmer) and Emma F. Smith (Milton); W - 22, shoeworker, b. Lebanon, ME, d/o Dana B. Hart (Milton, farmer) and Mattie A. Stevens (Middleton, shoeworker)

JENNESS,
Charles W. of Farmington m. Viola S. **Weymouth** of Farmington 5/12/1897; H - 53, lumber dealer, 2$^{nd}$, b. Rochester, s/o William Jenness (Rochester, mechanic) and Johanna Jenness (VT); W - 42, bookkeeper, b. Boston, d/o Charles L. Weymouth (ME, manufacturer) and Susan A. Twombly (E. Pittston, ME, housekeeper)

JESSEN,
John A. of Hartford, CT m. Christina **Durgin** of Farmington 9/11/1911; H - 29, elect. engineer, b. Copenhagen, s/o Frederick Jessen (Copenhagen, sea captain) and Annie Madsen (housewife); W - 31, stenographer, b. Belfast, Ireland, d/o Daniel Ferguson (Belfast, Ireland, miller) and Ellen McWha (Glasgow, Scotland, housewife)

**JEWELL,**
Arthur E. of Farmington m. Edna M. **Horne** of Farmington 11/16/1913; H - 30, steamfitter, 2nd, b. Joliet, IL, s/o George Jewell (Readfield, ME, carpenter) and Ada Read (OH); W - 2 shoeworker, b. Farmington, d/o Clarence E. Horne (wood dealer) and Agnes Moore (housekeeper)

**JOHNSON,**
Budd M. of Farmington m. Hittie R. **Cox** of Laconia 10/25/1905 in Laconia; H - 34, telegraph operator, b. St. Armond, Canada, s/o Parker S. Johnson (St. Armond, Canada, shoemaker) and Elizabeth J. Gilleland (St. Armond, Canada, shoe stitcher); W 34, telegraph operator, b. Meredith, d/o Benjamin F. Cox (Holderness, farmer) and Hannah E. Robinson (Meredith)

Charles W. of Farmington m. Mabel E. **Rich** of Farmington 9/15/1888; H - 21, shoe cutter, b. Farmington, s/o James M. (shoe finisher) and Mary L. (shoe stitcher); W - 19, shoe stitcher, b. Gouldsboro, ME, d/o Alfred (deceased) and Mary (housekeeper)

Fred A. of Farmington m. Susie **Higgins** of Farmington 5/3/1916; - 21, shoeworker, b. Farmington, s/o Frank Johnson and Bertha Wallace (Jackson, ME, housekeeper); W - 19, housekeeper, b. Farmington, d/o Leslie Higgins (Thorndike, ME, farmer) and Lydia Parker

Henry B. of Farmington m. Gertrude C. **Gardner** of Farmington 5/28/1927; H - 31, trucking, 3rd, b. Lynn, MA, s/o Charles A. Johnson (Sweden, shoemaker) and Ida M. Aderson (Sweden, housewife); W - 31, bookkeeper, 2nd, b. N. Adams, MA, d/o Henry Gardner (N. Adams, MA, real estate) and Mina Marcou (N. Adams, MA, housewife)

John C. of Farmington m. Ida S. **Meserve** of Dover 4/4/1888 in Dover; H - 22, truckman, b. Farmington, s/o John G. (Dover, sheriff) and Anstress R. (Milton, housekeeper); W - 18, housekeeper, b. Madbury, d/o George (Kingston, watchman) and Helen (Strafford, housekeeper)

John G. of Farmington m. Carrie **Willey** of New Durham 12/23/1897; H - 65, farmer, 2nd, b. Dover, s/o Dennis Johnson (Strafford, shoemaker) and Sarah Johnson (Kittery, ME, lady); W - 48, housework, 2nd, b. New Durham, d/o William H. Corson (New Durham, farmer) and Drucilla Corson (Middleton

**JONDR[E]Y,**
Arnold G. of Farmington m. Emeline K. **Tarbox** of Farmington 7/28/1928; H - 21, wood heel wkr., b. Elmore, VT, s/o Angus P. Jondrey (Bank Falls, NS, iceman) and Delia E. Harrison (Stow, VT, at home); W - 40, packer, $2^{nd}$, b. New York, NY, d/o William F. Kimball and Elizabeth Enders (see following entry)

Arnold G. of Farmington m. Emeline K. **Tarbox** of Farmington 1/20/1929; H - 22, wood heel wk., b. Elmore, VT, s/o Angus P. Jondry (Bank Falls, NS, iceman) and Della E. Honieson (Stowe, VT, at home); W - 40, packer, $2^{nd}$, b. New York City, d/o William F. Kimball and Elizabeth Enden (see preceding entry)

**JONES,**
Austin G. of Farmington m. Mary E. **Jones** of Farmington 12/8/1900; H - 54, farmer, $2^{nd}$, b. Boston, MA, s/o Ivory H. Jones (Alfred, ME, dead) and Nancy Hutchinson (Pepperell, MA, dead); W - 43, housekeeper, $2^{nd}$, b. Farmington, d/o Orrin K. Otis (Farmington, farmer) and Sarah Garland (Farmington, housekeeper)

John F. of Farmington m. Florence M. **Fernald** of Lee 6/22/1907 in Alton; H - 31, mill hand, b. Strafford, s/o William Jones (Strafford, mill hand) and Clara E. Emerson (Alton); W - 26, school teacher, b. Northwood, d/o Charles Fernald (Barrington, farmer) and Lizzie Randall (Lee)

Joseph W. of Rochester m. Hannah E. **Corson** of Farmington 6/16/1890; H - 28, shoe finisher, b. Rochester, s/o Cyrus W. Jones (Rochester, shoemaker) and Harriett M. (Rochester); W - 27, housekeeper, b. Barrington, d/o Belinda Robinson (Strafford, dead)

Onslow B. of Farmington m. Amy L. **Marston** of Alton 7/16/1891 in Portsmouth; H - 20, shoemaker, b. Alton, s/o Frank A. Jones (Alton, shoemaker); W - 18, housekeeper, b. Alton, d/o Frank F. Marston (Lawrence, MA, watchman)

Wilbur C. of Farmington m. L. Violet **Stanley** of Farmington 6/22/1910; H - 31, freight hand, b. New Durham, s/o Dana P. Jones (New Durham, farmer) and Fannie Dearborn (Lebanon, ME, housewife); W - 22, housekeeper, b. Springfield, MA, d/o Herbert Chapinze and Adelaide Rhines (New Durham, housekeeper)

**JORDAN,**

Charles A. of Farmington m. Maude V. **Livingstone** of Rochester 2/24/1909; H - 18, shoe worker, b. Beverly, MA, s/o Isaac Jordan (shoemaker) and Annie Moulton (Augusta, ME, shoe worker); W - 20, housekeeper, b. Rochester, d/o John E. Livingstone (Saco, ME, shoemaker) and Jennie M. Whitten (Saco, ME)

Charles A. of Farmington m. Alice N. **French** of Farmington 11/30/1916; H - 27, shoeworker, $2^{nd}$, b. Beverly, MA, s/o Isaac Jordan and Annie Morton (Augusta, ME); W - 32, shoeworker, $2^{nd}$, b. Rochester, d/o George Beacham (Rochester, shoeworker) and Ida Rhines (New Durham, housewife)

**JOY,**

Samuel O., Jr. of Farmington m. Mary H. P. **Cyr** of Farmington 7/20/1925; H - 27, mechanic, b. New Durham, s/o Samuel O. Joy (New Durham, RFD carrier) and Mary E. Berry (New Durham, housewife); W - 26, manicurist, b. Canada, d/o John Cyr (Canada, carpenter) and Mary Terren (Canada, housewife)

**JUNKINS,**

Willard R. of Farmington m. Carrie A. **Reed** of No. Hampton 9/3/1930 in Dover; H - 60, machinist, $2^{nd}$, b. York, ME, s/o Leonard R. Junkins and Ann Averill; W - 52, cook, $2^{nd}$, b. Houlton, ME, d/o James Armstrong and Abigail Thompson

**KEEHLWETTER,**

Franklin of Brookline, MA m. Jeannettie E. **Dame** of Farmington 2/2/1919; H - 22, electrician, b. Foxboro, MA, s/o Jacob Keehlwetter (Jamaica Plain, MA, paperhanger) and Julia A. Alexander (Foxboro, MA, clerk); W - 16, at home, b. Farmington, d/o Walter S. Dame (Farmington, foreman) and Ethel M. Young (Alton, housewife)

**KEITH,**

George E., Jr. of Farmington m. Barbara **Ferguson** of Peabody, MA 5/19/1936 in Concord; H - 21, shoeworker, b. Lynn, MA, s/o George E. Keith (Peabody, MA, shoeworker) and Beatrice Porter (Peabody, MA, housewife); W - 18, shoeworker, b. Peabody, MA, d/o Fred Ferguson (Peabody, MA, foundry worker) and Alice Gulica (Peabody, MA, housewife)

**KELLEHER,**
John J., Jr. of Newburyport, MA m. Mary **Orzechawski** of Newburyport, MA 8/5/1936; H - 25, chauffeur, b. Newburyport, MA, s/o John Kelleher (Newburyport, MA, shoeworker) and Mary A. Ryan (Newburyport, MA, at home); W - 23, shoeworker, b. Newburyport, MA, d/o S. Orzechawski (Russia, deceased) and M. Orzechawski (Russia, at home)

**KELLEY,**
Albert A. of Farmington m. Edith M. **Clark** of Farmington 7/1/1890 in New Durham; H - 20, shoemaker, b. Farmington, s/o Charles H. Kelley (dead) and Sarah A. (Farmington); W - 20, stitcher, b. Middleton, d/o James F. Clark (Lebanon, ME, laborer) and Lydia J.

Albert A. of Farmington m. Delma E. **Dame** of Farmington 10/5/1926; H - 56, shoeworker, $2^{nd}$, b. Farmington, s/o Charles H. Kelley and Sarah A. Horne; W - 23, housekeeper, b. Middleton, d/o Daniel E. Dame (postmaster) and Minnie Smith (shoeworker)

Everett B. of Farmington m. Emma F. **Harmon** of Farmington 2/14/1887; H - 18, shoemaker, b. Farmington, s/o Charles Kelley (Farmington) and Sarah Kelley; W - 18, d/o William Harmon (minister) and Lucy Harmon

James of Farmington m. Mrs. Carrie L. **Gilman** of Farmington 12/21/1902 in Dover; H - 57, farmer, $2^{nd}$, widower, b. Farmington, s/o Augustus S. Kelley (Dover, soap mfr.) and Mary C. Cole (Dover, housewife); W - 52, housekeeper, $2^{nd}$, widow, b. Gilmanton, d/o Moses Gilman (Gilmanton, farmer) and Rhoda Gilman (Gilmanton, housewife)

James of Farmington m. Delia A. **Cloutman** of Farmington 6/22/1904; H - 59, farmer, $3^{rd}$, widower, b. Dover, s/o Augustus Kelley (Dover, soap mfr.) and Mary C. Cole (Dover, housewife); W - 46, housekeeper, $3^{rd}$, widow, b. Farmington, d/o Thomas Pinkham (New Durham) and Adeline Hodgdon (Tuftonboro)

**KENNEY,**
Frank E. of Farmington m. Sybil P. **Bryant** of Somersworth 1/1/1895 in Somersworth; H - 29, shoeworker, b. Milton, s/o Edwin Kenney (Sebago, ME, merchant) and Mary A. Kenney (Middleton, housekeeper); W - 19, housekeeper, b.

Somersworth, d/o John D. Bryant (Somersworth, carpenter) and Marion B. Bryant (Lebanon, ME, housewife)

**KENT,**
John of Rochester m. Maria **Trask** of Farmington 2/25/1889 in Rochester; H - 66, farmer, 2nd, b. Rochester, s/o June Kent; W - 56, housekeeper, 2nd, b. Rochester, d/o Jane Otis

**KIMBALL,**
B. Frank of Alton m. Annie M. **Hill** of Alton 5/4/1898 in Alton; H - 34, shoe cutter, b. Farmington, s/o Daniel W. Kimball (Farmington, shoe cutter) and Mary A. Kimball (Farmington, housewife); W - 21, shoe stitcher, b. Canada, d/o Charles Hill (Alton, farmer) and Nellie Hill (Canada, housewife)

Carroll H. of Farmington m. Winnifred E. **Allen** of Farmington 10/21/1912; H - 27, clerk, b. Farmington, s/o Oscar F. Kimball (Haverhill, MA, retired) and Leanora Hayes (New Durham, housekeeper); W - 25, teacher, b. Farmington, d/o Peter D. Allen (carpenter) and Lillian F. Johnson (bookkeeper)

Charles H. of Farmington m. Augustia **York** of Farmington 3/8/1892; H - 40, shoemaker, b. Wolfeboro, s/o Nathaniel Kimball (dead) and Abagail Kimball (dead); W - 42, housekeeper, 2nd, widow, b. Concord, d/o Joseph P. Davis (Alexandria, farmer) and H. M. Davis (Gilford, housekeeper) of Farmington

F. Gordon of Farmington m. Margaret M. **Wiggin** of Portsmouth 1/23/1926 in Portsmouth; H - 23, accountant, b. Alton, s/o B. Frank Kimball (Farmington, shoeworker) and Annie H. Hill (Barnston, PQ, merchant); W - 24, stenographer, b. Portsmouth, d/o Austin C. Wiggin (Union, salesman) and Catherine M. White (Cambridge, housewife)

Fred of Farmington m. Elva F. **Purrington** of Tamworth 4/13/1907; H - 20, shoe cutter, b. Farmington, s/o David S. Kimball (Middleton, shoemaker) and Nellie Hanscombe (Middleton); W - 17, shoe worker, b. Farmington, d/o Daniel Purrington (farmer) and Flora Davis

Harry B. of Farmington m. Mabel M. **Dixon** of Farmington 9/17/1894; H - 22, engineer, b. Middleton, s/o Oscar F. Kimball (Haverhill, MA, beer bottling) and Leonore A. Kimball (New Durham, housekeeping); W - 22, b. Farmington, d/o Alvin Dixon (Eliot, ME, carpenter) and Mary A. Dixon (Eliot, ME)

John V. of Farmington m. Sayde J. **Gerrish** of Farmington 12/31/1913; H - 28, shoeworker, b. Farmington, s/o Samuel Kimball (Middleton, shoeworker) and Addie Young; W - 33, shoeworker, 2$^{nd}$, b. Haverhill, MA, d/o C. L. George (Haverhill, foreman) and Carrie Fisher (Hampstead, housekeeper)

Norman L. of Farmington m. Queenie G. **Hale** of Farmington 12/28/1918 in Rochester; H - 23, shoeworker, b. Farmington, s/o Harry B. Kimball (Middleton, clerk) and Mabel M. Dixon (Farmington, housewife); W - 22, shoeworker, b. New Durham, d/o Corey E. Hale and Ida M. Rhines (Rochester, housekeeper)

Verne I. of Berwick, ME m. Jennie M. **Barber** of Farmington 10/15/1932; H - 26, box shipper, b. Berwick, ME, s/o Elwood Kimball (Clifford, ME, machinist) and Lettie Goodwin (deceased); W - 20, shoeworker, b. Franklin, d/o Maurice Barber (Wheelock, VT, truck farmer) and Violet Ingalls (Walden, VT, housewife)

KING,

Charles A. of Dover m. Bernice **Wiggin** of Farmington 8/14/1920; H - 24, salesman, b. Calais, ME, s/o Henry B. King (Calais, ME, foreman) and Clara M. Stevens (Westfield, NB, housewife); W - 23, teacher, b. Farmington, d/o U. S. Wiggin (Dover, hotel keeper) and Bertha Ricker (Wolfeboro, housekeeper)

KIPP,

Albert W. of Arlington, MA m. Vivian **Graham** of Medford, MA 8/5/1933; H - 39, packer, b. Charlestown, MA, s/o Charles Kipp (Saugerties, NY, deceased) and Annie Norse (Boston, MA, deceased); W - 32, bookkeeper, b. Medford, MA, d/o John Graham (Scotland, towerman) and Fannie Murch (Somerville, MA, housekeeper)

**KIRIAPONTSOS,**

George of Farmington m. Eleanor **Witter** of Manchester 12/8/1933; H - 22, shoeworker, b. Lowell, MA, s/o John Kiriapontsos (Greece, mill worker) and Mary Pierakas (Greece, mill worker); W - 21, at home, b. Roxbury, MA, d/o Fredrick Witter (Douglas, NY, engineer) and Mabel Cooper (Croydon, secretary)

**KITCHEN,**

Paul A. of Farmington m. Abbie L. **Hanscum** of Farmington 5/28/1912; H - 23, shoeworker, b. Williamsport, PA, s/o Charles B. Kitchen (Cidan, PA, shoemaker) and Mary L. Lindaner (Cidan, PA, housekeeper); W - 26, housekeeper, 2nd b. Portsmouth, d/o George S. Hanscum (Portsmouth) and Mary Hanscum (Portsmouth, housekeeper)

**KNOX,**

Earl L. of Farmington m. Lillian A. **Stevens** of Rowley, MA 10/3/1933 in E. Rochester; H - 43, carpenter, 2nd, b. Ossipee, s/o Charles E. Knox (Berwick, ME, deceased) and Mary E. Chesley (Tamworth, deceased); W - 25, housewife, 2nd, b. Rowley, d/o Daniel Campbell (Glasgow, Scotland, deceased) and Grace A. Farley (Rowley, MA, cook)

Elmer S. of Farmington m. Carrie B. **White** of Farmington 8/20/1889 in Exeter; H - 27, shoemaker, b. Milton, s/o Jesse W. Knox (Milton, shoemaker) and Mary E. Knox (Lebanon, ME); W - 26, school teacher, b. Farmington, d/o Washington White (New Castle, carpenter) and Ann White (New Castle)

Elmer S. of Farmington m. Violet R. **Howard** of Farmington 11/2/1921; H - 59, shoeworker, 2nd, b. Milton, s/o Jessie W. Knox and Mary E. Canney; W - 40, housekeeper, 2nd, b. Montreal, Canada, d/o Alexander Ross (Scotland, retired) and Elizabeth Scott (Scotland, housewife)

Harry of Farmington m. Blanche **Rowe** of Farmington 2/12/1923; H - 28, carpenter, b. Farmington, s/o Ulysses S. Knox (Chatham, carpenter) and Addie Whitehouse (Middleton, housewife); W - 18, shoeworker, d/o Fred Rowe (Gilmanton, mill hand) and Minnie Burns (housekeeper)

John E. of Farmington m. Evelyn L. **Hersey** of Wolfeboro 12/25/1920 in Wolfeboro; H - 28, barber, b. Farmington, s/o Ulysses S. Knox (Farmington, carpenter) and Addie Whitehouse (Middleton, housewife); W - 28, at home, b. Wolfeboro, d/o Charles F. Hersey (Wolfeboro, salesman) and Nellie M. Black (Wolfeboro, housewife)

Leon E. of Farmington m. LaJoice **Jones** of Farmington 12/29/1888; H - 23, shoemaker, b. Lebanon, ME, s/o Jesse W. (Milton, shoe cutter) and Mary E. (Lebanon, ME, housekeeper); W - 19, shoe stitcher, b. Farmington, d/o Ezekiel (farmer) and Silence (Acton, ME, housekeeper)

Ulysses S. of Farmington m. Addie E. **Whitehouse** of Farmington 9/12/1891 in Milton; H - 27, carpenter, $2^{nd}$, b. Chatham, s/o Simeon P. Knox (Chatham, carpenter); W - 25, housekeeper, b. Middleton, d/o Warren H. Whitehouse (Middleton, shoemaker)

Ulysus S. of Farmington m. Mazuah H. **Johnson** of Farmington 2/11/1887; H - 23, carpenter, b. Chatham, s/o Simon Knox (Chatham, carpenter) and Sarah Knox; W - 20, housekeeper, b. Farmington, d/o Nathaniel Johnson (Farmington, shoemaker) and Julia Johnson

## KRANSBERG,

Harry L. of Beverly, MA m. Adrienne **Levesque** of Salem, MA 3/22/1937; H - 29, salesman, b. Beverly, MA, s/o Philip Kransberg (Russia, furniture store) and Esther Kransberg (Russia); W - 27, at home, b. Canada, d/o Marcel Levesque (Canada, machinist) and Laura Levesque (Canada)

## KROPP,

Maurice of Roxbury, MA m. Jessie **Batbal** of Beverly, MA 7/28/1934; H - 26, merchant, b. Boston, MA, s/o Nathan Kropp (Russia, retired) and Bessie Wise (Russia, at home); W - 26, clerk, b. Roxbury, MA, d/o Joseph Batbal (Spain, guard) and Josie Bebas (Spain, at home)

## LABONTA,

J. Edward of Farmington m. Eva R. **Strout** of Limington, ME 7/31/1902; H - 51, shoemaker, $4^{th}$, divorced, b. Canada, s/o J. B. LaBonta (Canada, dead) and Julia Collett (Canada, dead); W - 18, table waitress, b. Limington, ME, d/o Isaac H. Strout (Limington, ME, dead) and ----- (Limington, ME, cook)

## LABONTE,

Philip O. of Farmington m. Evelyn H. **Corliss** of Somersworth 4/9/1937 in Hampton; H - 33, shoeworker, b. Dover, s/o Peter Labonte (Canada, salesman) and Victoria Demars (Canada, at home); W - 30, shoeworker, b. Chicopee, MA, d/o George Corliss (Somersworth, painter) and Evelyn Bean (Berwick, ME, at home)

LACEY,

John E. of Farmington m. Katherine E. **Coyne** of Farmington 6/16/1934; H - 32, shoeworker, b. Cambridge, MA, s/o John A. Lacey (Arlington, MA, deceased) and Anna O'Connor (Cambridge, MA, at home); W - 27, at home, 2nd, b. Cambridge, MA, d/o Joseph P. Hogan (New York, deceased) and Anna A. O'Reilly (Cambridge, MA, housewife)

LAKE,

Frank E. of Loudon m. Jessie Martin **Keene** of Farmington 4/2/1921 in Rochester; H - 48, farmer, 2nd, b. Loudon, s/o James F. Lake (Loudon, farmer) and Sarah A. Sawyer (Loudon, housewife); W - 39, shoeworker, 2nd, b. E. Hiram, ME, d/o Eugene R. Martin (Kezar Falls, ME) and Euphemia Clark (Newbury, MA, housewife)

LAMONTAGNE,

Jerome of Rochester m. Evelyn C. **Colbath** of Farmington 6/12/1936 in Rochester; H - 24, shoeworker, b. Rochester, s/o H. LaMontagne (Rochester, shoeworker) and Flora Cormier (Rochester, housewife); W - 22, housekeeper, b. Farmington, d/o Loring Colbath (Farmington, shoeworker) and Grace Thurston (No. Berwick, housewife)

LANDRY,

Ernest of Rochester m. Anna Belle **Belanger** of Farmington 4/25/1927; H - 27, shoe cutter, b. Rochester, s/o Joseph Landry (Canada, shoemaker) and Demerise Pare (Canada, housework); W - 19, shoeworker, b. Farmington, d/o William Belanger (Canada, shoeworker) and Delia Lepene (Canada, shoeworker)

Robert of Farmington m. Rita **Paquette** of Manchester 10/15/1938 in Manchester; H - 25, shoeworker, s/o Joseph Landry (Canada, mill op.) and F'raide Gazaille (Canada, housewife); W - 28, shoeworker, b. Manchester, d/o George Paquette (Sandown, retired) and Rose Richards (Fall River, MA, housewife)

LAPINE,

John E. of Farmington m. Hattie M. **Gray** of Alton 11/1/1908; H - 17, shoemaker, b. Farmington, s/o Peter Lapine (Canada, farmer) and Ellen Duclow; W - 19, housekeeper, b. Alton, d/o William Gray (blacksmith) and Sarah Pierce

**LAROCHE,**
Leonel of Farmington m. Ethel M. **Lord** of Farmington 7/3/1937; H - 20, shoeworker, b. PQ, s/o Willie Laroche (PQ, deceased) and Mary Tetreau (Rutland, VT, at home); W - 19, at home, b. Porter, ME, d/o Walter Lord (deceased) and Marion Whitten (at home)

**LARY,**
Greenleaf H. of Farmington m. Mabel F. **Smith** of Farmington 6/30/1888 in Rochester; H - 23, shoe cutter, b. Haverhill, MA, s/o Hosea B. (Freedom, carpenter) and Augusta G. (Searsport, ME, housekeeper); W - 19, box maker, b. Appleton, OH, d/o George (Nottingham, pump mfr.) and Maria (London, England, housekeeper)

**LAVALLEY,**
Eugene J. of Farmington m. Maud E. **Laken** of Farmington 6/17/1896; H - 23, shoemaker, b. Ashland, s/o Oliver La Valley (Canada, shoemaker) and Louisa La Valley (Sanbornton, housewife); W - 21, stitcher, b. Everett, MA, d/o Frank C. Laken (farmer) and Hattie E. Lakin (New Castle)

**LAVERDIERE,**
Wilfred of Rochester m. Arline E. **Knox** of Farmington 12/26/1936; H - 23, shoeworker, b. Rochester, s/o H. J. Laverdiere (N. Hartford, CT, shoeworker) and Laurel Robbins (Richmond, Quebec, at home); W - 19, at home, b. Farmington, d/o Fred L. Knox (Farmington, druggist) and Millie Leighton (Farmington, housewife)

**LAVERTUE,**
Ralph of Rochester m. Kathryn **Cathcart** of Farmington 12/24/1926 in Milton; H - 21, shoeworker, b. Rochester, s/o Henry Lavertue (Rochester, painter) and Flora Downs (Wakefield, at home); W - 18, clerk, b. Farmington, d/o Fred Cathcart (Farmington) and Bernice Haddock (Farmington, shoeworker)

**LAWRENCE,**
Abbott W. of Farmington m. Arline C. **Place** of Farmington 6/10/1926 in Alton; H - 27, shoeworker, b. Boston, MA, s/o Henry S. Lawrence (Fitchburg, MA, shoeworker) and Blanche Dix (VT, housewife); W - 19, bookkeeper, b. Union, d/o Percy Place (Farmington, shoeworker) and Freena Lover (Union, housewife)

Arthur F. of Farmington m. Ruth E. **Tilton** of Farmington 5/30/1938 H - 25, shoeworker, b. Somerville, MA, s/o Henry Lawrence (Fitchburg, MA, retired) and Blanche Dix (Whitingham, VT, housewife); W - 19, cashier, b. Farmington, d/o Charles Tilton (Deerfield, shoeworker) and Ruby Davis (Pittsfield, housewife)

Henry E., Jr. of Farmington m. Marion **Carey** of Farmington 10/12/1935; H - 25, shoeworker, b. Bridgewater, MA, s/o Henry Lawrence (Lynn, MA, shoeworker) and Blanch M. Dix (Barre, VT, housewife); W - 30, shoeworker, b. Lawrence, MA, d/o Frank Carey (Lawrence, MA, deceased) and Mary Finnins (Lawrence, MA, housewife)

John W. of Farmington m. Altice M. **Adams** of Farmington 7/9/1937 in Chichester; H - 26, shoeworker, b. E. Bridgewater, MA, s/o Henry Lawrence (Fitchburg, MA, shoeworker) and Blanche Dix (Whitingham, VT, housewife); W - 22, shoeworker, b. Farmington, d/o Frank Adams (W. Newbury, MA, deceased) and Rachel Leighton (Marblehead, MA, deceased)

**LAWTON,**
James of Farmington m. Ida **Theriault** of Farmington 8/21/1938 in Sanford, ME; H - 23, shoeworker, b. Rockport, MA, s/o E. J. Lawton (Augusta, ME, baker) and F. McCatherine (Gloucester, MA, housewife); W - 23, at home, $2^{nd}$, b. Canada, d/o Israel Theriault (Canada, deceased) and M. Desonourier (Canada, housewife)

**LEAHY,**
James F. of Farmington m. Marjorie **Remick** of Farmington 11/17/1925 in Dover; H - 23, shoeworker, b. Farmington, s/o Joseph Leahy (Farmington, shoeworker) and Alice Teague (Rochester, housewife); W - 19, shoeworker, b. Springvale, ME, d/o Nathaniel P. Remick (Sutton, MA, shoeworker) and Mary E. Sprague (Grafton, MA, housewife)

Joseph P. of Farmington m. Alice J. **Tague** of Rochester 10/23/1901 in Rochester; H - 33, shoe finisher, b. Farmington, s/o Michael Leahy (Ireland, dead) and Honore Conner (Fredericton, NB, dead); W - 31, shoe stitcher, b. Rochester, d/o James Tague (Ireland, dead) and Hannah M. Merriman (Ireland, dead)

**LEAVITT,**

Charles E. of Farmington m. Mintie J. **Cate** of Farmington 1/11/1892; H - 33, horse dealer, b. Wolfeboro, s/o John Leavitt (dead) and Betsey Leavitt (dead); W - 26, housekeeper, $2^{nd}$, divorced, b. Farmington, d/o Jared P. Tibbetts (Farmington, 55, undertaker) and Lizzie Tibbetts (Dover, 47, housewife) of Farmington

George A. of Saco, ME m. Anna E. **Welch** of Saco, ME 2/15/1888; H - 41, fisherman, $2^{nd}$, b. Boston, MA, s/o A. W. (Saco, ME, fisherman) and Ann M. (Boston, MA, deceased); W - 39, mill woman, $2^{nd}$

Sidney A. of Farmington m. Isabelle L. **Giles** of Northwood 11/29/1893; H - 20, clerk, b. Farmington, s/o Almon Leavitt (Effingham, blacksmith) and Sarah E. Leavitt (Alton, housewife); W - 18, teacher, b. Northwood, d/o B. Curtis Giles (Northwood, farmer) and Ellen F. Giles (Northwood, housewife)

**LEE,**

Karl Dayton of Leominster, MA m. Clara Bertha **Neal** of Farmington 9/8/1915; H - 22, principal, b. Hudson, s/o John Lee (Stratford on Avon, England, boss carder) and Mary E. Fuller (S. Reading, MA, housekeeper); W - 22, teacher, b. North Berwick, ME, d/o Harry Isaac Neal (N. Berwick, ME, teacher) and Carrie Belle Colby (Henniker, housekeeper)

Perley I. of Farmington m. Mabelle E. **Bennett** of Farmington 8/20/1937 in Chichester; H - 42, contractor, $3^{rd}$, b. Stark, s/o Henry Lee (Milan, florist) and Lillian Minor (Stark, deceased); W - 28, bookkeeper, b. Farmington, d/o Parker D. Bennett (Farmington, carpenter) and Grace Leighton (Dover, deceased)

**LEFAVOUR,**
Ernest E. of Farmington m. Harriett A. **Thayer** of Farmington 11/25/1922; H - 34, station agent, 2nd, b. Marblehead, s/o Robert H. Lefavour and Harriett Ethridge (Marblehead, housekeeper); W - 32, tel. operator, 2nd, b. Farmington, d/o Walter Thayer (Gray, ME, merchant) and Susan A. Lord (Lebanon, ME, housewife)

**LEIGH,**
Charles E. of Farmington m. Ida E. **Walker** of Dover 5/8/1889; H - 40, farmer, 2nd, b. Dover; W - 25, shoe stitcher, b. Boston, MA d/o John C. Walker (Barrington, farmer) and Matilda Walker (Halifax, NS)

**LEIGHTON,**
A. P. of Farmington m. Christine E. **Brooks** of Farmington 8/13/1910; H - 24, electrician, b. Charlestown, s/o Henry T. Leighton (W. Falmouth, ME, bus. man) and Maria J. Bakema (Bangor, ME, housewife); W - 20, shoeworker, b. Farmington, d/o Percey J. Brooks (Alton, shoemaker) and Edith E. Tibbett (Farmington, housewife)

Charles I. of Farmington m. Addie A. **Dow** of Barnstead 5/7/1892 in South Alton; H - 24, shoemaker, b. Farmington, s/o Amasa R. Leighton (Dover, 53, farmer) and Frances C. Leighton (Effingham, 43, housewife) of Farmington; W - 24, dressmaker, b. Barnstead, d/o Charles H. Dow (Barnstead, 60, farmer) and Lydia A. Dow (Barnstead, 50, housewife) of Barnstead

Earl D. of Farmington m. Alma A. **Perrault** of Farmington 11/11/1912 in Rochester; H - 19, shoeworker, b. Barnstead, s/o Charles I. Leighton (Farmington, shoecutter) and Addie A. Dow (Barnstead); W - 20, shoeworker, b. Rochester, d/o Peter Perrault (shoemaker) and Cleandie Perrault (housekeeper)

Fred M. of Farmington m. Lowea E. **French** of Farmington 7/5/1893; H - 25, stable keeper, b. Farmington, s/o Charles Leighton (dead) and Emma A. Leighton (Farmington, housekeeper); W - 23, lady, b. Farmington, d/o Charles H. French (Farmington, laborer) and Martha French (Haverhill, lady)

George F. of Farmington m. Mary A. **Ordway** of Farmington 6/28/1924 in Alton Bay; H - 53, foreman, b. Marblehead, s/o

George F. Leighton and Margaret Sandwich; W - 28, teacher, b. Epping, d/o Charles C. Ordway (Epping, farmer) and Carrie E. Parker (Nottingham, housewife)

John H. of Farmington m. Annie L. **Perkins** of Farmington 11/14/1895 in Alton; H - 21, shoemaker, b. Farmington, s/o George F. Leighton (Farmington) and Margaret Leighton (NS, housework); W - 20, shoe packer, b. Farmington, d/o Robert R. Perkins (farmer) and Mary Perkins (Farmington)

Mark F. of Farmington m. Fannie M. **Lord** of Farmington 11/28/1906; H - 54, shoe cutter, b. Farmington, s/o Moses C. Leighton (Farmington, carpenter) and Hannah E. Tanner (Farmington); W - 48, shoe worker, b. Lebanon, ME, d/o Luther Lord (Lebanon, farmer) and Susan Lord

Oscar W. of Middleton m. Bessie L. **Kerr** of Farmington 10/28/1917 in Milton; H - 28, shoeworker, $2^{nd}$, b. Middleton, s/o Charles H. Leighton (Middleton, farmer) and Lucy A. Drew (Eaton, housewife); W - 34, shoeworker, $2^{nd}$, b. Lovell, ME, d/o Alphonzo Charles (lumberman) and Luvett A. Heath (housewife)

Walter E. of Farmington m. G. Frances **Lamper** of Alton 9/24/1916 in Milton; H - 23, shoeworker, b. Rochester, s/o Walter Leighton (Middleton, carpenter) and Lizzie S. Drew (Middleton, housekeeper); W - 23, bookkeeper, d/o George Lamper (Alton, farmer) and Myrtle Hayes (Alton)

**LEMOINE,**

John of Nashua m. Nancy **Streeter** of Sanbornville 6/8/1900; H - 22, laborer, b. Concord, s/o Alfred Lemoine (dead) and Lucie Lemoine (dead); W - 18, housekeeper, b. Sanbornville, d/o Joseph Streeter (England, millman) and Velirea Streeter (Barnstead, housekeeper)

**LEON,**

Joseph T. of Ayer, MA m. Emma **Tanwalt** of Farmington 6/19/1920; H - 40, soldier, b. NY, s/o Joseph Leon and Blanche Puscha; W - 34, at home, $3^{rd}$, b. Moncton, NB, d/o William Reuton (Moncton, NB, farmer) and Catherine Crandall (Moncton, NB, housewife)

**LEONARD,**

Lester S. of Farmington m. Ruth E. **Davis** of Farmington 6/7/1924 in Dover; H - 24, shoe cutter, b. Omaha, NE, s/o John Leonard (North Adams, shoemaker) and Nellie F. Steen (Sanford, ME, housewife); W - 22, housekeeper, b. Farmington, d/o George Davis (Farmington, shoeworker) and Eliza Davis (Farmington, housewife)

**LEPAGE,**

Paul of Farmington m. Mary **Garrett** of Farmington 7/23/1919 in Sanbornville; H - 27, shoeworker, b. Canada, s/o Paul Lepage (Canada) and Jennie Lepage (Canada, housewife); W - 39, shoeworker, $2^{nd}$, b. Springvale, ME, d/o Michael Custon (watchman) and Marie Custon (housewife)

**LESPERANCE,**

Elwin of Farmington m. Pauline **Terrell** of Farmington 9/9/1927; H - 19, shoeworker, b. Lancaster, s/o Elwin Cardwell and Hattie Lesperance (Lancaster, housekeeper); W - 17, at home, b. Farmington, d/o Charles Tirrell (shoeworker) and Goldie Stanley (housewife)

**LESTER,**

Percy T. of Farmington m. May C. **Camm** of Rochester 7/23/1920 in Dover; H - 40, chauffeur, b. England, s/o Thomas Lester and Susan Lester (England); W - 23, bookkeeper, b. England, d/o Arthur Camm (England, shoeworker) and Caroline Shipley (England)

**LEVEILLE,**

Walter of Farmington m. Marie A. **Letourneau** of Farmington 6/20/1936; H - 23, millworker, b. Woonsocket, s/o Joseph Leveille (Canada, mill worker) and Phobe Leveille (Canada, deceased); W - 27, mill worker, b. Rochester, d/o Louis Letourneau (Canada, truckman) and Deana Marcoux (Rochester, mill worker)

**LEWIS,**

Arthur L. of Salem, MA m. Gertrude E. **Sweeney** of Salem, MA 11/24/1937; H - 27, truckman, $2^{nd}$, b. Danvers, MA, s/o

Linwood Lewis (Salem, MA, laundryman) and Emma Roberts (Milford, mill worker); W - 21, salesgirl, b. Salem, d/o Gene Sweeney (Salem, MA, elevator man) and ----- (shoeworker)

**LIBBEY,**
Charles of St. Stephens, NB m. Euphonia A. **Collins** of St. David's Ridge 11/22/1900; H - 33, farmer, b. St. Stephens, NB, s/o Asa Libbey (St. Stephens, NB, farmer) and Mary E. Hanover (Alexander, NB, housekeeper); W - 26, housekeeper, b. St. David's Ridge, d/o David Collins (St. David's Ridge, farmer) and Sarah A. Creasey (housekeeper)

Erving A. of Rangeley, ME m. Lucy A. **Harrington** of Farmington 12/22/1898; H - 23, physician, b. New Durham, s/o Asa E. Libbey (New Durham) and Emma J. Chesley (New Durham, housewife); W - 25, school teacher, b. Norfolk, ON, d/o John S. Harrington (ON, clergyman) and Elizabeth Harrington (ON, housewife)

**LIBERTY,**
Frederick P., Jr. of Farmington m. Margaret E. **Follansbee** of Haverhill, MA 3/2/1935 in Newton; H - 22, shoeworker, b. Haverhill, MA, s/o Frederick P. Liberty (Kenova, PA, deceased) and Sarah I. Page (Haverhill, MA, deceased); W - 22, nurse, b. Haverhill, MA, d/o Samuel Follansbee (Somersworth, shoe findings) and Florence Carlton (Haverhill, MA, housewife)

Normand P. of Farmington m. Violet E. **Howard** of Farmington 7/9/1927; H - 20, pattern designer, b. Haverhill, MA, s/o Frederick Liberty (Butler, PA, shoe mfgr.) and Sadie Page (Canada, housewife); W - 21, priv. stenographer, b. Cambridge, VT, d/o Loren R. Howard and Violet Ross (housewife)

**LIEBERT,**
Isaac of Revere, MA m. Caroline B. **Bradford** of Revere, MA 9/8/1934; H - 40, butcher, b. London, England, s/o Barney Liebert (London, England, deceased); W - 28, nurse, b. Middleton, d/o Bauryde Bradford (Portsmouth, deceased) and Annie Lawrence (Exeter, deceased)

**LINCOLN,**

Fred of Rochester m. Eunice **Dore** of Farmington 6/15/1925 in Rochester; H - 25, plumber, b. E. Rochester, s/o George Lincoln (Danvers, MA, laborer) and Susie E. Thompson (Kennebunkport, ME); W - 18, at home, b. Farmington, d/o Ernest Dore (Farmington, shoeworker) and Inez Clough (Wolfeboro, housewife)

**LITTLEFIELD,**

Donald A. of Dover m. Hilda M. **Senter** of Farmington 10/24/1932 in Dover; H - 23, truck driver, b. So. Berwick, ME, s/o Ernest A. Littlefield (Berwick, ME, deceased) and Myrtle E. Quint (So. Berwick, ME, housewife); W - 21, b. Kingston, d/o Walter H. Senter (Derry, carpenter) and Gertrude T. Stevens (Wakefield MA, housewife)

Fred A. of Farmington m. Almira F. **Kimball** of Farmington 5/15/1893; H - 24, conductor, b. MA, s/o Orin Littlefield (MA, tinsmith) and Clara A. Littlefield (MA, housewife); W - 20, lady, b. Middleton, d/o Oscar Kimball (Farmington, bottler) and Lenora Kimball (Haverhill, MA, housewife)

Joseph F. of Brookline, MA m. Hattie T. **Willson** of Boston, MA 1/14/1909; H - 67, merchant, widower, b. Wells, ME, s/o Joseph Littlefield (Wells, ME, farmer) and Josephine Levett (Wells, ME, housekeeper); W - 58, sewing, b. York, ME, d/o Theodore Willson (York, ME, teacher) and Elizabeth Talpey (York, ME, housekeeper)

**LORING,**

Rupert L. of Ossipee m. Mary Ella **Langley** of Farmington 2/6/1934; H - 24, clerk, b. Ossipee, s/o Ray E. Loring (Ossipee, merchant) and Helen Corson (Franklin, MA, housewife); W - 22, at home, b. Franklin, MA, d/o Allyn L. Langley (Brighton, MA, caretaker) and Leila H. Smith (Franklin, MA, housewife)

**LOUGEE,**

Allie A. of Farmington m. Amy **Roberts** of Dover 6/20/1904; H - 20, shoemaker, b. Farmington, s/o Nehemiah Lougee (Farmington, shoemaker) and Etta E. Place (Sandwich, housewife); W - 16, housekeeper, b. Dover, d/o Edward Roberts (farmer) and Eva G. Roberts

Allie A. of Farmington m. Carrie B. **Witham** of Farmington 4/27/1913 in Dover; H - 28, shoeworker, 2$^{nd}$, b. Farmington, s/o Nehemiah Lougee (Farmington, laborer) and Julia Place (Sandwich, housekeeper); W - 28, shoeworker, b. Dover, d/o Woodbury Witham (Milton, fireman) and Ada Ellis (Milton, housekeeper)

Ernest R. of Farmington m. Annie M. **Jordan** of Farmington 10/25/1897; H - 26, shoemaker, b. Farmington, s/o Almon S. Lougee (Chelsea, VT, farmer) and Jennie Lougee (Parsonsfield); W - 27, 2$^{nd}$, b. Augusta, ME, d/o Frederick Morton (Augusta, ME, painter) and Sarah H. Morton (Augusta, ME, housewife)

Harry C. of Farmington m. Marjorie **Martineau** of Farmington 11/26/1936; H - 26, shoeworker, b. Farmington, s/o Allie Lougee (Farmington, shoeworker) and Carrie B. Witham (Farmington, shoeworker); W - 28, at home, b. Rochester, d/o J. D. Martineau (Rochester, farmer) and Edith Wyatt (Farmington, at home)

Herbert C. of Farmington m. Yvonne **Labossiere** of Farmington 4/24/1920; H - 20, shoeworker, b. Farmington, s/o Nehemiah Lougee (Farmington, laborer) and Julia E. Place (Sandwich, housewife); W - 21, housekeeper, 2$^{nd}$, b. Marlboro, MA, d/o Cleophas Labossiere (Canada, shoeworker) and Emile Beauleau (Canada)

Hiram C. of Farmington m. Clara E. **Horne** of Farmington 2/22/1887; H - 39, teamster, 2$^{nd}$, widower, b. Chelsea, VT, s/o John Lougee and Polly Lougee; W - 39, 2$^{nd}$, widow, b. Farmington, d/o John B. Twombly and Eliza Twombly

Jacob A. of Farmington m. Bessie C. **Chandler** of PEI 9/1/1900; H - 21, shoe finisher, b. Farmington, s/o Nehemiah Lougee (Farmington, shoe finisher) and Etta E. Place (Sandwich, housekeeper); W - 20, housekeeper, b. NS, d/o Thomas Chandler (PEI, dead) and Bridget McKee (PEI, dead)

Jacob A. of Farmington m. Hattie M. **Dyer** of Milton 9/24/1902 in Milton; H - 23, shoe finisher, 2$^{nd}$, widower, b. Farmington, s/o Nehemiah Lougee (Farmington, shoe finisher) and Etta E. Place (Sandwich, housewife); W - 26, shoe stitcher, b. Sanbornville, d/o Charles H. Dyer (Brownfield, ME, farmer) and Martha A. Drew (Brookfield, housewife)

Walter S. of Farmington m. Lila S. **Saunders** of Farmington 8/21/1920; H - 39, foreman, b. Farmington, s/o Nehemiah

Lougee (Farmington, laborer) and Julia Place (Sandwich, housewife); W - 42, housekeeper, 2nd, b. Milton, d/o Moses Cook and Sally Downing

**LOVERING,**
George A. of Farmington m. Irma L. **Davis** of Farmington 7/23/1905; H - 24, clerk, b. Farmington, s/o Frank A. Lovering (Tuftonboro, merchant) and Etta H. Gammon (Naples, ME); W - 19, school teacher, b. Parsonsfield, ME, d/o James E. Davis (Alton, shoe foreman) and Lue M. Furber (Northwood)

**LOWELL,**
Llewellyn L. of Farmington m. Annie M. **Marcoux** of Farmington 8/31/1918 in Dover; H - 29, lumbering, b. New Durham, s/o James A. Lowell (Hiram, ME, farmer) and Johan Parker (Hiram, ME); W - 32, shoeworker, 2nd, b. Somersworth, d/o Henry Dubois (Canada) and Mary Gommea (Canada, housekeeper)

**LUCAS,**
Frank J. of New Durham m. Abbie J. **Curtis** of Farmington 10/20/1894 in Wolfeboro; H - 36, shoemaker, b. New Durham, s/o Daniel Lucas (Wolfeboro) and Sarah F. Lucas (Alton); W - 27, school teacher, b. Farmington, d/o William A. Curtis (Farmington, farmer) and Melissa S. Curtis (housekeeper)

**MACK,**
Michael of Farmington m. Clara E. **Smith** of Farmington 4/24/1907; H - 37, shoemaker, b. N. Adams, MA, s/o James Mack (Ireland, teamster) and Ellen Wall (Ireland); W - 34, shoe stitcher, b. Deer Isle, ME, d/o Edwin Smith (Litchfield, ME, stone paver) and Martha Thompson (Deer Isle, ME)

**MACKENZIE,**
Charles P. of Lynn, MA m. Marguerite **Pelley** of Lynn, MA 5/14/1927; H - 50, police officer, 2nd, b. Lynn, MA, s/o James L. Mackenzie and Ella Ceates (Lynn, MA); W - 26, at home, 2nd, b. Salem, MA, d/o Charles A. Smith (Salem, MA, real estate) and Mary H. Sinclair

**MADDOCKS,**
Perley W. of Farmington m. Florence M. **Evans** of Farmington 12/2/1907; H - 31, shoemaker, 2$^{nd}$, b. Ellsworth, ME, s/o Walter Maddocks (Ellsworth, ME, blacksmith) and Annie Denico (Ellsworth, ME); W - 19, shoemaker, b. Farmington, d/o George H. Evans (Rochester, printer) and Ida O. Corson (Farmington)

**MALONEY,**
James J. of Linwood, PA m. Dorothy P. **Pouliot** of Farmington 9/3/1934; H - 29, inspector, b. Philadelphia, PA, s/o James J. Maloney (Ireland, spinner) and Katherine Thomas (Landford, PA, at home); W - 23, at home, b. Farmington, d/o Edward Pouliot (Sanbornville, shoeworker) and Ezelia Sturgeon (Milton Mills, housewife)

John B. of Farmington m. Lee A. **Cushman** of Rochester 10/8/1929 in Rochester; H - 24, farmer, b. Norton, MA, s/o Edward Maloney (Ireland, farmer) and Sarah Michaud (Canada); W - 21, shoeworker, b. Brockton, MA, d/o Charles H. Cushman (Nantucket, MA, merchant) and Annie C. Lyon (Worcester, MA, nurse)

**MANGAR,**
James R. of Lyman, ME m. Charlotte M. **Cook** of Farmington 3/12/1910; H - 22, shoemaker, b. Bridgton, ME, s/o James H. Mangar (Lyman, ME, farmer) and Carrie M. Walker (Brownfield, ME, housewife); W - 16, housekeeper, b. Barnstead, d/o George W. Cook (Holderness, farmer) and Clara A. Hubbard (Center Harbor, shoeworker)

**MANSON,**
George H. of Farmington m. Leonora **Sands** of Farmington 9/14/1910; H - 63, shoeworker, divorced, b. Limerick, ME, s/o Samuel Manson (Limerick, ME, tanner) and Eliza R. Sawyer (Hollis, ME, housewife); W - 54, housekeeper, widow, b. Equmock, PA, d/o Job Price (Equmock, PA, blacksmith) and Delia Starks (Mt. Pleasant, PA, housewife)

**MARCHAND,**
Goodyear A. of Rochester m. Celia **Parent** of Farmington 10/12/1927; H - 26, barber, b. Milton, s/o Arthur Marchand

(Canada, barber) and Fannie Valley (Wolfeboro, housewife); W - 19, shoeworker, b. S. Berwick, ME, d/o Edward Parent (Canada, laborer) and Celina Carona (Canada, housewife)

**MARCHANT,**
Frank A. of Gloucester, MA m. Estella M. **Card** of Farmington 1/1/1928; H - 51, steamfitter, $2^{nd}$, s/o Lorenzo Marchant and Ellen Crosby; W - 25, teacher, b. Brockton, MA, d/o Burton Card and Mamie Haynes (Farmington, shoeworker)

**MARCOUX,**
Albert A. of Manchester m. Hazel **Whitehouse** of Farmington 11/29/1921; H - 21, Navy, b. Manchester, s/o Archille Marcoux (Canada, loomfixer) and Aldea St. Onge (Canada, housewife); W - 19, shoeworker, b. Somersworth, d/o Harry Whitehouse (Somersworth, painter) and Gertrude R. Blake (Belfast, ME, housewife)

Gideon of Farmington m. Estella M. **Lemire** of Farmington 12/22/1916 in Rochester; H - 21, shoeworker, b. Rochester, s/o Joseph D. Marcoux (Canada, laborer) and Adelaide Cyr (Canada, housekeeper); W - 17, shoeworker, d/o Theodore Lemire (shoeworker) and Mamie Belmont (housekeeper)

Odule of Farmington m. Lucy C. **Burleigh** of Farmington 7/6/1912 in Gonic; H - 24, shoemaker, b. Rochester, s/o Joseph Marcoux (Canada) and Adelaide Cyr (Canada, housekeeper); W - 22, shoemaker, b. Farmington, d/o Harry C. Burleigh (Portsmouth, shoemaker) and Estella Burleigh (Middleton, housekeeper)

**MARDANES,**
Louis of Farmington m. Fannie **Huckins** of Farmington 2/28/1937 in Wolfeboro; H - 20, shoeworker, b. Manchester, s/o Nickolas Mardanes (Greece, shoeworker) and Eva Keho (Greece, mill worker); W - 16, shoeworker, b. Strafford, d/o Edgar Huckins (deceased) and Addie Hill (deceased)

**MARDEN,**
Horton D. of Farmington m. Josephine H. **Coleman** of Farmington 7/24/1937 in Claremont; H - 66, farmer, $2^{nd}$, b. Rye Beach, s/o Thomas Marden (Rye, deceased) and Eliza McDaniels (So. Berwick, ME, deceased); W - 59, housekeeper, $2^{nd}$, b.

Oakland, CA, d/o George Francis (Boston, MA, deceased) and Julia Weeks (Greenland, deceased)

**MARR,**

Charles of Freeport, ME m. Pauline **Remick** of Farmington 8/18/1928 in Dover; H - 20, shoeworker, b. Freeport, ME, s/o Ora Marr (Durham, ME, farmer) and Lydia Stetson (Freeport, ME, housewife); W - 20, shoeworker, b. Farmington, d/o Nathaniel Remick (shoeworker) and Mary E. Sprague (Grafton, MA, housekeeper)

**MARSH,**

Herbert E. of Farmington m. Mertie K. **Bishop** of Farmington 12/25/1911; H - 22, weaver, b. S. Royalton, VT, s/o Stephen Marsh (mechanic) and Hattie Page (Barnard, VT, lady); W - 16, domestic, b. S. Woodstock, VT, d/o Addie Bishop (E. Woodstock, CT, domestic)

Ralph S. of Effingham Falls m. Mae E. **Connors** of Charlestown 6/5/1905 in W. Milton; H - 26, student, b. Effingham Falls, s/o Henry Marsh (Brookfield, MA, shoemaker) and DeEtta E. Dore (Effingham Falls); W - 27, b. Charlestown, MA, d/o James Conners (England, cabinet maker) and Annie Morrissey (at sea, English waters)

**MARSHALL,**

Chesley S. of Rollinsford m. E. Gertrude **Hooper** of Farmington 4/10/1917; H - 20, clerk, b. Dover, s/o St. Clair Marshall (carpenter) and Mary Gibson (NS, housewife); W - 30, at home, b. Amesbury, MA, d/o Frank Hooper (England, minister) and Delina Taylor (NS, housewife)

**MARSTON,**

Frank R. of Farmington m. E. Ellen **Davis** of Farmington 1/1/1905; H - 54, shoe mfr., 3rd, b. Parsonsfield, ME, s/o Jacob Marston (Parsonsfield, ME, farmer) and Martha Doe (Parsonsfield, ME); W - 37, shoe stitcher, 2nd, b. New Durham, d/o John Berry (New Durham, farmer) and Nancy M. Phelps (New Durham)

Fred B. of Farmington m. Hester A. **Bumpus** of Farmington 12/11/1893 in Turner, ME; H - 27, shoe foreman, b. Middleton, s/o Frank R. Marston (Middleton, shoe foreman) and Susan A.

Young (Alton, lady); W - 27, teacher, b. Turner, ME, d/o Marti
K. Bumpus (Hebron, ME, farmer) and Lydia J. Bumpus (East
Turner, ME, housewife)

**MARTINEAU,**

Joseph of Farmington m. Edith L. **Wyatt** of Farmington 7/5/1913 in Rochester; H - 28, millhand, b. Somersworth, s/o Peter Martineau (Canada) and Soffit Perrauet (Canada); W - 28, housekeeper, $2^{nd}$, b. Farmington, d/o Asa Wyatt (Farmington, farmer) and Belle Wyatt

Ramon of Farmington m. Muriel H. **Osgood** of Farmington 9/16/1938 in Dover; H - 29, teacher, b. Rochester, s/o F. Martineau (Canada, deceased) and P. Marcoux (Canada, deceased); W - 25, at home, b. Haverhill, MA, d/o George Osgood (Epping, shoeworker) and Mary Beede (Fremont, shoeworker)

**MATHEWS,**

Nelson H. of Farmington m. Alice **Pinkham** of Farmington 5/1/1895; H - 21, heelmaker, b. Rochester, s/o J. Frank Mathews (Dover, shoelaster) and Jennie E. Mathews (Alton, housewife); W - 20, housekeeper, b. Farmington, d/o John W. Pinkham (New Durham, farmer) and Eliza Pinkham (housewife)

**MAXFIELD,**

Edward R. of Rochester m. Marie D. A. **Duquette** of Farmington 4/4/1932 in Rochester; H - 23, shoe operative, b. Rochester, s/o Henry Maxfield (Rochester, retired) and Clara Jacques (Canada, housewife); W - 21, laundry, b. Rochester, d/o Adelard Duquette (Canada, deceased) and Albertine Lapoint (Canada, housewife)

**MAYOTT[E],**

Harry C. of Farmington m. Margaret C. **Bower** of Effingham 11/16/1935 in Ossipee; H - 19, shoeworker, b. Farmington, s/o Fred Mayott (shoeworker) and Lizzie Howard (Farmington); W - 15, at home, b. Effingham, d/o Howard Bower (NS, laborer) and Beatrice Davis (Effingham, housewife)

Harry C. of Farmington m. Marion A. **Wyatt** of Farmington 7/8/1938; H - 22, shoeworker, $2^{nd}$, b. Farmington, s/o Fred

Mayotte (Derry, shoeworker) and Elizabeth Howard (Farmington, housewife); W - 18, shoeworker, b. Farmington, d/o Ralph Wyatt (Farmington, laborer) and Ellen Thompson (Barrington, at home)

## McCARTHY,

George D. of Farmington m. Hilda **Tilton** of Farmington 3/14/1925 in Dover; H - 37, shoeworker, 2$^{nd}$, b. Rockland, s/o Thomas McCarthy (Ireland, barber) and Mary A. McDermit (Abington, MA, housewife); W - 30, shoeworker, 2$^{nd}$, b. Farmington, d/o Percy J. Brooks (Alton, shoemaker) and Edith Tibbetts

## McCOLLOUGH,

Robert J. of Farmington m. Sylvia **Foss** of Farmington 2/2/1924 in Rochester; H - 22, shoeworker, b. Springvale, ME, s/o Andrew McCollough (Ireland, farmer) and Elizabeth Herring; W - 20, bookkeeper, b. Machias, ME, d/o Charles Foss (Machias, ME, farmer) and Hattie Bryant (Machias, ME, housekeeper)

## McDONALD,

Daniel of Farmington m. Nellie M. **Whitehouse** of Farmington 6/6/1891; H - 26, carpenter, b. PEI, s/o John McDonald (PEI, farmer); W - 21, housekeeper, b. Farmington, d/o Warren H. Whitehouse (Middleton, shoemaker)

## McDUFFEE,

Frank P. of Farmington m. Edna I. H. **Peavey** of Farmington 7/23/1910; H - 52, farmer, widower, b. Rochester, s/o James McDuffee (Rochester, farmer) and Abbie Palmer (Rochester, housewife); W - 52, housekeeper, widow, b. Alton, d/o John I. Huckins (Madbury, farmer) and Abbie W. Whitehouse (Somersworth, housewife)

## McGIBBON,

James of Farmington m. Cora A. **Tibbetts** of Farmington 9/21/1892; H - 32, barber, b. Milton Mills, s/o William McGibbon (dead) and Mary McGibbon (dead); W - 34, shoe stitcher, 2$^{nd}$, divorced, b. Great Falls, d/o ----- (dead) and Amanda Tibbetts (Ossipee, 63, lady) of Farmington

**McGRATH,**
Leo F. of Peabody, MA m. Mary F. **Perkins** of Salem, MA 2/2/1924; H - 25, leatherworker, b. Peabody, MA, s/o Corneli McGrath (Ireland, leatherworker) and Jane Quail (Ireland, housewife); W - 26, bookkeeper, b. Salem, MA, d/o William Perkins (Gloucester, RR man) and Mary E. Caskin (VT, housewife)

**McGREGOR,**
George A. of Haverhill m. Ora A. **Whitney** of Farmington 1/24/1906; H - 29, clerk, b. Ellsworth, ME, s/o John B. McGregor (Eastport, ME, grocer) and Mary E. Reynolds (Plt. No. 14); W - 33, bookkeeper, b. Farmington, d/o William W. Whitney (Natick, MA, shoemaker) and Julia A. Pinkham (Farmington, dressmaker)

**McINTIRE,**
Frank B. of Lebanon, ME m. Grace M. **Downing** of Farmington 10/17/1903 in Rochester; H - 35, rail roading, 2$^{nd}$, b. Dover, s/ Samuel C. McIntire (Wolfeboro, farmer) and Isabelle A. Sanborn (Milton, housewife); W - 29, housekeeper, b. Farmington, d/o George T. Downing (Farmington, farmer) and Anna Akins (Barnstead, housewife)
John of York, ME m. Lois **Talpey** of York, ME 9/26/1930; H - 21, truck driver, b. York, ME, s/o Malcolm McIntye (York, ME, farmer) and Marion Bragdon (York, ME, housewife); W - 18, waitress, b. York, ME, d/o Albert Talpey (Ogunquit, ME, carpenter) and Lois Littlefield (Portsmouth, housewife)

**McKENNEY,**
Alfred R. of Rochester m. Ethel A. **Wallingford** of Farmington 11/2/1912 in Rochester; H - 34, mill hand, b. Scarboro, ME, s/ Alfred F. McKenney (Waterboro, ME, optician) and Lizzie S. Guptill (Waterboro, ME, housekeeper); W - 25, shoeworker, 2$^{nd}$, b. Rochester, d/o Charles O. Gray (farmer) and Emma Hall (Rochester, housekeeper)

**McLAUGHLIN,**
Joseph L. of Farmington m. Helen L. **Hayes** of Dover 9/11/1923 in Dover; H - 37, physician, b. Berwick, ME, s/o Frank McLaughlin (Berwick, ME, physician) and Medora Libbey (ME,

housekeeper); W - 31, bookkeeper, b. Dover, d/o Henry G. Hayes (NH, merchant) and Annie I. Hoitt (NH, housekeeper)

**McMULLEN,**
Albert A. of Quincy, MA m. Maude E. **Hodgdon** of Farmington 12/25/1906; H - 24, machinist, b. St. Stephens, NB, s/o John McMullen (Dublin, bookkeeper) and Elizabeth Murray (Canada); W - 25, bookkeeper, b. Farmington, d/o Westbury Hodgdon (Farmington, shoe cutter) and Ellen A. Colbath (Middleton)

**McNEIL,**
Joseph of Farmington m. Josephine **Lucier** of Farmington 5/17/1910; H - 25, shoemaker, b. Somersworth, s/o Daniel McNeil (Quebec, machinist) and Mary Paradis (Quebec, housewife); W - 30, shoestitcher, widow, d/o Joseph Lucier (carpenter) and Dolphene Granger (housewife)

**McPHAIL,**
Charles F. of Farmington m. Ada Dell **Cooke** of Farmington 2/16/1889 in Rochester; H - 21, ship carpenter, b. East Boston, MA, s/o John A. McPhail (PEI, ship carpenter) and Juliette McPhail; W - 27, shoe stitcher, b. Milton, d/o John I. Cooke (Wolfeboro, farmer) and Mary A. Cooke (Exeter)

**McROBERTS,**
John of Farmington m. Carrie M. **Fletcher** of Farmington 11/25/1908; H - 28, shoe cutter, b. Reading, MA, s/o William McRoberts (Liverpool, England, mill foreman) and Rosa E. Woodward (Chelsea, MA); W - 26, b. Farmington, d/o James A. Fletcher (Daycott, MA, gardener) and Elizabeth Miller (New Durham)

**MERRILL,**
Arthur of Farmington m. Alice **Stevens** of Farmington 6/23/1933 in Chichester; H - 21, shoeworker, b. Hamilton, MA, s/o Paul Merrill and Rachel Parker (housewife); W - 19, maid, b. Attleboro, MA, d/o Henry Stevens and Georgia Hutchinson (housewife)

Austin W. of Belmont m. Rose M. **Cook** of Farmington 9/27/1928; H - 56, farmer, $2^{nd}$, b. Thornton, s/o Walter C. Merrill

(Thornton, farmer) and Rachael Morse (Campton, housewife); W - 55, nurse, 2nd, b. Holderness, d/o John Brown (Holderness farmer) and Helen Downing (housewife)

Wilbur E. of Farmington m. Catherine F. **Roark** of Farmington 9/1/1928 in Rochester; H - 20, shoeworker, b. Wakefield, MA, s/o Paul B. Merrill and Rachael H. Parker (Melrose, MA); W - 17, shoeworker, b. Boston, MA, d/o John Roark (Albany, NY, watchman) and Elizabeth McCrillis (Meredith, married)

**MESERVE,**

Karl G. of Farmington m. Hildred C. **Peterson** of Farmington 2/12/1908; H - 19, shoemaker, b. Farmington, s/o Samuel Y. Meserve (Rochester) and Julia Gilman (Danvers, MA); W - 17, shoemaker, b. Brighton, NS, d/o Enos L. Peterson (Lockport, NS, merchant) and Sarah M. McDonald (Souris, PEI)

**MILLAR,**

William G. of Dover m. Faye **Card** of Farmington 9/17/1906; H - 21, hotel clerk, b. Dover, s/o Clifford Millar (Dover, farmer) and Mamie Edmonds (Suncook); W - 18, paper box maker, b. Farmington, d/o George V. Card (New Castle, heel cutter) and Nancy J. Sampson (Dexter, ME)

**MILLER,**

Charles H. of Farmington m. Jennela **Smart** of Farmington 11/3/1887; H - 39, shoemaker, 3rd, widower, b. Dover, s/o Jonathan Miller (blacksmith) and Lydia Miller; W - 29, 2nd, b. Raymond, d/o Samuel Smart (Raymond, jeweler) and Sarah Smart

John B. of Farmington m. Annie L. **McCormick** of Farmington 5/19/1888; H - 21, teamster, b. Middleton, s/o John C. (Middleton, farmer) and Annie A.; W - 30, lady, 2nd, b. England, d/o Frank (England) and Mary

Joseph of Farmington m. Gertrude I. **Montgomery** of Farmington 8/27/1910; H - 21, upholsterer, b. Boston, s/o Louis Miller (Russia, carpenter) and Brino Bahn (Russia, housewife); W - 17, shoeworker, b. Dover, d/o Fred E. Montgomery (Strafford, shoemaker) and Emma F. Hackett (Danvers, MA, housekeeper)

Ray S. of Farmington m. Elsie M. **Young** of Farmington 12/23/1927; H - 18, shoeworker, b. Farmington, s/o William

Miller (Dover, carpenter) and Faye Card (Farmington, housewife); W - 18, shoeworker, b. Farmington, d/o Charles T. Young (Farmington, laborer) and Daisy Drew (Sanbornville, housewife)

MITCHELL,
H. Fayette of Farmington m. Ruby **Chase** of Farmington 1/15/1931; H - 23, ch. store mgr., b. New Haven, CT, s/o Carl P. Mitchell (Shelburne Falls, MA, plumber) and Augustine Mitchell (Shelburne Falls, MA, housewife); W - 19, shoeworker, b. New Durham, d/o Fred Chase (woodturner) and Ella Davis (housewife)

MOISEN,
Fred of Farmington m. Clara **Boucher** of New Durham 12/16/1911 in New Durham; H - 28, lumberman, b. Canada, s/o John Moisen (Canada, carpenter) and ----- (Canada, housekeeper); W - 19, housekeeper, b. New Durham, d/o Leon Bucher (Canada, carpenter) and Melvan Lamen (Canada, housekeeper)

MONTGOMERY,
Melvin of Farmington m. Ruth E. **Wentworth** of Farmington 1/25/1935; H - 20, shoe worker, b. Farmington, s/o William Montgomery (Lynn, MA, shoeworker) and Lillian Pitts (Sanford, ME, deceased); W - 23, maid, b. Lebanon, ME, d/o Linwood Wentworth (Lebanon, ME, retired) and Carrie Wentworth (Acton, ME, housewife)

William P. of Farmington m. Lillie M. **Pitts** of Sanford, ME 6/15/1912; H - 20, shoeworker, b. Lynn, MA, s/o Fred Montgomery (Barrington, shoemaker) and Emma Hackett (Danvers, MA, housekeeper); W - 27, shoeworker, 2$^{nd}$, b. New Bedford, d/o George F. Pitts (Waterboro, salesman) and Clara H. Pitts (Skowhegan, ME, housekeeper)

William P. of Farmington m. Ida M. **Chase** of New Durham 9/26/1921; H - 31, shoeworker, 2$^{nd}$, b. Lynn, MA, s/o Fred Montgomery (Dover, shoeworker) and Emma Hackett (Lynn, MA, housewife); W - 18, at home, b. Dover, d/o Fred H. Chase (farmer) and Ella B. ----- (housewife)

**MORAYIANIS,**
Nikitas of Farmington m. Vas'ke **Apostolopoulos** of Dover 5/9/1937 in Dover; H - 37, merchant, $2^{nd}$, b. Greece, s/o Arthur Morayianis (Greece, farmer) and D'tra Gran'jopulos (Greece, housewife); W - 24, at home, b. Dover, d/o C. Apostopoulos (Greece, deceased) and Th'nie Kostopoulos (Greece, housewife)

**MORIN,**
Thomas J. of Farmington m. Ada L. **Couture** of Farmington 10/29/1932; H - 59, painter, $2^{nd}$, b. Canada, s/o Narcissus Morin (deceased) and Sophrina Boucher (deceased); W - 43, housewife, $2^{nd}$, b. Rochester, d/o Henry Corson (deceased) and Mary J. Gilbert (deceased)

**MOSHER,**
Harold W. of Farmington m. Alberta S. **Willard** of Farmington 9/5/1936 in Nashua; H - 21, shoeworker, b. Springfield, MA, s/o Eugene Mosher (Chicopee, MA, dairy farm) and Catherine Haley (Woburn, MA, housewife); W - 19, office, b. Alton, d/o Raymond Willard (Alton, shoeworker) and Sarah Glidden (Alton, deceased)

**MOTT,**
Clarence M. of Farmington m. Alma **Randell** of Farmington 2/22/1925; H - 23, shoeworker, b. E. Rochester, s/o Orrie W. Mott (Milton, shoeworker) and Aleatha Jones (East Rochester, housekeeper); W - 18, shoeworker, b. Greenville, ME, d/o Harry Randell (Greenville, ME) and Irene B. Randell (Canada, housekeeper)

Orrie W. of Farmington m. Evelyn **Elliott** of Farmington 12/14/1926; H - 48, shoeworker, $2^{nd}$, b. Milton, s/o P. F. Mott and Jennie E. Mason; W - 20, domestic, b. Farmington, d/o William A. Elliott and Florence Holmes (shoeworker)

**MOULTON,**
Chester A. of Farmington m. Edith **Ham** of Farmington 9/2/1899; H - 20, laborer, b. Farmington, s/o George E. Moulton (Ossipee, laborer) and Janet Moulton; W - 18, b. Farmington, d/o Clarence Ham (Farmington, laborer) and Jennie Ham (Tuftonboro, housewife)

Herbert of Farmington m. Ivadell M. **Nichols** of Farmington 4/11/1936; H - 35, shoeworker, 2$^{nd}$, b. Milton, s/o Chester Moulton (Farmington, laborer) and Edith Ham (Farmington, deceased); W - 32, shoeworker, 3$^{rd}$, b. Wolfeboro, d/o Albert Nichols (Ossipee, farmer) and Copelia M. Ash (Halifax, NS, deceased)

Herbert P. of Farmington m. Elizabeth A. **Carpenter** of N. Berwick, ME 7/14/1927; H - 26, laborer, b. Milton Mills, s/o Chester A. Moulton (laborer) and Edith Ham; W - 18, laborer, b. E. Rochester, d/o Harry Carpenter (Berwick, ME, laborer) and Eliza I. Shorey (E. Rochester, housewife)

Irving H. of Farmington m. Sarah J. **Hill** of Farmington 6/12/1911 in Somersworth; H - 28, shoemaker, b. Farmington, s/o George E. Moulton (Farmington, shoemaker) and Janet L. Hill (New Durham, housekeeper); W - 40, shoe liner, 2$^{nd}$, b. Wakefield, d/o Amnen Reed (Wakefield, carpenter) and Elizabeth Reed (Newfield, ME, housekeeper)

John P. of Farmington m. Martha A. **Babb** of Farmington 11/9/1895; H - 19, farming, b. Farmington, s/o Moses P. Moulton (Dover, farmer) and Laura F. Moulton (Milton, housework); W - 16, housework, b. New Durham, d/o Charles H. Babb (shoemaker) and Jennie D. Babb (Farmington, housewife)

**MUDGETT,**

Robert H. of Farmington m. Elizabeth W. **Carter** of Farmington 10/17/1937; H - 23, laborer, b. Ctr. Sandwich, s/o Frank Mudgett (Ctr. Sandwich, laborer) and Annie Mudgett (Roxbury, MA, housewife); W - 33, school teacher, b. Farmington, d/o Albert Carter (Wilton, ME, retired) and Elizabeth M. Carter (Farmington, retired)

**MURREY,**

Arnold L. of Farmington m. Lena M. **Robblee** of Farmington 7/10/1922; H - 32, auto mechanic, 2$^{nd}$, b. PEI, s/o Charles Murrey and Mary A. Frost; W - 35, housekeeper, 2$^{nd}$, b. Tilton, d/o William Walker and Leona Gomo

Charles F. of Newton, MA m. Esther **Adams** of Farmington 5/30/1937; H - 33, banker, b. Chicago, IL, s/o George Murrey (Scotland, salesman) and Louise Fillebrown (Newton, MA, housewife); W - 23, secretary, b. Beverly, MA, d/o Ellsworth

Adams (Danvers, MA, advertising) and Mildred Hayes (Lynn, MA, housewife)

**NANGLE,**
Philip A. of Rochester m. Marion M. **Parks** of Farmington 10/8/19? in Rochester; H - 25, clerk, b. Rochester, s/o John Nangle (Ireland, shoeworker) and Bridget Trainor (Ireland, housewife) W - 28, nurse, b. Pontiac, MI, d/o Elmer Parks (MI, painter) and Grace Bugbee (MI, housewife)

**NASON,**
Elbert I. of Bristol, CT m. Hattie E. **Marison** of Farmington 6/6/191 in Bristol, CT; H - 32, farmer, b. Farmington, s/o William H. S Nason and Ellen F. Gray; W - 27, trained nurse, b. Dover, d/o Marcellus Marison and Ida C. Hill

Laureston M. of Farmington m. Abbie M. **Ayers** of New Durham 1/1/1887 in Dover; H - 27, shoestitcher, b. Eaton, s/o Charles Nason (Freedom, farmer) and Dorcas Nason; W - 19, housekeeper, b. New Durham, d/o J. Frank Ayers (canvasser) and Hattie Ayers

Leslie I. of Farmington m. Rosa D. **Brouillard** of Rochester 2/6/1922 in Rochester; H - 31, printer, b. Farmington, s/o Laureston M. Nason (machinist) and Abbie M. Ayer (Wakefield, housekeeper); W - 25, shoemaker, b. Sanbornville, d/o Isidore Brouillard (Roxton Falls, Canada, sawyer) and Mary Imbeault (St. Felicite, Canada, housewife)

**NEDEAU,**
Ralph I. of Farmington m. Alda **Marcoux** of Farmington 5/8/1915; ? - 21, restaurant, b. Farmington, s/o Walter S. Nedeau (Farmington, shoeworker) and Bina Labonte (Farmington, shoeworker); W - 17, shoeworker, b. Farmington, d/o Joseph Marcoux (Canada, laborer) and Adelaide Cyr (Canada, housewife)

Walter S. of Farmington m. C. Bina **LaBonte** of Farmington 11/1/1892; H - 20, shoemaker, b. Farmington, s/o Joseph Nedeau (Farmington, 45, shoemaker) of Worcester, MA and Emma Nedeau (New Durham, 39, lady) of Farmington; W - 21 shoe stitcher, b. Farmington, d/o Albert LaBonte (Canada, 45, shoemaker) and Orissa LaBonte (Farmington, 40, housewife) of Farmington

Walter S. of Farmington m. Maude M. **Duntley** of Farmington 9/23/1926; H - 53, shoeworker, 2nd, b. Farmington, s/o Joseph Nedeau (Canada) and Emma J. Corson (New Durham); W - 49, shoeworker, 2nd, b. E. Cambridge, MA, d/o Charles H. Brown (Lisbon, VT) and Sarah Card (New Castle)

NEILL,

Roy V. of Farmington m. Lucina M. **Furber** of Farmington 4/26/1933 in Milton; H - 39, salesman, 2nd, b. Newington, s/o Andrew A. Neill (Calais, ME, deceased) and Amelia Rochmont (Newington, housewife); W - 38, saleslady, 3rd, b. St. Albans, VT, d/o John Bird (St. Albans, VT, hotel manager) and Lucina Curtis (St. Albans, VT, hotel housekeeper)

NELSON,

Fred W. of Farmington m. Charlotte S. **Burleigh** of Farmington 6/28/1907; H - 25, shoeworker, b. Manchester, s/o Frank B. Nelson (Canada, machinist) and Josephine Wilson (Hooksett); W - 31, shoeworker, b. Farmington, d/o Henry Burleigh (carpenter) and Lucy Chamberlin (Portsmouth)

William H. of Medford, MA m. Evelyn G. **Smith** of Melrose, MA 6/17/1938; H - 22, painter, b. Roxbury, MA, s/o Franc Nelson (Roxbury, MA, architect) and Nellie Cook (England, at home); W - 21, at home, b. E. Boston, MA, d/o Thomas Smith (Manchester, England, piano-tech) and G. Rodenhiser (Lunenburg, NS, at home)

NEVERS,

Clarence E. of Farmington m. Agnes E. **Pike** of Farmington 6/19/1920; H - 31, mechanic, b. Wakefield, s/o William Nevers and Augusta Farnham (Wakefield, NH, housekeeper); W - 39, shoeworker, 2nd, b. Farmington, d/o Irving C. Rhines (New Durham, shoeworker) and Angie Brown

NEWELL,

Ralph A. of Springfield m. Frances C. **Dow** of Gonic 9/22/1900; H - 20, shoe cutter, b. E. Burke, VT, s/o Frank A. Newell (E. Burke, VT, dead) and Celia C. Humphrey (E. Burke, VT, housekeeper); W - 20, housekeeper, b. Woodstock, NB, d/o Zeb Dow (Woodstock, NB, print dyer) and Florence Carney (Woodstock, NB, housekeeper)

**NEWLING,**
Charles H. of Farmington m. Etta M. **Babb** of Farmington 7/18/1891 in North Conway; H - 24, stone cutter, b. Effingham s/o John H. Newling (dead); W - 27, housekeeper, 2$^{nd}$, b. Farmington, d/o Dennis Straw (dead)

**NICHOLL,**
Francis J. of Lowell, MA m. Frances E. **Stanley** of Farmington 4/30/1916; H - 25, machinist, b. Albany, NY, s/o Francis Nicholl and Agnes Miles (lady); W - 18, lady, b. Newtonville, MA, d/o Edwin Stanley (Newton Ctr., MA, salesman) and Helen G. Blethen (Newton Ctr., MA, shoeworker)

**NICHOLS,**
Howard A. of Farmington m. Ada L. **Perkins** of Farmington 10/1/1928; H - 21, laborer, b. Pittsfield, s/o Joseph Nichols (Wolfeboro, laborer) and Leona M. Peavey (Alton, housewife); W - 27, shoeworker, 2$^{nd}$, b. Grafton, d/o Daniel W. Elliott (Rumney) and Bertha C. Elliott (W. Falley, VT)

**NIEFORTH,**
Stewart of Farmington m. Lillian **Perkins** of Lyman, ME 10/11/1900 in Rochester; H - 27, teamster, b. Halifax, NS, s/o Edward Nieforth (Halifax, NS, fisherman) and Mary A. Gates (Halifax, NS, housekeeper); W - 30, housekeeper, 2$^{nd}$, b. Biddeford, ME, d/o John Loren (dead) and Mary Loren (dead)

**NOYES,**
Everett N. of Georgetown, MA m. Henrietta **Johnson** of Farmington 11/27/1905 in Dover; H - 26, shoemaker, b. Farmington, s/o Charles F. Noyes (Ashland, MA, shoemaker) and Alice Nelson (W. Harwich, MA, heelmaker); W - 31, housekeeper, b. New Hampton, d/o Samuel C. Johnson (New Hampton, farmer) and Nancy J. Bickford (Alton, housekeeper)

William B. of Melrose, MA m. Susie Ethel **Dow** of Farmington 8/19/1897; H - 25, school teacher, b. Guilford, s/o William E. Noyes (Abington, MA, clergyman) and Alice J. Noyes (Stetson, ME, at home); W - 21, at home, b. Farmington, d/o Charles E. Dow (Northwood, shoe stitcher) and Susan C. Dow (Northwood, at home)

**NUTE,**
Charles F. of Farmington m. Agnes I. **Cleveland** of Portland, ME 3/19/1925; H - 65, shoeworker, 2nd, b. Farmington, s/o Rufus M. Nute and Susan G. Hurd; W - 45, nurse, 2nd, b. Rockland, ME, d/o John C. Cleveland and Margaret Brewster

Eri F. of Farmington m. Martha S. **Yeaton** of Dover 4/19/1898 in Dover; H - 62, shoe cutter, 2nd, b. Milton, s/o Moses Nute (Milton, farmer) and Eunice V. Nute (Milton); W - 63, housekeeper, 2nd, b. Farmington

Harry A. of Farmington m. Helen E. **Wadleigh** of Union 10/12/1918 in Union; H - 27, timekeeper, b. Farmington, s/o Eugene P. Nute (Farmington, insurance) and Nellie Parker (Wolfeboro, housewife); W - 23, nurse, b. Union, d/o Frank Wadleigh (Union, farmer) and Mary Gilmore (Spring Hill, NS, housewife)

Lewis S. of Farmington m. Sophia M. **Bailey** of N. Berwick, ME 3/13/1905; H - 28, shoe fitter, 2nd, b. Farmington, s/o J. Sidney Nute (Milton, barber) and Emma L. Moore (Philadelphia, PA); W - 22, housekeeper, b. Manchester, d/o Nelson Bailey (Canada, mason) and Mary Belhumer (Canada)

Ray H. of Milton m. Deloria **Ferland** of Farmington 12/23/1922 in Milton; H - 24, shoeworker, b. Alton, s/o Arthur H. Nute (Milton, farmer) and Clara Chamberlain (Alton, housewife); W - 20, shoeworker, b. Rochester, d/o Thomas Ferland (Canada, shoemaker) and Mary Marcoux (Rochester, housewife)

William H. of Farmington m. Lizzie **Emerson** of Farmington 12/31/1910; H - 38, shoe foreman, divorced, b. West Milton, s/o Sidney Nute (Dover, laborer) and Emma Moore (Dover, housewife); W - 38, housekeeper, divorced, b. Brentwood, d/o Loren Hunt (farmer) and Mattie Perkins (Brentwood, housewife)

**NUTTER,**
George W. of Farmington m. Araminta B. **Pierce** of Gilmanton 3/8/1891 in Pittsfield; H - 55, shoemaker, 2nd, b. Gilmanton, s/o John Nutter (dead); W - 46, housekeeper, 2nd, b. Manchester, d/o Levi T. Young (Gilmanton, dead)

Harry F. of Farmington m. Lucie B. **Bennett** of Farmington 3/6/1904; H - 21, clerk, b. Farmington, d/o Frank O. Nutter (Farmington, teamster) and Sarah W. Pike (Middleton, housewife); W - 20, teacher, b. Farmington, d/o John P.

Bennett (Northwood, merchant) and Flora E. Hamblin (Winslow, ME, housewife)

John M. of Farmington m. Edith M. **Brown** of Farmington 11/28/1888; H - 29, shoemaker, b. Milton, s/o Jethro (deceased) and Lucinda; W - 21, housekeeper, b. Farmington d/o John L. (shoe cutter) and Mary (housekeeper)

Joseph F. of Farmington m. Lilla E. **Babb** of Farmington 1/22/1898 H - 40, shoemaker, 2$^{nd}$, b. Gilmanton, s/o John Nutter (Gilmanton, stone cutter) and Mercy A. Nutter (Barnstead, housewife); W - 25, shoe stitcher, b. NS, d/o Solomon Babb (Farmington, laborer) and Emma Babb (NS, housewife)

Roger A. of Farmington m. Lucille **Ware** of Farmington 8/28/1936 in W. Milton; H - 23, shoeworker, b. Farmington, s/o Joseph Nutter (Gilmanton I.W., deceased) and Lilla Babb (NS, deceased); W - 22, shoeworker, b. Farmington, d/o Arthur Ware (Waterville, ME, deceased) and Nellie Leighton (Lynn, MA, housewife)

## O'BRIEN,

William T. of New Bedford, MA m. Helen L. **Laughlin** of New Bedford, MA 8/1/1931; H - 39, proprietor, 2$^{nd}$, b. New Bedford, MA, s/o John O'Brien (Ireland, blacksmith) and Hannah Donovan (Ireland); W - 38, 2$^{nd}$, b. Acushnet, MA, d/o Michael Mahoney (Ireland, retired) and Catherine Driscoll (Ireland)

## OIKLE,

John of Farmington m. Mabel Gerrish **Smith** of Alton 2/8/1914 in Alton; H - 29, lumberman, b. NS, s/o Allen Oikle (NS, millman) and Manda Stewart; W - 32, shoeworker, 2$^{nd}$, b. Milton, d/o George Gerrish (Milton, carpenter) and Isabelle Ellis (Alton, housekeeper)

## ONGLEY,

Frank C. of Farmington m. Minnie **Durant** of Farmington 9/24/1914; H - 23, mechanic, 2$^{nd}$, b. Farmington, s/o Frederick Ongley (England, mechanic) and Elizabeth Bogness (Halifax, NS, housewife); W - 28, eyelet operator, 2$^{nd}$, b. Farmington, d/o William Renton (Moncton, NB, farmer) and Catherine Crandall (Moncton, NB, housewife)

**OTIS,**

Albert J. of Farmington m. Leora F. **Horne** of Farmington 10/6/1903; H - 27, teamster, $2^{nd}$, b. Farmington, s/o Lorenzo D. Otis (Farmington, farmer) and Elizabeth Cater (Farmington, housewife); W - 19, lady, b. Farmington, d/o Clarence E. Horne (Farmington, farmer) and Agnes Moore (Natick, MA, shoe stitcher)

Albert M. of Farmington m. Julia **Emerson** of Farmington 10/17/1898; H - 23, farmer, b. Farmington, s/o Lorenzo D. Otis (Farmington, farmer) and Elizabeth F. Otis (Farmington, housewife); W - 14, b. Farmington, d/o Charles Emerson (Farmington, farmer) and Vienna Emerson (Hopkinton, housewife)

Alonzo S. of Farmington m. Carrie M. **Edgerly** of Farmington 10/7/1899 in Rochester; H - 28, shoemaker, b. Farmington, s/o Lorenzo D. Otis (Farmington, farmer) and Elizabeth Otis (Farmington, housewife); W - 30, shoe stitcher, $2^{nd}$, b. Farmington, d/o Ira A. Quint (Bromfield, ME, carpenter) and Annie Quint (Fryeburg, ME, housewife)

Everett E. of Farmington m. Gladys S. **Hall** of Rochester 12/10/1921 in Rochester; H - 19, boxmaker, b. Farmington, s/o George E. Otis (Farmington, farmer) and Naomi Babb (Strafford, housewife); W - 26, dressmaker, $2^{nd}$, b. Rochester, d/o Lester Remick (Milton, shoeworker) and Lotty Jones (E. Rochester, housekeeper)

Everett E. of Dover m. Iva M. **Nichols** of Farmington 9/10/1925; H - 23, painter, $2^{nd}$, b. Farmington, s/o George E. Otis and Naomi Babb (Strafford, housekeeper); W - 21, laundry work, $2^{nd}$, b. Wolfeboro, d/o Albert J. Nichols (Ossipee, laborer) and Cophelia Ash

George E. of Farmington m. Naomia M. **Babb** of Strafford 10/30/1901 in New Durham; H - 29, farmer, b. Farmington, s/o Orin K. Otis (Farmington, farmer) and Sarah A. Garland (Farmington); W - 20, housekeeper, b. Strafford, d/o Joseph D. Babb (Farmington, farmer) and Melvina Ham (Strafford)

Gerald E. of Farmington m. Jeanette E. **Carreau** of Goffstown 12/25/1937 in Chichester; H - 29, undertaker's asst., b. Farmington, s/o Albert J. Otis (Farmington, laborer) and Leora Horne (Alton, housewife); W - 24, housework, b. Canada, d/o Joseph Carreau (Canada, deceased) and Jennie Mongeau (Lowell, MA, housewife)

Levi of Rochester m. Nella M. **Garland** of Farmington 7/25/1907 i Gonic; H - 40, shoemaker, 2$^{nd}$, b. Rochester, d/o John Otis (Strafford, shoemaker) and Mary Howard (Rochester); W - 27 housekeeper, 2$^{nd}$, b. Farmington, d/o George Henderson (Farmington, mill operator) and Lewacsha Downs (Farmingto

Norman L. of Farmington m. Susie R. **Meserve** of Farmington 4/25/1906; H - 22, undertaker, b. Farmington, s/o Lorenzo D. Otis (Farmington, farmer) and Elizabeth A. Cater (Farmington housewife); W - 23, school teacher, b. Danvers, MA, d/o Samuel Y. Meserve (Farmington, shoemaker) and Julia Gilman (housewife)

**PACKER**,

Leroy of Farmington m. Dorothy **Rhodes** of Farmington 4/5/1924; H - 20, shoeworker, b. Haverhill, s/o Frank W. Packer (Taunton, shoeworker) and Florence Presby; W - 19, shoeworker, b. Portsmouth, d/o Nicholas Rhodes (merchant)

**PAGE**,

Charles H. of Farmington m. Mary L. **Wilson** of Farmington 8/27/1896; H - 26, laborer, b. Milton, s/o George Page (laborer and Elizabeth J. Page (Farmington); W - 34, housework, 2$^{nd}$, Sherbrooke, PQ, d/o Lewis Robie (Montreal, PQ) and Mary Robie (Montreal, PQ, housework)

**PAIGE**,

Earl T. of Providence, RI m. Ethel R. **Peck** of Providence, RI 8/17/1931; H - 24, insurance, b. Providence, RI, s/o Clifford D Paige (Worcester, MA, insurance) and Florence Lapham (Valley Falls, RI, housewife); W - 21, clerk, b. Providence, RI, d/o Charles C. Peck (Providence, RI) and Clara B. Roland (Providence, RI)

**PALMER**,

Charles E. of Farmington m. Maude A. **Hackett** of Farmington 2/4/1933 in Rochester; H - 35, carpenter, 2$^{nd}$, b. Gilmanton, s/o George L. Palmer (Dover, farmer) and Daisy M. Smith (Gilmanton, housewife); W - 38, shoeworker, 2$^{nd}$, b. Peabody, MA, d/o John L. Parker (Middletown, MA, deceased) and Martha M. Farley (Essex, MA, housewife)

Charles R. of Farmington m. Jennie E. **Lake** of Pittsfield 8/7/1888 in Barnstead; H - 26, plumber, b. Milford, s/o Rufus W. (Bradford, farmer) and Alma R. (Milford, housekeeper); W - 19, housekeeper, b. Pittsfield, d/o Alonzo (Chichester, deceased) and Betsey (Pittsfield, housekeeper)

Leon L. of Gilmanton m. Earline **Edgerly** of Farmington 10/12/1927; H - 24, farmer, b. Gilmanton, s/o George L. Palmer (Dover, farmer) and Daisy M. Smith (Gilmanton, housework); W - 18, housekeeper, b. Farmington, d/o Earl Edgerly (Farmington, shoeworker) and Ethel M. Drew (Farmington, housework)

**PARENT,**

Conrad O. of Farmington m. Jeanette A. **Desaulniers** of Rochester 10/2/1937 in Rochester; H - 21, truckman, b. Gonic, s/o Edward Parent (Canada, deceased) and Celina Coran (Canada, housework); W - 22, at home, b. Rochester, d/o Joseph Desaulniers (MI, deceased) and Olivene Custeau (Lawrence, MA, housework)

**PARKER,**

Frank S. of Farmington m. Katie M. **Carroll** of White River Jct., VT 5/9/1900 in White River Jct., VT; H - 34, shoe fitter, b. Wolfeboro, s/o Sewall H. Parker (So. Wolfeboro, shoemaker) and Alzina B. Parker (Wolfeboro, housekeeper); W - 31, housekeeper, b. White River Jct., VT, d/o Thomas Carroll (Cork, Ireland, RR laborer) and Mary Carroll (Cork, Ireland, dead)

Harry F. of Farmington m. Alice D. **Marston** of Chichester 10/7/1929 in Chichester; H - 25, clergyman, b. Rochester, s/o Ned L. Parker (Farmington, merchant) and Mary A. Hussey (Farmington, housewife); W - 20, stenographer, b. Chichester, d/o Nathan J. Marston (Chichester, farmer) and Alice Parsons (Harbor Grace, NF, housewife)

John C. of Farmington m. Jennie M. **Mirrless** of Farmington 6/15/1893; H - 29, physician, b. Lebanon, ME, s/o John S. Parker (Lebanon, ME, physician) and Maria M. Parker (Lebanon, ME, housewife); W - 20, lady, b. Providence, RI, d/o John Mirrless (dead) and Martha Mirrless (Scotland, lady)

Ned L. of Farmington m. Mary A. **Hussey** of Farmington 2/19/1896; H - 26, clerk, b. Farmington, s/o Harry S. Parker (Wolfeboro, shoe cutter) and Hester A. Parker; W - 27, school teacher, b. Farmington, d/o James F. Hussey (Farmington, shoe cutter) and Sarah A. Hussey (Dover, housewife)

**PARKHURST,**
Leroy W. of Farmington m. Cecilia G. **Ancoin** of Winchester, MA 6/13/1927 in Winchester, MA; H - 26, shoeworker, b. Stoneham, MA, s/o Frank W. Parkhurst and Isabel Dunn; W - 26, child's nurse, b. St. Andrews, NF, d/o Patrick Ancoin and Lucy Delaney

**PARROCK,**
William R. of Farmington m. Maude **Furber** of Farmington 2/2/1910; H - 28, shoe cutter, b. Cambridge, MA, s/o Russell Lufkin (reg. army) and Helena Parrock (Lancashire, England, housekeeper); W - 18, housekeeper, b. Farmington, d/o George E. Furber (Alton, farmer) and Ada A. Nutter (No. Barnstead, housekeeper)

**PARSHLEY,**
Richmond H. of Rochester m. Bernice L. **Adams** of Farmington 11/23/1924; H - 25, drug clerk, b. Strafford, s/o Charles E. Parshley (Strafford, retired) and Mary E. Jewell (Barrington, housewife); W - 23, teacher, b. Farmington, d/o Frank A. Adams (W. Newbury, MA, shoeworker) and Rachael Leighton (Marblehead, MA, housewife)

**PATTEN,**
Claude B. of Rochester m. Evelyn A. **Gilbert** of Farmington 3/25/1920 in Rochester; H -21, real estate, b. Webster, s/o J. William Patten (Danbury, farmer) and Georgia Powers (Alexandria, housewife); W - 18, at home, b. Milton, d/o Daniel Gilbert (Farmington, shoeworker) and Ida M. Duntley (Milton, housewife)

**PAULSON,**
John A. of Farmington m. Alice M. **Huckins** of Strafford 10/1/1913 in Rochester; H - 38, farmer, b. Sweden, s/o Samuel Paulson (Sweden, cabinet maker) and Carolena Wilson (Sweden, housekeeper); W - 31, housekeeper, b. Strafford, d/o Daniel Huckins (Strafford) and Mercy Yeaton (Strafford)

**PEARL,**

Harold H. of Farmington m. Eva **Parent** of Farmington 7/28/1921; H - 18, shoeworker, b. Farmington, s/o Hervey Pearl (Farmington, painter) and Ina Canney (New Durham, housewife); W - 15, shoeworker, d/o Edward Parent (Canada, laborer) and Celina Caron (Canada, housewife)

Hervey of Farmington m. Ina B. **Canney** of Farmington 12/23/1893 in New Durham; H - 30, painter, b. Farmington, s/o Levi Pearl (Farmington) and Louisa Pearl (Farmington, housewife); W - 25, lady, b. New Durham, d/o Thomas H. Canney (New Durham, farmer) and Belle R. Canney (New Durham, housewife)

Preston A. of Farmington m. Mattie A. **Burrows** of Farmington 3/3/1891; H - 33, coal dealer, $2^{nd}$, b. Farmington, s/o Levi Pearl, Jr. (Farmington, farmer); W - 26, housekeeper, $2^{nd}$, b. NS, d/o William D. Kearney (dead)

**PEARSON[S],**

Edwin L. of Farmington m. Mary J. **Henderson** of Farmington 9/6/1891; H - 20, shoemaker, b. New Durham, s/o Horace B. Pearsons (Alexandria, shoe cutter); W - 26, shoe fitter, b. Farmington, d/o Enoch Henderson (Farmington, dead)

Edwin L. of Farmington m. Nora M. **Grant** of Farmington 5/1/1916; H - 45, shoeworker, $2^{nd}$, b. New Durham, s/o Horace B. Pearson and Lovey J. Gray; W - 26, shoeworker, $2^{nd}$, b. Rochester, d/o Silas H. Dame (Rochester, ice dealer) and Sarah M. McDuffee (Rochester)

**PEAVEY,**

Ernest F. of Farmington m. Pansy E. **Wallace** of Farmington 3/8/1902; H - 43, shoe cutter, $2^{nd}$, divorced, b. Farmington, s/o Anthony Peavey (Farmington, dead) and Elizabeth T. Edgerly (New Durham, dead); W - 19, school teacher, b. Farmington, d/o Albert S. Wallace (Hanover, supt. streets) and Elvira E. Whitehouse (Middleton, housewife)

Ernest F. of Farmington m. Mary E. **Wiggin** of Farmington 7/17/1918; H - 60, shoeworker, $3^{rd}$, b. Farmington, s/o Anthony Peavey (Farmington, solecutter) and Elizabeth Edgerly (New Durham, housekeeper); W - 59, housekeeper, b. Farmington, d/o Lewis R. Wiggin (Moultonboro, merchant) and Delia Decature (New Durham, housekeeper)

Merton L. of Farmington m. Clara **McCombie** of Farmington 7/8/1922 in Rochester; H - 30, shoeworker, b. Farmington, s/o Will L. Peavey and Alice Leavitt (Farmington); W - 31, shoeworker, $2^{nd}$, b. Portsmouth, Leslie Whitehouse (RR)

Paul H. of Farmington m. Edna I. H. **Berry** of Farmington 7/28/1902; H - 56, stone cutter, b. Farmington, s/o John L. Peavey (Farmington, dead) and Emily Furber (Portsmouth, dead); W - 42, teacher, $2^{nd}$, divorced, b. Alton, d/o John I. Huckins (Madbury, farmer) and Abbie W. Whitehouse (Somersworth, dead)

**PELLERIN,**

Jesse L. of Farmington m. Cora E. **Stacy** of Manchester 6/18/1930 in Manchester; H - 27, teacher, b. Hanover, s/o Lewis Pellerin (Lyme, laborer) and Ethel Clark (Andover, MA, housewife); W - 22, teacher, b. Manchester, d/o George M. Stacy (Merrimac, MA, machinist) and Janet O. Muir (Manchester, housewife)

**PELLETIER,**

Louis P. of Farmington m. Marion **Blaisdell** of Farmington 12/29/1934; H - 23, shoeworker, b. Sanford, ME, s/o Samuel Pelletier (Westbrook, ME, merchant) and Caroline Parrell (Cape Ball, NB, at home); W - 19, shoeworker, b. Derry, d/o John Blaisdell (Lebanon, ME, garage man) and Bertha Cate (Newmarket, housewife)

Rene R. of Farmington m. Mary A. **Kaltsas** of Farmington 6/11/1938; H - 24, shoeworker, b. Springvale, ME, s/o Samuel Pelletier (Westbrook, ME, merchant) and Caroline Parell (Acadia, NB, housewife); W - 21, shoeworker, b. Manchester, d/o Charles Kaltsas (Greece, shoeworker) and Mariana Lavigne (Manchester, shoeworker)

**PENCE,**

David of Springvale, ME m. Mattie **Thompson** of Springvale, ME 8/5/1922; H - 18, shoeworker, b. NB, s/o Alfred Pence (Cutler, ME, mill operative) and Julia Plant (NB, at home); W - 21, shoeworker, $2^{nd}$, b. Brookfield, MA, d/o Milton Towle (Canada, RR man) and Mary L. Ouellette (NS, at home)

Horace of Farmington m. Bertha **Stanley** of Farmington 1/16/1910; H - 21, shoemaker, b. Farmington, s/o John Pence (Cutler, ME, sailor) and Lizzie Maher (Lubec, ME); W - 18, shoeworker, b. Farmington, d/o R. Stanley (Porter, ME) and Ida Bisbee (Ossipee)

**PERCIVAL,**
Roy S. of Farmington m. Blanche E. **Noyes** of Farmington 6/20/1903 in Alton; H - 26, RR fireman, b. Farmington, s/o John W. Percival (Cleveland, OH, plumber) and Sadie F. Peavey (Farmington, housewife); W - 26, school teacher, b. Ashland, MA, d/o Charles F. Noyes (Oakham, MA, shoemaker) and Alice E. Nelson (Southam, MA, heelmaker)

**PERKINS,**
Adam G. of Farmington m. Dorothy M. **Arnold** of Farmington 5/4/1934 in West Milton; H - 24, shoeworker, b. Milton, s/o Harry O. Perkins (Dover, laborer) and Lena LaBonta (Middleton, housewife); W - 18, shoeworker, b. Farmington, d/o Samuel V. Arnold (Brockton, MA, shoeworker) and Sarah Godfrey (PEI, housewife)

Alton M. of Farmington m. Myrtie M. **Lucas** of Farmington 6/12/1901; H - 20, cutter, b. Brookfield, s/o Charles M. Perkins (Middleton, shoemaker) and Sarah A. Abbott (No. Berwick, ME); W - 17, housekeeper, b. Farmington, d/o Freeman D. Lucas (New Durham, farmer) and Emma Whitehouse (Gonic)

Alton M. of Farmington m. Edwina C. **Hurd** of Acton, ME 5/22/1916 in Milton Mills; H - 35, shoeworker, 2$^{nd}$, b. Brookfield, s/o Charles M. Perkins (Middleton, cobbler) and Sarah A. Abbott (N. Berwick, ME, housekeeper); W - 19, housekeeper, b. Milton Mills, d/o Frank J. Hurd (Acton, ME, carpenter) and Cora Hurd (Acton, ME, housekeeper)

Arthur L. of Farmington m. Eleanor **Wells** of Melrose Highlands 6/18/1914 in Melrose, MA; H - 26, merchant, b. Berwick, ME, s/o George W. Perkins (No. Berwick, ME, cashier) and Bertha Whitten (No. Berwick, ME, housewife); W - 25, lady, d/o George F. Wells (Haydenville, MA, salesman) and Lucy Baker (Wellfleet, MA, housewife)

Charlie of Farmington m. Mary **Austin** of Farmington 10/21/1933; H - 28, laborer, 2$^{nd}$, b. Meredith, s/o George Perkins (Meredith, deceased) and Annie Clark (Oak Hill, deceased); W - 19, laborer, b. Canaan, d/o Roy E. Austin (Canaan, deceased) and Ella Kimball (Boston, MA, housewife)

Daniel M. of New Durham m. Olive B. **Weeks** of Farmington 6/11/1905 in New Durham; H - 43, farmer, 2$^{nd}$, b. Alton, s/o John M. Perkins (Alton, farmer) and Asenath M. Lang (Brookfield); W - 47, housekeeper, 2$^{nd}$, b. VT, d/o Joseph Brackett (VT, farmer) and Olive Disbump

George H. of Farmington m. Thirza B. **Elliott** of Farmington 5/27/1938 in Milton; H - 21, shoeworker, b. Milton Mills, s/o Lester Perkins (Wolfeboro, shoeworker) and Lizzie Lord (Acton, ME, deceased); W - 22, shoeworker, b. Wolfeboro, d/ Henry Elliott (Rumney, deceased) and Lizzie Elliott (Grafton, housewife)

George L. of Farmington m. Mamie B. **Roberts** of Rochester 11/27/1895 in Rochester; H - 23, clerk, b. Farmington, s/o Luther H. Perkins (Farmington, clerk) and Jennie L. Perkins (New Durham); W - 25, school teacher, b. Rochester, d/o Henry K. Roberts (Rochester, farmer) and Ellen A. Roberts (Dover)

Harold of Farmington m. Dorothy **Lynch** of Dover 2/10/1934 in Dover; H - 27, shoeworker, b. Ossipee, s/o Lydia Perkins (Bartlett, housewife); W - 21, shoeworker, b. Brunswick, ME, d/o Andrew Lynch (Lawrence, MA, invalid) and Celia Cloutier (Newburyport, MA, housewife)

James N. of Farmington m. Olie E. **Cater** of Farmington 6/11/1894 H - 23, clerk, b. Middleton, s/o Cyrus B. Perkins (New Durham shoemaker) and Mary A. Perkins (Wolfeboro, housewife); W - 18, b. Strafford, d/o Willis H. Cater (Strafford, shoemaker) and Annie M. Cater (Rochester, dressmaker)

John T. of Farmington m. Lizzie B. **Hanscam** of Rochester 10/3/1894; H - 45, shoecutter, 2$^{nd}$, widower, b. Milton, s/o Asa Perkins (Wolfeboro) and Eliza F. Perkins (Wolfeboro, housekeeping); W - 37, b. Lebanon, d/o Aaron H. Hanscom (North Berwick, ME) and Susan Hanscom (Lebanon, ME, housekeeping)

Lester A. of Farmington m. Blanche S. **Cook** of Farmington 9/10/1938 in W. Milton; H - 42, shoeworker, 2$^{nd}$, b. Wolfeboro, s/o Charles Perkins (Middleton, retired) and Mary J. Pipper (Ossipee, at home); W - 34, shoeworker, b. Ossipee, d/o ----- (deceased)

Llewellyn C. of Farmington m. Mary A. **Finigan** of Haverhill, MA 8/7/1900; H - 24, shoemaker, b. No. Berwick, ME, s/o Charles M. Perkins (Middleton, shoemaker) and Sarah A. Abbott (No.

Berwick, housekeeper); W - 22, waitress, b. Ireland, d/o James Finigan (Ireland, farmer) and Nellie Rattery (Ireland, housekeeper)

Luther E. of Farmington m. Rosetta **Varney** of Farmington 10/21/1922; H - 26, shoeworker, b. Farmington, s/o Luther Perkins (Farmington, carpenter) and Teresa MacDonald (PEI, shoeworker); W - 25, bookkeeper, 2nd, b. Farmington, d/o Fred S. Varney (Farmington, shoeworker) and Angie Corson (Barrington, housewife)

Malcolm R. of Farmington m. Marion Leslie **Chesley** of Farmington 2/28/1912; H - 22, carpenter, b. Farmington, s/o Luther H. Perkins (Milton, carpenter) and Teresa MacDonald (PEI, shoemaker); W - 22, shoemaker, b. Farmington, d/o George L. Chesley (Wolfeboro, engineer) and Joanna Stevens (Thomasville, GA, housekeeper)

**PHILLIPS,**
Wendell of Farmington m. Julia A. **Burke** of Farmington 7/4/1892; H - 27, engineer, b. MA; W - 22, shoe stitcher, b. Wolfeboro, d/o ----- (dead) and Mary J. Burke (53, lady) of Alton

**PIERCE,**
Walter Henry of Farmington m. Corabell **Pierson** of Laconia 4/18/1894 in Laconia; H - 24, dentist, 2nd, widower, b. Pittsfield, s/o George H. Pierce (Barnstead, dead) and Arimenti B. Nutter (Lower Gilmanton, housewife); W - 26, b. Pierrepont, NY, d/o Harlow Pierson (Pierrepont, NY, carpenter) and Helen Pierson (Watertown, NY, housewife)

**PIERCY,**
Alexander D. of Rochester m. Emily **Walker** of So. Berwick 7/8/1887; H - 28, shoemaker, b. Rochester, s/o Andrew Piercy (Scotland, carder) and Irving Piercy; W - 19, stitcher, b. So. Berwick, d/o ----- (England, RR conductor)

**PIKE,**
Edgar E. of Calais, ME m. Maud E. **Kenney** of Farmington 2/10/1897; H - 21, shoe cutter, b. St. Stephens, s/o Joseph A. Pike (St. Stephens, NB, mechanic) and Nettie Pike (St. Stephens, NB, housekeeper); W - 17, housework, b. Lebanon,

ME, d/o George Kenney (shoemaker) and Lula Remick (Farmington, housekeeper)

Harry of Farmington m. Florence G. **Dodge** of Farmington 6/25/1922 in Rochester; H - 28, shoeworker, b. Farmington, s/o Harris Pike (St. Stephens, NB, engineer) and Mary Bishop (Edmondston, NB, housewife); W - 20, shoeworker, b. Farmington, d/o Herbert Dodge and Alice Garland (Rochester, housekeeper)

Herman J. of Farmington m. Amanda E. **Churchill** of Farmington 12/23/1903; H - 36, shoemaker, b. Sandwich, s/o Jacob H. Pike (Middleton, retired) and Louisa Thompson (Sandwich); W - 29, housekeeper, 2$^{nd}$, b. Middleton, d/o William B. Place (Middleton, shoemaker) and Lydia A. Whitehouse (Middleton)

Irving F. of Farmington m. Agnes M. **Rhines** of Farmington 7/8/1905; H - 24, shoemaker, b. Farmington, s/o Edward E. Pike (Middleton, shoemaker) and Etta M. Pearl (Rochester); W - 24, shoe worker, b. Farmington, d/o Irving C. Rhines (New Durham, farmer) and Angie Brown (Limerick, ME)

John E. of Farmington m. E. Ellen **Cloutman** of Farmington 6/19/1907; H - 23, shoeworker, b. Farmington, s/o Edwin E. Pike (Milton, shoeworker) and Etta M. Pearl (Rochester); W - 27, bookkeeper, b. Farmington, d/o James A. Cloutman (New Durham) and Myra Rollins (Rollinsford)

John W. of Farmington m. Eva B. **Thurston** of Effingham 12/24/1890 in Wakefield

Randolph K. of Laconia m. Beatrice G. **Towle** of Farmington 5/11/1929; H - 28, contractor, 2$^{nd}$, b. Manchester, s/o Milo L. Pike (New Hampton, contractor) and Sadie Kelley (New Hampton, housewife); W - 22, shoeworker, b. Berwick, ME, d/o Tristram F. Towle (New Durham, painter) and Kate Earner (Ireland, housewife)

Raymond of Farmington m. Margaret **Stanhope** of Farmington 11/8/1933 in Rochester; H - 27, shoeworker, 2$^{nd}$, b. Wakefield, s/o David Pike (Middleton, deceased) and May Miller (Lawrence, MA, housewife); W - 18, shoeworker, b. Milton, d/o Otis Stanhope (Lebanon, ME, shoeworker) and Hattie Coran (Athol, MA, housewife)

Sumner E. of Farmington m. Edith C. **Cameron** of Farmington 4/29/1922; H - 33, shoeworker, 2$^{nd}$, b. Rochester, s/o Elmer E. Pike (Middleton, shoeworker) and Susan Wallingford; W - 21, shoeworker, b. Hoboken, NJ, d/o John B. Cameron (England, farmer) and Hilda Cameron (England, housewife)

**PINKHAM,**
Charles H. of Farmington m. Ellen **Ham** of Strafford 12/25/1905 in Strafford Corners; H - 34, farmer, 2nd, s/o Edward Pinkham (lumberman) and Mary A. Hussey (Rochester); W - 47, housekeeper, 2nd, b. Barnstead, d/o Paul J. Canney (Madbury, farmer) and Eliza Hanson (Barnstead)

Clifton S. of Farmington m. Mary **Anderson** of N. Conway 7/27/1907; H - 20, shoe cutter, b. Farmington, s/o Fred Pinkham (Farmington, farmer) and Flora Richards (Farmington, shoe stitcher); W - 21, shoe worker, b. N. Conway, d/o George Anderson (N. Conway, lumberman) and Mary Miller (N. Conway)

Clifton S. of Farmington m. Emily C. **Duplessis** of Farmington 6/26/1915; H - 28, shoecutter, 2nd, b. Pittsfield, s/o Fred Pinkham (Farmington, laborer) and Flora Richards (Farmington, shoeworker); W - 24, waitress, 2nd, b. Montpelier, VT, d/o Francis Duplessis (Meriden, VT) and Mary Buckner

Fred of Alton m. Eva M. **Rollins** of Farmington 11/18/1920; H - 55, painter, 2nd, b. Farmington, s/o John W. Pinkham (New Durham, farmer) and Eliza Pinkham (New Durham, housewife); W - 44, shoeworker, 2nd, b. Farmington, d/o Stephen W. Berry (ME, farmer) and Hannah J. Edgerly (Middleton, housewife)

Seth H. of Farmington m. Nellie M. **Davis** of Farmington 12/10/1887; H - 22, shoemaker, b. Alton, s/o Andrew J. Pinkham (shoemaker) and Abbie Pinkham; W - 17, shoestitcher, b. Northwood, d/o Fred. A. Davis and Abbie Davis

**PIPER,**
Lloyd L. of Portland, ME m. Vera S. **Wing** of Portland, ME 8/2/1933; H - 23, soldier, b. Meredith, s/o Oscar Piper (Meredith Center, merchant) and Grace Bartlett (Tuftonboro, housewife); W - 25, housekeeper, 2nd, b. Great Works, ME, d/o Harry Smart (Bangor, ME, deceased) and Maude Duplissa (Orono, ME, housewife)

**PLACE,**

Dean A. of Farmington m. Lena **Batchelder** of Farmington 12/30/1911 in Springvale, ME; H - 20, shoemaker, b. Middleton, s/o William Place (Middleton, shoemaker) and Lydia Whitehouse (Middleton); W - 22, shoemaker, d/o George A. Batchelder (Shapleigh, ME, machinist) and Sarah Fernald (Shapleigh, ME, housekeeper)

Norman W. of Farmington m. Alma P. **Hill** of Farmington 7/1/1933 H - 22, shoeworker, b. Wakefield, s/o Percy Place (Farmington, shoeworker) and Frena Lover (Wakefield, deceased); W - 18, at home, b. Northwood, d/o Howard Parsons (Lynn, MA) and Ethel Richardson (Northwood, shoeworker)

Percy of Farmington m. Esther B. **Dore** of Farmington 11/8/1930 in Rochester; H - 46, shoeworker, $2^{nd}$, b. Farmington, s/o William Place and Lydia Whitehouse; W - 21, shoeworker, b. Farmington, d/o Ernest Dore (Milton, shoeworker) and Inez Clough (Rochester)

Ulysses I. of Farmington m. Flora R. G. **Carter** of Farmington 7/7/1906; H - 38, liquor dealer, b. Middleton, s/o William B. Place (Middleton, shoemaker) and Carrie A. Whitehouse (Middleton); W - 30, housekeeper, b. E. Hampton, MA, d/o Sheldon H. Gifford (Bridgewater, CT, farmer) and Lydia Elliott (E. Hampton, MA)

**PLAGMAN,**

George E. of S. Effingham m. Iva B. **Grace** of Farmington 3/1/1917 in Rochester; H - 55, steamfitter, $2^{nd}$, b. Boston, MA, s/o Henry Plagman (Boston, MA, wheelwright) and Mary E. Durgin (Boston, MA, housekeeper); W - 40, school teacher, $2^{nd}$, b. Farmington, d/o Benjamin Grace and Adeline Frost (Middleton housekeeper)

**PLUFF,**

William J. of Derry m. Arthana **Garland** of Farmington 9/11/1917; H - 21, shoeworker, b. Lewiston, MA, s/o Frank Pluff and Selina Howard (Lewiston, ME, housekeeper); W - 17, shoeworker, b. Alton, d/o Eli Garland and Fannie Garland (shoeworker)

**POLLARD,**
Richard of Farmington m. Mary B. **Blaisdell** of Farmington 4/2/1920; H - 32, shoeworker, 2nd, b. Millis, MA, s/o Harry Pollard (England, farmer) and Elizabeth Barrett (England, housewife); W - 26, shoeworker, 2nd, b. Waterboro, ME, d/o Fred C. Bickford (Parsonsfield, ME) and Maria E. Osborne (Stowe, ME, shoeworker)

**PORTER,**
Wallace N. of Farmington m. Minnie W. **Towns** of Brockton, MA 12/13/1890 in Rochester; H - 25, salesman, b. Bridgewater, MA, s/o Cephas A. Porter (Bridgewater, MA, farmer) and Betsey J. (Bridgewater, MA); W - 19, housekeeper, b. Plymouth, MA, d/o Charles B. Towns (pedler) and Abbie

**POTTER,**
Marshall W. of Springfield, MA m. Alice **Abbott** of Springfield, MA 8/25/1928; H - 27, machinist, b. Springfield, MA, s/o Marshall W. Potter (Montague, MA, retired) and Mary Cone; W - 26, teacher, b. Worcester, MA, d/o Daniel Abbott (Ossipee, retired) and Hannah Dand (Marlboro, MA, housewife)

**PRATT,**
Lester A. of Pittsburgh, PA m. Ardena B. **Perkins** of Farmington 8/2/1914; H - 28, chemist, b. Manchester, s/o Albert G. Pratt (Manchester, postal clerk) and Augusta Goldthwaite (Stoneham, MA, housewife); W - 27, teacher, b. Farmington, d/o Benjamin F. Perkins (Strafford Centre, undertaker) and Lucy Stiles (Strafford Center, housewife)

**PRESCOTT,**
Roscoe D. of Alton m. Florence P. **Tebbetts** of Farmington 3/24/1917; H - 19, clerk, b. Alton, s/o George R. Prescott (Alton, carpenter) and Lillian M. Jones (Alton, housewife); W - 22, shoeworker, b. New Durham, d/o Albinus P. Tebbetts (New Durham, farmer) and Mary F. Amazeen (Milton, housewife)
Roscoe D. of Farmington m. Emma **Marchand** of Rochester 12/18/1938 in Wolfeboro; H - 40, shoeworker, 2nd, b. Alton, s/o George Prescott (Alton, carpenter) and Lillian Jones (Alton, deceased); W - 42, laundress, 2nd, b. Dover, d/o Frank

Morrison (Dunbarton, laundry) and Mary Wingate (Somersworth, housewife)

**PRESTON,**

James D. of Farmington m. Nettie **DeWitt** of Snowville 1/4/1908; - 24, shoemaker, b. Muskegon, MI, s/o James F. Preston (Three Rivers, Canada, mill hand) and Elizabeth Ash (Three Rivers, Canada); W - 21, housekeeper, b. Snowville, d/o Jerome DeWitt (farmer) and Ella Stuart (Freedom)

Kenneth H. of Rochester m. Priscilla **Littlefield** of Farmington 1/22/1938 in E. Rochester; H - 28, mill operative, b. E. Rochester, s/o Herbert Preston (Barrington, shoeworker) and Gertrude Jacobs (E. Rochester, housewife); W - 24, housekeeper, b. Alfred, ME, d/o Charles Littlefield (Alfred, ME deceased) and Ida Maxfield (Alfred, ME, deceased)

**PRICE,**

Osborne W. of Farmington m. S. Evannah **Stiles** of Strafford 12/25/1888 in Strafford; H - 27, clerk, b. Gilmanton, s/o Amos R. (farmer) and Sarah C. (Gilmanton, housekeeper); W - 26, teacher, b. Strafford, d/o Joseph (Strafford, farmer) and Hannah (Strafford, housekeeper)

**PRIDE,**

Henry W. of Farmington m. Rosalie **Henaff** of Montreal, Canada 4/30/1895 in Laconia; H - 36, stonecutter, b. Portland, ME, s/o Joshua T. Pride (Westbrook, stonecutter) and Mary J. Pride (Windham); W - 19, b. NS, d/o Frank L. Henaff (France, foreman) and Fanny E. Henaff (housewife)

James H. of Westbrook, ME m. Isadore **Tibbetts** of Farmington 2/15/1892; H - 22, granite cutter, b. Westbrook, ME, s/o William Pride (granite cutter, 62, Westbrook, ME) of Westbrook, ME; W - 19, shoe worker, b. Milton, d/o Eri Tibbetts (dead) and Eliza B. Tibbetts (housekeeper) of Milton

Joshua T. of Farmington m. Lucy J. **Smith** of Farmington 8/30/1890; H - 60, stone worker, $2^{nd}$, b. Westbrook, ME, s/o Alexander Pride (dead) and June; W - 45, housekeeper, $3^{rd}$, b. New Durham, d/o James Fletcher (Pelham, physician)

**PROCTOR,**
Nathan L. of Farmington m. Josephine A. **Jenness** of Barnstead 4/18/1891; H - 58, shoe cutter, $2^{nd}$, b. Charlestown, MA, s/o Nathan Proctor (Chelmsford, MA, farmer); W - 53, tailoress, $2^{nd}$, b. Portsmouth, d/o William Nutter (Barnstead, farmer)

Nathan L. of Farmington m. Katherine L. **Straw** of Farmington 3/20/1897; H - 60, shoe cutter, $3^{rd}$, b. Charlestown, s/o Nathan Proctor (Chelmsford, MA) and Nancy Proctor (Strafford); W - 44, dressmaker, $2^{nd}$, b. Westfield, MA, d/o William Rogers (Welk, England, clergyman) and Katherine Rogers (Bath, England)

**PROKAPIAN,**
John of Farmington m. Alexandra **Kehaidry** of Manchester 6/16/1935 in Somersworth; H - 44, merchant, $2^{nd}$, b. Greece, s/o Prok'sis Prokapian (Greece, retired) and Eleny Tsonas (Greece, at home); W - 37, merchant, $2^{nd}$, b. Greece, d/o And'a Kalumbucas (Greece, deceased)

**PULSIFER,**
Harry H. of Farmington m. Bernice **Batchelder** of Farmington 5/25/1909 in Farmington; H - 31, hack driver, b. Rochester, s/o Charles H. Pulsifer (Minot, ME, farmer) and Harriett E. Pinkham (Durham, housekeeper); W - 20, school girl, b. Farmington, d/o Ed K. Batchelder (clerk) and Inez Hussey (Rochester, housekeeper)

John L. of Farmington m. Ruby **Avery** of Farmington 7/25/1908 in Milton; H - 25, shoemaker, b. Milton, s/o Charles Pulsifer (Minot, ME, farmer) and Harriett E. Pinkham (Durham); W - 19, shoemaker, b. Farmington, d/o Frank L. Avery (Barnstead, janitor) and Sarah S. Berry (Strafford)

John L. of Farmington m. Rachael **Stanhope** of Farmington 2/27/1926 in Rochester; H - 43, shoeworker, $2^{nd}$, b. Milton, s/o Charles Pulsifer and Harriett Pinkham; W - 24, domestic, b. Edmonds, ME, d/o Lincoln Stanhope (lumberman) and Etta Hayward (housewife)

Walter H. of Farmington m. Helen **Lovering** of Farmington 1/1/1898; H - 30, clerk, b. Durham, s/o Charles H. Pulsifer (Minot, ME, farmer) and Harriet Pulsifer (Durham); W - 18, b. Farmington, d/o Frank H. Lovering (Tuftonboro, merchant) and Etta H. Lovering (Farmington, housewife)

**PUTNAM,**

Bernard C. of Peru, ME m. Myrtie L. **Dixon** of Farmington 4/19/1902; H - 21, farmer, b. Peru, ME, s/o Lewis C. Putnam (Franklin Plt., dead) and Ida Bisbee (Franklin Plt., housewife); W - 22, housekeeper, b. Farmington, d/o William Dixon (Eliot, ME, carpenter) and Josephine Leighton (Farmington, housewife)

**QUINT,**

Everett of Dover m. Mary E. **Derwin** of Farmington 12/15/1933 in Rochester; H - 51, farmer, $2^{nd}$, b. Sanford, ME, s/o William Quint (North Berwick, ME, retired) and Hattie Caston (deceased); W - 29, housewife, b. Ireland, d/o ----- (Ireland, deceased)

Nicholas I. of Farmington m. Nina G. **Favor** of Concord 10/4/1899 in Concord; H - 25, merchant, b. Strafford, s/o Daniel I. Quint and Rosa E. Quint; W - 27, bookkeeper, b. Bristol, d/o Moses W. Favor (Concord, engineer) and Mary G. Favor (Concord, housewife)

**RAAB,**

Adolph, Jr. of Farmington m. Marion **Blaisdell** of Farmington 3/10/1934; H - 21, laborer, b. Des Moines, IA, s/o Adolph Raab (Germany, farmer) and Marie Kopp (Des Moines, IA, at home); W - 18, at home, b. Farmington, d/o Ernest Blaisdell (Farmington, shoeworker) and Mary Bickford (Waterbury, ME, shoeworker)

Dwight of Farmington m. Helen **Laflamme** of Gonic 11/30/1933 in Gonic; H - 22, carpenter, b. Des Moines, IA, s/o Adolph Raab (Germany, carpenter) and Marie Kopp (Des Moines, IA, housewife); W - 25, mill operative, b. Gonic, d/o Adelard Laflamme (Canada, deceased) and Addie Bussiere (Gonic, housewife)

**RAMSEY,**

Lawrence of Milton m. Ruth E. **Stevens** of Farmington 6/4/1938 in Ogunquit, ME; H - 24, mill operator, b. Thompson, CT, s/o Frank Ramsey (Somersworth, farmer) and Sophie Smith (Schuyler, NE, housewife); W - 19, waitress, b. Nottingham, d/o Carl Stevens (Rochester, merchant) and Emma Hartford (Rochester, mill operative)

**RAND,**

David E. of Farmington m. Annie Belle **Sprague** of Farmington 1/2/1913; H - 44, cobbler, 2$^{nd}$, b. Randolph, s/o S. B. Rand (N. Gloucester, ME, axe handle mkr.) and Caroline Leighton (Randolph); W - 46, housekeeper, 2$^{nd}$, b. MN, d/o Alphonse James and Lucy Fogg

Ernest W. of Farmington m. Grace G. **Ham** of Farmington 7/19/1919 in Rochester; H - 23, shoeworker, b. Milton, s/o George W. Rand (Cambridge, MA, fireman) and Ida E. Moore (Milton, housekeeper); W - 25, shoeworker, b. Farmington, d/o Irving L. Ham (Farmington, shoeworker) and Carrie E. Wentworth (Farmington, housekeeper)

Raymond of Farmington m. Lucy M. **Works** of Farmington 7/22/1916; H - 28, shoeworker, b. Alton, s/o John Rand (Alton) and Dora J. Green (Old Town, ME); W - 29, shoeworker, b. Lebanon, ME, d/o James Works (blacksmith) and Mary Works (Berwick, ME, housekeeper)

**RANDALL,**

George F. of E. Rochester m. Esther **Charles** of Farmington 6/18/1930 in E. Rochester; H - 25, mason, b. Lebanon, ME, s/o William E. Randall (Rochester, teamster) and Rhoda M. Willey (Rochester, housekeeper); W - 21, housekeeper, b. Bridgton, ME, d/o Will Charles (Chatham, laborer) and Minnie Gilpatrick (Cornish, ME, shoeworker)

Walter L. of Farmington m. Nellie S. **Perkins** of Farmington 9/25/1896 in Alton; H - 25, shoemaker, b. Farmington, s/o Alexander T. Randall (Bolton, Canada, shoemaker) and Ardelia R. Randall (Milton, housewife); W - 27, shoe fitter, b. Middleton, d/o Cyrus B. Perkins (Middleton, farmer) and Mary Perkins (Wolfeboro, housewife)

Willie I. of Farmington m. Ella F. **Trafton** of Farmington 12/5/1906; H - 42, shoe worker, b. New Durham, s/o George W. Randall (Rochester, shoemaker) and Deborah E. Towle (Wolfeboro); W - 37, shoe worker, b. Somersworth, d/o Mark F. Trafton (Bangor, ME, engineer) and Amanda Goodwin (Lebanon, ME)

**REED,**

Edward J. of Sanford, ME m. Thelma L. **Whiting** of Sanford, ME 12/22/1934 in Wells, ME; H - 21, lumberman, b. Sanford, ME, s/o Arthur Philpot (Emery Mills, ME, deceased) and Idella

Reed, Sanford, ME, at home); W - 19, mill hand, b. Sanford, ME, d/o Herbert Whiting (Hartford, CT, musician) and Joseph Bradshaw (St. Johns, NB, at home)

**REEVES,**
Earle D. of Farmington m. Mary E. **Brannan** of E. Boston, MA 4/2/1931 in Rochester; H - 35, shoeworker, b. PEI, s/o David Reeves (PEI, engineer) and Mattie Barnes; W - 32, nurse, b. E. Boston, MA, d/o James Brannan (NS, barber) and Catherin Lynch (NS, housewife)

Howard V. of Farmington m. Eva G. **Dodge** of Farmington 12/30/1911; H - 22, shoemaker, b. PEI, s/o David Reeves (St. Johns, NB, liveryman) and Madeline Burns (PEI, housekeeper); W - 18, shoe stitcher, b. Barrington, d/o Frank S. Dodge (Alton, lumberman) and Rosilla Dodge (Rochester, housekeeper)

**REGIS,**
John D. of Farmington m. Bessie **Haddock** of Farmington 8/25/1914; H - 20, shoeworker, b. Nashua, s/o Joseph Regis (Canada, shoeworker) and Josephine Gaudet (Nashua, housekeeper); W - 23, lady, $2^{nd}$, b. Farmington, d/o Howard Haddock (Haverhill, MA, shoeworker) and Luella Tibbetts (Middleton, housekeeper)

**REID,**
Philip of Fairfield, ME m. Mabel **Stanley** of Farmington 6/24/1916; H - 23, shoeworker, b. Bersville, NB, s/o John Reid (Bersville, NB, truckman) and Louise Pyne (Main River, NB, housewife); W - 16, housework, b. Hampton, d/o Samuel Stanley (Seal Cove, ME, jobbing) and Elvira E. Oakes (Holden, ME, shoeworker)

**REMICK,**
Charles E. of Farmington m. Hattie M. **Hill** of Farmington 9/16/1917; H - 60, shoeworker, $2^{nd}$, b. Milton, s/o Moses Remick and Clara Wentworth; W - 32, housekeeper, $2^{nd}$, b. Farmington, d/o Samuel W. Kimball (Middleton, shoeworker) and Addie R. Young

Clayton S. of Farmington m. Elva P. **Holland** of Farmington 9/25/1926 in Rochester; H - 23, shoeworker, b. Springvale,

ME, s/o Nathaniel Remick (clerk) and Mary E. Sprague (Grafton, MA, housewife); W - 20, bookkeeper, b. W. Pembroke, ME, d/o John Holland (Pembroke, ME, laborer) and ----- (W. Pembroke, ME)

Edgar of Milton m. Beatrice P. **Morgan** of Farmington 3/9/1912; H - 18, shoemaker, b. Milton, s/o C. E. Remick (Milton, farmer) and Lula Wentworth (Farmington, housekeeper); W - 16, lady, b. Wolfeboro, d/o Melvin Morgan (Wolfeboro, stone mason) and Lois Durgin (Conway)

Fred W. of Farmington m. Ruth B. **Towle** of Farmington 11/20/1915 in Dover; H - 22, shoeworker, b. Lebanon, ME, s/o Charles E. Remick (Milton, farmer) and Lulah Wentworth (Farmington, shoeworker); W - 21, shoeworker, b. Farmington, d/o Tristram Towle (New Durham, painter) and Katherine Earner (Ireland, housekeeper)

George P. of Farmington m. Ethel M. **Ellis** of Milton 4/18/1917 in Milton; H - 24, shoeworker, b. Grafton, MA, s/o Nathaniel P. Remick (Sutton, MA, shoeworker) and Mary E. Sprague (Grafton, MA, housewife); W - 16, shoeworker, b. Milton, d/o George E. Ellis (Wolfeboro, shoeworker) and Gertrude I. Duntley (Milton, housewife)

Joseph F. of Farmington m. Vianna F. **Varney** of Farmington 6/20/1914; H - 21, shoeworker, b. Worcester, MA, s/o N. P. Remick (Sutton, MA, shoeworker) and Mary E. Sprague (Grafton, MA, housekeeper); W - 16, housekeeper, b. Farmington, d/o Fred Varney (Farmington, shoeworker) and Angeline Corson (Barrington, housekeeper)

**REYNOLDS,**

Elmer S. of Alton m. Gertrude M. **Patch** of Farmington 3/20/1917 in Bellows Falls, VT; H - 45, teamster, b. New Durham, s/o Jonas Reynolds (New Durham) and Caroline Crockett (Boston, MA); W - 38, 2nd, b. Gilmanton, d/o Frank Clark (Manchester) and Fanny Smith (Alton)

George D. of Farmington m. Frances **Perkins** of Farmington 8/12/1922 in Dover; H - 23, shoeworker, b. Lynn, MA, s/o Edward Reynolds (Danvers, MA, shoeworker) and Ella Hackett (housewife); W - 17, shoeworker, b. Farmington, d/o Llewellyn Perkins (Berwick, ME, horse dealer) and Mary ----- (Guam, Ireland, housekeeper)

**RHINES,**

Carl W. of Farmington m. Marjorie D. **Hayes** of Rochester 7/9/193 in Rochester; H - 29, merchant, b. New Durham, s/o Herman Rhines (New Durham, woodturner) and Lucy Dow (Bristol, at home); W - 38, beauty parlor, 2$^{nd}$, b. Milton Mills, d/o William Mickel (Milton Mills, shoeworker) and Clara Crugan (Union, at home)

Irving C. of Farmington m. Lydia A. **Hall** of Farmington 7/5/1906 in Alton Bay; H - 47, shoemaker, 2$^{nd}$, widower, b. New Durham, s/o Alvah C. Rhines (New Durham, farmer) and Lydia L. French (Alton); W - 56, housekeeper, 2$^{nd}$, widow, b. Farmington, d/o Hiram Canney (Farmington, farmer)

Willie E. of Farmington m. Belle G. **Ayer** of Farmington 6/28/1934 in Rochester; H - 64, trucking, 2$^{nd}$, b. New Durham, s/o Alvah H. Rhines (New Durham, deceased) and Lydia French (New Durham, deceased); W - 56, housekeeper, 2$^{nd}$, b. New Durham, d/o Russ Wallace (Middleton, shoeworker) and Rilla B. McKeen (Lebanon, ME, shoeworker)

**RHODES,**

Ethard A. of Raymond m. Bernice L. **Willard** of Farmington 3/31/1938; H - 38, shoeworker, 2$^{nd}$, b. Omaha, NE, s/o Clyde Rhodes (IN, deceased) and Jennie Blair (IN, housewife); W - 27, shoeworker, 2$^{nd}$, b. Beverly, MA, d/o John Christy (Beverly, MA, shoeworker) and Mildred Fielder (Beverly, MA, shoeworker)

**RICHARDS,**

Ernest W. of Haverhill, MA m. Pauline E. **Wason** of Haverhill, MA 8/4/1920; H - 28, shoecutter, 2$^{nd}$, b. Farmington, s/o Cylus F. Richards and Jennie M. Ford (Effingham Center, housewife); W - 25, bookkeeper, 2$^{nd}$, b. Bradford, MA, d/o Newman W. Watson (Haverhill, MA, shoecutter) and Teresa Driscoll (South Wales, housewife)

Ralph P. of Salem, MA m. Ella M. **Sabeau** of Salem, MA 12/20/1926; H - 32, manager, 2$^{nd}$, b. Farmington, s/o Silas F. Richards and Melissa Ford (Effingham, nurse); W - 28, at home, b. NS, d/o Boyd A. Sabeau (NS, claim adjuster) and Priscilla Dillihand (NS, housewife)

**RICHARDSON,**
Charles F. of Farmington m. Annie M. **Hayes** of Farmington 9/26/1912 in Dover; H - 35, shoeworker, 2nd, b. Melvin Village, s/o Fred Richardson (Tuftonboro, carpenter) and Eliza Bickford (Eastport, ME); W - 24, shoeworker, 2nd, b. Cambridge, MA, d/o Charles J. Norman (S. Berwick, ME, farmer) and Mary L. Nichols (housekeeper)

Ernest A. of Farmington m. Marion **Thompson** of Farmington 4/11/1914; H - 20, boxmaker, b. Northwood, s/o Bert Richardson (Northwood, farmer) and Alice Garland (Farmington, housekeeper); W - 16, at home, b. Farmington, d/o Hervey Thompson (New Durham, farmer) and Florence Foss (Rochester, housekeeper)

Leon A. of Farmington m. M. Elizabeth **Joyal** of Somersworth 9/4/1937 in Somersworth; H - 33, shoeworker, b. Rochester, s/o Lindsey Richardson (Canada, laborer) and Ninta Davis (Dover, housewife); W - 33, stenographer, b. Somersworth, d/o Joseph Joyal (Canada, machinist) and Emma Guilmette (Canada, housewife)

**RICKER,**
Augustus of Farmington m. Sarah B. **Lougee** of Farmington 11/7/1896; H - 50, shoemaker, 2nd, b. Brookfield, s/o Benjamin A. Ricker (Wolfeboro, farmer) and Nancy J. Ricker (Middleton); W - 49, housework, 2nd, b. Farmington, d/o Samuel Ham (Farmington) and Jane Ham (Farmington)

Bertred E. of Farmington m. Mattie A. **Pearl** of Farmington 9/15/1900; H - 26, shoe trimmer, b. Belmont, s/o James E. Ricker (shoe trimmer) and Helen N. Currier (Belmont, housekeeper); W - 34, housekeeper, 3rd, b. Grand Falls, NB, d/o William Carney (dead) and Martha Carney (dead)

Charles H. of Farmington m. Mary **Cloutman** of Farmington 11/19/1892; H - 37, shoemaker, 2nd, divorced, b. Wolfeboro, s/o Gustus Ricker (Wolfeboro, 65, farmer) of Gilmanton and Nancy J. Ricker (dead); W - 22, shoe stitcher, b. Farmington, d/o Gates Cloutman (dead) and Susan Cloutman (Farmington, 42, shoe worker) of Farmington

Chester C. of Farmington m. Jennie S. **Colomy** of Farmington 8/11/1888 in Belmont; H - 18, edge trimmer, b. Belmont, s/o James E. (Wolfeboro, edge trimmer) and Helen N. (Meredith, housekeeper); W - 16, housekeeper, b. Farmington, d/o John (Farmington, laborer) and Alice (New Castle, housekeeper)

Irving J. of Farmington m. Mabel G. **Ross** of Dover 5/25/1910 in Rochester; H - 23, musician, b. Farmington, s/o James E. Ricker (Alton, shoe op.) and Helen Currier (Belmont, housewife); W - 23, shoe operative, b. Acton, ME, d/o Charles E. Ross (Freeport, ME, shoe op.) and Cora B. Hussey (Acton, ME, shoe op.)

James M. of Farmington m. Sarah E. **Pinkham** of New Durham 2/26/1895; H - 55, laborer, $3^{rd}$, b. Wolfeboro, s/o William Ricker and Lucy Ricker (Wolfeboro); W - 52, $2^{nd}$, b. New Durham, d/o David Horne and Anis Horne (New Durham)

John Q. A. of Farmington m. Margaret **Lepine** of Farmington 4/21/1895; H - 62, farmer, $2^{nd}$, b. New Durham, s/o Luther Ricker; W - 62, housekeeper, $3^{rd}$, b. Canada

Walter D. of Farmington m. Edith B. **Hamblett** of Farmington 7/23/1921; H - 42, shoeworker, $2^{nd}$, b. Wolfeboro, s/o James M. Ricker and Annie S. Dore; W - 32, shoeworker, $2^{nd}$, b. Farmington, d/o Samuel Kimball (Middleton, shoeworker) and Addie R. Young

William H. of Farmington m. Adelaide M. **Quint** of Farmington 1/11/1902; H - 28, shoemaker, b. Wolfeboro, s/o James M. Ricker (Wolfeboro, dead) and Annie S. Dore (Ossipee, dead); W - 28, shoe stitcher, b. Milton, d/o Ira A. Quint (carpenter)

**RILEY,**

James of Augusta, ME m. Glenna **Edgerly** of Farmington 9/19/1936 in Sanford, ME; H - 23, shoeworker, b. Augusta, ME, s/o Edward Riley (Ireland, deceased) and Ann Gorman (Ireland, deceased); W - 18, at home, b. Farmington, d/o Clyde Edgerly (Farmington, shoeworker) and Mary Henderson (No. Conway, shoeworker)

**RING,**

John of Farmington m. Florence **Kimball** of Farmington 5/5/1917 in Rochester; H - 21, shoeworker, b. St. John, NF, s/o Patrick Ring (St. John, NF, engineer) and Nora Wiseman (St. John, NF, housewife); W - 23, shoeworker, b. Farmington, d/o Samuel Kimball (Middleton, shoeworker) and Addie Young (Farmington)

**ROBERTS,**
Charles W. of Farmington m. Alice N. **Fernald** of Farmington 10/1/1895; H - 39, shoecutter, 2$^{nd}$, b. Farmington, s/o Jeremiah Roberts (Farmington) and Clarissa H. Roberts (New Durham); W - 39, 2$^{nd}$, b. Farmington, d/o Jeremy O. Nute (Milton, shoecutter) and Martha E. Nute (Natick, MA)

Frank H. of Farmington m. Gertrude E. **Lunde** of Farmington 9/24/1891 in Rochester; H - 24, shoemaker, b. Farmington, s/o Henry L. Roberts (dead); W - 19, shoe stitcher, b. Warren, d/o James P. Lunde (dead)

Fred H. of Farmington m. Bessie W. **Evans** of Malden, MA 6/6/1906 in Malden, MA; H - 38, sawyer, b. Rochester, s/o Henry K. Roberts (Rochester, carpenter) and Ellen A. Kimball (Dover); W - 31, stenographer, b. Haverhill, MA, d/o Abram Evans (Derry, custom shoe mkr.) and Josephine E. Page (Derry)

George C. of Farmington m. Florence I. **Lougee** of Farmington 6/21/1909; H - 22, drug clerk, b. Farmington, s/o William W. Roberts (Farmington, druggist) and Eloise A. Flanders (Danbury, housewife); W - 20, music teacher, b. Farmington, d/o Wilbur S. Lougee (Alton, shoemaker) and A. Jennie Berry (New Durham, housewife)

George G. of Farmington m. Rowena **Powell** of Alfred, ME 9/20/1930 in Rochester; H - 30, farmer, b. Derry, s/o Frank A. Roberts (Fryeburg, ME, farmer) and Annie A. Peavey (Derry); W - 18, at home, b. Alfred, ME, d/o William Powell (mill worker) and Rose ----- (housewife)

Harry F. of Farmington m. Edith F. **Connor** of Rochester 12/23/1905; H - 19, lineman, b. Rochester, s/o John P. Roberts (Rochester, farmer) and Irene Tibbetts (New Durham); W - 19, housekeeper, b. Farmington, d/o Charles E. Conner (Farmington, shoe cutter) and Florence Miller (New Durham, shoe stitcher)

John P. of Farmington m. Lillian A. **Hayes** of Farmington 4/22/1916; H - 62, shoeworker, 2$^{nd}$, b. Farmington, s/o Benjamin Roberts (Rochester, farmer) and Mary Place (Farmington, housekeeper); W - 56, shoeworker, 3$^{rd}$, b. Alton, d/o Solomon Rollins and Lucinda Tufts

John P. B. of Farmington m. Luella **Tanner** of Farmington 9/6/1903; H - 27, clerk, b. Farmington, s/o H. L. Roberts (Farmington, shoemaker) and Anna M. E. Towle (Winslow,

ME, housewife); W - 17, lady, b. Farmington, d/o John F. Tanner (Farmington, farmer) and Angelia L. Rand (Wolfeboro housewife)

John P. B. of Farmington m. Ethel M. **Blouin** of Farmington 1/31/1914 in Alton; H - 37, shoecutter, $2^{nd}$, b. Farmington, s/o Henry L. Roberts (shoe mfr.) and Anna M. E. Towle (NY, housekeeper); W - 26, housekeeper, $2^{nd}$, b. Moultonboro, d/o William Colby (farmer) and Josephine Browne (housekeeper)

**ROBINSON,**

Fred W. of Farmington m. Eva E. **Nutter** of Farmington 12/4/1892; H - 26, hotel clerk, b. Raymond, ME, s/o David S. Robinson (Raymond, ME, 49, farmer) and Abbie A. Robinson (Raymond ME, 48, housewife) of Raymond, ME; W - 19, lady, b. Farmington, d/o Mathew Nutter (Farmington, 45, shoemaker) and Roxie Nutter (Farmington, 43, housewife) of Farmington

Lew C. of Farmington m. Sadie F. **Plummer** of Farmington 3/17/1894 in Milton; H - 20, harness maker, b. Sanbornton, s/o Ira Robinson (Sanbornton, dead) and Caroline M. Robinson (Cambridge, MA, dead); W - 24, shoe fitter, b. Gilmanton, d/o Lorenzo C. Plumer (Farmington, shoemaker) and Ellen O. Plumer (Gilmanton, housekeeper)

**ROGERS,**

Charles C. of Farmington m. Ivy Alice **Roberts** of Farmington 12/22/1909; H - 33, physician, b. Windham, ME, s/o Albert T. Rogers (Standish, ME) and Lazella P. Hill (Naples, ME); W - 27, telephone op., b. Rochester, d/o Henry K. Roberts (Rochester, farmer) and Mabel R. Hill (Epping)

George C. of Farmington m. Ella F. **Trafton** of Farmington 10/20/1917; H - 31, section hand, b. Merrimac, MA, s/o Leonard Rogers and Jessie Jackson (Rowley, MA, housekeeper); W - 49, dressmaker, $2^{nd}$, b. Acton, ME, d/o William Hussey and Mary J. Hammett

**ROLLINS,**

Arthur S. of Alton m. A. Bernice **Currier** of Farmington 8/10/1912; H - 24, teacher, b. Salem, MA, s/o William H. Rollins (West Alton, station agent) and Lillie A. Sederquist (NS, housekeeper); W - 26, housekeeper, b. Farmington, d/o Burns

Currier (Farmington, shoemaker) and Sadie A. Lary (Somersworth, shoemaker)

Charles I. of Farmington m. Emma **Chatman** of Rockland, ME 5/19/1896; H - 33, shoe laster, 3rd, b. Farmington, s/o Perkins Rollins (Alton, lumberman) and Martha C. Rollins (housewife); W - 29, housekeeper, 2nd, b. Rockland, ME

Cyrus, Jr. of Farmington m. Maggie A. **Burke** of Farmington 1/23/1910 in Rochester; H - 18, clerk, b. Somersworth, s/o Cyrus Rollins (Lebanon, ME) and Augusta Towle; W - 17, shoeworker, b. Wolfeboro, d/o Edward Burke (Wolfeboro, shoemaker) and Estel Rollins

Edwin F. of Farmington m. Vinnie **Burnham** of Farmington 3/29/1892; H - 23, teamster, b. New Durham, s/o Cyrus C. Rollins (Alton, 56, farmer) of New Durham and Laura J. Rollins (dead); W - 18, lady, b. Farmington, d/o Charles S. Burnham (Farmington, 50, shoemaker) and Ellen Burnham (Farmington, 45, housewife) of Farmington

Ernest E. of Farmington m. Julia M. **Burrows** of Farmington 6/15/1921; H - 24, woodturner, b. N. Alton, s/o Elmer Rollins (New Durham) and Ella M. Dore (New Durham, housekeeper); W - 22, housekeeper, b. Union, d/o Isiah Burrows (Middleton) and Mamie Batersby

Ervin H. of Farmington m. Hattie F. **Clarke** of Farmington 6/23/1902; H - 37, laborer, 2nd, widower, b. Alton, s/o Isaac C. Rollins (New Durham, dead) and Abbie J. Watson (Alton, housekeeper); W - 17, housekeeper, b. Alton, d/o Frank Clark (Manchester, laborer) and Fannie Smith (Alton, housewife)

Harold C. of Farmington m. Ella C. **Winn** of New Durham 2/23/1920 in Rochester; H - 28, woodturner, b. Farmington, s/o John A. Rollins (New Durham, shoeworker) and Ruth L. Towle (New Durham, housewife); W - 20, at home, b. New Durham, d/o George E. Winn (Farmington, lumberman) and Helen Barker (Farmington, housewife)

Herbert S. of Farmington m. Alice B. **Gilman** of Farmington 6/1/1895 in Milton; H - 23, shoemaker, b. New Durham, s/o Samuel Rollins (Rochester, shoemaker) and Hattie Rollins (Alton); W - 19, b. Hallowell, ME, d/o William H. Gilman (Hallowell, ME, carpenter) and Emerline B. Gilman (Augusta, ME, housewife)

Leon P. of Farmington m. Violet May **Scott** of Farmington 9/15/1917; H - 25, shoeworker, b. Farmington, s/o Charles

Rollins and Nettie Tufts (New Durham, housekeeper); W - 18, shoeworker, b. Dalton, MA, d/o Joseph Scott (Dalton, MA, shoeworker) and Adelaide Scott (Lenox, MA, housekeeper)

Winslow C. of Farmington m. Beatrice **Coffin** of New Durham 8/31/1929; H - 48, laborer, 2nd, b. Caratunk, ME, s/o Dudley L. Rollins (Pleasant Ridge, ME) and Elizabeth R. Doile (Carryang, ME); W - 22, domestic, b. Berwick, ME, d/o Charles H. Coffin (Berwick, ME, milkman) and Cora R. Remick (Somersworth, housewife)

**ROUSSEAU,**

Frank of Farmington m. Harriette **Dwyer** of Farmington 10/27/191 in Gonic; H - 22, shoeworker, b. St. Medele, NB, s/o Edward Rousseau (farmer) and Atvea Roy (housekeeper); W - 21, shoeworker, b. Rogerville, NB, d/o Peter Dwyer (carpenter) and Maggie Collins (housekeeper)

**ROWE,**

Lyman L. of Farmington m. C. Isabelle **Brooks** of Farmington 5/28/1937 in Rochester; H - 22, shoeworker, b. Buxton, ME, s/o Daniel H. Rowe (Porter, ME, farmer) and Mary E. Pease (Conway, at home); W - 22, bookkeeper, b. Freedom, d/o Ralph M. Brooks (Eaton, farmer) and Hattie M. Stuart (Eaton, housewife)

**ROY,**

Arsene of Farmington m. Vinnie **Goodrow** of New Durham 4/6/1929; H - 35, laborer, b. Canada, s/o Leon Ray (Canada, farmer) and Mary Caureau (Canada, housewife); W - 44, housework, 2nd, b. Berwick, d/o Joseph Nalar (Canada, laborer) and Nellie Mayo (Canada, housewife)

**RUNDLETT,**

Rufus W. of Farmington m. Blanche A. **Roy** of Farmington 7/3/1932; H - 25, barber, b. Newburyport, MA, s/o Charles L. Rundlett (deceased) and Estella Bartlett (Brookline, MA, housekeeper); W - 21, bookkeeper, b. Farmington, d/o Romeo Roy (Canada, shoeworker) and Lea Jarvis (Canada, housekeeper)

**RUNNALS,**
Forest M. of Farmington m. Ida M. **Champion** of Parsonsfield, ME 5/24/1888; H - 30, shoemaker, b. New Durham, s/o Paul M. (New Durham, farmer) and Mary J. (deceased); W - 21, housekeeper, b. Wakefield, d/o Samuel (Effingham) and Mary (Boston, MA)

**RUNNELS,**
Paul M., Jr. of New Durham m. Blanche B. **White** of New Durham 1/19/1902; H - 25, farmer, b, New Durham, s/o P. M. Runnells (New Durham, farmer) and Mary J. Colomy (New Durham, dead); W - 17, housekeeper, b. New Durham, d/o George W. White (Marlboro, motorman) and Carrie Griffith (Keene, housekeeper)

**RUSSELL,**
Verdrum W. of Farmington m. Evelyn **Rhodes** of Farmington 10/30/1920; H - 19, shoeworker, b. Lynn, MA, s/o Frank S. Russell (Middleton, MA, shoeworker) and Nellie F. Russell (Portland, ME, housewife); W - 20, shoeworker, b. Portsmouth, d/o Nicholas Rhodes (Oswego, NY, shoeworker) and Ada M. Rhodes (PEI, housewife)

Warren B. of Farmington m. Bertha A. **Trusselle** of Farmington 9/2/1910; H - 26, shoeworker, b. Farmington, s/o Frank S. Russell (Middleton, MA, shoemaker) and Nellie E. Wells (Bath, ME, housekeeper); W - 32, shoeworker, b. Sandwich, d/o David Trusselle (Boscawen, case maker) and Mary E. Smith (Sandwich, housekeeper)

**ST. GERMAIN,**
Narcisse of Milton Mills m. Beulah **Manson** of Milton Mills 8/13/1909; H - 32, clerk, b. Haverhill, MA, s/o Narcisse St. Germain (wheelwright) and Margette Bouvier (Plattsburgh, NY, housewife); W - 19, weaver, b. Beverly, MA, d/o George H. Manson (Limerick, ME, shoemaker) and Lizzie Longfellow (Boston, MA, housekeeper)

**SAL[I]SBURY,**
Clifford K. of Brewer, ME m. Nina **Young** of Farmington 5/7/1914; H - 28, harness maker, 2$^{nd}$, b. Otis, ME, s/o Horace T. Salisbury (Otis, ME, laborer) and Rose Stanley (Tremont, ME,

housewife); W - 23, shoe stitcher, 2nd, b. Middleboro, MA, d/o Charles Richardson (meatcutter) and Gertrude Card (Farmington, nurse)

Lyndall C. of Farmington m. Olive J. **Reynolds** of Farmington 11/9/1935 in Rochester; H - 21, laborer, b. Farmington, s/o Clifford Salsbury (Otis, ME, carpenter) and Nina Richardson (Middleboro, MA, shoeworker); W - 19, shoeworker, b. Saugus MA, d/o James Reynolds (Danvers, MA, shoeworker) and Bertha Taysch (Germany, forelady)

**SANBORN,**

Almon C. of Wentworth m. Emma A. **Richardson** of Farmington 10/1/1889; H - 27, shoemaker, b. Gilmanton, s/o Isaac S. Sanborn (Gilmanton, farmer) and Nancy J. Sanborn (Lake Village); W - 23, stitcher, b. Farmington, d/o Charles Richardson (dead) and Charlotte Richardson (Alton)

Roland B. of Farmington m. Viola A. **Wood** of Rochester 9/26/1923 in Rochester; H - 30, mechanic, 2nd, b. Rochester, s/o George A. Sanborn (Rochester, farmer) and Nellie D. W. Winn (Hinsdale, housekeeper); W - 27, shoeworker, 2nd, b. Barrington, d/o George H. Wiggin (Barrington, farmer) and Marcille B. Verne (Beverly, MA, housekeeper)

Roland R. of Farmington m. Alice Mabel **Gray** of Farmington 6/28/1913; H - 20, farmer, b. Rochester, s/o George A. Sanborn (Rochester, farmer) and Nellie D. Winn (teacher); W - 23, lady, b. Farmington, d/o John I. Gray (farmer) and Ellen Varney (housekeeper)

**SANDERS,**

William M. of Farmington m. Nellie S. **Randall** of Farmington 5/18/1904; H - 30, merchant, 2nd, divorced, b. Farmington, s/o David B. Sanders (Ossipee, merchant) and Mary E. Kelley (No. Adams, MA); W - 34, shoeworker, 2nd, divorced, b. Middleton, d/o Cyrus B. Perkins (New Durham, farmer) and Mary A. Kimball (Wolfeboro, housewife)

**SANSOUCIE,**

Joseph of Farmington m. Lizzie E. **Drapeau** of Farmington 1/16/1897; H - 26, shoemaker, b. Worcester, s/o Joseph Sansoucie (Canada) and Leone Sansoucie (Canada); W - 14, housekeeper, b. Strafford, d/o Cleophas P. Drapeau (Canada East, section hand) and Rosalie Drapeau

William of Farmington m. Mary A. **Wentworth** of Farmington 1/28/1897 in Gonic; H - 29, shoemaker, b. Plaistow, s/o Peter Sansoucie (Warwick, Canada, grocer) and Mary Ann Sansoucie (Warwick, Canada, housekeeper); W - 21, table girl, b. Farmington, d/o Austin N. Wentworth (Barrington, heel cutter) and Abbie Wentworth (Farmington, housekeeper)

## SAUNDERS,

George H. of So. Windham, ME m. Aurilla J. **Walker** of Farmington 7/7/1908; H - 23, farmer, b. Milton, s/o Herbert C. Saunders (Lowell, MA, fireman) and Rhuhama Cook; W - 19, housekeeper, b. Milton, d/o John P. Walker (Thorndike, farmer) and Aurilla P. Palmer (Plymouth, ME)

## SAWYER,

Clifford L. of Farmington m. Minnie F. **Charles** of Farmington 11/10/1934; H - 49, laborer, $2^{nd}$, b. ME, s/o Jacob Sawyer (deceased) and Harriett York (deceased); W - 48, shoeworker, $2^{nd}$, b. ME, d/o Oris Gilpatrick (deceased) and Emily J. Sawyer (Hiramful, housewife)

Horatio M. of Farmington m. Adelina **Fountaine** of Lawrence 3/31/1912; H - 51, laborer, $3^{rd}$, b. Milbridge, ME, s/o Sewell B. Sawyer (farmer) and Martha J. Hall (housekeeper); W - 37, dressmaker, $2^{nd}$

Roscoe I. of Farmington m. Venna M. **Rollins** of Farmington 10/20/1935; H - 25, shoeworker, b. Farmington, s/o Horatio Sawyer (Brookfield, MA, deceased) and May L. Drew (Wakefield, MA, shoeworker); W - 24, shoeworker, $2^{nd}$, b. Farmington, d/o Irving Rollins (Alton) and Hattie Clark (Alton, deceased)

Sewell B. of Farmington m. Gertrude **Mitchell** of Gilmanton 2/23/1916; H - 20, teamster, b. LaGrange, ME, s/o Horatio Sawyer (laborer) and Cora Sawyer; W - 25, housekeeper, $2^{nd}$, b. Gilmanton, d/o William Downes (farmer) and Mary Randall

Walter F. of Farmington m. Alice J. **Dyer** of Farmington 8/10/1889; H - 40, truckman, b. Methuen, MA; W - 30, housekeeper, b. Rochester

Walter F. of Farmington m. Katie T. **Clough** of Farmington 6/17/1893; H - 35, laborer, $2^{nd}$, b. MA, s/o Francis Sawyer (MA,

farmer) and Adeline Sawyer (dead); W - 16, lady, b. Alton, d/o
Daniel B. Clough (Farmington, shoemaker) and Frances
Clough (Alton, housekeeper)

**SCHLENKER,**
John of Farmington m. Lizzie M. **Pike** of Farmington 1/14/1888 in
Milton; H - 35, baker, 2$^{nd}$, b. Germany, s/o John (Germany,
cooper) and Cristina; W - 25, shoe stitcher, b. Middleton, d/o
John S. (Middleton, farmer) and Mary M. (housekeeper)

**SCHOCH,**
Edgar of Farmington m. Mary Agnes **Nixon** of Farmington
12/26/1913; H - 23, shoeworker, b. Reading, PA, s/o Edward
A. Schoch (Stroudsburg, PA, printer) and Mary A. Surrell
(Reading, PA, housekeeper); W - 19, stenographer, b. Gonic,
d/o John Nixon (Somersworth, mill operator) and Martha A.
Conley (Stamford, CT, housewife)

**SCOTT,**
Joseph A. of Farmington m. Florence **Williams** of Freeport, ME
6/30/1929; H - 21, shoeworker, b. Farmington, s/o Joseph
Scott (Feeding Hills, MA, shoeworker) and Adelaide Davis
(Windsor, MA, shoeworker); W - 18, shoeworker, b. Amity,
ME, d/o Ray Williams (Amity, ME, foreman) and Hannah
Greenleaf (housewife)

**SCRUTON,**
Arthur G. of Farmington m. Mabel G. **Farnum** of Farmington
2/5/1921; H - 39, farmer, b. Farmington, s/o John F. Scruton
(Strafford, farmer) and Lydia A. Varney; W - 39, housekeeper,
2$^{nd}$, b. Ossipee, d/o William Kendall and Amanda Mills
(Woodstock, housekeeper)
Gilbert P. of Farmington m. Esta M. **Whitehouse** of Farmington
8/28/1929; H - 27, woodturner, b. Farmington, s/o James I.
Scruton (Farmington, merchant) and Sarah E. Preston
(Canada, housekeeper); W - 24, shoeworker, b. Somersworth,
d/o Harry Whitehouse and Lillian Blake (Belfast, ME,
housekeeper)
J. Irving of Farmington m. Lizzie **Preston** of Farmington 7/22/1899
in Milton; H - 25, laborer, b. Farmington, s/o James M. Scruton
(Farmington, butcher) and Sarah Scruton; W - 21, lady, b.

Canada, d/o James Preston (Sanford, ME, laborer) and Elizabeth Preston (Sanford, ME, housewife)

Jerold F. of Farmington m. Laura E. **Hayes** of Farmington 1/27/1922; H - 21, RR mail clerk, b. Farmington, s/o James I. Scruton (Farmington, meat cutter) and Elizabeth Preston (Fox River, Canada, housewife); W - 20, at home, b. Farmington, d/o Alphonzo C. Hayes (Farmington, brushmaker) and Eva B. Caswell (Barnstead)

Orin A. of Milton m. Ina G. **Duntley** of Farmington 6/14/1892; H - 26, mill worker, b. Farmington, s/o James M. Scruton (Farmington, 62, butcher) and Sarah A. Scruton (Barnstead, 58, housewife) of Farmington; W - 16, lady, b. Milton, d/o John Duntley (Milton, 48, shoemaker) and Elizabeth Duntley (Milton, 45, housewife) of Milton

Russell G. of Farmington m. Helen A. **Cotton** of Farmington 10/17/1901; H - 31, teamster, b. Farmington, s/o James M. Scruton (Farmington, farmer) and Sarah Hall (Strafford, dead); W - 17, housekeeper, b., Farmington, d/o Charles H. Cotton (Wolfeboro, dead) and Viola A. Edgerly (New Durham, laundress)

**SEAVEY,**

Edwin A. of Farmington m. Susie **Tibbetts** of Wakefield 10/29/1887; H - 36, carpenter, 2$^{nd}$, b. Boston, MA, s/o Samuel A. Seavey (Pittsfield) and Hannah S. Seavey; W - 20, b. Wakefield, d/o Benjamin F. Tibbetts (RR man) and Emily J. Tibbetts

Joseph E. of Farmington m. Nellie S. **Jones** of Gilmanton 6/17/1890 in Gilmanton; H - 39, farmer, 2$^{nd}$, b. Alexandria, s/o Calvin Seavey (Farmington, farmer) and Hyrena (Farmington); W - 39, housekeeper, b. Farmington, d/o Richard Jones (Gilmanton, farmer) and Annie (Gilmanton)

**SENTER,**

Clarence W. of Farmington m. Aurlie M. **Edgerly** of Farmington 4/8/1933; H - 22, shoeworker, b. West Kingston, s/o Walter H. Senter (West Kingston, shoeworker) and Gertrude F. Stevens (Lynn, MA, housewife); W - 18, shoeworker, b. Farmington, d/o Clyde Edgerly (Farmington, shoeworker) and Mary Anderson (Conway, shoeworker)

Lawrence P. of Farmington m. Margarete N. **Burke** of Rochester 1/15/1937; H - 31, chef, 2nd, b. Lynn, MA, s/o Walter H. Sente (Derry, shoeworker) and Gertrude F. Stevens (Malden, MA, housewife); W - 37, cook, 2nd, b. Gilmanton, d/o Edwin Nelso (Rochester, farmer) and Helen Nelson (No. Woodstock, housewife)

**SHACKFORD,**

John S. of Farmington m. Lena F. **Whitehouse** of Farmington 11/24/1897 in Milton; H - 22, photographer, b. Barnstead, s/o Amasa W. Shackford (Barnstead, photographer) and Clara A Shackford (Barnstead, housekeeper); W - 21, lining maker, b Farmington, d/o Warren H. Whitehouse (Middleton, shoe laster) and Emma A. Whitehouse (lining maker)

**SHANNON,**

Leander of So. Wolfeboro m. Gladys **Kimball** of Farmington 3/21/1910; H - 21, machinist, b. Alton, s/o Stephen Shannon (NY State, farmer) and Nellie Rollins (Alton); W - 20, housekeeper, b. So. Wolfeboro, d/o George D. Kimball (So. Wolfeboro, mill op.) and Grace Newman (Washington)

**SHAPLEIGH,**

Frank of Farmington m. Alice M. **Garland** of Farmington 8/9/1887 in Kennebunk, ME; H - 20, assistant postmaster, b. Middleton s/o Reuben Lougee (Middleton, trader) and Jennie Lougee; W - 24, stitcher, 2nd, widow, b. Middleton, d/o Joseph C. Miller (Middleton, shoemaker) and Annie A. Miller

**SHAW,**

William H. of Farmington m. Mabel **Ricker** of Farmington 7/9/1923 H - 43, cobbler, 2nd, b. Farmington, s/o Albert C. Shaw and Marilla Wentworth; W - 20, housekeeper, b. Farmington, d/o Charles H. Ricker and Mary A. Cloutman

**SHEEHAN,**

Henry J. of Milton m. Grace E. **Pike** of Farmington 8/23/1905; H - 21, farmer, b. Natick, s/o Daniel D. Sheehan (Natick, farmer) and Margarette A. Neal (Boston); W - 16, housekeeper, b. Farmington, d/o John C. Pike (Middleton, farmer) and Alice Arnold (Wells, ME)

Henry J. of Farmington m. Marietta **Emery** of Manchester 7/5/1923 in Hinsdale; H - 39, salesman, 2$^{nd}$, b. Natick, MA, s/o D. D. Sheehan (Natick, MA, retired) and Margaret A. Neal; W - 33, stenographer, b. N. Abington, MA, d/o Ralph C. Emery and Marietta Churchill (W. Abington, housekeeper)

**SILVIA,**

John J. of Farmington m. Gladys T. **Wilkes** of Farmington 8/12/1922 in Dover; H - 23, shoeworker, b. Oakland, CA, s/o Benjamin Silvia (CA, farmer) and Mary Pementel (CA, housewife); W - 17, at home, b. Barnstead, d/o George Wilkes (Putnam, CT, lumberman) and Bertha Coman (Putnam, CT, housewife)

John J. of Farmington m. Alice M. **Pinkham** of New Durham 1/25/1936 in Alton; H - 36, shoeworker, 2$^{nd}$, b. Oakland, CA, s/o Bernard P. Silvia (San Jose, CA) and Mary Perry (Alameda, CA); W - 23, housekeeper, b. Alton, d/o Clifton Pinkham (Farmington, woodworker) and Ella Emerson (N. Lebanon, ME, housewife)

**SIMONDS,**

Frank E. of Alton m. Marguerite A. **Ware** of Farmington 10/15/1927 in Alton Bay; H - 19, laborer, b. Farmington, s/o Eugene F. Simonds (Sharon, VT, merchant) and Cynthia J. Davis (Alton, housewife); W - 22, shoeworker, b. Farmington, d/o Arthur A. Ware (Waterville, ME, shoeworker) and Margaret Leighton (Lynn, MA, housekeeper)

**SINNIGER,**

Herbert of Farmington m. Helen S. **Pidgeon** of Melrose, MA 9/16/1935 in Hampton; H - 21, vaudeville, b. Worcester, MA, s/o Herbert Sinniger (So. Berwick, ME, carpenter) and Agnes Finley (Scotland, housewife); W - 21, at home, b. Boston, MA, d/o Ernest Pigeon (Franklin, MA, mechanic) and Helen Shellaber (New Orleans, housewife)

**SKILLINGS,**

John of Lawrence, MA m. Cristina M. **Morrison** of Farmington 2/1/1888 in Lawrence, MA; H - 26, merchant, b. Scotland, s/o William (Scotland, overseer) and Annie (housekeeper); W -

28, lady, b. Andover, MA, d/o Andrew (gardener) and Agnes (housekeeper)

**SLOAN,**

Benjamin B. of Farmington m. Adelaide C. **Waldron** of Farmington 9/13/1892; H - 22, druggist, b. Barre, VT, s/o David C. Sloan (Shoreham, VT, 44, merchant) of Chicago, IL and Hannah B. Sloan (Barre, VT, 42, lady) of Barre, VT; W - 20, lady, b. Milton, d/o John Waldron (Farmington, 45, shoemaker) and Adelaide C. Waldron (Manchester, 45, lady) of Farmington

**SMALL,**

Edwin E. of Farmington m. Harriet F. **Averill** of Farmington 9/7/1891 in Rochester; H - **44**, journalist, $2^{nd}$, b. Concord, s/o James B. Small (Phippsburg, MA, cabinet maker); W - 37, housekeeper, b. Farmington, d/o Bernard Averill (dead)

Isaac H. of Boston, MA m. Lula M. **Heath** of Boston, MA 3/4/1893; H - 25, clerk, b. NY, s/o Isaac H. Small (dead) and Jennie Young (Scotland, housewife); W - 20, clerk, b. Ashland, d/o Henry C. Heath (Ashland, farmer) and Ella J. Heath (Ashland, housewife)

**SMART,**

Harry P. of Ossipee m. Harriet R. **Colomy** of Farmington 10/24/1905; H - 23, clerk, b. Ossipee, s/o Charles H. Smart (Campton, mfr.) and Helen A. Folsome (Tamworth); W - 22, school teacher, b. Farmington, d/o George A. Colomy (Farmington, shoemaker) and Belle Jones (Berwick, ME)

Jerry E. of Farmington m. Ada F. **Barsantee** of Farmington 4/24/1926; H - 30, shoeworker, $2^{nd}$, b. Farmington, s/o Joel Smart and Mary Smith (Dover, housewife); W - 19, shoeworker, b. Portsmouth, d/o Albert Barsantee (Portsmouth, shoeworker) and Nellie Swinnerton (Somersworth, housewife)

John W. of Farmington m. Annie **James** of Farmington 4/6/1920; H - 38, shoeworker, b. Dover, s/o Joel Smart and Mary Smith (Dover, housekeeper); W - 51, housekeeper, $3^{rd}$, b. Sauk Rapids, MI, d/o Alphonzo James and Lucy Fogg

**SMITH,**

Albert M. of Farmington m. Eleanor V. **Fowler** of Seabrook 4/18/1934 in Rochester; H - 30, mechanic, b. Farmington, s/o

William A. Smith (Gilmanton I.W., box maker) and Iona B. Knight (Norton Mills, housewife); W - 18, at home, b. Seabrook, d/o Charles A. Fowler (Seabrook, fisherman) and Mary A. Jamorin (Newburyport, MA, deceased)

Arthur H. of Farmington m. Blanche M. **Miller** of Farmington 1/17/1925 in Rochester; H - 28, hotel clerk, 2nd, b. Lunenburg, MA, s/o Henry A. Smith (MA, farmer) and Eva Balentine (MA); W - 33, waitress, 2nd, b. Farmington, d/o Daniel B. Clough (Alton) and Lydia F. Young (Alton)

Chester F. of Farmington m. Evelyn B. **Brooks** of Farmington 10/25/1919 in Rochester; H - 23, woodturner, b. Alton, s/o Frank Smith (Alton, woodturner) and Alice Brooks (Dorchester, housewife); W - 21, at home, b. Farmington, d/o Percy J. Brooks (Alton, shoeworker) and Edith Tibbetts (Farmington)

Corran M. of Farmington m. Isabelle **White** of Stanley, NB 9/24/1904; H - 29, teamster, b. Gilmanton, s/o Warren M. Smith (Gilmanton, farmer) and Mary A. Howard (Gilmanton, housewife); W - 34, housekeeper, b. Stanley, NB, d/o James F. White (Stanley, NB, farmer) and Sarah Dennis (Stanley, NB, housewife)

Daniel C. of New Durham m. Viola C. **Libbey** of Farmington 11/3/1898 in New Durham; H - 55, farmer, b. Ipswich, MA, s/o Miah Smith (dead) and Emily Smith (dead); W - 44, b. New Durham, d/o Isaac C. Libbey (dead) and Clara S. Libbey (dead)

Edmund L. of Farmington m. Madeleine **Hayes** of Rochester 9/29/1931 in Rochester; H - 24, b. Farmington, s/o William A. Smith (Alton, sawmill) and Cora B. Knight (Nortonville, housewife); W - 20, b. Rochester, d/o Walter E. Hayes (Farmington, laborer) and Etta E. Roberts (Farmington, shoe operative)

Elbridge G. of Farmington m. Sarah **Horne** of Farmington 8/17/1894 in East Rochester; H - 41, shoemaker, 2nd, widower, b. Charlestown, s/o David M. Smith (Buxton, ME, farmer) and Nancy Smith (Alton, housewife); W - 45, housekeeping, 3rd, widow, b. Holderness, d/o Thomas Curry (Holderness) and Eleanor Curry (Holderness)

Harry A. of Farmington m. Hazel L. **Hussey** of Rochester 6/2/1909; H - 26, mill planer op., b. Boston; W - 17, housekeeper, b. Rochester, d/o John W. Hussey (Rochester, carpenter) and Sadie E. Garland (Rochester, housekeeper)

Horace H. of Farmington m. Estella M. **Card** of Farmington 10/20/1897; H - 26, blacksmith, b. Gilmanton, s/o Edward E. Smith (Ipswich, MA, teamster) and Jane H. Smith (Moultonboro, housewife); W - 23, school teacher, b. Farmington, d/o Thomas F. Card (New Castle, shoemaker) and Mary J. Card (New Durham, housekeeper)

James A. of Farmington m. Mary E. **Nutter** of Farmington 7/12/1919; H - 29, steamfitter, $2^{nd}$, b. York, ME, s/o Albert S. Smith (York, ME, farmer) and Hannah Jenkins (N. Berwick, ME); W - 34, bookkeeper, $2^{nd}$, b. Farmington, d/o Frank O. Nutter (teamster) and Sarah E. Pike (Middleton, housewife)

Samuel L. of Farmington m. Grace **Ward** of Farmington 1/4/1899; H - 48, hotel keeper, $3^{rd}$, b. Biddeford, ME, s/o Mark Smith and Anis Smith; W - 28, lady, $2^{nd}$, b. Bangor, ME

William of Union m. Gertrude **Huckins** of Farmington 3/20/1926 in Rochester; H - 25, mill worker, b. Acton, ME, s/o Charles Smith and Amanda M. Hussey (Shapleigh, ME, housekeeper); W - 21, bookkeeper, b. Strafford, d/o Edgar E. Huckins and Addie M. Hill (Strafford, housewife)

William C. of Farmington m. Fannie **Drew** of Union 11/25/1911; H - 26, laborer, b. Charlestown, MA, s/o William Smith (Manchester, England, engineer) and Mary Clark (Manchester, England, housekeeper); W - 16, lady, b. Sanbornville, d/o James Drew (Brookfield, teamster) and Clara Glidden (Alton, housekeeper)

William H. of Farmington m. Della **Hapgood** of Worcester, MA 1/27/1930; H - 44, painter, $2^{nd}$, b. Everett, MA, s/o Edgar Smith and Flora Prescott; W - 50, housekeeper, $2^{nd}$, b. Eaton, Canada, d/o Charles F. Kelsea and Rose A. Wheeler

William H. of Brockton, MA m. Margaret M. **Buckley** of Brockton, MA 5/20/1933; H - 22, shoeworker, b. Brockton, MA, s/o James Smith (Ireland, stone mason) and Rose Gay (Fall River, MA, housewife); W - 22, stenographer, b. Brockton, MA, d/o John T. Buckley (Bridgewater, laborer) and Mary J. Cook (Manchester, England, housewife)

William R. of Portland, ME m. Doris P. **Hurd** of Portland, ME 10/11/1937; H - 26, dist. manager, b. Portland, ME, s/o William Smith (Portland, ME, deceased) and Annie Cummings (England, deceased); W - 29, secretary, b. Alton Bay, d/o John P. Hurd (Milton, merchant) and Grace B. Hayes (Rochester, at home)

**SOUTER,**
William of Farmington m. Lillian Eileen **Mathews** of Farmington 11/20/1934 in Berwick, ME; H - 22, shoeworker, b. Somerville, MA, s/o Thomas Souter (Scotland, carpenter) and W'msena Swerns'n (Scotland, housewife); W - 16, at home, b. Lynn, MA, d/o Earle Mathews (Farmington, chef) and Gertrude Mathews (Farmington, housekeeper)

**SPEAR,**
Fred R. of Farmington m. Ruth **Gordon** of Farmington 6/29/1912 in Rochester; H - 24, shoemaker, b. East Boston, s/o Edwin C. Spear (E. Boston, MA, grocer) and Madge Tredhope (E. Boston, MA, housekeeper); W - 18, lady, b. Manchester, d/o Karl J. Brummer (tailor) and Lucia Gordon (Lyman, housekeeper)

Fred R. of Farmington m. Viola M. **Pike** of Farmington 6/30/1920; H - 30, shoeworker, 2nd, b. Boston, MA, s/o Edwin C. Spear (Boston, MA, shoeworker) and Madge T. Jameson (Boston, MA, housewife); W - 23, shoeworker, b. Farmington, d/o John C. Pike (Middleton, laborer) and Alice Pike (Wells, ME, housewife)

Howard M. of Farmington m. Ruth **Carpenter** of Farmington 4/21/1917; H - 24, shoeworker, b. East Boston, MA, s/o Edwin C. Spear (East Boston, MA, shoeworker) and Madge T. Jameson (East Boston, MA, housewife); W - 24, 2nd

**SPRAGUE,**
Verney of Farmington m. Ella May **Cook** of Farmington 7/1/1914; H - 22, shoeworker, b. Newfields, ME, s/o Simon Sprague (Newfields, ME, farmer) and Annie James (Black Hills, SD, housekeeper); W - 21, shoeworker, b. Meredith, d/o Nathaniel Cook (Barnstead, farmer) and Helen Browne (Holderness, housekeeper)

**STANLEY,**
Ernest of Farmington m. Clara A. **Downing** of Farmington 10/28/1916; H - 26, farmer, 2nd, b. Hollis, ME, s/o R. L. Stanley (Porter, ME, laborer) and Ida B. Bisby (Ossipee, housewife); W - 25, housekeeper, b. Middleton, d/o Charles W. Downing (Milton, laborer) and Sarah J. ----- (Farmington, housewife)

Irving of Farmington m. Emma **Roberts** of Hamilton, NH 10/1/191
in Hampton; H - 21, shoemaker, b. Kezar Falls, s/o Randall
Stanley (Kezar Falls, ME, teamster) and Ida Bisbee
(Parsonsfield, ME, housekeeper); W - 17, housekeeper, b.
Hamilton, d/o A. J. Roberts (Exeter, section hand)

Samuel S., Jr. of Farmington m. ----- 8/30/1919 in Rochester; H -
21, shoeworker, b. Deering, ME, s/o Samuel S. Stanley
(Holden, ME, laborer) [record of wife missing]

## STAPLES,

Clarence V. of Farmington m. Elsie A. **Roberge** of Wolfeboro
1/16/1926 in Wolfeboro; H - 20, shoeworker, b. Tuftonboro, d.
Frank Staples (Ossipee, laborer) and Inez Piper; W - 18, at
home, b. Manchester, d/o Louis Roberge (teamster) and
Bessie A. Elliott (housewife)

## STEELE,

Alfred D. of Farmington m. Rose **Ouellette** of Rochester
12/30/1934 in Rochester; H - 20, shoeworker, b. Lynn, MA, s/o
Alfred T. Steele (Haverhill, MA, shoeworker) and Caroline
Donaghy (Canada, shoeworker); W - 26, shoeworker, b.
Rochester, d/o Joseph Ouellette (Canada, deceased) and
Philouise Lefebre (Canada, housework)

## STEVENS,

Edgar N. of Farmington m. Viola J. **Colbath** of Farmington
11/20/1909; H - 43, mill hand, divorced, b. Middleton, s/o
James F. D. Stevens (Middleton, farmer) and Lydia F. Brown
(Benton, ME); W - 42, shoe stitcher, widow, b. Farmington, d/o
Charles C. Dudley (Somersworth, farmer) and Lydia A.
Tibbetts (Tamworth, housewife)

Ernest W. of Saco, ME m. Marion E. **Treamer** of Kennebunk
11/11/1936 in Rochester; H - 31, mechanic, b. W. Kennebunk,
s/o Orrin H. Stevens (Kennebunk, deceased) and Georgie
Noble (Kennebunk, deceased); W - 33, at home, b.
Kennebunk, d/o Charles Treamer (Berlin, foreman) and
Katherine Hall (Stanstead, housewife)

Guy Edward of Farmington m. Nellie **Haines** of Farmington
8/9/1913 in Rochester; H - 23, shoeworker, b. Wakefield, s/o
Edgar N. Stevens (Middleton, shoemaker) and Annie M.
Cleveland (Concord, housekeeper); W - 23, shoeworker, 2$^{nd}$, b

Farmington, d/o James Albert Place (Farmington, carpenter) and Mary Austin (Dover, housekeeper)

James of Farmington m. Frances **Manley** of London 7/29/1933 in Rochester; H - 20, farmer, b. Farmington, s/o Phil Stevens (Biddeford, ME, shoeworker) and Helen Brooks (Farmington, deceased); W - 18, maid, b. Barnesville, ME, d/o Thomas Manley (Barnesville, ME, mill worker) and Grace Gilmore (NS, maid)

Leon B. of Manchester m. Eliza E. **Berry** of Farmington 6/29/1919; H - 40, clerk, $2^{nd}$, b. W. Fairlee, VT, s/o Samuel Stevens and Martha E. Smith (Unity, housekeeper); W - 28, lady, $2^{nd}$, b. S. Berwick, ME, d/o Frank P. Berry (Portland, ME, shoeworker) and Emma I. Davis (S. Alton, housewife)

Percy E. of Farmington m. Mary K. **Yandoh** of Farmington 5/26/1927 in Somersworth; H - 40, foreman, $2^{nd}$, b. Farmington, s/o James E. Stevens (Milton, retired) and Etta E. Everett; W - 28, forelady, $2^{nd}$, b. Aberdeen, Scotland, d/o Albert Davidson and Jennie Reed (Aberdeen, Scotland, housewife)

Philemon E. of Farmington m. Helen **Brooks** of Farmington 8/19/1909; H - 22, shoeworker, b. Biddeford, ME, s/o James B. Stevens (Biddeford, ME, machinist) and Cora B. Billings (Biddeford, ME); W - 20, housekeeper, b. Farmington, d/o Percy Brooks (Alton, shoemaker) and Edith Tibbetts (Farmington)

Rockwell J. of Farmington m. Abbie F. **Leeds** of Farmington 6/7/1887 in Rochester; H - 31, shoemaker, b. Middleton, s/o Thomas J. Stevens (Middleton, farmer) and Mary E. Stevens; W - 33, stitcher, $2^{nd}$, b. Alton, d/o George F. Leeds (Alton, carpenter) and Dorothy Leeds

Ronello A. of Farmington m. Nellie **Abbott** of Farmington 5/30/1908; H - 22, farmer, b. Farmington, s/o John B. Stevens (Concord, farmer) and Carrie E. Canney (Farmington); W - 20, housekeeper, b. Farmington, d/o James Abbott (Farmington, farmer) and Emma Jordan (Farmington)

Sylvester E. of Farmington m. Reta A. **Eldridge** of Farmington 4/17/1933; H - 22, mechanic, b. Farmington, s/o Willis R. Stevens (Farmington, mechanic) and Blanch Elmer (Pennetwo, PA, waitress); W - 21, housewife, b. Ctr. Ossipee, d/o Everett Eldridge (Ossipee, carpenter) and Nettie Pike (Ossipee, housewife)

William C. of Farmington m. Lillian M. **Arnold** of Farmington 9/27/1922; H - 23, shoeworker, s/o Harry Stevens and Kate Felt; W - 18, shoeworker, b. Deerfield, d/o Samuel V. Arnold (Brockton, MA, shoeworker) and Sarah Godfrey (PEI, housewife)

Willis R. of Farmington m. Lura S. **Philbrick** of Farmington 12/19/1904; H - 22, machinist, b. Farmington, s/o John B. Stevens (W. Concord, millwright) and Carrie E. Canney (Farmington, housewife); W - 24, housekeeper, $2^{nd}$, divorced, b. No. Sutton, d/o William K. Philbrick (Antrim, farmer) and Ann E. Fiske (No. Sutton, housewife)

Willis R. of Farmington m. Blanche M. **Elmer** of Copeland, PA 1/28/1911; H - 28, farmer, $2^{nd}$, b. Farmington, s/o John B., Stevens (W. Concord, doctor) and Carrie E. Canney (Farmington, housekeeper); W - 22, housekeeper, b. Copeland, PA, d/o John J. Elmer (Baltimore, MD, farmer) and Sarah A. Eisenheth (Copeland, PA, housekeeper)

## STODDARD,

Guy H. of Farmington m. Ethel G. **Roberts** of Farmington 6/2/1906; H - 34, shoe cutter, b. Candor, NY, s/o Hermon Stoddard (Ithaca, NY, express agent) and Mary Van Vleck (Candor, NY); W - 24, clerk, b. Farmington, d/o John P. Roberts (Farmington, farmer) and Irene Tibbetts (New Durham)

## SULLIVAN,

Cornelius H. of Farmington m. Maxine G. **Long** of Farmington 3/22/1924 in Rochester; H - 21, shoeworker, b. Manchester, s/o Cornelius Sullivan and Annie Keaney; W - 19, bookkeeper, b. Snowville, d/o William Long (Eaton, painter) and Nina E. Dennett (W. Brownfield, housewife)

William L. of East Orange m. Rosa H. **Keyes** of Farmington 8/22/1936; H - 34, instructor, b. Beverly, MA, s/o Patrick Sullivan (Beverly, MA, meat cutter) and Mary Fitzpatrick (Salem, MA, housewife); W - 31, bank clerk, b. Peabody, MA, d/o William Keyes (Bridgewater, MA, retired) and Ellen Lawney (Plymouth, MA, at home)

## SWINERTON,

Herbert B. of Milton m. Esther **Blaisdell** of Farmington 12/24/1899 in Milton; H - 21, shoemaker, b. Milton, s/o R. G. Swinerton

(Newfield, farmer) and Augusta Swinerton (Somersworth, housewife); W - 19, b. Farmington, d/o Orin Blaisdell (Lebanon, ME, shoemaker) and Ada Blaisdell (Farmington, housewife)

**SYZE,**
Albert of Yorktown Heights, NY m. Laura S. **Huckins** of Farmington 6/12/1901 in Milton; H - 33, clergyman, b. Baldwin Place, NY, s/o James F. Syze (Jefferson Valley, NY, lumberman) and Martha B. Griffin (Baldwin Place, NY); W - 33, school teacher, b. Farmington, d/o John I. Huckins (Madbury, farmer) and Abbie W. Whitehouse (Somersworth)

**TANNER,**
Clarence J. of Alton m. Grace E. **Tilton** of Farmington 12/17/1918 in New Durham; H - 41, teamster, $2^{nd}$, b. Farmington, s/o Frank Tanner (Farmington, farmer) and Angelia Rand (New Durham, housekeeper); W - 25, housekeeper, $2^{nd}$, b. Farmington, d/o John K. Babb (Farmington, laborer) and Edith D. Elger (Barrington, housework)

Everett C. of Farmington m. Cressie B. **Kenney** of Farmington 1/21/1905; H - 26, shoemaker, b. Farmington, s/o George W. Tanner (Exeter, shoemaker) and Ellen F. Young (Middleton); W - 20, shoe stitcher, b. Farmington, d/o George Kenney (Lebanon, ME, shoemaker) and Lula Wentworth (Farmington)

Frank W. of Kennebunkport, ME m. Minnie M. **Emmons** of Saco, ME 4/4/1896; H - 32, fishing, $2^{nd}$, b. Kennebunkport, ME, s/o John V. Tanner (NS) and Hannah J. Tanner (Lyman, ME); W - 25, b. Saco, ME, d/o Francis Emmons (Kennebunkport, ME, farmer) and Mary Emmons (Kennebunkport, ME, housewife)

George I. of Farmington m. Gertrude M. **Smart** of Farmington 1/8/1910; H - 30, shoemaker, b. Farmington, s/o Henry H. Tanner (Farmington, farmer) and Martha A. Giles (Lebanon, ME, housekeeper); W - 17, housekeeper, b. Farmington, d/o Joel Smart (Maxwell, ME, farmer) and Mary A. Smith (Dover, housewife)

Hervey E. of Farmington m. Mary A. **O'Hara** of Farmington 9/1/1887 in Rochester; H - 24, shoemaker, b. Farmington; W - 22, b. Belfast, Ireland

Lincoln G. of Farmington m. Delia A. **Downing** of Farmington 12/28/1904; H - 22, B&M fireman, b. Chicago, IL, s/o Henry H.

Tanner (Sandwich, farmer) and Minnie McDonald (WV, housewife); W - 25, housekeeper, b. Farmington, d/o James Downing (Farmington, farmer) and Addie Smith (Rochester, housewife)

**TASH,**
Ernest L. of Farmington m. Nettie F. **Garland** of Farmington 9/9/1910; H - 20, electrician, b. Dover, s/o James F. Tash (New Durham, shoemaker) and Carrie Billings (Rochester, housewife); W - 24, shoeworker, b. Rochester, d/o C. I. Garland (Rochester, baker) and Ada Horne (Rochester, housewife)

**TASKER,**
Edgar E. of Orlando, FL m. Bertha E. **Davis** of Montville, ME 6/1/1926; H - 52, contractor, $2^{nd}$, b. Montville, ME, s/o Spofford J. Tasker (Montville, ME, farmer) and Andomer Rowell (Knox, ME, housewife); W - 49, housekeeper, $2^{nd}$, b. Montville, ME, d/o Benjamin Bointon (Washington, ME, farmer) and Nancy Griffin (Liberty, ME, housewife)

**TEAGUE,**
Ralph E. of Beverly, MA m. Helen **Merrow** of Farmington 10/25/1916; H - 27, B&M employee, b. Beverly, MA, s/o George E. Teague (Beverly, MA, salesman) and Abbie L. Langmaid (Exeter, housewife); W - 23, at home, b. Milton, d/o Wilbur S. Merrow (Ossipee, foreman) and Elizabeth Mitchell (Middleton, housewife)

**TEBBETTS,**
Fred N. of Farmington m. Lizzie **Armstrong** of Farmington 12/31/1902; H - 25, painter, b. Farmington, s/o Leander Tibbetts (Wakefield, farmer) and Delia A. Cloutman (Farmington, housewife); W - 27, shoeworker, $2^{nd}$, divorced, b. Farmington, d/o George H. Leighton (Farmington, shoemaker) and Marguerite Sandwich (NS, housekeeper)

Fred O. of Farmington m. Elna V. **Armstrong** of Farmington 7/26/1917; H - 27, shoeworker, b. Epping, s/o Manfred Tebbetts (Milton, shoeworker) and Nellie Densmore; W - 21, shoeworker, $2^{nd}$, b. Farmington, d/o Winthrop Armstrong (Farmington, shoeworker) and Elizabeth Leighton (Farmington)

Manfred of Haverhill, MA m. Mary **Leighton** of Farmington 12/24/1914; H - 51, shoeworker, 2nd, b. Milton, s/o Eri F. Tebbetts (Milton, shoemaker, farmer) and Eliza B. Pinkham (New Durham, housewife); W - 46, shoeworker, b. Marblehead, MA, d/o George Leighton (Farmington, shoemaker) and Margaret Sandwich (Halifax, housewife)

Rodney A. of Farmington m. Doris P. **Rhodes** of Farmington 1/1/1933 in Laconia; H - 34, fur farmer, b. New Durham, s/o Albinus B. Tebbets (deceased) and Mary F. Amazeen (Milton, housewife); W - 25, shoeworker, 2nd, b. Alton, d/o George Prescott (Alton, carpenter) and Lillian Jones (deceased)

Warren E. of Farmington m. Katherine A. **Corson** of Rochester 3/29/1934; H - 51, farmer, b. New Durham, s/o Albinus B. Tebbets (New Durham, deceased) and Mary F. Amazeen (Milton, housewife); W - 46, housewife, 2nd, b. Dover, d/o Mike Burns (Ireland, deceased) and Katherine Murry (Ireland, deceased)

**TEMPLE,**

Fred of Farmington m. Ida **Ham** of Farmington 4/1/1904; H - 32, laster, 2nd, widower, b. Texas Valley, NY, s/o Henry Temple (NY, blacksmith) and Elnora Brown (No. Adams, MA, housewife); W - 28, housekeeper, 2nd, widow, b. Concord, d/o Martin B. Stevens (Alton, laborer) and Malinda S. Taylor (Alton, housewife)

**TERRELL,**

Earle W. of Farmington m. Marie **Cooley** of Lynn, MA 12/10/1927 in Rochester; H - 33, carpenter, b. Milton, s/o Charles Tirrell and Annie J. Tuttle (Newmarket, housekeeper); W - 28, laundress, 2nd, b. Malden, MA, d/o Frank W. Garland (Moncton, NB, carpenter) and Clara B. Steves (Moncton, NB, housewife)

**THAYER,**

Elmer F. of Alton m. Annie M. **Edgerly** of Farmington 6/18/1905; H - 43, shoe mfr., b. S. Weymouth, s/o N. B. Thayer (So. Weymouth, MA, shoe mfr.) and Laura M. Newcomb (Holbrook, MA); W - 34, bank clerk, b. Farmington, d/o James B. Edgerly (Farmington, bank cashier) and Maria J. Fernald (So. Berwick, ME)

Fred I. of Farmington m. A. Lillian **Hayes** of Farmington 6/28/1904 H - 25, electrician, b. Westbrook, ME, s/o William F. Thayer (Gray, ME, merchant) and Ida B. Whitehouse (Alton, housewife); W - 19, lady, b. New Durham, d/o Seth W. Hayes (Farmington, salesman) and Luella Tash (New Durham)

Fred I. of Farmington m. Viola E. **Jackson** of Iselin, NJ 9/25/1920 in Rochester; H - 41, lumber mfg., 2$^{nd}$, b. Highland Lake, s/o William F. Thayer and Ida B. Whitehouse (Middleton, at home); W - 22, lady, b. Long Island, NY, d/o Harry M. Jackson (Stamford, CT, electrician) and Flora Stewart (Stockton, England, housewife)

James E. of Farmington m. Beulah L. **Perkins** of Alton 6/14/1934 Bedford; H - 26, cashier, b. Farmington, s/o Elmer F. Thayer (So. Weymouth, MA, deceased) and Annie M. Edgerly (Farmington, at home); W - 21, teacher, b. Alton, d/o Benjam Perkins (Alton, mason) and Winnifred Crocker (Rochester, at home)

Lawrence E. of Newport, VT m. Alice J. **Wheatley** of Brookfield, V 9/19/1893; H - 46, photographer, 2$^{nd}$, b. Brookfield, VT, s/o Edwin O. Thayer (dead) and Matilda Thayer (dead); W - 45, lady, b. Brookfield, VT, d/o Nathaniel Wheatley (Brookfield, VT) and Betsey W. Wheatley (dead)

## THEBERGE,

Wilfred J. of Amesbury, MA m. Ruth A. **Norris** of Amesbury, MA 1/4/1921; H - 28, merchant, 2$^{nd}$, b. Amesbury, MA, s/o Thomas Theberge (Canada, electrician) and Amanda Baron (Canada, housewife); W - 20, housekeeper, b. Malden, MA, d/o Elmer Norris (Malden, MA, farmer) and Eva Hall (ME, housewife)

## THERRIEN,

Edward of Farmington m. Edith E. **Armstrong** of Farmington 6/4/1926; H - 27, shoeworker, b. Farmington, s/o John Therrie and Clara Lessard; W - 27, furrier, b. Manchester, d/o Mortimer Armstrong (Farmington, shoeworker) and Mildred Whitlock (NB, furrier)

## THOMAS,

Carl Shipman of Farmington m. Bernice **Gilman** of Farmington 7/10/1908; H - 25, printer, b. St. Albans, VT, s/o Edwin H. Thomas (Lawrence, NY, publisher) and Jennie I. Shipman

(Hardwick, VT); W - 22, book keeper, b. Farmington, d/o
Charles B. Gilman (Farmington, painter) and Abbie B. Stevens
(Farmington, dressmaker)

**THOMPSON,**
Andrew N. of Farmington m. Flora **Wadleigh** of Somersworth
6/19/1909; H - 30, farmer, divorced, b. Porter, ME, s/o Alonzo
Thompson (Porter, ME, farmer) and Hannah Baston (Porter,
ME); W - 23, housekeeping, b. Somersworth, d/o Charles
Wadleigh (Somersworth, farmer) and Mary Moore

Elmer E. of Farmington m. Marian C. **Tuttle** of Independence, OH
11/7/1925; H - 20, farmer, b. New Durham, s/o John C.
Thompson (Concord, carpenter) and Julia E. Emerson
(Farmington, housewife); W - 23, teacher, b. Barrington, d/o
Owen Tuttle (Strafford, farmer) and Nettie Foss (Strafford,
housewife)

Ernest H. of Farmington m. Eva F. **Bryant** of Farmington 9/1/1927
in Rochester; H - 48, shoeworker, 2$^{nd}$, b. Strafford, s/o Hiram
Thompson and Nellie H. Frost; W - 46, housekeeper, 2$^{nd}$, b.
Manchester, d/o Charles O. Wallace (Boston, MA, painter) and
Eva A. -----

Eugene H. of Farmington m. Edna M. **Davis** of Farmington
7/2/1910 in Rochester; H - 27, meat cutter, b. Farmington, s/o
George L. Thompson (Farmington, farmer) and Hattie J.
Chesley (Farmington, housewife); W - 22, shoeworker, b.
Farmington, d/o Charles E. Davis (Wolfeboro, laborer) and
Ella Bunker (Farmington, housewife)

James H. of Center Harbor m. Lilla H. **Cook** of Farmington
6/20/1891; H - 34, carpenter, 2$^{nd}$, b. Center Harbor, s/o James
G. Thompson (Center Harbor, farmer); W - 23, housekeeper,
3$^{rd}$, b. Middleton, d/o Moses Cook (dead)

James R. of Ishpeming, MI m. Helen H. **Pearl** of Farmington
11/20/1893; H - 28, civil engineer, b. Burlington, WI, s/o James
Thompson (dead) and M. R. Thompson (Ishpeming, MI,
housekeeper); W - 33, music teacher, b. Farmington, d/o
Eleazer Pearl (Farmington, farmer) and Ann B. Pearl
(Farmington, housekeeper)

Winslow P. of Farmington m. Georgia I. **Colomy** of Farmington
11/28/1901; H - 22, farmer, b. Farmington, s/o John W.
Thompson (Farmington, farmer) and Jennie D. Hall
(Farmington); W - 21, shoeworker, b. Farmington, d/o George

A. Colomy (Farmington, shoemaker) and Eliza B. Jones (Somersworth)

**THURSTON,**

Clifton M. of Farmington m. Zelma **Nutter** of Farmington 3/28/1925 in Dover; H - 25, mechanic, b. Effingham, s/o William Thurston (Effingham, farmer) and Annie E. Merrill (Freedom, housewife); W - 23, stenographer, b. Farmington, d/o Joseph F. Nutter (Gilmanton, shoeworker) and Lilla Babb (NS, housewife)

Hanis of Farmington m. Alte F. **Littlefield** of Farmington 10/18/1925; H - 20, laborer, b. Plymouth, s/o Herbert Thurston (Milton, barber) and Ethel R. Higgins (Gorham, housewife); W - 27, stenographer, b. Farmington, d/o Fred A. Littlefield (insurance agt.) and Alma A. Kimball (housewife)

Herbert H. of Farmington m. Ethel **Higgin** of Springvale, ME 9/28/1903 in Milton; H - 23, barber, b. West Milton, s/o Charles Thurston (Strafford, shoemaker) and Cora J. Howe (West Milton, housewife); W - 17, lady, b. No. Gorham, ME, d/o Leslie Higgin (Thorndike, ME, carpenter) and Lydia Piper (No. Gorham, ME, housewife)

Percy L. of Farmington m. Grace E. **Hayden** of Farmington 8/29/1925 in Somersworth; H - 21, woodworker, b. Effingham Falls, s/o Martin V. Thurston (Broomfield, ME, farmer) and Clara M. Carlin (Chelsea, MA, housewife); W - 18, shoeworker, b. Freedom, d/o Mahlon Hayden (Fairfield, ME, carpenter) and Gertrude Kimball (Ossipee, shoeworker)

**TIBBETTS,**

Frank E. of Farmington m. Carrie B. **Hodgdon** of Alton 6/16/1888 in Somersworth; H - 23, shoemaker, 2nd, b. Rochester, s/o George (Lebanon, shoemaker) and Emma J. (Rochester, deceased); W - 22, housekeeper, b. Barnstead, d/o John D. (Barnstead, shoemaker) and Ellen J. (Alton, deceased)

Frank G. of Farmington m. Mary G. **Cloutman** of Farmington 9/12/1887; H - 28, merchant, b. Gilmanton I. W., s/o Reuben E. Tibbetts (Gilmanton I.W.) and Martha J. Tibbetts; W - 24, b. Farmington, d/o Jerrie E. Cloutman (New Durham) and Caroline A. Cloutman

Frank M. of Farmington m. Annie M. **Howard** of Milton 4/30/1892; H - 24, teamster, b. Milton, s/o Luke Tibbetts (Milton, 55, farmer) and Abbie Tibbetts (Milton, 57, housewife) of Milton; W - 28, housekeeper, 2nd, divorced, b. Barrington, d/o Ira Howard (dead) and Sarah Howard (dead)

Harris C. of Farmington m. Inez J. **Ham** of Farmington 1/14/1900 in Alton; H - 33, shoemaker, b. Farmington, s/o Timothy Tibbetts and Malvina Tibbetts; W - 22, lady, b. Farmington

Henry A. of Farmington m. Bertena J. **Smith** of Farmington 3/22/1907; H - 44, shoe cutter, 2nd, b. Farmington, s/o George F. Tebbetts (Farmington, blacksmith) and Betsey Place (Farmington); W - 29, shoe stitcher, b. Deer Isle, ME, d/o Edwin Smith (Litchfield, ME, stone paver) and Martha Thompson (N. Deer Isle, ME)

**TIERNEY,**

Joseph O. of Farmington m. Abbie B. **Hart** of Farmington 7/1/1915 in Rochester; H - 24, shoeworker, b. Providence, RI, s/o Robert W. Tierney (Providence, RI, sailmaker) and Mary A. Sloan (Providence, RI); W - 20, shoeworker, b. Lebanon, ME, d/o Dana Hart (foreman) and Mattie J. Stevens (housekeeper)

**TILTON,**

Sumner of Farmington m. Hildred **Brooks** of Farmington 7/28/1913; H - 22, shoeworker, b. E. Rochester, s/o Clark Tilton (W. Concord, VT, meat cutter) and Celia Jones (E. Rochester, housekeeper); W - 18, shoeworker, b. Farmington, d/o P. J. Brooks (Alton, shoeworker) and Edith Tibbetts (housekeeper)

**TIRRELL,**

Harold A. of Farmington m. Helen W. **Earle** of Alton 4/23/1927 in Alton; H - 18, baker, b. Springvale, ME, s/o Charles W. Tirrell (Boston, MA, laborer) and Annie Tuttle (Newmarket, housekeeper); W - 17, at home, b. Alton, d/o James A. Earle (Hartford, CT, laborer) and Nellie A. Jones (New Durham, housewife)

Melvin S. of Farmington m. Mardell E. **Howard** of Farmington 8/30/1912 in Rochester; H - 19, shoeworker, b. Lebanon, ME, s/o Charles Terrell (shoemaker); W - 18, shoeworker, b. Dover, d/o Herbert Howard (shoemaker) and Lizzie Miller (Dover, housekeeper)

Oscar L. of Lynn, MA m. Nellie G. **Orr** of Worcester, MA 8/27/1927 H - 39, shoeworker, 2nd, b. Melrose, MA, s/o Charles W. Tirrel and Annie Tuttle (Newmarket, housekeeper); W - 38, housekeeper, 2nd, b. Ireland, d/o Patrick Moen and Mary Boulon (Ireland)

**TOBY,**
Eddie E. of Farmington m. Gracie L. **Smith** of Farmington 11/6/1887; H - 20, shoemaker, b. Kittery Point, ME, s/o John E. Toby (Kittery Point, fisherman) and Martha A. Toby; W - 21 2nd, widow, b. Fryeburg, ME, d/o James McKeen (Fryeburg, ME, farmer) and Mary A. McKeen

**TOMLINSON,**
Enoch L. of Farmington m. Jennie B. **Hall** of E. Jefferson, ME 1/24/1895; H - 22, shoe laster, b. Nobleboro, ME, s/o James H Tomlinson (laborer) and Arlittie M. Tomlinson (Nobleboro); W 22, shoe fitter, b. E. Jefferson, ME, d/o Benjamin F. Hall (E. Jefferson, farmer) and Arabelle Hall (Wolfeboro, housekeeper)

**TOOTHAKER,**
Curtis C. of Rockland, MA m. Beatrice S. **Currul** of Rockland, MA 10/24/1931; H - 21, salesman, b. Berlin, s/o O. H. Toothaker (Harpswell, ME, salesman) and Grace M. Meade (Strafford, CT, housewife); W - 19, stenographer, b. Portland, ME, d/o Harry W. Currul (Halifax, NS, foreman) and Helen M. Hamilton (housewife)

**TORNO,**
Charles of Farmington m. Eliza E. **Berry** of Farmington 6/27/1912; H - 21, shoeworker, b. Germany, s/o Charles Torno (Germany) and Alvina Heubner (Germany, housekeeper); W - 21, lady, b. S. Berwick, ME, s/o Frank Berry (Portland, ME, shoemaker) and Emma Davis (South Alton, housekeeper)

**TOWLE,**
Floyd R. of Farmington m. Marion **Holder** of Farmington 12/23/1922 in Rochester; H - 24, shoeworker, b. New Durham, s/o Charles F. Towle (New Durham, shoeworker) and Henrietta Woodman (Alton, housewife); W - 16, shoeworker, b. Millis,

MA, d/o Irving C. Holder (foreman) and Annette Vinney (housewife)

George W. of Farmington m. Phebe **Leighton** of Farmington 9/12/1893; H - 22, shoemaker, b. Farmington, s/o Charles F. Towle (New Durham, shoemaker) and Emma Towle (New Durham, housewife); W - 19, lady, b. Farmington, d/o Charles H. Leighton (dead) and Emma A. Leighton (Farmington, housekeeper)

Tris S. of Farmington m. Adrienne **Langeoin** of Rochester 1/23/1937 in Rochester; H - 21, shoeworker, b. Dover, s/o Tristram Towle (New Durham, shoeworker) and Katherine Earner (Ireland, housewife); W - 19, shoeworker, b. Rochester, d/o Joseph Langeoin (Canada, deceased) and Zensida Langeoin (Canada, deceased)

Tristram F. of Farmington m. Annie B. **Trafton** of Farmington 2/18/1888; H - 20, shoemaker, b. New Durham, s/o Henry W. (Wolfeboro, shoemaker) and Emily M. (New Durham, housekeeper); W - 21, shoe stitcher, b. Great Falls, d/o Mark (Bangor, ME, engineer) and Amanda (W. Lebanon, ME, housekeeper)

**TRASK,**

Ralph C. of Farmington m. Helen D. **Yeaton** of Dover 6/1/1920 in Dover; H - 28, shoeworker, b. Farmington, s/o Lyman W. Trask (Strafford, shoeworker) and Ida E. Whitehouse (New Durham, housewife); W - 22, at home, b. Wakefield, d/o William A. Yeaton (Seabrook, RR engineer) and Lottie Palmer (Ellsworth, housewife)

**TRIPP,**

Charles H. of Farmington m. Ella N. **Bickford** of Farmington 4/22/1896 in Rochester; H - 29, farmer, b. Springvale, ME, s/o Charles H. Tripp (Springvale, ME, farmer) and Clara A. Tripp (Hiram, ME, housewife); W - 27, school teacher, b. Farmington, d/o John T. Bickford (Rochester, farmer) and Phebe H. Bickford (Gilford)

F. Leroy of Farmington m. Laura J. **Webster** of Farmington 5/1/1937 in Rochester; H - 44, shoeworker, 3rd, b. Milton, s/o Edwin Tripp (Sanford, ME, shoeworker) and Lucy Howe (Milton, deceased); W - 22, clerk, b. Farmington, d/o Charles

Webster (East Kingston, deceased) and Annie Gray (Merrimac, MA, at home)

**TUCKER,**
Charles P. of Boston, MA m. Grace A. **Gilman** of Farmington 6/30/1896; H - 24, salesman, b. S. Boston, MA, s/o Henry Tucker (Kittery, ME) and Mary A. Tucker (Tamworth); W - 19 b. Farmington, d/o Winslow H. Gilman (Farmington, shoe cutter) and Lydia F. Gilman (Farmington, housewife)

**TUFTS,**
Leon G. of Middleton m. Addie **Kimball** of Farmington 8/17/1901; - 22, farmer, b. Middleton, s/o George J. Tufts (Middleton, farmer) and Emma F. Whitehouse (Middleton); W - 17, housekeeper, b. Middleton, d/o David Kimball (Middleton, dead) and Nellie Hanscomb (Middleton)

**TURCOTTE,**
Oliver J. of Farmington m. Janet P. **Brown** of Conway 5/1/1937 in Rochester; H - 22, shoeworker, b. Bath, ME, s/o Oliver Turcot (Canada, mill) and Georgianna Dube (Canada, at home); W - 18, shoeworker, b. Albany, d/o Ford Brown (teamster) and Minnie Hammond (Albany, at home)

**TURMELLE,**
Edmond of Rochester m. Helen **Belanger** of Farmington 4/25/1927; H - 24, shoeworker, b. Rochester, s/o Athenase Turmelle (Canada, retired) and Athemise Ruel (Canada, housewife); W 20, housekeeper, b. Farmington, d/o William Belanger (Canada, shoemaker) and Delia Lepene (Canada, shoemaker)
Ethelbert of Rochester m. Beatrice **Belanger** of Farmington 7/27/1929; H - 24, shoeworker, b. Rochester, s/o Athanase Turmelle (Canada, shoemaker) and Athanise Ruel (Canada, housewife); W - 19, shoeworker, b. Gonic, d/o William Belanger (Canada, shoemaker) and Delia Lepine (Farmington housewife)

**TUTTLE,**
Charles E. of Farmington m. Rosetta **Dore** of Milton 9/28/1887 in Rochester; H - 36, sawyer, 2$^{nd}$, b. Middleton, s/o Ivory Tuttle

(Milton) and Malinda Tuttle; W - 22, operator, b. Milton, s/o Stephen Dore

Eugene A. of Farmington m. Maggie E. **Brawn** of Farmington 8/1/1895 in Strafford Corners; H - 19, shoemaker, b. Alton, s/o Stephen M. Tuttle (New Durham, laborer) and Eliza J. Tuttle (Rochester); W - 17, housekeeper, b. Dover, d/o Barney Reading (Dover, police officer) and Lizzie Reading (Dover, housewife)

Eugene A. of Rochester m. Maude R. **Bartlett** of Farmington 8/9/1926 in Seabrook; H - 48, fireman, 2$^{nd}$, b. Alton, s/o Stephen M. Tuttle (New Durham, carpenter) and Eliza J. Howard (Strafford, housewife); W - 38, housework, 3$^{rd}$, b. Farmington, d/o Joel Smart (Howland, ME, farmer) and Mary A. Smith (Dover, housewife)

Fred A. of Farmington m. Uraine B. **Leighton** of Farmington 3/4/1914; H - 35, shoeworker, 2$^{nd}$, b. ME, s/o H. V. Tuttle (ME, police) and Abbie B. Tuttle; W - 34, shoeworker, 2$^{nd}$, b. Farmington, d/o Charles H. Leighton (Farmington) and Emma A. Leighton (Natick)

Lester G. of Farmington m. Fannie **Smith** of Farmington 10/22/1914; H - 25, teamster, b. Epping, s/o Bert Tuttle (Nottingham, shoemaker) and Annie Hill (Epping, housekeeper); W - 18, shoeworker, 2$^{nd}$, b. Sanbornville, d/o James Drew (Brookfield, teamster) and Clara A. Glidden (Alton, housekeeper)

Willie M. of Farmington m. Ida M. **Averill** of Wolfeboro 6/16/1895 in Rochester; H - 24, laborer, b. Rochester, s/o Stephen M. Tuttle (New Durham, laborer) and Eliza J. Tuttle (Rochester); W - 23, housework, 2$^{nd}$, b. Wolfeboro, d/o Richard Kent (Wolfeboro) and Harriet Kent (Washington, DC)

**TWOMBLY,**

Fred J. of Farmington m. Martha A. **Marston** of Farmington 4/22/1899 in Alton; H - 26, shoemaker, b. Haverhill, MA, s/o Peter Twombly and Annie Twombly (Haverhill, MA); W - 32, shoe stitcher, b. Farmington, d/o Frank R. Marston (Farmington, shoe mfg.) and Susan Marston (Alton, lady)

Horne of Farmington m. Lydia M. **Shirley** of New Durham 4/1/1887 in New Durham; H - 73, farmer, 2$^{nd}$, widower, b. Farmington; W - 65, 2$^{nd}$, widow, b. Rochester

Laurel F. of Farmington m. Carrie **Thompson** of Farmington 10/11/1891; H - 42, farmer, b. Farmington, s/o John E. Twombly (dead); W - 41, housekeeper, 2$^{nd}$, b. Pittsfield, d/o Asa Varney (dead)

William of Sanbornville m. Frances **Derby** of Farmington 3/26/1933; H - 20, farmer, b. Union, s/o Clarence Twombly (Conway) and Bessie Downs (Wolfeboro, housewife); W - 20, shoeworker, b. Barnstead, d/o Charlie Derby (Montpelier, VT, carpenter) and Sylvia Cook (Barnstead, housewife)

**UNDERHILL,**

George E. of Tamworth m. Mary P. **Stacy** of Farmington 1/20/1935; H - 31, truck driver, b. Madison, s/o Everett Underhill (Chester, deceased) and Edna Mason (Madison, deceased); W - 31, maid, b. Sharon, VT, d/o George Stacy (Merrimac, MA, mechanic) and Janet G. Muir (Manchester, housewife)

**VALLANCOURT,**

Alfred of Rochester m. Madelaine **Cathcart** of Farmington 12/21/1934 in Rochester; H - 28, box maker, b. Lowell, MA, s/o Alexander Vallancourt (Gorham, deceased) and Melina Lachapelle (Canada, housework); W - 20, at home, b. Farmington, d/o Fred Cathcart (E. Rochester, shoeworker) and Bernice Haddock (Farmington, shoeworker)

**VAN VLECK,**

John F. of Farmington m. Helen P. **Colbath** of Farmington 8/4/1923; H - 21, shoeworker, b. Baltimore, s/o G. B. Van Vleck (Brooklyn, NY, shoeworker) and Blanche N. Schock (Philadelphia, housekeeper); W - 20, shoeworker, b. Portsmouth, d/o Fred Colbath (shoeworker) and Elizabeth ----- (Portsmouth, housekeeper)

**VANASSE,**

Armand L. of Farmington m. Doris **Tracy** of Rochester 8/25/1934 in Laconia; H - 25, shoeworker, b. Canada, s/o Avitis Vanasse (Canada, shoeworker) and Georgana Roberts (Laconia, beauty parlor); W - 22, shoeworker, b. Ipswich, MA, d/o John Tracy (Poland, caretaker) and Sophia Kotton (Poland, at home)

**VARNEY,**
Albert L. of Farmington m. Edith L. **Wyatt** of Farmington 1/18/1908 in Rochester; H - 21, teamster, b. Milford, MA, s/o Arthur N. Varney (Farmington, janitor) and Hattie King (Newark, NJ); W - 23, housekeeper, $2^{nd}$, b. Farmington, d/o Asa L. Wyatt (Farmington, teamster) and Bell Wyatt (Farmington)

Albert L. of Farmington m. Doris J. **Moulton** of Farmington 10/16/1915; H - 30, teamster, $2^{nd}$, b. Millville, MA, s/o Arthur M. Varney (Farmington, janitor) and Hattie King (Newark, NJ); W - 15, b. Farmington, d/o John P. Moulton (Farmington, farmer) and Martha A. Babb (New Durham, housekeeper)

Alvord O. of Farmington m. Hellena M. **Coombs** of Derry 9/28/1887; H - 33, shoecutter, $2^{nd}$, b. Alton, s/o Paul F. Varney (Alton, carpenter) and Lydia A. Varney; W - 20, shoefitter, b. Derry, d/o Joseph Coombs (farmer) and Harriet Coombs

Arthur F. of Farmington m. Stella P. **Bickford** of Farmington 4/4/1923 in Rochester; H - 26, farmer, b. Dover, s/o J. Fred Varney (Lebanon, ME, farmer) and Eva Foss (Strafford, housekeeper); W - 26, housekeeper, b. Farmington, d/o Walter H. Bickford (Rochester, farmer) and Mary Varney (Farmington, housekeeper)

Benjamin E. W. of New Durham m. Esther E. **Thompson** of Farmington 11/16/1916; H - 20, farmer, b. Farmington, s/o Albert D. Varney (Farmington, farmer) and Lula E. Brackett (Lowell, MA, housekeeper); W - 17, at home, b. New Durham, d/o Hervey J. Thompson (Farmington, farmer) and Florence J. Foss (Rochester, housekeeper)

Chester C. of Alton m. Helen A. **Geary** of Farmington 7/12/1929 in Sanbornville; H - 21, RR employee, b. Alton, s/o Albert D. Varney (Farmington, farmer) and Lulu Brackett (Lowell, retired); W - 18, shoeworker, b. Milton, d/o Anthony W. Geary (ME, lumberman) and Alice Perkins (Milton, housewife)

Daniel of Farmington m. Nellie **Whitehouse** of Farmington 5/15/1894; H - 47, laborer, $2^{nd}$, divorced, b. Tuftonboro, s/o Daniel Varney (Wakefield) and Lucy Varney (Rochester); W - 32, $2^{nd}$, widow, b. Belfast, ME, d/o Charles Shattock (Belfast, ME) and Mary Shattock (London, England)

Elvin V. of Farmington m. Eldora B. **Glidden** of Farmington 7/13/1901; H - 28, shoemaker, b. Farmington, s/o Ira E. Varney (Milton, dead) and Tamson E. Varney (Farmington, dead); W - 28, housekeeper, 2nd, b. Alton, d/o Henry A. Brown (VT, dead) and ----- (Alton)

Fred L. of Farmington m. Florence M. **Kendall** of Strafford, VT 6/12/1895 in Strafford, VT; H - 29, shoe stitcher, b. Milton, s/o John O. Varney (Milton, farmer) and Hannah L. Varney (Farmington, housewife); W - 26, housekeeper, b. Strafford, VT, d/o John K. Kendall (Strafford, VT, teamster) and Lucy Kendall (Strafford, VT)

Fred S. of Farmington m. Angie E. **Corson** of Farmington 2/4/1895 H - 21, shoemaker, b. Tuftonboro, s/o Daniel Varney (Tuftonboro, laborer) and Laurette I. Varney (New Durham); W - 23, housework, b. Barrington, d/o Lorenzo D. Corson (Lebanon) and Belinda Robinson (Strafford, housekeeper)

John F. of Farmington m. Ellen M. **Foss** of Dover 9/10/1893 in Barnstead; H - 61, farmer, 3rd, b. Farmington, s/o Phineas Varney (dead) and Huldah Varney (dead); W - 30, lady, 3rd, b. Stowe, ME, d/o George Johnson (dead) and Nancy Johnson (lady)

Lewis N. of Farmington m. Grace T. **Pinkham** of Middleton 10/30/1901 in Berwick, ME; H - 24, farmer, b. Farmington, s/o John F. Varney (Farmington, farmer) and Emma Cotton (Milton); W - 20, housekeeper, b. Middleton, d/o George Pinkham (Middleton, farmer) and Laura Maine (Milton)

Linnie V. of Farmington m. Ruth E. **Nourse** of Ashby, MA 1/1/1925 in Ashby, MA; H - 22, clerk, b. Farmington, s/o Elvin V. Varney (Farmington, shoeworker) and Eldora B. Brown (Alton, housewife); W - 23, teacher, b. Fitchburg, MA, d/o Albert F. Nourse and Myra E. Hager

Oe of Farmington m. Carrie A. **Edgerly** of Durham 1/3/1891 in Newmarket; H - 17, shoemaker, b. Alton, s/o Elisha Varney (dead); W - 18, housekeeper, b. Durham, d/o Elisha Edgerly (Durham, farmer)

Owen M. of Farmington m. Lillian B. **Downing** of Farmington 7/31/1887 in Pittsfield; H - 34, farmer, b. Farmington, s/o Othniel Varney (Farmington, farmer) and Kezra F. Varney; W - 20, b. Farmington, d/o James H. Downing (Farmington, farmer) and Adeline Downing

Ralph George of Farmington m. Kathleen **Thurston** of Farmington 12/22/1928 in Lebanon, ME; H - 20, shoeworker, b. Farmington, s/o Lewis N. Varney (Farmington, shoe operative) and Florence Pinkham (Middleton, housewife); W - 16, at home, b. Farmington, d/o Herbert Thurston (Plymouth, barber) and Ethel Higgins (Gorham, ME, housewife)

Walter E. of Farmington m. Emma E. **Ellis** of Alton 9/29/1923 in Rochester; H - 24, mechanic, b. Farmington, s/o Fred S. Varney (Farmington, shoemaker) and Angie Corson (Barrington, housekeeper); W - 18, shoeworker, b. Alton, d/o Ersmus Ellis (Gilmanton, carpenter) and Frances Jones (Alton, housewife)

## VICKERS,

Charles S., Jr. of Farmington m. Delia **Beaulieu** of Cambridge, MA 9/3/1933 in Rochester; H - 29, electrician, b. Sheffield, England, s/o Charles Vickers (Dranfield, England, retired) and Lilly Stuart (deceased); W - 18, housework, b. Limestone, ME, d/o Pierre Beaulieu (mill worker) and Annaise Dupont (deceased)

William J. of Farmington m. Della F. **Glidden** of New Durham 6/30/1923 in Dover; H - 20, electrician, b. England, s/o Charles Vickers (England, shoemaker) and Lill Stewart; W - 20, b. New Durham, d/o Harry Glidden (New Durham, woodturner) and Lila B. Randall (New Durham, housekeeper)

## WALDEN,

William A. of Farmington m. Doris O. **Nutter** of Farmington 11/24/1932 in Rochester; H - 27, garage, b. Weirs, s/o Gilbert Waldren (deceased) and Clara E. Bailey (Manchester, nurse); W - 23, nurse, b. Gilford, d/o J. Freeman Nutter (Gilmanton I.W. shoe foreman) and Lilla M. Babb (deceased)

## WALDRON,

Arthur F. of Farmington m. E. Grace **Herring** of Farmington 3/2/1887; H - 33, manufacturer, 2$^{nd}$, widower, b. Farmington, s/o Jeremiah W. Waldron (Farmington, manufacturer) and Mary E. Waldron; W - 32, b. Farmington, d/o George M. Herring (Framingham, MA) and Ellen E. Herring

Augustus S. of Farmington m. Sarah H. **Mullen** of Farmington 1/11/1888 in Great Falls; H - 41, harness maker, 2$^{nd}$, b. Farmington, s/o James H. (Farmington, deceased) and Abigail J. (New Durham, housekeeper); W - 35, tailoress, b. Acton, ME, d/o John and Mary M. (Acton, ME, housekeeper)

Donald H. of Farmington m. Gladys A. **Prescott** of Alton 11/19/1910 in Alton; H - 25, mill hand, b. Farmington, s/o Arthur F. Waldron (Farmington, sawyer) and Hannah A. Hall (Canaan, housewife); W - 19, housekeeper, b. Alton, d/o George R. Prescott (Alton, carpenter) and Lillian A. Jones (Alton, housewife)

Harrison G. of Farmington m. Marion D. **Atwood** of Farmington 5/29/1924 in Dover; H - 38, insurance, 2$^{nd}$, b. Farmington, s/o Samuel Waldron (Farmington, farmer) and Margaret Worster (Somersworth, housewife); W - 26, nurse, b. Hudson, MA, d/o George W. Atwood (Abington, MA, mfg. shoe factory) and Ma B. Dunbar (Bridgewater, MA, housewife)

Robert of Farmington m. Evelyn **Pinkham** of New Durham 12/31/1936; H - 23, shoeworker, b. Farmington, s/o Donald Waldron (Farmington, mill worker) and Gladys Prescott (Alton at home); W - 25, shoeworker, b. No. Lebanon, d/o Clifton Pinkham (Farmington, wood worker) and Ella Emerson (N. Lebanon, ME, housewife)

## WALKER,

Charles M. of Whitinsville, MA m. Marjorie L. **Eaton** of Melrose, M 10/1/1932; H - 22, teacher, b. Leominster, MA, s/o Charles H. Walker (Mechanic Falls, ME, school supt.) and Lillian Rainey (Hooksett, housekeeper); W - 20, student, b. Salisbury, MA, d/o Harlon Eaton (Salisbury, MA, adv. manager) and Evelyn True (Salisbury, MA, housekeeper)

Joseph F. of Farmington m. Alice **Marshall** of New Durham 11/12/1933; H - 57, jobber, 2$^{nd}$, b. Carlton, England, s/o Josep Walker (Carlton, England, deceased) and Jane Johnson (Norton, England, deceased); W - 55, matron, 2$^{nd}$, b. Farmington, d/o Hiram Brackett (Ossipee, deceased) and Augusta French (Farmington, at home)

## WALLACE,

Edgar F. of Farmington m. Clara E. **Littlefield** of Fitchburg, MA 1/1/1887 in Fitchburg, MA; H - 26, shoemaker, b. New Durham, s/o George N. Wallace (Ossipee) and Abbie A. Wallace; W - 24, teacher, b. Westford, MA, d/o Orrin Littlefield (Wells, ME, tinman) and Augusta Littlefield

George M. of Farmington m. Lucy M. **Berry** of Farmington 1/31/1913; H - 53, shoeworker, 2$^{nd}$, b. New Durham, s/o

George N. Wallace (Wakefield) and Abigail A. Runnals (New Durham); W - 76, housekeeper, 2nd

George M. of Farmington m. Augusta J. **Berry** of Dover 6/14/1921 in Dover; H - 62, shoeworker, 3rd, b. New Durham, s/o George M. Wallace and Abigail A. Runnells; W - 52, housekeeper, 2nd, b. New Durham, d/o Elwin A. Berry and Emma J. Hurd (Farmington)

Walter S. of Farmington m. Etta **Carter** of Farmington 7/4/1907 in Milton; H - 24, shoeworker, b. Middleton, s/o Charles F. Wallace (Middleton, laborer) and Dora Perkins (Middleton); W - 35, seamstress, 2nd, b. New Durham, d/o Lewis Valley (Canada, laborer)

William of Exeter m. Fannie **Clark** of Farmington 7/15/1920; H - 55, farmer, 2nd, b. Marlboro, MA, s/o William Wallace and Harriet Post; W - 60, housekeeper, 2nd, b. Alton, d/o James F. Smith and Jerusha Glidden

**WALLINGFORD,**

Calvin of Farmington m. Ethel A. **Gray** of Strafford 4/28/1907; H - 18, hostler, b. Farmington, s/o Charles Wallingford (Alton, shoemaker) and Carrie Randall (Rochester); W - 19, housekeeper, b. Strafford, d/o Charles Gray (Strafford, farmer) and Emma Hall (Strafford)

William J. of Farmington m. Rena S. **Bean** of Wolfeboro Falls 7/13/1937 in Somersworth; H - 25, carpenter, b. E. Derry, s/o Charles Wallingford (laborer) and Rosana Dermont (at home); W - 18, shoeworker, b. Freedom, d/o Willis H. Bean (Conway, carpenter) and Ellen Thompson (Eaton, at home)

**WALSH,**

John R. of Lebanon m. Amelia A. **Martineau** of Farmington 8/9/1930; H - 22, shoe operative, b. Lebanon, s/o John E. Walsh (Somersworth, shoe operative) and Grace M. Smith (Pittsfield, MA, housewife); W - 19, shoe operative, b. Rochester, d/o Frank Martineau (Canada, RR employee) and Jennie Marcoux (Canada, housewife)

Leroy F. of Farmington m. Arlene F. **Gibbs** of Farmington 8/21/1920; H - 24, shoeworker, 2nd, b. Bridgewater, s/o Frank Walsh (Somersworth, superintendent) and Eva McGrillis (East Rochester, housewife); W - 16, at home, b. Farmington, d/o

Ralph P. Gibbs (Bridgewater, MA, foreman) and Grace Emery (Farmington, housewife)

**WARD,**

Donald of Rochester m. Jeanette **Blouin** of Rochester 5/7/1933; H - 25, mill worker, b. Rochester, s/o Frank Ward (Rochester, hostler) and Mary Jane Jacques (Rochester, housewife); W - 22, b. Lebanon, ME, d/o Louis Blouin (Canada, millworker) and Eva Langlois (Lowell, MA, deceased)

**WARE,**

Arthur A. of Farmington m. Nellie M. **Leighton** of Farmington 1/20/1906; H - 29, shoe stock fitter, $2^{nd}$, widower, b. Waterville ME, s/o Charles Ware (Webster, ME, brick mfr.) and Eliza Golden (Lewiston, ME); W - 28, shoe worker, b. Lynn, d/o George Leighton (Farmington, shoemaker) and Margaret Sandwich (NS)

William V. of Farmington m. Lizzie J. **Varney** of Farmington 12/10/1903 in Rochester; H - 41, farmer, b. Salem, MA, s/o Alfred F. Ware (Salem, MA, farmer) and Hannah E. Varney (Farmington, housewife); W - 39, school teacher, b. Farmington, d/o Ivory Varney (Farmington, farmer) and Elina M. Varney (Gilmanton, housewife)

**WARREN,**

Buckley J. of Norwalk, CT m. Marion C. **Montgomery** of Farmington 3/18/1932; H - 25, none, b. Tombstone, AZ, s/o Buckley J. Warren (deceased) and Helen M. Callahan (deceased); W - 18, at home, b. Farmington, d/o William P. Montgomery (Farmington, shoeworker) and Lillian Pitts (deceased)

**WASHBURN,**

David L. of Springfield, MA m. Elizabeth N. **Fernald** of Farmington 9/24/1907; H - 28, dentist, b. Natick, MA, s/o Oscar Washburn (Milton, dentist) and Emma J. Leland (Eden, ME); W - 28, school teacher, b. Farmington, d/o George W. Fernald (Farmington, card engraver) and Alice Nute (Farmington)

**WATSON,**
Carl L. of Farmington m. Ruth C. **Cardinal** of Farmington 5/3/1938;
H - 22, shoeworker, b. Sanford, ME, s/o Frank Watson
(Bridgton, ME, shoeworker) and Clara Foss (Garland, ME,
housewife); W - 23, shoeworker, 2$^{nd}$, b. Farmington, d/o Solon
Wilkins (Ossipee, shoeworker) and Grace Haddock (Ossipee,
shoeworker)

**WATTON,**
Wilbur of Farmington m. Fannie **Wyatt** of Farmington 6/4/1917 in
Rochester; H - 23, farmer, b. ME; W - 23, teacher, b.
Farmington, d/o George Wyatt (Farmington, mill operative)
and Alice True

**WAUGH,**
Charles M. of Cambridgeport, MA m. Evelyn Marie **Proctor** of
Farmington 11/26/1896; H - 30, trav. salesman, b.
Cambridgeport, MA, s/o William A. Waugh (carriage mfr.) and
Mary J. Waugh (Boston, MA, housewife); W - 19, b.
Farmington, d/o Nathan L. Proctor (Charlestown, MA, shoe
cutter) and Melinda J. Proctor (New Durham)

**WEBBER,**
Horace E. of Farmington m. Annie M. **Richardson** of Farmington
10/18/1913; H - 18, RR section hand, b. Brockton, MA, s/o
George K. Webber (foreman) and Mary M. West
(housekeeper); W - 16, shoeworker, b. Farmington, d/o Ai
Richardson (mason) and Lydia Richardson (housekeeper)

**WEBSTER,**
Charles W. of Farmington m. Dorothy L. **Gilson** of Farmington
12/25/1933; H - 29, mail carrier, b. Farmington, s/o Charles
Webster (East Kingston, deceased) and Annie Gray
(Merrimac, MA, housewife); W - 21, at home, b. Boston, MA,
d/o Lewis F. Gilson (Farmington, gen. agt. B&M) and Lillian
Chesley (Farmington, housewife)

Frank E. of Farmington m. Ruth E. **Henderson** of Rochester
2/3/1900 in Rochester; H - 27, clerk, b. Farmington, s/o Joseph
F. Webster (Farmington, farmer) and Sarah L. Webster
(Farmington, housewife); W - 21, teacher, b. Rochester, d/o

Frank D. Henderson (Rochester, farmer) and Eliza A. Henderson (Rochester, housewife)

Frank E. of Farmington m. Georgie **Thompson** of Farmington 9/30/1938; H - 66, real estate, 2nd, b. Farmington, s/o Joseph Webster (Newmarket, deceased) and Sarah Avery (Epsom, deceased); W - 59, housewife, 2nd, b. Farmington, d/o George Colomy (Farmington, retired) and Eliza B. Jones (Farmington housewife)

George A. of Farmington m. Mary W. **Arnold** of Farmington 6/18/1921; H - 21, shoeworker, b. Haverhill, MA, s/o Charles L Webster (E. Kingston, shoeworker) and Annie M. Gray (Merrimac, MA, housewife); W - 18, shoeworker, b. PEI, d/o Samuel V. Arnold (Brockton, MA, shoeworker) and Sarah Godfrey (PEI, housewife)

## WEEDEN,

Wilbur N. of Lynn, MA m. Ida E. **Linscott** of Lynn, MA 11/6/1907; H - 21, teamster, b. Lynn, MA, s/o Forest A. Weeden (Danvers, MA, lunchroom prop.) and Alta Newhall (Lynn, MA); W - 21, operative, b. Farmington, d/o James Linscott (Farmington, shoeworker) and Ida Lord (Farmington)

## WELCH,

Carroll C. of Ossipee m. Sara Elizabeth **Scruton** of Farmington 9/1/1928 in Ctr. Conway; H - 21, clerk, b. Ossipee, s/o Walter S. Welch (Ossipee, merchant) and Cora B. Davis (Ossipee, housewife); W - 20, stenographer, b. Farmington, d/o J. Irving Scruton (Farmington, fruit dealer) and Elizabeth Preston (Fox River, Canada, housewife)

## WELLS,

Fred W. of Farmington m. Georgie A. **Mitchell** of NY 7/5/1910; H - 22, civil engineer, b. Danville, Canada, s/o W. H. Wells (Rumney, merchant) and Minnie Williamson (Danville, Canada, housewife); W - 19, school girl, b. NY, d/o ----- (NY, jeweler) and ----- (NY, housewife)

## WENTWORTH,

Alvin H. of Farmington m. Abbie J. **Evans** of Farmington 11/11/1904; H - 70, heelmaker, 2nd, widower, b. Middleton, s/o David Wentworth (Farmington, farmer) and Charlotte Corson

(Middleton, housewife); W - 60, housekeeper, 2$^{nd}$, widow, b. Alton

Alvin S. of Farmington m. Mary A. **Evans** of Farmington 12/4/1897; H - 24, heel cutter, b. Farmington, s/o Alvin H. Wentworth (Gilmanton, s. leather cutter) and Henrietta Wentworth (Gilmanton, housekeeper); W - 20, heel maker, b. Farmington, d/o James I. Evans (Alton, section boss) and Augusta Evans (housekeeper)

Charles W. of Farmington m. Ida B. **Clark** of Farmington 7/19/1923; H - 74, boxmaker, 3$^{rd}$, b. Dover, s/o Henry Wentworth and Eliza Littlefield; W - 42, housekeeper, b. Alton, d/o Frank Clark and Fannie S. Smith (Alton, housekeeper)

George E. of Wolfeboro m. Lillian V. **Crockett** of Georgetown, MA 5/1/1897 in Wolfeboro; H - 30, shoemaker, b. Wolfeboro, s/o Morris Wentworth (Wakefield, shoemaker) and Annie E. Wentworth (Tuftonboro, housekeeper); W - 22, housework, b. Cambridgeport, MA, d/o George W. Crockett (Rollinsford, carpenter) and Mary E. Crockett (Lowell, MA, housekeeper)

John E. of Farmington m. Cynthia **Cook** of Farmington 6/27/1922 in East Rochester; H - 58, laborer, b. Rochester, s/o George Wentworth and Hannah Bickford; W - 47, housekeeper, b. Barnstead

Joseph D. of Farmington m. Jennie May **Savoir** of Farmington 10/17/1914; H - 24, shoeworker, b. Farmington, s/o Joseph Wentworth (Farmington, shoeworker) and Martha Wentworth (Farmington, shoeworker); W - 16, at home, b. Dover, d/o Joseph Savoir (Canada, conductor) and Delia Savoir (Canada, housekeeper)

Laurence of Farmington m. Marguerite L. **Carty** of Gilmanton I.W. 8/26/1937 in Laconia; H - 20, shoeworker, b. Middleton, s/o Joseph Wentworth (Middleton, shoeworker) and Jennie Savoie (Dover, clerk); W - 21, hairdresser, b. New York City, d/o Edward Carty (NY, milkman) and Bernice Brown (Plymouth, at home)

Loren G. of Wolfeboro m. Nellie F. **Randall** of Wolfeboro 7/14/1888; H - 26, stock fitter, b. Milton, s/o Albert F. (Milton, deceased) and Mary A.; W - 21, housekeeper, b. New Durham, d/o George W. (stock fitter) and Elizabeth (housekeeper)

Reginald R. of Farmington m. Mary E. **Ham** of Farmington 4/26/1919; H - 18, shoeworker, b. New Durham, s/o Gertrude

Ham; W - 20, bookkeeper, b. Farmington, d/o Clarence Ham (laborer) and Mary Peavey (housewife)

**WESSEL,**
George W. of Farmington m. Eugenie **Flanders** of Farmington 8/1/1888 in Rochester; H - 22, shoemaker, b. Danvers, MA, s Joseph (shoemaker) and Catherine (housekeeper); W - 18, housekeeper, b. Farmington, d/o Samuel B. (deceased) and Marcia A. (housekeeper)

**WESTERBURG,**
George L. of Farmington m. Mabel M. **Lewis** of Farmington 8/25/1928 in Rochester; H - 28, shoeworker, $2^{nd}$, b. Malden, MA, s/o Leonard Westerburg (Sweden, shoeworker) and Emma Frederickson; W - 28, shoeworker, $2^{nd}$, b. Hampton, d/ Samuel Stanley (Bangor, ME, watchman) and Elvira E. Oake (Waltham, ME, housewife)

**WEYMOUTH,**
Carl H. of Farmington m. Theora **Hayes** of Farmington 11/24/1929 in Portsmouth; H - 20, salesman, b. Farmington, s/o Harold Weymouth (Boston, MA, truckman) and Winnie Nutter (Farmington, forelady); W - 19, clerk, b. Farmington, d/o Arth G. Hayes (New Durham, shoeworker) and Ethel Brooks (Farmington, housewife)

Edwin L. of Farmington m. Genevieve **Cilley** of Farmington 4/30/1930; H - 55, farmer, b. Boston, MA, s/o Daniel Drew (Barnstead, farmer) and Sarah E. Hall (Barnstead, housekeeper); W - 51, housekeeper, b. Farmington, d/o Danie P. Cilley (Boston, MA, physician) and Velma A. Waldron (Farmington, housekeeper)

Harold E. of Farmington m. Vera W. **Cate** of Rochester 1/22/1920 in Rochester; H - 33, laundryman, $2^{nd}$, b. Boston, MA, s/o Theodore Weymouth (Boston, MA, expressman) and Lizzie F Eagles (NS, housewife); W - 25, stenographer, b. Brookfield, d/o Harry W. Cate (Brookfield, farmer) and Amy Burgess (New Orleans, LA, housewife)

**WHEATLEY,**
Hannibal P. of Farmington m. Hattie N. **Tibbetts** of Farmington 1/8/1908; H - 59, physician, $3^{rd}$, b. Brookfield, VT, s/o

Nathaniel Wheatley (Brookfield, VT, farmer) and Betsey P. Wood (Westford, VT); W - 40, 2$^{nd}$, b. Farmington, d/o Freeman P. Howe (Farmington, farmer) and Adeline P. Roberts (Farmington)

**WHEELER,**
Courtland of Farmington m. Olive A. **Swinerton** of Milton 4/26/1891 in Milton; H - 29, shoemaker, b. Isle La Motte, VT, s/o Edward Wheeler (dead); W - 16, housekeeper, b. Great Falls, d/o Richard G. Swinerton (Newfield, farmer)

Frank E. of Farmington m. Myra B. **Tuttle** of Farmington 6/1/1898 in Alton; H - 27, hotel keeper, b. Natick, MA, s/o Darwin E. Wheeler (Ashland, MA, lumberman) and Angeline Wheeler (Alton, housekeeper); W - 21, school teacher, b. Farmington, d/o Daniel Tuttle (Barnstead, lumber dealer) and Ruth A. Tibbetts (Farmington, school teacher)

**WHITE,**
Charles W. of Gilford m. Annie **Davis** of Gilford 4/30/1892; H - 21, blacksmith, b. Farmington, s/o Llewellyn White (New Castle, 43, shoemaker) of Farmington and Mary A. White (Rochester, 40, housewife) of Gilford; W - 18, lady, b. Gilford, d/o Arthur Davis (Gilford, 49, carpenter) and Alice Davis (Gilford, 47, housewife) of Gilford

George A. of Farmington m. Ida B. **Carr** of New Durham 4/15/1913 in Rochester; H - 37, shoeworker, 2$^{nd}$, b. Beverly, MA, s/o Stephen D. White (milkman) and Katie Fernald (housekeeper); W - 40, housekeeper, 2$^{nd}$, b. New Durham, d/o Ira Rand (farmer) and Abigail Savage

George A. of Bristol, VT m. Gertrude J. **Whiting** of Sanford, ME 5/20/1933 in Dover; H - 20, roofer, 2$^{nd}$, b. Bristol, VT, s/o Ira White (Bristol, VT, mason) and Dora Ward (Bristol, VT, housewife); W - 20, millworker, b. Sanford, ME, d/o Herbert Whiting (Hartford, CT, musician) and Josephine Bradshaw (Canada, housewife)

George Arthur of East Boston m. Josie Ella **Averill** of Farmington 4/17/1897; H - 21, fireman, b. Beverly, MA, s/o Stephen D. White (Beverly, MA, milkman); W - 18, b. Farmington, d/o Trask Averill (Farmington, farmer) and Almena Averill (New Durham, housekeeper)

George I. of Farmington m. Bessie E. **Leighton** of Farmington 6/25/1896; H - 25, express agent, b. Farmington, s/o Washington White (New Castle, carpenter) and Sarah A. White (Dover, housewife); W - 22, milliner, b. Farmington, d/o Amasa R. Leighton (Effingham, farmer) and Francena B. Leighton (Portsmouth, housewife)

George W. of Portland, ME m. Helen H. **Horne** of Portland, ME 8/16/1937; H - 22, b. Revere, MA, s/o Joseph White (Hyde Park, MA, carpenter) and Rena Bowering (Revere, MA, at home); W - 20, at home, b. Dorchester, MA, d/o Herbert Horne (Wolfeboro, optician) and Hazel Foster (Dorchester, MA, at home)

Harley C. of Farmington m. Eunice L. **Dudley** of New Durham 6/5/1905 in New Durham; H - 56, farmer, $2^{nd}$, b. Wenham, s/o Samuel White (Hope, ME) and Marie Curtis (Salem, MA); W - 35, housekeeper, $2^{nd}$, b. New Durham, d/o Iva Rand (Alton, farmer) and Abigail Ham

Melvin J. of Farmington m. Jessie Maude **Dustin** of Plymouth 8/9/1904 in Plymouth; H - 27, school teacher, b. Farmington, s/o Harley C. White (Wenham, MA, farmer) and Mary E. Johnson (Farmington, housewife); W - 23, teacher, b. Hebron, d/o Robert Dustin (Bristol, stone contractor) and Ida A. Nelson (Plymouth, teacher)

**WHITEHOUSE,**

C. W. of Farmington m. Addie M. **Canney** of Farmington 5/10/1890; H - 26, shoe cutter, b. Middleton, s/o W. H. Whitehouse (Middleton, shoemaker) and Emma A. (Newmarket); W - 28, housekeeper, b. Farmington, d/o Edmund B. Canney (Farmington, farmer) and Lydia M. (Tamworth)

Charles of Farmington m. Annie A. **Averill** of Farmington 11/5/1902 in Rochester; H - 27, shoe cutter, b. Farmington, s/o Charles M. Whitehouse (Milton, farmer) and Ida B. Colbath (Dover, heelmaker); W - 23, shoe stitcher, b. Farmington, d/o Trask W. Averill (Farmington, farmer) and Augusta Wallace (housewife)

Ellwood K. of Farmington m. Nellie **Shattuck** of Farmington 4/23/1887; H - 25, laster, b. New Durham, s/o Thomas Whitehouse (Middleton) and Ellen Whitehouse; W - 25, b. Belfast, ME, d/o Charles Shattuck (Belfast, ME) and Mary Shattuck

Frank I. of Farmington m. Fannie C. **Fall** of Farmington 7/6/1908; H - 23, clerk, b. Farmington, s/o Daniel P. Whitehouse (Middleton, shoeworker) and Marilla J. Howard (Farmington); W - 20, book keeper, b. Farmington, d/o Charles T. Fall (Farmington, shoeworker) and Emma Richardson (Farmington, shoeworker)

Fred of Farmington m. Laura A. **Cloutman** of Farmington 4/25/1898; H - 49, shoemaker, b. Dover, s/o Charles S. Whitehouse and Mary Whitehouse; W - 49, housekeeper, 2$^{nd}$, b. Alton, d/o Samuel Ham and Jane Ham

Fred of Wellesley, MA m. Mildred M. **Stillings** of Natick, MA 8/28/1905; H - 28, electrician, b. Ossipee, s/o F. P. Whitehouse (Ossipee, clerk) and Sarah Whitehouse (Tuftonboro); W - 21, cashier, b. Farmington, d/o Calvin Stillings (Jackson, salesman) and Edith Tibbetts (Farmington)

Fred L. of Farmington m. Ellen M. **Tufts** of Middleton 5/28/1938 in Milton; H - 19, boxmaker, b. Rochester, s/o F. Whitehouse (Strafford, boxmaker) and Georgie Berry (Farmington, deceased); W - 20, shoeworker, b. Middleton, d/o Leon Tufts (Middleton, millhand) and Addie M. Kimball (Middleton, housewife)

Harvey, Jr. of Middleton m. Annie H. **Wallace** of Farmington 2/15/1916 in Rochester; H - 20, farmer, b. Rochester, s/o Harvey Whitehouse (Middleton, farmer) and Isabelle Ellis (Rochester, housekeeper); W - 23, shoeworker, b. Middleton, d/o Charles F. Wallace (Middleton, shoeworker) and Dora Perkins (Middleton, housekeeper)

Perley E. of Farmington m. Victoria M. **DuQuette** of Milton 10/7/1911; H - 24, shoe cutter, b. Farmington, s/o Daniel Whitehouse (Middleton, shoe laster) and Marilla Howard (Farmington, housewife); W - 18, shoeworker, b. Union, d/o Leon DuQuette (Canada, fireman) and Emma Hall (Canada, housewife)

**WHITNEY,**

Myron H. of Farmington m. Vivian H. **Allen** of Rochester 3/17/1938 in Auburn; H - 30, carpenter, 2$^{nd}$, b. Bridgton, ME, s/o John Whitney (Boston, MA, laborer) and Ida Hanscomb (Chatham, merchant); W - 37, housekeeper, 2$^{nd}$, b. Rochester, d/o Orin Grant (Acton, ME, deceased) and Jennie Emerson (Northwood, housewife)

Will E. of Farmington m. Winnie M. **Wiggin** of Farmington 11/14/1901; H - 24, printer, b. Farmington, s/o William W. Whitney (Natick, MA, shoemaker) and Julia A. Pinkham (Farmington, dressmaker); W - 25, shoeworker, 2$^{nd}$, b. Farmington, d/o Otis W. Fall (Alton, dead) and Mary A. Beck (Alton)

**WHITTEN,**

James B. of Farmington m. Flora L. **Osgood** of Farmington 8/19/1915; H - 58, mason, 2$^{nd}$, b. Wolfeboro, s/o Augustus Whitten (Wolfeboro, mason) and Lydia Kent (Canada); W - 46 housekeeper, 2$^{nd}$, b. Springfield, MA, d/o Abbie H. Judd

**WIGGIN,**

Archie C. of Farmington m. Maude R. **Smart** of Farmington 4/10/1909 in Dover; H - 32, laborer, b. Farmington, s/o Lewis R. Wiggin (Tuftonboro) and Martha Tanner (Farmington); W - 22, housekeeper, b. Farmington, d/o Joel Smart (Maxwell, ME farmer) and Mary A. Smith (Dover, housewife)

Fred N. of Farmington m. Inez **Place** of Middleton 12/24/1895 in Dover; H - 22, hackman, b. Farmington, s/o Lewis R. Wiggin (Moultonborough) and Martha A. Wiggin (Farmington, housewife); W - 19, shoe fitter, b. Middleton, d/o William B. Place (Middleton, shoemaker) and Lydia A. Place (Middleton, housewife)

Fred N. of Farmington m. Annie L. **Moore** of Portland, ME 10/11/1915; H - 43, chauffeur, 2$^{nd}$, b. Farmington, s/o Lewis R. Wiggin (Tuftonboro, miner) and Martha E. Tanner (Farmington); W - 44, housekeeper, 2$^{nd}$, b. Whitneyville, ME, d/o David Hurlburt (NS, farmer) and Louisa Gray (NS, housekeeper)

Fred N. of Farmington m. Anna B. **Batchelder** of Farmington 11/16/1918; H - 45, chauffeur, 3$^{rd}$, b. Farmington, s/o Lewis R. Wiggin and Martha A. Tanner (Farmington, housekeeper); W - 46, dressmaker, b. Haverhill, MA, d/o John Batchelder and Maria A. Bartlett

Uriah S. of Farmington m. Bertha M. **Ricker** of Farmington 11/24/1894; H - 24, foreman factory, b. Dover, s/o Albert H. Wiggin (Dover) and Rebecca S. Wiggin (Biddeford, ME, housekeeper); W - 18, housekeeper, b. Wolfeboro, d/o James

M. Ricker (Wolfeboro, shoemaker) and Annie S. Ricker (Ossipee)

**WILKINS,**
Leslie O. of Farmington m. Geraldine **Abbott** of Ctr. Ossipee 1/9/1927; H - 32, barber, 2nd, b. Wolfeboro, s/o William E. Wilkins and Marion A. Hartford (Ireland, housekeeper); W - 24, shoeworker, b. Ossipee, d/o Lyford Abbott (mill hand) and Etta ----- (housewife)

Robert of Farmington m. Arline **Richardson** of Farmington 4/19/1932; H - 21, soldier, b. Farmington, s/o Solon Wilkins (deceased) and Grace Haddock (Ossipee, housewife); W - 18, waitress, b. Farmington, d/o Ernest Richardson (Northwood, laborer) and Marion Thompson (Farmington, housewife)

Robert R. of Portsmouth m. Irma **Place** of Farmington 10/27/1935 in Wolfeboro; H - 22, electrician, 2nd, b. Farmington, s/o Solon Wilkins (Wolfeboro, deceased) and Grace Haddock (Ossipee, housewife); W - 18, at home, b. Springvale, ME, d/o Dean Place (Middleton, shoeworker) and Lena Batchelder (Springvale, ME, at home)

**WILKINSON,**
Edward W. of Farmington m. Iva M. **Chandler** of Northwood 11/21/1925; H - 33, shoeworker, 2nd, b. Auburn, ME, s/o Henry Wilkinson (England, textile worker) and Emma Wood (England, housewife); W - 24, shoeworker, 2nd, b. Chichester, d/o Charles Presby (Chichester, carpenter) and Lillian Edmonds (Chichester, housewife)

**WILLARD,**
Clyde A. of Farmington m. Mildred A. **Christie** of Farmington 7/5/1926; H - 24, shoeworker, b. Alton, s/o Smith A. Willard (Alton, police officer) and Sadie E. Lamper; W - 30, shoeworker, 2nd, b. Beverly, MA, d/o Albert W. Fielder and Alice M. Caswell (Beverly, MA, forelady)

Frank B. of Springfield, MA m. Clara A. **Small** of Farmington 4/22/1895; H - 32, salesman, 2nd, b. Franklin, VT, s/o Frank B. Willard and Laura M. Robis (Franklin, VT); W - 22, b. North Gray, ME, d/o Marcus W. Small (Raymond) and Helen A. Goff

Frank N. of Farmington m. Etola **Bubier** of Alton 8/10/1925; H - 20, shoeworker, b. Alton, s/o Smith Willard (Alton, shoeworker)

and Sadie Lamper; W - 18, at home, b. Newport, ME, d/o Sc[?]
Bubier (Hudson, ME, mill operative) and Belle Bubier (Alton,
housewife)

Maurice S. of Alton m. Bernice L. **Christie** of Farmington 9/1/192[?]
H - 19, shoeworker, b. Alton, s/o Smith Willard (Alton, clerk)
and Sadie Lamper (Alton, housewife); W - 17, at home, b.
Beverly, MA, d/o John Christie (Lynn, MA, shoeworker) and
Mildred Fielder (Beverly, MA, shoeworker)

Maurice S. of Farmington m. Irene M. **Mosher** of Farmington
4/27/1934 in Rochester; H - 24, shoemaker, $2^{nd}$, b. Alton, s/o
Smith A. Willard (Alton, real estate) and Sadie Lamper (Alton
at home); W - 23, bookkeeper, d/o Eugene Mosher
(Springfield, MA, farmer) and Catherine Haley (Woburn, MA,
housewife)

Raymond C. of Farmington m. Annie B. **Elliott** of Farmington
6/23/1924; H - 31, lumberman, $2^{nd}$, b. Alton, s/o Smith Willard
(Alton, shoeworker) and Sadie Lamper (Alton, housewife); W
30, shoeworker, $3^{rd}$, b. Ogunquit, ME, d/o Aaron Dunnell and
Clara Gerald (York, ME, housekeeper)

Smith A. of Alton m. Gertie E. **Carter** of Farmington 4/25/1916; H -
48, shoeworker, $2^{nd}$, b. Alton, s/o William Willard (farmer) and
Maria S. Perkins (Thorington); W - 31, housekeeper, $3^{rd}$, b. N.
Scituate, d/o Robert C. Bishop (Johnston, RI) and Hannah F.
Kimball (Scituate, RI, housekeeper)

**WILLEY,**

Almon E. of Farmington m. Ester U. **Cilley** of New Durham
9/14/1901 in New Durham; H - 45, shoemaker, $2^{nd}$, b. New
Durham, s/o Samuel Willey (New Durham, dead) and Mary A.
Coburn (Pelham); W - 19, housekeeper, b. Coldrain, MA, d/o
Daniel F. Cilley (Coldrain, MA, engineer) and Ida Hathaway
(Coldrain, MA, dead)

Burnes C. of S. Lebanon, ME m. Addie M. **Rhines** of Farmington
9/30/1911; H - 21, blacksmith, b. S. Lebanon, ME, s/o Eben
Willey (Alton, farmer) and Mattie Stevens (S. Lebanon, ME,
housekeeper); W - 26, shoe cutter, b. New Durham, d/o Irving
C. Rhines (New Durham, farmer) and Angie Brown (Limerick,
ME, housekeeper)

Charles D. of Farmington m. Pauline J. **Worster** of Farmington
7/9/1932 in Alton; H - 25, shoeworker, b. Farmington, s/o John
D. Willey (Middleton, retired) and Celia R. Lougee (Gilmanton,

housekeeper); W - 22, shoeworker, b. Farmington, d/o Henry Worster (Berwick, ME, shoeworker) and Clara Leclair (Dover, housekeeper)

Charles H. of Farmington m. Mary Edna **Berry** of New Durham 5/21/1902 in New Durham; H - 73, farmer, 2nd, widower, b. Brookfield, s/o John Willey (Brookfield, dead) and Betsey Jones (Wolfeboro, dead); W - 41, housekeeper, b. New Durham, d/o John Berry (New Durham, dead) and Nancy M. Phelps (Sutton, housekeeper)

Charles R. of Farmington m. Etta B. **Aspinwall** of Farmington 1/27/1889 in New Durham; H - 25, shoemaker, b. New Durham, s/o Ruel W. Willey (farmer) and Mary E. Willey (New Durham); W - 19, shoe fitter, b. New Durham, d/o John G. Aspinwall (Dover, shoemaker) and Frances P. Aspinwall (Middleton)

Charles R. of Farmington m. Nellie M. **Smith** of New Durham 9/30/1891; H - 28, shoemaker, 2nd, b. New Durham, s/o Ruel W. Willey (New Durham, farmer); W - 30, housekeeper, 2nd, d/o John Smith (dead)

Frank E. of Farmington m. Abbie D. **Laurens** of Farmington 5/24/1889; H - 31, shoe cutter, 3rd, b. Middleton, s/o Benjamin Willey (New Durham, laborer) and Lydia E. Willey; W - 19, shoe fitter, b. Farmington, d/o Isaac Laurens (dead) and Susan Laurens

George E. of Farmington m. Margueret E. **Brough** of Farmington 5/16/1936; H - 25, shoeworker, b. Farmington, s/o John Willey (Middleton, retired) and Celia Lougee (Gilmanton, housewife); W - 18, shoeworker, b. Laconia, d/o Nathaniel Brough (Randolph, deceased) and Alice Danforth (Belmont, shoeworker)

Herbert A. of Farmington m. Emma L. **Montee** of Farmington 5/20/1905; H - 23, moulder, b. New Durham, s/o Charles P. Willey (New Durham, farmer) and Carrie Corson (New Durham); W - 20, shoe stitcher, b. Farmington, d/o John Montee (St. Canos, Canada, shoemaker) and Lucy Winter (Gorham, ME, shoe stitcher)

John D. of Farmington m. Celia R. **Downs** of Farmington 5/20/1906 in New Durham; H - 53, farmer, 2nd, divorced, b. Middleton, s/o Charles W. Willey (Middleton, farmer) and Abigail Grace (New Durham); W - 19, housekeeper, 2nd, widow, b. Gilmanton, d/o A. P. Lougee and Ella Watson

**WILLSON,**

Charles W. T. of Farmington m. Nellie M. **Joy** of New Durham 8/14/1907 in New Durham; H - 23, clerk, b. Farmington, s/o Edward Willson (York, ME, merchant) and M. Emma Hayes (Farmington); W - 19, school teacher, b. Findley, MN, d/o S. Orrin Joy (farmer) and Mary E. Berry (New Durham)

Edward T. of Farmington m. Jessie L. **Hayes** of Boone, IA 8/29/1906; H - 52, merchant, 2$^{nd}$, widower, b. York, ME, s/o Theodore Willson (York, ME, farmer) and Elizabeth S. Talpey (York, ME); W - 41, 2$^{nd}$, widow, b. Sigourney, IA, d/o Warren Havens (OH, editor) and Jenney Dunn (Bridgton, IL)

Paul J. of Farmington m. Vera **DeMeritt** of Milton 12/30/1934; H - 21, clerk, b. Farmington, s/o Charles W. T. Willson (Farmington, janitor) and Nellie M. Joy (St. Paul, MN, housewife); W - 23, shoeworker, b. Milton, d/o Bertold DeMerit (Newfields, ME, foreman) and Musetta Dorr (Dover, housewife)

**WILSON,**

Orville A. of Farmington m. Mary L. **Robie** of Farmington 10/3/1895; H - 58, vet. surgeon, 2$^{nd}$, b. Bennington, s/o Wesley Wilson (Bennington) and Rachel Wilson (Bennington); W - 33, housework, b. Shelbrook, Canada, d/o Lewis Robie (Montreal, Canada) and Mary Robie (Montreal, Canada)

**WINGATE,**

Arthur R. of Farmington m. L. Clarabell **Barr** of Alton 5/29/1899 in Alton; H - 23, shoemaker, b. Farmington, s/o Charles W. Wingate and Mary E. Wingate (Farmington, housekeeper); W - 21, lady, b. NS, d/o Charles H. Barr (NS, farmer)

Henry S. of Farmington m. Lizzie M. **Chadwick** of Alton 6/16/1889 in Alton; H - 23, clerk, b. Rochester, s/o Joseph Wingate (Berwick, ME, merchant) and Sally R. Wingate (Rochester); W - 17, housekeeper, b. Chelsea, MA, d/o Benjamin F. Chadwick (Nantasket, MA, dead) and Eunice A. Chadwick (Nantasket, MA)

**WINN,**

George E. of Farmington m. Helen **Barker** of Farmington 1/11/1896; H - 21, farmer, b. W. Lebanon, ME, s/o Caleb W. Winn (W. Lebanon, ME, farmer) and Sarah W. Winn (W.

Lebanon, ME, housewife); W - 21, b. Farmington, d/o John H. Barker (Farmington, merchant) and Ella Barker

**WOODMAN,**
Jesse of Farmington m. Evelyn J. **Curtis** of Farmington 8/30/1930; H - 27, shoe operative, b. Middleton, s/o Frank Woodman and Lavona Drew (housewife); W - 22, at home, b. Farmington, d/o Fred Curtis (Milton, shoeworker) and Carrie Howard (Farmington, housewife)

Willis of Farmington m. Ida **Ham** of Farmington 11/16/1907; H - 31, mill hand, 2$^{nd}$, b. Alton, s/o Leroy Woodman (Alton, farmer) and Abbie Davis (Alton); W - 32, shop hand, 3$^{rd}$, d/o ----- (Alton)

**WOODROW,**
Edward of Farmington m. Maurial **Patrick** of Alton 12/20/1913; H - 25, lumberman, b. Bartlett, s/o David Woodrow (laborer) and Mary Goodblood; W - 16, at home, d/o Curt Patrick

**WOODWORTH,**
Leland L. of Farmington m. F. Mildred **Mack** of N. Easton, MA 6/25/1926; H - 24, pattern maker, b. Hillsboro, NS, d/o John C. Woodworth (NS, carpenter) and Eva Caswell; W - 21, stenographer, b. Boston, MA, d/o Abbott P. Mack and Rowena B. Fox (NS, housewife)

**WORCESTER** [see Worster],
George W. of Farmington m. Ida Mildred **Keniston** of Dover 10/3/1917 in Dover; H - 19, second-hand dealer, b. Somersworth, s/o Kirk Worcester (Somersworth, farmer) and Harriett Perkins; W - 21, saleslady, b. Newmarket, d/o Charles Keniston (Groton, tailor) and Marion Doeg

Robert A. of Farmington m. Mabel **Reynolds** of Farmington 3/7/1936 in Rochester; H - 22, shoeworker, b. Farmington, s/o Henry Worcester (Berwick, ME, shoeworker) and Clara LaClair (Dover, shoeworker); W - 23, shoeworker, b. Saugus, MA, d/o James Reynolds (Danvers, MA, shoeworker) and Bertha Tansch (Germany, shoeworker)

**WORSTER** [see Worcester],

Herbert of Farmington m. Lillian M. **Morrill** of Newburyport 10/15/1927; H - 51, painter, 2nd, b. Somersworth, s/o George Worster and Eliza J. Hartford; W - 43, laundress, 3rd, b. Bartlett, d/o John F. Tracey and Mary E. Tracey

Wilfred H. of Farmington m. Laura M. **Hussey** of Farmington 1/21/1934 in Alton; H - 22, shoeworker, b. Farmington, s/o Henry H. Worster (Somersworth, shoeworker) and Clara LeClare (Danville, housewife); W - 19, at home, b. Springvale ME, d/o Charles S. Hussey (So. Sanford, ME, deceased) and Ethel M. Reynolds (Shapleigh, ME, housewife)

**WOTTON**,

Robert M. of Farmington m. Flora V. **Charles** of Jackson 9/24/1938 in Jackson; H - 18, farmer, b. Whittier, CA, s/o Wilbur Wotton (Thomaston, ME, fireman) and Fannie Wyatt (Farmington, housewife); W - 25, teacher, b. Jackson, d/o Rodney Charles (Chatham, garageman) and Ruth Stilphen (Glen, housewife)

**WRIGHT**,

Frank C. of New Durham m. Anna A. **Downing** of Farmington 6/29/1914 in Dover; H - 27, farmer, b. Crescent City, CA, s/o Frank I. Wright (Alton, shoemaker) and Abbie C. Jenkins; W - 24, teacher, b. Farmington, d/o George T. Downing (Farmington, farmer) and Etta Chamberlain (housekeeper)

**WYATT**,

Asa of Farmington m. Amanda M. **Kendall** of Farmington 1/24/1914; H - 65, farmer, 2nd, b. Farmington, s/o Ira Wyatt (MA) and Louisa Wingate (Farmington); W - 61, housekeeper, 2nd, b. NS, d/o David Mills (Bangor, ME) and Eliza Fuller (NS)

Charles F. of Farmington m. Rose R. **Henderson** of Farmington 4/30/1897 in Rochester; H - 20, farming, b. Farmington, s/o Lyman Wyatt (Farmington, farmer) and Mary H. Wyatt (Farmington); W - 14, housework, b. Farmington, d/o George Henderson (Farmington, farmer) and Achsa M. Henderson (Farmington, housekeeper)

Charles F. of Farmington m. Addie L. **Chesley** of Farmington 3/19/1905 in Rochester; H - 27, teamster, 2nd, b. Farmington, s/o Lyman Wyatt (Farmington, teamster) and Mary Wyatt

(Farmington); W - 15, b. Farmington, d/o Frank B. Chesley (Farmington, farmer) and Sadie Foss (Rochester)

George H. of Farmington m. Alice L. **True** of Yarmouth, ME 5/9/1888; H - 22, farmer, s/o Lyman (Farmington, farmer) and Mary H. (deceased); W - 24, housekeeper, d/o William W. and Alice F. (New York City, housekeeper)

George H. of Wells, ME m. Adelaide E. **Mutch** of Swampscott 12/29/1929; H - 64, farmer, 2nd, b. Farmington, s/o Lyman Wyatt (Wenham, MA) and Mary Garland (Farmington); W - 53, housekeeper, 2nd, b. Wenham, MA, d/o George H. Wyatt (Wenham, MA, grocer) and Adelaide Batchelder (Beverly Farms, MA)

Henry I. of Farmington m. Clara A. **Varney** of Farmington 12/18/1894 in Rochester; H - 25, farmer, b. Farmington, s/o Lyman A. Wyatt (Farmington, farmer) and Mary L. Wyatt (Farmington); W - 24, b. Farmington, d/o Ivory Varney and Elma Varney (housekeeper)

Lyman of Farmington m. Ida **Gilpatrick** of Farmington 12/13/1897 in Rochester; H - 58, farmer, 3rd, b. Wenham, s/o Ira Wyatt (Wenham, MA, farmer) and Louisa Wingate (Farmington, housewife); W - 35, housekeeper, 2nd, b. Barrington, d/o Stephen Boston (York, ME, farmer) and Hannah Giles (Barrington, housewife)

Ralph F. of Farmington m. Ellen E. **Thompson** of Barrington 6/30/1917 in Rochester; H - 19, farmer, b. Farmington, s/o George H. Wyatt (Farmington, lumberman) and Alice True; W - 20, housekeeper, b. Barrington, d/o Tilghman Thompson (Barrington, farmer) and Lanzarah Raynes (Bangor, ME)

**YEATON,**

Joseph W. of Springvale, ME m. Jessie E. **Dike** of Stoneham, MA 4/25/1895; H - 32, shoemaker, 2nd, b. Alfred, ME, s/o Joseph Yeaton (Alfred, ME) and Nancy Yeaton; W - 36, shoemaker, b. Stoneham, d/o Charles C. Dike and Susan F. Dike (Lemington, ME)

**YERKS,**

Cassius J. of Lynn, MA m. Mary S. **Burrows** of Lynn, MA 6/10/1922; H - 54, salesman, 2nd, b. Chappaqua, NY, s/o Alexandra Yerks and Catherine Yerks; W - 46, shoeworker, 2nd, b. Farmington, d/o Daniel Burrows and Frances French

**YORK,**

Charles F. of Farmington m. Lizzie M. **Bickford** of Farmington 11/20/1889; H - 32, teamster, b. Middleton, s/o Amos W. York (dead) and Mary B. York; W - 33, housekeeper, b. Dover, d/o John T. Bickford (Rochester, farmer) and Phoebe Bickford (Strafford)

George A. of New Durham m. Barbara T. **Wyatt** of Farmington 4/22/1936 in New Durham; H - 18, laborer, b. Belmont, s/o Raymond York (Belmont, woodturner) and Caroline Jones (Gilmanton, housewife); W - 18, housework, b. Barrington, d/o Ralph Wyatt (Farmington, laborer) and Ellen Thompson (Barrington, housewife)

**YOUNG,**

Alvah H. of Farmington m. Gertie M. **Swinerton** of Milton 2/4/1906 in Milton; H - 19, mill hand, b. Farmington, s/o Herbert S. Young (Alton, mill hand) and Susie E. Pettigrew (Farmington) W - 16, b. Worcester, d/o Jacob M. Swinerton (Milton, shoemaker) and Emma A. Melville (Braintree, MA)

Carlton C. of Rochester m. Dorothy **Davis** of Farmington 6/9/1926; H - 17, soldier, b. Rochester, s/o Fred G. Young (shoeworker) and Edna Bennett (Rochester, housewife); W - 18, at home, b Farmington, d/o Earl Davis (shoeworker) and Bessie Haddock (Farmington, housewife)

Charles H. of Farmington m. Etta M. **Young** of Middleton 8/4/1888 in Milton; H - 36, stock fitter, 2$^{nd}$, b. Middleton, s/o Samuel (New Durham, farmer) and Martha (Middleton, deceased); W 24, housekeeper, b. Middleton, d/o J. Henry (Tuftonboro, farmer) and Mary E. (Middleton, housekeeper)

Charles T. of Farmington m. Alice **Gray** of Haverhill, MA 3/13/1889 H - 31, farmer, b. Farmington, s/o Hiram Young (dead) and Judith Young (Barnstead); W - 21, housekeeper, b. Dover, d/o John Gray (Dover, shoemaker) and Clara Gray (Strafford)

Charles T. of Farmington m. Daisy **Drew** of Sanbornville 6/14/1901 in New Durham; H - 43, farmer, 2$^{nd}$, b. Farmington, s/o Hiram Young (dead) and Judith Davis (dead); W - 18, d/o James Drew (lumberman) and Clara Gledden

Eugene C. of Farmington m. Mina A. **Brackett** of Farmington 7/21/1897 in Boston; H - 29, hotel clerk, b. Newark, NJ, s/o Charles Young (Scotland) and Catherine Brien (Ireland, housekeeper); W - 24, saleslady, b. New Durham, d/o Hiram

A. Brackett (Ossipee, shoemaker) and Augusta French (Farmington, housekeeper)

Frank E. of Farmington m. Elora E. **Shorey** of Rochester 2/25/1892 in Gilmanton; H - 29, shoemaker, $2^{nd}$, divorced, b. Alton, s/o Charles E. Young (Alton, 58, farmer) and Hannah Young (Alton, 52, housekeeper) of Alton; W - 29, shoe stitcher, $2^{nd}$, divorced, b. New Durham, d/o Samuel Randall (New Durham, 60, teamster) of Rochester and Lugatha Randall (dead)

Fred of Farmington m. Maude M. **Young** of Middleton 6/19/1909; H - 21, teamster, b. Farmington, s/o Frank V. Young (Farmington, farmer) and Mary Varney (New Durham, housekeeper); W - 20, housekeeper, b. Haverhill, d/o Charles H. Young (Farmington, shoemaker) and Etta M. Young (New Durham, housekeeper)

Malcolm J. of Farmington m. Ethel E. **McCullough** of Farmington 10/22/1927 in Hampton Falls; H - 25, shoeworker, b. Farmington, s/o Eugene Young and Mina Brackett (Farmington, shoeworker); W - 23, shoeworker, b. Rochester, d/o Andrew McCullough (Ireland, farmer) and Elizabeth Herron (Ireland)

Nathaniel H. of Farmington m. Josephine A. **Bradbury** of Farmington 11/11/1915; H - 60, farmer, b. Farmington, s/o Hiram A. Young (Wakefield, farmer) and Judith A. Davis (Barnstead, housekeeper); W - 64, housekeeper, $2^{nd}$, b. Middleton, d/o Jeremiah Downing (Middleton, farmer) and Sarah Whitehouse (Middleton, housekeeper)

Abbott, Alice - Potter, Marshall W.
Abbott, Geraldine - Wilkins, Leslie O.
Abbott, Mildred I. - Allen, Charles L.
Abbott, Nellie - Stevens, Ronello A.
Abbott, Rena M. - Douglass, Robert R.
Adams, Alice M. - Lawrence, John W.
Adams, Bernice L. - Parshley, Richmond H.
Adams, Esther - Murrey, Charles F.
Adams, Jeanette E. - Howard, Emery E.
Adams, Leila B. (Davis) - Carter, William
Ainsley, Ella E. - Gowin, William L.
Akerley, Martha E. H. (Hazel) - Davis, John B.
Allen, Ruth Elizabeth - Babbitt, Will Crane
Allen, Vivian H. (Grant) - Whitney, Myron H.
Allen, Winnifred E. - Kimball, Carroll H.
Amazeen, Hattie B. - Curtis, Irving S.
Ames, Madeline - Howard, Fred W.
Ancoin, Cecilia G. - Parkhurst, Leroy W.
Anderson, Mary - Pinkham, Clifton S.
Anderson, Mary V. - Edgerly, Clyde H.
Angevine, Ella (Robbins) - Dexter, Owen S.
Apostolopoulos, Vas'ke - Morayianis, Nikitas
Armstrong, Edith E. - Therrien, Edward
Armstrong, Elna V. - Tebbetts, Fred O.
Armstrong, Lizzie (Leighton) - Tebbetts, Fred N.
Arnold, Doris - Beckwith, Frederick M.
Arnold, Dorothy M. - Perkins, Adam G.
Arnold, Floretta L. C. - Hutchins, William R.
Arnold, Lillian M. - Stevens, William C.
Arnold, Mary W. - Webster, George A.
Aspinwall, Cora E. - Edwards, Charles M.
Aspinwall, Etta B. - Willey, Charles R.
Atwood, Marion D. - Waldron, Harrison G.
Auclair, Irene Celia - Bridges, Lawrence
Auclair, Irene M. - Douglass, Donald R.
Augustine, Isola G. - Batchelder, Ralph M.
Austin, Dora Evelyn - Bartle, Carl Raymond
Austin, Mary - Perkins, Charlie
Averill, Annie A. - Whitehouse, Charles
Averill, Flora M. - Haynes, Frank H.
Averill, Harriet F. - Small, Edwin E.

Averill, Ida M. (Kent) - Tuttle, Willie M.
Averill, Josie Ella - White, George Arthur
Avery, Grace L. - Boyd, Charles M.
Avery, Ruby - Pulsifer, John L.
Avery, Winnifred M. - Benson, Perley H.
Ayer, Belle G. (Wallace) - Rhines, Willie E.
Ayers, Abbie M. - Nason, Laureston M.

Babb, Eleanor W. - Currier, Fred E., Jr.
Babb, Etta M. (Straw) - Newling, Charles H.
Babb, Hazel M. - Hancock, Frank A.
Babb, Lilla E. - Nutter, Joseph F.
Babb, Martha A. - Moulton, John P.
Babb, Naomia M. - Otis, George E.
Bachelder, Anna B. - Wiggin, Fred N.
Bailey, Fannie J. (Drew) - Goodwin, Charles E.
Bailey, Sophia M. - Nute, Lewis S.
Barber, Jennie M. - Kimball, Verne I.
Barker, Amy L. - Horne, Herbert F.
Barker, Clara - Berry, Charles H.
Barker, Helen - Winn, George E.
Barr, L. Clarabell - Wingate, Arthur R.
Barsantee, Ada F. - Smart, Jerry E.
Bartlett, Maude R. (Smart) - Tuttle, Eugene A.
Barton, Marguerite A. - Foster, Kenneth R.
Batbal, Jessie - Kropp, Maurice
Batchelder, Bernice - Pulsifer, Harry H.
Batchelder, Clara (Eastman) - Cook, Ansel P.
Batchelder, Grace - Davis, Carl T.
Batchelder, Lena - Place, Dean A.
Bean, Rena S. - Wallingford, William J.
Beattie, Elenora - Jackson, Harry S.
Beaulieu, Delia - Vickers, Charles S., Jr.
Belanger, Anna Belle - Landry, Ernest
Belanger, Beatrice - Turmelle, Ethelbert
Belanger, Helen - Turmelle, Edmond
Bennett, Lucie B. - Nutter, Harry F.
Bennett, Mabelle E. - Lee, Perley I.
Berry, Ardena - Breen, Timothy E.
Berry, Augusta J. - Flanders, Herman F.
Berry, Augusta J. - Wallace, George M.

Berry, Edna I. H. (Huckins) - Peavey, Paul H.
Berry, Eliza E. - Torno, Charles
Berry, Eliza E. - Stevens, Leon B.
Berry, Elsie M. H. - Gray, George R.
Berry, Emma E. - Horne, Everett E.
Berry, Eugenie L. (Landry) - Beaulieu, Joseph C.
Berry, Fannie B. (Clough) - Baxter, Daniel Forest
Berry, Gertrude M. - Berry, Joseph E.
Berry, Laura A. (Straw) - Edgerly, George W.
Berry, Lucy M. - Wallace, George M.
Berry, Mary Edna - Willey, Charles H.
Berry, Thelma - Gray, Irving A.
Bickford, Annie - Anderson, John F.
Bickford, Ella N. - Tripp, Charles H.
Bickford, Lizzie M. - York, Charles F.
Bickford, Mary B. - Blaisdell, Ernest O.
Bickford, Stella P. - Varney, Arthur F.
Billings, Virginia I. - Bobineau, William
Bird, Lucina M. - Furber, John E.
Bishop, Alice R. - Howes, Leroy F.
Bishop, Mertie K. - Marsh, Herbert E.
Blaisdell, Ada Estella - Curtis, Asa A.
Blaisdell, Bernice F. - Card, William L.
Blaisdell, Eleanor F. - Hull, Walter F.
Blaisdell, Eleanor F. - Glass, Eugene
Blaisdell, Esther - Swinerton, Herbert B.
Blaisdell, Marion - Raab, Adolph, Jr.
Blaisdell, Marion - Pelletier, Louis P.
Blaisdell, Marjorie - Canney, Mervale
Blaisdell, Mary V. (Bickford) - Pollard, Richard
Blatchford, Clara I. - Chesley, Norman
Blouin, Ethel M. (Colby) - Roberts, John P. B.
Blouin, Jeanette - Ward, Donald
Boucher, Clara - Moisen, Fred
Bowden, Elizabeth H. (Morrison) - Downing, Jeremiah W.
Bower, Margaret C. - Mayott, Harry C.
Brackett, Mina A. - Young, Eugene C.
Bradbury, Josephine A. (Downing) - Young, Nathaniel H.
Bradford, Caroline B. - Liebert, Isaac
Bradley, Marion J. - Abbott, Walter D.
Brainard, Augusta A. (Thayer) - Fletcher, Fred P.

Branna, Mary E. - Reeves, Earle D.
Brawn, Maggie E. - Tuttle, Eugene A.
Brock, Evelyn M. - Foss, Sumner H.
Brock, Helen A. - Amazeen, Walter M.
Brooks, Addie F. - Furber, John C.
Brooks, C. Isabelle - Rowe, Lyman L.
Brooks, Christine E. - Leighton, A. P.
Brooks, Crissie C. - Drew, Clifford T.
Brooks, Ethel M. - Hayes, Arthur G.
Brooks, Evelyn B. - Smith, Chester F.
Brooks, Helen - Stevens, Phileman E.
Brooks, Hildred - Tilton, Sumner
Brooks, Lila I. - Hale, Morton H.
Brough, Marcia L. - Clark, Albert H.
Brough, Margueret E. - Willey, George E.
Brouillard, Rosa D. - Nason, Leslie I.
Brown, Cora E. - Hurd, George
Brown, Edith M. - Nutter, John M.
Brown, Ellen M. (Smith) - Bailey, Rufus
Brown, Etta L. - Davis, Frank M.
Brown, Ida J. - Aspinwall, Cyrus G.
Brown, Janet P. - Turcotte, Oliver J.
Browne, Ella J. - Chandler, Willis C.
Browne, Eva N. - Cox, Herbert M
Bryant, Eva F. (Wallace) - Thompson, Ernest H.
Bryant, Sybil P. - Kenney, Frank E.
Bubier, Etola - Willard, Frank N.
Buckley, Margaret M. - Smith, William H.
Bumpus, Hester A. - Marston, Fred B.
Bunker, Merle E. - Currier, Charles F.
Burke, Julia A. - Phillips, Wendell
Burke, Maggie A. - Rollins, Cyrus, Jr.
Burke, Margarete N. (Nelson) - Senter, Lawrence P.
Burleigh, Charlotte S. - Nelson, Fred W.
Burleigh, Lucy C. - Marcoux, Odule
Burnham, Vinnie - Rollins, Edwin F.
Burroughs, Ida B. - Currier, John T.
Burrows, Addie - Ham, Edwin
Burrows, Helen R. - Cardinal, Jonny B.
Burrows, Julia M. - Rollins, Ernest E.
Burrows, Mary S. - Yerks, Cassius J.

Burrows, Mattie A. (Kearney) - Pearl, Preston A.
Burrows, Maude E. - Dufresne, Harry D.
Burrows, Nellie B. - Fall, Horace P.
Bush, Leona M. (Rollins) - Gagnon, Joseph E. A.
Butler, Irene F. (Furber) - Dole, George E.

Cameron, Edith C. - Pike, Sumner E.
Camm, Elsie - Auclair, Dorilla
Camm, May C. - Lester, Percy T.
Campbell, Laura S. - Davis, George F.
Canney, Addie M. - Whitehouse, C. W.
Canney, Cora P. - Hurd, Harry W.
Canney, Florence E. (Leighton) - Gelinas, William E.
Canney, Grace R. - Hall, Fred W.
Canney, Ina B. - Pearl, Hervey
Canney, Mary W. (Wilson) - Hill, Horace G.
Card, Estella M. - Smith, Horace H.
Card, Estella M. - Marchant, Frank A.
Card, Ethel V. - Browne, Henry A.
Card, Faye - Miller, William G.
Cardinal, Ruth C. (Wilkins) - Watson, Carl L.
Carey, Marion - Lawrence, Henry E., Jr.
Carpenter, Elizabeth A. - Moulton, Herbert P.
Carpenter, Ruth - Spear, Howard M.
Carr, Ida B. (Rand) - White, George A.
Carreau, Jeanette E. - Otis, Gerald E.
Carroll, Katie M. - Parker, Frank S.
Carter, Elizabeth W. - Mudgett, Robert H.
Carter, Etta (Valley) - Wallace, Walter S.
Carter, Flora R. G. - Place, Ulysses I.
Carter, Gertie E. (Bishop) - Willard, Smith A.
Carter, Helen W. - Gilman, Lloyd M.
Carty, Marguerite L. - Wentworth, Laurence
Cassidy, Ora E. - Cate, John H.
Caswell, Eva B. - Hayes, Alphonzo C.
Cate, Mintie J. (Tibbetts) - Leavitt, Charles E.
Cate, Vera W. - Weymouth, Harold E.
Cater, Olie E. - Perkins, James N.
Cathcart, Kathryn - Lavertue, Ralph
Cathcart, Madelaine - Vaillancourt, Alfred
Cave, Cora E. - Evans, James E.

Caverly, Cynthia - Cook, Nathaniel P.
Chadwick, Lizzie M. - Wingate, Henry S.
Chamberlin, Alice D. - Davis, Harry W.
Champion, Ida M. - Runnals, Forrest L.
Chandler, Bessie C. - Lougee, Jacob A.
Chandler, Iva M. (Presby) - Wilkinson, Edward W.
Charles, Esther - Randall, George F.
Charles, Flora V. - Wotton, Robert M.
Charles, Minnie D. (Gilpatrick) - Sawyer, Clifford L.
Chartier, Louise - Goodrow, Middie
Chase, Ida M. - Montgomery, William P.
Chase, Ruby - Mitchell, H. Fayette
Chatman, Emma - Rollins, Charles I.
Cheney, Georgia F. (Hurd) - Aiken, Vaughn N.
Chesley, Addie L. - Wyatt, Charles F.
Chesley, Bessie M. - Dickey, Howard A.
Chesley, Clara M. (Towle) - Burnham, Charles T.
Chesley, Edna M. - Garland, J. Weston
Chesley, Georgie M. - Holmes, Charles W.
Chesley, Lillian M. - Gilson, Lewis F.
Chesley, Marion Leslie - Perkins, Malcolm R.
Chesley, Mertie - Goodwin, Charles E.
Christie, Bernice L. - Willard, Maurice S.
Christie, Mildred A. (Fielder) - Willard, Clyde A.
Churchill, Amanda E. - Pike, Herman J.
Churchill, Catherine M. - Barbour, George J.
Cilley, Ester U. - Willey, Almon E.
Cilley, Genevieve - Weymouth, Edwin L.
Clancy, Ardella L. - Beers, Alfred W.
Clare, Agnes - Gouin, Walter J.
Clark, Edith M. - Kelley, Albert A.
Clark, Fannie (Smith) - Wallace, William
Clark, Florence E. - Connor, Charles E.
Clark, Ida B. - Wentworth, Charles W.
Clark, Sarah (Riley) - French, Bert L.
Clarke, Bertha - Connor, George W.
Clarke, Hattie F. - Rollins, Ervin H.
Cleveland, Agnes I. - Nute, Charles F.
Clough, Inez B. - Dore, Ernest
Clough, Katie R. - Sawyer, Walter F.
Clough, Velma L. - Curtis, Clarence L., Jr.

Cloutman, Delia A. - Kelley, James
Cloutman, E. Ellen - Pike, John E.
Cloutman, Laura A. (Ham) - Whitehouse, Fred
Cloutman, Mary - Ricker, Charles H.
Cloutman, Mary A. - Tibbetts, Frank G.
Cloutman, Nellie A. - Allen, W. Dean
Coaty, Emma (Ham) - Hubbard, Harry I.
Coburn, Mamie - Cameron, Allen
Coffin, Beatrice - Rollins, Winslow C.
Colbath, Ada B. - Hill, Loren S.
Colbath, Annie M. - Canney, Isaac A.
Colbath, Blanche A. - Bubier, Victor J.
Colbath, Evelyn C. - LaMontagne, Jerome
Colbath, Helen P. - Van Vleck, John F.
Colbath, Prue A. - Card, Edward F.
Colbath, Viola J. (Dudley) - Stevens, Edgar N.
Colbath, Vonie - Colbath, Willie L.
Coleman, Josephine H. (Francis) - Marden, Horton D.
Collins, Euphonia A. - Libbey, Charles
Collins, Eva M. - Blanchard, Carl C.
Collins, Helen - Helm, Harold
Colomy, Clara (Kimball) - Bunker, Charles T.
Colomy, Clara (Kimball) - Drake, Raymond P. R.
Colomy, Georgia I. - Thompson, Winslow P.
Colomy, Harriet R. - Smart, Harry P.
Colomy, Ida M. - Cobb, Walter P.
Colomy, Jennie S. - Ricker, Chester C.
Conner, Edith F. - Roberts, Harry F.
Conner, Lillian M. - Currier, Ray B.
Connor, Florence F. - Bickford, Charles L.
Connor, Ida E. - Hayes, Frank C.
Connor, Marion E. - Hogan, Francis J.
Connors, Mae E. - Marsh, Ralph S.
Constant, Laura D. - Crowell, Saul J.
Cook, Anna R. - Elkins, Bert H.
Cook, Blanche S. - Perkins, Lester A.
Cook, Charlotte M. - Mangar, James R.
Cook, Cynthia - Wentworth, John E.
Cook, Edith M. (Carleton) - Bowers, Charles A.
Cook, Ella May - Sprague, Verney
Cook, Lilla H. - Thompson, James H.

Cook, Rose M. (Brown) - Merrill, Austin W.
Cook, Rose M. - Elwell, George F.
Cook, Selvia V. - Derby, Charles L.
Cooke, Ada Dell - McPhail, Charles F.
Cooley, Marie (Garland) - Terrell, Earle W.
Cooley, Mary A. - Elkins, Bert H.
Coombs, Hellena M. - Varney, Alvord O.
Cooper, Freda (Dwyer) - Bouvier, William
Corliss, Evelyn H. - Labonte, Philip O.
Corpening, Callie J. (Jenkins) - Berry, Joseph E.
Corson, Angie E. - Varney, Fred S.
Corson, Bessie - Duquette, Lewis J.
Corson, Doris (Rouckey) - Burnham, Ralph H.
Corson, Estella M. (Tuttle) - Burleigh, Henry A.
Corson, Eva B. - Hayes, Thomas T.
Corson, Hannah E. - Jones, Joseph W.
Corson, Katherine A. (Burns) - Tebbets, Warren E.
Corson, Mattie A. - Edgerly, Willie H.
Cotton, Helen A. - Scruton, Russell G.
Cotton, Viola (Edgerly) - Emery, Edwin A.
Coulombe, Jeanette - Aiken, George
Coulombe, Jeanette - Cardinal, Leo H.
Coulombe, Rita B. - Cardinal, Raymond
Couture, Ada L. (Corson) - Morin, Thomas J.
Cox, Hittie R. - Johnson, Budd M.
Coyne, Katherine E. (Hogan) - Lacey, John E.
Crane, Pearl - Diemer, Spero
Creager, Clara V. - Collins, Eugene F.
Crockett, Lillian V. - Wentworth, George E.
Cronk, Ruby R. - Harriman, Stanley
Crouse, Leona B. - Arnold, Samuel V., Jr.
Currier, A. Bernice - Rollins, Arthur S.
Currier, Catherine M. - Goodell, James H.
Currier, Elfreda M. - Baston, Burton W.
Currier, Etta May (Davis) - Evans, Elmer E.
Currier, Margaret L. - Cilley, Clifton H.
Currier, Nancy B. - Corson, Walter N.
Currul, Beatrice S. - Toothaker, Curtis C.
Curtis, Abbie J. - Lucas, Frank J.
Curtis, Evelyn J. - Woodman, Jesse
Cushman, Lee A. - Maloney, John B.

Cyr, Mary H. P. - Joy, Samuel O., Jr.

Dame, Delma E. - Kelley, Albert A.
Dame, Iris St. Helena - Furnans, John E.
Dame, Jeannette E. - Keehlwetter, Franklin
Daudelin, June L. - Folger, Anton W.
Daudelin, Maxine E. - Dierauer, William
Davidson, Fannie L. - Hall, John E. S.
Davis, Anne P. - Bannon, John P.
Davis, Annie - White, Charles W.
Davis, Arazona M. - Brown, Vinal H.
Davis, Bertha E. (Bointon) - Tasker, Edgar E.
Davis, Charlotta E. - Drawbridge, Robert W.
Davis, Dorothy - Young, Carlton C.
Davis, E. Ellen (Berry) - Marston, Frank R.
Davis, Edna M. - Thompson, Eugene H.
Davis, Emma I. (Gilman) - Giles, Fred A.
Davis, Etta K. - Hayes, Winfield S.
Davis, Eliza - Davis, George A.
Davis, Irma L. - Lovering, George A.
Davis, Leiler B. - Adams, John G.
Davis, Lucie M. (Furber) - Goodwin, Richard J. P.
Davis, Melinda Frances - Gilman, Ruel P.
Davis, Minnie P. - Barker, Charles B.
Davis, Nellie M. - Pinkham, Seth H.
Davis, Ruth E. - Leonard, Lester S.
Davis, Sadie L. (Shortridge) - Dore, Daniel C.
Day, Madaline A. - Burton, Henry A.
Dean, Goldie M. - Abbott, Edward P.
DeMeritt, Vera - Willson, Paul J.
DePatra, Doris - Harriman, Cyrus
Derby, Frances - Twombly, William
Derwin, Mary E. - Quint, Everett
Desaulniers, Jeanette A. - Parent, Conrad O.
DeWitt, Nettie - Preston, James D.
Dexter, Martha E. - Ham, Eric N.
Dike, Jessie E. - Yeaton, Joseph W.
Dixon, Cora (Maine) - Hodgdon, Ellsworth A.
Dixon, Mabel M. - Kimball, Harry B.
Dixon, Myrtle L. (Leighton) - Putnam, Bernard C.
Dodge, Eva G. - Reeves, Howard V.

Dodge, Florence G. - Pike, Harry
Donaldson, Nora (LaPrice) - Durgin, Benjamin F.
Dore, Augustia D. - Brown, John W.
Dore, Esther B. - Place, Percy
Dore, Eunice - Lincoln, Fred
Dore, Lillian R. - Curtis, Reginald W.
Dore, Rosetta - Tuttle, Charles E.
Dore, Sadie L. (Shortridge) - Call, Louis
Doughty, Isabelle - Davis, John F.
Douglas, Virginia B. - Hoadley, J. Emery
Dow, Addie A. - Leighton, Charles I.
Dow, Frances C. - Newell, Ralph A.
Dow, Nettie I. - Chesley, Walter L.
Dow, Susie Ethel - Noyes, William B.
Downes, Emma L. - Connor, Charles F.
Downing, Anna A. - Wright, Frank C.
Downing, Clara A. - Stanley, Ernest
Downing, Delia A. - Tanner, Lincoln G.
Downing, Eva - Hurd, William R.
Downing, Grace M. - McIntire, Frank B.
Downing, Lillian B. - Varney, Owen M.
Downing, S. Alice - Gilson, Levi H.
Downs, Celia R. (Lougee) - Willey, John D.
Drapeau, Lizzie E. - Sansoucie, Joseph
Drew, Daisy - Young, Charles T.
Drew, Ethel M. - Edgerly, Earle M.
Drew, Fannie - Smith, William C.
Drew, Gertie M. - Hall, Frank A.
Drew, Mary E. (Childs) - Drew, George F.
DuBois, Leanor M. - Haddock, Hector R.
Dudley, Eunice L. (Rand) - White, Harley C.
Dudley, Viola - Colbath, Irving E.
Dufrane, Maude E. (Burrows) - Alvcy, Walter M.
Dunn, Lillian F. - Currier, George Richard
Dunn, M. Delia - Hussey, Leland M.
Dunn, Nellie M. - Armstrong, Roy L.
Duntley, Ina G. - Scruton, Orin A.
Duntley, Maude M. (Brown) - Nedeau, Walter S.
Dupere, Alice B. - Hart, Donald B.
Duplessis, Emily C. - Pinkham, Clifton S.
DuQuette, Lena - Howe, Frank R.

Duquette, Marie D. A. - Maxfield, Edward R.
DuQuette, Victoria M. - Whitehouse, Perley E.
Durant, Minnie (Renton) - Ongley, Frank C.
Durgin, Christina - Jessen, John A.
Dustin, Jessie Maude - White, Melvin J.
Duval, Cora - Doucette, Alexander
Dwyer, Harriette - Rousseau, Frank
Dyer, Alice J. - Sawyer, Walter F.
Dyer, Hattie M. - Lougee, Jacob A.

Eagan, Mary - Jenkins, Alfred T.
Earle, Helen W. - Tirrell, Harold A.
Eaton, E. Annabelle - Huckins, J. Leslie
Eaton, Marjorie L. - Walker, Charles M.
Edgerly, Annie M. - Thayer, Elmer F.
Edgerly, Aurlie M. - Senter, Clarence W.
Edgerly, Beatrice Janet - Ellison, William Henry
Edgerly, Carrie A. - Varney, Oe
Edgerly, Carrie M. (Quint) - Otis, Alonzo S.
Edgerly, Doris E. - Bailey, George E.
Edgerly, Earline - Palmer, Leon L.
Edgerly, Glenna - Riley, James
Edgerly, Velda M. - Cardinal, Ernest
Eldridge, Emily B. - Griswold, Horace D.
Eldridge, Reta A. - Stevens, Sylvester E.
Elkins, Flossie (Sinniger) - Drew, William D.
Elliott, Annie B. (Dunnell) - Willard, Raymond C.
Elliott, Evelyn - Mott, Orrie W.
Elliott, Thirza B. - Perkins, George H.
Ellis, Elizabeth T. - Drew, Clifton H.
Ellis, Emma E. - Varney, Walter E.
Ellis, Ethel M. - Remick, George P.
Elmer, Blanche M. - Stevens, Willis R.
Emerson, Bessie F. - Gillis, George A.
Emerson, Julia - Otis, Albert M.
Emerson, Lizzie (Hunt) - Nute, William H.
Emery, Grace B. - Gibbs, Ralph P.
Emery, Marietta - Sheehan, Henry J.
Emery, Sadie (Haywood) - Hackett, William
Emmons, Minnie M. - Tanner, Frank W.
Estes, Cora (Flagg) - Curtis, Chester F.

Ettinger, Gertrude - Garland, John
Evans, Abbie J. - Wentworth, Alvin H.
Evans, Bessie W. - Roberts, Fred H.
Evans, Florence M. - Maddocks, Perley W.
Evans, Mary A. - Wentworth, Alvin S.
Everett, Mary D. - Hayes, Ira C.

Fall, Fannie C. - Whitehouse, Frank I.
Farnam, Emmeline L. - Dodge, Kenneth W.
Farnham, Sarah N. (Jones) - Furber, Will E.
Farnum, Mabel G. (Kendell) - Scruton, Arthur G.
Farrington, Carrie - Burrows, Alverton
Faulkner, Lilla - Crockett, Willard E.
Favor, Nina G. - Quint, Nicholas I.
Felker, Charlotte D. - Bagley, Newman V.
Ferguson, Barbara - Keith, George E., Jr.
Ferland, Delda - Caulstone, Emile A.
Ferland, Deloria - Nute, Ray H.
Fernald, Alice N. (Nute) - Roberts, Charles W.
Fernald, Elizabeth N. - Washburn, David L.
Fernald, Florence M. - Jones, John F.
Finigan, Mary A. - Perkins, Llewellyn C.
Finnegan, Katherine T. - Drew, John J.
Flanders, Eugenie - Wessel, George W.
Flanders, Lennar G. (Lucas) - Brandis, Arthur E.
Flanders, Manetta E. - Berry, Frank H.
Fletcher, Carrie M. - McRoberts, John
Follansbee, Margaret E. - Liberty, Fredrick P., Jr.
Foss, Alice M. - Foss, Harold J.
Foss, Ellen M. (Johnson) - Varney, John F.
Foss, Erline M. (Terrill) - Gray, Frank P.
Foss, Sadie - Chesley, Frank B.
Foss, Sylvia - McCollough, Robert J.
Fountain, Adelina - Sawyer, Horatio M.
Fowler, Eleanor V. - Smith, Albert M.
French, Alice N. (Beacham) - Jordon, Charles A.
French, Lowea E. - Leighton, Fred M.
French, Mildred F. - Ingerson, Edgar A., Jr.
Furber, Irene - Butler, George F.
Furber, Lucina M. (Bird) - Neill, Roy V.
Furber, Maude - Parrock, William R.

Furbish, Millie L. - Elwell, Charles F.

Gadd, Marcia R. - Canney, Merlin H.
Gardner, Gertrude C. - Johnson, Henry B.
Garland, Alice M. (Miller) - Shapleigh, Frank
Garland, Arthana - Pluff, William J.
Garland, E. Maude - Gilman, John S.
Garland, Nella M. (Henderson) - Otis, Levi
Garland, Nettie F. - Tash, Ernest L.
Garrett, Mary - Lepage, Paul
Garvis, Mary I. (Hayes) - Hayes, Winfield A.
Gault, Ethel L. (Perkins) - Fisher, Ira
Gault, Hazel - Dexter, Owen S.
Geary, Barbara (Remick) - Bowden, Winslow
Geary, Helen A. - Varney, Chester C.
Geddis, Reta B. - Davis, Albert M.
Gerrish, Sayde J. (George) - Kimball, John V.
Gibbs, Arlene F. - Walsh, Leroy F.
Gilbert, Evelyn A. - Patten, Claude V.
Giles, Isabelle L. - Leavitt, Sidney A.
Gilman, Alice B. - Rollins, Herbert S.
Gilman, Bernice - Thomas, Carl Shipman
Gilman, Bessie J. - Curtis, William B.
Gilman, Carrie L. (Gilman) - Kelley, James
Gilman, Cora E. - Flanders, Arthur W.
Gilman, Grace A. - Tucker, Charles P.
Gilpatrick, Ida (Boston) - Wyatt, Lyman
Gilson, Dorothy L. - Webster, Charles W.
Glidden, Bernice L. - Blaisdell, Ernest O.
Glidden, Della F. - Vickers, William J.
Glidden, Eldora B. (Brown) - Varney, Elvin V.
Glidden, Grace M. - Bunker, Forest W.
Glidden, Gretchen L. - Grondin, Raymond P.
Golder, Ada A. - Aubin, Edwin S.
Goldsmith, Addie - Glidden, Stanley
Gooch, Evelyn L. - Bragdon, Harold I.
Gooch, Velma I. - Hackett, George E.
Goodrich, Caroline E. - Gilman, Leo D.
Goodrow, Vinnie (Nalar) - Roy, Arsene
Goodwin, Anna - Burke, Edmund A.
Goodwin, Annie B. (Dunnell) - Elliott, William A.

Goodwin, Cora E. - Davis, Alonzo I.
Goodwin, Lucia H. - Bickford, Sylvester R.
Gordon, Ruth - Spear, Fred R.
Grace, Flora M. - Grace, John A.
Grace, Iva B. - Plagman, George E.
Graham, Vivian - Kipp, Albert W.
Grant, Nora M. (Dame) - Pearson, Edwin L.
Granville, Lucinda R. - Harmon, John H.
Gray, Alice - Young, Charles T.
Gray, Alice Mabel - Sanborn, Roland R.
Gray, Dorothy H. - Gardner, Uel A.
Gray, Edith B. - Babb, John K.
Gray, Ethel A. - Wallingford, Calvin
Gray, Hattie M. - Lapine, John E.
Gray, Lillian E. - Garland, Wilfred E.
Gray, Lizzie A. (York) - Davis, John F.
Gray, Nellie - Bickford, Edward H.
Gray, Pearl - Ham, Irving C.
Greene, Doris L. - Bartlett, Matthew J.
Greene, Evelyn May - Gray, John Ivory
Greene, Gretchen - Bridges, Henry L.
Greene, Lillian M. - Gray, Arthur M.
Greene, Thelma V. - Blake, George O.
Greenier, Lola E. - Geary, Richard A.
Grey, Carrie S. - Hartford, Edwin L.
Grover, Lizzie - Babb, Charles H.
Guay, Catherine - Card, Ralph H.
Guilbault, Parmelia - Elliott, Ernest E.

Hackett, Maude A. (Parker) - Palmer, Charles E.
Haddock, Bessie - Regis, John D.
Haddock, Bessie S. - Davis, Earle R.
Haddock, Lura B. - Cathcart, Fred F.
Hagan, Prudence A. - Colbath, William L.
Haines, Nellie (Place) - Stevens, Guy Edward
Hale, Doris V. - Dore, Leon
Hale, Ida May (Rhines) - Bowers, Charles A.
Hale, Magean E. - Berry, Zanello D.
Hale, Queenie G. - Kimball, Norman L.
Hall, Gladys S. (Remick) - Otis, Everett E.
Hall, Isabelle A. - Evans, Wilbur J.

Hall, Jennie B. - Tomlinson, Enoch L.
Hall, Lydia A. (Canney) - Rhines, Irving C.
Hall, Marion E. - Hayes, A. Fred
Ham, Beth Lydia - Briggs, Allen S.
Ham, Edith - Moulton, Chester A.
Ham, Ellen (Canney) - Pinkham, Charles H.
Ham, Grace G. - Rand, Ernest W.
Ham, Ida - Woodman, Willis
Ham, Ida (Stevens) - Temple, Fred
Ham, Inez J. - Tibbetts, Harris C.
Ham, Mabel - Abbott, Ernest R.
Ham, Mary E. - Wentworth, Reginald R.
Hamblett, Edith B. (Kimball) - Ricker, Walter D.
Hamilton, Beatrice - Boisvert, Arthur
Hamilton, Rena - Bennett, Orville D.
Hanscam, Lizzie B. - Perkins, John T.
Hanscom, Marion - Fuller, Perley
Hanscum, Abbie L. - Kitchen, Paul A.
Hanson, Marion - Grenier, Alfred J.
Hapgood, Della (Kelsea) - Smith, William H.
Harding, Olive L. - Brooks, Frank W.
Harding, Ruby M. - Davis, George W.
Harmon, Emma F. - Kelley, Everett B.
Harriman, Grace - Hill, Ivan L.
Harriman, Rebecca E. - Baldwin, Frank L.
Harrington, Laura M. - Batchelder, Albert M.
Harrington, Lucy A. - Libbey, Erving A.
Harrison, Lulu I. - Colbath, Guy S.
Hart, Abbie B. - Tierney, Joseph O.
Hart, Althea M. - Boucher, Lucian
Hart, Bernice M. - Jenkins, Ralph C.
Hartfiel, Beatrice M. - Bickford, Robert G.
Hartford, Mattie C. - Bickford, George F.
Hartsford, Etta M. (Merrow) - Elkins, Charles
Havens, Jessie L. - Willson, Edward T.
Hawkes, Mildred - Arnold, Ralph
Hawkes, Violet E. (Clark) - Huntington, Harold
Hayden, Grace E. - Thurston, Percy L.
Hayes, A. Lillian - Thayer, Fred I.
Hayes, Adelaide E. (Putnam) - Chesley, Benjamin P.
Hayes, Annie M. (Norman) - Richardson, Charles F.

Hayes, Clara Maude - Hayes, Guy Golden
Hayes, Enid - Cook, Ernest P.
Hayes, Ethel Maude - Canney, Ralph W.
Hayes, Helen L. - McLaughlin, Joseph L.
Hayes, Jennie B. - Browne, Fred W.
Hayes, Laura E. - Scruton, Jerold F.
Hayes, Lillian A. (Rollins) - Roberts, John P.
Hayes, Marjorie D. (Mickel) - Rhines, Carl W.
Hayes, Martha B. - Glidden, Howard C.
Hayes, Mary I. - Hayes, Winfield S.
Hayes, Maud - Grenier, Alfred
Hayes, Mildred E. - Edwards, Glenn
Hayes, Roberta T. - Goodwin, Ralph L.
Hayes, Sadie E. - Emerson, Horten C.
Hayes, Theora - Weymouth, Carl H.
Haynes, Mamie A. - Card, Berton B.
Head, Mabel G. (Gerald) - Foster, William C.
Heath, Lula M. - Small, Isaac H.
Hemingway, Elizabeth (Gorman) - Ferris, Harry J.
Henaff, Rosalie - Pride, Henry W.
Henderson, Mary J. - Pearsons, Edwin L.
Henderson, Nellie M. - Garland, James M.
Henderson, Rose R. - Wyatt, Charles F.
Henderson, Ruth E. - Webster, Frank E.
Herring, E. Grace - Waldron, Arthur F.
Hersey, Evelyn L. - Knox, John E.
Higgin, Ethel - Thurston, Herbert H.
Higgins, Susie - Johnson, Fred A.
Hill, Alma P. - Place, Norman W.
Hill, Annie M. - Kimball, B. Frank
Hill, Hattie M. (Kimball) - Remick, Charles E.
Hill, Persis A. - Berry, Elverton C.
Hill, Sarah J. (Reed) - Moulton, Irving H.
Hillman, Marion R. R. - Aiken, Percy G.
Hobbs, Katie M. - Foss, James W.
Hodgdon, Carrie B. - Tibbetts, Frank E.
Hodgdon, Maude E. - McMullen, Albert A.
Hodgdon, Nellie G. - Burbank, Lindley A.
Hodgkins, Ruby J. - Callender, Willard D.
Hogan, Margaret A. - Davis, Harry F.
Holder, Marion - Towle, Floyd R.

Holland, Elva P. - Remick, Clayton S.
Holmes, Florence E. - Elliott, William A.
Holmes, Ida M. - Horne, Izah A.
Hooper, E. Gertrude - Marshall, Chesley S.
Horne, Agnes G. - Bean, Frank L.
Horne, Allie A. - Grace, Irving S.
Horne, Clara E. (Twombly) - Lougee, Hiram C.
Horne, Edna M. - Jewell, Arthur F.
Horne, Eva M. - Henderson, Lewis F.
Horne, Helen H. - White, George W.
Horne, Idana - Currier, George W.
Horne, Lena G. (Lucas) - Flanders, Herman F.
Horne, Leora F. - Otis, Albert J.
Horne, Mary A. (Kaine) - Davis, Hiram A.
Horne, Sarah (Curry) - Smith, Elbridge G.
Howard, Annie M. - Tibbetts, Frank M.
Howard, Carrie E. - Curtis, Fred
Howard, Carrie M. (Stevens) - Card, Alvin W.
Howard, Eva M. (Burgoyne) - Currier, Albert E.
Howard, Mardell E. - Tirrell, Melvin S.
Howard, Violet E. - Liberty, Normand P.
Howard, Violet R. (Ross) - Knox, Elmer S.
Howland, Olivine F. - Frost, Wendell
Hoyt, Helen A. - Goodwin, John F.
Huckins, Abbie - Fernald, Winfield G.
Huckins, Addie M. (Hill) - Hayes, Harry I.
Huckins, Alice M. - Paulson, John A.
Huckins, Fannie - Mardanes, Louis
Huckins, Gertrude - Smith, William
Huckins, Laura S. - Syze, Albert
Huckins, Mary A. - Cate, David W.
Hughs, Mary E. - Brough, Marshall
Hunt, Margaret A. - Butler, George F.
Huppe, Mary Leda - Belanger, William Eugene
Hurd, Bernice T. - Curtis, Norman W.
Hurd, Charlotte S. - Davis, Albert H.
Hurd, Doris P. - Smith, William R.
Hurd, Edwina C. - Perkins, Alton M.
Hurd, Flora B. - Emerson, Augustus S.
Hurd, Georgia M. - Cheney, Owen W.
Hurd, Lillian - Emery, George

Hurd, Mary J. - Emery, Clifton E.
Hurlburt, Alice L. - Burnham, Robert T.
Hussey, Grace P. (Plimpton) - Huntress, Ralph
Hussey, Hazel L. - Smith, Harry A.
Hussey, Laura M. - Worster, Wilfred H.
Hussey, Mary A. - Parker, Ned L.
Hutchinson, Lizzie D. - Burke, Stephen

Jackson, Annie B. - Crouse, Henry A.
Jackson, Viola E. - Thayer, Fred I.
James, Annie - Smart, John W.
Jenkins, Emma F. (Smith) - Bradshaw, Frank H.
Jenness, Josephine A. (Nutter) - Proctor, Nathan L.
Johnson, Alice C. - Claflin, Clyde P.
Johnson, Flora B. - Hale, C. Edgar
Johnson, Henrietta - Noyes, Everett N.
Johnson, Lura S. - Hayes, John R.
Johnson, Mazuah H. - Knox, Ulysus S.
Jones, Clara - Eaton, Almon W.
Jones, LaJoice - Knox, Leon E.
Jones, Lizzie A. - Berry, Irving N.
Jones, Mary E. (Otis) - Jones, Austin G.
Jones, Nellie S. - Seavey, Joseph E.
Jordan, Annie M. (Morton) - Lougee, Ernest R.
Joy, Annette E. - Howard, Everett A.
Joy, Lucy M. - Clay, Franklin B.
Joy, Nellie M. - Willson, Charles W. T.
Joyal, M. Elizabeth - Richardson, Leon A.

Kaltsas, Mary A. - Pelletier, Rene R.
Keene, Jessie (Martin) - Lake, Frank E.
Kehaidry, Alexandra (Tsonas) - Prokapian, John
Kelley, Emma L. - Colbath, Bert D.
Kendall, Amanda M. (Mills) - Wyatt, Asa
Kendall, Florence M. - Varney, Fred L.
Keniston, Ida Mildred - Worcester, George W.
Kenney, Cressie B. - Tanner, Everett C.
Kenney, Maud E. - Pike, Edgar E.
Kerr, Bessie L. (Charles) - Leighton, Oscar W.
Keyes, Rosa H. - Sullivan, William L.
Kimball, Addie - Tufts, Leon G.

Kimball, Almira F. - Littlefield, Fred A.
Kimball, Annie M. - Chesley, Herbert J.
Kimball, Annie M. - Bickford, Harry G.
Kimball, Clara B. - Colomy, Horatio S.
Kimball, Edith B. - Hamblett, Charles H.
Kimball, Edna M. - Emerson, Everett W.
Kimball, Elaine M. - Hunt, Loren D.
Kimball, Florence - Ring, John
Kimball, Florence M. - Hogan, Edward F.
Kimball, Gladys - Shannon, Leander
Kimball, Hattie M. - Hill, Jonathan S.
King, Grace - Brouillard, Henry
Kittredge, Eldie - Burleigh, Harry A., Jr.
Knox, Annie M. - Dame, Frank H.
Knox, Arline E. - Laverdiere, Wilfred
Knox, Mildred - Brown, Ira S.

LaBonte, C. Bina - Nedeau, Walter S.
Labossiere, Yvonne - Lougee, Herbert C.
Laflamme, Helen - Raab, Dwight
Lajoie, Melina (Coutois) - Guilmet, Napoleon
Lake, Jennie E. - Palmer, Charles R.
Laken, Maud E. - LaValley, Eugene J.
Lamper, G. Frances - Leighton, Walter E.
Lane, Cora E. - Berry, Arthur E.
Laney, Pauline - Cathcart, Herbert R.
Langeoin, Adrienne - Towle, Tris S.
Langford, Olga I. - Elkins, Arthur A.
Langley, Mary A. - Emerson, William I.
Langley, Mary Ella - Loring, Rupert L.
Lapine, Delia - Belanger, William
Larochelle, Florence M. (Ranney) - Clarke, Clarence B.
Laughlin, Helen L. (Mahoney) - O'Brien, William T.
Laurens, Abbie D. - Willey, Frank E.
Lawton, Katherine E. - Bennett, Roland F.
Leeds, Abbie F. - Stevens, Rockwell J.
Leighton, Alta F. - Barker, Will T.
Leighton, Bessie E. - White, George I.
Leighton, Doris L. - Canney, Merlin H.
Leighton, Grace M. - Bennett, Parker D.
Leighton, Grace M. - Chesley, Harry M.

Leighton, Lizzie - Armstrong, Winthrop C.
Leighton, Lizzie N. - Avery, James F.
Leighton, Mary - Tebbetts, Manfred
Leighton, Nellie M. - Ware, Arthur A.
Leighton, Phebe - Towle, George W.
Leighton, Rachel - Adams, Frank A.
Leighton, Uraine B. - Tuttle, Fred A.
Leighton, Violet M. - Davis, Norman G.
Leithhead, Agnes - Cave, Clinton J.
Lemire, Estella M. - Marcoux, Gideon
Leonard, Nellie F. (Steen) - Armstrong, Harry W.
Lepine, Margaret - Ricker, John Q. A.
LeTair, Minnie A. (Humphrey) - Hurd, J. G.
Letourneau, Juliet L. - Belleville, Ernest L.
Letourneau, Marie A. - Leveille, Walter
Levesque, Adrienne - Kransberg, Harry L.
Lewis, Mabel M. (Stanley) - Westerburg, George L.
Libbey, Viola C. - Smith, Daniel C.
Linscott, Ida E. - Weeden, Wilbur N.
Linscott, Mary A. - Cotton, Joseph W.
Littlefield, Alte F. - Thurston, Hanis
Littlefield, Bertha A. - Gibbs, Marshall P.
Littlefield, Clara E. - Wallace, Edgar F.
Littlefield, Gladys E. - Irish, Earle W.
Littlefield, Maude A. - Elkins, Leroy T.
Littlefield, Priscilla - Preston, Kenneth H.
Littlefield, Serena J. (Murrey) - Edgerly, Frank H.
Livingstone, Maude V. - Jordan, Charles A.
Long, Maxine G. - Sullivan, Cornelius H.
Lord, Aurie P. - Holmes, Ralph L.
Lord, Aurie P. - Currier, George R.
Lord, Eleanor - Brown, Listan M.
Lord, Ethel M. - LaRoche, Leonel
Lord, Fannie M. - Leighton, Mark F.
Lougee, Florence I. - Roberts, George C.
Lougee, Martha E. - Gilman, Erman F.
Lougee, Sarah B. (Ham) - Ricker, Augustus
Lovering, Helen - Pulsifer, Walter H.
Lovering, Madaline - Dame, Kenneth O.
Lovejoy, Maud A. - Hayes, Eugene B.
Lowell, Eleanora E. D. - Carr, Ai

Lucas, Abbie E. - Dustin, Fred A.
Lucas, Abbie E. - Emmond, Henry B.
Lucas, Carrie E. (Sawyer) - Barrett, James O.
Lucas, Lena G. - Horne, Irving E.
Lucas, Myrtie M. - Perkins, Alton M.
Lucier, Josephine - McNeil, Joseph
Ludden, Anna E. - Connors, Joseph N., Jr.
Lufkins, Cora E. (Ballard) - Hovey, Charles N.
Lunde, Gertrude E. - Roberts, Frank H.
Lydecker, Martha A. - Amazeen, R. Alden
Lynch, Dorothy - Perkins, Harold

MacDonald, Addie S. - Hayes, Maurice W.
Mack, F. Mildred - Woodworth, Leland L.
Manchester, Harriet E. - Fisher, John E.
Manley, Frances - Stevens, James
Manson, Beulah - St. Germain, Narcisse
Marchand, Emma (Morrison) - Prescott, Roscoe D.
Marcoux, Alda - Nedeau, Ralph I.
Marcoux, Annie M. (Dubois) - Lowell, Llewellyn L.
Marcoux, Estella (Lemire) - Cardinal, Leon J.
Marison, Hattie E. - Nason, Elbert I.
Marquise, Florence (Clark) - Doucette, Alex
Marsh, Grace J. - Henderson, Herbert J.
Marshall, Alice (Brackett) - Walker, Joseph F.
Marston, Alice D. - Parker, Harry F.
Marston, Amy L. - Jones, Onslow B.
Marston, Mamie E. (Swan) - Benson, Warren
Marston, Martha A. - Twombly, Fred J.
Marston, Myrtle - Freelove, William B.
Martineau, Amelia A. - Walsh, John R.
Martineau, Marjorie - Lougee, Harry C.
Mason, Ethel - Aikens, Percy G.
Mathews, Lillian Eileen - Souter, William
McAllister, Lillian G. - Foster, Kenneth R.
McAskill, Annie - Drue, Joseph
McCarthy, Eleanor (Zacharias) - Gleason, Charles S.
McCarty, Martha E. - Cummisky, Peter M.
McCombie, Clara (Whitehouse) - Peavey, Merton L.
McCormick, Annie L. - Miller, John B.
McCullough, Elsie I. - Hatch, Frank David

McCullough, Ethel E. - Young, Malcolm J.
McKennay, Flora - Bergstrom, Leroy
Meader, Leola M. - Gray, Clyde S.
Melvin, Mary J. - Hannaford, Thomas H.
Merrow, Helen - Teague, Ralph E.
Merrow, Mary E. - Hartford, Edwin L.
Meserve, Ida S. - Johnson, John C.
Meserve, Susie R. - Otis, Norman L.
Metcalf, Mary J. - Fanning, John A.
Miller, Blanche M. (Clough) - Smith, Arthur H.
Miller, Florette P. - Card, Alvin W.
Miller, Katie C. - Downing, Edward J.
Mirrless, Jennie M. - Parker, John C.
Mitchell, Georgie A. - Wells, Fred W.
Mitchell, Gertrude (Downes) - Sawyer, Sewell B.
Moisan, Leona F. - Elliott, Jesse
Montee, Carrie M. - Gilman, Leon E.
Montee, Emma L. - Willey, Herbert A.
Montee, Florence M. - Armstrong, Roy
Montgomery, Gertrude - Burke, Dana L.
Montgomery, Gertrude I. - Miller, Joseph
Montgomery, Marion - Carey, Marcus P.
Montgomery, Marion C. - Warren, Buckley J.
Moore, Annie L. (Hurlburt) - Wiggin, Fred N.
Moore, Gladys - Champagne, Francois
Moore, Mrs. Lizzie (Woodis) - Howard, Elroy C.
Moore, Melissa E. - Gilman, Frank I.
Morgan, Beatrice P. - Remick, Edgar
Morgan, Jessie L. - Berry, Elverton C.
Morgan, Lois I. (Durgin) - Chesley, George L.
Morrill, Lillian M. (Tracey) - Worster, Herbert
Morrill, Nellie M. (Whitehouse) - Doty, Benjamin F.
Morris, Lizzie - Colbath, Clarence E.
Morrison, Cristina M. - Skillings, John
Mosher, Irene M. - Willard, Maurice S.
Moulton, Amy E. - Cates, Charles E.
Moulton, Celia E. - Ham, William M.
Moulton, Doris J. - Varney, Albert L.
Moulton, Ethel B. - Auclair, Albany
Mullen, Sarah H. - Waldron, Augustus H.
Mutch, Adelaide E. (Wyatt) - Wyatt, George H.

Neal, Clara Bertha - Lee, Karl Dayton
Newcome, Rosa L. - Crowther, Dyson
Nichols, Iva M. - Otis, Everett E.
Nichols, Ivadell M. - Cotton, Harry E.
Nichols, Ivadell M. - Moulton, Herbert
Nichols, Mildred - Carter, William C.
Nims, Estelle C. - Crane, Donald P.
Nixon, Mary Agnes - Schoch, Edgar
Norman, Annie M. - Hayes, Harry I.
Norris, Ruth A. - Theberge, Wilfred J.
Nourse, Ruth E. - Varney, Linnie V.
Noyes, Blanche E. - Percival, Roy S.
Nunan, Bertha G. - Clough, Percy B.
Nute, Edith M. - Brawn, Fred L.
Nutter, Christa A. - Dore, Clarence M.
Nutter, Cora E. - Dexter, James R.
Nutter, Doris O. - Walden, William A.
Nutter, Eva E. - Robinson, Fred W.
Nutter, Julie E. (Greenlaw) - Downing, Woodbury H.
Nutter, Mary E. - Butler, Cleveland
Nutter, Mary E. - Smith, James A.
Nutter, Zelma - Thurston, Clifton M.

O'Connor, Mary - Carter, Wilfred
O'Hara, Mary - Tanner, Hervey E.
Ordway, Mary A. - Leighton, George F.
Orr, Nellie G. (Moen) - Tirrell, Oscar L.
Orzechawski, Mary - Kelleher, John J., Jr.
Osgood, Alberta L. - Ferland, Robert W.
Osgood, Flora L. - Whitten, James B.
Osgood, Muriel H. - Martineau, Ramon
Otis, Esther E. - Davenport, Hollis L.
Otis, Evelyn - Glidden, Ernest E.
Otis, Florence - Dexter, Fred
Otis, Gertrude B. - Colbath, Frank N.
Ouellette, Rose - Steele, Alfred D.

Paquette, Rita - Landry, Robert
Parent, Alice E. - Brooks, Vincent Y.
Parent, Celia - Marchand, Goodyear A.
Parent, Eva - Pearl, Harold H.

Parkhurst, Dorothy - Emerson, J. Ralph
Parkhurst, Lillian F. - Amazeen, Walter
Parks, Marion M. - Nangle, Philip A.
Parrock, Maude F. (Furber) - Edgerly, Walter C.
Parshley, Marion M. - Fowler, Clarence D.
Patch, Gertrude M. (Clark) - Reynolds, Elmer S.
Patch, Gladys L. - Berry, Arthur L.
Patch, Mamie - Howard, Herbert, Jr.
Patnande, Marie R. - Glidden, Frank E.
Patrick, Murial - Woodrow, Edward
Pearl, Helen H. - Thompson, James R.
Pearl, Mattie A. - Ricker, Bertred E.
Peavey, Edna I. H. (Huckins) - McDuffee, Frank P.
Peck, Ethel R. - Paige, Earl T.
Pelletier, Mary M. - Cutting, Walter L.
Pelley, Marguerite (Smith) - Mackenzie, Charles P.
Perkins, Ada L. - Nichols, Howard A.
Perkins, Annie L. - Leighton, John H.
Perkins, Ardena B. - Pratt, Lester A.
Perkins, Beulah L. - Thayer, James E.
Perkins, Frances - Reynolds, George D.
Perkins, Hazel A. - Anderson, Leslie W.
Perkins, Kate M. - Brackett, Erwin H.
Perkins, Lillian - Nieforth, Stewart
Perkins, Mary F. - McGrath, Leo F.
Perkins, Mildred - Horne, William H.
Perkins, Nellie M. - Burnham, Charles T.
Perkins, Nellie S. - Randall, Walter L.
Perrault, Alma A. - Leighton, Earl D.
Perrino, Mary A. - Adams, Walter W.
Peterson, Hildred C. - Meserve, Karl G.
Philbrick, Lura S. - Stevens, Willis R.
Pidgeon, Helen S. - Sinniger, Herbert
Pierce, Araminta B. (Young) - Nutter, George W.
Pierson, Corabell - Pierce, Walter Henry
Pike, Agnes (Wiggin) - French, Leslie
Pike, Agnes E. (Rhines) - Nevers, Clarence E.
Pike, Bertha - Dexter, Frank L.
Pike, Francis (Clough) - Ferland, Emile A.
Pike, Grace E. - Sheehan, Henry J.
Pike, Lizzie M. - Schlenker, John

Pike, Viola M. - Spear, Fred R.
Pinkham, Alice - Mathews, Nelson H.
Pinkham, Alice M. - Silvia, John J.
Pinkham, Edith A. - Herring, William M.
Pinkham, Evelyn - Waldron, Robert
Pinkham, Georgia E. - Colbath, Clarence E.
Pinkham, Grace T. - Varney, Lewis N.
Pinkham, Mary A. (Hussey) - Gray, Joseph L.
Pinkham, Sarah E. (Horne) - Ricker, James M.
Pinkham, Shirley - Dickie, Ralph
Pitman, Minnie L. - Holmes, Fred W.
Pitts, Lillie M. - Montgomery, William P.
Place, Arline C. - Lawrence, Abbott W.
Place, Eva May - Burnham, Leroy L.
Place, Inez - Wiggin, Fred N.
Place, Irma - Wilkins, Robert R.
Place, Nellie - Haynes, Roland
Plummer, Marie V. - Crosby, Charles M.
Plummer, Sadie F. - Robinson, Lew C.
Pouliot, Dorothy P. - Maloney, James J.
Powell, Rowena - Roberts, George G.
Power, Florence (Pray) - Emery, William
Pratt, Teresa A. - Babb, Fred O.
Prescott, Gladys A. - Waldron, Donald H.
Prescott, Rita M. - Clements, Charles G.
Preston, Lizzie - Scruton, J. Irving
Proctor, Evelyn Marie - Waugh, Charles M.
Pulsifer, Ruby (Avery) - Gravelle, Arthur
Purrington, Elvaa F. - Kimball, Fred
Putney, Florence V. - Ferguson, Arthur C.

Quile, Lydia - Bardis, Peter M.
Quint, Adelaide M. - Ricker, William H.

Raab, Edna - Hebert, Placide
Racine, Philura A. D. (Davidson) - Herrman, John
Raitt, Nellie M. - Fernald, Frank G.
Rand, Sadie - Corson, Walter N.
Randall, Nellie F. - Wentworth, Loren G.
Randall, Nellie S. (Perkins) - Sanders, William M.
Randall, Nettie A. (Page) - Hadley, Eugene P.

Randell, Alma - Mott, Clarence M.
Reed, Carrie A. (Armstrong) - Junkins, Willard R.
Regis, Marie Malina - Harrison, William J.
Remick, Annie - Blaisdell, Frank D.
Remick, Marjorie - Leahy, James F.
Remick, Pauline - Marr, Charles
Remick, Ruth E. - Dexter, Ernest F.
Remick, Vera M. - Gilbert, Wilfred
Reynolds, Alice (Stowell) - Dailey, Frank
Reynolds, Gertrude - Hayes, Arthur S.
Reynolds, Mabel - Worcester, Robert A.
Reynolds, Olive J. - Salsbury, Lyndall C.
Rhines, Ada M. - Averill, John W.
Rhines, Addie M. - Willey, Burnes C.
Rhines, Agnes M. - Pike, Irving F.
Rhines, Lucretta I. - Cathcart, Fred J.
Rhines, Ruth L. - Currier, Herbert H.
Rhodes, Doris P. (Prescott) - Tebbets, Rodney A.
Rhodes, Dorothy - Packer, Leroy
Rhodes, Evelyn - Russell, Verdrum W.
Rich, Mabel E. - Johnson, Charles W.
Richards, Jennie M. F. (Ford) - Brown, Leander F.
Richardson, Annie M. - Webber, Horace E.
Richardson, Annie W. - Andrews, Fred A.
Richardson, Arline - Wilkins, Robert
Richardson, Elizabeth - Chabot, Alfred
Richardson, Emma A. - Sanborn, Almon C.
Richardson, Lizzie M. - Foss, Charles A.
Richardson, Olive D. - Corson, George A.
Ricker, Bertha M. - Wiggin, Uriah S.
Ricker, Blanch G. - Hamel, Henry T.
Ricker, Edith A. - Davis, Arthur N.
Ricker, Helen A. - Drew, Philip L.
Ricker, Mabel - Shaw, William H.
Ricker, Nettie A. - Edgerly, Frank E.
Riley, Catherine A. (Hannagan) - Clements, Ralph W.
Rines, Ida M. - Hale, Corie E.
Ring, Mary A. - Currier, Charles V.
Ring, Mary C. - Guilmet, Rudolph
Ripley, Emily - Contois, Raymond E.
Roark, Catherine F. - Merrill, Wilbur E.

Robblee, Lena M. (Walker) - Murrey, Arnold L.
Roberge, Elsie A. - Staples, Clarence V.
Roberts, Amy - Lougee, Allie A.
Roberts, Arolin A. - Bickford, Moses R.
Roberts, Edith F. (Connor) - Hall, Errol S.
Roberts, Ella A. - Davis, Ralph E.
Roberts, Emma - Stanley, Irving
Roberts, Ethel G. - Stoddard, Guy H.
Roberts, Inez A. - Hayes, William T.
Roberts, Ivy Alice - Rogers, Charles C.
Roberts, Lena M. - Ham, Charles E.
Roberts, Mamie B. - Perkins, George L.
Robie, Mary L. - Wilson, Orville A.
Robinson, Susan E. - Durant, Harry E.
Rodden, Ella M. - Downing, Henry H.
Rogers, Althea V. - Gilman, Ernest F.
Rogers, Caroline S. (Place) - Burleigh, Henry
Rogers, Ethel E. (O'Neal) - Emery, Alden C.
Rogers, Violetta P. - Davis, Russell A.
Rollins, Eva M. (Berry) - Pinkham, Fred
Rollins, Flora E. - Hayes, Forrest H.
Rollins, Reta - Glidden, Clyde R.
Rollins, Venna - Hogan, Joseph
Rollins, Venna M. - Sawyer, Roscoe I.
Ross, Mabel G. - Ricker, Irving J.
Rowe, Blanche - Knox, Harry
Rowohlt, Violet T. - Brown, Albert J.
Roy, Blanche A. - Rundlett, Rufus W.
Runnells, Lizzie M. - Curtis, Henry B.
Russell, Anna A. - Armstrong, John M.
Russell, Annie - Bready, Frank A.
Ryan, Lillian E. - Elliott, William A.

St. Laurence, Jean A. - Holmes, Ralph L.
St. Pierre, Geraldine - Duperre, Raymond
Sabeau, Ella M. - Richardson, Ralph P.
Sanborn, Lucy H. (Watson) - Davis, John M.
Sands, Leonora (Price) - Manson, George H.
Saunders, Lila S. (Cook) - Lougee, Walter S.
Savage, Marion (Grimes) - Horne, Fred I.
Savoir, Jennie May - Wentworth, Joseph D.

Scott, Addie May (Leathers) - Ham, George W.
Scott, Violet E. - Burleigh, Charles P.
Scott, Violet May - Rollins, Leon P.
Scruton, Addie L. - Burnham, George H.
Scruton, Bessie L. - Coleman, Ira
Scruton, Laura - Freethy, Wilbert A.
Scruton, Sara Elizabeth - Welch, Carroll C.
Secord, Eleanor D. - Barker, Hiram L.
Senter, Gertrude F. (Stevens) - Berry, Charles M.
Senter, Hilda M. - Littlefield, Donald A.
Shattuck, Nellie - Whitehouse, Ellwood K.
Shaw, Vivian M. - Hayes, Arthur J.
Sherman, Mabel E. (Leavitt) - Horne, William H.
Shipley, Carolina - Davis, John
Shirley, Lydia M. - Twombly, Horne
Shorey, Elora E. (Randall) - Young, Frank E.
Simonds, Florence (Richardson) - Cates, Alfred A.
Simonds, Harriett B. - Hanson, Julian R.
Small, Jennie A. - Babb, Horatio N.
Smallman, Ida (Lutz) - Irving, Charles J.
Smart, Gertrude M. - Tanner, George I.
Smart, Grace C. - Burnham, Frank
Smart, Jennela - Miller, Charles H.
Smart, Maude R. - Wiggin, Archie C.
Smart, Minnie F. - Eaton, Charles C.
Smith, Alice N. - Fowler, Clarence D.
Smith, Bertena J. - Tibbetts, Henry A.
Smith, Clara E. - Mack, Michael
Smith, Emma - Davis, George H.
Smith, Evelyn G. - Nelson, William H.
Smith, Fannie (Drew) - Tuttle, Lester G.
Smith, Gracie L. (McKeen) - Toby, Eddie E.
Smith, Josephine S. - Foster, Charles A.
Smith, Lucy J. (Fletcher) - Pride, Joshua T.
Smith, Mabel F. - Lary, Greenleaf H.
Smith, Mabel Gerrish (Gerrish) - Oikle, John
Smith, Maud J. - Hanson, Julian R.
Smith, Nellie M. - Willey, Charles R.
Spear, Charlotte G. - Armstrong, Winthrop C.
Spence, Mary - Glidden, Augustus
Sprague, Annie Belle (James) - Rand, David E.

Stacy, Cora E. - Pellerin, Jesse L.
Stacy, Mary P. - Underhill, George E.
Stanhope, Margaret - Pike, Raymond
Stanhope, Rachael - Pulsifer, John L.
Stanhope, Ruth (Peoples) - Coleman, Harold L.
Stanley, Bertha - Pence, Horace
Stanley, Frances E. - Nicholl, Francis J.
Stanley, L. Violet - Jones, Wilbur C.
Stanley, Mabel - Reid, Philip
Staples, Alfreda J. - Ham, John H.
Steadman, Gertrude E. (Bishop) - Carter, Joseph P.
Stevens, Alice - Merrill, Arthur
Stevens, Bernice L. - Goodwin, Eugene T.
Stevens, Edna H. - Camm, Stewart A.
Stevens, Ida B. - Ham, Herman
Stevens, Lillian A. (Campbell) - Knox, Earl L.
Stevens, Marguerite F. - Furber, Myron
Stevens, Ruth E. - Ramsey, Lawrence
Stiles, S. Evannah - Price, Osborne W.
Stillings, Edith E. (Tibbetts) - Brooks, Pierce J.
Stillings, Mildred M. - Whitehouse, Fred
Stott, Georgie M. - Dallen, Frank A.
Strainge, Nellie F. - Cate, Frank O.
Straw, Katherine L. (Rogers) - Proctor, Nathan L.
Streeter, Nancy - Lemoine, John
Strout, Eva R. - LaBonta, J. Edward
Sullivan, Katie - Hayes, Nehemiah B.
Sutton, Edith M. (Carleton) - Cook, Henry N.
Sweeney, Gertrude E. - Lewis, Arthur L.
Swinerton, Alice L. - Canney, Carl B.
Swinerton, Edith - Bowley, Fred E.
Swinerton, Ella F. - Blaisdell, Clarence L.
Swinerton, Estella A. - Durkee, Porter J.
Swinerton, Gertie M. - Young, Alvah H.
Swinerton, Olive A. - Wheeler, Courtland

Taber, Emma J. - Ham, Benjamin
Tague, Alice J. - Leahy, Joseph P.
Talpey, Lois - McIntire, John
Tanguay, Mary J. - Crosby, George M.
Tanner, Adella G. - Banks, Frank E.

Tanner, Evelyn - Furber, Otto J.
Tanner, Grace L. - Allen, C. R.
Tanner, Luella - Roberts, John P. B.
Tanwalt, Emma (Reuton) - Leon, Joseph T.
Tarbox, Emeline K. (Kimball) - Jondrey, Arnold G.
Tarbox, Emeline K. (Kimball) - Jondry, Arnold G.
Tasker, Emma A. - Hanson, Chester H.
Tauwalt, Emma (Renton) - Hurlburt, Charles W.
Tebbetts, Florence P. - Prescott, Roscoe D.
Tebbetts, Marion Ruth - Cheney, Morris Emery
Terrell, Pauline - Lesperance, Elwin
Thayer, Harriet A. - Colomy, Ralph S.
Thayer, Harriett A. - Lefavour, Ernest E.
Theriault, Ida - Lawton, James
Thompson, Carrie (Varney) - Twombly, Laurel F.
Thompson, Ellen E. - Wyatt, Ralph F.
Thompson, Esther E. - Varney, Benjamin E. W.
Thompson, Ethel M. - Chesley, Ralph J.
Thompson, Georgie (Colomy) - Webster, Frank E.
Thompson, Louisa - Hanson, Frederick J.
Thompson, Marion - Richardson, Ernest A.
Thompson, Mattie (Towle) - Pence, Daniel
Thurston, Eva B. - Pike, John W.
Thurston, Grace G. - Colbath, Lauren G.
Thurston, Kathleen - Varney, Ralph George
Tibbetts, Alice M. - Evans, Charles W.
Tibbetts, Alice M. - Brown, John A.
Tibbetts, Amanda (Lee) - Cramer, William A.
Tibbetts, Cassandra M. - Hurd, Thomas
Tibbetts, Cora - McGibbon, James
Tibbetts, Florence F. - Colomy, Horatio S.
Tibbetts, Grace M. - Haynes, John L.
Tibbetts, Hattie N. (Howe) - Wheatley, Hannibal P.
Tibbetts, Isadore - Pride, James H.
Tibbetts, Phebe L. - Ham, Charles E.
Tibbetts, Susie - Seavey, Edwin A.
Tilton, Grace E. (Babb) - Tanner, Clarence J.
Tilton, Hilda (Brooks) - McCarthy, George D.
Tilton, Ruth E. - Lawrence, Arthur F.
Towle, Annie L. - Dixon, Elmore H.
Towle, Annie M. - Bodwell, William S.

Towle, Beatrice G. - Pike, Randolph K.
Towle, Bernice P. - Cheney, Arnold J. H.
Towle, Ruth B. - Remick, Fred W.
Towns, Minnie W. - Porter, Wallace N.
Tracy, Doris - Vanasse, Armand L.
Trafton, Annie B. - Towle, Tristram F.
Trafton, Ella F. - Randall, Willie I.
Trafton, Ella F. (Hussey) - Rogers, George C.
Trafton, Katherine H. - Casey, Gordon W.
Trainor, Marion E. - Ashland, George
Trask, Ida B. - Goodrum, William
Trask, Maria (Otis) - Kent, John
Treamer, Marion E. - Stevens, Ernest W.
Trefethen, Myra F. - Amazeen, R. Alden
Tripp, Helen W. - Flanders, Herman T.
True, Alice L. - Wyatt, George H.
Trusselle, Bertha A. - Russell, Warren B.
Tufts, Dorothea - Aichler, Alonzo
Tufts, Ellen M. - Whitehouse, Fred L.
Tufts, Mary E. - Collins, Stephen
Tufts, Ruth - Hartfiel, Roy
Turcott, Mary Ann - Garland, Edgar E.
Tuttle, Fannie (Drew) - Bailey, Nelson
Tuttle, Lilla - Gilbert, George
Tuttle, Marian C. - Thompson, Elmer E.
Tuttle, Mildred A. - Burleigh, Harry A., Jr.
Tuttle, Minnie E. - Foss, Wilbur E.
Tuttle, Myra B. - Wheeler, Frank E.
Tweedy, Maude D. - Hoyt, Lindsay F.

Varney, Clara A. - Wyatt, Henry I.
Varney, Ellen E. - Haynes, John S.
Varney, Esther E. (Thompson) - Boyd, John A.
Varney, Lizzie J. - Ware, William V.
Varney, Mary A. - Bickford, Walter H.
Varney, Rose E. - Fall, Henry S.
Varney, Rosetta - Perkins, Luther E.
Varney, Vianna D. - Remick, Joseph F.
Vickers, Gladys - Jackson, William H.

Wadleigh, Flora - Thompson, Andrew N.

Wadleigh, Helen E. - Nute, Harry A.
Waldron, Adelaide C. - Sloan, Benjamin B.
Walker, Angie - Farwell, Fred T.
Walker, Aurilla J. - Saunders, George H.
Walker, Emily - Piercy, Alexander D.
Walker, Ida E. - Leigh, Charles E.
Wallace, Annie J. - Whitehouse, Harvey, Jr.
Wallace, Pansy E. - Peavey, Ernest F.
Wallingford, Ethel A. (Gray) - McKenney, Alfred R.
Walton, Carrie D. - Adams, Eugene I.
Warburton, Gladys G. (Armstrong) - Hodgens, James T.
Ward, Grace - Smith, Samuel L.
Ware, Lucille - Nutter, Roger A.
Ware, Marguerite A. - Simonds, Frank E.
Warren, Addie S. (Dunlley) - Davis, George F.
Watson, Pauline E. - Richards, Ernest W.
Webster, Effie A. (Willey) - Davis, Charles S.
Webster, Fannie E. - Curtis, Sylvester R.
Webster, Laura J. - Tripp, F. Leroy
Webster, Ruth - Eldridge, Lester
Wedgwood, Ursula B. - Hayes, William T.
Weeks, Emma M. - Blaisdell, Archie M.
Weeks, Olive B. (Brackett) - Perkins, Daniel M.
Welch, Anna E. - Leavitt, George A.
Welch, Phyllis (Carpenter) - Dickie, Kenneth W.
Wells, Eleanor - Perkins, Arthur L.
Wentworth, Annie J. - Curtis, Everett I.
Wentworth, Bessie E. - Cloutman, John F., Jr.
Wentworth, Carrie E. - Ham, Irving L.
Wentworth, Gladys I. - Amazeen, Clarence A.
Wentworth, Hazel F. - Burleigh, Ray C.
Wentworth, Liberty W. - Cooke, John H.
Wentworth, Mary A. - Sansoucie, William L.
Wentworth, Maybelle - Huckins, Walter
Wentworth, Ruth E. - Montgomery, Melvin
Weymouth, Viola S. - Jenness, Charles W.
Wheatley, Alice J. - Thayer, Lawrence E.
White, Blanche B. - Runnels, Paul M., Jr.
White, Carrie B. - Knox, Elmer S.
White, Fannie M. - Hayes, Charles L.
White, Isabelle - Smith, Corran M.

White, Nellie A. (Rowe) - Fall, William A.
White, Reta M. - Beck, Charles W.
Whitehouse, Addie E. - Knox, Ulysses S.
Whitehouse, Esta M. - Scruton, Gilbert P.
Whitehouse, Hazel - Marcoux, Albert A.
Whitehouse, Jennie M. - Horne, Izah A.
Whitehouse, Lena F. - Shackford, John S.
Whitehouse, Martha J. - Dudley, Horace I.
Whitehouse, Nellie (Shattock) - Varney, Daniel
Whitehouse, Nellie M. - McDonald, Daniel
Whitehouse, Pauline - Hayden, Everett
Whitehouse, Sadie E. - Bunker, Cyrus S.
Whitehouse, Susan J. (Amazeen) - Garey, Newman A.
Whiting, Gertrude J. - White, George A.
Whiting, Thelma L. - Reed, Edward J.
Whitney, Ora A. - McGregor, George A.
Whitten, Carrie E. (Joy) - Elkins, Cyrus
Wiggin, Bernice - King, Charles A.
Wiggin, Margaret M. - Kimball, F. Gordon
Wiggin, Mary E. - Peavey, Ernest F.
Wiggin, Winnie M. (Fall) - Whitney, Will E.
Wilkes, Gladys T. - Silvia, John J.
Wilkins, Arline (Richardson) - Goodstone, John
Wilkins, Ruth C. - Cardinal, Carroll C.
Willard, Alberta S. - Mosher, Harold W.
Willard, Bernice L. (Christy) - Rhodes, Ethard A.
Willey, Abbie D. (Laurens) - Banks, Edward
Willey, Carrie (Corson) - Johnson, John G.
Willey, Lillian A. (Rollins) - Hayes, Seth W.
Willey, Lizzie A. - Currier, Fred E.
Willey, Verna - Adams, Edgar N.
Williams, Florence - Scott, Joseph A.
Willson, Hattie T. - Littlefield, Joseph F.
Wilson, Mary E. - Canney, Henry J.
Wilson, Mary L. (Robie) - Page, Charles H.
Wing, Vera S. (Smart) - Piper, Lloyd L.
Wingate, Lillian M. - Browne, Lindley R.
Winn, Ella C. - Rollins, Harold C.
Witham, Carrie B. - Lougee, Allie A.
Witt, Ada L. - Butler, Thomas E.
Witter, Eleanor - Kiriapontos, George

Wood, Elizabeth A. - Copp, Arthur Leroy
Wood, Lizzie May - Carter, Albert E.
Wood, Nellie M. (Tucker) - Bunker, Sidney P.
Wood, Viola A. (Wiggin) - Sanborn, Roland B.
Works, Emma L. - Berry, George H.
Works, Lucy M. - Rand, Raymond
Wormstead, Doris L. - Gray, Ernest L.
Worster, Pauline J. - Willey, Charles D.
Wyatt, Barbara T. - York, George A.
Wyatt, Edith L. - Varney, Albert L.
Wyatt, Edith L. - Martineau, Joseph
Wyatt, Fannie - Watton, Wilbur
Wyatt, Ida M. - Bean, Ivan A.
Wyatt, Marion A. - Mayotte, Harry C.
Wyeik, Mary - Coulombe, Almanzor

Yandoh, Mary K. (Davidson) - Stevens, Percy E.
Yeaton, Helen D. - Trask, Ralph C.
Yeaton, Martha S. - Nute, Eri S.
Yeaton, Minnie E. - Card, Oliver H.
York, Augustia (Davis) - Kimball, Charles H.
York, Fannie - Doty, Benjamin
York, Nellie - Doty, Benjamin F.
Young, Daisy (Drew) - Davis, John F.
Young, Ella M. - Bishop, Everett J.
Young, Elsie M. - Miller, Ray S.
Young, Ethel M. - Dame, Walter S.
Young, Etta M. - Young, Charles H.
Young, Lizzie M. - Forsaith, Samuel S.
Young, Maude M. - Young, Fred
Young, Nellie - Gordon, Frank
Young, Nina (Richardson) - Salisbury, Clifford K.

# DEATHS

**ABBOTT,**

Daniel H., d. 8/21/1930 at 67/4/16; retired; widower; b. Ossipee; Lemuel Abbott (Ossipee) and Abbie Peavey (Ossipee)

Eugene, d. 4/5/1919 at 68/2/22; farmer; married; b. Ossipee; Asa Abbott (Ossipee) and Sarah Moody (Ossipee)

Hannah A., d. 6/14/1930 at 59/3/29; housekeeper; married; b. Marlboro, MA; James C. Dand (NS) and Annie Bruce (NS)

Laura A., d. 7/16/1928 at 76/1/9; housekeeper; widow; b. Ossipee; Lemuel Abbott (Ossipee) and Abbie Peavey (Ossipee)

Leslie E., d. 3/28/1922 at 0/4/16; b. Farmington; Ernest R. Abbott (Concord) and Mabel Ham (Milton)

Sarah, d. 9/30/1905 at 86/10/12; cancer of liver; widow; b. Ossipee; Clemency Moody (Ossipee) and Mary Cooley (Ossipee)

**ADAMS,**

Eliza B., d. 7/29/1893 at 77/5/15; heart disease; housekeeper; widow; b. Alexander; James B. Adams (Alexandra)

Floyd A., d. 11/24/1911 at –; stillborn; b. Farmington; Frank E. Adams (MA, shoe operative) and Rachel Leighton (MA)

Frank A., d. 8/28/1932 at 71/7/7 in Rochester; retired; married; b. W. Newbury, MA; Jerry Adams (York, ME) and Mary Brock (W. Newbury, MA)

Rachel K., d. 11/3/1936 at 67/3/29; at home; widow; b. Marblehead, MA; George F. Leighton (Farmington) and Margaret Sandwich (Halifax, NS)

William R., d. 1/13/1912 at 58/0/30; cerebral hemorrhage; shoemaker; married; b. Randolph, MA; Richard Adams (coal dealer) and Eliza J. Remick (Gardiner, ME)

**AIKEN,**

Edith, d. 11/29/1920 at 34; housewife; married; b. Quincy, MA; John Masson (Scotland) and Isabelle McDonald (Scotland)

Mary A., d. 6/23/1938 at 63/8/5; housewife; married; b. NB; Charles McKennelley (NB) and Lois Clark (NB)

Percy G., d. 7/4/1929 at 38/1/13; horse dealer; widower; b. Barnstead; David L. Aiken (Barnstead) and Annie F. Shaw (Concord)

**ALLEN,**
Almira P., d. 6/13/1925 at 79/0/17; housekeeper; widow; b. Limerick, ME; Joseph Harmon (Limerick, ME) and Susan Philpot (Limerick, ME)
George, d. 1/8/1912 at 0/0/1; inanition; b. Farmington; Peter Allen (Greece, shoemaker) and Rose Garrett (Canada)
Lester H., d. 8/15/1888 at 44/2; meningitis; machinist; married; b. Chelsea, MA; George Allen (VT) and Alma Dinsmore (VT)
Lillian F., d. 5/19/1919 at 55/3/29; bookkeeper; widow; b. Farmington; James Johnson (Strafford) and Mary L. Watson (Gilmanton)
Nellie A., d. 12/28/1934 at 60/7; at home; married; b. Farmington; John F. Cloutman and Ellen E. Kimball
Peter, Jr., d. 1/8/1912 at 0/0/1; inanition; b. Farmington; Peter Allen (Greece, shoemaker) and Rose Garrett (Canada)
Peter D., d. 6/18/1906 at 58/0/15; carcinoma lower lip; carpenter; married; b. Quebec

**ALVEY,**
son, d. 2/9/1922 at –; b. Farmington; Walter N. Alvey (Milton) and Maude Burrows (Appomattox)

**AMAZEEN,**
Caroline B., d. 9/17/1894 at 77/9/24; asthenia; housewife; married; b. Portsmouth; Daniel Sherburn and Jane Colbath
Charles H., d. 2/12/1934 at 85/10/16; farmer; widower; b. Farmington; Henry C. Amazeen (New Castle) and Abagail Wentworth (Milton)
Emily Louise, d. 1/19/1910 at 69/7/26; broncho pneumonia; housewife; married; b. Worcester, MA; Frederick Johnson (Worcester, MA) and Eunice Kellogg (Stonington, CT)
Emma, d. 2/12/1930 at 79/6/7; housewife; married; b. Standish, ME; Alvah Rollins and Abigail Colomy
George E., d. 10/6/1923 at 79/7/16; shoecutter; married; b. Newcastle, ME; Rufus Amazeen and Caroline Sherman
Lillian, d. 11/25/1935 at 41/5/18 in Rochester; housewife; married; b. Lynnhurst; Frank Parkhurst (Amherst) and Isabelle F. Dunn (Wakefield, MA)
Maria, d. 6/6/1925 at 85/10/11

Myra F., d. 1/16/1896 at 35/5/18; typhoid fever; housewife; married b. New Castle; Llewellyn Trefethen (New Castle) and Dorothy Randall (New Castle)

Nellie K., d. 3/27/1888 at 0/11; innatrition; b. Farmington, A. R. Amazeen (Farmington) and Nellie E. Knox (Milton)

Rufus, d. 12/29/1912 at 99/5/18; old age; farmer; widower; b. New Castle; William Amazeen (New Castle, farmer)

Rufus A., d. 1/21/1938 at 83/1/1; coppersmith; married; b. Newington; Rufus Amazeen (Portsmouth) and Caroline Sherburn (Portsmouth)

Warren K., d. 5/14/1929 at 7/11/21 in Milton; b. Milton; Walter Amazeen (Milton) and Lillian F. Parkhurst (Lynnhurst, MA)

**ANDERSON,**

Bertha, d. 10/4/1920 at 22/8/17; bookkeeper; single; b. Wakefield, MA; Walter Anderson (Stoneham, MA) and Evelyn Hicks (Robbins, ME)

Carl, d. 5/15/1922 at 73; farmer; widower; b. Sweden; Catherine Anderson (Sweden)

Ernest, d. 2/14/1916 at 0/0/1; b. Farmington; Walter Anderson (Stoneham, MA) and Evelyn E. Hicks (Robbinston, ME)

Evelyn E., d. 8/14/1935 at 63/2/20 in Portland, ME; housework; widow; b. Robbinston, ME; Valentine Hicks and Mary E. Madden

Matilda, d. 4/2/1922 at 72/11/21; housewife; married; b. Sweden

Phyllis E., d. 8/16/1930 at 9/7/6 in Rochester; b. Milton; Leslie Anderson (Stoneham, MA) and Hazel A. Perkins (Middleton)

**ANDREWS,**

Agnes, d. 3/16/1899 at 0/1/16; anaemia; b. Farmington; Joseph Andrews (Oldtown, ME) and ----- (NS)

Esther, d. 3/12/1899 at 29/4/11; pulmonisis; basket maker; married

John, d. 9/10/1902 at 11/8/10; unknown; student; single; Joe Andrews and Agnes Andrews

Oliver E., d. 11/17/1891 at 69/11/19; pneumonia; farmer; widower; b. Berwick, ME; Benjamin Andrews and Mercy Randall

**ANGEL,**

Charles, d. 6/19/1928 at 63/6/24; retired; married; b. Woodstock, VT; David Angel (Woodstock, VT)

**ANNIS,**
Charles, d. 5/4/1938 at 88/8/24; foreman p. mill; married; b. Naples, ME; John G. Annis (Bethel, ME) and Mary Edgerly

**ARMSTRONG,**
Alice, d. 10/17/1927 at 78/7/20; housekeeper; widow; b. Somersworth; William B. Martin (Somersworth) and Clara Wallingford (Lowell, MA)
C. M., d. 11/4/1908 at 62/4; cerebral hemorrhage; shoemaker; married; b. Scotland
Florence, d. 2/3/1920 at 31/5
Harry W., d. 9/4/1933 at 64/3/8; janitor; divorced; b. Somersworth; Charles M. Armstrong (Scotland) and Alice E. Martin (Somersworth)

**ARNOLD,**
Mary A., d. 1/27/1887 at 74/7/7; housekeeper; widow; b. RI
Sarah, d. 1/10/1935 at 54/0/1; housewife; married; b. PEI; Noah Godfrey (PEI) and Mary Clow (PEI)

**ARSENAULT,**
Jane E., d. 9/26/1932 at 72/9/26; housekeeper; widow; b. Canada; Hosea Collette (Canada) and Marie Ducette (Canada)

**ASPINALL,**
Cyrus G., d. 6/14/1898 at 30/9; suicide; laborer; married; b. Middleton; John Aspinall

**ATHERTON,**
Helen P., d. 9/6/1918 at 30/6/10; housewife; married; b. Exeter; S. A. Lawrence (NH) and Augusta Horne (Middleton)

**ATWOOD,**
May B., d. 12/4/1938 at 78/6/16; housewife; married; b. Bridgewater, MA; Lucius Dunbar (Bridgewater, MA) and Lucinda Packard (E. Boston, MA)

**AUCLAIR[E],**
Clarinor, d. 5/7/1925 at 53; shoeworker; widow; b. Canada

Existe, d. 10/25/1917 at 45/9/9; mgr. of sawmill; married; b. Fossdale, RI; Trefflie Auclaire (Canada) and Louise Venson (Canada)

Felix, d. 4/7/1937 at 65/7/11; shoeworker; married; b. Canada; Francois Auclair (Canada) and Rose Auclair (Canada)

**AUSTIN,**

Charles H., d. 10/24/1887 at 49/8/27; shoemaker; married; b. Somersworth; Benjamin Austin and Polly Worster

Mary E., d. 8/29/1905 at 66; shock; housekeeper; widow; b. New Durham; J. L. Pinkham (New Durham) and Betsey M. Adams (Barnstead)

**AVERILL,**

Almena, d. 11/7/1925 at 74/2/24; housewife; married; b. New Durham; George Wallace and Abigail Runnells

Elizabeth N., d. 1/15/1922 at 73/2/6; widow; b. N. Sharon, ME; John Hutchinson (Danvers, MA) and Susan Y. Butler (Waterville, ME)

Ernest N., d. 12/7/1888 at 0/3/23; hydercophalus; b. Farmington; T W. Averill (Farmington) and Augusta A. Wallace

George E., d. 2/21/1895 at 17/7/14; accidental shooting; farming; single; b. Farmington; Trask Averill (Farmington) and Augusta A. Runnells (New Durham)

John W., d. 4/7/1929 at 53/10/18; shoeworker; married; b. Farmington; Trask W. Averill and Augusta Wallace

Laura E., d. 4/5/1899 at 54; anaemia; housewife; single; b. Mt. Vernon; Barnard Averill (Mt. Vernon) and Harriet Richardson

Mary B., d. 7/13/1890 at 0/7/1; pneumonia; b. Farmington; Trask W. Averill and Augusta Runnells

Trask W., d. 1/28/1929 at 86/10/18; farmer; widower; b. Farmington; Bernard Averill

**AVERY,**

daughter, d. 12/21/1890 at –; stillborn; b. Farmington; Frank L. Avery (Barnstead) and Sarah S. Berry (Strafford)

Ann C., d. 9/22/1893 at 86/4/6; old age; lady; widow; b. Epsom; Robert McDaniel and Nancy Keniston

Elbridge T., d. 9/27/1910 at 74/4; car. of bladder; painter; single; b. S. Wolfeboro; John Avery

Frank L., d. 12/27/1917 at 77/10/11; retired; married; b. Barnstead; Stephen Avery (Barnstead) and Ann McDaniels (Epsom)

Lizzie N., d. 11/17/1912 at 40/5/14; tuberculosis; married; b. Farmington; H. C. Leighton (shoemaker) and Georgia Rhines

Sarah S., d. 4/19/1938 at 83/7/20; housewife; widow; b. Strafford; Benjamin Berry (Strafford) and Nancy Hanscom (Strafford)

Solomon, d. 7/1/1926 at 83/11/14; farmer; widower; b. NH; Samuel Avery (VT) and Lucinda Holmes (NH)

**AYERS,**

Adeline A., d. 2/17/1911 at 67/2/20; pneumonia; married; b. Kittery, ME; Nathan Pettigrew (New Castle, ME, fisherman) and ----- (Kittery, ME)

Charles E., d. 5/10/1927 at 54/2/28; postmaster; single; b. New Durham; John O. Ayers (Kittery, ME) and Addie Pettigrew (Kittery, ME)

John O., d. 2/6/1927 at 86/8/25; widower

Mary E., d. 5/24/1929 at 80/7/17; widow; b. New Durham; Lewis Sumner and Elmira -----

**BABB,**

George M., d. 10/15/1897 at 30/2/15; phthisis pulmonalis; merchant; single; b. Bangor; Andrew N. Babb (Orono, ME) and Annie M. Peterson (Boston)

John K., d. 12/21/1936 at 75/7/6 in Rochester; laborer; widower; b. Farmington; Leonard Babb and Martha Cook

Leonard, d. 9/8/1888 at 65/4/24; mortification; shoemaker; married; Jethro Babb (Strafford) and Sally Drew (Strafford)

Martha, d. 1/13/1908 at 84/2/15; fracture of hip; housekeeper; widow; b. Northwood; Richard Emerson and Delia Goss

Mary E., d. 10/2/1928 at 80

Mary O., d. 3/28/1931 at 92/7/1; widow; b. Amherst, NS; Thomas Coates and Jane Embree

Matilda R., d. 6/18/1894 at 45/9/14; cancer; millhand; widow; b. Farmington; Isaac Canney and Matilda Reed (Farmington)

Melvin E., d. 8/31/1930 at 74/9/22; wheelwright; divorced; b. Strafford; Samson H. Babb and Elmira Evans

Solomon H., d. 7/14/1918 at 72/10/12; shoeworker; married; b. Farmington; Leonard P. Babb (Farmington) and ----- Emerson (Northwood)

Sophia L., d. 11/3/1907 at 79/11/29; senectus; widow; b. Barrington; ----- Raynolds (farmer) and Mary L. Locke (Barrington)

**BACHELDER,**
Angie, d. 7/21/1888 at 58; peritonitis; housekeeper; married; b. Alton
Roy E., d. 6/26/1888 at 6/3; phthisis; b. Farmington; E. K. Bachelder and Inez Hussey

**BAGLEY,**
son, d. 12/12/1935 at –; b. Farmington; Victor Bagley (Whiting, ME) and Elizabeth Bryant (Princeton, ME)

**BAILEY,**
Doris E., d. 9/1/1933 at 20/4/9; housewife; married; b. Farmington; Earle M. Edgerly (Farmington) and Ethel Drew (Farmington)
Everett M., d. 9/28/1922 at 68; shoeworker; single; b. Farmington; Dexter Bailey and Mary -----
George H., d. 12/25/1935 at 51 in Dedham, MA; retired; married; b. Middleboro, MA; George Bailey (Portland, ME) and Lillian Shaw (Middleboro, MA)
Mary K., d. 4/11/1903 at 72/2; pneumonia; housewife; widow; b. Farmington; ----- Bacon and ----- Harmond

**BAKER,**
George E., d. 4/22/1916 at 60/7/5; merchant; married; b. S. Lawrence, MA; Asa F. Baker (Dover)
Georgia A., d. 12/4/1928 at 73/11/18; housekeeper; widow; b. Bradford; Albert Bartlett and Sarah Cook

**BANFIELD,**
stillborn son, d. 2/19/1933 at – in Rochester; b. Rochester; Ralph Banfield (Conway) and Violet Dow (Farmington)

**BANFILL,**
Wilber, d. 8/18/1905 at 0/11/21; convulsions; b. Nashua; W. S. L. Banfill (Ossipee) and Rosie LaForge (Canada)

**BANKS,**
Abbie L., d. 6/5/1900 at 30/5/21; consumption; housekeeper; married; b. Farmington; Isaac Lawrence (Tuftonboro) and Sarah Ransom (Farmington)

**BANNISTER,**
Ann A., d. 9/8/1891 at 74/1/19; cancer; housekeeper; widow; b. Derry

**BARKER,**
Ella May, d. 6/20/1931 at 77/0/15; widow; b. Farmington; Robert K. Peavey (Farmington) and Mary A. Beals (Natick, MA)

Emily M., d. 2/14/1901 at 81/9/15; tuberculosis of lung; widow; b. Farmington; Josiah Edgerly (New Durham) and Mary Tash (Durham)

George W., d. 2/21/1903 at 50/3/26; heart failure; farmer; single; John Barker (Epping) and Emily M. Edgerly (Farmington)

Hiram, d. 3/26/1887 at 71/3/5; broker; widower; b. Alton; John Barker and Sally Davis (Alton)

Hiram E., d. 2/21/1902 at 23/2/4; tuberculosis; student; single; b. Farmington; Hiram H. Barker (Farmington) and Ella M. Peavey (Farmington)

Hiram H., d. 11/15/1915 at 63/11/13; retired; married; b. Farmington; Hiram Barker (Alton) and Maria Hayes (New Durham)

John, d. 5/22/1893 at 92/2/27; old age; broker; married; b. Epping; John Barker (Epping) and Sally Davis (Alton)

John H., d. 5/8/1919 at 79; storekeeper; widower; b. Wolfeboro; John Barker (Epping) and Emily Edgerly (NH)

Louis H., d. 5/6/1902 at 15/6/7; pulmonary tuberculosis; student; single; b. Farmington; Hiram H. Barker (Farmington) and Ella M. Peavey (Farmington)

Luella T., d. 12/28/1888 at 35/8/7; septicemia; housekeeper; married; John P. Kilroy (Ireland) and Hannah B. Leighton

Mary E., d. 4/8/1901 at 58/2/4; congestion of brain; single; b. Farmington; John Barker (Epping) and Emc M. Edgerly (Farmington)

Mary E., d. 9/11/1901 at 17/3/6; tubercular meningitis; student; single; b. Farmington; Hiram H. Barker (Farmington) and Ella M. Peavey (Farmington)

Will T., d. 8/19/1936 at 58/9/8; retired; married; b. Farmington; Hiram H. Barker (Farmington) and Ella M. Peavey (Farmington)

**BARNABY,**
William, d. 3/16/1917 at 0/2/14; b. Tilton; Rudolph Barnaby (Worcester, MA) and Mabel R. Eckles (Plymouth)

**BARNES,**
son, d. 3/11/1908 at –; stillborn; b. Farmington; Arland Barnes (N. Salem, MA) and Rose Dilange (Lowell, MA)

**BARRETT,**
Abbie C., d. 1/8/1889 at 84/10/19; old age

Alexander, d. 8/5/1907 at 80/8/13; cerebral hemorrhage; retired; widower; b. ME; Alexander Barrett (ME, farmer) and Abbie C. Hersey

Carrie E., d. 6/17/1932 at 68/2/11 in Standish; housework; widow; b Quincy, MA; Harry M. Sawyer (ME) and Caroline Barrett (Quincy, MA)

Frank A., d. 2/8/1917 at 54/11/16; lumberman; married; b. Francestown; Charles A. Barrett (Lancaster) and Ann B. Butler (Antrim)

Helen A., d. 8/10/1922 at 75/4/29; housewife; married; b. New London; J. R. Phillips and Julia A. Phillips

James O., d. 4/6/1931 at 89/3/23; retired; married; b. Hinsdale; Ira Barrett

Sarah R., d. 12/30/1904 at 75/8/25; senectus; housewife; married; b. Alfred, ME; James Randall (N. Berwick, ME) and Hannah Hanson (N. Berwick, ME)

**BARRY,**
John, d. 10/3/1925 at 65; shoeworker; widower; b. Marblehead; Henry Barry (Ireland) and Margaret Brown (Ireland)

**BARSANTEE,**
Nellie, d. 2/2/1937 at 69/10/23; housewife; married; b. Somersworth; Richard Swinerton (Newfield, ME) and Maria Whitehouse

**BASTON,**
Carrie B., d. 11/8/1919 at 48/8/3; housewife; married; b. Henniker; Newton G. Colby (Henniker) and Clara A. Johnson (Groton, MA)

**BATCHELDER,**
Albert, d. 8/11/1928 at 70/1/16; shoeworker; married; b. New Durham; Mayhew Batchelder (Eaton) and Angie Gilman (Alton)

Betsey, d. 9/3/1914 at 99/7/20; old age; widow; b. Farmington; Anthony Peavey (Rochester, farmer) and Susan Knight (Rochester)

Edward, d. 8/19/1926 at 79/11/19; agent; married; b. Somersworth; Jeremiah Batchelder and Elizabeth Peavey (Farmington)

**BAXTER,**
son, d. 8/23/1914 at 0/0/0; stillborn; b. Farmington; D. Forest Baxter (Brockton, shoemaker) and Fannie B. Clough (Alton)

**BEAN,**
son, d. 3/10/1900 at –; stillborn; b. Farmington; Ivory U. Bean (Farmington) and Ida M. Wyatt (Farmington)

Charles F., d. 9/2/1914 at 64/1/19; tuberculosis; shoemaker; married; b. Milton; George W. Bean (Acton, ME, mechanic) and Susan Grant (W. Lebanon)

George W., d. 6/11/1900 at 52/9/27; cerebral hemorrhage; horsetrainer; married; b. Rochester; George J. Bean (Carroll Co.) and Susan Grant (Farmington)

Hannah W., d. 7/26/1914 at 76/11/22; arteriosclerosis; married; b. Milton; Hiram Cook (Milton, farmer) and Hannah Wiggin

Lewis L., d. 11/11/1915 at 81/11; engineer; widower; b. Waterboro, ME; Elijah Beane (Waterboro, ME) and Susan Hanson

**BEAUPRE,**
Frederick, d. 3/8/1908 at 25; hemorrhage wound; woodchopper; single; b. Canada; Thomas Beaupre (Canada)

**BECK,**
Reta M., d. 6/19/1934 at 50/11/1; housewife; married; b. Farmington; Harley C. White (Danvers, MA) and Mary E. Johnson (Farmington)

**BENNETT,**
Amanda, d. 4/13/1920 at 83/11/9; housekeeper; single; b. Farmington; William Bennett (Farmington) and Mary Wingate (Farmington)

Edith E., d. 11/20/1932 at 77/1/5 in New Durham; housewife; married; b. Farmington; Richard Colbath (Tuftonboro) and Susan Peavey (Tuftonboro)

Ella, d. 6/6/1937 at 72/4/26 in Dover; retired; widow; b. New Hampton; Alvin Hoyt (Salisbury) and Jennie Fifield (New Hampton)

Emily M., d. 1/24/1925 at 84; retired; widow; b. Farmington

Flora E., d. 9/16/1929 at 71/10/14; housewife; married; b. Albion, ME; Alexander Hamlin and Abbie Wentworth

Florence G., d. 10/1/1938 at 58/1/2; domestic; single; b. Hiram, ME Orrin E. Bennett (Fryeburg, ME) and Ida E. Lowell (Hiram, ME

George W., d. 2/8/1929 at 75/2/29; shoeworker; married; b. Dover

Grace M., d. 12/24/1933 at 58/0/12; housewife; married; b. Dover; Samuel Leighton (Farmington) and Ellen Colbath (Farmington

Ida M., d. 11/24/1933 at 73/5/7; at home; divorced; b. Hiram, ME; Milo Lowell (Hiram, ME) and Lucille Hatch (Hiram, ME)

John L., d. 10/25/1911 at 37/2/10; spinal sclerosis; farmer; single; b Farmington; Stephen Bennett (Farmington, farmer) and Emily Leighton (Farmington)

John P., d. 9/1/1931 at 84/2/25; retired; widower; b. Northwood; Plummer Bennett and Susan Chesley (Northwood)

Mary A., d. 1/17/1921 at 86/10/25; dressmaker; single; b. Farmington; William Bennett and Mary Wingate

Procinda, d. 1/16/1921 at 90/0/6; housekeeper; widow; b. Farmington; David Roberts and Elizabeth Canney

S. W., Jr., d. 11/1/1889 at 25/1/27; suicide; farmer; b. Farmington; Stephen W. Bennett

Sherebiah, d. 4/6/1897 at 72/4/22; heart failure; farmer; married; b. Farmington; William Bennett (Farmington) and Mary Wingate (Farmington)

Stephen, d. 5/29/1922 at 45/5/4; married; b. Wells, ME; Stephen Bennett (Wells, ME)

Stephen W., d. 4/2/1901 at 69/7/28; cerebral apoplexy; farmer; married; b. Farmington; William Bennett and Mary Wingate

**BENSON,**
Horace T., d. 3/15/1926 at 39/2/15; married

Lillian, d. 1/28/1908 at 0/0/2; cerebral hemorrhage; b. Farmington; Perley Benson (Biddeford, ME) and Winnie M. Avery (Farmington)

Susan C., d. 3/23/1909 at 86/2/24; mitral regurgitation; housekeeper; b. Hollis, ME; James Chadbourne (Lyman, ME) and Susan Chadbourne

Winnifred M., d. 1/30/1908 at 21/2/23; org. heart disease; housewife; married; b. Farmington; Frank L. Avery (Barnstead) and Sarah S. Berry (Strafford)

**BENTON,**

Lois, d. 8/5/1889 at 80/2; old age; housekeeper; b. Colebrook; Eleazer Benton and Sarah Selham

**BERGERON,**

Amelia, d. 11/13/1925 at 56; housewife; married; b. Suncook; John Larond

**BERRY,**

Abbie A. E., d. 10/31/1901 at 59/9/23; tumor with oper.; widow; b. Barnstead; Levi F. French (Barnstead) and Hannah Peavey (Barnstead)

Arthur, Jr., d. 9/30/1927 at –; b. Rochester; Arthur L. Berry (New Durham) and Gladys L. Patch (Rochester)

Calista, d. 10/28/1917 at 83/7/7; housewife; widow; b. Farmington; Nicholas Colbath (Rochester) and Keziah Rand (Rochester)

Celestia A., d. 5/16/1912 at 70/5/11; nephritis; housekeeper; single; b. Barnstead; John Berry (Alton, farmer) and Sally Chamberlin (Alton)

Charles H., d. 7/5/1936 at 77/2/28; retired; widower; b. Barnstead; Plummer O. Berry (Barnstead) and Abbie A. French (Barnstead)

Clara B., d. 6/27/1912 at 72/4/13; cerebral softening; married; b. Farmington; Hiram Barker (Alton, banker) and Maria Hayes (New Durham)

Clifton E., d. 1/15/1930 at 48/6 in Belmont, MA; ladies apparel; single; b. Farmington; John M. Berry (Moultonboro) and Leah Roberts (Farmington)

Edwin E., d. 3/1/1891 at 39/10/23; consumption; shoe cutter; married; b. New Durham; Enoch Berry (New Durham) and Eliza Hurd (Dover)

Eleanor, d. 7/8/1892 at 63/2/2; cancer of stomach; housewife; married; b. Middleton; Joseph Varney (Farmington, farmer) and Rebecca Ferm (MA); burial - Strafford

Eliza S., d. 1/3/1913 at 87/1/19; cholangetis; housework; widow; b. Parsonsfield, ME; William Emery and Jane Brown

Emma, d. 8/2/1892 at 23/11/10; acute bronchitis; housewife; married; b. Farmington; George T. Works (Sanford, ME, blacksmith) and Unice Wallingford (Lebanon, ME)

Emma J., d. 1/25/1926 at 81/5/20; housewife; widow; b. Farmington; John S. Hurd (New Durham) and Susan A. Dame (Farmington)

Hattie S., d. 11/30/1915 at 60/9/13; widow; b. Alton

John L., d. 3/3/1910 at 31/5/29; pneumonia; shoemaker; b. New Durham; John K. Berry (New Durham) and Carrie M. Savage (New Durham)

John M., 2$^{nd}$, d. 8/4/1893 at 49/1/22; consumption; farmer; married; b. Barnstead; Peter Berry (Strafford) and Susan Babb (Strafford)

Lulie M., d. 11/12/1935 at 58/3/11; housewife; widow; b. Danvers, MA; John Foss and Ella Watson (Gilmanton)

Lyman E., d. 3/4/1926 at 62/5/26; married; b. New Durham; Eben E. Berry (New Durham) and Lucy M. Chesley (New Durham)

May A., d. 7/3/1932 at 40/9/3 in New Durham; at home; single; Willis E. Berry (New Durham) and Watie Joy (New Durham)

Mehitable, d. 3/3/1892 at 83/8/1; pneumonia; housewife; widow; b. Farmington; Ichabod Hayes

Myra F., d. 3/27/1917 at 0/0/13; b. Rochester; Irving Berry (Farmington) and Lizzie A. Jones

Nancy M., d. 1/16/1917 at 82/2/17; housewife; widow; b. Sutton; Nathan Phelps and Lucy Wilkins

Nathaniel H., d. 1/15/1908 at 90/5/15; old age; shoemaker; widower; b. Moultonboro; Benjamin Berry

Olive S., d. 4/17/1906 at 85/10/2; old age; housewife; married; b. Middleton; Moses Place (Farmington) and Keziah Hayes (Farmington)

Percy C., d. 6/8/1909 at 37/11/8; spastic paraphlegia; b. New Durham; Eben E. Berry (New Durham) and Lucy Chesley (New Durham)

Plummer O., d. 4/11/1887 at 56/4/2; farmer; married; b. Strafford; Peter Berry and Susan Babb

Ralph L., d. 11/22/1918 at 34/4/5; none; single; b. Strafford; Dana R. Berry (Strafford) and Edna H. Huckins

Sally, d. 2/25/1897 at 85/2/14; old age; housekeeper; widow; b. Alton; George Chamberlin (Alton) and Sarah Furber (Farmington)

Watie M., d. 10/23/1935 at 72/11/8 in New Durham; at home; widow; b. New Durham; Samuel Joy (New Durham) and Mary A. Evans (New Durham)

William L., d. 6/25/1890 at 63/5/28; chronic bronchitis; shoe cutter; married; b. Moultonboro; Benjamin Berry (Rye) and Abigail Locke (Rye)

William L., d. 2/11/1928 at 73/2/8; bank clerk; single; b. Farmington; William L. Berry (Moultonboro) and Calista Colbath (Farmington)

Zanello Delson, d. 11/24/1931 at 74/6/16 in Rochester; married; b. New Durham; Ichabod Berry (New Durham) and Almira T. Gooch (Alton)

**BERTHIAUME,**
Joseph, d. 10/16/1918 at 39/11/4; teamster; married; b. Canada

**BEVILLE,**
Jennie L., d. 9/26/1937 at 54/0/19; housewife; married; b. Lynn, MA; Thomas A. Barrows (Andover, MA) and Annie Devine (Salem, MA)

**BICKFORD,**
son, d. 3/31/1901 at –; stillborn; b. Farmington; W. H. Bickford (Rochester) and Mary A. Varney (Farmington)

Arolin, d. 2/8/1938 at 85/9/13; housewife; widow; b. New Durham; Samuel Roberts and Rhoda Berry

Brad. G., d. 3/13/1893 at 81/5/13; cerebral apoplexy; blacksmith; married; b. Northwood; Jesse Bickford (Northwood) and Mary Gove

Cora B., d. 2/21/1900 at 28/0/10; chronic gastritis; married; b. Farmington; John Bickford (Rochester) and Phoebe Hayes (Strafford)

David C., d. 12/5/1920 at 75/8/10; farmer; widower; b. Rochester; John F. Bickford (Rochester) and Hannah Dunerell (Farmington)

Eunice, d. 9/25/1889 at 64/2/5; dropsy; housekeeper

Herbert, d. 10/7/1918 at 63/0/13; laborer; single; b. Rochester; John Bickford (Rochester) and Hannah Demeritt (Farmington)

Isaac, d. 6/4/1904 at 74/10/4; dilation of heart; farmer; widower; b. Rochester; David Bickford (Rochester) and Elizabeth Jenness (Rochester)

John T., d. 3/15/1923 at 91/3/4; retired; widower; b. Rochester; James Bickford (Rochester) and Elizabeth Hussey (Farmington)

Julia A., d. 6/12/1903 at 64/8; chronic bronchitis; housewife; married; Jabez W. Hatch (VT) and Sarah Robinson (VT)

Linwood, d. 11/1/1918 at 15/2/4; student; single; b. Moultonboro; George O. Bickford (Moultonboro) and Margaret Hudson (NS)

Moses R., d. 1/9/1926 at 79/8; retired; married; b. Freedom; Horatio Bickford and Lucy Rumney

Phebe H., d. 12/7/1895 at 67/0/14; pulmonary hemorrhage; housekeeper; married; b. Strafford; Ebenezer Hayes (Strafford) and Margarett Hayes (Alton)

Walter H., d. 7/24/1935 at 74/11/29; farmer; married; b. Dover; John T. Bickford (Rochester) and Phobie Hayes (Strafford)

## BIRCH,

Charles A., d. 10/11/1925 at 56/11/20; retired navy; married; b. Germany; Adolph Birch and Amanda Clements

## BISHOP,

Lizzie H., d. 8/10/1923 at 50/4/5; housewife; married; b. Hardwick, VT; George Page and Jennie Young (Farmington)

## BLACKINGTON,

Charles, d. 3/28/1919 at 65/9/21; shoeworker; married; b. E. Union, ME; Gilbert Blackington (E. Union, ME) and Ann Hull

## BLAISDELL,

son, d. 9/6/1896 at 0/0/15; heart failure; b. Farmington; Orin P. Blaisdell (Lebanon, ME) and Ada Jones (New Durham)

Clarence, d. 9/26/1934 at 61/10/14; shoeworker; married; b. Lebanon, ME; Orrin M. Blaisdell (Lebanon, ME) and Jane Hersom (Lebanon, ME)

George E., d. 2/8/1933 at 81 in Concord; carpenter; widower; b. Barrington; Oliver Blaisdell (NH)

Lewis F., d. 4/17/1903 at 5/5/5; cerebro spinal fever; Orrin M. Blaisdell (Lebanon, ME) and Ada Jones (So. Abbington)

Mary L., d. 7/24/1928 at 71/2/14; married; b. Strafford

Orin E., d. 10/16/1921 at 0/1/21; b. Farmington; Ernest Blaisdell (Farmington) and Bernice Glidden (Farmington)

Orrin M., d. 5/11/1928 at 78/4/29; shoeworker; married; b. Lebanon, ME; Thomas Blaisdell (Lebanon, ME) and Eliza Manson (Limerick, ME)

R. H., d. 8/13/1901 at 1/5/1; pyemia; b. Farmington; C. L. Blaisdell (Lebanon, ME) and Ella F. Swinerton (Somersworth)

**BLAKE,**

Emma L., d. 3/14/1933 at 72/11/8; at home; widow; b. Middleton; John W. Horne (Middleton) and Sarah Garland (Middleton)

George, d. 12/22/1893 at 79/11/22; pneumonia; farmer; married; b. Milton; James Hayes (Milton) and Dorothea Leighton

Mary T., d. 3/11/1894 at 70; old age; housekeeper; widow; b. New Durham; George Leighton and ----- Edgerly

**BLANCHARD,**

G. B., d. 1/14/1900 at 72/6/4; cerebral congestion; hotel keeper; married; b. E. Stoughton; Isaac Blanchard (E. Stoughton) and Eunice Beals (Randolph, MA)

Sarah E., d. 2/11/1913 at 47/3/24; kidney insufficiency; housekeeper; married; b. Rutland, VT; George M. Chase (Bradford, VT) and Nancy Sleeper (Bradford, VT)

Walter I., d. 10/31/1922 at 60; physician, surgeon; married; b. Concord; Amos Blanchard (Methuen, MA) and Adelaide Morse (Francestown)

**BLOOD,**

Mary E., d. 11/25/1937 at 86/9/16; at home; widow; b. Somersworth; William B. Martin (Somersworth) and Clara Wallingford (Lowell, MA)

**BOLO,**

Charles B., d. 11/25/1890 at 22/5/22; consumption; laborer; single; b. Farmington; Jack Bolo and Susan Rollins (Standish)

**BONO,**
daughter, d. 9/23/1889 at –; stillborn; b. Farmington; Charles Bono (Canada) and Rosa Stone (Morey, ME)

**BOODEY,**
Horace P., d. 4/1/1930 at 85/11/18 in New Durham; farmer; married; b. Alton; Harrison Boodey (New Durham) and Tamson Ham (New Durham)

**BOODY,**
Mary C., d. 2/24/1936 at 84/6 in New Durham; at home; widow; b. Farmington; ----- Killroy and Anna B. Leighton (Farmington)
Robert, d. 10/31/1895 at 81/8; blood poisoning; farmer; widower; b. Barrington; John Boody and Susanna Hayes (Nottingham)

**BOUDREAU,**
Alfred, d. 5/19/1925 at –; single
Cora M., d. 5/30/1908 at 22/1/23; tuberculosis; married; b. Holderness; Levi Gault (Holderness) and ----- (Sandwich)
Gladys, d. 9/4/1906 at 0/2/11; entiro-colitis; b. Farmington; Lafayette Boudreau (Wheelock, VT) and Eva Drew (Holderness)
Leon, d. 7/25/1907 at 0/0/22; illiocolitis; b. Farmington; L. Boudreau (Wheelock, VT, laborer) and Eva Drew (Holderness)

**BOWERS,**
Harry, d. 9/26/1922 at 65/11/21; cigar mfgr.; widower; b. Columbus, OH; Philip Bowers (Bavaria) and Elizabeth Buchanan (France)

**BOWMAN,**
John, Jr., d. 2/12/1897 at 80/6; phthisis; showman; married; b. Boston; John Bowman (Lexington)

**BOYER,**
son, d. 1/8/1909 at –; premature birth; b. Farmington; Alfred Boyer and Mary E. Cole (Madbury)

**BRACKETT,**
Augusta, d. 2/28/1937 at 87/11/1; at home; widow; b. Farmington; Jeremiah French (Farmington) and Mary Hodgdon (Farmington)

Hiram, d. 9/29/1923 at 83/10/19; farmer; married; b. Ossipee; Levi Brackett (Ossipee) and Susan Edwards (Parsonsfield, ME)
James, d. 12/27/1926 at 86/2/7; retired; widower; b. Portland, ME
Joseph, d. 4/23/1920 at 82/10/3; farmer; widower; b. Ossipee; Levi Brackett (Ossipee) and Susan Edwards (Parsonsfield, ME)

**BRADBURY,**
George W., d. 6/14/1913 at 64/6/26; gunshot wound; shoemaker; married; b. Brookfield; John Bradbury and Pauline Ellis

**BRADEEN,**
Sarah F., d. 7/2/1915 at 71/8/12; housekeeper; widow; b. Limerick, ME

**BRADSHAW,**
Frank H., d. 3/27/1936 at 72/8/23 in Rochester; retired; married; b. Charlestown, MA; Isaac Bradshaw (NB) and Sarah Harding (NB)
Martha, d. 4/30/1924 at 74/8/10; widow; b. Chelsea, MA; Ephraim Hubbard (Bangor, ME) and Sapphira Lyons

**BRAGDON,**
Stephen M., d. 3/4/1909 at 72/2/8; heart disease; farmer; b. Milton; George L. Bragdon and Betsey Henderson (Milton)

**BRAINARD,**
Aroline, d. 12/9/1921 at 67/5/26; housewife; married; b. Hanson, MA; Henry Thyger and Mary Turner
Mary E., d. 7/21/1910 at 18/8/27; struck by lightning; shoeworker; single; b. Plymouth; Alvin C. Brainard (Holderness) and Mary Gibbins (Ireland)
William S., d. 11/12/1929 at 80/2/11 in Rochester; mill worker; married; b. Bridgewater, MA; John Brainard and Nancy Sampson

**BRAWN,**
Edith M., d. 10/5/1918 at 43/5/24; housekeeper; married; b. Milton; George E. Nute (Milton) and Abbie M. Russell (Clinton, MA)

**BREEN,**
Timothy E., d. 3/23/1912 at 50/9/28; suicide; baker; married; b. Rockville, CT; ----- (Ireland)

**BROCK,**
Harold S., d. 11/16/1918 at 14/10/4; student; single; b. Strafford; Roscoe A. Brock (Rochester) and Jennie Bickford (Rochester)

**BROOKS,**
son, d. 7/24/1893 at –; stillborn; b. Farmington; Percy Brooks (Alton) and Edith Tibbetts (Farmington)
daughter, d. 11/21/1925 at --; b. Farmington; William Brooks (England) and Annie Harrison (England)
Abbie G., d. 10/9/1927 at 62/7/6; housewife; married; b. Loudon; Romeyn B. Hurd (Alton) and S. Frances Varney (Wolfeboro)
Alonzo S., d. 8/12/1935 at 75/9/1; shoeworker; widower; b. Alton; David K. Brooks (Alton) and Sophia Langley (Alton)
Edith, d. 5/1/1919 at 54/1/13; housekeeper; married; b. Farmington; Alvin Tibbetts and Eliza Otis (Strafford)
Fredrick E., d. 3/16/1933 at 59/3/12; clergyman; married; b. Vernon VT; George Brooks (Vernon, VT) and Nancy Morgan (Northfield, MA)
Percy, d. 11/9/1933 at 77/6/27; retired; widower; b. Alton; David P. Brooks (Augusta, ME) and Sophia Langley (Alton)

**BROWN,**
son, d. 2/26/1893 at –; anaemia; b. Farmington; Joseph W. Brown (Newark, NJ) and Agnes Paterson (Windsor, PQ)
Augusta D., d. 6/27/1909 at 42/3/18; cerebral hemorrhage; b. Milton; Stephen Dorr (Milton) and Malvina Staples (Milton)
Bernice H., d. 3/4/1931 at 54/11/7; housewife; married; b. Milton; John Hart
Clarissa, d. 6/16/1888 at 68; worn out; housekeeper; widow; b. Barrington; ----- Hodgkins and ----- Howard
Isadore E., d. 3/22/1895 at 45/2/4; change of life; housewife; married; b. New Durham; George Preston and Margaret Lougee
John, d. 9/13/1892 at 72/5/8; asthenia; shoemaker; widower; b. Cornish, ME; John Brown (Cornish, ME, farmer) and Mary Heart (Cornish, ME)

John W., d. 11/9/1930 at 71/9/19; shoeworker; widower; b. Milton; Joseph E. Brown (Milton) and Elizabeth Varney (Milton)

Joseph E., d. 12/26/1900 at 66/4/25; dropsy; farmer; widower; b. Wolfeboro; Moses Brown

Leander F., d. 2/3/1921 at 64/10/28; farmer; married; b. W. Newbury, MA; Osgood Brown (Bethel, ME) and Anna Chase (W. Newbury)

Lillian B., d. 6/9/1895 at 25/9/3; apoplexy; housework; married; b. Rochester; Orin W. Gray (Barrington) and Carrie O. Carter (Dover)

Lizzie J., d. 4/4/1906 at 60/2/10; la grippe; housekeeper; married; b. Dover; Joseph A. Nute (Dover) and Hannah C. Nutter (Dover)

Louis B., d. 9/11/1931 at 63/2/28 in Rochester; shoeworker; single; b. Farmington; John L. Brown (Wilmot) and Mary E. Twombly (Farmington)

Lydia F., d. 4/3/1904 at 50/1/28; enteroiotitis; married; b. New Durham; John Davis, Jr. (New Durham)

Mary, d. 3/14/1910 at 74/2/14; pneumonia; housekeeper; widow; b. Farmington; Alvah Twombly and Prescilla Thompson

Mary A., d. 11/1/1933 at 85/2 in Rochester; housekeeper; widow; b. Rochester; William Jenness (Rochester) and Joanna Thresher (Sandwich)

Mary E., d. 6/27/1921 at 64/7/27

Rainsford W., d. 4/5/1932 at 68/1/26; shoeworker; widower; b. St. John, NB; Silas H. Brown and Sarah C. Brown

Sarah E., d. 10/8/1898 at 54/9/15; angina pectoris; lodging house keeper; widow; b. Boston, MA; George F. Leeds (Boston, MA) and Harriet Mellows (Alton)

Walter, d. 5/20/1938 at 60 in Dover; laborer; single; b. Farmington; John Brown (Wilmot) and Mary Twombly (Farmington)

**BROWNE,**

Almeda, d. 5/29/1937 at 88/6/29; none; widow; b. Acton, ME; Joseph Sanborn (Acton, ME) and Abigail Varney

Charles H., d. 2/21/1928 at 81/11/15; shoeworker; married; b. New Durham; Charles Browne and Adeline Pinkham

John B., d. 12/10/1916 at 66/8/17; shoeworker; widower; b. Brighton, ME; John Brown (ME) and Martha L. Rand (ME)

John L., d. 9/1/1908 at 76/8/2; harmaturia; farmer; married; b. Wilmont; Joseph Browne

Lillian M., d. 8/22/1919 at 53/4/11; married; b. Farmington; William Wingate (Farmington) and Eliza Wingate (Farmington)

**BRUCE,**
Robert W. S., d. 10/2/1922 at 60/1/5; shoeworker; widower; b. Hudson, MA; Walter Bruce (Montpelier, VT) and Nancy Grant (Frankfort, ME)
Thomas Kitson, d. 1/22/1897 at 1/1/16; not known; b. Wentworth; Thomas Kitson Bruce (Chelsea) and Katie B. Jewett (Laconia)

**BUCKLEY,**
Timothy E., d. 1/17/1916 at 48/10/15; hotel clerk; married; b. Ireland; John Buckley (Ireland) and Margaret Murray (Ireland)

**BUKER,**
son, d. 12/10/1916 at 0/0/1; b. Farmington; W. H. Buker (ME) and Alice A. Foss (NH)

**BULLARD,**
James, d. 8/26/1894 at 61/11/12; Bright's disease; widower; b. Boston; Francis Bullard (Walford) and Harriet Manson (New Haven, CT)

**BUNKER,**
Ann F., d. 3/10/1913 at 64/3/20; valvular heart disease; housewife; married; b. Dover; John D. Rollins (Wolfeboro, shoemaker) and Patience Colomy (Farmington)
Elizabeth A., d. 11/27/1902 at 76/9/27; chronic gastritis; housewife; widow; b. Alton; William Stevens (Alton) and Abigail Stevens (Rochester)
Forrest L., d. 3/31/1935 at 46/9/22; shoeworker; married; b. Farmington; Cyrus Bunker and Sadie Whitehouse
Henry, d. 5/4/1929 at 80/1/23; farmer; widower; b. Farmington; Levi Bunker (Farmington) and Elizabeth Stevens (Alton)
Joseph S., d. 7/29/1907 at 88/4/20; old age; farmer; widower; b. Farmington; Benjamin Bunker
Mary A., d. 12/27/1895 at 77/3/15; senectus; housewife; widow; b. Farmington; Benjamin Ham (Farmington) and Abagail Gray (Lebanon, ME)
Relief R., d. 6/29/1900 at 71/1/23; heart disease; housewife; married; b. Farmington; Jeremiah Horne (Farmington)

**BURBANK,**
Nellie G., d. 7/31/1936 at 58/9/8; housewife; married; b. Farmington; W. G. Hodgdon (Farmington) and Ellen Colbath (Middleton)

**BURKE,**
Ethel E., d. 5/29/1922 at 46/5/28; housekeeper; widow; b. Wolfeboro

**BURLEIGH,**
daughter, b. 7/22/1895 at –; stillborn; b. Farmington; Harry Burleigh (Farmington) and Estella M. Tuttle (Middleton)
Caroline S., d. 1/27/1902 at 64/3/22; heart disease; housewife; married; b. Bartlett; Ira Place (Bartlett) and Nancy Robinson (Farmington)
Estella M., d. 5/30/1931 at 71/11/29; housewife; married; b. New Durham; Stephen Tuttle (Middleton) and Mary A. Berry (New Durham)
Henry, d. 7/24/1906 at 72/11/29; softening of brain; carpenter; widower; b. Boston; Henry Burleigh (Newmarket) and Sarah Alexander (Boston)

**BURNHAM,**
Alice C., d. 6/23/1913 at 48/1; multiple sclerosis; single; b. Farmington; Charles F. Burnham (New Durham, carpenter) and Betsey J. Tufts (Farmington)
Betsey, d. 5/18/1919 at 89/7/3; housekeeper; widow; b. Farmington; David Tufts and Charlotte -----
Carrie, d. 2/5/1926 at 57/1/27; restaurant keeper; married; b. Keene; Edward Griffith (Keene) and Hattie J. Prescott (Charlestown, MA)
Charles F., d. 9/28/1894 at 66/8; carcinoma axxela; leather cutter; married; b. New Durham; G. W. Burnham (New Durham) and Sarah M. Davis (New Durham)
Charles S., d. 4/24/1918 at 73/6; shoemaker; married; b. Middleton; Thomas Burnham (Durham) and Eliza Ham (New Durham)
Effie L., d. 12/19/1937 at 63/9/11; bookkeeper; divorced; b. Watertown, MA; Fred C. Keyser (Bristol) and Elizabeth Lyons (Wolfeboro)
Ellen H., d. 1/23/1927 at 78/4/11; housekeeper; widow; b. Farmington; Thomas Pinkham and Adeline -----

Florence, d. 4/9/1928 at 65/2/30; school teacher; single; b. Farmington; Charles F. Burnham (Farmington) and Betsy Tut (Farmington)

George W., d. 9/27/1903 at 72/4/10; cancer of stomach; artist; married; George Burnham (New Durham) and Sarah Burnham (Farmington)

Grace G., d. 11/14/1931 at 52/0/7; housewife; married; b. Dover; Joel Smart and Mary Smith

James M., d. 8/5/1909 at 76/7/21; heart disease; shoe cutter; b. New Durham; George W. Burnham (New Durham) and Sarah Davis (New Durham)

Joseph W., d. 1/22/1906 at 67/11/27; broncho pneumonia; laborer married; b. New Durham; Thomas Burnham (New Durham) and Eliza M. Ham (Durham)

Lucina F., d. 3/2/1909 at 73/10/18; grippe; housekeeper; b. Farmington; Peter Pearl and Pamelia Berry

Nancy, d. 4/3/1896 at 67/9/29; cancer; housekeeper; married; b. Farmington; Levi Pearl (Farmington) and Clarissa French (Farmington)

Nellie M., d. 10/27/1905 at 29/7/4; diabetes mellitus; shoeworker; single; b. Farmington; James G. Perkins (Lebanon) and Mary F. Dixon (W. Lebanon, ME)

Robert T., d. 2/24/1913 at 76/9/9; cardiac dilation; shoemaker; married; b. New Durham; Thomas Burnham and Eliza Ham

Ruth E., d. 6/12/1891 at 80/4; paralysis; housekeeper; widow; b. New Durham; George Davis and Patience Elkins

Velma, d. 12/20/1919 at 0/5/11; b. Farmington; Leroy Burnham (Farmington) and Eva M. Place (Middleton)

William H., d. 8/4/1928 at 93/3/13; musician; widower; b. Stoneham, MA; George Burnham (Brookfield) and Sarah Davis (Barnstead)

**BURROUGHS,**

Giles, d. 8/9/1900 at 79/0/28; valvular disease of heart; farmer; widower; b. Lebanon

**BURROWS,**

Emma S., d. 5/10/1921 at 50/8/16; housewife; married; Joseph Knowles (Milton) and Martha Whitehouse (Middleton)

William E., d. 6/6/1907 at 78/9/15; bronchopneumonia; pedler; married; b. Middleton; William E. Burrows (farmer) and Sarah Burrows

Willie H., d. 4/27/1890 at 31/8/19; consumption; shoemaker; married; b. Natick, MA; William E. Burrows (Middleton) and Mercie Howard (Strafford)

BUSS,

George E., d. 7/15/1900 at 42/7/9; la grippe; laborer; married; b. W. Boylston; Edward Buss (Sterling, MA) and Olive K. Davis (N. Braintree)

BUTLER,

J. Frank, d. 9/15/1922 at 59; musician; single; b. Farmington; John Butler (Ireland) and Ann Leader (Ireland)

James, d. 4/20/1900 at 35/9/16; influenza; upholsterer; single; b. Farmington; John W. Butler and Ann Leeder

John N., d. 9/20/1905 at 73/10/16; jaundice; stone mason; widower

Robert E., d. 4/26/1937 at 0/2/21; b. Rochester; George F. Butler (Derry) and Margaret Hunt (Farmington)

Thomas E., d. 7/21/1933 at 72/7/13; shoeworker; widower; b. Farmington; John Butler (Ireland) and Ann Leader (Ireland)

BUZZELL,

Josie M., d. 4/8/1914 at 76/7/9; heart failure; widow; b. Wolfeboro; Jonathan Fernald (Brookfield, farmer) and Mary C. Pike (Middleton)

Samuel H., d. 10/14/1911 at 74/0/1; heart failure; shoe cutter; married; b. Middleton; Jacob Buzzell (Middleton) and Marion Stanton (Wakefield)

CADY,

Emma A., d. 1/22/1921 at 53/3/21; housewife; married; b. Sweden; Lars F. Nilsson (Sweden) and Ingrid Nilsson (Sweden)

Henry F., d. 1/27/1930 at 59/9/25; laborer; divorced; b. Provincetown, MA; Frank Cady (Provincetown) and Viola Hayne (Provincetown)

CAHILL,

Ellen T., d. 1/4/1919 at 42/3/27; housewife; married; b. Providence, RI; Owen Nealy (Ireland) and Margaret Glennon (Ireland)

**CALEF,**
Emily, d. 9/14/1901 at 72/11/10; heart disease; married; b. Sandwich; Thomas Ricker and Lydia Thompson
Everett, d. 2/17/1898 at 39/5/25; dropsy; farmer; married; b. Farmington; James Calef (Rochester) and Emily Ricker (Sandwich)

**CALL,**
Louis, d. 9/6/1925 at 62/0/27; carpenter; married; b. Concord; Horace Call (Concord) and Emeline Smart (Concord)

**CAMPBELL,**
son, d. 10/20/1924 at –; b. Farmington; Arthur Campbell (PEI) and Rosina Bailey (MA)
Arthur E., d. 5/5/1929 at 5/4/13; b. Lynn, MA; Arthur B. Campbell (Alberton, PEI) and Rosina L. Bailey (Gloucester, MA)
May E., d. 6/15/1918 at 49/5/21; housewife; married; b. Acton, ME; George Perkins (Middleton) and Sarah Bodwell

**CANNEY,**
son, d. 12/18/1894 at –; b. Farmington; I. A. Canney (Farmington) and Annie Colbath (Farmington)
Belle R., d. 10/18/1917 at 73/5/12; housewife; widow; b. Hopkinton; Isaac Dolby (Hopkinton) and Hannah Nutter
Charles H., d. 5/2/1892 at 55; pneumonia; single; b. Wolfeboro
Edmund, d. 12/3/1907 at 81/0/10; natural causes; widower; b. Farmington; Edmond Canney (Farmington, farmer) and ----- Brewster (Strafford)
Hannah E., d. 6/5/1897 at 68/6/13; neurasthenia; widow; b. Farmington; Otis Scruton (Farmington)
John H., d. 9/25/1917 at 59/9/10; shoemaker; single; b. Strafford; William Canney (Farmington) and Sarah Downs (Farmington)
Laban L., d. 8/5/1912 at 90/10/7; cirrhosis of liver; farmer; married; b. Farmington; Issac Canney (Farmington, farmer) and Berthana Allard (Farmington)
Lydia M., d. 9/23/1896 at -5/4/15; general debility; housewife; married; b. Tamworth; Joseph Pease
Marjorie, d. 7/6/1922 at 0/0/1; b. Farmington; Ralph W. Canney (New Durham) and Ethel M. Hayes (Milton)

Rachael, d. 6/2/1917 at 93/2/18; housewife; widow; b. Somersworth; Benjamin Andrews (Somersworth) and Mary Teat

Sharonton H., d. 3/6/1897 at 69/0/1; heart disease and dropsy; farmer; married; b. Farmington; I. D. Canney (Madbury) and Matilda Read (Farmington)

Thomas, d. 6/21/1917 at 79/8/3; farmer; married; b. New Durham; Benjamin Canney (New Durham) and Margaret Henderson (Rochester)

Ursula, d. 9/9/1924 at 1/5/14; b. Farmington; Merlin Canney (Gilmanton) and Doris Leighton (Farmington)

**CARD,**

Abram A., d. 11/26/1904 at 77/2/8; heart disease; shoemaker; widower; b. New Castle; James Card (New Castle) and Sally Amazeen (New Castle)

Berton B., d. 8/14/1912 at 42/4/3; tuberculosis; store keeper; married; b. Farmington; Thomas F. Card (New Castle) and Mary J. Smith

Caroline J., d. 5/25/1924 at 83/4/27; housewife; widow; b. Portland, ME; Levi Gilson (Poland, ME) and Martha Perkins (Kittery, ME)

Edward F., d. 8/8/1938 at 68/1/16; laborer; divorced; b. Farmington; George V. Card (New Castle) and Nancy Sampson (Dexter, ME)

Floretta P., d. 4/25/1906 at 32/6/29; scarlet fever; housewife; married; b. New Durham; James A. Miller (New Durham) and Grace Ham (Alton)

George V., d. 1/17/1938 at 95/5/20; shoeworker; widower; b. New Castle; Edward Card (New Castle) and F. A. Francis (New Castle)

James W., d. 3/28/1932 at 87/;9/14; retired; married; b. New Castle; Thomas Card and Frances A. Frances

Lillian E., d. 3/27/1920 at 57/4/1; single; b. New Castle; William W. Card (New Castle) and Caroline J. Gilson (Portland, ME)

Mary Ellen, d. 1/8/1934 at 85/8/24; at home; widow; b. Farmington; Alvin C. Tibbetts (Berwick, ME) and Eliza Otis (Strafford)

Mary J., d. 10/22/1935 at 86/8; at home; widow; b. New Durham; George K. Smith (Newburyport) and Hannah Colomy (New Durham)

Nancy J., d. 6/27/1927 at 84; married; b. Dexter, ME; William Sampson and Jane Hibbard

Thomas F., d. 4/24/1905 at 66/9/5; Bright's disease; shoemaker; married; b. New Castle; Edward S. Card (New Castle) and Frances A. Francis (Portsmouth)

William W., d. 11/4/1909 at 73/1/26; chr. val. dis. heart; shoecutter b. New Castle; Edward Card and Frances Francis

**CAREY,**

Guy R., d. 7/8/1935 at 48/9/11 in Tilton; shoeworker; divorced; b. Farmington; Elisha S. Carey (ME) and Nellie Blanchard

Michael, d. 10/3/1890 at 90; paralysis; laborer; single; b. Ireland

**CARLETON,**

Charles G., d. 5/3/1906 at 53/4/0; bronchial hemorrhage; single; b. Rochester; Ralph Carleton (New Durham) and Amanda M. Pearl (Farmington)

**CARLTON,**

Amanda, d. 8/10/1903 at 70/9/25; shock; widow; Jonathan Pearl (Rochester) and Amanda Pearl (Rochester)

Carey F., d. 9/18/1911 at 76/11; cerebral hemorrhage; farmer; widower; b. Bradford, MA

Mary E., d. 9/17/1902 at 65/1/7; heart disease; housewife; married; b. Farmington; Benjamin Downing and Trephina Califf

Walter, d. 8/18/1923 at 66/9/27; shoemaker; widower; b. Rochester Ralph Carlton and Amanda Pearl

**CARPENTER,**

son, d. 4/25/1934 at –; b. Farmington; Phyllis Carpenter (E. Rochester)

**CARR,**

Ira, d. 10/15/1924 at 2/5/2; b. N. Berwick, ME; Charles R. Carr (Brownfield, ME) and Emma Boulet (Rochester)

**CARTER,**

Albert E., d. 1/1/1938 at 86/11/13; merchant; married; b. Wilton, ME; Hiram Carter (Bow) and Hannah Mayhew (Livermore, ME)

Fred A., d. 2/27/1901 at 21/2/23; pneumonia; drug clerk; single; b. Farmington; A. E. Carter (Wilton, ME) and Katie A. Dame (Farmington)

Joseph P., d. 2/22/1913 at 30/8/22; pulmonary tuberculosis; meat cutter; married; b. N. Conway; William Carter (Newport, VT, stone mason) and Abbie J. Emery (Bartlett)

Katie A., d. 3/7/1897 at 36/2/8; neuralgia of the heart; housewife; married; b. Farmington; Elihu N. Dame (Farmington) and Martha A. Dame (Farmington)

Leila B., d. 9/17/1930 at 61/8 in Manchester; widow; b. Farmington; George M. Davis (Farmington) and Angelia Small (Durham)

**CASWELL,**

Laura A., d. 8/29/1918 at 78/11/28; housewife; widow; b. Barnstead; Joseph Young (Barnstead) and Lydia Lougee (Barnstead)

Maud L., d. 3/16/1925 at 51/2/6; shoeworker; single; b. Barnstead; Samuel Caswell (Barnstead) and Laura Young (Barnstead)

**CATE,**

Belle V., d. 9/13/1910 at 49/2/18; secondary anemia; dressmaker; married; b. Madbury; John B. Huckins (Madbury) and Mary A. Morrison (Alton)

Mary A., d. 4/17/1920 at 51/0/27; housekeeper; widow; b. Madbury; John B. Huckins (Madbury) and Mary A. Morrison (Alton)

**CATES,**

Philena E., d. 9/5/1920 at 83/10/15; housekeeper; married; b. Naples, ME; Jethro Libby and Olive Floyd

**CATHCART,**

daughter, d. 2/19/1917 at 0/0/0; b. Farmington; Fred F. Cathcart (E. Rochester) and Bernice Haddock (Farmington)

daughter, d. 9/4/1918 at 0/1; b. Farmington; Fred Cathcart (Rochester) and Bernice Haddock (Farmington)

Alice M., d. 2/25/1902 at 35/11/11; cancer; housewife; married; b. Portland, ME; William Reddy (Portland) and Mary Haggerty (Ireland)

Fred J., d. 3/22/1937 at 70/8/17; barber; widower; b. Brookline; Allen Cathcart (Ireland) and Mary Lynch (Ireland)

Lurietta, d. 10/24/1918 at 43/9/15; housewife; married; b. New Durham; Alvah C. Rhines (New Durham) and Lydia French (New Durham)

Ruth E., d. 5/19/1911 at 1/2/4; pertussis; b. Farmington; Fred F. Cathcart (E. Rochester, shoemaker) and Bernice Haddock (Farmington)

**CAULSTONE,**

Frances D., d. 12/28/1931 at 5/10/17 in Rochester; b. Farmington; Emile A. Caulstone (Cape Breton) and Delda L. Ferland (NH)

**CAVE,**

Byron, d. 5/4/1917 at 22; laborer; single; b. Rochester; John Cave (England) and Georgia Downing (Rochester)

John J., d. 7/8/1930 at 70/1/10 in Concord; married; b. England; Thomas Cave (England) and Mary Jones (England)

Minnie F., d. 8/19/1917 at 20/10/28; single; b. Berwick, ME; John Cave (Northampton, England) and Georgia Downing (Farmington)

**CAVERLY,**

Almira B., d. 1/12/1892 at 68/7/3; paralysis; housekeeper; single; b. New Durham; John Caverly (New Durham, farmer) and Dorothy Caverly (Alton)

S. F. P. [female], d. 1/6/1913 at 79/10/1; uremia; school teacher; single; Thomas Caverly (New Durham, farmer) and Eliza Pierce (Lebanon, ME)

**CHAMBERLIN,**

Belinda, d. 2/16/1897 at 84/9/7; senile debility; widow; b. ME; Christopher Bryant (ME) and Susan Swan (MA)

George, d. 6/8/1904 at 89/7/10; catarrh bilary ducts; farmer; widower; b. Alton; George Chamberlin and Sarah Furber

Philina, d. 12/4/1891 at 72/3/11; cerebral softening; housekeeper; widow

William, d. 6/25/1894 at 65/6/19; cystitis; farmer; married; William Chamberlin and Hannah Davis (New Durham)

**CHAPPRON,**

Matt, d. 2/24/1912 at 41/3; acute alcoholism; shoemaker; married; b. NY; ----- (undertaker) and Mary -----

**CHASE,**
Jennie F., d. 11/12/1932 at 46/6/10; shoeworker; divorced; b. Milan; Lorenzo Chase (Albany) and Carrie Parrish (Albany)
Laban W., d. 12/5/1919 at 19/1/21; laborer; single; b. Dighton, MA; Benjamin S. Chase (Dighton, MA) and Alice A. Dunbar
Otis W., d. 4/24/1926 at 72/9/22; farmer; married; b. Maidstone, VT; Albert S. Chase (NH) and Lydia O. Hawkins (VT)

**CHENEY,**
Owen W., d. 4/10/1931 at 60/3/16; shoeworker; married; b. Wells, ME; James Cheney

**CHESLEY,**
daughter, d. 5/23/1922 at –; b. Farmington; Harold J. Chesley (Farmington) and Ruby A. Burnham (Boston, MA)
A. E., d. 5/9/1913 at 72/3/23; peritonitis and anemia; housekeeper; widow; b. Danvers, MA; Orin Putnam (Danvers, farmer) and Sally P. Nourse (Danvers)
Benjamin, d. 11/17/1890 at 72/3/8; heart disease; farmer; widower; b. Farmington; Samuel Chesley (Farmington) and Polly Furber (Wolfeboro)
Benjamin P., d. 2/9/1906 at 83/8/0; shock; retired farmer; married; b. Middleton; Benjamin Chesley (Durham) and Abigail Page (Rochester)
Emma, d. 4/7/1921 at 66/5/19; housewife; married; b. New Durham; Joseph Y. Berry (New Durham) and Betsey D. Scruton (Strafford)
Evelyn, d. 12/10/1896 at 1/4/6; pneumonia; b. Alton; Herbert Chesley (New Durham) and Annie M. Kimball (Wolfeboro)
Frank B., d. 5/29/1927 at 70/6/2; farmer; widower; b. Farmington; John F. Chesley and Hannah Garland
G. E., d. 2/6/1900 at 0/10/3; broncho pneumonia; b. Farmington; Herbert Chesley (New Durham) and Annie Kimball (Wolfeboro)
George L., d. 4/5/1913 at 59/11/6; hemorrhage of brain; engineer; widower; b. Brookfield; James Chesley and Sarah Lord
George Washington, d. 12/19/1897 at 62/10/4; uremic coma; shoemaker; divorced; b. Farmington; Lemuel Chesley (Farmington) and Mary Furber (Wolfeboro)
Hannah, d. 3/13/1907 at 74/1/6; pneumonia; widow; b. Farmington; John Garland (Rochester, farmer) and Mary Ham (Barrington)

Joanna J., d. 8/28/1901 at 43/10/15; pulmonary tuberculosis; married; b. Thomasville, GA; John Stevens (Thomasville, GA) and Cynthia E. Page (So. States)

John F., d. 9/10/1900 at 72/5/25; angina pectoris; farmer; married; b. Farmington; Lemuel Chesley (Farmington) and Mary Furber (Wolfeboro)

Marion L., d. 4/12/1936 at 46/1/27; clerk; divorced; b. Farmington; George L. Chesley (Brookfield) and Joanna J. Stevens (Thomasville, GA)

Nettie I., d. 10/25/1919 at 53/1/26; bookkeeper; married; b. Northwood; Samuel T. Dow (Northwood) and Lucy A. Yeaton (Epsom)

Sadie B., d. 2/21/1900 at 29/4/11; consumption; housewife; married; b. Rochester; Luther J. Foss (Rochester) and Ada Wentworth (Rochester)

Salome, d. 2/27/1892 at 81/10/27; heart failure; lady; widow; b. Alton; John Jones (Farmington, farmer) and Mary Watson (Farmington)

Walter L., d. 8/24/1933 at 67/7/4; retired; widower; b. Wolfeboro; John F. Chesley (New Durham) and Lydia F. Ward (Wayland, MA)

**CHILD[S],**

Donald, d. 1/9/1915 at 0/0/1; b. Farmington; Charles E. Child (Farmington) and N. Susie Fletcher (Hollis, ME)

Dora, d. 2/4/1915 at 0/0/26; b. Farmington; Charles E. Child (Farmington) and N. Susie Fletcher (Hollis, ME)

Ethel, d. 3/24/1934 at 17/10/26 in Rochester; student; single; b. Farmington; Charles E. Child (Farmington) and N. Susan Fletcher (Hollis, ME)

James E., d. 12/12/1918 at 63/9/11; farmer; married; b. Milton; James S. Child (Cambridge, MA) and Mary Goodwin (Lebanon, ME)

James S., d. 2/15/1896 at 74/10/27; heart failure; carpenter; widower; b. Cambridge, MA; James Child

N. Susan, d. 6/12/1933 at 54/9/3 in Barnstead; housewife; married; b. Farmington; Prisham Fletcher (New Durham) and Emily Bensa (Hollis, ME)

**CHUBBUCK,**
son, d. 7/16/1902 at –; stillborn; b. Farmington; Walter Chubbuck (Somerville) and Grace Cleveland (Hubbardston)

**CILLEY,**
Adelaide A., d. 4/20/1896 at 83/3/7; apoplexy; widow; b. Canterbury; Abner Haines (Canterbury) and Elizabeth Ayers (Canterbury)
Daniel P., d. 11/14/1888 at 82/5/13; heart disease; preacher; married; b. Epsom; Daniel Cilley
George J., d. 10/20/1936 at 62/3/2; lumberman; married; b. Nottingham; David T. Cilley (Nottingham) and Sylvania Tuttle (Nottingham)
Velma A. W., d. 8/6/1937 at 85/8/12; at home; widow; b. Farmington; Jeremiah Waldron (Farmington) and Mary E. Knight (Farmington)

**CLAPP,**
Rosamond, d. 11/5/1911 at 0/0/6; inanition; b. Farmington; Lawrence Clapp (Cambridge, physician) and Helen W. Rhone (Wilkes-Barre)

**CLARK,**
son, d. 12/9/1919 at 0/0/2; b. Farmington; Florence Clark (Alton)
Clarence, d. 5/1/1930 at 54/1/25; laborer; widower; b. Gilmanton; Frank Clark (Manchester) and Fannie Smith (Alton)
Frank, d. 3/26/1917 at 58/5/3; none; married; b. Manchester
George G., d. 8/22/1937 at 15/8/1; student; single; b. Washington; Daniel Clark (Brookfield, NY) and Ruth G. Clark (Friendship, NY)
James F., d. 4/28/1913 at 77/9/19; cerebral softening; farmer; married; b. Rochester; Moses Clark (farmer) and Olive Clark
Jane I., d. 10/23/1906 at 89/2/26; heart disease; widow; b. Berwick; Clark J. Wentworth (Berwick, ME) and Elenor Lord (Berwick, ME)

**CLARKE,**
Flora M., d. 7/2/1918 at 38; housewife; married; b. Brockton, MA; Samuel Reynolds (Canada) and Lina Gilman (Canada)
Lydia J., d. 4/11/1916 at 68/1/3; housekeeper; widow; b. Middleton; Ivory Tuttle (Middleton) and Belinda J. Cook (Milton)

**CLOUGH,**
Lucy P., d. 4/24/1888 at 81/0/13; broken femur; housekeeper; widow; b. Wolfeboro; Richard Rust (Wolfeboro) and Sally Thurston (Wolfeboro)

**CLOUTMAN,**
Edwin, d. 1/14/1890 at 41/7/4; pneumonia; lawyer; married; b. Alton; Jeremiah A. Cloutman (New Durham) and Caroline Davis (Alton)
Ellen E., d. 2/27/1897 at 59/0/14; pneumonia; housekeeper; married; b. Bradford; Samuel A. Kimball and Ann M. Griffin
Emma S., d. 12/26/1938 at 87/7/27; housewife; widow; b. Milton; Henry Downs (Canada) and Elizabeth Drew (Dover)
H. G., d. 7/1/1888 at 54/5/26; labial paralysis; shoemaker; married; b. New Durham; John Cloutman (New Durham) and Patience T. Edgerly (New Durham)
Herman, d. 5/6/1924 at 63/8/27
Hersey, d. 3/29/1890 at 76/9/15; apoplexy; carpenter; widower; b. Wakefield; John Cloutman (Wakefield) and Hannah Folsom
J. F., d. 12/7/1905 at 73/11/10; angina pectoris; shoe mfg'r; widower; b. New Durham; John F. Cloutman (Wakefield) and Patience Edgerly (New Durham)
Jeremiah A., d. 2/1/1889 at 73/2; heart disease; shoe cutter; b. New Durham; John Cloutman and Harriet Folsom
John F., d. 1/17/1904 at 0/4/10; meningitis; b. Farmington; John Cloutman, Jr. (Farmington) and Bessie Wentworth (Middleton)
Lovina, d. 8/11/1915 at 58/1/26; housekeeper; widow; b. Rollinsford; E. D. T. Rollins and Sallie R. Speed
Patience, d. 12/13/1894 at 91/6/20; old age; widow; b. New Durham; Andrew Edgerly (New Durham) and Nancy Tash (New Durham)
Samuel S., d. 10/11/1896 at –/3; apoplexy; carpenter; married

**CLUFF,**
Asa F., d. 3/28/1936 at 74/3/25 in Dover; lumberman; married; b. Alfred, ME; Ebenezer Cluff (Alfred, ME) and Arabella Johnson (Stowe, ME)

**COATY,**
Edward, d. 8/27/1912 at 23/0/13; suicide by shooting; shoemaker; single; b. Farmington; Edward Coaty (Canada) and Emma Ham (Barnstead)

**COBURN,**
Frank W., d. 9/6/1918 at 61/9/3; kinfe mfgr.; married; b. New Durham; Frank W. Coburn (Pelham) and Susan Willey (New Durham)
Leona, d. 5/12/1936 at 81/0/11; at home; widow; b. Milton Mills; James Smith and Ann Ricker

**COFFIN,**
Cora E., d. 5/15/1921 at 38/4/5; shoeworker; married; b. Alton; John C. Young
I. G., d. 5/15/1921 at 48/4/1; shoeworker; married; b. Rochester; George E. Coffin (Milton) and Ella Hurd (Farmington)

**COGHLIN,**
George W., d. 5/22/1897 at 0/3/15; peritonitis; b. Farmington; Francis Coghlin (Boston) and Annie A. Moran (Boston)

**COLBATH,**
Angie E., d. 2/12/1911 at 32/8/9; chronic nephritis; shoe stitcher; married; David Tufts and Corine Berry (Strafford)
Arthur L., d. 12/8/1917 at 0/5/1; b. Farmington; Lauren Colbath (Farmington) and Grace G. Thurston (N. Berwick, ME)
Bert D., d. 4/18/1935 at 59/11/11; fireman; married; b. Farmington; Dudley J. Colbath (Alton) and Sarah L. Colbath (Middleton)
Betsey, d. 9/9/1895 at 101/1/4; old age; widow; b. Strafford; Andrew Foss (Strafford)
David R., d. 4/15/1887 at 59/9/12; shoemaker; widower; b. Farmington, Nicholas Colbath (Farmington) and Kezia Rand (Barnstead)
Dorothy A., d. 4/7/1908 at 73/5/15; abscess of liver; housekeeper; widow; b. New Castle; Henry Amazeen (New Castle) and Louisa Rand (Rye)
Eleazer, d. 12/12/1909 at 81/5; ch. val. dis. heart; shoemaker; b. Barnstead; Dudley G. Colbath (Newington) and Betsey Pickerig (Barnstead)

Elmira C., d. 9/2/1899 at 52/5/20; nephritis of intestines; housewife married; b. Middleton; Wingate Whitehouse (Middleton) and Eliza Colbath (Middleton)

Elmira E., d. 12/21/1900 at 63/4/5; diabetes; housewife; married; b New Durham; John Willey (New Durham) and Lovey Watson (New Durham)

Florence, d. 12/5/1937 at 81/6/25 in Methuen, MA; at home; single b. Farmington; Richard Colbath (Farmington) and Hannah Parker (Chester)

Freeman, d. 4/30/1898 at 77/4; old age; farmer; widower

George H., d. 2/7/1917 at 80/0/29; none; single; b. Dorchester, MA, Leighton Colbath (Middleton) and Hannah Graham (NH)

Georgia E., d. 10/25/1928 at 72/11/29; housewife; married; b. Dover

Hannah, d. 1/3/1892 at 71/4/13; pneumonia; housewife; widow; b. Chester; Almont Parker (Windsor, VT, clergyman) and Anchol Taylor

Hannah, d. 1/4/1895 at 81/8/7; pneumonia; housework; widow; b. E Concord; Asa Garland (E. Concord) and Hannah Graham (Chester)

Jane, d. 5/27/1893 at 79/2/23; dropsy; lady; widow; b. Farmington

Jeremiah H., d. 11/24/1895 at 51/7; accident; shoemaker; single; b New Durham; George W. Colbath (Middleton) and Jane Varney (Rochester)

John L., d. 10/14/1927 at 79/11/27; shoemaker; widower; b. Farmington; Lyman A. Colbath and Paulina Wentworth (Lebanon, ME)

John W., d. 11/19/1928 at 79/5/29; farmer; widower; b. Middleton; Leighton Colbath (Middleton) and Hannah Graham (Concord)

Lawrence, d. 3/12/1925 at 0/0/1; b. Farmington; Lauren Colbath (Farmington) and Grace E. Thurston (N. Berwick, ME)

Lucinda, d. 9/29/1908 at 80/0/21; old age; housekeeper; married; b. Pittston, ME; Silas Hunt

Lulu I., d. 3/10/1922 at 28/8/10; housewife; married; b. St. George, ME; James Harrison (Scotland) and Mary Monoghan (Scotland)

Lyman A., d. 1/23/1899 at 76/1/23; heart failure; farmer; widower; Nicholas Colbath (Rochester) and Keziah Rand (Durham)

Mary C., d. 10/5/1932 at 75/10/7 in Haverhill, MA; housekeeper; single; b. Farmington; Lyman A. Colbath (Farmington) and Paulina Wentworth (Lebanon, ME)

May E., d. 10/6/1927 at 69/9/27; housekeeper; widow; b. Middleton; George W. Downing (Middleton) and Caroline Colbath (Middleton)

Richmond E., d. 3/8/1899 at 80/5/10; Bright's disease; farmer; widower; b. Farmington; Nicholas Colbath (Farmington) and Kezia Rand (Farmington)

Susan, d. 5/26/1905 at 85/1/30; old age; widow; b. Ossipee; James Peavey (Tuftonboro) and Mary Wiggin (Portsmouth)

Urania B., d. 2/5/1896 at 73/4; apoplexy; housewife; married; b. Lyme; Calvin Beal (Lyme) and Sally Franklin (Norton, MA)

Vonia N., d. 2/19/1937 at 84/6/21 in New Durham; housekeeper; widow; b. New Durham; Hiram S. Lee and Maria Sumner

Warren, d. 10/3/1907 at 71/8/15; consumption; engineer; married; b. Middleton; Benjamin Colbath (Middleton) and Wealthy Page (Rochester)

Willey L., d. 12/28/1922 at 60/3/11; farmer; married; b. Middleton; Lauren Colbath (Middleton) and Elmira E. Willey (Middleton)

**COLE,**

Leon, d. 7/9/1888 at 0/1/5; hemorrhage; b. Farmington; Frank Cole (Dover) and Nellie Wakeham (Milton)

Loren J., d. 4/13/1937 at 88/10/21; retired; widower; b. Brownfield, ME; Josiah Cole (Brownfield, ME) and Nancy Linscott (Brownfield, ME)

**COL[E]MAN,**

Charles D., d. 3/6/1930 at 65/2/28 in Rochester; widower; b. Royalston, MA; Joel Coleman and Laura Kratt

Helen B., d. 3/17/1928 at 0/0/1; b. Nashua; Charles Colman (Rochester) and Lila Bessey (Dover)

Helen C., d. 9/2/1924 at 56/4/7; housewife; married; b. Dover; James W. Kingsbury (Dover) and Geogina Thomas (Ansona, MA)

Joseph W., d. 12/19/1915 at 91/10/0; retired; married; b. Dover; Calvin Coleman (Dover) and Phoebe Card (New Castle)

Mary A., d. 10/7/1921 at 74/8; housekeeper; widow; b. Farmington; Freeman Howe (Farmington) and Adeline Roberts (Farmington)

**COLLINS,**
- Mary E., d. 9/4/1935 at 68/7/5; housewife; widow; b. Alton; Samuel Tufts (Middleton) and Susan Chamberlin (Alton)
- Stephen, d. 8/11/1926 at 66/5/22; lumberman; married; b. NS; John Collins (NS) and Eliza Hutchinson (NS)

**COLOMY,**
- Alice J., d. 1/26/1917 at 76/4/16; housekeeper; widow; b. New Castle; Benjamin Curtis (New Castle) and Sarah Amazeen (New Castle)
- Alphonzo E., d. 8/14/1930 at 71/11/3; farmer; widower; b. Farmington; John F. Colomy (Farmington) and Alice J. Curtis (New Castle)
- Ethel W., d. 1/12/1890 at 7/8/1; convulsions; b. Farmington; William H. W. Colomy (Middleton) and Matilda Wakeman (Milton)
- Horatio, d. 2/23/1906 at 36/0/14; influenza; shoemaker; married; b. Farmington; John F. Colomy (Farmington) and Alice Curtis (New Castle)
- John F., d. 10/14/1892 at 57/4/27; catarrhal phthisis; shoemaker; married; b. Farmington; Richard Colomy (Farmington, shoemaker) and Mary Colbath (Middleton)
- Jonas H., d. 2/2/1910 at 81/9; paresis; shoe stitcher; married; b. New Durham; Daniel Colomy and Rebecca Pinkham
- Maria A., d. 8/20/1914 at 81/8/3; dilation of heart; housekeeper; widow; b. New Durham; Ephraim Pinkham (farmer) and Sarah Chase
- Matilda, d. 5/22/1921 at 65/0/18; housewife; married; b. Milton; Simeon Wakeham and Mary Wentworth (Middleton)
- Sarah G., d. 3/9/1925 at 69; shoeworker; married; b. Farmington; Charles C. Dudley (Somersworth) and Lydia H. Tibbetts (Tamworth)
- W. Clifford, d. 1/22/1892 at 15/0/20; inflammation of the bowels; single; b. Farmington; W. Henry W. Colomy (Middleton, shoemaker) and Matilda E. Wakeham (Milton)
- William H. W., d. 11/23/1927 at 83/5/19; retired; widower; b. Middleton; Richard Colomy and Mary Colbath

**COMMUSKY,**
- daughter, d. 5/21/1890 at –; stillborn; b. Farmington; T. Cummusky (PEI) and Delia Fitzgerald (Ireland)

**CONNAUGHTON,**
R. [male], d. 5/29/1924 at 44; shoemaker; single; b. Clinton, MA; L. Connaughton (Ireland) and Ellen McNulty (Dedham, MA)

**CONNELL,**
James, d. 1/24/1892 at 16/9; hip joint disease; single; b. Ireland; John Connell (Ireland, carpenter) and Mary J. Carr (Ireland); burial - Strafford

**CONNOR,**
Abbie M., d. 7/23/1908 at 49/2/16; pul. consumption; widow; b. Farmington; J. P. Richardson (New Durham) and Mary E. Lougee (Gilmanton)

Bertha, d. 11/26/1921 at 29/4/13; housewife; married; b. Alton; Frank Clark (Manchester) and Fannie Smith (Alton)

Bridget, d. 9/3/1892 at 74/6/24; old age; housekeeper; widow; b. County Claire, Ireland; John Noonon (Ireland, farmer) and Mary Noonon (Ireland); burial - Dover

Charles, d. 2/6/1901 at 65/5/20; tuberculosis; laborer; single; b. Fredericton, NB; Francis Connor (Ireland) and Bridget Noonan (Ireland)

Charles E., d. 1/30/1917 at 58/5/24; shoemaker; married; b. Gilmanton; William E. Connor (Gilmanton) and Mary S. Gilman (Gilmanton)

Edward C., d. 3/4/1916 at 31/2/7; shoemaker; married; b. Farmington; Michael Connor (NB) and Abbie Richardson (Farmington)

Ellen, d. 12/3/1917 at 0/11/23; b. Farmington; Charles E. Connor (Farmington) and Florence E. Clark (Alton)

Ellen E., d. 4/18/1894 at 54; paralytic shock; single; b. Pittsfield; William Connor (Pittsfield) and Mary Batchelder

Florence, d. 1/14/1926 at 35/6/2; shoeworker; widow; b. Alton; Frank Clark (Manchester) and Fannie Smith (Alton)

Florence, d. 4/5/1926 at 64/10/5; housekeeper; widow; b. New Durham; James A. Miller (New Durham) and Lydia Austin

Fred C., d. 7/22/1931 at 63/6/10; shoeworker; single; b. Gilmanton; William A. Connor (Gilmanton) and Mary S. Gilman (Gilmanton)

John F., d. 2/10/1909 at 28/11/19; consumption; shoecutter; b. Farmington; Michael Connor and Abbie Richardson

Mary S., d. 1/24/1917 at 81/2/24; housewife; widow; b. Gilmanton; Moses Gilman (Gilmanton) and Rhoda Gilman (East Alton)

Michael, d. 3/9/1901 at 55/7/22; moist gangrene; shoemaker; married; b. Fredericton, NB; Francis Connor (Ireland) and Bridget Noonan (Ireland)

Patrick P., d. 7/20/1912 at 63/5/20; paresis; engineer; single; b. Fredericton; Frank Connor (Ireland, farmer) and Bridget Smith (Ireland)

Wilbur H., d. 3/10/1910 at 20/2/22; tuberculosis; shoemaker; single b. Dover; Michael Connor (NB) and Abbie Richardson (Farmington)

William A., d. 12/2/1901 at 80/9/4; int'nl hemorrhage; farmer; married; William Connor (Gilmanton) and Eliza Batchelder (Gilmanton)

**CONSTANT,**

Joseph, d. 11/30/1903 at 2/6; broncho pneumonia; Almon Constant (Canada) and Mary A. Matchey (Canada)

**COOK,**

daughter, d. 5/31/1929 at 0/0/4 in Rochester; b. Rochester; Clarence E. Cook (Middleton) and Pauline Tufts (Middleton)

George W., d. 12/9/1938 at 76/11/29; farmer; widower; b. Holderness; Moses Cook (Bridgton, ME) and Freelove Downing (Holderness)

Henry M., d. 4/23/1932 at 74/11/28 in Rochester; b. Milton; Moses Cook (Milton) and Trisla Downing (NH)

**COOKE,**

Gladys, d. 12/29/1895 at 1/10/10; bronchial pneumonia; b. Farmington; Charles H. Cook (Brockton) and Addie Burnham (Farmington)

**COOKSON,**

Abraham, d. 4/21/1898 at 67/4/4; heart disease; farmer; widower; b. Unity, ME; Josiah Cookson (Unity, ME) and Mary Blake (Unity, ME)

George W., d. 7/1/1927 at 72/9/15; carpenter; married; b. Warren; Abram Cookson and Harriett Jackson

Susie M., d. 12/9/1897 at 13/6/1; abdominal tumor; school girl; b. Warren; Abram Cookson (Plymouth) and Hattie Ford (Warren)

**COPP,**

Belinda, d. 8/7/1900 at 68/6/1; endocarditis; housekeeper; single; b. West Lebanon; Isaac Copp (W. Lebanon) and Betsey Wentworth (W. Lebanon)

Charles T., d. 12/31/1926 at 80/6/14; farmer; single; b. Middleton; Samuel Copp (Middleton) and Rose Tibbetts (Farmington)

Edna Rixford, d. 8/23/1929 at 79/5/15 in Pittsfield, MA; widow; b. N. Barnstead; William Rixford (Boston, MA) and Mary Ann Locke (Strafford)

Frank O., d. 8/25/1934 at 81/4/16 in Rochester; retired; married; b. Wakefield; Samuel Copp (Middleton) and Rose Tibbetts (Middleton)

Laura A., d. 10/6/1936 at 81/4/13; at home; widow; b. Methuen, MA; Charles V. Butler (Pelham) and Laura Jewett (Sunapee)

**CORLEY,**

Marian, d. 4/12/1893 at 1/1; acute meningitis; b. Farmington; Frank Corley (Canada) and Amelia Preston (Canada)

**CORSON,**

son, d. 2/23/1918 at –; b. Farmington; Walter N. Corson (Farmington) and Nancy B. Currier (Amesbury, MA)

Betsey D., d. 7/5/1897 at 70/0/7; concussion of brain; housework; married; b. New Durham; Nathaniel Ham (New Durham) and Clarisy Chamberlin

George H., d. 1/7/1888 at 27/10/27; consumption; shoemaker; Albert Corson and Betsey Ham (New Durham)

Grace E., d. 6/26/1888 at 0/5/2; pneumonia; b. Middleton; Charles Corson (Farmington) and Estella Tuttle (Farmington)

Levina, d. 1/10/1895 at 86/5/24; widow; b. Middleton

Lorana, d. 1/11/1911 at 61/10/4; bronchitis; married; b. Milton; Hazen Duntley (Bow, blacksmith) and Phoebe Leighton (Rochester)

Mary J., d. 7/10/1931 at 76/0/22; widow; b. Farmington

Melissa F., d. 4/19/1921 at 55/6/17; housewife; married; b. Alton; William B. Durgin and Martha Durgin

Walter M., d. 8/7/1923 at 39/10/14; laborer; married; b. Farmington; Charles Corson (Farmington) and Estella Tuttle (Middleton)

**COTE,**
Edward, d. 4/27/1899 at 65/9/23; typhoid fever; laborer; married; b Canada

**COTTON,**
Arthur I., d. 2/2/1917 at 27/11/7; shoeworker; single; b. Farmington Charles Cotton (Wolfeboro) and Viola Edgerly (New Durham)

**COTTULI,**
Charles F., d. 9/16/1919 at 59
Josephine, d. 4/18/1921 at 63/4; kitchen helper; widow; b. New Durham; Joseph Berry (New Durham) and Laurentina Glidder (New Durham)

**CRAM,**
Georgie M., d. 12/19/1916 at 32/0/13; housekeeper; married; b. Farmington; Charles E. Connor (Gilmanton) and Florence A. Miller (New Durham)

**CREDEFORD,**
Betsey, d. 8/28/1903 at 60/6/22; cancer of liver; housekeeper; widow; Steven Wallingford (Lebanon, ME) and Mercy Wallingford (Lebanon, ME)

**CROCKETT,**
John, d. 11/30/1915 at 97/3/16; farmer; widower; b. Middleton; ----- Crockett and ----- Main (Rochester)

**CROSBY,**
Addie E., d. 12/28/1920 at 63/11; housekeeper; married; b. New Castle; John W. Martin (New Castle) and Eliza Averill (Mt. Vernon)
Charles W., d. 9/27/1931 at 76/8/23; shoeworker; widower; b. Dover; Orin Crosby and Mary T. -----
Ida M., d. 9/17/1904 at 32/3/26; lobular cor'lsis liver; shoe stitcher; single; b. Barnstead; John Q. Crosby (Gilford) and Melissa Pitman (Barnstead)
Melissa A., d. 7/21/1917 at 76/10/4; housewife; widow; b. Barnstead; Henry Pitman (Barnstead) and Druzilla Miles (Sheffield, VT)

**CROSS,**
Norma L., d. 4/2/1933 at 0/6; b. Farmington; Frank S. Cross (Meredith) and Doris Jenness (Lynn, MA)

**CROUGHAN,**
Charles J., d. 4/20/1923 at 45/11/20; foreman; single; b. Lynn, MA; James Croughan (Ireland) and Mary Scanlon (Ireland)

**CURRIER,**
son, d. 6/2/1902 at –; stillborn; b. Farmington; Charles V. Currier (Farmington) and Mary Ring (Farmington)
son, d. 10/6/1904 at –; stillborn; b. Farmington; Fred E. Currier (Farmington) and Abbie Willey (New Durham)
Eva B., d. 4/23/1938 at 24/10/14 in Pembroke; shoeworker; married; b. Venburn, ME; Denis Bourgeon (Venburn, ME) and Annie Albert (NB)
George E., d. 6/22/1912 at 76/9/30; arteriosclerosis; farmer; widower; b. Holliston; Richard Currier (Canaan, carpenter) and Lucretia Abby
George W., d. 7/28/1935 at 71/7/24 in Rochester; farmer; widower; b. Farmington; George E. Currier (Holliston, MA) and Mary C. Plummer (Farmington)
Idana, d. 11/7/1934 at 73/9/20; at home; married; b. Strafford; Samuel Foss and Sarah Berry
Lillian T., d. 7/31/1916 at 21/7/6; shoeworker; married; b. Hudson, MA; Jeremiah Dunn (Brookfield, MA) and Nellie Cochrane (Cork, Ireland)
Mary C., d. 3/21/1896 at 62/2/19; paralysis; housekeeper; married; b. Farmington; William Plummer (ME) and Polly Ham (Farmington)
Perry N., d. 9/24/1900 at 0/9/4; tuberculosis of bowels; b. Farmington; F. E. Currier (Farmington) and Abbie Willey (New Durham)
Ruth L., d. 8/12/1934 at 20/0/8; housewife; married; b. New Durham; Herman Rhines (New Durham) and Lucy Dow (Dorchester)

**CURTIS,**
daughter, d. 6/26/1889 at –; blue baby; b. Farmington; Edwin Curtis (Farmington) and Jennie O. Rollins (Farmington)

Ada E., d. 3/23/1902 at 18/1/21; acute general peritonitis; housewife; married; b. Farmington; Orrin M. Blaisdell (Lebanon, ME) and Ada E. Jones (Abington)

Cora, d. 11/4/1926 at 34/6/2; shoeworker; married; b. Belmont, ME Fidelphus Flagg (Belmont, ME) and Hattie Jackson (Belmont, ME)

Edward A., d. 12/8/1932 at 75/10/28; farmer; widower; b. Middleton Rufus Curtis (New Castle) and Adeline Place (Middleton)

Elison O., d. 7/15/1893 at 75/8; Bright's disease; shoe manufact.; married; b. New Castle; Thomas Curtis (Kittery, ME) and Catharina Berry (Portsmouth)

George F., d. 5/28/1910 at 44; acute alcoholism; laborer; single; Rufus Curtis

Irving S., d. 4/21/1932 at 69/0/24; farmer; divorced; b. Farmington; William A. Curtis (New Castle) and Melissa S. Pinkham (Farmington)

James C., d. 11/30/1892 at 44/2/21; empyema; shoemaker; married; b. New Castle; E. O. Curtis (New Castle, shoe manufacturer) and Matilda White (New Castle)

Jessie B., d. 4/28/1894 at 0/10; pneumonia; b. Farmington; J. Clinton Curtis (New Castle) and Lizzie Leighton (Farmington)

Juiletta F., d. 5/16/1929 at 69/3/10; widow; b. Holderness; Moses Cook and Freelove Downing

Juna O., d. 6/25/1928 at 69/2/12; housewife; married; b. Farmington; Alvah Rollins (Wolfeboro) and Abigail Colomy (Farmington)

L. Ella, d. 4/1/1925 at 73/5/27; artist; single; b. Farmington; Ellison A. Curtis (New Castle) and Matilda White (New Castle)

Mary, d. 5/6/1888 at 1/9/21; spinal meningitis; b. Farmington; J. Clinton Curtis (Farmington) and S. Ellen Leighton (Farmington)

Matilda A., d. 12/31/1905 at 79/6; cerebral softening; widow; b. New Castle; Thomas White (New Castle) and Julia White (Eliot, ME)

Melissa S., d. 2/17/1917 at 74/3/6; housewife; married; b. Farmington; William Pinkham (Farmington) and Sabrina Colbath (New Durham)

Moses, d. 3/29/1921 at 67/5/13; shoeworker; widower; b. Milton; Rufus Curtis (New Castle) and Adeline Place (Middleton)

Muriel, d. 10/15/1921 at 6

Sylvester, d. 12/8/1919 at 59/11/18; shoeworker; married; b. Farmington; Rufus Curtis (New Castle) and Adeline Place (Middleton)

Thomas C., d. 3/18/1903 at 25/11/18; pneumonia; leather skiver; single; b. Haverhill, MA; James C. Curtis (Eliot, ME) and Lizzie Leighton (Farmington)

William A., d. 4/5/1932 at 93/7/4; farmer; widower; b. New Castle; Benjamin Curtis (New Castle) and Sarah Amazeen (New Castle)

**CUSHMAN,**

Henry T., d. 10/12/1930 at 72/7/11; shoeworker; married; b. Sumner, ME; Isaac Cushman and Nancy Ricker

**CYR,**

Paul, d. 6/27/1922 at 37/1/4; laborer; single; b. Rochester; John Cyr (Canada) and Delan Therrien (Canada)

**DAME,**

Abigail R., d. 2/24/1892 at 82/10/10; paralysis; housekeeper; widow; b. Rochester; Stephen Ham (Rochester)

Adeline A., d. 5/10/1901 at 51/11; cancer; married; b. Farmington; David S. Roberts (Farmington) and Sabrina Lord (ME)

Albert W., d. 5/20/1903 at 61/8/15; pulmonary tuberculosis; shoe cutter; widower; Emory J. Dame (Farmington) and Louis G. Watson (Alton)

Caroline, d. 5/27/1903 at 87/11/20; bronchitis; retired; widow; Benjamin Parker (Salem, MA) and Lucy Dow (Beverly, MA)

Erving W., d. 2/24/1913 at 0/10/30; broncho pneumonia; b. Farmington; Walter S. Dame (Farmington, shoemaker) and Ethel M. Young (Alton)

Helen, d. 7/10/1936 at 57/1/27 in Rochester; at home; married; b. Ossipee; William Haynes (England) and Laura Abbott (Wolfeboro)

Ida F., d. 12/1/1892 at 14/6/5; phronic nephritis; b. Farmington; Charles H. Dame (New Castle, farmer) and Annie P. Nute (New Castle)

John U., d. 9/9/1893 at 85/11/6; old age; farmer; married; b. Farmington; Moses Dame (Durham) and Deborah Furber (Newington)

Jonathan, d. 5/4/1890 at 65/9; heart failure; shoe cutter; married; b
Farmington; Edward Dame (Farmington) and Cathrine Miller

Lydia A., d. 3/9/1891 at 60/4/9; heart failure; housekeeper; widow;
b. Fitchburg, MA; Joseph Chase (Fitchburg, MA) and Harriett
Phelps (Sutton)

Martha A., d. 2/4/1906 at 74/7/24; shock; widow; b. Farmington;
Jeremiah Dame (Farmington) and Susan Horne

Norton E., d. 1/8/1888 at 62/5/10; Bright's disease; farmer; married
b. Farmington; Edward Dame (Farmington) and Catherine
Wilson (Farmington)

Royal M., d. 12/28/1893 at 75; shock; laborer; widower; b. Dover;
Joseph Dame (Farmington)

**DAVIDSON,**

Emma, d. 4/11/1926 at 75/10/11; housekeeper; widow; b.
Gilmanton; Joseph Watson (Gilmanton) and Sally Piper
(Gilmanton)

Karleen B., d. 9/11/1933 at 0/0/18 in Rochester; b. Farmington;
Walter Davidson (Belfast, Ireland) and Corine Thurston
(Farmington)

Katherleen, d. 12/13/1934 at 1/3/20; b. Farmington; Walter
Davidson (Belfast, ME) and Corine Thurston (Farmington)

Newell, d. 2/25/1918 at 74/9/2; shoemaker; married; b. Newton,
MA; John B. Davidson (Holderness) and Sarah H. Loud
(Holderness)

**DAVIS,**

son, d. 7/28/1901 at –; not known; b. Farmington; Charles E. Davis
(Wolfeboro) and Ella A. Bunker (Farmington)

Angelia A., d. 8/27/1921 at 91/2/18; widow; b. Madbury; ----- Small
and ----- Greenough

Annie M., d. 8/8/1938 at 77/11/27 in Dover; housewife; married; b.
Harrisburg, PA; John Wilson (England) and Elizabeth Wilson
(Scotland)

Arianna P., d. 4/25/1911 at 61/11/29; septicemia; widow; b.
Farmington; Martin L. Hayes (Farmington, shoe mfgr.) and
Eliza Pearl (Farmington)

Caroline B., d. 5/15/1902 at 73/3/24; shock; widow; b. Farmington;
Joseph Hayes (Alton) and Betsy Brewster (Wolfeboro)

Charles E., d. 6/10/1917 at 68; clerk; widower; b. Saco, ME

Charles E., d. 1/24/1932 at 67/9/8; shoeworker; married; b. Farmington; Alsefron Davis (Newfield, ME) and Sylvia Berry (Alexandria)

Charles E., d. 9/11/1935 at 80/6/21; none; widower; b. Wolfeboro; Sewall Davis (Wolfeboro) and Mary Fuller (Wolfeboro)

Charles W., d. 9/10/1938 at 91/8/27; carpenter; widower; b. Barrington; Daniel W. Davis (Barrington) and Mary A. Corson (Rochester)

Clara Bell, d. 2/20/1911 at 50/8/1; pneumonia; milliner; married; Everett Leighton (shoemaker) and Alice Edgerly (New Durham)

Edgar R., d. 12/23/1910 at 0/2/20; asphyxia; b. Farmington; Earl R. Davis (Dover) and Bessie Haddock (Farmington)

Effie C., d. 1/24/1923 at 55; housewife; married; b. Lebanon, ME; George Goodwin (W. Lebanon, ME) and Hannah Connachee (St. George, NB)

Elizabeth C., d. 7/16/1913 at 90/7/15; cerebral softening; widow; b. Farmington; Henry Seward (merchant) and Mary Canney (Farmington)

Elizabeth G., d. 2/11/1915 at 14/4/10; b. Farmington; Alonso I. Davis (New Durham) and Effie C. Goodwin (W. Lebanon, ME)

Ella A., d. 11/11/1922 at 57/11/27; housewife; married; b. Farmington; Sherburn Bunker (Farmington) and Relief Horne (Farmington)

Ella R., d. 3/6/1930 at 63/9/25; widow; b. Farmington; Joseph A. Roberts (Farmington) and Phoebe Chesley (NH)

Emily H., d. 4/23/1900 at 81/6/15; senectus; housekeeper; single; b. Alton; John Davis (Alton) and Mary McDuffee (Alton)

Emma A., d. 12/23/1897 at 37/1/4; endocarditis; housewife; married; b. Farmington; Nathaniel R. Hurd (Farmington) and Elizabeth J. Babb (Barrington)

Eric N., d. 11/22/1899 at 7/2/8; cardiac asthma; b. Farmington; Samuel Y. Davis (Farmington) and Nellie M. Berry (New Durham)

Fred William, d. 1/18/1915 at 56/6/27; shoeworker; married; b. Farmington; Joseph P. Davis (NH) and Hope M. Eaton (NH)

George F., d. 12/9/1933 at 66/6/21 in Auburn, ME; shoeworker; married; b. Farmington; George Frank Davis (NH) and ----- Locke (NH)

George N., d. 1/26/1908 at 74/2/6; acute insanity; farmer; married; b. Barnstead; Timothy Davis

Harry K., d. 2/18/1936 at 52 in Rochester; shoeworker; married; b. Turkey; David Davis (Turkey)

Henry S., d. 4/12/1930 at 80/10/21 in Concord; clerk; widower; b. New Durham; Thomas M. Davis (NH) and Elizabeth Seaward (NH)

Ida M., d. 10/8/1923 at 63/9/7; widow; b. Farmington; James D. Place (Bartlett) and Jane Ricker (New Durham)

Ira S., d. 8/25/1889 at 77/3/20; consumption of the bowels; shoe cutter; b. Alton; Jacob Davis (Alton) and Lois Hadley (Gilmanton)

Isabella, d. 7/15/1918 at 42/2/16; housewife; married; b. Harpswell ME; John Avis

James, d. 4/3/1889 at 64/9/13; pneumonia; shoemaker; b. Alton; Eleazer Davis (Alton) and Polly Sanborn (Sanbornton)

James, d. 12/15/1921 at 73

James E., d. 9/26/1901 at 50/5/3; hep. cirrhosis; foreman; married; b. Alton; James Davis (Alton) and M. E. Cloutman (New Durham)

John B., d. 3/15/1924 at 88/2/23; laborer; widower; Timothy Davis and Anna Applebee

Linnie R., d. 8/2/1888 at 1/7; meningitis; b. Farmington; John F. Davis (Farmington) and Ida Place (Farmington)

Martha E., d. 6/25/1888 at 58/9/10; enlargement of heart; housekeeper; married; b. New Durham; John Cloutman (New Durham) and Patience T. Edgerly (New Durham)

Mary E., d. 1/2/1903 at 87/9/12; old age; retired; widow; b. Farmington; ----- Floyd

Meander H., d. 5/16/1931 at 70/7/10; retired; married; b. Middleton; Charles W. Davis (Tuftonboro) and Emily C. French (Middleton)

Nellie M., d. 12/13/1925 at 70/9/19; librarian; married; b. New Durham; Daniel Lucas (New Durham) and Sarah Chesley (New Durham)

Patience D., d. 3/26/1899 at 69/11/12; paralysis; housewife; married; b. Farmington; Thomas Colomy (Farmington) and Annie Colomy (Farmington)

Sadie G., d. 10/2/1899 at 0/1/12; consumption; b. Farmington; Charles E. Davis (Wolfeboro) and Ella A. Bunker (Farmington)

Samuel, d. 12/10/1888 at 67/3/4; pneumonia; farmer; married; b. Farmington; Samuel Davis (Eliot, ME) and Abigail Tibbetts (Farmington)

Timothy, d. 5/14/1921 at 57/7/13; laborer; married; b. Farmington; Nathaniel Davis (Barnstead) and Amanda Richardson (Woburn, MA)

**DAVY,**
Ina M., d. 4/25/1937 at 41/1/23 in Laconia; housewife; married; b. Exeter; Almon Sanborn (Gilmanton) and Emma Richardson (Farmington)

**DAY,**
Frank B., d. 8/20/1919 at 51/7/9; shoeworker; married; b. Shapleigh, ME; Benjamin Day and Aurena Goodwin (Augusta, ME)

**DEARBORN,**
Emma, d. 1/3/1927 at 76/11/2; single; b. W. Lebanon, ME

**DE[A]LAND,**
Elmira E., d. 8/22/1895 at 72/4/7; org. dis. of heart; housework; married; b. Wolfeboro; Joshua Pierce (Lebanon, ME) and Sarah Ricker (Brookfield)
Hannah, d. 5/3/1921 at 77/2/23; housekeeper; single; b. Wolfeboro; John Dealand (New Durham) and Elmira Pierce (Wolfeboro)
John, d. 8/27/1895 at 84/2/11; hemorrhage of kidney; farmer; widower; b. New Durham; Robert Deland (Barrington) and Hannah Tuttle (Milton)

**DELANO,**
Andy S., d. 4/19/1930 at 62/2/12; laborer; married; b. ME; Alcando Delano and Elethea Morse
Ella, d. 7/15/1930 at 60/1/20; at home; widow; b. Chester, VT

**DELPE,**
Janet, d. 8/19/1911 at 10/8/27; peritonitis; b. Manchester; Lewis Delpe (Canada, shoemaker) and Lea Gervais (Canada)

**DEMERITT,**
John F., d. 6/14/1904 at 82/2/14; heart disease; farmer; widower; b. Farmington; Paul Demeritt (Farmington) and Abigail Leighton (Farmington)

Joseph L., d. 10/28/1915 at 84/5/6; farmer; single; b. Farmington;
   Mark Demeritt (Farmington) and Abigail Leighton (Farmington
Mark L., d. 8/13/1895 at 48/10/9; neuralgia of heart; shoemaker;
   married; John F. Demeritt (Farmington) and Charlotta Lang
   (Farmington)

**DENNEY,**
Carrie, d. 11/1/1909 at –; apoplexy; shoe operator

**DERBY,**
Verlie, d. 3/29/1934 at 18/7/22; at home; single; b. Barnstead;
   Charles Derby (Montpelier, VT) and Sylvia Cook (Barnstead)

**DEROY,**
daughter, d. 8/11/1934 at – in Rochester; b. Rochester; Richard
   DeRoy (Canada) and Florence Belanger (Ipswich, MA)
Lucille Loraine, d. 4/16/1929 at 0/8/14 in Rochester; b. Rochester;
   Adelard Deroy (Canada) and Florence Belanger (Ipswich, MA)
Philomene, d. 4/8/1923 at 52/3/25; housewife; married; b. Canada;
   Celestine Smith (Canada) and Marie Paradis (Canada)

**DEVITT,**
Charles, d. 9/13/1926 at 67/4/1; retired; single; b. Ireland

**DEXTER,**
Frank L., d. 3/25/1932 at 45/10/13 in Keene; shoe cutter; married;
   b. NS; Louis L. Dexter (NS) and Jennie Croll (NS)

**DICEY,**
George R., d. 10/17/1890 at 32/11/8; consumption; shoemaker;
   married; b. Alton; Stephen G. Dicey (Gilmanton) and A. J.
   Wallace (Kempton, C.E.)
Nellie F., d. 5/15/1897 at 36/3/3; consumption; shoestitcher; widow;
   b. Alton; Perley W. Prescott (Alton) and Anna M. Dudley
   (Barnstead)

**DICKIE,**
Deidre, d. 10/5/1936 at –; b. Farmington; Ralph I. Dickie
   (Farmington) and Shirley Pinkham (Milton)

**DIERAUER,**
Harry, d. 10/13/1937 at 45/6/21; shoeworker; married; b. Salamanca, NY; Augustus Dierauer (Switzerland) and Katherine Grob (Switzerland)

**DIMMOCK,**
Annie M., d. 11/28/1929 at 86/7/1; widow; b. Glasgow, Scotland; Donald Buchanan (Scotland) and Elizabeth Clink (Scotland)
William, d. 8/3/1929 at 85/10/1; retired; married; b. Ferrisburg, VT; Thomas Dimmock (England) and Anna Dalrymple (VT)

**DINSMORE,**
M. D. L., d. 7/25/1901 at 74/8; disease of heart; engineer; married; b. Conway; Dean Dinsmore (Conway) and Hannah Burbank

**DIXON,**
Alte M., d. 6/27/1934 at 58/5/25; shoeworker; single; b. Farmington; Alvin Dixon (Eliot, ME) and Mary Libby (Eliot, ME)
Alvin, d. 12/22/1911 at 71/8/3; enlarged prostate; carpenter; widower; b. Eliot, ME; Stephen Dixon and Abigail -----
Ashbel A., d. 1/9/1897 at 26/11/17; disease of nephritis; iron worker; married; b. W. Lebanon; Stephen Dixon (W. Lebanon) and Alma Hurd (N. Berwick)
Elmore H., d. 11/15/1909 at 42/4/12; diabetes mellitus; shoe operator; b. Eliot, ME; Alvin H. Dixon and Mary Libby
George M., d. 1/19/1890 at 62/6/10; pneumonia; carpenter; widower; b. Eliot, ME; William Dixon (Eliot, ME)
Mary A., d. 3/5/1893 at 53/11/19; pneumonia; housewife; married; b. Eliot, ME; Alexander Libbey (Eliot, ME) and Deborah Chick (Eliot, ME)

**DOCKHAM,**
Viola, d. 11/12/1937 at 88/3/3; at home; widow; b. Provincetown, MA; Naham Haynes (Concord, MA) and Sophronia Parks (Concord, MA)

**DODGE,**
Bertha F., d. 7/19/1904 at 26/8/19; Bright's disease; housewife; married; b. Farmington; Charles L. Garland (Rochester) and Mary E. Sullivan (Rochester)

**DOLAN,**
Rena B., d. 2/10/1928 at 61

**DOLBY,**
Agnes M., d. 9/12/1892 at 0/0/24; cerebral inflammation; b. Farmington; Arthur P. Dolby (Alton, shoemaker) and Mary A. Hoye (Dover)

**DOLLIVER,**
Fred B., d. 1/31/1927 at 80/7/27; carpenter; widower; b. NS
Mary, d. 6/22/1902 at 43/7/14; septic peritonitis; housewife; married; b. Dover; Terrance Ring (Ireland) and Bridget Cannor (Ireland)

**DONNELL,**
Aaron J., d. 8/28/1922 at 80/0/30; farmer; married; b. Wells; Jacob Donnell (N. Berwick) and Harriett Jacobs (Wells)

**DORE,**
son, d. 2/23/1888 at 0/0/1; paralysis; b, Farmington; Herbert W. Dore (Wakefield) and Flora E. Burnham (Farmington)
Charles W., d. 4/27/1921 at 74/5/24; laborer; married; b. Alton; Benjamin Dore and Deborah Ricker
Clara A., d. 1/30/1927 at 66/7/14; housekeeper; single; b. Farmington; Henry Dore (Alton) and Susan C. Rollins (Alton)
Daniel C., d. 10/7/1915 at 69/3/22; shoeworker; married; b. Alton; Henry Dore (Alton) and Susanna Rollins (Alton)
George A., d. 6/1/1913 at 38; natural causes; shoemaker; divorced; b. Alton; Alvin H. Dore (Alton, laborer) and Flora L. Hill (Canada)
Henry, d. 1/7/1908 at 92/9/7; old age; laborer; widower; b. Alton; Abijah Dore (Lebanon, ME) and Eunice LeGro (Lebanon, ME)
Herbert B., d. 3/23/1888 at 0/1/1; spasms; b. Farmington; Herbert W. Dore (Wakefield) and Flora E. Burnham (Farmington)
Mary A., d. 12/28/1900 at 66/6/16; spinal sclerosis; housewife; widow; b. Somersworth; G. Morrison
Mary E., d. 10/3/1923 at 72/0/29; housekeeper; single; b. Milton; Henry Dore (Alton) and Susan B. Allen (Middleton)
Susan L., d. 3/24/1904 at 81/11/19; hyp. congestion lung; housewife; married; b. Alton; John Rollins (Alton) and Mary Perkins (Middleton)

**DORR,**
Roy E., d. 12/20/1933 at 34/11/18; laborer; married; b. Cherryfield, ME; Millard Dorr (Cherryfield, ME) and Clara Kilton (Harrington, ME)

**DOTY,**
Nellie M., d. 3/30/1924 at 54/0/12; housewife; married; b. Middleton; Warren Whitehouse (Middleton) and Ella A. York (Middleton)
Nellie V., d. 12/2/1914 at 44/8/4; nervous shock; housewife; married; b. Middleton; Joseph York (Middleton, shoemaker) and Augusta Davis

**DOW,**
C. D., d. 6/5/1893 at 51; heart disease; salesman
William L., d. 2/15/1935 at 86/7/23; retired; widower; b. Moultonboro; Perkins Dow (Ossipee) and Eunice Brown (Wolfeboro)

**DOWNES,**
Laura A., d. 11/20/1933 at 88/9/15 in Laconia; widow; b. Gilford; Elisha Eaton (Pittsfield) and Betsey Brown (Gilford)
Lewis, d. 6/15/1918 at 81/10; farmer; widower; b. Farmington; John H. Downes (Farmington) and Mary B. Roberts (Rochester)

**DOWNING,**
son, d. 4/16/1897 at –; stillborn; b. Farmington; Edward J. Downing (Farmington) and Katie C. Miller (LaGrange)
Alonzo, d. 9/21/1919 at 72; shoemaker; married; b. Holderness; Royal Downing (Holderness) and Fannie Prescott
Angie J., d. 10/25/1933 at 79/8/2; widow; b. Auburn, ME; Gilbert Chamberlain (Bryant Pond, ME) and Belinda Bryant (Bryants Pond, ME)
Eliza D., d. 3/30/1892 at 74/10; paralysis; housekeeper; married; b. Middleton; Amasa Whitehouse (Middleton, farmer) and Abigail Cotton (Wolfeboro)
Elizabeth, d. 9/4/1900 at 72/3/12; tuberculosis of lung; housekeeper; widow; b. Somersworth; G. Morrison
George T., d. 12/3/1915 at 68/0/5; farmer; married; b. Farmington; Benjamin Downing (Farmington) and Tryphemia Calef (Rochester)

J. M., d. 10/2/1898 at 78/9/8; heart disease; farmer; married; b. Middleton

Jomes, d. 11/26/1907 at 66/7/6; locomotor ataxia; widower; b. Farmington; Benjamin Downey (Farmington, farmer) and Tuphenia Calif

Julia A., d. 10/7/1904 at 62/8/18; cancer; married; b. Rochester; Timothy Linscott and Johanna Meader

Samuel H., d. 11/8/1901 at 87/6/14; senectus; farmer; widower; b. Middleton; Samuel Downing (Somersworth) and Mary A. Davi (Alton)

Sarah G., d. 1/2/1888 at 66/5/12; pneumonia; housekeeper; married; b. Middleton; I. Whitehouse

T. B., d. 2/17/1896 at 87/2/20; pneumonia; widow; b. Rochester; John Calef and Betsey Burnham

Winnie E., d. 10/15/1890 at 18/2/13; typhoid fever; housekeeper; single; b. Farmington; James H. Downing (Farmington)

Winnie M., d. 7/26/1891 at 18/11/22; tuberculosis; housekeeper; married; b. Rochester; James Wormwood and Julia Linscott

**DOWNS,**

Maria H., d. 9/17/1911 at 72/8/11; heart failure; housewife; married b. Farmington; John G. Horne (Farmington, farmer) and Hannah Whitehouse (New Durham)

Winona, d. 4/29/1933 at 11/2/13; b. Milton; Perley E. Downes (Madison) and Helena Thompson (Silver Lake)

**DRAKE,**

Mercy, d. 10/27/1903 at 84/0/5; old age; housewife; widow; William Bennett (Farmington) and Mary Wingate (Farmington)

**DRAPEAU** [see Dropean],

son, d. 1/5/1893 at –; b. Farmington; Cleophas Drapeau (PQ) and Rose Duclos (PQ)

Cleophas, d. 1/19/1930 at 76/10/3; laborer; widower; b. Canada

**DREW,**

daughter, d. 11/6/1903 at –; stillborn; Charles E. Drew (Alton) and Lizzie M. Whittier (Barrington)

son, d. 1/27/1936 at –; b. Farmington; Robert B. Drew (Middleton) and Grace M. Drew (W. Lebanon)

Abigail R., d. 1/19/1907 at 91/7/22; bronchial pneumonia; housekeeper; widow; b. Parsonsfield, ME; William Rumery (Saco, ME, farmer) and Margaret McGrath (Saco, ME)

Alice L., d. 6/14/1906 at 16/6/17; phthisis pulmonalis; school girl; single; b. Farmington; Frank J. Drew (Gilmanton) and Lizzie H. Young (Dover)

Annie, d. 11/2/1931 at 92/5/13 in New Durham; widow; b. PEI

Blanch I., d. 3/16/1889 at 12/8/4; pulmonary phthisis

Charles E., d. 10/5/1931 at 56/2/16; shoeworker; married; b. Alton; Charles Drew (Alton) and Anna Watson (ME)

Clifford T., d. 7/7/1926 at 35/11/27; shoeworker; married; b. Middleton; Horace Drew (Eaton) and Maggie Walker (England)

Elizabeth M., d. 6/20/1934 at 83; housewife; widow; b. Milton; James S. Child and Mary Goodwin

Ellsworth, d. 7/12/1922 at 52/7/19; farmer; married; b. Eaton; Thomas Drew (Eaton) and Sarah Bryant (Eaton)

Florence V., d. 4/27/1921 at 43/10/11; at home; married; b. Boston, MA; Alfred Putney and Susan Peaks (Cohasset)

Frank W., d. 2/25/1900 at 4/8; acute nephritis; b. Farmington; Frank Drew (Alton) and Lizzie H. Young (Dover)

George F., d. 9/19/1921 at 67/11/13; shoeworker; married; b. Farmington; Alonzo Drew (MA) and Mary E. Place (Somersworth)

Irvin E., d. 1/24/1889 at 1/6; typhoid pneumonia; b. Farmington; Frank J. Drew (Gilmanton) and Lizzie H. Young (Dover)

James, d. 5/13/1932 at 82 in Concord; bobbin mill; widower; b. Brookfield; James Drew and Abbie Richard

Joseph, d. 1/2/1909 at 84/2/12; senile dementia; farmer; widower; b. Alton; John Drew and Lottie Davis

Lizzie, d. 9/29/1898 at 43/0/9; diabetes gangrene; housewife; married; b. Middleton; Wingate Whitehouse (Middleton) and Eliza Colbath (Farmington)

Lizzie W., d. 4/20/1911 at 59/9/6; chronic nephritis; shoeworker; married; b. Dover; Samuel N. Warren and Mary ----- (Eliot, ME)

Lucy T., d. 5/3/1891 at 29/7/19; pneumonia; housekeeper; married; b. Berwick, ME; Nathaniel M. Young (Gilmanton) and Hannah Harriman (Bartlett)

Mary E., d. 3/19/1887 at 55/8; housekeeper; married; b. Lebanon, ME; Aaron D. Place and Mary R. Place

Sarah E. H., d. 2/28/1923 at 83/2; housewife; widow; b. Barnstead; Joseph Hall (Barnstead) and Betsey Drew (Alton)

Wesley, d. 9/27/1936 at 74/11/29; at home; widower; b. Eaton; Thomas Drew and Sarah Bryant

**DROPEAN** [see Drapeau],
child, d. 4/3/1890 at –; stillborn; b. Farmington; Cleophas Dropean (Canada) and Rosie Dropean (Canada)

**DUCLOS,**
Mary, d. 2/24/1893 at 57/10/13; pneumonia; housewife; married; b. Canada; Antonie Poinier (Canada) and Josie Lebair (Canada)

**DUDLEY,**
Charles C., d. 3/3/1905 at 74/8/10; shock; farmer; married; b. Somersworth; Stephen Dudley (Alton) and Sarah S. Garland (Ossipee)

Eben A., d. 2/21/1908 at 48/2/23; epilepsy; laborer; single; b. Farmington; Charles C. Dudley (Somersworth) and Lydia Tibbetts (Tamworth)

Fred E., d. 3/25/1938 at 66/1/19; laborer; single; b. Farmington; Charles Dudley (Somersworth) and Lydia Tibbetts (Tamworth)

George A., d. 1/24/1938 at 68/10/27 in Derry; jeweler; widower; b. Farmington; Charles Dudley (Somersworth) and Lydia Tibbetts (Tamworth)

Lydia A., d. 10/27/1908 at 78/4/5; bronchitis; housekeeper; widow; b. Tamworth; Moses Tibbetts (Wolfeboro) and Sarah York (Tamworth)

Nathaniel S., d. 10/15/1889 at 70/10/26; cerebral apoplexy; blacksmith; b. Gilmanton; Nathaniel Dudley (Gilmanton) and Mary Smith (Gilmanton)

Oscar S., d. 10/11/1933 at 79/5/8; farmer; married; b. Wolfeboro; Charles Dudley (East Rochester) and Lydia Tebbets (Tamworth)

**DUFRESNE,**
Marie, d. 2/2/1915 at 0/4/4; b. Springvale, ME; Harry Dufresne (VT) and Maud E. Burrows (Milton)

**DUNN,**
Nellie B., d. 10/2/1904 at 36; nortic insufficiency; housewife; married; b. Ireland; Thomas Cochrain (Ireland) and Nellie Osborne (Ireland)

**DUNNELL,**
Augusta, d. 12/12/1935 at 83/9/25; at home; widow; b. York, ME

**DUNTLEY,**
Charles A., d. 2/25/1926 at 59/11/3; shoeworker; married; b. Alton; Charles W. Duntley (Sandwich) and Levina Watson (Gilmanton)
Lena F., d. 10/29/1932 at 53/9/20; housewife; married; b. New Durham; Frank Hayes (New Durham) and Lena F. Hayes (New Durham)
Livona, d. 7/2/1892 at 55/11/28; enclocaeles; housewife; married; b. Gilmanton; Joseph Watson (Middleton, farmer) and Mary Spencer (Strafford)

**DUPUIS,**
Lydia, d. 4/16/1911 at 27/11; suicide, drowning; housewife; married; b. Canada; Joseph Marcoux (Canada, laborer) and Adelaide Cyr (Canada)

**DUQUETTE,**
Adelarde, d. 1/24/1928 at 46/11/12; police officer; married; b. Canada; Joseph Duquette (Canada) and Caroline Corrineau (Canada)
Leon, d. 3/25/1936 at 42/1/13 in Concord; none; single; b. Canada; Leon Duquette (Canada)

**DURGIN,**
Mehitable C., d. 4/7/1908 at 73; cerebral hemorrhage; housekeeper; widow; b. Conway; Robert Allard and Rebecca C. Moulton
Nathan, d. 2/26/1898 at 82/5/26; heart disease; farmer; widower

**DUSTIN,**
son, d. 12/27/1891 at –; stillborn; b. Farmington; Fred R. Dustin and Abbie E. Lucas (Farmington)

**EALY,**
　Lillian A., d. 10/24/1903 at 25/2/1; consumption; housewife; widow; Onslow S. Smith (Conway) and Nellie M. Smith (Waterboro, ME)

**EASTMAN,**
　Edward E., d. 5/25/1931 at 47/2/9; junk dealer; married; b. Bartlett; Eldwin Eastman and Mary J. Odway
　Ellen F., d. 10/29/1896 at –/4; cancer of bone; housekeeper; widow b. Laconia; Benjamin R. Gilman (Gilmanton) and Caroline Chase (Laconia)
　George N., d. 4/28/1892 at 72/3/4; pneumonia; lawyer; married; b. Farmington; Nehemiah Eastman (Gilmanton, lawyer) and A. B Woodman (Farmington)
　George W., d. 12/12/1927 at 88/4/15; shoeworker; widower; b. Stowe

**EATON,**
　Philander, d. 9/13/1888 at 75/1/11; worn out; shoemaker; widower; b. Framingham; Silas Eaton, Jr. (Framingham) and Nancy Stone (Framingham)

**EDGERLY,**
　Dwight E., d. 4/8/1928 at 74/3/15; bank cashier; married; b. Gilmanton; Owen J. Edgerly (Gilmanton) and Mary Robinson (Meredith)
　Ella M., d. 7/8/1902 at 44/9/25; gangrene; single; b. Farmington; Hosea B. Edgerly (Farmington) and Maria McDuffee (Rochester)
　Ella R., d. 7/16/1920 at 44/11/3; housewife; married; b. Scotland
　Ethel M., d. 9/1/1915 at 26/3/15; housewife; married; b. Farmington; Charles E. Drew and Lizzie Child (Farmington)
　Fred E., d. 3/12/1890 at 31/2; chronic pleurisy; expressman; married; b. Gilmanton; Owen Edgerly (Gilmanton) and Mary E. Robinson (Meredith)
　Georgia, d. 11/5/1894 at 44/1; pneumonia; housewife; married; b. Lowell, MA; G. M. Garland (Ossipee) and Jane Moody (Wolfeboro)
　Helen P., d. 5/9/1892 at 0/8; peritonitis; b. Farmington; Willie Edgerly (Barrington, shoemaker) and Mattie A. Corson (Barrington)

Hosea B., d. 1/9/1892 at 69/3/15; apoplexy; shoe manufacturer; married; b. Farmington; Harriet Edgerly

James B., d. 11/1/1922 at 88/9/3; retired; widower; b. Farmington; Joseph B. Edgerly and Cordelia Waldron

John H., d. 6/1/1896 at 66/2/5; pneumonia; farmer; married; b. New Durham; John Edgerly (New Durham) and Tamson Doe (New Durham)

Johnnie, d. 9/9/1906 at 0/1/11; enteritis; b. Farmington; William H. Edgerly (Farmington) and Mattie A. Corson (Barrington)

Josiah B., d. 4/7/1888 at 87/7/27; old age; cabinet maker; widower; b. New Durham; Josiah Edgerly and Polly Tash

Maria, d. 12/10/1908 at 76/6/24; cancer; widow; b. Rochester; Thomas McDuffee and Hannah Pierce

Martha, d. 2/22/1920 at 51/0/18; housekeeper; widow; b. Barrington; L. D. Corson (Lebanon, ME) and Melinda Allen (Barrington)

Martha E., d. 2/23/1888 at 56/5/5; cancer; housekeeper; married; b. Great Falls; Robert Fernald (Shapleigh, ME) and Aphia Coffin (Shapleigh, ME)

Mary A., d. 3/1/1899 at 41/7/12; pneumonia; housewife; single; b. Farmington; Josiah B. Edgerly (Farmington) and Eliza J. Hayes (Farmington)

Maud A., d. 3/16/1897 at 11/4/3; urinic coma; b. Farmington; Erville Edgerly (Farmington) and Carrie Quint (Farmington)

Maude F., d. 9/1/1937 at 46/2/14; housewife; married; b. Alton; George E. Furber (Alton) and Ada A. Nutter (Barnstead)

Minnie E., d. 10/25/1938 at 77/1/8; housewife; married; b. Bridgton, ME; Charles Cates (Oxford, ME) and Philena Libby (Naples, ME)

Nellie A., d. 6/11/1900 at 43/0/23; endocarditis; dressmaker; widow; b. Farmington; Jacob P. Horne (Farmington) and Amanda Colbath (Farmington)

Tamson, d. 10/23/1888 at 89/4/6; old age; widow; b. Alton

Winfield, d. 9/10/1927 at 81/3/12; Brig. Gen. USA; married; b. Farmington; Josiah B. Edgerly (Farmington) and Cordelia Waldron (Farmington)

**EDMONDS,**

N. R., d. 9/30/1901 at 32/5/21; acute hepatitis; married; b. Doylestown, OH; William Tuttle and Eunice Tuttle (Akron, OH)

**ELKINS,**

Caroline, d. 6/4/1923 at 86/9/1; housekeeper; widow; b. Effingham John E. Lewis and Louise Leighton

Charles, d. 11/29/1933 at 73/4/26; shoeworker; divorced; b. Farmington; Ira Elkins (Farmington) and Caroline Lewis (Effingham)

Cyrus, d. 4/9/1902 at 57/5/7; heart disease; laborer; married; b. Farmington; John C. Elkins (VT) and A. Varney (Farmington)

George, d. 1/11/1917 at 67/6/2; patternmaker; married; b. Farmington; John C. Elkins (ME) and Axa Varney (NH)

Ira, d. 4/25/1923 at 90/5/22; retired; married; b. Farmington; John C. Elkins and Achsa Varney

Jeremiah S., d. 8/5/1905 at 57/9/19; nephritic cirrhosis; physician; married; b. Barnstead; John P. Elkins (Andover) and Sarah Pendergast (Barnstead)

John B., M.D., d. 9/8/1895 at 56/10/8; angina pectoris; physician; married; b. New Durham; John P. Elkins, M.D. (Andover) and Sara F. Pendergast (Barnstead)

Laura I., d. 11/27/1923 at 66/10/27; dressmaker; widow; b. Rochester

Mary E., d. 4/2/1892 at 85/9/12; pneumonia; housekeeper; widow; b. New Durham; Doctiver Pinkham (New Durham, farmer)

**ELLIOTT,**

stillborn son, d. 11/25/1932 at –; b. Farmington; Jesse Elliott and Leona F. Moisan (New Durham)

Catherine J., d. 8/31/1936 at 2/1/8; b. Hempstead, NY; Theodore Elliott (Bow) and Maybelle Swaine (Rochester)

Charles H., d. 7/9/1932 at 79/8/29 in Sanford, ME; mail carrier; married; b. Lisbon; Charles H. Elliott

Eddie, d. 11/19/1896 at 0/6/6; pneumonia; b. Farmington; George S. Elliott (Concord) and Ida Nealley (Lowell, MA)

Flora P., d. 12/31/1918 at 16/7/18; single; b. Alton; Charles F. Elliot (Rumney) and Martha J. Brock (Dorchester)

Jesse M., d. 2/23/1903 at 70/2/19; jaundice; carriage jobber; married; William Elliott (Barnstead) and Mary Emerson (Barnstead)

Mary E., d. 10/8/1898 at 19/11/1; consumption; single; b. Farmington; Jesse M. Elliott (Barrington) and Rosetta S. Otis (Farmington)

Maude, d. 8/8/1906 at 24/0/0; pulmonary tuberculosis; single; b. Farmington; Jesse M. Elliott and Rosetta Otis (Farmington)

Myrtle J., d. 3/15/1901 at 17/2/1; acute tuberculosis; school girl; single; b. Farmington; Jesse M. Elliott (Barrington) and Rosetta Otis (Farmington)

Rose L., d. 3/6/1900 at 2/0/5; tuberculosis; b. Farmington; James Stanton and Mary E. Elliott (Farmington)

Rosetta S., d. 4/1/1930 at 79/0/11; housekeeper; widow; b. Farmington; Orrin K. Otis (Farmington) and Sarah Garland (Farmington)

William A., d. 9/12/1922 at 51/6/18; mechanic; married; b. Farmington; Jesse M. Elliott (Strafford) and Rosetta Otis (Farmington)

William J., d. 2/28/1908 at 2/0/22; tubercular meningitis; b. Farmington; William A. Elliott (Farmington) and Florence E. Holmes

**ELLIS,**
Arthur W., d. 6/10/1919 at 7

**EMERSON,**
Bessie, d. 3/26/1911 at 0/1/26; colitis; b. Farmington; Berton Emerson (Raymond, sawyer) and Mary E. Kenney (NB)

Charles, d. 8/3/1911 at 71/5/8; heart disease; farmer; married; b. Farmington; Joseph Emerson (Farmington) and Lydia A. George (Barnstead)

Elizabeth, d. 2/24/1935 at 62 in Concord; school teacher; widow; b. Strafford; Daniel Quint (Canaan) and Rose Allard (Madison)

Frances, d. 7/19/1919 at 62/5/26; housekeeper; married; b. New Durham; William Chamberlain and Harriet Elkins

George R., d. 1/7/1935 at 68/0/13; grain dealer; married; b. Farmington; Charles Emerson (Farmington) and Vienna F. Dolby (Hopkinton)

Gerald M., d. 1/12/1910 at 0/0/20; pneumonia; b. Farmington; Bert E. Emerson (Chester) and Mary E. Kenney (NB)

**EMERY,**
daughter, d. 12/12/1897 at –; premature birth; b. Farmington; Edwin A. Emery (Middleton) and Viola A. Edgerly (New Durham)

E. Augustus, d. 3/4/1908 at 61/1/19; suicide shooting; laborer; widower; b. Middleton; Daniel C. Emery and Abigail Whitehouse (Middleton)

Ida Estella, d. 4/23/1897 at 5/6/27; typhoid fever; b. Farmington; Clifton E. Emery (Milton) and Mary J. Hurd (Farmington)

Sarah F., d. 7/2/1926 at 76/3/28; housewife; widow; b. West Milton; Zachens Gore (NH) and Hannah Green (NH)

Viola A., d. 4/8/1907 at 51/11/5; meningitis; married; b. New Durham; David Edgerly (New Durham, clergyman) and ----- (New Durham)

**EMMONS,**

Eunice, d. 1/13/1890 at 64/4/26; cerebral softening; housekeeper; married; b. New Durham; Timothy Horne (New Durham) and ----- Richardson (New Durham)

Hiram, d. 12/24/1897 at 75/1/14; malignant growth & age; farmer; widower; b. Farmington; Thomas Emmons (Kennebunkport) and Olive Perkins (Brownfield)

**ETHERIDGE,**

James, d. 6/15/1917 at 39; shoeworker; single; b. Farmington

Melinda M., d. 5/15/1889 at 39/2/10; albuminuria; housekeeper; b. New Castle; Ellerson O. Curtis (New Castle) and Matilda A. White (New Castle)

**EVANS,**

Abbie M., d. 9/14/1895 at 0/2/1; asthenia; b. Milton; Charles W. Evans (Alton) and Alice M. Tibbetts (Rochester)

Blanche I., d. 8/11/1920 at 30/0/29; housewife; married; b. Quebec; William O'Brien (Quebec) and Mary Stephen (Montreal, Canada)

Charles W., d. 2/23/1932 at 64/9/19; shoeworker; married; b. Alton; Robert W. Evans and Mary Colomy

Clara A., d. 8/27/1931 at 85/0/27 in Gonic; retired; widow; b. Farmington; Furber Young and Rhoda Goodall

Ezra H., d. 3/26/1904 at 63/10/20; double pneumonia; shoemaker; married; b. New Durham; Ezra Evans (New Durham) and Belinda York (New Durham)

Isabelle, d. 9/24/1936 at 64/0/5; at home; widow; b. Auburn, ME; Charles B. Hall (Portland, ME) and Adeline Newman (Portland, ME)

James I., d. 11/3/1915 at 64/8/20; section foreman; married; b. New Durham; Robert Evans (Alton) and Mary Colomy (New Durham)
Jeremiah D., d. 9/1/1887 at –; married
Marion L., d. 12/30/1936 at 39/3; housewife; married; b. Berwick, ME; Henry Whitehouse (Somersworth) and Gertrude Blake (Belfast, ME)
Wilbur J., d. 1/2/1916 at 52; druggist; married; b. Alton; Joseph Evans (Alton) and Ann French

**FALL,**
daughter, d. 2/13/1891 at –; stillborn; b. Farmington; William E. Fall (Farmington) and Nellie White (Rochester)
son, d. 6/25/1925 at –; b. Farmington; Leba Piper (Effingham Falls)
Charles T., d. 12/18/1930 at 77/0/15; retired; married; b. Farmington; Otis Fall and Rosillah Evans
Frank W., d. 4/27/1891 at 25/8/4; consumption; painter; single; b. Farmington; Otis W. Fall (Alton) and Rozellah Evans (CO)
Julia Emma, d. 6/19/1933 at 71/10/11; at home; widow; b. Farmington; Joshua Richardson (Derry) and Susan Wiggin (Moultonborough)
Lawrence R., d. 1/19/1916 at 0/0/5; b. Farmington; Henry S. Fall (Somersworth) and Rosie E. Varney (Farmington)
Louisa M., d. 3/19/1909 at 85/2/9; old age; b. Alton; Tristram Fall (Alton) and Sarah Wentworth (Middleton)
Orrin T., d. 5/30/1903 at 75/0/23; shock; shoemaker; divorced; Tristram Fall (Alton) and Sarah Wentworth (Middleton)
Otis W., d. 1/2/1892 at 69/5/6; Bright's disease; shoemaker; married; b. Alton; Trusham Fall (Middleton, farmer) and Sarah Wentworth (Alton)
Perley A., d. 9/3/1914 at 47/0/22; angina pectoris; woodsman; single; b. Lebanon, ME; Melvin Fall (Lebanon, farmer) and Mary E. Pierce (Lebanon)
Richard W., d. 1/5/1918 at 0/0/6; b. Farmington; Henry S. Fall (Somersworth) and Rosie E. Varney (Farmington)
Theresa G., d. 2/28/1924 at 0/2/15; b. Farmington; Louise Fall (Tuftonboro)

**FARWELL,**
Fred T., d. 11/23/1938 at 74/1/24 in Rochester; shoeworker; married; b. Wilmot; Thomas Farwell (New London) and Harriett Chase (Wilmot)
Susan E., d. 12/21/1932 at 71/4/25 in Tilton; retired; widow; b. Moultonboro; True Perkins Dow (Tuftonboro) and Eunice C. Brown (Wolfeboro)

**FAUCETT,**
Anna E., d. 6/29/1936 at 75/8/19 in New Durham; at home; single; b. Walpole, MA; William Faucett (St. Johns, NB) and Eliza Barry (Ireland)

**FERLAND,**
Elna A., d. 4/26/1915 at 0/0/23; b. Farmington; Thomas Ferland (Canada) and Mary D. Marcoux (Rochester)
Joseph, d. 4/3/1915 at 0/0/0; b. Farmington; Thomas Ferland (Canada) and Mary D. Marcoux (Rochester)
Thomas, d. 8/1/1930 at 60/3/7; shoeworker; married; b. Canada; George Ferland (Canada) and Marie Turmell (Canada)

**FERNALD,**
Caroline, d. 9/26/1920 at 80/0/18; retired; widow; b. Farmington; Benjamin Wingate (Farmington) and Lavinia Davis (Farmington)
George W., d. 11/2/1890 at 36/8/17; chr. albumenuria; civil engineer; married; b. Farmington; James E. Fernald (Springvale, ME) and Laura E. Whitehouse (Farmington)
James E., d. 7/28/1895 at 64/10; cystitis; merchant; married; b. Springvale; Robert Fernald (Shapleigh) and Apphia Coffin
Jonathan, d. 4/21/1893 at 95/4/21; old age; farmer; widower; b. Wolfeboro; William J. Fernald (Brookfield) and Betsey Johnson (Andover, MA)
Laura A., d. 3/14/1913 at 85/4; influenza; widow; b. Farmington; G. L. Whitehouse (Middleton, civil engineer) and Liberty N. Dame (Rochester)

**FERRETTI,**
son, d. 2/26/1905 at –; premature birth; b. Farmington; Ralph A. Ferretti (Italy) and Fannie L. Casassa (Italy)

**FERRIN,**
Belle, d. 11/12/1930 at 77/9/25; housewife; married; b. Bethlehem; Jasper Nourse (Littleton) and Miranda Farr (ME)

**FIFIELD,**
Herman, d. 8/26/1937 at 21/7/29 in Sanford, ME; shoeworker; single; b. Wakefield; George R. Fifield (Conway) and Blanche Phinney (Porter, ME)

Phoebe J., d. 1/14/1931 at 67/4/21; housekeeper; married; b. Farmington; Charles H. Kelley and Sarah A. Horne

**FLANAGAN,**
Lucy, d. 3/24/1931 at 75/0/2; housekeeper; widow; b. Shapleigh, ME; Benjamin Day and Aurena Goodwin

**FLANDERS,**
Arthur, d. 2/7/1906 at 49/4/4; tuberculosis of lung; last mfgr.; b. Concord; Langdon Flanders (Concord) and Eliza A. Smith (Hopkinton)

Arthur L., d. 3/11/1936 at 81 in Boston, MA; druggist; single; b. NH; Samuel Flanders (NH) and Marcia A. Brown (NH)

Eliza A., d. 1/25/1924 at 88/9/17; housekeeper; widow; b. Hopkinton; Andrew Smith and Eliza Sherburn

Herman T., d. 2/24/1934 at 71/7/21; shoeworker; married; b. Farmington; Samuel B. Flanders and Marcia Brown

Langdon S., d. 3/8/1899 at 80/1/15; Bright's disease; last manufacturing; married; b. Concord; Richard Flanders (Concord) and Abigail Furber (Newington)

Marcia, d. 3/13/1919 at 85/9/6; housewife; widow; b. Wilmot; Joseph Brown and Betsey Kimball

**FLETCHER,**
daughter, d. 11/6/1891 at –; no strength to breath; b. Farmington; Fred P. Fletcher (New Durham) and Ella R. Jones (Barnstead)

Elizabeth, d. 10/9/1914 at 74/1/7; cerebral hemorrhage; married; b. New Durham; Richard Miller (Milton, farmer) and Paulina Buzzell (Acton, ME)

Ellen R., d. 7/22/1894 at 30/8; consumption; housekeeper; married; b. Gilmanton; James Jones and Nancy Bunker (Barnstead)

Emily F., d. 3/22/1909 at 63/8/7; pericarditis and grippe; housekeeper; b. Hollis, ME; Daniel Benson (Hollis, ME) and Susan Chadbourne (Hollis, ME)

James A., d. 1/30/1917 at 79/4/7; florist; widower; b. Dracut, MA; James H. Fletcher (Pelham, MA) and Abigail H. Coburn (Pelham, MA)

John H., d. 11/25/1891 at 26/3/16; bronchitis; blacksmith; married; b. Hollis, ME; George W. Fletcher (New Durham) and Julia A Willey (New Durham)

Lillian, d. 10/13/1926 at 55/5/24; shoe forelady; widow; b. Nobleboro, ME; Thomas A. Kaler (Nobleboro, ME) and Sarah Nash (Nobleboro, ME)

Tristram, d. 7/12/1906 at 72/0/23; heart disease; shoemaker; married; b. Pelham; James A. Fletcher (Salem) and Abigail Coburn (Pelham)

**FLYNN,**

John H., d. 1/16/1926 at 68/4/11; shoeworker; single; b. Lynn, MA; James Flynn (Lynn, MA)

**FOOTE,**

Clarence M., d. 12/26/1895 at 42/9/13; septicemia; sailor; b. Portsmouth; Henry Foote (Danvers, MA) and Sarah P. Pease (Tamworth)

**FORD,**

Andrew J., d. 11/15/1902 at 73/11/9; cerebral apoplexy; widower

**FORTIN,**

May A., d. 5/17/1936 at 47/9/14 in Rochester; shoeworker; married; b. Lynn, MA; Peter Therrien (Milton, MA) and Matilda Garipay (Canada)

**FOSS,**

Adelaide, d. 9/14/1934 at 77/5/19 in Haworth, NJ; housekeeper; widow; b. VT; George Smith (VT)

Amy L., d. 3/3/1909 at 15/8/3; acute nephritis; schoolgirl; b. Farmington; James W. Foss (Rochester) and Katie M. Hobbs (Farmington)

Charles A., d. 4/29/1918 at 58/8/14; laborer; divorced; b. Farmington; William Foss (Farmington) and Charlotte Freeman (New York City)

Charlotte, d. 1/11/1896 at 61/9/16; bronchial pneumonia; housekeeper; widow; b. NY; Jesse Foman (England)

Charlotte S., d. 12/8/1899 at 57/5/15; malignant tumor; housewife; married; b. Strafford; Ezra T. Rumery (ME) and Charlotte Lougee (Strafford)

Clark, d. 8/27/1896 at 70/9/17; haematemesis; mason; married; b. Gilmanton; Clark Foss (Gilmanton) and Mehitable Stiles (Strafford)

Ellen C., d. 7/13/1938 at 81/1; housewife; widow; b. Barrington; David Ham (Barrington) and Hannah Varney (Barrington)

Etta M., d. 1/13/1917 at 48/5/8; shoeworker; married; b. Dover; George B. Tibbetts (Dover) and Abbie C. Drew (Dover)

Frank E., d. 10/18/1918 at 33/10/6; merchant; single; b. Rochester; James F. Foss (Rochester) and Ellen C. Ham (Barrington)

Harriett A., d. 8/26/1901 at 70/9/16; Bright's disease; widow; b. Dover; Lenard Shepard and Veronia Pierce (Worcester)

Henry I., d. 10/27/1902 at 38/5/12; alcoholism; laborer; married; b. Farmington; William H. Foss (Farmington) and Charlotte Foreman (Farmington)

Lena A., d. 5/3/1928 at 65/11/12; b. Middleton; Thomas Young (Middleton) and Levina Beady (Ireland)

Luther J., d. 6/3/1923 at 78/6/24; retired; widower; b. Rochester; Jeremiah Foss (Rochester) and Esther Berry (Strafford)

Martha L., d. 5/27/1920 at 51/11/23; housekeeper; widow; John P. Jones (W. Medway, MA) and Sarah J. ----- (Portsmouth)

Sally W., d. 12/31/1890 at 79/10/19; cancer of stomach; housekeeper; widow; b. Farmington; John Robinson (Milton) and Joan Ricker (Milton)

William M., d. 11/8/1916 at 59/11/14; blacksmith; married; b. Deerfield; William J. Foss (Gilmanton) and Jerusha Pettingill (Franklin)

Winnie E., d. 11/20/1923 at 47/11/15; single; b. Danvers, MA; John C. Foss (Alton) and Ella Watson (Alton)

**FOUNTAIN,**
Louis L., d. 2/25/1918 at 64/8/15; laborer; widower; b. Canada; Louis Fountain (Canada)

**FRAISER,**
Jack, d. 6/6/1938 at 73 in Dover; shoeworker; divorced; b. NS; Hugh Fraiser (NS) and Dorothy Fraiser (NS)

**FREEMAN,**
Gloria, d. 11/17/1936 at 0/8/1 in Boston, MA; b. Farmington; Maynard Freeman (Rockland, ME) and Lizzie Perry (Rochester)

**FRENCH,**
Amy W., d. 6/4/1898 at 83/3/7; old age; widow; b. Concord; John Wallace (Keene) and Nancy Darling (Keene)
Betsey, d. 2/8/1899 at 83/3/27; bronchitis; housewife; widow; b. Farmington; Benjamin Bunker (Farmington) and Hannah French (Farmington)
Byron P., d. 10/11/1889 at 35/6/3; pneumonia; shoemaker; b. Farmington; Stephen French (Farmington) and Mary E. Young (Farmington)
Charles C., d. 12/6/1936 at 64/3/6; shoeworker; widower; b. Farmington; Charles H. French (Farmington) and Martha Wentworth (Milton)
Charles H., d. 1/8/1916 at 74/3/28; laborer; widower; b. Farmington; Jeremiah French (Farmington) and Mary Hodgdon
Charles S., d. 3/27/1914 at 59/2/25; chronic nephritis; foreman; married; b. Newmarket; Fred French and Jane Tuttle
Clara B., d. 3/23/1915 at 65/8/26; housekeeper; single; b. Middleton; Charles French (Farmington) and Betsey Bunker (Farmington)
Ella A., d. 8/8/1929 at 69/0/26; shoeworker; widow; b. Farmington; Alexander T. Randall (Canada) and Ardelia R. Cook (Milton)
Evon, d. 10/9/1918 at 21/2/18; housewife; married; b. Plymouth, MA; Simon French (NS) and Lucretia Briggs (Plymouth, MA)
Frank E., d. 3/30/1935 at 83/8/26; livery; single; b. Middleton; Charles French and Betsey French
G. B., d. 3/11/1900 at 39/0/18; suicide shooting; teamster; widower; b. Farmington; Jerry French (Farmington)
Irving, d. 5/11/1935 at 60/3/28; shoeworker; married; b. Farmington; Charles H. French (Farmington) and Martha Wentworth (Milton)

Jeremiah, d. 6/1/1906 at 59/7/8; apoplexy; shoe cutter; married; b. Farmington; Jeremiah French (Farmington) and Peace Corson (Milton)

Levi F., d. 1/4/1889 at 80/11/21; heart disease; shoemaker; b. Farmington; David French and Abigail Roberts

Martha J., d. 5/22/1915 at 70/11/23; housewife; married; b. Milton; William Wentworth (Milton) and Susan Wentworth (Milton)

Mary E., d. 7/25/1893 at 72/6; apoplexy; lady; married; b. Farmington; Samuel Young (Farmington) and Abigail Rand (Farmington)

Mary H., d. 1/29/1889 at 44/3; cancer; housekeeper; b. Dover; Dudley Stanton and Mary Stanton

Pheobe J., d. 10/11/1897 at –; paralysis; housekeeper; widow; b. I. Oldtown

Stephen, d. 12/23/1889 at 75/5/26; Bright's disease; farmer; b. Farmington; Stephen French (Farmington) and Mary Pinkham (Dover)

Sylvester L., d. 1/25/1899 at 55/2/29; heart failure; shoemaker; widower; Charles French (Farmington) and Betsey Bunker

**FRYE,**

Eben, d. 5/2/1901 at 55/7; right pneumonia; carpenter; married; b. Eliot, ME; Topias Frye (Eliot, ME) and Mary J. Frye (Eliot, ME)

**FULLER,**

Ella A., d. 12/16/1928 at 76/0/23; housekeeper; widow; b. Farmington; Joseph Wiggin and Pelina Welch

George O., d. 12/10/1898 at 45/5/9; paralysis; blacksmith; married; b. Farmington; William Fuller

Henry T., d. 1/30/1924 at 60

Lulla M., d. 3/23/1897 at 66/3/7; heart failure; housewife; married; b. Rochester; Loraine Corson (Rochester)

William W., d. 5/8/1900 at 75/2; cerebral hemorrhage; shoemaker; widower; Asa Fuller and Dorothy Houghton

**FULLERTON,**

Charles E., d. 12/29/1936 at 85/11/5; shoeworker; widower; b. Wolfeboro; Andrew Fullerton (Wolfeboro) and Mary Getchell (Wolfeboro)

Emma C., d. 9/1/1931 at 74/9/26; housewife; married; b. Alton

**FULTON,**
James, d. 1/15/1937 at 51; shoeworker; widower; b. NS; Danforth Fulton (NS) and Catherine Hingley (NS)

**FURBER,**
Addie F., d. 10/22/1918 at 34/7/5; shoeworker; married; b. Alton; Alonzo S. Brooks (Alton) and Abbie G. Hurd (Alton)

Emerson, d. 7/2/1895 at 78/6/10; valv. dis. of heart; farmer; married; b. Farmington; Samuel Furber (Farmington) and Annie Leighton (Farmington)

Frank A., d. 12/10/1911 at 56/4/16; pneumonia; single; b. Farmington; Emerson Furber (Farmington, farmer) and Mary Young (Farmington)

George E., d. 5/12/1937 at 75/9; retired; married; b. Alton; Benjamin F. Furber (Alton) and Sarah Babb (Dover)

John, d. 6/27/1926 at 32/4/1; shoeworker; married; b. Alton; George Furber (Alton) and Ada Nutter (Barnstead)

Mary, d. 11/9/1901 at 87/7; cer. soft. and age; widow; b. Strafford; Benjamin Young (Alfred) and M. Montgomery (Strafford)

**GAGNON,**
Adolphus, d. 4/13/1934 at 72/7/27; watchmaker; b. Canada; Pierre Gagnon (Canada) and Marie Mercelle (Canada)

**GARLAND,**
son, d. 7/31/1904 at –; stillborn; b. Farmington; William P. Garland (Farmington) and Lona B. Gray (Farmington)

son, d. 7/11/1933 at –; Robert Garland (Rochester) and Annie Tarbox (Rochester)

daughter, d. 7/25/1934 at –; b. Farmington; Robert Garland (Rochester) and Annie Tarbox (Rochester)

Albert, d. 7/1/1912 at 60/10/26; cerebral hemorrhage; dentist; married; Isaac Garland (Barnstead, farmer) and Mary Rollins (Barnstead)

Ann A., d. 12/25/1921 at 84/3/21; housekeeper; widow; b. New Durham; Luther Pinkham

Charles L., d. 7/30/1910 at 58/7/16; sun stroke; laborer; married; b. Farmington; Sherebiah Garland (Rochester) and Eliza J. Hopkins (MA)

Darius E., d. 9/9/1910 at 75/2/28; mitral insufficiency; farmer; widower; b. Alton; Thomas Garland

Edna C., d. 2/2/1927 at 55/1/1; accountant; widow; b. Wolfeboro; John Chesley (New Durham) and Lydia Ward (Cochituate, MA)

Eleza J., d. 1/27/1919 at 88/4/22; retired; widow; b. Portsmouth; Elihu Hopkins and Eleza Smith

Eli, d. 6/7/1917 at 49/9/24; shoeworker; married; b. Alton; Eli Garland (Alton) and Susan Corson (Alton)

Ephraim, d. 12/25/1891 at 60/0/6; la grippe; farmer; widower; b. Farmington; John Garland

Fannie, d. 9/5/1906 at 1/1/27; entiro-colitis; b. Farmington; Eli Garland (Alton) and Fannie A. Kimball (Wolfeboro)

Frank R., d. 1/1/1920 at 47/6/12; single; b. Rochester; Sherebiah Garland (Rochester) and Eliza J. Hopkins (Portsmouth)

George A., d. 10/15/1922 at 72/0/10; shoeworker; married; b. Lowell, MA; George W. Garland and Joanna Moody

Hannah, d. 2/5/1888 at 82/7/4; apoplexy; b. Rochester

Ida F., d. 5/15/1938 at 86/3/14; housekeeper; widow; b. Gonic; William Babb (Gonic) and Sophia Locke

Joan, d. 2/15/1903 at 82/10/27; old age; retired; widow; Joseph Moody (Wolfeboro) and Joanna Meecham (Ossipee)

John F., d. 6/3/1925 at 90; farmer; single; b. Great Falls; Jacob Garland (Sanford, ME) and Mary Downing (Rochester)

John W., d. 12/14/1938 at 69/4/29; laborer; married; b. Alton; Eli Garland (Alton) and Mary J. Corson (Alton)

Lester E., d. 1/29/1930 at 53/9/14; shoeworker; b. Alton; Eli Garland and Mary J. Corson

Llewellyn D., d. 6/18/1929 at 72/1/3 in Milton; farmer; married; b. Farmington; J. Dudley Garland and Ann A. Pinkham

Lloyd E., d. 10/20/1903 at 0/3/20; convulsion; William P. Garland (Farmington) and Luna B. Gray (Farmington)

Mary A., d. 8/24/1895 at 83; housewife; widow

Mary E., d. 10/22/1927 at 70/4; housekeeper; widow; b. Rochester; John Sullivan and Mary Miles

Mildred M., d. 1/11/1930 at 0/2/12; b. Rochester; Wilfred E. Garland (Farmington) and Lillian Gray (Portsmouth)

Nathaniel, d. 2/2/1894 at 85/1 in Rochester; cerebral embolism; farmer; married; Tristram Garland and Elizabeth Garland

Norman C., d. 4/9/1899 at 1/1/11; bronchitis; b. Farmington; Joseph W. Garland (Rye) and Edna Chesley (Wolfeboro)

Sherebiah, d. 8/6/1906 at 85/1/0; old age; farmer; married; b. Rochester; Richard R. Garland and Mary Hurd (Rochester)

Wilfred, Jr., d. 7/16/1928 at 0/1/13; b. Farmington; Wilfred E. Garland

William L., d. 1/5/1908 at 72/9/8; pneumonia; widower; b. Farmington; John P. Garland (Barrington)

## GARNETT,

Stephen C. F., d. 4/30/1930 at 85/9/9 in Rochester; widower; b. Pembroke, ME; Joseph Garnett (Pembroke, ME)

## GARY,

Newman A., d. 4/12/1903 at 43/7/13; delirium tremens; grocer; married; Samuel Garey (Waterboro, ME) and Shuah Foss (Scarboro, ME)

## GEARY,

Susan J., d. 2/28/1933 at 79/0/2 in Milton; shoeworker; widow; b. Milton; Henry Amazeen (New Castle) and Abigail Wentworth (Milton)

## GERRISH,

Carrie L., d. 2/7/1930 at 73/8/15 in Brockton, MA; at home; married b. Union; Daniel Willey (NH)

Elisha P., d. 4/4/1913 at 77/6/17; cerebral softening; laborer; married; b. W. Lebanon; Nathaniel Gerrish (W. Lebanon, ME, farmer) and Fannie Willett (Gloucester)

## GILBERT,

Darrel, d. 4/4/1915 at 2/8; b. Milton; Daniel Gilbert (Farmington) and Ida M. Duntley (Milton)

John I., d. 7/3/1916 at 14/6/20; student; single; b. Milton; Daniel Gilbert (Farmington) and Ida M. Duntley (Farmington)

## GILES,

Amanda J., d. 2/7/1917 at 62/1/14; housewife; married; b. Alton; James W. Kimball (Alton) and Nancy Locke (Barnstead)

Clara S., d. 1/22/1925 at 85/9/23; housekeeper; widow; b. Epsom; George Grant

George S., d. 1/29/1908 at 67/8/17; chr. nephritis; single; Orrin P. Giles (Shapleigh, ME) and Alzire Emery

Perley C., d. 2/21/1915 at 81/9/30; farmer; married; b. Deerfield; Benjamin Giles and Lucinda Hoyt

**GILKERSON,**
Helen, d. 4/18/1906 at 4/0/20; scarlet fever; b. Alton; Harry N. Gilkerson (Stannard, VT) and Celia M. Flint (New Durham)

**GILMAN,**
Amanda M., d. 10/26/1902 at 66/1/8; cerebral apoplexy; widow; b. Danvers; Nathan R. Cross (Danvers) and Elizabeth Batchelder (Danvers)

Annie M., d. 8/2/1930 at 70/5/26; housewife; married; b. Farmington; Frank Avery and Annie Place

David, d. 3/28/1893 at 50/2/17; consumption; farmer; single; b. Farmington; Moses Gilman (Gilmanton) and Rhoda Gilman (Alton)

Ella A., d. 5/18/1935 at 81/7/22; retired; single; b. Alton; Manoah Gilman (Alton) and Mercy Grant (Gilford)

Etta M., d. 1/3/1897 at –; stillborn; b. Farmington; Warren E. Gilman (Kingston) and Maud A. Clark (St. Johns)

Frank I., d. 5/3/1938 at 69/4/26; painter; married; b. Farmington; Winslow Gilman (Tamworth) and L. Wentworth (Farmington)

Fred W., d. 7/2/1937 at 78/3/8; retired; married; b. Salisbury, MA; Samuel E. Gilman (Anson, ME) and Lucy Moodey

Helen W., d. 5/29/1930 at 38 in Windham, ME; housewife; married; b. Farmington; Albert E. Carter (ME) and Kate Dame (NH)

Jean F., d. 12/4/1918 at 46/3/7; housewife; married; b. Scotland; David Armstrong (Ireland) and Jean McMellen (Scotland)

Samuel E., d. 4/6/1932 at 97/6/29; farmer; widower; b. Anson, ME; Samuel Gilman (Anson, ME) and Mary Pike (Salisbury, MA)

Warren L., d. 9/13/1936 at 85/3/7; retired; widower; b. Alton; M. G. W. Gilman (Alton) and Mercy Grant (Gilford)

William, d. 1/25/1907 at 84/8/3; old age; married; b. Hallowell, ME; Moses B. Gilman (Gilmanton) and Nancy Brannard (Winthrop, MA)

Winslow H., d. 6/7/1900 at 64/5/21; pneumonia; shoecutter; married; b. Farmington; Josiah Gilman (Tamworth) and Abigail Hopgood (Tamworth)

**GILMORE,**
George A., d. 4/28/1887 at 65/10/14; trader; married

Jessie B., d. 9/14/1889 at 0/8/4; cholera infantum; b. Farmington; Frank S. Gilmore (Milton) and Mary J. Robinson (Farmington)

**GILMOUR,**
Walter P., d. 2/26/1919 at 26/3/4; bookkeeper; single; b. NS; William Gilmour (NS) and Priscilla Brown (NS)

**GILSON,**
Alice S., d. 10/12/1931 at 63/4/22 in Milton; widow; b. Farmington; James Downing (Farmington) and Addie Smith (Rochester)

Clara A., d. 8/31/1911 at 58/0/7; cerebral hemorrhage; housewife; married; b. Alton; Lewis F. Jones (New Durham, farmer) and Betsey Edgerly (New Durham)

Franklin, d. 11/11/1920 at 76/9/23; RR emp.; widower; b. Kittery, ME; Levi Gilson (Portland, ME) and Martha Perkins (Kittery, ME)

Josiah P., d. 3/17/1909 at 71/10/15; senile gangrene; b. Portland, ME; Levi Gilson (Belfast, ME) and Martha A. Perkins (Kittery, ME)

Levi H., d. 1/25/1929 at 79/3/17; shoecutter; married; b. Kittery, ME; Levi Gilson and Martha Perkins

**GLIDDEN,**
son, d. 8/2/1937 at –; b. Farmington; Ormand Glidden (Alton) and Elsie M. Fifield (Conway)

son, d. 8/2/1937 at –; b. Farmington; Ormand Glidden (Alton) and Elsie M. Fifield (Conway)

Augustus, d. 2/12/1903 at 47/8/3; tuberculosis; shoemaker; married; Levi Glidden (Effingham) and Levona Dore (Alton)

Dolly C., d. 5/25/1918 at 95; widow

Emma L., d. 6/3/1899 at 5/5/21; convulsions; b. Farmington; Ira W. Glidden (Parsonsfield, ME) and Nellie A. Watson (Wakefield)

Francis A., d. 3/11/1904 at 41/3/29; cancer; housewife; married; b. Farmington; Joshua Tibbetts (Farmington) and Mary Wentworth (Milton)

George W., d. 5/25/1923 at 29/2/2; farmer; married; b. Farmington; Herbert Glidden (Rochester) and Louise Wyatt (Farmington)

Hattie J., d. 1/11/1897 at 39/6/2; consumption; housekeeper; married; b. Farmington; Samuel Horne (Middleton) and Margaret Horne (Farmington)

Herbert G., d. 10/16/1936 at 82/6/19; shoeworker; single; b. Farmington; Isaac Glidden (Gilford) and Dolly Carter (Wellington)

Ira W., d. 1/30/1921 at 58/3/16; expressman; married; b. Parsonsfield, ME; Addison Glidden (Effingham) and Comfort Marston (Parsonsfield, ME)

Lila B., d. 6/10/1932 at 53/2/25 in Rochester; housewife; married; b. New Durham; Charles A. Randall (New Durham) and Martha J. Woodman (New Durham)

Marjorie, d. 4/1/1925 at 9/10/26; b. New Durham; Sidney Glidden (Farmington) and Alice F. Glidden (New Durham)

Mary I., d. 5/18/1926 at 80/0/11; housewife; married; b. New Durham; William H. Corson (New Durham) and Drusilla Jones (Middleton)

Winnifred, d. 9/20/1915 at 26/1/24; laborer; single; b. New Durham; John F. Glidden (Ashland) and Eldora B. Browne (Alton)

**GLIENICKI,**
M. Z., d. 7/22/1928 at 26

**GLINES,**
Hiram F., d. 6/22/1919 at 81/10/16

**GOOCH,**
John M., d. 2/22/1923 at 89/6/17; farmer; married; b. Alton; Joseph Gooch and Nancy N. Davis (Lee)

Sarah M., d. 6/27/1923 at 79; housewife; married; b. Steubenville, OH; T. W. Hearn (NH)

**GOODALL,**
Mark D., d. 1/9/1897 at 62; accident; farming; married; b. Farmington; Joseph Goodall (VT) and Margaret Horne (Farmington)

**GOODWIN,**
Elizabeth E., d. 11/15/1930 at 79/7/6; widow; b. Alton; Jonathan Sleeper (Alton) and Harriett Howe (New Boston)

Emily, d. 9/29/1924 at 72/0/13; single

Hannah, d. 3/4/1920 at 84/4/7; married; b. St. Johns, NB; David Comancher and Nancy Smith

Inez, d. 9/24/1933 at 55/3/16; housewife; married; b. Alton; Joseph B. Ham (Alton) and Christina Flanders (Gilmanton)

John F., d. 10/23/1934 at 69/3/21 in Rochester; shoeworker; widower; b. York, ME; Charles E. Goodwin (York, ME) and Mary J. Baston (S. Berwick, ME)

Lavina, d. 11/9/1904 at 67/5/3; shock; housekeeper; widow; b. Lebanon, ME; Stephen Wallingford (Lebanon, ME) and Mercy Wallingford (Lebanon, ME)

Lucy M., d. 2/17/1912 at 56/8/5; rectal cancer; housekeeper; married; b. Nottingham; John D. Furber (Newmarket, farmer) and L. T. Batchelder (N. Hampton)

Susan C., d. 8/9/1921 at 56/3; housekeeper; married; b. VT; ----- Smith

**GORDON,**

Alice R., d. 12/17/1937 at 78/3/2; at home; widow; b. Boston, MA; Fred C. Keyser (Bristol) and Elizabeth Lyons (Wolfeboro)

Francenia J., d. 5/1/1933 at 82/7/2; widow; b. New Durham; Lewis R. Sumner

Will H., d. 5/24/1931 at 71/8/19; retired; married; b. Medford, MA; Thomas A. Gordon (New Hampton) and Lucina Griffith (Dixfield, ME)

**GOULD,**

Abbie M., d. 9/3/1920 at 72/0/22; housekeeper; married; b. Alton; Jacob Glidden (Alton) and Lydia Hayes (Alton)

George D., d. 11/5/1928 at 69/5/21; minister; married; b. New Hudson, NY; Downing Gould and Keziah Guilford

**GRACE,**

Adelaide A., d. 4/15/1933 at 68/1/8; housewife; married; b. Middleton; John W. Horne (Middleton) and Sarah Garland (Middleton)

Benjamin, d. 7/5/1914 at 79/6/27; arteriosclerosis; married; b. New Durham; John Grace (Kittery, ME, farmer) and Deborah Willey (New Durham)

Betsey M., d. 8/10/1892 at 75/4/12; paralytic cerebral congestion; housewife; married; Stephen Davis (farmer) and Nancy Bickford

Lydia A., d. 4/8/1930 at 90/3/23; housekeeper; widow; b. Middleton; Samuel Frost and Adeline Horne

**GRAMOR,**
George W., d. 7/10/1916 at 21/10/24; shoeworker; single; b. Albania

**GRANFIEL,**
Robert C., d. 11/15/1934 at 76; retired; divorced; b. Montpelier, VT

**GRANVILLE,**
Mary M., d. 7/29/1930 at 95/10/20; widow; b. Effingham; Jacob Tuttle and Martha Brackett

**GRAY,**
Addie B., d. 6/6/1912 at 0/8/19; interitis; b. E. Rochester; Herbert J. Gray (Dover, laborer) and Dasie Emery

Addie E., d. 2/17/1893 at 24/9; tuberculosis; housewife; married; b. Pittsfield; James W. Pillsbury (Pittsfield) and Lizzie Keniston (Pittsfield)

Carrie O., d. 10/7/1894 at 41/4/27; consumption; housekeeper; widow; b. Dover; Richard D. Cater (Barrington) and Mahala Hayes (Dover)

Charles O., d. 2/25/1932 at 71/6/25; laborer; married; b. Strafford; Simon Gray and Lovey S. Jones

Cora E., d. 11/27/1891 at 32/1/12; hemorrhage of liver; housekeeper; married; b. Strafford; Mark F. Foss (Strafford) and Livonia Berry (Durham)

Diantha V., d. 11/3/1934 at 93/8/24; at home; widow; b. Alton; George Chamberlin (Alton) and Keziah Jenkins (New Durham)

Eliza J., d. 9/5/1910 at 80/7/7; fracture of hip; divorced; b. Farmington; James Gray (Farmington) and Annie Whitehouse (Farmington)

Ethel May, d. 2/3/1921 at 0/0/3; b. Farmington; Arthur Gray (Farmington) and Lillian Green (Alton)

Fred O., d. 9/26/1894 at 18; pneumonia; laborer; single; b. Barrington; Orin W. Gray (Barrington) and Carrie O. Cater (Dover)

George H., d. 4/23/1927 at 66/3/23; shoeworker; married; b. Alexandria; Stephen Gray and Ellen Seavey

Ina M., d. 7/29/1936 at 76/0/7; at home; widow; b. Milton; Henry Downs and Elizabeth Drew

Jerry L., d. 2/16/1912 at 73/11/6; angina pectoris; farmer; married; b. Strafford; Jethro L. Gray (Strafford, farmer) and Lucretia ----

Mary C., d. 10/8/1896 at --/4/15; cancer of breast; housewife; married; b. Farmington; Joseph B. Varney (Farmington) and Rebekah Fenr (Milton)

Mary E., d. 7/4/1924 at 73/10/23; housekeeper; widow; b. Portland, ME; James Berry (Buxton, ME) and Eliza Emery (Parsonsfield, ME)

Mary T., d. 4/3/1906 at 94/5/16; angina pectoris; housewife; widow; b. Alton; Jeremy Edgerly and Betsey Leighton

Myra C., d. 7/15/1938 at 79/10/29; housewife; widow; b. Marlow; Charles Elliott (Mason) and Anna Royce (Alstead)

Orin W., d. 9/18/1894 at 49/7/15; acute uraemia; worked in mill; married; b. Barrington; Joseph Gray (Barrington) and Susan Gray (Barrington)

Otis M., d. 9/24/1907 at 81/11/20; angina pectoris; carpenter; married; b. Strafford; Harry Gray (Barrington, farmer) and Dorothy Otis (Rye)

Patience K., d. 3/28/1912 at 71/8/20; pneumonia; housekeeper; married; b. Farmington; Otis Scruton (Farmington, farmer) and Mary Rogers (Acton, ME)

Robert A., d. 4/8/1932 at 1/2/19; b. Farmington; Everett L. Gray (Gorham) and Sadie Dewhurst (Newport)

Roland G., d. 3/28/1923 at 0/8/8; b. Farmington; George R. Gray (Grafton) and Elsie M. H. Berry (Farmington)

Samuel N., d. 3/4/1913 at 79/5/6; apoplexy; farmer; married; b. Farmington; James Gray (Farmington, farmer) and Annie Whitehouse (Farmington)

Samuel V., d. 11/12/1929 at 85/7/7 in Rochester; retired; married; b. Strafford; Simon Gray (Strafford) and Lovey Jones (Strafford)

Sarah E., d. 12/27/1914 at 78/8/22; diabetes; widow; b. Strafford; John Blake (painter) and Betsey Cornell

Sarah F., d. 6/23/1935 at 84/4/16; at home; widow; b. Orange; Jefferson Pierce and ----- Martin

Warren A., d. 7/10/1923 at 1/3/2; b. Grafton; Clifton W. Gray (New Durham) and Dora L. Bliss (Hooksett)

William A., d. 2/1/1928 at 81/10/20; retired; married; b. Alexandria; Samuel Gray and Mary Edgerly

**GREENE,**
Alexis C., d. 8/13/1932 at 71/1/26; retired; married; b. Skowhegan, ME; Witter Greene (Starks, ME) and Mary Quimby (Starks, ME)

**GRENIER,**
son, d. 9/13/1927 at –; b. Rochester; Alfred Grenier (Rochester) and Marian Hanson (Farmington)
Maude, d. 5/31/1923 at 36/11/12; housewife; married; b. Farmington; Arista Horne (Middleton) and Clara Parker (Farmington)

**GUILMET,**
Napoleon, d. 7/19/1934 at 70/9/19 in Methuen, MA; lumber dlr.; married; b. Canada; Pierre Guilmet (Canada) and Eulalie Aulie (Canada)

**GUISTINA,**
Daniel, d. 2/27/1922 at 0/0/9; b. Farmington; Daniel Guistina (Italy) and Pierina Pinbert (Italy)

**GUPTILL,**
Alvaro, d. 3/3/1935 at 82/11/8; retired; married; b. Lebanon, ME; Benjamin Guptill and Lydia A. Pray
Benjamin H., d. 12/14/1899 at 70/1/20; uraemia; shoemaker; married; b. Lebanon, ME; Moses Guptill (Newfield, ME) and Tamson Hodgdon (Ossipee)
Everett B., d. 2/23/1923 at 65/0/22; shoemaker; married; b. Lebanon, ME; Benjamin Guptill (Boston) and Lydia Evans (Lebanon, ME)

**HAAS,**
Elizabeth G., d. 9/17/1930 at 77/6/20; domestic; widow; b. Mt. Pleasant Mills, PA; Samuel Gosling (PA) and Carrie Haas (PA)

**HACKETT,**
Ira E., d. 1/7/1907 at 0/1/7; bronchitis; b. Farmington; Westley Hackett (Danvers, MA, RR section hand) and Gertrude Evans (Alton)
Olive J., d. 3/11/1933 at 89/8/18; widow; b. Pittsfield; Orin Marston (Pittsfield)

Raymond, d. 1/26/1916 at 18/0/16; student; single; b. Farmington; Wesley Hackett (Danvers, MA) and Gertrude Evans (Alton)

Selina, d. 1/7/1900 at 0/0/1; anaemia; b. Farmington; Wesley Hackett (Danvers) and Gertie N. Evans (Alton)

William R., d. 4/4/1926 at 83/0/22; laborer; married; b. Sandwich; William Hackett

**HADDOCK,**

Luella, d. 7/17/1926 at 63/0/7; housewife; married; b. Middleton; Timothy Tibbetts (Farmington) and Melvina Colbath (Middleton)

**HADLEY,**

Abby C., d. 7/28/1889 at 43/4/19; typhoid fever; housekeeper; b. Middleton; John Ricker (Somersworth) and Mary A. Garland (Middleton)

**HAGERTY,**

Mary, d. 1/16/1888 at 47/0/22; pul. phthisis; housekeeper; married; b. NS; John Cameron (Scotland) and Mary Frazier (Scotland)

Mary C., d. 1/7/1888 at 13/6; consumption of bowels; b. Weymouth, MA; Michael Hagerty (Ireland) and Mary Cameron (NS)

**HAGGETT,**

Mary E. J., d. 6/25/1893 at 73/11; cardiac dropsy; lady; widow; b. Farmington; Josiah Merrow (Farmington) and Nancy Hodgdon (Farmington)

**HAIGH,**

Jeffery G., d. 12/16/1922 at 67/0/11; clergyman; married; b. Canterbury, England

**HAINES,**

Charles N., d. 2/7/1888 at 47/1/11; Bright's disease; carpenter; married; b. Parsonsfield, ME; Simon Haines (Waterboro, ME) and Hannah Taylor (Effingham)

Harriot P., d. 7/11/1917 at 100/5/28; teacher; single; b. Canterbury; Abner Haines (Canterbury) and Elizabeth Ayers (Canterbury)

**HALE,**

Elinor R., d. 4/11/1890 at 67/7/7; consumption; housekeeper; married; b. Livermore, ME; James Ames (Lewiston, ME) and Margaret Randall (Lewiston, ME)

Merton H., d. 3/21/1936 at 39/1/15 in Boston, MA; laborer; married; b. New Durham; Edgar Hale and Ida M. Rhines (Rochester)

**HALEY,**

Lucy G., d. 3/6/1931 at 67/9/21; housewife; married; b. Rochester; Alvah Guptill (Cornish, ME) and Lydia A. Furlong (Limerick, ME)

**HALL,**

Asa A., d. 5/30/1923 at 93/4/8; carpenter; widower; b. Strafford; ----- Hall (MA) and ----- Demeritt (MA)

Emma F., d. 8/20/1924 at 72/4/29; housewife; widow; b. Boston, MA; Ivory Jones and Nancy Hutchins (Pembroke)

Fannie D., d. 3/5/1915 at 48/5/20; housekeeper; married; b. New Castle; Ralph Davidson (New London, CT) and Lucretia Harris (New London, CT)

Hannah J., d. 4/7/1898 at 77/0/20; pneumonia; widow; b. New Durham; Henry Gray (Barrington) and Dorothy Otis (Barrington)

John F., d. 6/10/1904 at 52/6/13; softening of brain; merchant; married; b. Barnstead; George Hall (Barnstead) and Sally Drew (Alton)

Maria A., d. 1/18/1900 at 68/3/27; gastritis; housewife; married; b. New Durham; Ephraim Stanton (Strafford) and Abigail Hayes (Barnstead)

Orin, d. 7/28/1896 at 69/3/19; apoplexy; farmer; widower; b. Strafford; Israel Hall (Strafford) and Mary Sanders (Strafford)

Solomon H., d. 5/22/1900 at 55/9/9; d. b. pneumonia; farmer; married; b. Farmington; Stacy Hall (Barnstead) and Hannah Gray (Strafford)

Stacy, d. 3/18/1894 at 81/2/18; gangrene; married; b. Barrington; Solomon Hall and Lydia Scruton

**HAM,**

son, d. 12/19/1899 at 0/0/4; hemorrhage of bowels; b. Farmington; Clarence Ham (Farmington) and Mary E. Peavey (Tuftonboro)

Addie Belle, d. 9/25/1897 at 24/10/5; consumption; housekeeper; married; b. Farmington; Daniel Burrows (Middleton) and Belle French (Farmington)

Blanche E., d. 7/29/1908 at 19/10/19; tuberculosis; single; b. Farmington; Irving L. Ham (Farmington) and C. E. Wentworth (Farmington)

Carrie N., d. 8/8/1906 at 46/5/27; heart disease; divorced; b. New Durham; Benjamin Savage and Abigail Ham (New Durham)

Clara E., d. 5/28/1902 at 46/1/19; anaemia; housewife; married; b. Farmington; Alexander T. Randall (Bolton, Canada) and Adeli R. Cook (Milton)

Clarence M., d. 5/4/1937 at 79/5/9; laborer; widower; b. Farmington William P. Ham and Hannah Cook

Cyrus A., d. 11/19/1933 at 67/7/11 in Rochester; widower; b. Farmington; Moses Ham (Farmington) and Mary E. Nutter (Barnstead)

Emma F., d. 12/19/1895 at 0/8/4; pneumonia; b. Farmington; Clarence M. Ham (Farmington) and Mary E. Peavey (Tuftonboro)

Frank, d. 12/2/1936 at 76; laborer; widower; b. Farmington; Moses Ham and Elizabeth Nutter

Herbert G., d. 3/2/1913 at 29; burns of 3$^{rd}$ degree; single; b. Farmington; Clarence M. Ham (Farmington, laborer) and Mary E. Peavey (Tuftonboro)

Herman, d. 1/5/1903 at 42; suicide by shooting; shoe finisher; married; Benjamin Ham (Farmington) and Wealthy Hutchins (ME)

James E., d. 4/24/1894 at 0/8/10; pneumonia; b. Farmington; Clarence M. Ham (Farmington) and Mary E. Peavey (Farmington)

James W., d. 4/30/1917 at 58/5/5; mechanic; widower; b. Barrington; David F. Ham (Rochester) and Hannah Varney (Barrington)

Justina, d. 3/19/1898 at 39/11/9; peritonitis; housekeeper; single; b. Dover; Benjamin Ham (Farmington) and Wealthy Hutchins (ME)

Martha E., d. 3/19/1938 at 49/7/7; shoeworker; married; b. Laconia; Caleb Dexter (NS) and Harriet Gault (Gilmanton)

Mary, d. 3/24/1908 at 88/5/4; acute uremia; widow; b. Barnstead; Kaleb Clough (Barnstead) and Sally Clarke (Barnstead)

Mary E., d. 4/6/1930 at 72/4/23; housewife; widow; b. Ossipee; Benjamin F. Peavey (Ossipee) and Abigail Aldrich (Ossipee)

Samuel D., d. 9/11/1897 at 86/10/24; senility; farmer; married; b. Rochester; Nathaniel Ham (Rochester) and Abigail Downing (Middleton)

Samuel D., d. 7/24/1931 at 63/11/25; shoeworker; married; b. N. Berwick, ME; Almira Ham (N. Berwick, ME)

Sarah E., d. 1/8/1935 at 85/11/19; housewife; widow; b. Belgrade, ME; Isaac Willey (New Durham) and Louisa Bickford (Belgrade, ME)

William M., d. 12/19/1934 at 57/11/3; shoeworker; divorced; b. Farmington; Clarence Ham (Farmington) and Mary E. Peavey (Tuftonboro)

William P., d. 5/25/1924 at 86/11/22; shoemaker; widower; b. Farmington; Samuel Ham (Farmington) and Jane Jenness (Wolfeboro)

**HAMMETT,**
Clifton, d. 12/3/1906 at 0/10/12; broncho-pneumonia; b. Lakeport; Peter Hammett (Wheelock, VT) and Emma Boudreau (Bellows Falls)

**HANCOCK,**
Georgia, d. 5/8/1921 at 1/2/18; Frank Hancock (Salem) and Hazel Babb (Farmington)

**HANSCOM,**
Harry S., d. 10/22/1918 at 34/4/16; shoeworker; single; b. Stratham; George S. E. Hanscom and Mary E. Moulton

**HANSEN,**
Clara Ellen, d. 2/15/1931 at 77/10/3 in Brockton, MA; housewife; widow; b. Farmington; ----- Horne (NH) and Nancy Burnham (Farmington)

**HANSON,**
child, d. 4/29/1893 at –; stillborn; b. Farmington; Alvin S. Hanson (Barnstead) and Mary E. Clough (Boston, MA)

Caleb, d. 3/25/1904 at 94/6/4; old age; farmer; married; b. Strafford; Ebenezer Hanson (Strafford) and Abigail Caverno (Lee)

Charles B., d. 1/30/1899 at 61/0/11; consumption; shoemaker; married; b. Rochester; John O. Hanson (Rochester) and Mary Goodwin (Rochester)

Eliza J., d. 12/17/1925 at 76/2/13; housewife; married; b. Essex, NY; Peter R. Kellum and Mary Brown

Fannie B., d. 4/17/1927 at 82; housekeeper; widow; Lewis Jones (New Durham) and Betsey Jones (New Durham)

Frances, d. 5/21/1919 at 66/2/13; widow; b. Somersworth; James Tucker (Salisbury, MA) and Mary E. Hall (Haverhill, MA)

Fred J., d. 1/25/1936 at 79/0/9; heel mfg.; married; b. Dover; Joseph H. Hanson (Dover) and Elizabeth Main (New Durham)

Herbert W., d. 2/4/1896 at 0/8/1; cong. gas. entes.; b. Farmington; Alvin Hanson (S. Barnstead) and Mary Clough (Boston, MA)

Louisa H., d. 4/16/1891 at 73/7; perilenitis; housekeeper; married; b. Strafford; Edward Evans (Strafford) and Dolly Hardy (Strafford)

Nancy, d. 3/6/1903 at 87/10; old age; widow; Jonathan Goodwin (Berwick, ME) and Betsy Andrews (Berwick, ME)

Orin B., d. 6/27/1891 at 42/11/14; apoplexy; physician; single; b. Strafford; Caleb Hanson (Strafford) and Louisa H. Evans (Strafford)

Sidney R., d. 9/29/1922 at 62/7/20; shoeworker; widower; b. Dover; Joseph H. Hanson (Dover) and Sarah E. Main (Farmington)

**HARMON,**

Charles A., d. 4/28/1925 at 70/4/2; shoeworker; widower; b. Limerick, ME; Joseph Harmon (Limerick, ME) and Susan Philpot (Limerick, ME)

Cinda K., d. 9/28/1925 at 67/3/17; housewife; married; b. Effingham; John Granville (Ossipee) and Mary Tuttle (Effingham)

Clara A., d. 10/20/1918 at 69/1/18; housewife; married; b. Farmington; Abram A. Card (New Castle) and Mary Pinkham (Farmington)

John H., d. 10/6/1930 at 72/2/27; retired; widower; b. Limerick, ME; Joseph G. Harmon and Susan Philpot

**HARRIMAN,**

daughter, d. 4/4/1911 at 0/0/1; premature birth; b. Farmington; Charles Harriman (Somersworth, laborer) and Alice M. Ham (Farmington)

Cyrus L., d. 4/15/1938 at 65/0/7; shoeworker; married; b. Eaton; Cyrus Harriman and Lavisa Glidden

**HARRINGTON,**
Ethel M., d. 7/5/1895 at 18/9/5; peritonitis; student; single; b. Hillsdale, MI; John S. Harrington (Zorra, ON) and Elb'n A. Bingham (Zorra, ON)

**HARRISON,**
Cora B., d. 12/3/1927 at 63/5/15

**HART,**
Delta C., d. 3/27/1926 at 64/4/24; shoe foreman; married; b. Milton; John F. Hart (Milton) and May A. Twombly (Milton)
Mattie J., d. 3/22/1922 at 54/3/20; housewife; married; b. Middleton; Jonathan Stevens and Sarah J. Garland (Union)

**HARTFIEL,**
Ellen, d. 4/14/1907 at 0/2/7; debility; b. Farmington; Roy Hartfiel (Dalton, KY, shoemaker) and Ruth Tufts (Middleton)
Ray, d. 12/6/1913 at 34/8/6; tuberculosis; shoemaker; married; b. Dayton, KY; Paul Hartfield and Mary Hartfiel

**HARTFORD,**
daughter, d. 9/20/1933 at 0/0/1; b. Farmington; Harold Hartford (East Rochester) and Eva M. Hughes (Barrington)
Annie M., d. 9/28/1933 at 0/0/8; b. Dover; Harold Hartford (East Rochester) and Eva M. Hughes (Barrington)
Carrie S., d. 10/15/1897 at 19/11/25; consumption; housekeeper; widow; b. Barrington; Orin Gray (Barrington) and Carrie Cator (Barrington)
Edwin L., d. 9/26/1897 at 30/3; cirrhosis of liver; shoemaker; married; b. Dover; George Hartford (Rochester) and Julia Palmer (Rochester)
Julia A., d. 3/17/1893 at 64/2; pneumonia; housekeeper; married; b. Effingham; Chris Palmer and Patience Hersom
Leroy L., d. 1/8/1897 at 2/0/5; pneumonia; b. Farmington; Edwin L. Hartford (Dover) and Carrie S. Gray
Maria, d. 12/26/1933 at 81/10/29; at home; widow; b. Middleton; George W. Downing (Middleton) and Carolyn Colbath (Middleton)

Nelson, d. 4/18/1921 at 71/6/17; laborer; married; b. Conway; Benjamin Hartford (Conway) and ----- Kelley (Conway)

**HARTWELL,**
Edith H., d. 7/4/1931 at 82/9/23; widow; b. Blue Hill, ME; Daniel B. Allen (Blue Hill, ME) and Mary E. Allen (Blue Hill, ME)
Isaac, d. 1/17/1929 at 66 in Concord; clerk; single; b. MA; Charles Hartwell (MA) and Rosina Packard (MA)

**HATCH,**
George A., d. 2/25/1924 at 80/10/1; shoemaker; married; b. N. Berwick, ME; Elijah Hatch and Eliza Harrison

**HAWKES,**
Philip L., d. 3/15/1890 at 39/11/10; pneumonia; shoemaker; married; b. Danvers, MA; Timothy Hawkes (Salem, MA) and Mary A. Smith

**HAYES,**
Abbie M., d. 1/6/1903 at 80/4/2; old age; retired; widow; Thomas Robbinson (Brentwood)
Ann F., d. 11/12/1889 at 73/11/18; heart disease; housekeeper; b. Farmington; Josiah Edgerly (Farmington) and Mary Tash (Madbury)
Augustus, d. 7/20/1901 at 70; apoplexy; farmer; single; b. Somersworth
Augustus, d. 12/18/1926 at 71/9/3; knife mfgr.; married; b. Alton; Samuel Hayes and Mary Whitehouse
Charles F., d. 3/6/1901 at 30/7/10; pneumonia; laborer; married; b. Alton; Charles P. Hayes (ME) and Ellen F. Dicey (Alton)
Charles H., d. 2/14/1899 at 63/8/20; pneumonia; farmer; married; b. Farmington; Aaron Hayes (Farmington) and Mary Rand (Farmington)
E. Pauline, d. 2/15/1932 at 23/1/20; bookkeeper; single; b. Farmington; William T. Hayes (Farmington) and Inez Roberts (Rochester)
E. Winslow, d. 12/4/1919 at 71/5/16; shoe mfg.; married; b. Farmington; Israel Hayes (Milton) and Ann F. Edgerly (Farmington)
Emma J., d. 1/16/1929 at 77/6/26 in New Durham; housewife; widow; b. Tuftonboro; Isaac Laurens

Eugene B., d. 10/26/1933 at 59/5/17; retired; married; b. Farmington; James E. Hayes (Farmington) and Mary E. Peavey (Farmington)

Eva B., d. 2/19/1905 at 27/0/21; meningitis; married; b. Barnstead; Samuel D. Caswell (Barnstead) and Laura A. Caswell (Barnstead)

Ezekiel C., d. 10/25/1906 at 74/0/16; arteriosclerosis; farmer; widower; b. Farmington; Daniel Hayes (Farmington) and Betsey Rundlett

F. P., d. 1/14/1900 at 48/10/11; pneumonia; hotel keeper; married; b. Alton; Samuel Hayes (New Durham) and Mary Whitehouse (Middleton)

Fannie E., d. 8/22/1914 at 55/3/13; carcinoma of uterus; stitcher; divorced; b. New Durham; Frank I. Hayes (New Durham, farmer) and Rebecca Gooch (Alton)

Fannie H., d. 5/8/1911 at 33/1/8; tuberculosis; shoeworker; single; b. Somersworth; Charles C. Hayes (Farmington) and Etta L. Jones (Somersworth)

Festus V., d. 10/16/1903 at 62; chronic nephritis; farmer; married; Ira Hayes and Mary Varney

Frank C., d. 4/11/1924 at 67/10/27

George L., d. 3/2/1934 at 70/2/25 in New Durham; retired; widower; b. Alton; Samuel Hayes (New Durham) and Mary Whitehouse (Middleton)

Georgia H., d. 8/17/1929 at 75/3/13; housekeeper; widow; b. Farmington; Freeman P. Howe (Farmington) and Adeline M. Roberts (Farmington)

Gertrude M., d. 10/10/1895 at 17/1/10; peritonitis; housewife; single; b. Belgrade, ME; George I. Hayes (New Durham) and Eva E. Goodwin (Belgrade, ME)

Harry I., d. 10/31/1936 at 57/11/20; laborer; widower; b. New Durham; Benjamin Randall (New Durham) and Fannie E. Hayes (New Durham)

Herbert E., d. 8/31/1927 at 61/2/24; brushmaker; single; b. New Durham; Nehemiah Hayes (New Durham) and Martha A. Durgin (New Durham)

Ira C., d. 4/13/1908 at 40/3/3; dilation of heart; machinist; married; b. New Durham; Franklin Hayes (Rochester) and Augusta Willey (New Durham)

Ira V., d. 10/8/1888 at 71/8; farmer; b. Farmington; Levi Hayes (Barrington) and Rhoda Hayes (Dover)

Iris Ella, d. 4/26/1911 at 0/1/10; enteritis; b. Farmington; Arthur G. Hayes (New Durham, shoeworker) and Ethel M. Brooks (Farmington)

Isaiah, d. 3/23/1888 at 85/2/2; erysipelas; farmer; widower; b. Farmington; Daniel Hayes (Farmington) and Olive French (Farmington)

Israel, d. 3/27/1898 at 81/10/16; senectus; shoe manufacturer; married; b. Milton; Ichabod Hayes (Madbury) and Sally Card (New Castle, ME)

James E., d. 3/22/1920 at 78/11/9; farmer; married; b. Farmington; Richard R. Hayes (Farmington) and Martha Edgerly (Farmington)

John R., d. 3/29/1912 at 31/6/23; cancer of liver; machinist; married; b. Farmington; James E. Hayes (Farmington, farmer) and Mary E. Peavey (Farmington)

Jonathan, d. 11/23/1911 at 86/9/6; senility; shoe mfgr.; single; b. Farmington; Daniel Hayes (Farmington, farmer) and Betsy Raulett (Farmington)

Levi F., d. 1/28/1898 at 52/9; seb. of blood vessels; shoe worker; married; b. S. Berwick, ME; Isaiah Hayes (Farmington) and Mary H. Rollins (Alton)

Lizzie M., d. 11/3/1922 at 67/7/26; housewife; married; b. Milton; Er Perkins (Alton) and Mary ----- (Wolfeboro)

Lydia H., d. 1/8/1892 at 56/0/20; heart disease; housewife; married; b. New Castle; W. M. Tarlton (New Castle, ship carpenter) and Hannah Twombly (New Castle)

Marion E., d. 4/7/1926 at 19/11/10; at home; single; b. Farmington; Arthur G. Hayes (New Durham) and Ethel Brooks (Farmington)

Mary A. P., d. 7/5/1898 at 76/11/28; old age; housekeeper; widow; b. Middleton; Amos Whitehouse (Middleton) and Abigail Cotton (Wolfeboro)

Mary E., d. 12/2/1894 at 81/7/4; heart disease; widow; b. Farmington; E. Rand (Farmington) and Sarah Thompson (Farmington)

Mary E., d. 10/12/1933 at 81/4/6; housekeeper; widow; b. Farmington; John Peavey (Farmington) and Emily Furber (Farmington)

Myra A., d. 5/22/1910 at 54/8/26; cancer of breast; shoeworker; divorced; b. Garland, ME; Harrison Knight and Ann Lougee (Sanbornville)

Nehemiah B., d. 3/19/1910 at 67/4/13; influenza; shoemaker; married; b. New Durham; Samuel Hayes (New Durham) and Mary Whitehouse (Middleton)

Rebecca P., d. 3/9/1915 at 87/8/11; widow; b. Alton; Joseph Gooch and Mary -----

Richard R., d. 4/4/1889 at 77/1/14; heart disease and pneumonia; farmer; b. Farmington; Daniel Hayes (Farmington) and Betsy Randlett (Farmington)

Sarah M., d. 4/26/1896 at 75/10/26; heart failure; single; b. Barrington; John Hayes (Barrington) and Hannah Clark

Seth C., d. 3/9/1927 at 72/5/12; painter; widower; b. Alton; Daniel Hayes (Alton) and Patience Evans (Alton)

Seth W., d. 3/29/1937 at 79/2/18; retired; divorced; b. Farmington; John F. Hayes (New Durham) and Ann Ricker (Rochester)

William T., d. 9/12/1932 at 66/0/13; clerk; married; b. Farmington; Ezekiel Hayes (New Castle) and Lydia Tarlton (New Castle)

William W., d. 4/3/1887 at 56/10/10; lumber mfr.; married; b. So. Barnstead; Watson Hayes (Rochester) and Joanna Winkley (Barrington)

## HAYNES,

Hannah E., d. 4/13/1931 at 81/4/23 in Gloucester, MA; widow; b. Springvale, ME; Hiram Lord (ME) and Mary Butler (ME)

John, d. 2/25/1896 at 85/5/6; old age; last manufacturer; widower; b. Canaan

John S., d. 4/25/1922 at 75/4/28; farmer; married; b. Concord; John Haynes and Lydia Fisher

Mary E., d. 3/16/1891 at 41/5/19; pneumonia; housekeeper; married; b. Farmington; Richmond E. Colbath (Farmington) and Hannah Parker (Chester)

## HAZEL,

daughter, d. 2/1/1904 at –; stillborn; b. Farmington; Walter Hazel (Gloucester) and Jennie P. Tarr (Gloucester)

## HECK,

Lyda C., d. 8/29/1938 at 75/8/13; housewife; widow; b. Farmington; Charles L. Pearl (Farmington) and E. A. Burnham (Alfred, ME)

**HENDERSON,**
Annie J., d. 6/26/1934 at 52/6/21 in Rochester; at home; married; Penacook; Edwin D. Ordway (Penacook) and Emerline Sanborn (Penacook)
Eliza A., d. 9/17/1928 at 84/11/14; housekeeper; widow; b. Boston MA; William Henderson (Dover) and Rebecca Richards (Dover)
Lewachra M., d. 3/12/1929 at 70/10/10; widow; b. Farmington; Lou Downs (Farmington) and Maria Horne (Farmington)
Ren'ld, d. 10/14/1907 at 0/6/15; intestinal indigestion; b. Acton, ME H. Henderson (Farmington, lumberman) and Grace Marsh (Acton, ME)
Sarah, d. 2/1/1905 at 79/10/17; la grippe; single; b. Farmington; Timothy Henderson (Rochester) and Olive Burnham (Farmington)

**HERRING,**
William M., d. 12/2/1900 at 41/9/21; pneumonia; clerk; married; b. Farmington; G. M. Herring (Framingham) and Ellen Eames (Framingham)

**HERSEY,**
John H., d. 1/17/1919 at 69/9/14

**HERSOM,**
Alice M., d. 2/14/1930 at 35 in Rochester; married; b. Farmington; Herbert Ham (Farmington) and Ardis Stevens (Alton)

**HILL,**
Harvey R., d. 11/28/1935 at 50/6/7 in Portsmouth; salesman; married; b. Portsmouth; Charles Hill (Eliot, ME) and Martha Gunnison (Kittery, ME)
Ivan L., d. 1/9/1907 at 30/10/10; heart failure; shoemaker; married; b. New Durham; Joseph Hilliard and Jennette Hill (New Durham)
Katherine, d. 7/1/1926 at 0/1/12; b. Farmington; Arthur Hill and Elena Tirrell (MI)

**HIRTH,**
John F., d. 4/14/1921 at 76/10/12; carpenter; married; b. Boston, MA; Daniel Hirth (Germany) and Maria Robbins (Hallowell, ME)

**HOAGE,**
Mary E., d. 1/4/1932 at 42/3/10; housewife; married; b. Fredericton, NB; John E. Vincent (NB) and Mary Robinsen (NB)
Newell H., d. 11/20/1933 at 18/3/7; student; single; b. Portland, ME; James Hoage (Portland, ME) and Lucille Hatch (Portland, ME)

**HODGDON,**
Cora A., d. 10/1/1934 at 73/4/29 in Milton; at home; married; b. Milton; Stephen W. Maine (Milton) and Hannah Horne (Middleton)
Ellen A., d. 12/21/1909 at 65/9/7; Bright's disease; housewife; b. Middleton; Leighton Colbath (Middleton) and Hannah Graham (Concord)
Wesbury, d. 4/18/1921 at 78/4/28; shoecutter; widower; b. Middleton; William Hodgdon and Nancy Ham (Farmington)

**HOITT,**
Livona T., d. 6/24/1892 at 78/9/11; heart disease; housekeeper; widow; b. North Hampton; Jacob Batchelder (farmer) and Abigail Tailor; burial - Northwood

**HOLLAND,**
Albert P., d. 9/15/1923 at 77/7/15; retired; widower; b. Pembroke, ME; John Holland and Sarah Mayhar
Hazel D., d. 11/7/1917 at 17/7/30; none; single; b. Pembroke, MA; Sadie E. Holland (Pembroke, MA)

**HOLMES,**
Asa L., d. 4/19/1907 at 84/1/16; gall stones; farmer; married; b. Farmington; Joseph Holmes (Strafford, farmer) and Polly Scruton (Farmington)
Dorothy, d. 9/3/1920 at 3/5/26
Eliza, d. 2/25/1892 at 87/6/15; heart failure; housewife; widow; b. Farmington; Lemuel C. Richard (farmer) and Mary Moore
Emma A., d. 9/2/1921 at 67/11/8; housewife; married; b. Moultonboro; Parker Payne (Sandwich) and Jennie Gray

Fannie A., d. 9/19/1893 at 27/6/3; tuberculosis; lady; single; b. Farmington; John R. Holmes (Farmington) and Fanny F. Fowler (Bristol, ME)

Fannie F., d. 4/23/1896 at 57/0/13; enten phthisis; housekeeper; married; b. Round Pond, ME; David Murphy (Round Pond, ME) and Hannah Carter (Round Pond, ME)

Henry H., d. 9/24/1923 at 76/2/2; farmer; widower; b. Jefferson; Nathan H. Holmes (Jefferson) and Lucinda Briant (ME)

Margaret, d. 1/21/1890 at 87/8/25; pneumonia; widow; b. Alton; Samuel Hayes

Sarah T., d. 1/13/1911 at 77/4/4; broncho pneumonia; housekeeper widow; b. Barnstead; Peter Berry (Barnstead, farmer) and Susan Babb (Barnstead)

Woodbury, d. 5/29/1902 at 79/2/19; old age; farmer; widower; b. Farmington

**HOLT,**
Alice L., d. 10/12/1934 at 82 in Rochester; at home; widow; b. Farmington; Aaron Hayes (Farmington) and Mary E. Hayes (Farmington)

**HORAN,**
Hester D., d. 1/7/1921 at 10/0/20

**HORNE,**
Amanda, d. 9/18/1898 at 69/1/5; heart disease; housekeeper; widow; b. Farmington; Nicholas Colbath (Rochester) and Keziah Rand (Farmington)

Charles A., d. 9/6/1933 at 46/2/17; farmer; single; b. Farmington; William H. Horne (Farmington) and Mary E. Colbath (Wakefield)

Charles F., d. 4/27/1906 at 0/0/0; stillborn; b. Farmington; Fred I. Horne (Farmington) and Marion Grimes (Dover)

Clara I., d. 5/20/1925 at 58/2/28; housekeeper; divorced; b. Farmington; Nathaniel Parker

Cynthia A., d. 5/13/1926 at 86/7/18; housekeeper; widow; b. Tuftonboro; William Ricker (Tuftonboro) and Lucy Whitten (Tuftonboro)

Elinore M., d. 4/29/1932 at 0/9/16; b. Somersworth; Newall Horne (Rochester) and Charlotte Whitehouse (Barrington)

Elizabeth, d. 3/16/1927 at 81/4/6; housewife; widow; b. Somersworth; Joseph H. Wiggin (Farmington) and Paulina A. Welch (York, ME)

Eunice, d. 3/25/1895 at 89/5/10; old age; widow; b. New Durham; Stephen Pinkham and Judith Pinkham

Frank, d. 7/25/1910 at 73/0/27; natural causes; laborer; married; b. Farmington; John Horne (Farmington) and Hannah Witham (Farmington)

Fred A., d. 2/7/1929 at 64/1/0; farmer; single; b. Farmington; John W. Horne (Farmington) and Elizabeth M. Wiggin (Somersworth)

George H., d. 11/29/1918 at 3/0/23; b. Farmington; William E. Horne (Farmington) and Mildred Perkins (Hampton)

Harry B., d. 6/17/1923 at 0/0/53 (sic); single; b. Farmington; Lorenzo A. Horne (Rochester) and Elsie M. Pinkham (Farmington)

Ida M., d. 11/12/1923 at 62/9/3; housewife; married; b. Strafford; William P. Holmes (Strafford) and Sarah Berry (Bangor, ME)

Izah, d. 1/3/1887 at 81/9/29; farmer; widowed; b. Farmington; Nathaniel Horne

Izah A., d. 3/3/1932 at 67/4/6; liveryman; married; b. Farmington; Stephen Horne (Farmington) and Nancy ----- (ME)

Izah N., d. 4/20/1936 at 62/1/22 in No. Barnstead; laborer; divorced; b. Farmington; Nathaniel Horne (Farmington) and ----- (Strafford)

John W., d. 10/27/1926 at 85/5/22; farmer; married; b. Farmington; Peter M. Horne (Farmington) and Mary Pendexter (Farmington)

Mary E., d. 7/10/1896 at 79/9/25; catarrhal pneumonia; housewife; married; b. Farmington; John Pendexter (Madbury) and Susan Davis (Rochester)

Mary E., d. 8/26/1931 at 67/9/13; widow; b. Wakefield; Colman Colbath and Cinda Hunt (Providence, RI)

Mary J., d. 3/29/1896 at 82/5/10; cardiac weakness; widow; b. Rochester; John Califf (Rochester) and Betsey Burnham (Farmington)

Matilda, d. 4/19/1904 at 71/0/12; gangrene of foot; married; b. Dover; Jonathan Watson (Sandwich) and Adeline Tibbetts (Dover)

Nathaniel, d. 9/23/1892 at 65/4/11; blood poison; farmer; widower; b. Farmington; Izah Horne (Farmington, farmer) and Deborah French (Farmington)

Peter M., d. 3/30/1898 at 82/10/17; accident; farmer; widower; b. Farmington; William Horne (Dover) and Susan Worth (Loudor

Stephen, d. 7/18/1907 at 64/2/1; heart failure; divorced; b. New Durham; Benjamin Horne (Farmington, farmer) and Eunice Pinkham (New Durham)

Stephen F., d. 1/7/1895 at 63/9/16; cerebral hemorrhage; farmer; single; b. Farmington; Izah Horne (Farmington) and Deborah French (Farmington)

Sybil, d. 2/28/1894 at 77/11/4; heart disease; retired; widow; b. Sweden, NY; Andrew Wentworth (Berwick, ME) and Ruth Spooner (Still Water, NY)

William H., d. 7/28/1922 at 66/11/19; farmer; married; b. Farmington; William H. Horne (Farmington) and Lydia J. Pinkham (Farmington)

William H., d. 7/3/1934 at 49/4/9; farmer; divorced; b. Farmington; William H. Horne (Farmington) and Mary E. Colbath (Wakefield)

**HOVEY,**

Charles N., d. 5/15/1936 at 72/9/29 in Morristown, NJ; retired; married; b. Charlestown, MA; George Hovey (MA) and Melissa Davis (NH)

**HOWARD,**

daughter, d. 10/17/1891 at –; stillborn; b. Farmington; John W. Howard (Barrington) and Annie Ferrell (Boston, MA)

son, d. 11/29/1908 at –; stillborn; b. Farmington; Herbert O. Howard (Gonic) and Elizabeth Miller (Dover)

daughter, d. 10/26/1911 at –; hemorrhage; b. Farmington; Herbert Howard (Gonic, shoemaker) and Lizzie T. Mills (Dover)

Annie M., d. 2/6/1922 at 50/2/14; single; b. Farmington; Emery Howard and Mary E. Dame (Farmington)

Clayton E., d. 11/14/1929 at 0/0/0 in Rochester; b. Rochester; Everett A. Howard (Farmington) and Annette Joy (Union)

Eva M., d. 11/14/1888 at 0/11/19; scarletina; b. Farmington; Emory Howard

Hannah, d. 4/30/1919 at 85/0/24; housekeeper; widow; b. Rochester; Joseph Brown (Rochester) and Jane Hodgdon (Rochester)

Ida B., d. 2/23/1932 at 52/5/21 in Rochester; at home; married; b. Alton; Frank Clark (Manchester) and Fannie Smith (Alton)

Lawrence, d. 9/7/1917 at 0/1/16; b. Farmington; Herbert Howard (Dover) and Mamie Patch (Alton)

Lillian P., d. 3/13/1916 at 0/2/19; b. Milton; Herbert Howard (Dover) and Mary Patch (Milton)

Mabel, d. 7/31/1903 at 0/0/1; congenital debility; Herbert Howard (Rochester) and Lizzie Miller (Dover)

Mary E., d. 5/2/1899 at 66/6/21; heart disease; housewife; widow; b. Farmington; Daniel Dame and Abigail Ham

Shirley M., d. 4/17/1934 at 13/2/2; b. Springfield, MA; Herbert F. Howard (Dover) and Celinda Myers (Shelburne, VT)

**HOWE,**

Adeline A., d. 12/21/1900 at 76/7; heart disease; housewife; widow; b. Farmington; Hanson Roberts (Farmington) and E. C. Kimball (Farmington)

Charles W., d. 3/10/1905 at 53/2; heart disease; teamster; married; b. Farmington; Freeman P. Howe (Farmington) and Adeline A. Roberts (Farmington)

Mary Ann, d. 11/8/1922 at 90/10/27; housewife; widow; b. Milton; James Plummer (Milton) and Betsey Dealand (Wakefield)

**HOWLAND,**

Vianna, d. 3/24/1923 at 82/3/28; housekeeper; widow; b. W. Dennis, MA; Aaron Baker (W. Dennis, MA) and Esther Chase (W. Harwich, MA)

**HOYT,**

Judith, d. 1/21/1890 at 75/5; cancer; widow; b. Northwood; Reuben Hoyt (Northwood) and Nancy Robinson

**HUBBARD,**

John, d. 3/8/1937 at 73/1/8 in Dover; laborer; single; b. Farmington; George W. Hubbard (Brookfield) and Marie Hubbard (Mt. Vernon)

**HUCKINS,**
Abbie W., d. 1/25/1898 at 66/6/15; heart disease; housewife; married; Andrew Whitehouse (Rollinsford) and Mary T. Wise (Sanford, ME)
Georgianna, d. 1/23/1933 at 77/7/21; housewife; married; b. Wilmot; John Berry (New Durham) and Nancy Phelps (Wilmo
John A., d. 5/24/1930 at 64/3/1; farmer; married; b. Farmington; John I. Huckins (Madbury) and Abby Whitehouse (Sanford, ME)
John B., d. 8/6/1913 at 85/9/7; old age; farmer; widower; b. Madbury; Robert L. Huckins (Madbury) and Mary Daniels (Alton)
John Ira, d. 11/8/1911 at 81/9/23; gangrene; farmer; widower; b. Madbury; John D. Huckins (Madbury, farmer) and Mary Locke (Barrington)

**HULL,**
Elizabeth A., d. 12/24/1913 at 79/11/23; cancer of liver; widow; b. Salisbury, MA; Samuel Willey and Lovey Hanscom
Marjorie A., d. 8/7/1913 at 0/0/1; asphyxia; b. Farmington; Walter F Hull (Dover, shoemaker) and Eleanor T. Blaisdell (Farmingtor

**HUNT,**
Wilfred, d. 3/11/1929 at 0/1/14; b. Rochester; William Hunt (NY) and Margaret Bonney (Kingston, MA)

**HUNTRESS,**
Abram, d. 1/25/1904 at 43/5/5; pneumonia; shoemaker; divorced
Eugene, d. 5/20/1922 at –; physician; married; b. Portsmouth; Seth W. Huntress (Portsmouth) and Catherine Palmer (Sutton)

**HURD,**
daughter, d. 2/1/1903 at –; anaemia; Willie G. Hurd (Milton) and Nellie A. Varney (Farmington)
son, d. 5/16/1907 at –; stillborn; b. Farmington; Will G. Hurd (Milton, farmer) and Nellie A. Varney (Farmington)
Edith, d. 12/18/1893 at 8; diphtheria; b. Farmington; George Hurd (Farmington) and Sophia J. Foss (Strafford)
Eliza S., d. 3/22/1889 at 73/9/7; pulmonary phthisis; housekeeper; b. Cherry Valley, NY; Daniel Sanborn (Sanbornton) and Sarah Butler

George H., d. 1/14/1920 at 52/7/14; machinist; married; b. Alton; Marcus M. Hurd (Alton) and Mary Hanscam (Alton)

George W., d. 3/19/1906 at 60/7/11; cancer; farmer; married; b. Farmington; John Hurd (Ossipee) and Josie Nutter

Henry, d. 2/4/1921 at 79/10/18; farmer; widower; b. Farmington; Jonathan Hurd (Farmington) and Abigail Rand (Farmington)

Henry B., d. 7/23/1907 at 10/10/12; diphtheria; b. Farmington; Will G. Hurd (Milton, teamster) and Nellie A. Varney (Farmington)

Jeremiah R., d. 1/23/1912 at 89/2/1; bronchial pneumonia; farmer; married; b. Farmington; Jonathan Hurd (farmer) and Abigail Hurd (Farmington)

Margaret O., d. 2/27/1920 at 59/5/27; housekeeper; widow; b. Eliot, ME; James M. Raitt and Margaret P. Munro

Mary A., d. 1/14/1924 at 86/10/2; housekeeper; widow; b. Milton; Offin Merrow and Salona Jones

Sarah E., d. 12/19/1914 at 77/5/29; hypostatic pneumonia; widow; b. Farmington; John Place (Farmington, farmer) and ----- Henderson

Timothy W., d. 1/14/1893 at 84/9/3; nervous prostration; farmer; widower; b. New Durham; John Hurd (Dover) and Abigail Walker

**HUSSEY,**

Charles W., d. 9/24/1888 at 65/8/14; consumption; farmer; married; b. Rochester; Jonathan Hussey (Rochester) and Mary Hayes (Farmington)

James F., d. 9/30/1921 at 89/2/28; shoeworker; widower; b. Farmington; Jeremy Hussey (Farmington) and Abigail Leighton (Farmington)

Lucy A., d. 10/16/1916 at 57/11/6; married; b. Lyman, ME; Jacob Goodwin and Roda Smith

Nancy B., d. 12/18/1895 at 69/11; heart disease; housewife; widow; b. New Durham; Stephen T. Davis (Kittery, ME) and Nancy Bickford (New Durham)

Sarah A., d. 7/31/1918 at 84/1/18; housewife; married; b. Wolfeboro; Nathaniel Edgerly (Wolfeboro) and Mary Furber (Wolfeboro)

Stephen, d. 3/9/1920 at 83

**HUTCHINS,**
Florence, d. 9/15/1904 at 31/2/13; general tuberculosis; milliner; single; b. Lebanon, ME; S. L. Hutchins (Lebanon, ME) and Sarah Mace (Lebanon, ME)
J. Frank, d. 2/23/1923 at 60/7/18; painter; married; b. Madison; John Hutchins (Madison) and Frances White (Madison)
Sarah A., d. 12/27/1910 at 76/5/17; bronchitis; married; b. Lebanon Joseph C. Mace (Rye) and Abigail Pray (Berwick, ME)
Solomon, d. 5/9/1917 at 79/7/24; shoeworker; widower; b. Lebanon, ME; Simon Hutchins (Wakefield) and Dorothy Farnham (Acton, ME)

**HUTCHINSON,**
John F., d. 7/3/1902 at 84/9/27; old age; shoemaker; widower

**HYDE,**
Sally, d. 3/24/1904 at 83/9/14; acute indigestion; widow; b. Middleton; John York and Sarah Lord

**HYLAND,**
Nelson S., d. 9/17/1912 at 40/8/10; heart failure; shoemaker; married; b. Newport, VT; Jesse Hyland (VT, farmer) and Ruby ----- (VT)

**IRISH,**
Carrie E., d. 12/1/1915 at 53/7/28; housewife; married; b. Albany, NY; John Parrish and Joanna -----

**JACKSON,**
George H., d. 9/10/1913 at 52/0/0; suicide, shooting; cobbler; single; b. New Durham; Jacob A. Jackson (New Durham, carpenter) and Mary J. Critchett (Alton)
Jacob A., d. 7/7/1899 at 84/0/25; paralysis; laborer; widower; b. Somerville, MA; Mary Burnham (New Durham)
Mary A., d. 6/18/1926 at 66/10/9; widow; b. New Durham; Jacob A. Jackson (New Durham) and Mary Critchett (Alton)
Mary J., d. 8/31/1902 at 77/8/23; old age; housewife; widow; b. Alton; Lemuel Critchet (Alton) and ----- Cooper (Alton)
Vianna, d. 2/16 or 17/1930 at 84/6/1; at home; widow; b. Farmington; Charles Gage and Martha York

**JAFFERY,**
Emily F., d. 4/15/1917 at 69; housewife; married; John Brown (Cornish, ME) and Hannah Brown (Cornish, ME)

**JAMESON,**
Sarah A., d. 6/26/1921 at 78; housekeeper; widow; b. St. Johns, NB; John Willson (Scotland)

**JEFFERSON,**
Donald, d. 12/28/1912 at 0/0/24; cellulitis; b. Farmington; C. D. Jefferson (Roxbury, MA, expressman) and Stella M. Stackpole (E. Lebanon, ME)

**JENKINS,**
Clara A., d. 7/5/1919 at 83/11/28; housekeeper; widow; b. Barnstead; Trueworthy Chamberlain and Hannah Hayes (Dover)
Dana, d. 12/15/1926 at 69/3/5; shoeworker; single; b. Lebanon, ME
Henry A., d. 11/30/1889 at 55/5/10; pneumonia; shoe fitter; b. New Durham; Elijah Jenkins (New Durham) and Abigail Drew (Dover)

**JENNESS,**
Edward, d. 3/7/1922 at 49/7/17; caretaker; married; b. S. Berwick, ME; John H. Jenness and Harriett S. Brown
Frank P., d. 8/20/1897 at 43/7/21; heart failure; single; b. Somersworth; Parker A. Jenness (Rochester) and Elizabeth J. Morrison (Somersworth)
Joanna, d. 7/23/1888 at 75/2; paralysis; housekeeper; married; H. Thrasher
John H., d. 6/12/1931 at 79/0/26; retired; single; b. Rochester; William Jenness (Rochester) and Joanna Thresher (Sandwich)
Viola S., d. 10/11/1935 at 80/6/24; at home; widow; b. Boston; Charles Weymouth and Susan A. Hunt (ME)
William, d. 12/11/1905 at 90/7/24; senectus; farmer; widower; b. Rochester; John Jenness (Dover) and Lydia Johnson

**JEWELL,**
George W., d. 11/28/1925 at 86/1/18; prison guard; widower; David Jewell (ME)

**JOHNSON,**

daughter, d. 1/10/1938 at –; b. Farmington; William Johnson (Dover) and Grace Merrill (MA)

Angie P., d. 3/28/1925 at 81/9/17; housekeeper; widow; b. Farmington; ----- French

Beatrice A., d. 12/8/1889 at 20/1/24; Bright's disease; stitcher; b. Farmington; N. C. Johnson (Stowe, ME) and Julia A. Wentworth (Farmington)

Budd M., d. 3/27/1923 at 51/6/20; station agent; married; b. St. Armand, PQ; Parker S. Johnson (St. Arnold, PQ) and Elizabeth Gilliland (Farmington)

Charles W., d. 12/11/1928 at 61/10/4; shoeworker; widower; b. Farmington; James M. Johnson (Strafford) and Mary L. Watson (Gilmanton)

George B., d. 6/30/1902 at 66/10/17; heart failure; shoemaker; married; b. Wolfeboro; Ezra Johnson (Wolfeboro) and Nancy Perkins (Wolfeboro)

Hannah, d. 10/21/1906 at 86/9/20; shock; widow; b. Brookfield; Moses Perkins (Brookfield)

Harold D., d. 2/26/1919 at 44/0/15; RR conductor; married; b. Milton; James Johnson (New Durham) and Julia Hatch (N. Berwick, ME)

Ida S., d. 7/27/1921 at 51/1/18; housekeeper; married; b. Madbury; George W. Meserve (Lee) and Ellen M. Stanton (Strafford)

James M., d. 10/19/1905 at 64/1/28; cirrhosis of liver; farmer; widower; b. Strafford; David Johnson (Fryeburg) and Hannah McKeene (Fryeburg)

James W., d. 9/5/1920 at 82/9/27; farmer; widower; b. Wolfeboro; Ezra Johnson and Mary Perkins (New Durham)

Jennie Bell, d. 10/2/1892 at 0/6/12; whooping cough; b. Farmington; John C. Johnson (Farmington, farmer) and Ida S. Meserve (Madbury)

John, d. 6/20/1907 at 75/8/28; uriniaia; farmer; married; b. Dover; Dennis Johnson and Sarah Weeks (Kittery, ME)

John C., d. 2/5/1926 at 59/11/3; farmer; widower; b. Farmington; John G. Johnson (Dover) and Anstress Rogers (Farmington)

Joseph W., d. 10/26/1930 at 96/0/27; widower; b. Wolfeboro; Joseph Johnson and Lurana Y. Whitten

Mary L., d. 10/4/1904 at 58/5/16; uteris cancer; housewife; married; b. Gilmanton; Joseph Wilson (Gilmanton) and Sally Piper (Gilmanton)

Mildred J., d. 4/30/1894 at 1/10/10; hydrocephalus; b. Lynn, MA; Charles Johnson and Annie Tupper (Gilmanton)

Nathaniel C., d. 4/13/1902 at 62/11/19; heart disease; shoemaker; married; b. Stowe, ME; David Johnson (Fryeburg, ME) and Hannah McKeen (Fryeburg, ME)

Parker S., d. 5/29/1920 at 74/7/7; carpenter; widower; b. Canada; Ira Johnson (Canada) and Sally Coffin (Canada)

Ruth S., d. 3/31/1897 at 90/1/26; old age; widow; b. Hiram, ME; John Pierce and Rebecca Simons

Sophia J., d. 5/29/1916 at 79/9/11; housewife; married; b. Wolfeboro; Moses Tibbetts and Sarah York

Wilder, d. 12/26/1905 at 74/0/10; Bright's disease; stone cutter; widower; b. Bangor, ME

**JONES,**

son, d. 6/8/1892 at 0/0/1; heart failure; b. Farmington; Onslow B. Jones (Alton, shoemaker) and Amy L. Marston (Alton)

Annie M., d. 4/1/1921 at 67/9; housewife; widow; b. Wolfeboro; Benjamin F. Blaisdell (Wolfeboro) and ----- Pierce (Wolfeboro)

Arthur R., d. 1/11/1933 at 49/4/18; married; b. New Durham; Howard S. Jones (Boston, MA) and Ella M. Davis (Alton)

Austin J., d. 11/27/1901 at 55/10/9; fat. degen. of heart; married; b. Boston; Ivory H. Jones (Hanover) and N. Hutchinson (Pepperell)

Betsey L., d. 3/28/1898 at 88/9/5; cerebral softening; widow; b. Alton; Jeremiah Edgerly (Durham) and Betsey Leighton (Wolfeboro)

Bettsy B., d. 1/2/1897 at 78/0/14; heart trouble; housewife; married; b. New Durham; Joseph Boody

Clara A., d. 7/9/1918 at 63/6/18; hotel prop.; married; b. Rochester; Joseph Young (Middleton) and Julia Rollins (Rochester)

Clara E., d. 12/27/1913 at 60/3/24; carcinoma of stomach; housekeeper; single; b. Alton; Seth R. Emerson (Alton, shoemaker) and Emily Rollins (Alton)

Dana P., d. 6/18/1937 at 84/7/18; retired; widower; b. New Durham; John Jones (New Durham) and Ann Berry (New Durham)

Edwin, d. 12/19/1901 at 47; heart disease; shoemaker; single; b. Acton; Waterman Jones and Elizabeth Perkins (Alton)

Ella M., d. 7/13/1922 at 68/11/5; housewife; married; b. Alton; James Davis (Alton) and Martha Cloutman (New Durham)

Ezekiel R., d. 1/8/1904 at 76/11/9; old age infirmities; blacksmith; married; b. Lebanon, ME; Isaac Jones (Lebanon, ME) and Betsey Roberts (Lebanon, ME)

Georgia A., d. 11/13/1924 at 78/7/27; housewife; widow; b. Lawrence, MA; Stephen Lawrence

Isaac, d. 6/24/1899 at 79; old age; farmer; widower; b. Barrington

Lewis, d. 2/14/1887 at 73/6/12; farmer; married; b. New Durham; William Jones and ----- Edgerly (New Durham)

Lewis F., d. 1/26/1920 at 80/4/17; engineer; married; b. Alton; Lew Jones (Alton) and Betsey Edgerly (New Durham)

Lydia J., d. 3/7/1892 at 86/5/18; old age; housewife; married

Marilla F., d. 7/30/1920 at 84/7/29

Mary E., d. 1/10/1920 at 73/5/18; housewife; married; b. Farmington; Rufus Amazeen (New Castle) and Carolin Sherburn (Portsmouth)

Melissa S., d. 3/3/1887 at 50/0/2; housekeeper; married; b. Farmington; George Garland (Rochester) and Lucinda Downing (Farmington)

Nancy, d. 7/30/1900 at 86/4/11; anaemia; housekeeper; widow; b. Pepperell; Tim Hutchinson (Pepperell) and Jenette Robinson (Pembroke)

Samuel H., d. 8/4/1897 at 50/3/11; cancer in throat; laborer; married; b. Barnstead; Enos Jones and Sarah Twombley

Silence, d. 3/3/1926 at 90/7/18; housewife; widow; b. Canaan, ME; Isaac Lord (ME) and Eliza Hussey (ME)

Ulysses S., d. 2/10/1893 at – in Dover; burned; single; Lewis F. Jones (New Durham) and Susan A. Tailor

William, d. 10/17/1920 at 69; watch repairer; widower; b. Middleton John Jones (Middleton) and Mary S. Burrows (Middleton)

William W., d. 6/4/1929 at 56/11/0; shoeworker; single; b. Alton; Willie Jones (Alton) and Helen Flanders (Alton)

**JORDAN,**

Charles A., d. 7/29/1936 at 48/5/13; shoeworker; married; b. Beverly, MA; Isaac Jordan and Annioe Morton (Augusta, ME)

George C., d. 12/18/1889 at 73/1/20; heart disease; farmer; b. Farmington; Simon Jordan (Denmark, ME) and Hannah Walker (Farmington)

Sarah J., d. 9/29/1920 at 69/2/6; housekeeper; single; b. Farmington; George Jordan (Farmington) and Lydia Thompsor (Farmington)

**JOY,**
son, d. 1/11/1928 at –; b. Rochester; Samuel O. Joy, Jr. (New Durham) and Hedwidge Cyr (Canada)
Flora B., d. 2/23/1888 at 15/5/9; anaemia; houseekeper; single; Cynthia Joy
Maria, d. 3/4/1914 at 86/6/3; apoplexy; widow; b. Yarmouth, NS
Mary E., d. 6/12/1935 at 71/3/3 in New Durham; at home; widow; b. New Durham; Joseph Y. Berry (New Durham) and Betsey Scruton (Strafford)
Samuel O., d. 8/22/1934 at 74/11/20 in New Durham; farmer; married; b. New Durham; Samuel W. Joy (New Durham) and Mary A. Evans (New Durham)

**JUNKINS,**
Abbie J., d. 3/5/1929 at 70/3/5; housewife; married; b. Brentwood; Henry Orne and Elizabeth Hall

**KELLEY,**
Abbie, d. 2/3/1931 at 72/3/6; housekeeper; widow; b. Farmington; Thomas Pinkham (New Durham) and Adelaide Hodgdon (Farmington)
Albert, Jr., d. 4/23/1927 at –; b. Farmington; Albert A. Kelley (Farmington) and Delma E. Dame (Wakefield)
Delma E., d. 4/23/1927 at 23/8/24; housewife; married; b. Wakefield; Daniel E. Dame (Portsmouth) and Minnie M. Smith (Wakefield)
Edith M., d. 11/23/1923 at 54/3/10; housewife; married; b. Middleton; James F. Clark and Lydia J. Tuttle (Middleton)
Ella D., d. 2/19/1937 at 71/2/2; lodging house; widow; b. Tracy, NB; Ephraim Nason (Tracy, NB) and Elizabeth Gray (Amherst, NS)
Harry A., d. 4/12/1891 at 0/8/13; infantile colic; b. Farmington; James R. Kelley (Derby, VT) and Ella D. Nason (Pracy, NB)
James A., d. 3/11/1923 at 77/3/20; farmer; married; b. Dover; Augustus Kelley (Dover) and Mary Cole (Springvale, ME)
James E., d. 7/8/1933 at 84/6/16; retired; widower; b. Derby, VT; John Kelley (St. Johnsbury, VT) and Melina Roberts (Alton)
Lydia C., d. 5/28/1903 at 55/3/6; epilepsy; housewife; married; Moses Gilman (Gilmanton) and Rhoda Gilman (Alton)
Sarah A., d. 8/24/1918 at 88/8/14; housekeeper; widow; b. Farmington; Barzillai Horne and Lucy French

**KELSEA,**
Sarah G., d. 11/9/1903 at 43/4/27; anaemia; dressmaker; divorced; George W. Burnham (New Durham) and L. F. Pearl (Farmington)

**KENDALL,**
William, d. 4/10/1911 at 70; cancer of liver; retired; married; b. Concord; Prescott Kendall and Mary Dow

**KENNEY,**
Edmund, d. 1/26/1917 at 78/9/22; trader; widower; b. Lisbon, ME
Frank E., d. 4/14/1933 at 69; shoeworker; divorced; b. Milton
Mary A., d. 10/27/1902 at 78/1/23; old age; housewife; married; b. Middleton; Ebenezer Wentworth and Sophia Roberts

**KENNISTON,**
Martha, d. 12/13/1907 at 73/9/21; influenza; housekeeper; widow; b. Lebanon, ME; J. Wallingford (farmer) and Susan Wallingford

**KENT,**
John, d. 4/27/1905 at 83/0/26; accidental; farmer; widower

**KIMBALL,**
son, d. 9/8/1893 at 0/4/5; pneumonia; b. Farmington; David S. Kimball (Middleton) and Nellie Hanscom (Dover)
daughter, d. 7/30/1901 at 0/0/13; heart trouble; b. Farmington; M. S. H. Kimball (Alton) and Alice M. Hurd (Alton)
Addie R., d. 10/30/1897 at 32/3/23; consumption and heart disease; housekeeper; married; b. Farmington; Alamander Young (Farmington) and Rebecca Keniston
Annie, d. 8/29/1897 at 1/3/21; consumption caused dropsy brain; b. Farmington; Samuel W. Kimball (Middleton) and Addie R. Young (Farmington)
Annie M., d. 4/23/1897 at 36/9/20; epilepsy; single; b. Farmington; Daniel W. Kimball (Bradford) and Mary A. Wingate (Farmington)
Augusta, d. 5/24/1922 at 72/10/15; housewife; married; b. Concord; Joseph P. Davis and Hope M. Eaton
Charles, d. 1/17/1928 at 71; retired lea. dlr.; married; b. Amesbury, MA; Thomas Kimball

Charles H., d. 8/3/1938 at 87/9; laborer; widower; b. Wolfeboro; Nathaniel Kimball (Wolfeboro) and Abagail Willey (Wolfeboro)

Clara E., d. 4/16/1935 at 76/10; at home; single; b. Farmington; Daniel Kimball (Groveland, MA) and Mary A. Wingate (Farmington)

Daniel, d. 6/7/1918 at 84/1/22; shoeworker; married; b. Bradford, MA; Samuel Kimball (Goffstown) and Anna M. Griffin (Groveland, MA)

Daniel J., d. 1/15/1913 at 64/8/0; cancer of stomach; laborer; married; b. Parsonsfield, ME; Daniel N. Kimball (Parsonsfield, ME, farmer) and Lulema Clough (Parsonsfield)

David S., d. 9/15/1897 at 45/9/16; consumption; shoemaker; married; b. Middleton; N. W. Kimball (Middleton) and Martha B. Ham (New Durham)

Ernest, d. 4/8/1896 at 1/0/9; pneumonia; b. Farmington; Clara Kimball (Middleton)

Frank A., d. 3/21/1896 at 28/11/1; consumption; shoemaker; married; Oscar Kimball (Haverhill, MA) and Leonora A. Hayes (New Durham)

George C., d. 6/16/1918 at 55/2/18; merchant; married; b. Farmington; Jeremiah Kimball (Alton) and Naomi Elkins (Farmington)

Georgie A., d. 7/18/1889 at 16/6/15; chlorosis; David S. Kimball (Middleton) and Nellie M. Hanscomb (Dover)

Harry B., d. 5/12/1924 at 52/7/5; clerk; married; b. Middleton; Oscar F. Kimball (Haverhill, MA) and Leonora Hayes (New Durham)

Irene, d. 10/20/1898 at 62; accident; housekeeper; widow; b. Rochester; Jacob Garland (Rochester) and Sabina Brewster (Barrington)

Leonora, d. 4/13/1919 at 74/4/1; housewife; married; b. New Durham; Samuel Hayes (New Durham) and Mary Whitehouse (Middleton)

M. Florence, d. 12/24/1921 at 60/8; nurse; widow; b. Rumford, ME; William Hutchinson (NY) and Phoebe M. Lufkin (Rumford, ME)

Mary A., d. 2/28/1923 at 84/8/23; housewife; widow; b. Farmington; Benjamin Wingate (Farmington) and Lavina Davis (Farmington)

Mary E., d. 3/18/1935 at 58/4/7; at home; single; b. Farmington; Daniel W. Kimball (Groveland, MA) and Mary A. Wingate (Farmington)

Nellie M., d. 10/28/1909 at 57/3/12; apoplexy; housekeeper; b.
　　Dover; John W. Hanscom (Newmarket) and Marie Stevens
　　(Middleton)
Oris S., d. 11/4/1907 at 0/4/19; inflammation; b. Farmington; A. E.
　　Kimball (Middleton, laborer) and Myrtie Glidden (New Durham
Oscar F., d. 2/17/1929 at 81/7/8; shoeworker; widower; b. Haverhill
　　MA; Nehemiah Kimball and Martha Ham
Samuel, d. 3/11/1924 at 63/11/14; shoemaker; widower; b.
　　Middleton; N. W. Kimball (Middleton) and Martha Ham (Alton)
Samuel A., d. 5/18/1894 at 88/2; paralysis and age; widower; b.
　　Bradford; Samuel Kimball and Nancy Smith
Susan M., d. 5/15/1891 at 41/2/11; heart failure; housekeeper;
　　married; b. Standish, ME; John T. Rollins (Wolfeboro) and
　　Patience Colomy (Farmington)

**KING,**
son, d. 8/19/1927 at –; b. Farmington; Charles A. King (Calais, ME)
　　and Bernice Wiggin (Bangor, ME)
Virginia, d. 5/19/1936 at 6/5 in Boston, MA; b. Farmington; Stephen
　　King (Calais, ME) and Harriet Brooks (Marlboro, MA)

**KINGSBURY,**
Georgina, d. 3/12/1918 at 71/10/3; housekeeper; married; b.
　　Hanson, MA; Hale S. Thomas (Hanson, MA) and Julia D. Snell
　　(Boston)
James A., d. 10/14/1928 at 85/3/25; retired; widower; b. Dover

**KITCHEN,**
Norma L., d. 7/22/1919 at 6/3/28; b. Farmington

**KITTREDGE,**
Charles E., d. 5/4/1932 at 73/0/29; gas sta. prop.; married; b.
　　Stoneham, MA; Joseph B. Kittredge (Woburn, MA) and
　　Celistia Evans (Moultonboro)

**KNIGHT,**
Elbridge, d. 11/16/1920 at 71/0/6; retired; single; b. Milton; Stephen
　　Knight (Brooks, ME) and Louise Clary (Farmington)
John W., d. 10/26/1904 at 82/5/29; senectus; physician; widower; b.
　　Farmington; William Knight (Kittery, ME) and Mary Pearl
　　(Farmington)

Louisa, d. 6/8/1899 at 78/11/20; heart failure; housewife; widow; b. Brooks, ME; Joshua Clay (Brooks, ME) and Nancy Rich (Brooks, ME)

**KNOWLES,**
Joseph F., d. 8/15/1930 at 1/10/26 in No. Rochester; b. Rochester; Joseph F. Knowles (Middleton) and Frances McNeil (Central Falls, RI)
Roberta M., d. 10/24/1932 at 5/5/7 in Rochester; b. Rochester; Joseph F. Knowles (Middleton) and Frances M. McNeal (Central Falls, RI)

**KNOX,**
Addie E., d. 8/17/1930 at 64/11/26; housekeeper; widow; b. Middleton; Warren Whitehouse (Middleton) and Emma York (Middleton)
Annette, d. 2/25/1910 at 67/4/6; gastric carcinoma; housewife; b. Farmington; Nathan Durgin and Mary Trickey
Carrie W., d. 9/13/1907 at 44/5/28; carcinoma of breast; school teacher; married; b. Farmington; Washington White (New Castle) and Ann S. Card (New Castle)
Eliza, d. 2/17/1931 at 70; housekeeper; widow; b. England; George Turner (England)
Eva B., d. 5/181/933 at 45/3/28; housewife; married; b. Rochester; Charles Bickford (Groton) and Ellen M. Perham (Derry)
James R., d. 12/25/1915 at 77/9; retired; widower; b. Milton; Jesse Knox (Milton) and Lydia Dorr (Milton)
Jesse W., d. 2/23/1903 at 69/6/16; meningitis; shoemaker; married; Jesse Knox (Milton) and Lydia Dore (Milton)
Lojoyce J., d. 1/30/1918 at 48/4/28; housewife; married; b. Farmington; Ezekiel Jones (Lebanon, ME) and Silence Lord (Canaan, ME)
Mary E., d. 11/20/1915 at 75/7/8; widow; b. Lebanon, ME; Samuel Kenney
Simeon P., d. 8/17/1918 at 87/4/17; carpenter; widower; b. Chatham; Samuel Knox (Cornish, ME) and Olive Lord (Parsonsfield, ME)
Ulysses S., d. 5/25/1923 at 59/3/7; carpenter; married; b. Stowe, ME; Simeon Knox and Sarah Bickford
Violet A., d. 4/19/1931 at 47/10/26; housewife; married; b. Montreal; Alexander Ross (Scotland) and Elizabeth Scott (Scotland)

**LABONTE,**
A. Guy, d. 5/5/1934 at 61/1/20; shoeworker; single; b. Farmington; Albert Labonte (Canada) and Orissa Boody (Berwick, ME)
Albert, d. 5/30/1915 at 73/9/7; laborer; widower; b. Canada; John B LaBonte (Canada) and Julia Collet (Canada)
Edward J., d. 5/29/1914 at 63/0/18; suicide, shooting; shoemaker; widower; b. Canada; John B. Labonte (Canada, coover) and Julia Collet (Canada)
Julie, d. 2/27/1894 at 87; old age; widow
Orissa A., d. 7/24/1908 at 61/9/29; myocarditis; housekeeper; married; b. Berwick, ME; Harrison S. Boody (New Durham) and Tonison Ham (New Durham)

**LACEY,**
John E., d. 12/29/1934 at 32/11 in Rochester; shoeworker; married b. Cambridge, MA; John E. Lacey (Arlington, MA) and Hannal Connors

**LAGACY,**
Joseph, d. 1/3/1936 at 90/9/1 in Dover; laborer; single; b. Canada; Frank Legacy (Canada) and Jasten Dube (Canada)

**LAMARCHE,**
Leon, d. 10/23/1933 at 77/2/29; retired; widower; b. Canada; ----- Lamarche (Canada)
Virginia, d. 8/30/1929 at 69/9/28; housewife; married; b. Canada; Edward Prescott (Canada) and Mary Prescott (Canada)

**LANE,**
Levi, d. 10/15/1890 at 76/5/10; paralysis; farmer; widower; b. Chichester

**LANG,**
Martin V. B., d. 9/8/1899 at 63/5/15; paralysis; farmer; widower; b. Alton; John Lang (Alton) and Mary J. Webb (Portsmouth)
Mary A., d. 11/16/1902 at 58/8/13; apoplexy; housewife; married; b. Barnstead; Sampson B. Lock (Barnstead) and Esther Nutter (Barnstead)

**LANGLEY,**
Alonzo D., d. 5/22/1923 at 57/7; laborer; single; b. Acton, ME; John W. Langley (Acton, ME) and Nancy S. Dunnell (Newfield, ME)

**LAPHAM,**
Bertha, d. 11/16/1937 at 69/1/1; domestic; widow; b. New Durham; Albert Labonte (Canada) and Orissa Boody (Berwick, ME)

**LAPINE** [see Lepine],
Matilda, d. 7/3/1894 at 7/4/13; fever; b. Farmington; Peter Lepine (Montreal, Canada) and Ellen Fitzgerald (Sherbrooke, Canada)

**LARY,**
Hosea B., d. 8/7/1915 at 80/3/9; carpenter; married; b. Freedom; Samuel Lary and Sally Rundall
Lydia F., d. 6/3/1924 at 85/9/9; housekeeper; widow; b. Farmington; David Wentworth and Charlotte Carsen
Mary L., d. 2/11/1889 at 24/4/1; albuminuria of pregnancy; housekeeper; b. Wolfeboro; George E. Tibbetts and S. Victoria Tibbetts

**LASALLE,**
Joseph D., d. 3/22/1906 at 1/7/29; cholera infantum; b. Farmington; Joseph I. LaSalle (Carthage, NY) and Clara Hudson (Hermon, NY)
Lucy S., d. 10/3/1905 at 0/3/27; cholera infantum; b. Farmington; Joseph S. LaSalle (Carthage, NY) and Clara H. Hudson (Herman, NY)

**LASHON,**
Charles F., d. 11/25/1920 at 41/4/21; shoeworker; married; b. Skowhegan; John Lashon (Madison, ME) and Sarah Chafin (St. John, Canada)

**LAURENS,**
Sarah S., d. 5/9/1903 at 76/11/5; valvular disease of heart; widow; Samuel Ransom (Dover) and Abigail Holmes (Farmington)

**LAWRENCE,**
son, d. 8/17/1927 at 0/0/1; b. Farmington; Abbott Lawrence (Boston) and Arlene C. Place (Milton)
Samuel, d. 3/10/1935 at 75/11/25; county commissioner; married; b. Meredith; Samuel A. Lawrence and Anna V. Hunt

**LEAH[E]Y,**
Hanorah, d. 3/3/1917 at 74/6/12; housewife; widow; b. NB; Francis Connor (Ireland) and Bridget Noonan (Ireland)
Michael, d. 9/30/1892 at 70; old age; laborer; married; b. Ireland; Dennis Leahey (Ireland, laborer); burial - Dover
William, d. 9/20/1887 at 28/10/13; shoemaker; single; b. Farmington; Michael Leahy (Ireland) and Hannora Connor (NB)

**LEAVITT,**
Almon, d. 1/19/1916 at 77/2/13; retired; married; b. Effingham; Samuel Leavitt and Elizabeth Brackett
Nellie S., d. 5/3/1929 at 83/1/27; widow; b. Alton; Lewis Jones and Betsey Edgerly
Sidney, d. 1/17/1931 at 58/1/12 in Concord; storekeeper; married; b. NH; Almon Leavitt (NH) and Nellie Jones (NH)

**LEBELLE,**
infant, d. 2/17/1930 at –; b. Farmington; Alfred LeBelle (Haverhill, MA) and Blanche Marcotte (Salmon Falls)

**LECLAIR,**
Alfred, d. 3/3/1934 at 78/1/20; laborer; widower; b. Jamestown, Canada

**LEE,**
Sim, d. 10/26/1918 at 30/11/25; "yellow"; laundryman; single; b. San Francisco; Lee Fung (China) and Eng Sue (China)

**LEGRO,**
Edwin, d. 3/11/1930 at 76/6/13; married; b. Farmington; James LeGro (Rochester) and Ellen Waldron (Rochester)
Ellen A., d. 10/26/1897 at 75/9/7; broncho-pneumonia and old age; housekeeper; widow; b. Rochester; Daniel Waldron (Rochester) and Elizabeth Page (Rochester)

Lydia A., d. 12/22/1926 at 80/1; housekeeper; widow; b. Wolfeboro; John C. Drew (Wolfeboro) and Sarah Lucas (Wolfeboro)

**LEIGHTON,**
Addie A., d. 12/20/1907 at 40/4/3; pomition anemia; dressmaker; married; b. Barnstead; Charles H. Dow (Barnstead, farmer) and Lydia Shackford (Barnstead)

Alice O., d. 2/16/1908 at 84/11; old age; housekeeper; widow; b. New Durham; Jonathan Edgerly

Amasa R., d. 1/18/1899 at 60/4/4; pneumonia; farmer; married; b. Farmington; George Leighton (Farmington) and Emily Roberts

Charles, d. 9/7/1890 at 43/10/4; consumption; shoe cutter; married; b. Farmington; M. C. Leighton (Farmington) and Hannah E. Tanner (Farmington)

Charles F., d. 5/24/1900 at 24/1/5; phthisis pulmonalis; shoemaker; single; b. Farmington; H. Leighton (Farmington) and Emma Colbath (Farmington)

Charles I., d. 1/28/1926 at 58/2/5; widower

Charles W., d. 12/1/1932 at 78/6/17; retired; married; b. Farmington; John W. Leighton (Farmington) and Susan C. Bennett (Farmington)

Clara S., d. 9/16/1930 at 79/9/11; widow; b. Farmington; George K. Smith (Rowley, MA) and Hannah Colomy

Dorris, d. 9/2/1900 at 0/8/11; cholera infantum; b. Farmington; John Leighton (Farmington) and Annie Perkins (Farmington)

E. Ann, d. 3/14/1901 at 61/0/20; cer. spin. sclerosis; divorced; b. Farmington; Emerson Furber (Farmington) and Mary Young (Farmington)

Elizabeth, d. 3/14/1909 at 83/11/26; influenza; b. Portsmouth; Daniel Sherburn (Portsmouth) and Jane Colbath (Barnstead)

Emma A., d. 2/12/1895 at 47/11/30; pneumonia; housework; widow; b. Natick, MA; Freeman Colbath (Farmington) and Urana Neal (Farmington)

Francina, d. 4/1/1919 at 71; housekeeper; widow; b. Effingham; Jeremiah Brown (Effingham) and Susan Moulton (Freedom)

Frank, d. 10/15/1898 at 70/3/4; heart disease; painter; married

Fred M., d. 6/24/1923 at 55/8/19; liveryman; divorced; b. Farmington; Charles Leighton and Emma Colbath (Natick, MA)

George, d. 2/20/1904 at 0/1/14; la grippe; b. Farmington; Harry Leighton (Farmington) and Maggie Troy (Danvers, MA)

George, d. 3/30/1907 at 63/2/24; cancer; shoemaker; married; b. Farmington; Moses Leighton (Rochester, carpenter) and Hannah Tanner (Rochester)

Georgia A., d. 5/20/1936 at 84/5/15; at home; widow; b. New Durham; Samuel Rhines (New Durham) and Charlotte Evans (New Durham)

Guy F., d. 6/29/1935 at 50/4/3; shoeworker; single; b. Farmington; Charles H. Leighton and Emma A. Beal

Hannah, d. 8/3/1906 at 83/7/5; chronic nephritis; widower; b. Farmington; John Tanner (Rochester) and Mary Thompson (Farmington)

Hannah B., d. 4/23/1904 at 82/1/2; bronchial pneumonia; married; b. Farmington; Levi W. Leighton (Farmington) and T. Chamberlin (New Durham)

Harry I., d. 6/3/1905 at 36/2/18; heart failure; shoe cutter; married; Charles M. Leighton (Farmington) and Emma A. Colbath (Natick)

Henry C., d. 7/14/1931 at 82/9/20; dairyman; married; b. Farmington; Samuel Leighton (Farmington) and Elizabeth Sherburn (Portsmouth)

John B., d. 1/6/1925 at 76/1/10; farmer; widower; b. Farmington; John W. Leighton (Farmington) and Susan D. Bennett (Farmington)

John H., d. 1/8/1936 at 61/6; shoe worker; married; b. Farmington; George F. Leighton (Farmington) and Margaret Sandwich (Halifax, NS)

John W., d. 10/8/1920 at 72/1/18; shoeworker; married; b. Farmington; Moses C. Leighton and Hannah Tanner (Farmington)

Joseph J., d. 12/9/1891 at 75/7/10; heart disease; contractor; married; b. Farmington; Richard Leighton and Mary Kimball

Levi W., d. 8/9/1888 at 58/5/3; dropsy; farmer; married; b. Farmington; Levi Leighton

Lucy A., d. 3/1/1938 at 86/0/13; housewife; widow; b. Eaton; Thomas Drew and Sarah Bryant

Margaret, d. 5/19/1913 at 73/2/2; dilation of heart; housekeeper; widow; b. Halifax; James Sandwich (England, farmer) and Mary Cary (Halifax)

Mark F., d. 7/3/1911 at 59/5; alcoholism; shoe cutter; widower; b. Farmington; Moses C. Leighton (Farmington, carpenter) and Hannah E. Tanner (Farmington)

Mary Susan, d. 10/9/1929 at 79/2/20 in Marblehead, MA; at home; widow; b. Swampscott, MA; John Leavitt (Swampscott) and Nora Sweet (Marblehead)

Mrs. V., d. 5/21/1895 at 58/1/20; asthenia; housewife; married; b. Lowell; David Burnham (Alexandria) and Dorcas Horace (Berwick, ME)

Olive S., d. 5/20/1923 at 35/8; shoeworker; b. Farmington; George Otis (Farmington) and Clara Pinkham (Farmington)

Ray E., d. 1/20/1902 at 0/2/10; brain fever; b. Farmington; Harry I. Leighton (Farmington) and Maggie Troy (Danvers)

Samuel J., d. 12/27/1894 at 75/7/8; softening of brain; farmer; married; b. Farmington; Richard Leighton (Farmington) and Rachel Kimball (Alton)

Sarah C., d. 9/1/1899 at 77/1/1; old age; housewife; married; b. Farmington; William Bennett (Farmington) and Mary Wingate (Farmington)

Sophie, d. 4/29/1922 at 88/4/12; widow; b. Mt. Vernon; Bernard Averill (Mt. Vernon) and Harriet Richardson (Farmington)

Susan I., d. 4/3/1931 at 70/2/6; housekeeper; widow; b. Barnstead; Plummer O. Berry (Barnstead) and Abbie A. E. French (Barnstead)

Varnum H., d. 4/23/1902 at 83/4/7; acute congestion liver; widower; b. Strafford; Sarah Winkley (Strafford)

Wilbur S., d. 3/21/1928 at 72/9/5; laborer; single; b. Farmington; Moses C. Leighton (Farmington) and Hannah E. Tanner (Farmington)

**LEMIRE,**
Mamie M., d. 3/26/1935 at 60/11/15 in Derry; at home; married; b. Canada; George Bellmore (Canada) and Mary ----- (Canada)

**LEONARD,**
Harriett J., d. 6/18/1928 at 85/11/12; widow; b. NY; Hezekiah Murdock (NY) and Sylvia Mallory (No. Adams, MA)

**LEPINE** [see Lapine],
Ellen, d. 10/25/1894 at 42/9/22; cardiac dropsy; housekeeper; married; b. Canada; Thomas Fitzgerald (Ireland) and Mary Laungean (Canada)

Margaret, d. 6/30/1903 at 68; nutral insufficiency; housekeeper; widow

Peter, d. 12/25/1911 at 66/1; chronic nephritis; farmer; married; b. Canada; Peter Lepine (Canada, farmer) and Margaret V. ----- (Canada)

**LESPERANCE,**
Richard, d. 1/7/1934 at 0/6/12 in Dover; b. Farmington; Edwin Lesperance (Lancaster) and Pauline Tirrell (Springvale, ME)

**LESSARD,**
Amanda, d. 10/28/1911 at 48/7/16; pneumonia; housekeeper; widow; b. Canada; Nazurie Nedeau (Canada) and Celina Gagni (Canada)

**LEVESQUE,**
Joseph, d. 3/8/1924 at 0/0/1; b. Farmington; Joseph Levesque (Lowell, MA) and Aurel Scott (Milton)

**LEWIS,**
Electa A., d. 6/29/1919 at 65/5/29; housewife; married; b. Ellensburg, NY; Jacob Aiken and Abbie Langley
George M., d. 10/14/1919 at 72/2/3; shoeworker; widower; b. Effingham; John Lewis (NH) and Eliza Leighton (NH)
John E., d. 10/10/1888 at 49/11/10; phthisis; machinist; married; b. Ossipee; John Lewis (Portsmouth) and Louisa Leighton (Effingham)
Louise, d. 5/7/1890 at 78/1/26; phthisis; housekeeper; widow; b. Effingham; Isaac Leighton (Barrington) and Sarah Buzzell

**LIBBEY,**
Caroline, d. 1/2/1899 at 83/3/27; pneumonia; housewife; single; b. Eliot, ME
Elizabeth G., d. 5/20/1922 at 91/5/19; housewife; widow; b. New Durham; Joseph Chamberlain (Farmington) and Sarah Holmes (Farmington)
Joseph T., d. 3/22/1921 at 93/0/24; retired, farmer; married; b. New Durham; Asa Libbey (New Durham) and Nancy Clough (Alton)

**LIBBY,**
son, d. 7/22/1923 at –; b. Farmington; Joshua Libby (Evansham) and Mabel Stanley (Evansham)

**LINSCOTT,**
George H., d. 2/21/1898 at 53/2/28; apoplexy; chief of police; married; b. Sanford, ME; Timothy Linscott (Sanford, ME) and Joanna Meader (Rochester)

**LITTLEFIELD,**
Alma F., d. 8/8/1928 at 54/10/12; housewife; married; b. Middleton; Oscar F. Kimball and Lenora Hayes
Fred A., d. 11/5/1931 at 62/3/16; insurance; widower; b. Fitchburg, MA; Orin Littlefield (Wells, ME) and Clara Walker (New York, NY)
John C., d. 3/2/1889 at 68/6; heart failure; tailor; Theodore Littlefield
Jothan, d. 5/27/1925 at 69/7/20; fish dealer; married; b. Ogunquit, ME; Jothan Littlefield

**LOCKE,**
Ellen C., d. 6/25/1934 at 82/4/20; at home; b. Hanson, MA; Henry Thayer and Mary Turner
Emma F., d. 9/23/1907 at 12/8/1; a'm ambust'n b'l'a; school girl; b. Exeter; Oliver A. Locke (Dover, carpenter) and Mary Flagg (Exeter)
James W., d. 12/23/1924 at 66/4/19; married
Luella A., d. 5/12/1893 at 3/0/24; scarlet fever; b. Farmington; Henry P. Locke (Gilmanton) and Jennie Foss (Strafford)

**LOONEY,**
Adelaide, d. 1/21/1925 at 52/7/4; housekeeper; divorced; b. Farmington; James Waldron (Farmington) and Adelaide Cilley (Manchester)

**LORD,**
daughter, d. 12/17/1926 at –; b. Farmington; William Lord (Rochester) and Elsie Pope (Wells, ME)
Catherine H., d. 11/15/1898 at 66/6/14; housewife; married; b. Sutton; Nathaniel Palmer (Sutton) and ----- (Warren)
Harold, d. 9/30/1918 at 21; woodturner; single; b. E. Rochester; Fessenden Lord
Hattie B., d. 8/19/1930 at 68/3/27; housewife; married; b. W. Lebanon, ME

James J., d. 4/10/1908 at 68/1/3; uremia; married; b. Berwick, ME; Samuel Lord (Berwick, ME) and Hannah Hutchins (Wells, ME)

Josephine, d. 3/25/1938 at 77/11/24; widow; b. Exeter

Susan E., d. 6/23/1898 at 69/7/14; malignant growth in side; housekeeper; widow; b. Rochester; Daniel Grant and Susan Foss (Lebanon)

**LOUGEE,**

daughter, d. 12/25/1904 at –; stillborn; b. Farmington; Jacob Lougee (Farmington) and Hattie Dyer (Sanbornville)

Almon S., d. 10/9/1913 at 70/0/4; nephritis; shoemaker; widower; b. Washington, VT; Jacob S. Lougee (Moultonboro, farmer) and Abigail Marsh (Loudon)

Annie, d. 3/25/1897 at 49; housewife; married; b. Cornish; William Pendexter

Annie D., d. 9/24/1919 at 55/11/28; shoeworker; widow; b. Augusta, ME; Fred Morton (Augusta, ME) and Sarah Rankins (Augusta, ME)

Chester N., d. 7/11/1899 at 58/0/12; albuminuria; laborer; single; b. Farmington

Effie M., d. 8/28/1903 at 0/1/9; gastro enteritis; Jacob Lougee (Farmington) and Hattie M. Dyer (Sanbornville)

Ernest K., d. 12/16/1903 at 32/8/29; pulmonary tuberculosis; shoemaker; married; b. Farmington; Almon S. Lougee (Chester, VT) and Jennie Durgin (Parsonsfield, ME)

Hiram C., d. 3/16/1892 at 44/1; albumenura; teamster; married; b. Chelsea, MA; John H. Lougee (Moultonboro, farmer) and Polly Durmore (Chelsea, MA)

Jennie B., d. 8/30/1936 at 77/10/28; housewife; married; b. New Durham; John Berry (New Durham) and Nancy M. Phelps (Wilmot)

June C., d. 2/23/1920 at 1/8; b. Farmington; Herbert Lougee (Farmington) and Evon Gardaria (Manchester)

Lillian R., d. 12/2/1938 at 70/2/12; housewife; married; b. Milton; Moses Cook (Bridgton, ME) and Freelove Downing (Holderness)

Nehemiah, d. 1/29/1928 at 72/6/16; retired; married; b. Farmington; Jacob Lougee and Abigail Horne

Reuben P., d. 2/11/1910 at 69/6/27; tuberculosis; trader; widower; b. Gilmanton

Simeon, d. 5/22/1891 at 85/8/29; congestion of lungs; carpenter; widower; b. New Gloucester; Simeon Lougee (Gilmanton) and Mary Smith (Parsonsfield)

**LOVERING,**
Etta H., d. 9/11/1930 at 83/8/19; housekeeper; widow; b. Naples, ME; George Gammon and Abbie Lord

F. A., d. 11/23/1905 at 58/11/15; fatty deg. of heart; merchant; married; b. Tuftonboro; Plumer D. Lovering (Tuftonboro) and Lydia Burbank (Tuftonboro)

Frank E., d. 7/22/1936 at 24/3/28 in Rochester; shoeworker; single; b. Farmington; George A. Lovering (Wakefield) and Irma T. Davis (Farmington)

**LOWELL,**
Alonzo J., d. 2/19/1930 at 87/4/3; retired; widower; b. Hiram, ME; Nial Lowell (Baldwin, ME) and Rachael Storer (Hiram, ME)

Ethel M., d. 5/25/1890 at 1/6/20; tuberculosis; b. Farmington; Stillman R. Lowell (Hiram, ME) and Cora E. Willey (New Durham)

Fred C., d. 12/23/1927 at 0/0/23; b. Rochester; Fred C. Lowell (Lebanon, ME) and Marjorie Ryan (Kennebunk, ME)

Mary J., d. 2/22/1929 at 53/8/13; housewife; married; b. Farmington; George Hurd (Farmington) and Sophia Foss (Strafford)

Philemon, d. 7/29/1937 at 64/0/28 in New Durham; sawyer; widower; b. Hiram, ME; James A. Lowell (Hiram, ME) and Joanna Parker (Hiram, ME)

Sherwood A., d. 3/3/1934 at 0/0/21 in New Durham; b. New Durham; Fred C. Lowell (Lebanon, ME) and Marjorie Ryan (Kennebunk, ME)

**LUCAS,**
Emma F., d. 10/25/1918 at 63/6/25; shoeworker; widow; b. Rochester; George Whitehouse (Strafford) and Lydia Ransome (Strafford)

**LYSTER,**
Lawrence, d. 9/3/1920 at 1/3/17; b. Norris Bend, O; Frederick Lyster (Kirkdale, PQ) and Mary Lillian Law (Richmond, PQ)

**MAGEE,**
Charles, d. 6/25/1938 at 43/7/9 in Alton Bay; shoeworker; married; b. Manchester; George Magee (Scotland) and Ida Wyman (Goffstown)
George W., d. 2/14/1927 at 0/10/10; b. Farmington; Charles A. Magee (Manchester) and Cecilia Lawrence (Jamaica Plains, MA)

**MAIN,**
Stephen W., d. 3/31/1915 at 83; shoemaker; widower; b. Milton; Stephen Main and Mary Downs (Milton)

**MALONEY,**
James F., d. 8/2/1930 at 16 in Rochester; student; single; b. AR; Edward Maloney (Ireland) and Sarah Marchand (Canada)
Sarah, d. 3/4/1927 at 51; housewife; married; b. Canada; Louis Marchand (Canada) and Rebecca Palmer (Canada)

**MANSFIELD,**
Grace, d. 9/25/1930 at 43/10/2 in Concord; shoemaker; divorced; b NH; George M. Nutter (NH) and Leah Hayes (NH)

**MANSON,**
George H., d. 1/19/1914 at 66/7/11; cerebral softening; shoemaker; married; b. Limerick, ME; Samuel Manson (Limerick, ME, farmer) and Eliza Sawyer (Hollis, ME)
George H., Jr., d. 10/5/1911 at 26/11/22; diabetic melliter; shoe operator; single; b. Farmington; George H. Manson (Limerick, ME, shoe operator) and Lizzie Longfellow (Boston, MA)

**MARCHAND,**
Harry, d. 8/27/1918 at 34/3/10; farmer; single; b. Somersworth; Eugene Marchand (Canada) and Emma J. Preu (Boston)

**MARCOUX,**
Arthur J., d. 10/28/1935 at 49; laborer; single; b. Rochester; Joseph Marcoux (Canada) and Adelaide Cyr (Canada)
Gideon, d. 5/31/1925 at 30/5/16; shoemaker; married; b. Rochester; Joseph Marcoux (Canada) and Adelaide C. (Canada)
Harry T., d. 5/9/1908 at 1/2/9; croup; b. Milton; Joseph E. Marcoux (Thetford, PQ) and Annie D. Wood (Somersworth)

Joseph E., d. 1/10/1913 at 32/3/17; tubercular meningitis; shoe operator; married; b. Canada; Joseph D. Marcoux (Canada, laborer) and Adelaide Cyr (Canada)

**MARDEN,**
Abbie O., d. 4/12/1890 at 26/0/6; inflammation of bowels; cook; married; b. Wolfeboro; James Marden (Wolfeboro) and Lucinda Warren (Brookfield)

**MARSH,**
Etta V., d. 5/31/1924 at 67/3/13; housewife; married; b. Littleton; Augustus Streeter (Littleton) and Lydia Phillips (Littleton)

**MARSTON,**
Ada L., d. 6/22/1902 at 53/4/10; septicemia; housewife; married; b. Alton; James Davis and Martha Cloutman
Charles, d. 11/19/1926 at 72/0/8; machinist; married; b. Chichester; Oliver Marston (Pittsfield) and Jennie Sherburn (Pittsfield)

**MARTIN,**
son, d. 2/23/1938 at –; b. Farmington; Theodore Martin (Cambridge, MA) and Beatrice Maly (Cambridge, MA)
Elisha H., d. 9/13/1931 at 41/9 in Athol, MA; shoeworker; married; b. Gardner, MA

**MARTINEAU,**
Edmund, d. 6/2/1938 at 68/1/5; B & M RR; widower; b. Canada; Pierre Martineau (Canada) and Sophia Perrault (Canada)
Phil'ise, d. 9/13/1936 at 59/3/11; housewife; married; b. Rochester; Joseph Marcoux (Canada) and Adelaide Cyr (Canada)

**MASON,**
John W., d. 12/2/1928 at 88/0/21; farmer; single; b. Portsmouth; Benjamin Mason and Sally Brackett (Ossipee)

**MATHEWS,**
Alice, d. 2/14/1906 at 31/6/17; tuberculosis of lung; married; b. Farmington; John W. Pinkham (New Durham) and Eliza Pinkham (New Durham)
J. Francis, d. 2/14/1927 at 76/1/14; widower

Jennie L., d. 2/3/1905 at 6/6/9; stoppage of liver; b. Farmington; Nelson H. Mathews (Farmington) and Alice Pinkham (Farmington)

Neal, d. 2/18/1901 at 0/6/2; pneumonia; b. Farmington; Nel H. Mathews (Rochester) and Alice Pinkham (Farmington)

Sumner F., d. 1/22/1909 at 34/0/10; suicide by shooting; laborer; b. Rochester; Frank Mathews (Burke, VT) and Jennie E. Donnel (Alton)

## MATTHEWS,

Jennie, d. 4/16/1900 at 46/9/12; suicide; housewife; widow; b. Alto John Donelly (St. Johns, NB) and Sarah Brown (Hiram, ME)

## MAXFIELD,

Alp'ri'h, d. 9/21/1899 at 57/4/17; typhoid fever; housewife; widow; b. Wentworth; Lebina Page (Wentworth) and Betsey Merrill (Wentworth)

## MAYNARD,

Christopher, d. 2/7/1902 at 81/11/1; old age; farmer; widower; b. Stow, MA; Uriah Maynard (Stow, MA) and Mary Maynard (Stow, MA)

Mary J., d. 1/26/1892 at 51/9/17; paralysis; housewife; married; b. Farmington, John Walker (Farmington, farmer) and Eliza Furber (Farmington)

## MAYO,

Caroline, d. 12/26/1891 at 83/4/27; chronic bronchitis; housekeepe widow; b. Chatham, MA; Samuel Emery (Chatham, MA) and Jerusha Chase

## McANNIS,

Gertrude L., d. 9/22/1891 at 0/7/22; consumption; b. Boston, MA; Janet L. McAnnis (Boston, MA)

## McCARTHY,

Charles E., d. 12/18/1925 at 57/7/26; shoecutter; single; b. Lynn, MA; Dennis McCarthy (Ireland) and Hannah McDonald (Ireland)

**McCORMICK,**
daughter, d. 1/30/1890 at 0/4/7; tuberculosis; b. Farmington; Thomas J. McCormick (Malden, MA) and Helen L. Tanner (Farmington)
H[elen]., d. 3/15/1890 at 23/8/15; pulmonary phthisis; housekeeper; married; b. Farmington; John F. Tanner (Farmington) and Angelina L. Rand (New Durham)

**McDAVID,**
Rosina, d. 2/22/1936 at 82 in Dedham, MA; at home; widow; b. Scotland; John Blaine (Scotland) and J. McLaughlin (Scotland)

**McDONALD,**
John, d. 8/28/1894 at 76/9/15; paralysis; farmer; married; b. PEI; Dane MacDonald (Scotland) and Mary Macdonald (Scotland)

**McDUFFEE,**
Edna, d. 4/28/1926 at 67/11/17; retired; married; b. Alton; John I. Huckins (Madbury) and Abbie Whitehouse (Sanford, ME)
Frank P., d. 5/30/1932 at 74/3/12 in So. Paris, ME; teamster; widower; b. Rochester; James McDuffie (Rochester) and Abbie Palmer (Rochester)
Mabel, d. 4/6/1907 at 40/6/23; tuberculosis; shoestitcher; married; b. Alton; Lewis A. Proctor (Alton, farmer) and Sarah A. Collins (Barnstead)

**McEACHERN,**
F. A., d. 9/15/1938 at 89/10/13; housewife; widow; b. PEI; Douglas McPhee (PEI) and M. McKinnon (PEI)

**McFARLEAN,**
Mary, d. 8/9/1920 at 61/5/5; housewife; married; b. PEI; ----- Clough

**McGREGOR,**
Minnie, d. 10/14/1918 at 33/6/3; housewife; married; b. Greenville; Jeremiah Chadbourne (Waterboro, ME) and Mary F. Mack (Bradford, MA)
Nellie, d. 11/12/1915 at 42/5/1; housewife; married; b. NS; Melbourne Phinney (NS) and Eliza Baker (NS)

**McINTYRE,**
Arlie, d. 10/29/1931 at 60 in Boston, MA; housewife; married; b. IA; James Davis (Waldoboro, ME) and Angeline Engley (Waldoboro, ME)

**McNAYR,**
Sarah W., d. 12/16/1931 at 64/1/22; housekeeper; widow; b. Salem MA; Alfred Nason and Sarah Poole

**McNEAL,**
Albion J., d. 5/28/1936 at 81/9/10 in Barnstead; farmer; married; b. Barnstead; Jonathan McNeal (Barnstead) and Sarah J. Garland (Barnstead)
Ida J., d. 11/11/1938 at 84/2/13 in Sanford, ME; housewife; widow; b. Farmington; Reuben Copp (Farmington)

**McWHITNEY,**
Andrew B., d. 9/25/1931 at 40/5; married; b. Concord; William J. McWhitney (Ireland) and Sarah A. Smith (Newfields)

**MEADER,**
Jessie B., d. 7/17/1924 at 68/0/14; housekeeper; married; b. Farmington; Asa B. Hayes (Farmington) and Sarah Berry (Strafford)

**MELLOWS,**
Adriana, d. 7/31/1897 at 62/8; malig. growth in rectum; housewife; widow; b. Gorham; Stephen Libbey (Gorham) and Mary Loe (Gray, ME)
Daniel C., d. 5/15/1891 at 67/8/7; fever and abscess; shoe cutter; married; b. Alton; Samuel Mellows and Patience Leighton (Strafford)

**MERRILL,**
Hannah J., d. 7/6/1896 at 87/4/29; heart disease; housekeeper; widow; b. S. Berwick, ME; Edmund Lord (S. Berwick, ME) and Philomela Emery (S. Berwick, ME)

**MESERVE,**

Charles F., d. 9/27/1927 at 80/9/11; shoemaker; widower; b. Farmington; Samuel Meserve (Rochester) and Belinda French (Middleton)

Clifton E., d. 9/23/1921 at 0/4/2; b. Ossipee; Frank C. Meserve (Freedom) and Ruby Ryer

Florence A., d. 9/16/1894 at 3/6/10; convulsions; b. Farmington; Samuel Meserve (Rochester) and Julia Gilman (Danvers, MA)

George W., d. 9/5/1926 at 80/1/14; retired; married; b. Lee; Charles Meserve and Sophronia Tucker (Grafton)

Julia G., d. 12/21/1928 at 70/8/25; widow; b. Danvers, MA; Stephen Gilman (Alton) and Amanda Cross (Danvers, MA)

Samuel, d. 7/9/1918 at 95/3/29; McKay stitcher; married; b. Rochester; Stephen Meserve (Milton) and Susan Henderson (Gonic)

**MILLER,**

Carrie T., d. 5/18/1905 at 69/7/24; cancer of stomach; housekeeper; single; b. New Durham; Richard Miller (Milton) and Paulina Buzzell (Acton, ME)

Charles H., d. 3/25/1904 at 55; structural brain disease; laborer; widower

Henry B., d. 3/12/1922 at 64/10/26; knife mfgr.; married; b. New Durham; James A. Miller (New Durham)

Jencella S., d. 10/26/1896 at 39; neuralgia of heart; housewife; married; b. Raymond; Samuel Smart and Sarah J. Smart

John B., d. 12/31/1933 at 68/7/4 in Dover; farmer; widower; b. Middleton; Joseph C. Miller (Middleton) and Augusta Horne (Middleton)

Joseph B., d. 5/25/1912 at 81/0/22; heart failure; farmer; widower; b. Milton; Richard Miller (Milton, farmer) and Paulina Buzzell (Acton, ME)

Joseph C., d. 4/6/1900 at –; acute nephritis; laborer; widower; b. Middleton; Bartholomew Miller and Paulina Miller

Mary A., d. 1/19/1914 at 71/11/11; cerebrospinal de'n; housekeeper; single; b. New Durham; Richard Miller (Milton, farmer) and Paulina Buzzell (Acton, ME)

Paulina, d. 11/5/1897 at 88/0/23; paralysis; housewife; divorced; b. Milton; Henry Miller (Milton) and Molly Rines (Milton)

Pauline, d. 9/11/1888 at 86/8/13; cholera morbus; b. Acton, ME; James Buzzell (Wells, ME) and Tabatha Allen (York, ME)

Richard, d. 12/25/1891 at 90/4/21; hemorrhage of the kidneys; farmer; widower; b. New Durham

Russell R., d. 2/25/1938 at 92/3/16; farmer; widower; b. New Durham; Richard Miller (Milton) and Paulina Buzzell (Acton, ME)

**MILLINER,**

George, d. 5/7/1919 at 77/4/15; laborer; widower; b. Sackville, NB; Robert Milliner and Emily Purdy

**MILLS,**

Charles E., d. 1/30/1924 at 76/9/5; mechanic; widower; b. Hudson, MA; George Mills (Portland, ME) and Elizabeth Stickney

Joseph F., d. 7/4/1910 at 70/7/12; Bright's disease; farmer; married; b. Strafford; Jeremiah Mills (Durham) and Sarah Foss (Strafford)

Olive W., d. 4/23/1911 at 71/0/13; pneumonia; retired; widow; b. Dover; Isaac D. Canney (Madbury, farmer) and Matilda Reed (Farmington)

S. Josephine, d. 12/10/1918 at 50/6/1; housewife; married; b. New Durham; John Davis (New Durham)

**MOISAN,**

Edgar, d. 10/30/1931 at 51/2/18; mill operative; single; b. Canada; Pierre Moisan (Canada) and Obeline Ferland (Canada)

**MONTEE,**

Lucy E., d. 6/8/1906 at 47/2/5; brain fever; stitcher; married; Charles Winter

**MONTGOMERY,**

Lillian, d. 4/22/1918 at 32/5/23; housewife; married; b. Watertown, ME; George F. Pitts and Clara Lindall

Sarah A., d. 8/23/1913 at 72/3/5; arteriosclerosis; widow; b. Strafford; William Perry (Strafford) and Sarah Hall

**MOONEY,**

Elizabeth, d. 2/24/1925 at 65; housewife; married; b. Wendell, MA; Cornelius Bresnahan and Mary McCarthy (Ireland)

Frank E., d. 7/25/1934 at 75/2/5; merchant; married; b. Alton; Edwin P. Mooney (Alton) and Tamson Leighton (Farmington)

Sarah E., d. 1/1/1922 at 70/5/17; widow; b. Wolfeboro; John C. Drew (Wolfeboro) and Sarah Lucas (Wolfeboro)

Tamson A., d. 4/8/1920 at 85/8/22; housewife; widow; b. Farmington; Levi Leighton (Farmington) and Tamson Chamberlin (New Durham)

**MOORE,**

Abbie H., d. 4/18/1923 at 77/3/9; widow; b. Danvers, MA; Timothy Hawes and Mary -----

W. H., d. 4/23/1900 at 56/9; cerebral apoplexy; shoemaker; married; b. Boston; Horace Moore (Henniker) and Nancy J. Knight (Wayne, ME)

**MORRILL,**

C. J., d. 3/13/1912 at 41/9/18; tuberculosis; foreman; married; b. Sherbrook, PQ; William Morrill (Tuftonboro, farmer) and Susan Brown (Tuftonboro)

**MORRISON,**

Mary E., d. 12/24/1933 at 1/2/7; b. Rochester; Roger H. Morrison (Boston, MA) and Mary Corson (Milton)

**MORSE,**

Harold E., d. 3/12/1907 at 11/6/3; general peritonitis; school boy; b. N. Bedford, MA; William T. Morse (Rochester, N. Bedford, MA, shoemaker) and Adelaide Elsbree (Taunton, MA)

**MORTON,**

Annie M., d. 4/15/1926 at 34/8/26; housewife; married; b. Gorham, ME; William Skillings (Gorham, ME) and ----- (NS)

**MOULTON,**

daughter, d. 10/23/1899 at –; stillborn; b. Farmington; Justin C. Moulton (Farmington) and Mamie M. Ham (Farmington)

Addie J., d. 11/9/1888 at 0/6/5; infl. of bowels; b. Farmington; George E. Moulton (Tamworth) and Jeanette S. Hill (New Durham)

Arabell, d. 4/14/1887 at 0/3; b. Farmington; George E. Moulton (Tamworth) and Janette Hill (New Durham)

Edwin P., d. 3/11/1931 at 82/5; clergyman; married; b. VT

Harold, d. 12/15/1900 at 0/2/19; syphilis; b. Farmington; C. A. Moulton (Farmington) and Edith Ham (Farmington)
Harriet, d. 11/4/1917 at 85/0/2; housewife; widow; b. Tamworth; Daniel Remick and Esther Nickerson
J. C. S., d. 7/29/1893 at 37/0/24; hemorrhage; housewife; married b. New Durham; Joseph Hill (Rockport, ME) and Maria Simmers (New Durham)
Joseph P., d. 11/19/1912 at 87/10/7; old age; shoemaker; married b. Milton; James Moulton
Laura S., d. 5/2/1909 at 54/1/2; erysipelas; housewife; b. W. Milton Josiah Witham and Susan Place (Farmington)
Lillian, d. 7/27/1903 at 20/4/20; tuberculosis of lungs; single; George Moulton (Tamworth) and Jennette Hill (New Durham)
Mary E., d. 7/7/1929 at 76/11/27; housewife; married; b. Tilton; Loren Foss and May A. Mason
Moses P., d. 4/10/1915 at 71/6/14; farmer; widower; b. Diamonds Cr.

## MUNROE,
George, d. 7/22/1928 at 21

## MURPHY,
Estella, d. 5/16/1895 at 0/4/21; marasmus; b. Farmington; Samuel Murphy (Dover) and Mary M. Harding (P. Herbert, NS)

## MURTAUGH,
Patrick, d. 11/15/1888 at 51; cirrhosis of liver; shoemaker; married; b. Ireland

## NASON,
Laureston, d. 10/26/1903 at 41/0/21; muscular rheumatism; machinist; married; Charles Nason and Ann Durgin

## NEDEAU,
son, d. 3/4/1916 at –; b. Farmington; Ralph I. Nedeau (Farmington) and Alda A. Marcoux (Rochester)
Dorothy, d. 6/23/1915 at 0/0/18; b. Farmington; Ralph I. Nedeau (Farmington) and Alda A. Marcoux (Rochester)
Emma J., d. 11/27/1929 at 75/11/17; shoeworker; widow; b. Farmington; Albert Corson and Betsey D. Ham (New Durham)

**NELSON,**
Jothan, d. 4/3/1895 at 86/7; farmer; single; b. China, ME

**NEWELL,**
Cora E., d. 12/8/1916 at 31/9/24; married; b. Ferrisburgh, VT; Ira J. Brydia (Ferrisburgh, VT) and Carrie Dayfoot (Lansing, MI)

**NILSSON,**
Lars F., d. 4/23/1920 at 79/2/1; potter; married; b. Sweden

**NOLAN,**
Thomas, d. 8/30/1907 at 80; congestion of brain; retired soldier; widower; b. Killoney, Ireland

**NOURSE,**
daughter, d. 1/31/1908 at –; stillborn; b. Farmington; Ernest Nourse (Medway, MA) and Grace O'Connell (Medway, MA)

**NOYES,**
Alice E., d. 2/3/1923 at 63/3/21; housewife; married; b. Oakham, MA; James B. Nelson (MA) and Ellen Cram (MA)
Charles F., d. 2/13/1935 at 80 in So. Portland, ME; retired; widower; b. Oakham, MA; William Hayes (sic) (Oakham, MA) and Harriett A. Fitts
Henry J., d. 4/30/1925 at 67/0/23; clerk; married; b. Anawan, IL; James B. Noyes (NH) and Sibbil Wentworth (NY)
Inez M., d. 7/26/1925 at 64/11/13; housewife; married; b. Middleton; Charles Whitehouse (Middleton) and Mary Brooks (Lebanon, ME)
Mary A., d. 9/17/1925 at 68/6/18; at home; widow; b. Farmington; Peter M. Horne (Farmington) and Mary Pendexter (Rochester)
William, d. 2/16/1911 at 88/3/7; heart failure; laborer; widower; b. Oakham, MA

**NUTE,**
Agnes C., d. 9/13/1938 at 58/2/15; nurse; married; b. Rockland, ME; John Cleveland (Rockport, ME) and Margaret Brewster (Rockport, ME)
Alcena M., d. 9/7/1921 at 61/7/27; housewife; married; b. Saco, ME; George W. Marshall (Biddeford, ME) and Cynthia Hutchins (China, ME)

Alonzo, d. 12/24/1892 at 66/10/12; malarial blood poison; shoe manufacturer; married; b. Milton; David Nute (Milton, farmer) and Lavina Cook (Wakefield)

Alonzo E., d. 4/1/1921 at 73; farmer; single; b. Dover; Stephen Nute (Milton) and Eleanor Abbott (Tuftonboro)

Alonzo I., d. 12/5/1923 at 73; accountant; single; b. Farmington; Alonzo Nute (Milton) and Mary Pearl (New Durham)

Arthur H., d. 9/7/1932 at 65/9/26 in Milton; farmer; widower; b. Milton; Stephen Nute (Milton) and Mary Abbott (Tuftonboro)

Byron P., d. 11/5/1921 at 62/1/28; freight agent; married; b. Farmington; Eri F. Nute (Milton) and Mary Rollins (Somersworth)

Charles W., d. 8/23/1926 at 80/7/17; shoeworker; married; b. Dover; Stephen Nute and Eleanor Abbott

Clara B., d. 9/6/1921 at 58/0/17; housewife; married; b. Alton; William Chamberlin (Alton) and Sarah Tufts (Middleton)

Clara M., d. 1/15/1937 at 77/11/17; at home; widow; b. Milton; James M. Varney (Milton) and Mary E. Jones (Milton)

David H., d. 3/20/1889 at 53/8; phthisis, pneumonia and chronic dirrhoea; shoemaker; David Nute

Elizabeth H., d. 1/19/1900 at 62/0/26; inflammation of brain; milliner; widow; b. Bangor, ME; Alva Huntress (Sanford, ME) and Emma Ross (Portland)

Eri F., d. 2/20/1910 at 75/0/18; acute indigestion; shoe cutter; widower; b. Milton; Moses Nute and Eunice Varney

Eugene P., d. 5/16/1922 at 69/11/2; insurance; married; b. Farmington; Alonzo Nute (Milton) and Mary Pearl (Farmington)

Hannah L., d. 12/18/1898 at 85/5/23; old age; widow; b. Alton; Robert Hayes (Barrington) and Phebe Holmes (Barrington)

John S., d. 4/23/1933 at 86/3/9; retired; widower; b. Dover; Hopley Y. Nute (Dover) and Sarah Pinder

Mary C., d. 8/3/1892 at 62/5/22; unknown; housewife; married; b. Lebanon, ME; Moses Rollins (Lebanon, ME, farmer) and Alice Shapley (Lebanon, ME)

Mary Pearl, d. 6/29/1912 at 83/2; old age; widow; b. Farmington; Joseph Pearl (Farmington, farmer) and Betsey Hayes (Milton)

Nellie S. P., d. 3/25/1928 at 70/9/25; widow; b. S. Wolfeboro; Harry S. Parker (Wolfeboro) and Hester A. Stevens (Orford)

Nettie M., d. 4/3/1910 at 51/3/25; val. disease of heart; housewife; b. Alton; Charles Pickering (Gilmanton) and Mary Place

Rufus M., d. 3/11/1887 at 64/8; manufacturer; married; b. Milton

Russell F., d. 6/7/1892 at 76/2/21; pneumonia; currier; married; b. Milton; Jacob Nute (Madbury, farmer) and Hannah Young (Dover)

Sophia M., d. 1/2/1922 at 37/7/26; shoeworker; married; b. Manchester; Nelson Bailey (Canada) and Mary Belmere (Canada)

Susan G., d. 10/22/1924 at 87/8/8; housewife; widow; b. Milton; Jonathan Hurd and Abigail Rand (Farmington)

Willis J., d. 1/6/1891 at 0/2/25; congestion of lungs; b. Alton; Gardiner Nute (Dover) and Clara Chamberlin (Middleton)

**NUTTER,**

Almena, d. 7/3/1926 at 89/3/2; widow; b. No. Ware

Arabella, d. 4/5/1918 at 66/10/7; housewife; widow; b. Farmington; John W. Leighton (Farmington) and Susan C. Bennett (Farmington)

Charles E., d. 4/27/1905 at 55/2/11; heart disease; liquor dealer; widower; b. Barnstead; Joseph Nutter (Farmington) and Sophronia Drew (Alton)

Edith M., d. 3/2/1889 at 22/6/15; childbirth; housekeeper; b. Farmington; John L. Brown (Wilton) and Mary E. Twombly (Farmington)

Eliza J., d. 7/11/1892 at 42/11/29; peritonitis; housewife; married; b. Rochester; Locke Howard (Rochester, stone cutter) and Lydia S. Brown (Rochester); burial - Strafford

Elizabeth W., d. 4/27/1905 at 92/10/13; nat. insufficiency; widow; b. Rochester; Toby Hanson (Rochester) and ----- (Brookfield)

Frank O., d. 2/23/1935 at 80/6/28; truckman; widower; b. Farmington; James O. Nutter (Barnstead) and Mary A. Horne (Barnstead)

Henry C., d. 11/9/1914 at 68/11/6; gangrene of leg; farmer; married; b. Farmington; Richard Nutter (Farmington, farmer) and Arsenath D. ----- (Rochester)

James M., d. 7/7/1900 at 49/10/22; apoplectic shock; shoemaker; widower; b. Milton; Thomas Nutter (Milton) and Mary Pinkham (Milton)

John M., d. 5/21/1928 at 69/4/22; farmer; married; b. Milton; Jethro Nutter and Lucinda Maine

Joseph F., d. 12/23/1933 at 76/6/5 in Haverhill; janitor; widower; b. Gilmanton; John Nutter (Barnstead) and Mercy Berry (Barnstead)

Lettie K., d. 10/29/1914 at 51/1/11; cerebral hemorrhage; married; b. Farmington; Charles H. Hayes (Farmington, mill hand) and Frances Amazeen (New Castle)

Lilla E., d. 6/30/1929 at 56/11/9; housewife; married; b. River Philip NS; Solomon H. Babb (Farmington) and Martha E. Davidson (NS)

Lizzie A., d. 1/13/1926 at 65/1/17; shoeworker; divorced; b. Middleton; Solomon Rollins (New Durham) and Lucinda Tufts (Middleton)

Lucinda, d. 3/3/1890 at 53/8/8; Bright's disease; housekeeper; married; b. Gilmanton; Ezra S. Nutter (Barnstead) and Jane S Young (Gilmanton)

Roxie, d. 7/24/1896 at 44/11/19; consumption; housekeeper; married; b. Farmington; Charles T. Gage (Dover) and Martha F. York (Canterbury)

Sarah E., d. 3/4/1915 at 77/10/0; housekeeper; widow; b. Tamworth; Daniel Roberts and Sarah Parrott

Sarah W., d. 7/23/1934 at 75/8/27; at home; married; b. Middleton; Ebenezer S. Pike and Drusilla Hodge

Stephen, d. 2/25/1895 at 59/11/1; pnuemonia; married; b. Farmington; Naham Nutter (Farmington) and Esther W. Horne (Farmington)

Wesley I., d. 9/20/1926 at 66/4/8; married; b. Farmington; Stephen Nutter (W. Ossipee) and Sarah Roberts (Tamworth)

**O'BRIEN,**

Nellie, d. 12/11/1897 at 32/8/7; tuberculosis pulmonary; housewife; married; b. Ireland; Timothy O'Brien (England) and Nora Fittspatrick (Ireland)

**O'GRADY,**

Martin, d. 11/6/1912 at 27/4; accidental; shoemaker; single; b. Ireland

**ORDWAY,**

Carrie E., d. 5/19/1933 at 64/8/29; at home; widow; b. Nottingham; William Parker (Merrimac) and Agnes Cutler (Bedford)

**OSBORN,**
Addie B., d. 12/6/1894 at 39/5/10; peritonitis; housewife; married; b. Farmington; Furber Young (Farmington) and E. R. Goodall (Farmington)

**OSBORNE,**
Florence, d. 6/11/1925 at 46/8/13; housekeeper; married; b. PEI; Charles Jenkins (PEI) and Agnes Norton (PEI)

Maria E., d. 8/22/1929 at 59/8/24; shoeworker; married; b. Stowe, ME; Aaron Smith (Stowe, ME) and Mary Cole (Hiram, ME)

Martha A., d. 12/6/1934 at 70/2; at home; married; b. Effingham; Hiram Towle (Lee) and Rose Blodgett (Naples, ME)

**OTIS,**
Ai D., d. 8/16/1906 at 71/4/7; pernicious anemia; farmer; married; b. Farmington; William A. Otis (Farmington) and Sarah W. Deland (Brookfield)

Alonzo S., d. 8/23/1926 at 55/0/13; shoeworker; married; b. Farmington; Lorenzo D. Otis (Farmington) and Elizabeth Cator (Farmington)

Clara E., d. 12/17/1896 at 41/5/3; consumption; housewife; married; b. Farmington; John W. Pinkham (New Durham) and Eliza Pinkham (New Durham)

Elizabeth F., d. 5/20/1911 at 72/4/26; chronic nephritis; widow; b. Farmington; Otis Cater and Lovey Canney

George E., d. 2/21/1925 at 52/5/29; farmer; married; b. Farmington; Orrin K. Otis (Farmington) and Sarah Garland (Farmington)

George Washington, d. 6/17/1897 at 60/11/21; cerebral softening; farmer; married; b. Farmington; William W. Otis (Farmington) and Sarah Deland (Brookfield)

John D., d. 2/2/1905 at 55/0/18; pneumonia; blacksmith; married; b. Farmington; William Otis (Farmington) and Sarah Deland (Wolfeboro)

Josephine J., d. 11/13/1916 at 30/0/10; housewife; married; b. Newfoundland; William Sullivan (Newfoundland) and Bridget McClue (Newfoundland)

Lorenzo D., d. 10/12/1907 at 72/3/23; chronic gastritis; farmer; married; b. Farmington; William Otis (Farmington, farmer) and ----- Nutter (Farmington)

Orrin K., d. 5/30/1904 at 76/9/8; old age; farmer; married; b. Farmington; Thomas J. Otis (Farmington) and Susan Nutter (Farmington)

Sarah A., d. 4/5/1910 at 80/8/25; influenza; housewife; widow; b. Barrington; John Garland

Serena H., d. 3/24/1897 at 53/7/5; pneumonia; housekeeper; single b. Farmington; William A. Otis (Farmington) and Sarah W. Dealand (Brookfield)

**OUILETTE,**
Andre, d. 4/20/1927 at 58; laborer; b. Canada

**PAGE,**
Elizabeth J., d. 10/27/1890 at 56/6/16; consumption; housekeeper; married; b. Farmington; Hiram Young (Farmington) and Margaret Ham (New Durham)

Ethel G., d. 11/4/1931 at 56/9/29; housewife; single; b. Hampstead George Page (Sandown) and Almena Bragg (Hampstead)

Harold, d. 7/20/1906 at 5/11/23; tubercular meningitis; Walter E. Page (Manchester)

Munroe M., d. 4/25/1915 at 74/3/29; laborer; single; b. Wentworth; Zebina Page and Betsey Merrill

Joseph, d. 4/10/1929 at 0/0/1 in Rochester; b. Rochester; Harold Page (Dover) and Lydia W. Ferland (Rochester)

Lydia W., d. 4/10/1929 at 28/5/2 in Rochester; b. Rochester; Thomas Ferland (Canada) and Mary Marcoux (Rochester)

Walter E., d. 7/29/1906 at 32/3/6; general tuberculosis; shoe cutter married; b. Manchester; Charles E. Page (Manchester) and Angie Brunell (Plaistow)

**PAGGETT,**
Reginald, d. 7/22/1928 at 21

**PALGIAN,**
Phillip, d. 6/25/1938 at 51/11/10 in Pembroke; shoeworker; single; b. Armenia; Harry Palgian (Armenia)

**PARENT,**
daughter, d. 8/26/1925 at 0/0/1; b. Farmington; Edward Parent (Canada) and Celam Carron (Canada)

Edward, d. 4/23/1935 at 58/11/21 in Rochester; wood dealer; married; b. Canada; Paul Parent (Canada) and Philemen Caron (Canada)

Evelyn, d. 11/11/1917 at 0/0/0; b. Farmington; Edward Parent (Canada) and Celavaire Carron (Canada)

Robert G., d. 9/30/1931 at 5/0/21 in Rochester; b. Rochester; Edward Parent (Canada) and Salina Coran (Canada)

**PARKER,**

David T., d. 12/1/1888 at 75/8; pneumonia; physician; married; b. Bradford, VT; C. Parker

Harry S., d. 1/16/1912 at 79/10/29; chronic myocarditis; mechanic; widower; b. Wolfeboro; Samuel S. Parker (Wolfeboro, farmer) and Jane T. Cate (Brookfield)

Hester A., d. 4/15/1892 at 63/7/6; sementus uteria; housewife; married; b. Orford; Marvley Stevens (Warren, stone cutter) and Livonia Davis (Orford)

Lucy A., d. 12/24/1891 at 62/11; paralysis; housekeeper; widow; b. Lebanon, ME; Seth Wentworth (Lebanon, ME) and Mary Chamberlin (Lebanon, ME)

Mary A., d. 6/6/1929 at 60/10/5; housewife; married; b. Farmington; James F. Hussey (Farmington) and Sarah Edgerly (Dover)

Mary E., d. 11/3/1938 at 83/3/8; housewife; widow; b. Farmington; Jacob Horne (Middleton) and Amanda Colbath (Farmington)

Percy F., d. 9/27/1929 at 68/9/24 in Coronado, CA; b. Wolfeboro; Harry S. Parker (Wolfeboro) and Hester A. Stevens (Oxford)

Ramona C., d. 11/8/1931 at 15/7/9 in Rochester; at home; single; b. Haverhill, MA; Stewart Parker and Reta White (Farmington)

Samuel S., d. 9/8/1931 at 76/3/29; attorney; married; b. Wolfeboro; Harry S. Parker (Wolfeboro) and Hester R. Stevens

Sewall H., d. 12/29/1911 at 75/5/15; hemorrhage; shoemaker; married; Mathew S. Parker (Wolfeboro, blacksmith) and Clara C. Blake (Wolfeboro)

**PAULSON,**

Charles, d. 3/5/1918 at 0/1/9; b. Farmington; John A. Paulson (Sweden) and Alice M. Huckins (Strafford)

**PAYNE,**

Beatrice L., d. 9/2/1905 at 21/1/22; Bright's disease; housekeeper; single; b. Lynn; George H. Payne (Lynn, MA) and Beatrice C. Thorn (NB)

Susie M., d. 7/3/1922 at 73; housekeeper; single; b. Moultonboro; Parker Payne (Sandwich) and Jennie Guy

**PEABODY,**

Carrie L., d. 5/27/1921 at 64/8/23; housekeeper; single; b. Lawrence; Amaza Peabody (Beverly, MA) and Caroline Cummings (Methuen, MA)

**PEARL,**

Ann B., d. 9/23/1918 at 85/6/15; housewife; widow; b. Palmyra, ME; Henry Pendleton (ME) and Eunice Goodwin (ME)

Charles L., d. 11/4/1927 at 68/0/9; shoemaker; single; b. Farmington; Charles L. Pearl (Farmington) and Elizabeth Burnham (Alfred)

Eleazer, d. 1/21/1916 at 88/0/1; retired; married; b. Farmington; Peter Y. Pearl (Farmington) and Pamela Berry (New Durham)

Elizabeth A., d. 10/1/1894 at 65/7/20; disease of heart; housekeeper; widow; b. Alfred, ME; George Burnham (Kennebunk) and Celia White (Alfred, ME)

Florence H., d. 4/16/1904 at 5/5/3; tubercular meningitis; b. Farmington; Preston Pearl (Farmington) and Mattie Keaney (NS)

Fred L., d. 1/12/1931 at 70/9/4; painter; single; b. Farmington; Levi Pearl (Strafford) and Louisa Johnson (Strafford)

Isaac E., d. 8/21/1895 at 57/10/26; phthisis pulmonalis; lawyer; married; b. Farmington; Eleazer Pearl (Farmington) and Barbara Emerson (Palmyra, ME)

Levi, d. 4/5/1895 at 89/7; lumberman; widower; b. Farmington; Eleazer Pearl

Levi, d. 3/27/1899 at 64/6/15; paralysis; lumber dealer; married; b. Farmington; Levi Pearl (Farmington) and Clarisy French (Farmington)

Louisa M., d. 9/12/1907 at 70/6/17; apoplexy; widow; b. Ossipee; David Johnson and Hannah Johnson

Louise A., d. 3/12/1900 at 24/5/22; shot by revolver; shoestitcher; single; b. Rochester; George Pearl (Farmington) and Martha Willson (Scotland)

Lydia B., d. 9/25/1895 at 79/10/6; pneumonia; widow; b. New Durham; Samuel Jones and Nancy Bennett

Mary J., d. 3/27/1895 at 74/1/14; bronchial pneumonia; housewife; married; b. Wayne, ME; William Knight

Preston A., d. 8/28/1898 at 40/6/21; locomotor ataxia; coal dealer; married; b. Farmington; Levi Pearl (Farmington)

Rufus K., d. 1/11/1889 at 50/4/17; Bright's disease; bookkeeper; b. Farmington; Peter Pearl (Farmington) and Pauline Berry (New Durham)

Sophronia L., d. 8/13/1910 at 65/5/12; burn and auto inf'e; housekeeper; widow; b. Sudbury, MA; Hersey Cloutman (New Durham) and Lydia Haines (Sudbury, MA)

## PEARSON,

son, d. 7/27/1899 at 0/0/6; meningitis; b. Farmington; Frank Pearson (Newburyport) and Rose Sanborn (Holderness)

Agnes T., d. 4/25/1911 at 1/8; scarlet fever; b. Sanford; Theodore Pearson (Canada, lumberman) and Delphine Belanger (Canada)

Edwin L., d. 11/17/1937 at 67/1/13; shoeworker; married; b. New Durham; Horace Pearson (Alexandria) and Lovey J. Gray (Farmington)

Frank M., d. 4/28/1934 at 75/1/9; shoeworker; widower; b. New Durham; Horace B. Pearson (Alexandria) and Lovey J. Gray (Farmington)

Lovey J., d. 11/11/1906 at 73/4/8; angina pectoris; housewife; married; b. Farmington; Samuel Gray (Farmington) and ----- Edgerly (Alton)

## PEARSONS,

Annie A., d. 4/6/1931 at 68/4/14 in Haverhill, MA; housewife; widow; b. Farmington; Charles Anthony (Providence, RI)

Loren A., d. 2/12/1919 at 65/7/25; married

Mary J., d. 5/21/1915 at 50/11/3; shoeworker; married; b. Farmington; Enoch Henderson and Sarah J. Ellis

## PEAVEY,

son, d. 5/16/1903 at 0/0/7; heart failure; Ernest Peavey (Farmington) and Pansy Wallace (Farmington)

Alfred S., d. 1/29/1890 at 56; paralysis; shoemaker; married; Enoch E. Peavey

Alice E., d. 11/8/1930 at 61/4/21; domestic; divorced; b.
Farmington; Almon Leavitt (Effingham) and Nellie Jones
Clara E., d. 7/1/1930 at 38/0/6 in Rochester; shoeworker; married;
b. Portsmouth; Leslie Whitehouse and Phoebe Faulkner
Mary A., d. 3/21/1904 at 67/5/4; angina pectoris; housekeeper;
widow; b. Woodstock, CT; Calvin Beal (Lyme) and Sally Franklin
William C., d. 9/28/1938 at 87/1/8 in New Durham; farmer; married
b. New Durham

**PELLETIER,**

Mary J., d. 9/12/1913 at 2/6/23; acute inte'l dis.; b. Sanford, ME;
George J. Pelletier (Springvale, ME, grocer) and Valeda St. Pierre (Frazerville, PQ)

**PENCE,**

Horace C., d. 7/15/1929 at 38/10/22; shoeworker; married; b.
Cutler, ME; John Pence (Cutler, ME) and Lizzie Maher (Lubec, ME)

**PENDEXTER,**

George W., d. 11/16/1916 at 78/11/13; mechanic; single; b.
Farmington; John Pendexter (Madbury) and Susan Davis (Farmington)

**PERKINS,**

son, d. 6/8/1891 at –; stillborn; b. Farmington; B. Frank Perkins (Strafford) and Lucy A. Stiles (Strafford)
son, d. 7/20/1901 at –; prematurity; b. Farmington; L. C. Perkins (N. Berwick, ME) and M. A. Finnegan (Ireland)
Abbie G., d. 4/22/1912 at 00; premature birth; b. Farmington; E. C. Perkins (Berwick, ME, physician) and Louise M. Todd (Rowley, MA)
Albert H., d. 7/7/1892 at 44/1/6; albumenura; shoe cutter; married; b. Milton; Asa Perkins (Wolfeboro, farmer) and Eliza Perkins (Wolfeboro)
Asenath J., d. 1/9/1914 at 81/10/25; chronic uremia; domestic; widow; b. Brookfield; Reuben Lang (Brookfield, farmer) and ---- (Brookfield)
Augusta, d. 1/19/1927 at 76/6/6

Benjamin F., d. 5/2/1927 at 71/0/1; undertaker; married; b. Strafford; Paul Perkins (Strafford) and Mary S. Perkins (Strafford)

Charles E., d. 6/18/1928 at 77/6/15; retired; widower; b. Strafford; Asa Perkins (Strafford) and Deborah Young (Strafford)

Charles H., d. 1/18/1921 at 68/9/2; retired; widower; b. Milton; Eri S. Perkins (Wolfeboro) and Mary A. Dow (Wolfeboro)

Charles M., d. 6/10/1931 at 79/9/29; widower; b. Middleton; John D. Perkins (Middleton) and Harriet A. Garland (Middleton)

Cora E., d. 5/23/1919 at 58/9/14; housewife; married; b. New Durham; Jerome Witham (New Durham) and Mary Randall (New Durham)

Cyrus B., d. 5/2/1916 at 72/11/14; shoeworker; married; b. Middleton; James Perkins (New Durham) and Polly Davis (New Durham)

Daniel M., d. 7/4/1935 at 73/8/28; retired; widower; b. Alton; James M. Perkins (Alton) and Asenith J. Lang (Brookfield)

Edwina, d. 12/9/1918 at 22/0/1; housewife; married; b. Milton Mills; Frank Hurd and Cora Hurd

Grace, d. 3/17/1903 at 23/11/17; diabetes; school teacher; single; b. Whitefield; John F. Perkins and Augusta Cloutman

Harriet E., d. 9/7/1890 at 55/2/4; shock; housekeeper; married; b. Fitchburg, MA; Joseph Chase (Fitchburg, MA) and Harriet Phelps (Sutton)

James H., d. 7/27/1903 at 60/7/22; chronic chol'ng'ts; shoemaker; widower; James Perkins (Hallowell, ME) and Susan Downs (Rochester)

John J., d. 1/9/1935 at 89 in Arlington, MA; shoeworker; widower; b. Wolfeboro; John Perkins (Wolfeboro) and Mary Doe (Wolfeboro)

John M., d. 1/22/1911 at 85/1/21; broncho pneumonia; farmer; married; b. Alton; John Perkins (farmer) and Sarah Libby (New Durham)

L. M. T., d. 4/26/1912 at 38/3/25; erysipelas; housekeeper; married; b. Rowley, MA; Daniel G. Todd (Rowley, MA, farmer) and Abbie G. Hackett (Auburn, ME)

Lena G., d. 6/23/1938 at 57/10/15 in Wakefield; housewife; divorced; b. Middleton; Ned Labonta (Canada) and Annie Willey (Milton)

Llewellyn, d. 2/3/1935 at 58/5/27; fish dealer; married; b. No. Berwick, ME; Charles Perkins (Middleton) and Sarah Abbott (N. Berwick, ME)

Lucy A., d. 2/19/1934 at 78/7/21 in Winchester, MA; housewife; widow; b. Farmington; Joseph Stiles (Strafford) and Hannah W. Foss (Strafford)

Luther H., d. 2/10/1929 at 80/8/14; carpenter; married; b. Milton; Ephraim Perkins and Susan Wentworth

Mary A., d. 12/24/1907 at 70/5/11; influenza; widow; b. Boston, MA

Mary A., d. 3/6/1938 at 88/5/24; housewife; widow; b. Wolfeboro; Nathaniel Kimball (Wolfeboro) and Abigail Willey (Wolfeboro)

Mary F., d. 6/10/1901 at 48/9/13; meningitis; married; b. Lebanon, ME; Luther Dixon (Lebanon, ME) and Elizabeth Berry (Stratham)

Mary O., d. 7/23/1922 at 62/3/3; housewife; married; b. Washington, VT; Joseph Brackett

Mildred, d. 9/7/1937 at 38/8/6 in Concord; none; divorced; b. Scotland

Robert R., d. 7/7/1907 at 70/1/2; dropsy; widower; b. Farmington; Ephraim Perkins (Farmington, farmer) and Susan Wentworth (ME)

Sarah A., d. 7/29/1918 at 70/8/4; housewife; married; b. N. Berwick ME; ----- Abbott (N. Berwick, ME) and Sophia Remick (N. Berwick, ME)

Sarah R., d. 5/13/1908 at 62/10/23; heart disease; widow; b. Wolfeboro; John Deland (New Durham) and Elmira Pierce (Wolfeboro)

Teresa, d. 3/9/1936 at 76/8/21; at home; widow; b. PEI; Daniel McDonald

Willie L., d. 12/8/1922 at 65/10/24; farmer; single; b. Farmington; Robert Perkins (Farmington) and Mary Wiggin (Farmington)

**PERR[E]AULT,**

Eva M., d. 10/6/1918 at 19/3/27; waitress; married; b. Everett, MA; Ronald McGregor (Wakefield) and Nellie T. Phinney (NS)

Joseph, d. 9/28/1924 at 49/4/5; shoemaker; widower; b. Canada; France Perreault (Canada) and Caroline Laplante (Canada)

**PETERSON,**
Enos L., d. 6/27/1913 at 47/9/8; uremia; machinist; married; b. Lockport, NS; David Peterson (Gordon, NS, sailmaker) and Margaret A. Buckley (Gordon, NS)
Hazel, d. 3/7/1896 at 0/9; pneumonia; b. Farmington; Enos L. Peterson (Lockport, NS) and Sadie McDonald (PEI)
Lindsey V., d. 3/14/1909 at 1/7; cerebro spinal meningitis; b. Farmington; Enos L. Peterson (NS) and Sarah McDonald (PEI)

**PETTIGREW,**
Clarinda, d. 9/16/1898 at 53; Bright's disease; housekeeper; married; b. New Castle; Samuel Batson (New Castle) and Mary L. Neal (New Castle)
Fabius B., d. 5/12/1896 at 40/7; consumption; shoe cutter; married; b. New Castle; C. H. Pettigrew and Susan E. Card
Mary B., d. 1/24/1892 at 17/9/24; albumenura; single; b. Farmington, Charles H. Pettigrew (Kittery, ME, shoemaker) and ----- (New Castle)

**PEVERLY,**
Phronia, d. 10/1/1909 at 69/5/14; old age; housekeeper; b. Middleton; John D. Horne (Middleton) and Mary Chase (New Durham)

**PHELPS,**
Jerome, d. 3/23/1937 at 82/6/10; widower; b. Danvers, MA; Joseph Phelps (Northfield) and Eliza Townsend (Salem, MA)

**PHILBRICK,**
Edith M., d. 6/6/1934 at 61/7/27; at home; married; b. Ossipee; James R. B. Cook (Tamworth) and Mary A. Bunker

**PIERCE,**
Viola B., d. 11/22/1892 at 22; poison resulting from insanity; housewife; married; b. Wonaske Falls, VT; Oliver Devine (Stowe, VT, carpenter) and Melvina Buckford; burial - Pittsfield

**PIKE,**
Amanda E., d. 3/6/1922 at 48/0/18; housewife; married; b. Middleton; William B. Place (Middleton) and Lydia Whitehouse (Middleton)

Irving F., d. 2/24/1910 at 28/11/9; pul. consumption; heel burnisher married; b. Farmington; Edwin E. Pike (Milton) and Etta M. Pearl (Rochester)

Jacob H., d. 2/28/1915 at 87/3/4; shoemaker; widower; b. Middleton; Jacob Pike (Middleton) and Hannah Burnham (Middleton)

John C., d. 2/17/1929 at 63/2/19; janitor; married; b. Middleton; John S. Pike and Mary Cloutman

Josephine R., d. 3/25/1906 at 4/4/1; d'rm'tis a'b's e'h'a; b. Farmington; John C. Pike (Middleton) and Alice M. Arnold (Wells, ME)

Leonore M., d. 6/28/1927 at 0/0/17; b. Rochester; Cecil M. Pike (Brookfield) and Lua M. Berry (New Durham)

Mary Alice, d. 12/16/1892 at 1/9/8; meningitis; b. Farmington; Harris Pike (New Britton, laborer) and Ada Livock (PQ); burial - Rochester

Maude E., d. 12/6/1938 at 57 in Jamaica Plain, MA; housewife; widow; b. Lebanon, ME; George Kenney (Lebanon, ME) and Lulu Wentworth (Farmington)

Miriam E., d. 7/20/1919 at 86/9/20

Susie F., d. 11/3/1938 at 72/6/19 in Rochester; housewife; married; b. Shapleigh, ME; Benjamin Day and Aurena Goodwin

**PINKHAM,**

son, d. 10/12/1892 at –; lack of vitality; b. Farmington; David T. Pinkham (Farmington, peddler) and Hattie T. Goodwin (Milton Mills); burial - Milton Mills

son, d. 9/26/1895 at –; stillborn; b. Farmington; A. R. Pinkham (Hollis, ME) and Georgie Wigglesworth (Farmington)

son, d. 6/1/1909 at –; stillborn; b. Farmington; Clifton Pinkham (Pittsfield) and Mary Anderson (No. Conway)

Abbie, d. 4/23/1909 at 78; senile debility; housekeeper; Bart Willey (New Durham) and Pauline Willey (New Durham)

Alphonzo, d. 3/28/1918 at 63/7/28; shoemaker; married; b. Hollis, ME; Ira F. Pinkham and Lizzie Kimball

Austin, d. 9/26/1918 at 40/11/17; prop. apt. house; married; b. Farmington; Alphonzo Pinkham (Hollis, ME) and Georgia Wigglesworth (Farmington)

Clifton S., d. 7/16/1908 at –; shock; single; b. Farmington; Clifton S. Pinkham (Pittsfield) and Mary Anderson (Conway)

David T., d. 3/23/1897 at 25/2/13; consumption; shoemaker; single; b. Farmington; Edwin Pinkham (New Durham) and Abigail Willey (New Durham)

Eliza, d. 6/20/1907 at 74/10/2; apoplexy; widow; b. Farmington; S. W. Pinkham (farmer)

Esther E., d. 7/30/1900 at 64/9/5; heart disease; housekeeper; married; b. Brownfield; John Kimball (Brownfield) and Elvia Merryfield (Brownfield)

Etta L., d. 9/13/1929 at 69/6/6 in Rochester; domestic; widow; b. Farmington; John Brown and Clarissa Brown

Eva M., d. 10/7/1935 at 58/10/26 in New Durham; housewife; married; b. Farmington; Stephen W. Berry (Bangor, ME) and Hannah Edgerly (Middleton)

Frank, d. 11/2/1902 at 44/8/5; unknown; grocery clerk; married; b. New Durham; John Pinkham (New Durham) and Eliza Pinkham (New Durham)

George B., d. 4/29/1888 at 27/1/22; consumption; laborer; married; b. Farmington; E. Pinkham (New Durham) and Abbie Willey (New Durham)

George W., d. 10/24/1903 at 62/6; cancer; shoe cutter; married; John L. Pinkham (New Durham) and Betsey M. Adams (Barnstead)

Ira F., d. 4/21/1916 at 95/2/10; shoemaker; married; b. New Durham

James, d. 8/4/1906 at 54/7/14; dysentery; shoe buffer; married; b. Wolfeboro; William Pinkham and Mary F. Chase

John F., d. 10/8/1887 at 38/9/5; shoemaker; married; b. Middleton; Stephen F. Pinkham (Farmington) and Abigail Tufts (Middleton)

John L., d. 3/21/1887 at 73/7/2; carpenter; married; b. New Durham; D. Pinkham

John W., d. 9/7/1898 at 66/8/24; consumption; farmer; married; b. New Durham; William Pinkham (New Durham)

Leander, d. 5/7/1887 at 17/9/20; laborer; single; b. Farmington; Edwin Pinkham (New Durham) and Abigail Willey (New Durham)

Levi L., d. 3/30/1899 at 63/10; paralysis; shoe dealer; married; b. New Durham; Levi H. Pinkham and Maria T. Leighton

Mary J., d. 2/19/1892 at 78/11/13; old age; housekeeper; widow; b. Farmington; M. Hussey (farmer) and ----- Hanson

Mary P., d. 12/27/1889 at 81/3/23; erysipelas; invalid; b. Farmington; Levi Pinkham (Farmington) and Sally Pearl (Farmington)

Samuel W., d. 1/11/1891 at 82/7/24; heart failure; farmer; widower Stephen Pinkham and Judith White

Sarah A., d. 8/15/1919 at 75/10/7; housekeeper; widow; b. Farmington; Thomas Pinkham (New Durham) and Adeline Hodgdon (Farmington)

Stephen, d. 10/29/1897 at 83; old age; farmer; widower; b. Farmington; Samuel Pinkham (Farmington) and Leah French (Farmington)

Walter, d. 1/15/1895 at 20/6/26; tuberculosis; shoemaker; single; b. Farmington; Edwin Pinkham (New Durham) and Abbie Willey (New Durham)

William I., d. 11/27/1928 at 50; salesman; married; b. Middleton; George E. Pinkham (Farmington) and Laura J. Main (West Milton)

**PIPER,**

George G., d. 3/18/1932 at 75/11/9; farmer; widower; b. Tuftonboro George W. Piper (Alton) and Mary E. Burke (Alton)

Ruth F., d. 4/12/1934 at 24/3/22 in Manchester; teacher; single; b. N. Abington, MA; Bernard L. Piper (Milton Mills) and Harriett Emerson (Farmington)

**PIPPIN,**

Eva B., d. 7/22/1915 at 0/2/23; b. Milton Mills; Charles Pippin (Union) and Florida Currier

**PITMAN,**

Ann S., d. 12/19/1895 at 72/8/26; pneumonia; housewife; widow; b. Farmington; Moses Jenness (Rochester) and Susan Berry (Strafford)

Charles H., d. 12/2/1926 at 82/4/19; insurance agt.; married; b. Barnstead; Henry Pitman (Barnstead) and Drucilla Miles (VT)

Eben, d. 1/25/1923 at 70/11/18; tailor; widower; b. Barnstead; Edward Pitman (Barnstead) and Ann S. Jenness (Rochester)

Frank D., d. 8/24/1921 at 78/7/28; shoeworker; married; b. Barnstead; Daniel Pitman (Barnstead) and Betsey Pitman (Rumney)

Lizzie S., d. 7/11/1931 at 81/2/22; widow; b. New Durham; Daniel Lucas (Canada) and Sarah F. Chesley (New Durham)

**PLACE,**
Clifton W., d. 1/7/1903 at 22/1/21; typhoid fever; shoemaker; single; William B. Place (Middleton) and Lydia Whitehouse (Middleton)
Freena L., d. 8/12/1929 at 46/0/9; housewife; married; b. Wakefield; Augustin J. Lover (Canada) and Celina Clouthie (Canada)
George K., d. 3/22/1906 at 78/1/1; remittent fever; farmer; single; b. Farmington; Ira Place and Nancy Robinson
Isaiah H., d. 4/24/1895 at 70/3/11; pneumonia; farmer; widower; b. Middleton; Moses Place and Keziah Hayes
John F., d. 7/10/1903 at 36/2/25; tuberculosis; blacksmith; single; -- Robbins and Lydia P. Place (Barnstead)
Lydia A., d. 5/24/1900 at 51/5/24; abscess of pharynx; housekeeper; married; b. Middleton; A. W. Whitehouse (Middleton) and Eliza Colbath (Middleton)
Martha Jane, d. 12/26/1929 at 15/7/20; student; b. Tampa, FL; John M. Place (Middleton) and Maude Blake (Lowell, MA)
Ulysses I., d. 3/22/1907 at 38/8/18; cirrhosis of liver; saloon keeper; married; b. Middleton; William B. Place (Middleton, shoemaker) and Lydia Whitehouse (Middleton)

**PLUMMER,**
William H., d. 4/14/1912 at 77/2/8; cerebral hemorrhage; widower; b. Farmington; William Plummer and Polly Ham (Farmington)

**POLLARD,**
Richard, d. 5/17/1923 at 0/0/21; b. Farmington; Richard Pollard (Millis, MA) and Mary Bickford (Waterville, ME)

**POULIOT,**
Exzelia, d. 12/3/1936 at 54/5/16; housewife; married; b. Milton Mills; Henry Sturgeon (Canada) and Dorothy Sturgeon (Canada)

**PRAY,**
Capitola E., d. 3/25/1921 at 59/7/23
Frances F., d. 9/10/1896 at 71/8/4; cold and old age; single; b. Rochester; Samuel Pray and Sarah W. Farnham

**PRESCOTT,**
Ann M., d. 12/28/1896 at 56/5/24; cancer; housewife; married; b. Barnstead; William Dudley (Barnstead) and Harriet Dudley (Barnstead)
Crosby, d. 12/8/1921 at 71/2/1; janitor; married; b. Acton, ME; Sewell Prescott (Acton) and Marilla Hersom (Lebanon)
Harriett, d. 3/19/1923 at 79/0/22; housekeeper; widow; b. Charlestown, MA; Charles Sapham (Dorchester, MA) and Jemima Prescott (Sandwich)

**PRESTON,**
Elizabeth D., d. 5/5/1934 at 79/11/3; at home; widow; b. Canada

**PRICE,**
Mary C., d. 6/3/1929 at 75/3/17; housekeeper; widow; b. New Durham; Miles Chesley (New Durham) and Maria Hurd (New Durham)

**PRIDE,**
Amy, d. 2/8/1912 at 43/3; surgical shocks; housewife; married; b. England; ----- (Manchester, England)
Ernest T., d. 2/7/1896 at –; heart failure; b. Farmington; Henry W. Pride (Portland, ME) and Rosalie Henraff (Sidney, CB)
Joshua T., d. 5/24/1912 at 82/1/15; apoplexy; granite cutter; widower; b. Windham, ME; Elich Pride (ME, farmer)
Lucy J., d. 12/5/1911 at 65; angina pectoris; housewife; married

**PROCTOR,**
Charlotte M., d. 8/9/1893 at 58; nervous shock; dressmaker; single b. Charlestown; Nathan Proctor (Kingsboro, MA) and Nancy Langley (Strafford)
Katherine L., d. 6/2/1934 at 82/0/10 in New Durham; at home; widow; b. Westfield, NJ; William Rogers (London, England) and Catherine Barrett (Wells, England)
Malinda J., d. 5/12/1890 at 50/0/29; rupture of intestines; housekeeper; married; b. New Durham; John Elkins (New Durham) and Mary Pinkham (New Durham)
Nathan L., d. 4/12/1914 at 81/0/26; cerebral degen.; married; b. Somerville, MA; Nathan Proctor and Nancy Langley

**PULSIFER,**
son, d. 8/24/1907 at –; stillborn; b. Farmington; W. H. Pulsifer (Madbury, merchant) and Helen Lovering (Farmington)
Harriet E., d. 11/9/1905 at 63/6/2; cerebral softening; widow; b. Durham; Alfred Pinkham (Durham) and Harriett Bunker (Durham)
Hattie I., d. 10/18/1917 at 44; teacher; single; b. Rochester; Charles Pulsifer (Minot, ME) and Harriet Pinkham (Durham)
Helen L., d. 9/27/1927 at 47/9/18; housewife; married; b. Farmington; Frank Lovering and Etta Gammon

**PUTNAM,**
Albert E., d. 10/5/1917 at 71/11/1; merchant; married; b. Danvers, MA; Orin Putnam (Danvers, MA) and Sally P. Nourse (Danvers, MA)

**PUTNEY,**
Susie M., d. 10/19/1890 at 38/7/19; consumption; housekeeper; married; b. Cohasset, MA; John Q. Peeks (C'mpt'n, MA) and Mary S. Jones (Cohasset, MA)

**QUINT,**
Ira A., d. 4/9/1917 at 82/7/25; carpenter; widower; b. ME
Sophia A., d. 7/19/1914 at 80; senile dementia; housewife; married; b. Corena, ME; Jacob Leighton

**RADFORD,**
Nellie A., d. 8/25/1935 at 62/4/28; housewife; married; b. Plainfield, NJ; John Burnham (Standish, ME) and Adelia Champlin (Kingston, RI)

**RAND,**
Annah S., d. 6/3/1924 at 67/6/19; housekeeper; widow; b. Farmington; Isaac Willey and Louisa Bickford
Carrie I., d. 8/10/1906 at 55/6/28; pulmonary tuberculosis; housewife; married; b. Randolph; Robert Leighton (Randolph) and Mary Willey (Conway)
Ernest W., d. 7/27/1924 at 29/11/21; shoemaker; married; b. Milton; George W. Rand (Cambridge, MA) and Ida Moore (Milton)
Ira, d. 8/19/1922 at 79/2/19; married; b. Alton; Burnham Rand

James M., d. 7/12/1932 at 59/0/7; brakeman; married; b. Strafford; Bickford Rand (Rochester) and Mary A. Berry (Strafford)

Jeremiah, d. 5/30/1904 at 76/2/27; internal hemorrhage; shoe cutter; married; b. Alton; Mary Rand (Alton)

Lois D., d. 10/20/1887 at 78/3/11; housekeeper; single; b. Farmington

Louisa, d. 12/17/1908 at 79; chronic Bright's disease; widow; b. Farmington; Isaiah Peavey

Mary, d. 7/28/1938 at 69/11/14; housewife; divorced; b. Canada; Peter Lesard (Canada) and Agustine Gravelle (Canada)

Ora May, d. 9/25/1920 at 1/3/1; b. Gonic; Natt Rand (New Durham) and Alta May Dore (Milton)

**RANDALL,**

A. Leon, d. 11/11/1895 at 29/3/11; epilepsy; single; b. Farmington; Alex T. Randall (Bolton, PQ) and Adelia Cooke (Milton)

Adelia R., d. 3/24/1907 at 73/11/9; pernicious anemia; housekeeper; widow; b. Milton; Hiram Cook (Milton, farmer) and Hannah Rhines (Milton)

Alexander T., d. 12/5/1897 at 68/7; uremia; shoemaker; married; b. Bolton, Canada; George Randall (Moultonboro) and Hannah Magoon (Canada)

Alma O., d. 12/5/1894 at 22/2/8; consumption; shoe stitcher; single; b. Farmington; A. T. Randall (Bolton, PQ) and Ardelia Cook (Milton)

Clara A., d. 6/8/1917 at 44/2/11; housewife; married; b. Farmington; Charles Wiggins and Abbie E. Dame

Clarence, d. 8/14/1937 at 49/10/11 in Wolfeboro; laborer; single; b. Brownfield, ME

Deborah, d. 9/21/1906 at 65/7/0; gall stones; housekeeper; married; b. Wolfeboro; William Towle (Alton) and Ruth L. Doe (Kensington)

George W., d. 6/8/1902 at 70/7/2; tuberculosis; shoemaker; married; b. Rochester; James Randall and Hannah Dugene

Ina M., d. 7/17/1935 at 49/9/23; housekeeper; married; b. Farmington; Martin Glidden (Alton) and Frances Tibbetts (Farmington)

Lavina N., d. 3/27/1916 at 65/3/24; housekeeper; widow; b. Lebanon, ME; Richard H. Foss (Rochester) and Lydia Durgin (Chatham)

Lydia A., d. 1/23/1933 at 75/11/3; housekeeper; widow; b. NS

Mark W., d. 8/19/1900 at 0/7/9; cholera infantum; b. Manchester; H. E. Randall (Farmington) and Mildred Griffin (Portsmouth)
William I., d. 11/15/1938 at 74/3/1 in Concord; shoeworker; married; b. New Durham; George Randall and Elizabeth Towle

RANSOM,
Isaac, d. 2/22/1891 at 61/11/9; pneumonia; shoemaker; widower; b. Farmington; Samuel Ransom (Dover) and Abigail Holmes (Farmington)

READY,
George W., d. 2/20/1920 at 88/1/19; sailor; widower

REED,
William K., d. 7/31/1888 at 24/7; typhoid fever; shoemaker; married; b. Marblehead, MA; A. W. Reed (Topsham, ME) and Mary Walford (Marblehead, MA)

REEVES,
Beulah M., d. 11/15/1922 at –; Howard Reeves (PEI) and Eva G. Dodge (Barrington)

REGIS,
Elda, d. 2/23/1919 at 0/0/1; b. Farmington; John D. Regis (Nashua) and Bessie Haddock (Farmington)

REMICK,
daughter, d. 10/19/1924 at 0/0/1; b. Milton; Edgar A. Remick (Milton) and Carrie E. Grace (Albany)
infant, d. 4/10/1927 at –; b. Farmington; Clayton Remick (ME) and Elva P. Holland (ME)
Charles D., d. 8/5/1905 at 72/1/21; heart failure; farmer; widower; b. Acton, ME; Joseph Remick (Acton, ME) and Abigail Bean (Acton, ME)
Charles E., d. 2/11/1936 at 76/9/17; retired; widower; b. Milton; Moses Remick and Clara Wentworth
Cora E., d. 11/16/1937 at 77/0/19; at home; widow; b. Farmington; John F. Colomy (Farmington) and Alice Curtis (New Castle)
Edgar, d. 2/20/1920 at 0/0/13

Everett, d. 4/14/1913 at 1/3/3; entero-colitis; b. Farmington; Nathaniel P. Remick (Sutton, MA, shoemaker) and Mary E. Sprague (Grafton, MA)

George P., d. 10/14/1918 at 25/1/17; shoemaker; married; b. Grafton, MA; Nathaniel P. Remick (Sutton, MA) and Mary E. Sprague (Grafton, MA)

Harold L., d. 4/12/1921 at 0/0/1; b. Milton; Edgar B. Remick (Milton) and Carrie E. Grace (Albany)

Lula E., d. 7/30/1935 at 75/1/20 in Medway, MA; none; divorced; b. Farmington; Alvin Wentworth (Farmington) and Henrietta Pickering (Farmington)

Nathaniel, d. 6/30/1911 at 16/2/14; chronic nephritis; single; Nathaniel P. Remick (shoemaker)

Nathaniel, d. 2/4/1929 at 65/10/11 in Goffstown; shoeworker; married; b. Sutton, MA; Nathaniel Remick (ME) and Matilda Young (ME)

Robert W., d. 1/28/1923 at 0/0/1; b. Farmington; Edgar Remick (Milton) and Carrie Grace (Albany)

Susan J., d. 5/25/1903 at 64/1/6; pneumonia; housewife; married; John Smallcorn (Barrington) and Lucy Seavey (Barrington)

William E., d. 2/11/1921 at 66/10/10; shoeworker; married; b. Somersworth; Timothy Remick

William H., d. 11/24/1891 at 63/9/10; cancer; farmer; single; b. Tamworth; Nathaniel Remick (Lebanon) and Etta Nickerson (Tamworth)

William L., d. 2/16/1908 at 7/9/27; paralysis; b. Putnam, CT; Nathaniel P. Remick (Sutton, MA) and Mary E. Sprague (Grafton, MA)

**RESTELLI,**

Ida, d. 6/10/1889 at 0/3; meningitis; b. Concord; Caesar Restelli (Italy)

**REYNOLDS,**

Edward, d. 4/30/1932 at 65/5/29; shoemaker; married; b. Salem, MA; William Reynolds (Ireland) and Mary Rowe (Ireland)

George W., d. 2/15/1921 at 0/0/1; b. Farmington; E. S. Reynolds (New Durham) and Gertrude Clark (Gilmanton)

Richard A., d. 5/22/1897 at 1/3/18; cerebro spinal meningitis; b. Springvale; Elmer S. Reynolds (New Durham) and Clara M. Goodwin (Springvale)

**RHINES,**
Alvah H., d. 4/2/1923 at 66/6/22; shoemaker; married; b. New Durham; Alvah C. Rhines (New Durham) and Lydia French
Edith M., d. 5/5/1917 at 27/2/19; none; single; b. New Durham; Irving C. Rhines (New Durham) and Angie S. Brown (Cornish, ME)
Evelyn A., d. 10/12/1922 at 16/2/28; single; b. New Durham; Herman Rhines (New Durham) and Lucy B. Dow (Dorchester)
Genevra, d. 10/20/1918 at 46/6/9; room girl; single; b. New Durham; Alvah C. Rhines (New Durham) and Lydia French (New Durham)
Lydia A., d. 10/11/1909 at 59/3/24; cancer; nurse; b. Farmington; --- -- Canney
Lydia L., d. 7/25/1909 at 74/10/3; senility; housekeeper; b. New Durham; Levi French (New Durham) and Betsey Willey (New Durham)
Willie E., d. 12/4/1934 at 64/1/18; trucking; married; b. New Durham; Alvah Rhines (New Durham)

**RICH,**
Alfred L., d. 10/18/1891 at 19/2/28; pulmonary tuberculosis; clerk; single; b. Gouldsboro, ME; Alfred Rich (Isle au Haut) and Mary E. Joy (Steuben, ME)
James E., d. 4/29/1919 at 79; sea captain; widower; b. N. Truro, MA
Mary E., d. 10/18/1893 at 49/3; dropsy; lady; widow

**RICHARDS,**
S. F., d. 4/25/1900 at 54/3/21; pneumonia; painter; married; b. Weld, ME; Liberty Richards (Salem, ME) and Abigail Baker (Hooksett)

**RICHARDSON,**
Albert, d. 10/13/1918 at 18/8/24; shoemaker; single; b. Northwood; Herbert Richardson and Alice Garland (Farmington)
Omosey, d. 2/2/1891 at 0/8/3; whooping cough; b. Auburn, ME; Ai J. Richardson (Upton, ME) and Lydia Holden (Stewartstown)
Susan, d. 10/31/1903 at 71/9/7; premature senility; housekeeper; widow; Stephen Wiggin (Alton) and Sarah Leighton (Farmington)

**RICKER,**
son, d. 7/28/1894 at 0/0/3; hemorrhage; b. Farmington; Charles H. Ricker (Wolfeboro) and Mary Cloutman (Farmington)

daughter, d. 7/15/1903 at –; hydramnios; Bertred E. Ricker (Farmington) and Mattie Kearney (St. Stephens, NB)

son, d. 6/22/1906 at 0/0/0; stillborn; b. Farmington; B. E. Ricker (Farmington) and Mattie Kearney (Fredericton, NB)

daughter, d. 4/11/1911 at 0/0/0; stillborn; b. Farmington; Irving J. Ricker (Farmington, musician) and Mabel G. Ross (Acton, ME

Annie, d. 10/15/1897 at 93/6/16; thrombosis and old age; housekeeper; widow; b. Farmington; Moses Whitehouse (Farmington) and Nancy Page (Rochester)

Annie S., d. 11/5/1889 at 44/7/3; internal hemorrhage; housekeeper; b. Ossipee; Alvah Dore

Augusta, d. 6/28/1887 at 40/10/18; housekeeper; married; b. Concord; Samuel L. Currier (Gilmanton) and Hannah K. Smith (Canterbury)

Augustus, d. 2/3/1903 at 57/4/24; heart disease; shoemaker; widower; Benjamin A. Ricker (Wolfeboro) and Nancy J. Colbath (Brookfield)

Benjamin A., d. 5/25/1905 at 79/1/1; cirrhosis of liver; married; b. Wolfeboro; Benjamin Ricker and Mary Wiggin

Charles E., d. 12/25/1896 at 63; pneumonia; farmer; widower; Luther Ricker and Louisa Witham (New Durham)

Christina B., d. 12/23/1905 at 52/10/16; cancer; widow; b. Gilmanton; J. A. Flanders (Gilmanton) and Susan H. Plummer (Gilmanton)

Eugene, d. 3/29/1910 at 52/1/3; Bright's disease; shoemaker; b. Alton; George Ricker (Alton) and Augusta Rollins (Alton)

George, d. 11/16/1895 at 0/1/22; septicemia; b. Farmington; Charles H. Ricker (Wolfeboro) and Mary Cloutman (Farmington)

Harriet L., d. 12/28/1913 at 0/0/24; malnutrition; b. Farmington; Harry W. Ricker (Wolfeboro, clerk) and Addie M. Quint (Milton)

Helen G., d. 11/8/1924 at 74/0/20; housewife; married; b. Tilton; Samuel Currier and Hannah Smith

Ira O., d. 3/17/1929 at 77/3/2; shoeworker; married; b. Barrington; Ira S. Ricker (Dover) and Mary E. Hall (Barrington)

James E., d. 8/20/1929 at 81/1/3; shoeworker; widower; b. New Durham; Benjamin A. Ricker and Nancy C. Colbath

John, d. 3/28/1898 at –; infancy; b. Farmington; Charles H. Ricker (Wolfeboro) and Mary A. Cloutman (Farmington)

John Q. A., d. 7/18/1895 at 68/1/1; blood poison; shoemaker; married; b. New Durham; Luther Ricker and Louisa Witham (New Durham)

Leslie W., d. 1/15/1932 at 71/6/19 in New Durham; retired; widower; b. New Durham; Ira S. Ricker (Barrington) and Mary E. Hall (Dover)

Mabel, d. 6/24/1899 at 0/1/1; anaemia; b. Farmington; Charles H. Ricker (Wolfeboro) and Mary A. Cloutman (Farmington)

Mamie, d. 3/11/1919 at 49/0/6; shoeworker; widow; Emma Lawrence

Mary E. H., d. 5/4/1904 at 77/7/4; apoplexy; housewife; widow; b. Barrington; Daniel Hall and Nancy Brown

Mary H., d. 12/8/1919 at 64/11/11; housekeeper; single; b. Melrose, MA; Ira S. Ricker (Dover) and Mary E. Hall (Barrington)

Mehitable, d. 1/20/1895 at 85/4/27; bronchial pneumonia; widow; b. Alton; Jedidiah Flanders (Alton) and Lucy Hatch (Gilmanton)

N. Franklin, d. 1/19/1895 at 67/5/24; cancer of bladder; farmer; married; Thomas Ricker (Sandwich) and Lydea Thompson (Farmington)

Randall L., d. 10/24/1930 at 24/10; single; b. Farmington; William H. Ricker and Addie Quint

Sarah B., d. 11/8/1902 at 55/2/4; cancer; housewife; married; b. Farmington; Samuel Ham and Jane Jenness

Sarah E., d. 1/15/1891 at 49/7/4; acute uraemia; housekeeper; married; b. Great Falls; Martin Jenkins (Berwick, ME) and Sophia M. Curtis (Sanford, ME)

Walter D., d. 6/12/1935 at 56/6/11; shoeworker; divorced; b. Wolfeboro; James M. Ricker (Tuftonboro) and Annie S. Dorr (Ossipee)

Wendella, d. 11/1/1927 at 59/4/12; housewife; married; b. New Durham; John F. Tash (New Durham) and Almira B. Ham (Alton)

**RIDLEY,**

Etta F., d. 12/16/1894 at 41/11/16; cancer; housewife; married; b. Ossipee; Ephraim Tibbetts (New Durham) and Amanda Cooley (Holland, VT)

James, d. 12/29/1932 at 56/7/5; laborer; single; b. Alfred, ME; John C. Ridley (Alfred, ME) and Mary F. Knights (Kennebunk, ME)

**RING,**
- Alice E., d. 2/2/1906 at 32/8/3; shock; single; b. Farmington; Dennis Ring (Ireland) and Annie M. Conner (NB)
- Annie M., d. 12/17/1921 at 76/10/18; housekeeper; widow; b. Fredericton, NB; Francis Connor and Bridget Noonan
- Dennis, d. 12/4/1921 at 77/2/22; blacksmith; married; b. Ireland; Terrence Ring (Ireland) and Bridget Connor (Ireland)
- Dennis J., d. 9/6/1890 at 8/1/29; typhoid fever; b. Farmington; Dennis Ring (Ireland) and ----- (NB)

**RIOUX,**
- Irene, d. 8/9/1913 at 3/11/23; brain fever; b. St. Johnsbury, VT; Alfred Rioux (Canada, brickmaker) and Emily Moran (Canada)

**ROBERTS,**
- son, d. 9/26/1889 at –; stillborn; b. Farmington; Charles W. Roberts (Farmington) and Carrie E. Cloutman (Alton)
- A. Allura, d. 10/15/1896 at 35/–/21; vesicular emp'ena; musician; single; b. Farmington; Henry L. Roberts (Farmington) and Anna M. Tole (Winslow, ME)
- Alice N., d. 3/17/1929 at 73/6/7 in Ware, MA
- Anna M., d. 4/7/1915 at 78/9/16; widow; b. ME; Philip Towle (ME) and Deborah Towle (ME)
- Arthur, d. 7/30/1907 at 54/4; intestinal obstruction; laborer; single; b. Farmington; Ira Roberts (Middleton, carpenter) and Belinda Roberts
- Benjamin, d. 1/5/1900 at 71/6; syncope of heart; farmer; married; b. Rochester; Caleb Roberts (Dover) and Rhoda Roberts (Farmington)
- Betsey, d. 4/29/1900 at 71/19/19 (sic); la grippe; housekeeper; b. Gilmanton; Nehemiah Lougee (Gilmanton) and Doratha Hull (Tuftonboro)
- Carrie E., d. 9/26/1889 at 31/8/10; post partum hemorrhage; b. Alton; Jeremiah A. Cloutman (New Durham) and Caroline A. Davis (Alton)
- Charles E., d. 12/2/1908 at 64/2/5; heart failure; real estate agt.; widower; b. Boston, MA; John Roberts (Wakefield) and Ruth Bowker
- Charles W., d. 2/14/1931 at 74/7/8 in Ware, MA; widower
- Clara I., d. 7/2/1906 at 45/4/9; coma; married; b. New Durham; Silas Tibbetts (New Durham) and Louise Grace (New Durham)

Clyde S., d. 5/16/1930 at 25/9/12 in Rochester; mill hand; married; b. Rochester; Herman C. Roberts (Alexandria) and Susanna Warbrick (England)

David S., d. 10/28/1909 at 87/1/6; ursinia; farmer; b. Farmington; Hanson Roberts (Farmington) and Elenor Kimball (Farmington)

Deborah, d. 7/30/1894 at 85/6/11; old age; housekeeper; widow; b. Farmington; William Fernald (Durham) and Betsey Johnson (Brookfield)

Ella P., d. 2/17/1924 at 73/4/11; housekeeper; widow; b. Farmington; Daniel Pearl (Milton) and Lydia Jones (New Durham)

Eloise A., d. 11/28/1897 at 40/9/7; tuberculosis; housewife; married; b. Danbury; Samuel B. Flanders (Danbury) and Marcia A. Brown (Danbury)

Frank H., d. 3/15/1907 at 40/0/23; pulmonary tuberculosis; shoe laster; widower; b. Farmington; Henry L. Roberts (Farmington, shoe mfgr.) and A. M. E. Towle (Winslow)

George E., d. 11/2/1890 at 61/1/28; phthisis pulmonalis; shoe manufacturer; married; b. Farmington; John Roberts (Farmington) and Abigail Wingate (Farmington)

Gertrude E., d. 10/8/1897 at 25/1/23; uremia and convulsions; housekeeper; married; b. Warren; James Lund (Warren) and Ada Cookson (Warren)

Harry H., d. 3/5/1903 at 59/7/16; malignant jaundice; carpenter; married; Asa Roberts (Rochester) and Elizabeth Tibbetts (Rochester)

Helen A., d. 2/13/1930 at 76/2/5; housewife; married; b. Minneapolis, MN; Benjamin Murch (Kittery, ME) and Mary Trefetheren (Kittery, ME)

Herman C., d. 2/1/1931 at 66/7/8 in Rochester; farmer; widower; b. Alexandria; Samuel Roberts (Rochester) and Patience Ackerman (Alexandria)

Herman W., d. 9/5/1892 at 45/6; typhoid fever; grain dealer; married; b. Rochester; John L. Roberts (Rochester, farmer) and Rebecca Haines (Farmington); burial - Rochester

Horace, d. 3/4/1921 at 66/3/1; farmer; married; b. Farmington; Benjamin Roberts and Mary E. Place (Farmington)

Horatio G., d. 3/24/1895 at 43/0/5; consumption; shoemaker; single; b. Farmington; George E. Roberts (Farmington) and Ella E. Roberts (Farmington)

James M., d. 3/14/1892 at 83/8/10; la grippe; farmer; widower; b. Farmington; Joseph Roberts (Rochester, farmer) and Elizabet Dame (Rochester)

Jeremiah, d. 3/9/1892 at 87/3/11; heart disease; farmer; widower; b Farmington; Joseph Roberts (Rochester, farmer) and Elizabet Dame (Rochester)

Jeremiah B., d. 7/6/1894 at 54/3/24; chronic diarrhea; shoe stitcher married; b. Farmington; Jeremiah Roberts (Farmington) and Clarissa Edgerly (New Durham)

John D., d. 12/20/1902 at 80/7/16; old age; farmer; widower; b. Middleton; John Roberts (Middleton) and Polly Davis (Middleton)

John P., d. 7/30/1927 at 75/6/2; retired; divorced; b. Farmington; Benjamin Roberts (Rochester) and Mary E. Place (Farmington

John S., d. 1/22/1907 at 58/3/15; valvular disease of heart; farmer; married; b. Milton; James C. Roberts (Milton, farmer) and Lydia K. Skates (Milton)

Joseph A., d. 8/31/1904 at 77/11/6; tumor of brain; shoe business; widower; b. Farmington; John Roberts (Farmington) and Abigail Wingate (Farmington)

Lelia, d. 12/29/1888 at 25/6/14; heart disease; housekeeper; married; b. Lewiston, ME; John Holland (Lewiston) and Emily S. Welch (Milton, ME)

Lillian A., d. 8/16/1933 at 73/10/2; at home; divorced; b. New Durham; Solomon P. Rollins and Lucinda Tufts

Lydia B. F., d. 11/16/1893 at 75/7/6; shock; housewife; married; b. Middleton; Nathaniel Frost (Middleton) and Samantha Buzzell (Middleton)

Lydia E., d. 4/8/1900 at 68/6/21; paralysis; widow; b. Farmington; Joseph Roberts (Farmington) and Sarah Knight (Farmington)

Mary E., d. 11/3/1918 at 84/3/11; housekeeper; widow; b. Farmington; Jonathan Place (Milton) and Abigail Henderson (Rochester)

Mary E., d. 12/19/1931 at 76/0/28; housekeeper; widow; b. Anawan, IL; James B. Noyes (Franklin) and Sybil Wentworth (Sweden)

Natt F., d. 5/4/1934 at 79/3/24; retired; widower; b. Middleton; John D. Roberts (Middleton) and Lydia Frost (Middleton)

Oceanna, d. 4/30/1922 at 70/6/21; housewife; widow; b. Farmington; Otis Fall (Wolfeboro) and Rosillah Evans (Canada)

Samuel B., d. 1/20/1901 at 90/11/15; heart disease; farmer; widower; b. Tuftonboro; Silas Roberts and Sarah Beck

Sarah A., d. 5/3/1917 at 68/4/19; shoeworker; widow; b. Alton; Henry Dore (Alton) and Susana Rollins (Alton)

Sarah E., d. 8/22/1918 at 75/3/10; housekeeper; widow; b. Moultonboro; Jeremiah Willey (New Durham) and Betsey Webster (New Durham)

Susannah, d. 6/12/1925 at 59/2/29; housekeeper; married; b. NS

William C., d. 10/11/1901 at 74/0/7; ac. regurgitation; janitor; widower; b. Farmington; Natt Roberts (Farmington)

William W., d. 2/7/1933 at 82/11; druggist; widower; b. Farmington; Joseph A. Roberts (Farmington) and Phoebe Chesley (Farmington)

Winfield, d. 4/12/1911 at 63; intestinal obstruction; laborer; single; b. Middleton; Ira Roberts (Middleton, farmer) and Belinda ----- (MA)

Winfield, d. 7/22/1926 at 75/0/5; retired; widower; b. New Durham; David S. Roberts (New Durham) and Sabrina Lord (Canaan, ME)

**ROBINSON,**

Allison, d. 9/2/1938 at 61/2/22; merchant; married; b. Haverhill, MA; George Robinson (Reading, MA) and Mary Spaulding (Wilmington, MA)

Alphonzo R., d. 3/31/1919 at 68/6/23; farmer; married; b. CT; Humphrey Robinson (Baldwin, ME)

Andrew J., d. 4/4/1899 at 63; pulmonisis; farmer; married; b. Farmington, ME; Lemuel Robinson (Farmington) and Martha J. Foss (Farmington)

Eliza A., d. 8/7/1892 at 46/2/4; inflammation; housewife; married; b. Barrington; John Bowen (Barrington, farmer) and Clarace Hodgdon (Barrington)

Lemuel, d. 8/8/1896 at 86/8/18; senile gangrene; farmer; widower; b. Farmington; John Robinson and Johanna Ricker (Milton)

Mary E., d. 2/9/1919 at 72/2/15; widow; b. Wilmington, MA; Maynard Spaulding and Ellen Bond

Melinda, d. 1/14/1905 at 75; cerebral hemorrhage; widow; b. Barrington; Daniel Allen (Barrington) and Annie Rowe (Barrington)

Sybil B., d. 10/1/1929 at 46/9/2 in Rochester; married; b. Rochester; J. Frank Otis (Farmington) and Ida J. Garland (Rochester)

William E., d. 5/17/1927 at 56/11/17; laborer; married; b. Farmington; George W. Robinson (Farmington) and Elizabeth Weeks (Farmington)

**ROGERS,**
Charles C., d. 6/1/1930 at 53/3/7; physician; married; b. Windham ME; Albert P. Rogers (Standish, ME) and Livella Hill (Naples, ME)
Eldon R., d. 2/3/1911 at 0/0/11; jaundice; b. Farmington; Charles C. Rogers (Windham, ME, physic., surgeon) and Alice I. Roberts (Rochester)
Georgietta, d. 10/7/1895 at 46/0/19; cerebral congestion; housekeeper; married; b. Somersworth; David Harriman (Conway) and Hannah Goodwin (Baldwin)

**ROLLINS,**
son, d. 7/23/1890 at --; stillborn; b. Farmington; Irving Rollins and Annie Hubbard
daughter, d. 12/29/1913 at 0/0/0; prematurity; b. Farmington; Cyrus Rollins, Jr. and Nellie Chandler
Abbie E., d. 10/19/1902 at 0/3/2; malnutrition; b. Farmington; Irving H. Rollins (Alton) and Hattie F. Clark (Alton)
Abbie J., d. 5/2/1892 at 0/1; brain fever; b. Farmington; Irving H. Rollins (Alton, shoemaker) and Annie M. Hubbard (Farmington)
Addie F., d. 2/19/1920 at 33/5/19; housewife; married; b. Alton; Frank Clark (Manchester) and Fannie Smith (Alton)
Annie, d. 4/30/1900 at 46/6/29; pneumonia apoplexy; housekeeper, married; b. Farmington; G. W. Hubbard (Wakefield) and Maria A. Averill (Mt. Vernon)
Charles I., d. 12/10/1905 at 44/9/1; chro. Bright's disease; shoemaker; widower; b. Farmington; John P. Rollins (Alton) and Martha C. Rollins (Alton)
Cyrus, d. 3/30/1917 at 61/11/17; hotelkeeper; married; b. New Durham; Perkins Rollins and Martha -----
Edna A., d. 3/22/1897 at 1/2/2; pneumonia; b. Farmington; Herbert S. Rollins (New Durham) and Alice B. Gilman (Hallowell)
Elmer, d. 12/12/1937 at 66/4/10; poultryman; married; b. New Durham; Cyrus C. Rollins (Alton) and Laura French (Farmington)

Elsie F., d. 4/7/1898 at 8/4/11; meningitis; b. Farmington; John A. Rollins (Rochester) and Ruth L. Towle (New Durham)

Etta F., d. 2/12/1925 at –; domestic; divorced; b. Wolfeboro

Grover T., d. 6/14/1897 at 8/9/3; drowning; b. Farmington; Irving H. Rollins (Alton) and Anna Hubbard (Farmington)

John A., d. 9/5/1932 at 74/3/2; retired; married; b. Rochester; John P. Rollins (Alton) and Martha C. Rollins (Alton)

Martha C., d. 5/30/1896 at 70/2; paralysis; housewife; married; b. Alton; Richard Rollins

Roland, d. 9/12/1904 at 0/3/25; indigestion; b. Farmington; Irving H. Rollins (Alton) and Hattie Clark (Alton)

William A., d. 11/8/1891 at 34/10/6; suffocation; laborer; single; b. Standish, ME; John T. Rollins (Wolfeboro) and Patience Colomy (Farmington)

**ROSE,**
Vessie I., d. 2/11/1923 at 72/5; housekeeper; widow; b. New Castle; Josiah Trefethen (Kittery, ME) and Isabelle Curtis (New Castle)

**ROSS,**
Alexander, d. 12/26/1928 at 76/7/23; farmer; married; b. Scotland; James Ross (Scotland)

**ROUCKEY,**
son, d. 7/3/1929 at 0/0/0; b. Farmington; George A. Rouckey (Lebanon, ME) and Gertrude E. Ricker (New Durham)

**ROWE,**
Estella I., d. 4/3/1933 at 72/11/27; shoeworker; widow; b. Lebanon, ME; Nathaniel J. Canney (Lebanon, ME) and Araminta Wentworth (Milton)

**ROWELL,**
Ralph J., d. 3/30/1926 at 67/11/2; salesman; married; b. Springfield, MA

**RUNNELLS,**
daughter, d. 6/13/1892 at –; stillborn; b. Farmington; Forrest L. Runnells (New Durham, shoe laster) and Ida M. Champion (East Wakefield)

Laurentina, d. 11/26/1922 at 95/3; widow; b. Alton; Benjamin
 Glidden (Farmington) and Betsey Burnham (Farmington)
Paul M., d. 8/23/1915 at 83/4/9; farmer; widower; b. New Durham;
 Samuel Runnals (New Durham) and Eliza Ricker (New
 Durham)

**RUSSELL,**
Frank S., d. 1/3/1928 at 81/8/0; shoeworker; married; b. Middleton,
 MA; Samuel Russell
George F., d. 8/4/1928 at 88/10/12; farmer; widower; b. Utica, NY;
 Frank Russell
Lottie A., d. 7/26/1932 at 68/1/18; housekeeper; widow; b. Alton;
 Charles H. Chamberlin and Mary E. Wallace
Theresa, d. 4/20/1892 at 0/7/28; meningitis; b. Farmington; George
 F. Russell (Utica, NY, shoe cutter) and Lottie A. Chamberlin
 (Alton)

**SAMPSON,**
Jane A., d. 5/20/1896 at 79/8; old age; widow; b. Dexter, ME; -----
 Hibbard

**SANBORN,**
daughter, d. 9/12/1890 at 0/0/26; premature birth; b. Farmington;
 Almon C. Sanborn (Sanbornton) and Emma Richardson
Abigail, d. 11/16/1906 at 81/0/1; old age; housewife; widow; b.
 Milton; Richard Varney and Comfort Place
Alice M., d. 5/5/1923 at 33/8/1; housekeeper; married; b.
 Farmington; John I. Gray (Farmington) and Ellen Varney
 (Farmington)
Hannah, d. 4/28/1927 at 91/5/15; widow; b. Farmington; Alvah
 Varney (Farmington) and Abigail Hanson (Brookfield)
Harriett, d. 5/2/1921 at 78/7/24; housekeeper; widow; b.
 Farmington; Charles Gage (Dover) and Martha York (New
 Durham)
Harry, d. 11/15/1917 at 48/6/24; shoeworker; married; b.
 Farmington; Isaac Sanborn (Somersworth) and Ellen S.
 Linscott (Berwick, ME)
John E., d. 8/9/1918 at 77/3/13; boxmaker; married; b. Wolfeboro
Lutheria A., d. 10/27/1895 at 55/1; cancer in stomach; housework;
 married; Solomon Tanner (Groton, MA) and Elizabeth A.
 Dudley (Wayland, MA)

Marjorie, d. 4/11/1919 at 0/0/1; b. Farmington; Roland Sanborn (Rochester) and Alice M. Gray (Farmington)

Nathan, d. 2/17/1920 at 82/11/1; farmer; married; b. Tamworth; Simon Sanborn (Tamworth) and Hannah Pratt (VT)

Nellie Winn, d. 10/8/1931 at – in Rochester; b. Rochester; Roland Sanborn (Rochester) and Grace Haddock (Ossipee)

## SANDERS,

David B., d. 4/5/1893 at 43/6/6; shock; gentleman; married; b. Ossipee; Robert Sanders (Effingham) and Lavina Philbrick (Effingham)

Hannah B., d. 3/8/1897 at 77/4/4; old age; housekeeper; single; b. Farmington; Joseph Sanders (Strafford) and Sarah Beck (Farmington)

## SANSOUCIE,

Joseph L., d. 8/10/1897 at 0/0/29; anaesthesia; b. Farmington; Joseph Sansoucie (Worcester) and Lizzie E. Drapeau (Strafford)

## SARGENT,

Edwin, d. 7/2/1898 at 62/8; organic disease spinal cord; farmer; married; b. Merrimac, MA; Orlando Sargent (Merrimac, MA) and Abigail Patten (Amesbury, MA)

## SAUNDERS,

Mary F., d. 12/9/1909 at 48/8/10; Bright's disease; housewife; b. Salem; Charles E. Butler (Calhoun) and Laura Jewett (New London)

## SAWYER,

Alice J., d. 2/21/1891 at 31/2/3; hemorrhage; housekeeper; married; b. Rochester; John B. Spinney (York, ME) and Lizzie M. Bickford (Rochester)

Clifford L., d. 1/4/1936 at 57/9/12; laborer; married; b. York, ME; Jacob Sawyer and Harriett Sawyer

## SCHLENKER,

Elizabeth, d. 4/22/1920 at 57/9/7; retired; widow; b. Middleton; John Pike and Mary Cloutman

Josephine, d. 6/28/1911 at 29/8/16; tuberculosis; bookkeeper; single; b. Rochester; Agatha Schlenker (Germany)

**SCHOCH,**
daughter, d. 7/28/1915 at 0/0/0; b. Farmington; Edgar Schoch (Reading, PA) and Mary A. Nixon (Rochester)

**SCHREITER,**
Bernard, d. 4/9/1922 at 0/0/3; b. Boston; Wilhelmina Schreiter (Portsmouth)

**SCOTT,**
daughter, d. 7/4/1891 at –; stillborn; b. Farmington; Edward J. Scott (NB) and Angie Yeaton (Alfred, ME)
Joseph W., d. 4/16/1931 at 53/11/23 in Rochester; shoeworker; married; b. Feeding Hills, MA; Frank Scott (Washington, MA) and Melvina San Souci (Canada)
Leon, d. 6/20/1890 at 0/7; cholera infantum; b. Farmington; Edward J. Scott (NB) and Argie Yeaton (Alfred, ME)
Walter E., d. 1/20/1889 at 0/5/20; cerebral inflammation; b. Springvale, ME; Edward J. Scott (NB) and Angie G. Yeaton (Springvale)

**SCRIVER,**
Adeline, d. 7/30/1929 at 87/10/2 in Boston, MA; at home; widow; b. Tuftonboro; John Tibbetts (Tuftonboro) and Catherine Leathers (Tuftonboro)

**SCRUTON,**
son, d. 11/8/1905 at –; immaturity; b. Farmington; Irving Scruton (Farmington) and Lizzie Preston (Fall River)
Charles M., d. 3/25/1905 at 52/6/25; Bright's disease; farmer; married; b. Farmington; Miles Scruton (Farmington) and Lydia Yeaton (Strafford)
Edward J., d. 6/27/1920 at 63/7/24; married
Frank M., d. 10/3/1898 at 22/5/19; typhoid malarial; soldier; single; b. Farmington; James M. Scruton (Strafford) and Sarah Hall (Strafford)
Ida M., d. 4/11/1905 at 46/9/16; acute insanity; married; b. Farmington; Stacy Hall (Barnstead) and Hannah J. Gray (Strafford)

Joan Marie, d. 6/9/1934 at 0/0/2 in Rochester; Gerald Scruton (Farmington) and Esther Whitehouse (Somersworth)

John F., d. 5/11/1927 at 85/6/3; farmer; widower; b. Strafford; Joseph Scruton and Louisa Brock

Lois, d. 1/12/1887 at 80/6; housekeeper; married; b. New Durham

Lydia A., d. 9/26/1898 at 72/2/18; diabetes; housekeeper; widow; b. Strafford; William Yeaton (Strafford) and Abbie Ham (Strafford)

Lydia L., d. 3/30/1915 at 74/7/12; housekeeper; married; b. Farmington; Amos Varney (Farmington) and Annie Locke (Rochester)

Miles, d. 2/13/1893 at 101/2/17; old age; farmer; widower; b. Strafford; Patience Allard

Miles, d. 9/24/1901 at 76/11/15; paralysis; farmer; widower; b. Farmington; Miles Scruton (Farmington) and Sarah Canney (Alexandria)

Sarah A., d. 1/23/1899 at 64/5/29; dropsy; housewife; married

Thomas C., d. 3/12/1887 at 65/3; farmer; married; Miles Scruton and Salley Canney

**SEARS,**
Arthur V., d. 11/19/1910 at 35/8/24; tuberculosis; laborer; single; b. NS; John W. Sears (NS) and Catherine McKenna (NS)

**SEAVEY,**
Hyrena, d. 3/5/1890 at 73/2/22; paralysis; housekeeper; widow; b. Nottingham; Taylor Clark

Inez A., d. 10/20/1894 at 3/2/9; scarlet fever; b. Gilmanton; Joseph E. Seavey (Alexandria) and Nellie Jones (Gilmanton)

Marion, d. 10/17/1894 at 0/8/21; bronchitis; b. Farmington; Joseph E. Seavey (Alexandria) and Nellie Jones (Gilmanton)

**SENTER,**
Walter, d. 3/30/1938 at 67/4/15 in Dover; shoeworker; married; b. Derry; Frank Senter (Derry) and Mary E. Davis (Derry)

**SHACKFORD,**
Clara, d. 3/26/1936 at 91/5/19 in Rochester; at home; widow; b. Barnstead; Simeon Lougee (Barnstead) and Mary Tibbetts (Barnstead)

John S., d. 6/28/1900 at 25/2/18; tubercular meningitis; artist; married; b. Barnstead; A. W. Shackford (Barnstead) and Clar Lougee (Barnstead)

**SHAW,**
Kate M., d. 9/1/1935 at 58/3/11; housewife; married; b. Farmington Robert R. Perkins (Farmington) and Mary J. Wiggin (Farmington)
Sue Lee, d. 1/27/1923 at 48/11/21; housewife; married; b. Roanok VA; ---- Ward

**SHEEHAN,**
Grace E., d. 9/18/1922 at 33/1/20; housewife; married; b. Farmington; George C. Pike (Middleton) and Mary A. Arnold (ME)

**SHELDON,**
Linda M., d. 1/3/1924 at 70/2/15; at home; married; b. Parsonsfield ME; John Brown (Parsonsfield, ME) and Hannah Brown (ME)

**SHEPARD,**
John J., d. 2/11/1938 at 53/7/2 in Rochester; shoeworker; divorced b. Holyoke, MA

**SHEVENELL,**
Edward, d. 6/9/1903 at 0/4; acute nephritis; Charles Shevenell (Biddeford) and Trixy Broderick (Lawrence)

**SHOREY,**
Catherine, d. 9/11/1907 at 63/5/6; apoplexy; housekeeper; divorced; b. NS; Fredric Lynch (Fredericton, NB, farmer)

**SIDNEY,**
Elizabeth, d. 5/17/1938 at 60/4/8; housekeeper; widow; b. Canada; John Mahew (Ireland)

**SIMPSON,**
Georgia, d. 10/18/1924 at 71/7/9; housewife; married; b. Cumberland; Seward Shaw and Abigail Shaw
William M., d. 2/14/1933 at 82/1/30; retired; widower; b. Leistershire, England; retired; widower

**SMALL,**
- Hattie E., d. 12/8/1930 at 79 in Rochester; domestic; widow; b. Farmington; Bernard Averill
- Isaac H., d. 7/18/1915 at 47/11/8; dentist; widower; b. New Rochelle, NY; Isaac H. Small (Limerick, ME) and Jennie M. McKay (Edinburgh, Scotland)
- Lucy A., d. 12/4/1907 at 70/0/20; heart disease; milliner; widow; b. Alton; David Ricker (Gilmanton, farmer) and Mehitable Flanders (Gilmanton)
- Nellie C., d. 3/23/1935 at 72/6/23; at home; single; Isaac H. Small and Jennie M. Mackay (Scotland)

**SMART,**
- son, d. 12/17/1927 at –; b. Rochester; Jeremiah Smart (Farmington) and Ada F. Barsantee (Portsmouth)
- son, d. 1/4/1930 at – in Rochester; b. Rochester; Jerry Smart (Farmington) and Ada Barsantee (Portsmouth)
- daughter, d. 6/9/1937 at – in Rochester; b. Rochester; Jerry Smart (Farmington) and Ada Barsantee (Portsmouth)
- Annie B., d. 4/14/1924 at 58/3/19; housewife; married; b. MN; Alphonzo James and Lucy Fogg
- Joel, d. 10/9/1910 at 65/9/19; dysentery; farmer; married; b. Maxfield, ME; John Smart
- Mary A., d. 12/29/1936 at 82/1/26; at home; widow; b. Dover; Alonzo Smith and Hannah Kelly

**SMITH,**
- son, d. 2/24/1923 at –; b. Farmington; Irving Smith (NH) and Beatrice Glidden (NH)
- Ada E., d. 3/18/1926 at 71/6/4; housekeeper; widow; b. Wolfeboro; Abram Cookson (ME) and Harriet Jackson (Warren)
- Annie, d. 10/20/1910 at 81; gastroenteritis; widow; b. England; Rev. Wm. Rogers (England) and Katherine Barrett (England)
- Annie R., d. 8/28/1934 at 73/3/2; housekeeper; divorced; b. W. Lebanon, ME; Jacob Smith (Tamworth) and Betsey E. Gerrish (Lebanon, ME)
- Annie S., d. 8/14/1894 at 42/3/14; intestinal obstruction; shoestitcher; divorced; b. Farmington; Stephen French (Farmington) and Mary E. Young (Farmington)

Charles F., d. 8/11/1911 at 55/2/10; tuberculosis; salesman; married; b. Farmington; George K. Smith (Groveland, MA, shoemaker) and Hannah Colomy

Clara A., d. 11/25/1916 at 63/2/8; housewife; married; b. Farmington; Moses Leighton (Farmington) and Hannah Tanner (Farmington)

Clarence L., d. 12/2/1918 at 12/2/15; student; single; b. Rochester; Leland C. Smith (Moultonboro) and Alice M. Jones (Farmington)

Daniel H., d. 1/28/1919 at 70/7/12; painter; married; b. Moultonboro; Eliphalet Smith

Ellen S., d. 2/8/1922 at 76/4/22; housewife; widow; b. Sandwich; ---- Moulton and Sophronia Ricker

Estella M., d. 12/29/1933 at 59/6/18; housewife; married; b. Farmington; Thomas F. Card (New Castle) and Mary J. Smith (New Durham)

Frank J., d. 5/4/1925 at 68/7/6; shoeworker; married; b. Danbury; George H. Smith (Randolph, VT) and Marion Brown (Wilmot)

George E., d. 10/22/1889 at 36/11/20; pulmonary tuberculosis; shoemaker; b. Farmington; George K. Smith (W. Newbury, MA) and Hannah Colomy (New Durham)

George E., d. 9/11/1927 at 80; shoeworker; married; b. Charlestown, MA; David M. Smith and Nancy Varney

George K., d. 12/29/1902 at 76/10/27; apoplexy; shoemaker; widower; b. Newburyport

Horace H., d. 5/29/1935 at 63/10/10; retired; widower; b. Gilmanton; Edward E. Smith (MA) and Jane Evans (Ossipee)

Irving W., d. 7/1/1935 at 68/1/3 in Rochester; boxmaker; widower; b. Farmington; George K. Smith (Newburyport, MA) and Hannah Colomy (New Durham)

Julia M. R., d. 1/31/1932 at 95/4/16 in Springfield, MA; housewife; widow; b. Farmington; Jeremiah Roberts (Farmington) and Clarissa H. Edgerly (Farmington)

May J., d. 6/4/1918 at 42/3/1; housewife; married; b. Kittery, ME; Oliver S. Curtis (Kittery, ME) and Martha Picott (Kittery, ME)

Nancy, d. 11/23/1894 at 67/10/4; pneumonia; housewife; married; b. Rochester; David Varney (Wakefield) and Lucy Smith (Rochester)

Sarah, d. 4/23/1932 at 86/9 in Rochester; housekeeper; widow; b. Holderness; Thomas Curry and Eleanor Poole

Sarah A., d. 4/17/1928 at 74/6/15; housewife; married; b. Alton

Simeon F., d. 6/3/1936 at 85/9/13 in Rochester; widower; b. Rochester; James Smith and Sarah Flanders

**SNELL,**
Stillman L., d. 4/13/1887 at 55/1/6; shoemaker; married; b. Poland, ME; Job Snell (Poland, ME) and Lydia Starbird (Gray, ME)

**SOUCY,**
son, d. 1/21/1925 at 0/0/1; b. Farmington; Alma Soucy (NH)

**SPEAR,**
Dorothy, d. 3/14/1913 at 0/0/2; premature birth; b. Farmington; Fred R. Spear (E. Boston, MA, shoecutter) and Ruth T. Gordon (Manchester)
Edwin C., d. 8/20/1928 at 67/3/10; shoeworker; married; b. East Boston, MA; Robert Spear (Eastport, ME) and Ann Winchester (Eastport, ME)

**STACEY,**
Georgia H., d. 4/17/1931 at 56/7/6; housewife; married; b. Deerfield Parade; George H. Marston and Jennie -----

**STANLEY,**
Alvira E., d. 3/10/1934 at 61/9/13; shoeworker; widow; b. Clifton, ME; John Oakes (Dexter, ME) and Nancy Rich (Bangor, ME)
Helen P., d. 10/17/1912 at 19/2/19; pneumonia; b. Farmington; Edward Stanley (Newton Ctr., salesman) and Helen Blethen (Newton Ctr.)
Samuel S., d. 3/6/1933 at 71/11/3; laborer; married; b. Sealcove, ME; George S. Stanley (Sealcove, ME) and Susan Reed (Sealcove, ME)

**STAPLES,**
Eliza, d. 6/8/1903 at 35; puerperal elmp'sia; housewife; married; Robert H. Acorn (PEI) and Catherine Stewart (Scotland)
Florence M., d. 5/26/1910 at 26/11/7; miscarriage; housewife; married; b. Tuftonboro; George Piper and Etta Piper (Tuftonboro)
Frank M., d. 4/2/1899 at 31; pulmonisis; shoe cutter; divorced; b. Kittery, ME; Melson Staples and Fannie Briggs

**STETSON,**
Aldena S., d. 4/26/1891 at 55/1/2; albumenuria; housekeeper; widow; b. Warren, ME; John Crawford (Warren, ME) and Mahala Russell (Warren, ME)

**STEVENS,**
son, d. 12/12/1914 at 0/0/0; stillborn; b. Farmington; Philemon Stevens (Biddeford, shoeworker) and Helen S. Brooks (Farmington)

Abbie L., d. 5/8/1892 at 38/0/11; chronic supperative overitis; housewife; married; b. Alton; George T. Leeds (Boston, MA, carpenter) and Dorothy Langley (Lee)

Abigail, d. 2/9/1898 at 93/9; old age; widow; b. Rochester; Jonathan Stevens (Rochester) and Mary Horne (Rochester)

Charlotte A., d. 12/22/1909 at 74/1/28; ephidroma of nose; housewife; b. Canton, MA; Daniel Wallace and Betsey Benton

Helen S., d. 6/7/1919 at 30/5/2; housewife; married; b. Farmington; Percy J. Brooks (Alton) and Edith Tibbetts (Farmington)

Hiram J., d. 12/26/1916 at 84/5/29; shoeworker; widower; b. Alton; William Stevens (Alton) and Abigail Richards (Alton)

J. Oscar, d. 4/30/1894 at 36/0/24; consumption; shoemaker; single; b. Middleton; B. F. B. Stevens (Middleton) and Statora Wilson (Freeport, ME)

James E., d. 9/2/1935 at 76/9/22; retired; widower; b. Milton; James Stevens (Middleton) and Lydia Brown (Middleton)

John B., d. 5/8/1909 at 77/2/16; chronic cohitis; physician; b. Concord; John G. Stevens

Linnie G., d. 7/21/1917 at 7/10/27; Ronello Stevens (Farmington) and Nellie F. Abbott (Farmington)

Lydia A., d. 6/25/1911 at 68/2; hemo. of kidney; housekeeper; widow; b. New Durham; Samuel Roberts (millman) and Rhoda Berry (New Durham)

**STIMPSON,**
Ralph W., d. 10/7/1934 at 47/1/7; shoeworker; married; b. Dresden, ME; George Stimpson and Jennie L. Auben

**STRAW,**
Alonzo, d. 5/27/1907 at 85/2; pneumonia; blacksmith; widower; b. Barnstead; Samuel Straw (farmer) and Elizabeth Eastman (Barnstead)

Harriet A., d. 5/11/1889 at 56/6; pneumonia; housekeeper; b. Farmington; Lemuel Richardson and Margaret Downs

**STUART,**
Lucy E., d. 4/30/1888 at 29/4/15; typhoid fever; housekeeper; married; b. Bridgewater; Moses Tirrell (Bridgewater) and Maria Peasley (Bridgewater)

**SUTHERLAND,**
Hugh M., d. 4/29/1891 at 44/5/2; rheumatism of heart; shoe cutter; married; b. Boston, MA; Murdock Sutherland (Scotland) and Annie Frasin (Scotland)
Lucy A., d. 7/3/1897 at 49/2/24; phthisis; housekeeper; widow; b. Orleans; Elisha Mayo and Caroline Emery
Robert W., d. 10/14/1889 at 18/11/12; phthisis; last maker; b. Hanover, MA; H. M. Sutherland (Boston, MA) and Lucy A. Mayo (Orleans)
Roline, d. 12/30/1902 at 19/5/22; typhoid fever; student; single; b. No. Hanover; Hugh Sutherland (Boston, MA) and Lucy A. Mayo (Orleans, MA)

**SWINERTON,**
Emma, d. 7/16/1936 at 68/8/21 in Milton; at home; widow; b. Braintree, MA; Charles A. Melville and Rhoda McKenistry
Jacob, d. 12/31/1923 at 64/8; shoemaker; married; b. Rochester; Richard Swinerton (Newfield, ME) and Augusta Whitehouse
James, d. 7/31/1928 at 81/10; farmer; widower; b. Somersworth; Andrew Swinnerton (Newfield, ME) and Phydelia Stone (Sanford, ME)
Maria, d. 5/25/1925 at 83/1/26; housekeeper; widow; b. Somersworth; Jacob Whitehouse (Gonic) and Lydia Horne
Reginald, d. 4/25/1917 at 13/11/30; b. Milton; Jacob Swinerton (Rochester) and Emma A. Melville (N. Braintree, MA)

**SYLVIA,**
Priscilla, d. 9/15/1932 at 5/5/29 in Barnstead; b. Farmington; John Sylvia (Oakland, CA) and Gladys Wilkes (Barnstead)

**TALBOT,**
    Henry W., d. 3/25/1936 at 71/9/16; shoeworker; married; b. Brooklyn, NY; Mark Talbot (Scotland) and Margaret Stocker (Scotland)

**TALPEY,**
    Charles W., d. 12/25/1905 at 70/1/9; cancer of stomach; bank cashier; married; b. York, ME; Jonathan Talpey (York) and Elizabeth Carlyle (York)

**TANNER,**
Angelina, d. 7/19/1919 at 72/3/5

Austin D., d. 10/9/1909 at 0/1; ilio-colitis; b. Farmington; Herbert E Tanner (Farmington) and Marie A. Devaney (Ireland)

Charles H., d. 8/27/1890 at 24/11/20; phthisis pulmonalis; shoemaker; single; b. Farmington; William H. Tanner (Farmington) and Martha A. Giles (Acton, ME)

Ellen F., d. 12/27/1916 at 64; widow; b. Union; Joseph Young and Julia Rollins

George W., d. 7/31/1914 at 71/3/12; mitral regurgitation; shoemaker; married; b. Exeter; Seth Tanner (sailor and mason)

Henry H., d. 1/10/1918 at 77/6/2; farmer; widower; b. Sandwich; Joshua Tanner (Farmington) and Sarah Ham (Farmington)

Horatio G., d. 8/13/1888 at 46/4/9; bronchitis; farmer; single; b. Sandwich; J. W. Tanner (Farmington) and Sarah Ham (Farmington)

John E., d. 5/16/1903 at 57/3/22; catarrh of bowels; farmer; married; Ira Tanner and Eliza Tanner

Joseph, d. 2/13/1910 at 80; ch. Bright's disease; laborer; single; b. Farmington; John Tanner and Mary Thompson

Leona A., d. 4/14/1911 at 0/0/6; enterculitis; b. Farmington; George I. Tanner (Farmington, shoemaker) and Gertrude Smart (Farmington)

Lincoln G., d. 8/20/1932 at 50/6/3 in Boston, MA; engineer; married b. Chicago, IL; Henry A. Tanner (Sandwich) and Minnie MacDonald (AR)

Martha A., d. 12/24/1918 at 74/11/24; housewife; widow; b. Lebanon, ME; Orrin P. Giles and ----- Emery

Sarah, d. 4/1/1890 at 76/1/11; phthisis; housekeeper; widow; b. Farmington; Thomas Ham (Farmington) and Elizabeth Pinkham (Farmington)

William H., d. 2/10/1906 at 80/3/4; malignant jaundice; farmer; married; b. Farmington; John Tanner (Farmington) and Mary Thompson (Farmington)

**TANWALT** [see Tauwalt],

William H., d. 9/3/1910 at 25/2/26; pul. tuberculosis; hotel clerk; married; b. Cambridge, MA; Henry T. Tanwalt (Cambridge, MA) and Dora Haynes (Provincetown, MA)

**TARL[E]TON,**

Dolly C., d. 10/28/1903 at 84/11/26; shock; housewife; widow; William Tarleton (New Castle) and Marian Trefethen (Skowhegan)

George, d. 8/26/1902 at 88/1/20; hemorrhage of brain; expressman; married; b. New Castle; Elias Tarlton (New Castle) and Elizabeth Tarlton (New Castle)

**TASH,**

John N., d. 6/26/1932 at 66/2/29 in New Durham; farmer; married; b. New Durham; John F. Tash (New Durham) and Almira B. Ham (Alton)

**TAUWALT** [see Tanwalt],

Henry, d. 10/25/1929 at 63/1/17 in Rochester; teamster; married; b. Cambridge, MA; William Tauwalt (Cambridge) and Catharine Tauwalt (Cambridge)

**TAYLOR,**

Margaret M., d. 6/20/1895 at 70/9/20; widow; b. St. Johns, NB

**TEBBETTS,**

Albinus B., d. 10/15/1930 at 78/11/17; farmer; married; b. New Durham; Baalis B. Tebbets (Farmington) and Hannah J. Grace (New Durham)

Ernest, d. 10/6/1918 at 26/6/19; farmer; single; b. New Durham; Albinus Tebbetts (New Durham) and Mary F. Amazeen (Milton)

Harris, d. 5/4/1907 at 40/4/4; tubelar laringitis; teamster; married; b Farmington; T. J. Tebbetts (Berwick, farmer) and Melvina Colbath (Middleton)

Mary E., d. 5/12/1937 at 81/0/22; at home; widow; b. West Milton; Harry Amazeen (New Castle) and Abigail Wentworth (West Milton)

**TERRIER,**

Clara L., d. 8/26/1900 at 26; septicemia; housewife; single; b. Barton, Canada; Eczavi Lessard (St. Frederick) and Justine Gravelle (St. Fredericks)

**THAYER,**

Alice J. W., d. 11/12/1904 at 56/10/28; fatty deg. of heart; saleswoman; divorced; b. E. Brookfield, VT; Nathaniel Wheatley (Brookfield, VT) and Betsey P. Wood (Westford, VT)

Elmer F., d. 5/14/1926 at 64/8/13; shoe mfgr.; married; b. S. Weymouth, MA; Noah B. Thayer (S. Weymouth, MA) and Lucy Newcomb (Randolph, MA)

Ida B., d. 3/31/1929 at 74/7/7; widow; b. Alton; Charles Whitehouse

Susan, d. 9/6/1923 at 63/1/15; housewife; married; b. Farmington; Luther Lord and Susan E. Grant (Lebanon)

William F., d. 11/13/1913 at 58/2/19; chronic Bright's disease; lumber dealer; married; b. Gray, ME; Edward F. Thayer (Gray, ME, carpenter) and Elmeda Purington (Windham, ME)

**THOMPSON,**

Almira B., d. 10/27/1889 at 68/8/4; disease of brain; housekeeper; b. Farmington; Miles Thompson (Farmington) and Sally Hanson (Farmington)

Charles, d. 10/3/1937 at 81/6/6; retired; married; b. Farmington; Joseph P. Thompson (Farmington) and Melissa W. Cater (Farmington)

Frank N., d. 8/28/1894 at 48/10/27; cancer; laborer; married; b. Rochester

George W., d. 9/1/1895 at 72/5/6; valv. dis. of heart; farmer; married

H. M., d. 12/26/1901 at 78/9/3; old age; widow; b. Farmington; Miles Thompson (Farmington) and Sally Hanson (Farmington)

Hannah, d. 7/9/1915 at 83/4/29; widow; b. Tuftonboro; Ephraim Tibbetts (Farmington) and Mary Rand (Farmington)

Hattie, d. 9/26/1918 at 57/3/14; housewife; married; b. Farmington; Benjamin Chesley (Farmington) and ----- Gray (New Durham)

James H., d. 3/30/1932 at 73/7/19 in Keene; janitor; married; b. Farmington; James L. Thompson (NH) and Hannah Tibbetts (NH)

James L., d. 11/19/1887 at 62/0/4; farmer; married; b. Farmington

Jennie, d. 11/20/1909 at 62/6/27; apoplexy; housewife; b. Farmington; Stacey Hall (Barnstead) and Hannah J. Gray (New Durham)

John, d. 8/12/1924 at 78/10/9; farmer; widower; b. Farmington; George W. Thompson and Elizabeth Canney

L. M., d. 3/13/1913 at 58/6/18; cancer of stomach; housewife; married; b. Farmington; John F. Chesley (Farmington, farmer) and Hannah Garland (Farmington)

Melissa, d. 1/8/1891 at 60/5; gastroenteritis; housekeeper; married; b. Farmington; Otis Cater (Farmington) and Lovey Cater (Farmington)

Sara G., d. 2/21/1928 at 78/2/24; housewife; married; b. Deblois, ME; Jacob Gould and Rebecca Cates (Machias, ME)

Winslow, d. 1/1/1935 at 55/2/22; farmer; married; b. Farmington; John W. Thompson (Farmington) and Dorothy J. Hall (Farmington)

**THURSTON,**

Bernice, d. 4/19/1906 at 0/0/21; cahexnia; b. Farmington; Willie Thurston (Newton, MA) and Grace Ham (Milton)

Clarence, d. 1/6/1924 at 21/11/3; farmer; single; b. Effingham; Martin Thurston (Brownfield, ME) and Clara M. Carlis (Chelsea, MA)

**TIBBETTS,**

son, d. 4/21/1902 at –; stillborn; b. Farmington; William Pond (W. Medway) and Cassie Tibbetts (Farmington)

daughter, d. 9/30/1904 at 0/0/2; internal hemorrhage; b. Farmington; Harris C. Tibbetts (Farmington) and Inez Ham (Gilmanton)

Alvin C., d. 2/25/1890 at 64/4/22; typhoid pneumonia; carpenter; married; b. Farmington; Charles Tibbetts (Rochester) and Nancy Jordan (Parsonsfield, ME)

Angie, d. 10/10/1901 at 36/5/24; consumption; b. Alton; James B. Tibbetts (Alton) and Hannah Lucas (Alton)

Anstress, d. 4/21/1896 at 59/1/3; softening of brain; housekeeper; widow; b. Middleton; Moses Place (Middleton) and Caziah Hayes (Farmington)

Betsey, d. 7/29/1895 at 74/2; old age; housewife; married; b. Farmington; Aaron Place (Farmington) and Mary R. Stephens (Farmington)

Carrie B., d. 3/29/1935 at 69/0/3; housewife; married; b. Barnstead John H. Hodgdon (Barnstead) and Ellen Nute (Alton)

Charles W., d. 12/14/1918 at 60/10/19; farmer; single; b. Middleton Timothy Tibbetts (Farmington) and Malina Colbath (Middleton)

Eliza J., d. 2/2/1892 at 67; erysipelas; housekeeper; widow; b. Strafford

Emma M., d. 5/15/1891 at 40/9/6; paralytic shock; housekeeper; single; b. Farmington; George F. Tibbetts (Farmington) and Betsey Place (Farmington)

Frank E., d. 4/2/1935 at 69/9/1; laborer; widower; b. Berwick, ME

George F., d. 2/8/1897 at 73/10/26; cerebral hemorrhage; blacksmith; widower; b. Farmington; Joseph Tibbetts (Sandwich) and Elanor Pearl (Sandwich)

George F., d. 4/16/1901 at 41/6/20; multiple sclerosis; hotel clerk; married; b. Farmington; George F. Tibbetts (Farmington) and Betsy Place (Farmington)

George M., d. 7/20/1892 at 42/9/25; consumption; farmer; married; b. Farmington; Eri F. Tibbetts (Farmington, farmer) and Eliona Colbath (Farmington)

Guy C., d. 6/15/1891 at 7/5/18; drowned; b. Farmington; George F. Tibbetts, Jr. (Farmington) and Etta M. Chesley (Farmington)

Henry A., d. 2/20/1932 at 69/9/14; shoeworker; married; b. Farmington; George F. Tibbetts and Betsy Place

Jared P., d. 12/8/1896 at 60/8/27; acute pneumonia; undertaker; married; Charles Tibbetts (Berwick, ME) and Nancy Jordan (Berwick, ME)

Joshua A., d. 6/14/1892 at 72/11/23; rheumatism of the heart; farmer; widower; b. Farmington; Joshua Tibbetts (Farmington, farmer) and Elizabeth Stevens (Farmington)

Leonard T., d. 7/8/1902 at 75/1/13; old age; farmer; widower

Mary A., d. 4/6/1889 at 65/6/26; hernia; housekeeper; b. Milton; William Wentworth (Milton) and Susan Wentworth (Milton)

Mary E., d. 5/9/1894 at 50/2/6; pneumonia; housekeeper; married; b. Dover; Ethernal Streeter (W. Concord, VT) and Julia A. Drew (W. Concord, VT)

Mary E., d. 12/31/1938 at 85/3/15; at home; widow; b. Farmington; Charles A. Kelley and Sarah A. Horne

Melvina E., d. 8/15/1896 at 56/6; apoplexy; housekeeper; widow; b. Middleton; Benjamin R. Colbath (Middleton) and Wealthy Page (Rochester)

Sarah A., d. 10/1/1899 at 54/10/12; cardiac asthma; housewife; married; b. Farmington; Joshua A. Tibbetts (Farmington) and Mary Wentworth (Milton)

Thelma, d. 11/14/1919 at 0/3/1; b. Farmington; Grace Tibbetts (Farmington)

## TITCOMB,

Elizabeth, d. 5/31/1906 at 73/10/21; liver trouble; married; b. New Durham; Benjamin Canney and Margaret Henderson

## TNEEY,

Joseph, d. 10/12/1906 at 0/2/0; enteritis; b. Farmington; George Tneey (Exeter) and Edith Ricker (Strafford)

## TOWLE,

Bessie W., d. 7/24/1890 at 0/3/15; congestion of lungs; b. Farmington; Tristram F. Towle (New Durham) and Annie B. Trafton (Great Falls)

Emily M., d. 12/22/1922 at 71/6/29; widow; b. New Durham; James H. Fletcher (New Durham) and Abigail Colman (New Durham)

Emma F., d. 6/19/1938 at 84/9/23; housewife; widow; b. New Durham; Jerome Witham (New Durham) and Mary Randall (New Durham)

Fred A., d. 4/3/1892 at 10/3; acute meningitis; b. Farmington; Tristram F. Towle (New Durham, painter) and Annie B. Trafton (Great Falls)

George S., d. 3/26/1898 at 26/9/1; consumption; shoe worker; married; b. New Durham; Charles F. Towle (New Durham) and Eliza Witham (New Durham)

Harold J., Jr., d. 9/6/1932 at 8/6/26 in Rochester; student; b. Boston, MA; Harold J. Towle (Bristol) and Agnes O'Connor (Cambridge, MA)

Henry W., d. 9/2/1904 at 60/6/16; apoplexy; shoemaker; married; b. Farmington; William Towle (Alton) and Ruth Doe (Bennington)

Irene H., d. 2/13/1889 at 0/0/3; debility; b. Farmington; Tristram F. Towle (New Durham) and Annie B. Trafton (Great Falls)

John W., d. 4/24/1889 at 59/5/6; inflammation of kidneys

Phoebe E., d. 2/3/1915 at 40/6/11; shoestitcher; widow; b. Farmington; Charles H. Leighton (Farmington) and Emma A. Colbath (Natick, MA)

Sarah E., d. 4/7/1911 at 63; pneumonia; housewife; widow; b. Alto Mary J. Evans (Alton)

Tristram, d. 1/5/1937 at 67/6/12; painter; married; b; New Durham; Henry W. Towle (Dover) and Emily Fletcher (New Durham)

## TOZER,

Maretta M., d. 7/16/1932 at 66/3/1; housekeeper; widow; b. NS; John McCullin (NS) and Mary Schurman (NS)

William E., d. 1/21/1914 at 3/9/21; heart failure; b. Milton; Granvill Tozer (Danvers, MA, shoemaker) and Annie M. Wiggin (Milton)

## TRAFTON,

Amanda F., d. 10/9/1895 at 63/11/23; diabetes; housework; widow; b. Lebanon, ME; Daniel Goodwin (Lebanon, ME) and Polly Fa (Lebanon, ME)

Charles, d. 10/17/1907 at –; deletion of heart; widower

Mark, d. 2/27/1918 at 82; engineer; widower; b. Bangor, ME; Theodore Trafton and Elizabeth Rogers

## TRASK,

Charles H., d. 11/28/1889 at 26/5/12; phthisis pulmonalis; shoemaker; b. Strafford; Ansel K. Trask (Mt. Vernon, ME) and Maria Otis (Rochester)

Edward E., d. 5/19/1902 at 28/1/9; phthisis pulmonalis; shoecutter; single

Lyman W., d. 3/16/1929 at 71/0/13; married; b. Strafford; Ansil K. Trask (Strafford) and Maria Otis (Strafford)

Maria, d. 8/28/1919 at 85/11/17

Patricia, d. 1/3/1930 at 0/0/10; b. Farmington; Ralph C. Trask (Farmington) and Helen D. Yeaton (Wakefield)

## TRIPP,

Florence A., d. 12/1/1931 at 48/9/29 in Milton; housewife; married; b. Milton; Charles Hayes (Milton) and Nellie Parmenter (Dover

**TUCKER,**
Alice J., d. 10/24/1937 at 56/10/1; housewife; married; b. Fitchburg, MA; Robert M. Jones (Holliston, MA) and Emma Cushing (Fitchburg, MA)

**TUFTS,**
Carleton W., d. 8/1/1922 at 0/8/8; b. Farmington; Isaac F. Tufts (Middleton) and Lucy Goodwin (Alton)
John R., d. 5/14 or 15/1928 at 63; farmer; widower; b. Alton; Samuel S. Tufts and Susan Chamberlin

**TURCOTTE,**
daughter, d. 12/2/1937 at – in New Durham; b. New Durham; Thomas Turcotte (Canada) and Leona Marcou (Woltan, VT)

**TURNER,**
Llewellyn, d. 12/1/1927 at 76/3/23; farmer; married; b. W. Washington, ME; Nehemiah Turner (Vanceboro, ME) and Elizabeth Williams (Vassalboro, ME)

**TUTTLE,**
son, d. 5/25/1924 at –; b. Farmington; Earle Tuttle (NH) and Margaret Clowney (SC)
A. Fred, d. 10/6/1936 at 58/7/13; shoeworker; married; b. Buckfield, ME; Velorus H. Tuttle and Abbie Fuller
Abbie, d. 5/5/1925 at 78; at home; married; b. Nottingham; John Furber (NH) and Vina Batchelder (NH)
Barbara, d. 3/7/1926 at 0/4/26; single; b. Farmington; Archie M. Tuttle (Boston) and Lena Lesperance (Lancaster)
Charles I., d. 6/20/1931 at 81/9/22 in Manchester; shoe cutter; widower; b. Nottingham; Nathaniel Tuttle (Nottingham) and Martha Ham (Nottingham)
John, d. 1/27/1927 at 93/1/16; shoeworker; widower; b. Barnstead; Hanson Tuttle (Barnstead) and Sally Mills (Alton)
Malinda J., d. 2/3/1888 at 56/9/23; anaemia; widow; b. Milton; Hiram W. Cooke (Milton) and Hannah Rines (Milton)
Shirley M., d. 2/14/1929 at 51/3/15; shoeworker; married; b. Buckfield, ME; Hiram Tuttle
Stanley R., d. 5/25/1908 at 0/5; convulsions; b. Farmington

**TWOMBL[E]Y,**
C. M., d. 12/30/1912 at 62/11/25; angina pectoris; housewife; married; b. Gilmanton; Asa Varney and Alice Estes
Georgia, d. 1/23/1930 at 56/0/28; housekeeper; widow; b. Canada; Peter Lessard (Canada) and Agustine Gravel (Canada)
Jennie, d. 1/6/1887 at 38/1; housekeeper; married
John E., d. 8/31/1891 at 69/4/22; heart disease; farmer; widower; b. Farmington; Peter Twombly
John W., d. 6/26/1891 at 56/11; cinosis wepatis; shoemaker; married; b. Middleton; Samuel Twombly (Milton) and Eliza Works (Middleton)
Laurel, d. 2/22/1920 at 71; farmer; widower; b. Farmington; John Twombly and Drucilla R. Chesley (New Durham)
Susan H., d. 7/28/1923 at 88/1/11; housewife; widow; b. E. Pittston, ME; Silas Hunt and Lucy Cressey

**VACHON,**
Emile, d. 10/8/1932 at 27/6/12 in Rochester; leatherboard; married; b. Somersworth; Joseph Vachon (Canada) and Demerise Gosselin (Canada)
Josephine M., d. 11/6/1933 at 3/0/20; b. Alton; Joseph Vachon (Lancaster) and Inez Elliott (Gilmanton)

**VARNEY,**
Abram, d. 1/15/1888 at 84/8/19; paralysis; widower
Alice M., d. 2/25/1895 at 83/0/9; old age; housewife; widow; b. No. Berwick; Jedidiah Estes (No. Berwick) and Esther Osborne (Danvers, MA)
Anstress R., d. 7/6/1892 at 58/3/16; nervous prostration; housewife; married; b. Farmington; Mordicia Varney (Farmington, farmer) and Mary Wocester (Middleton)
Beard P., d. 6/18/1908 at 71/6/26; heart disease; farmer; widower; b. Farmington; Mordecai Varney
Belle, d. 3/8/1929 at 38/0/1; single; b. Farmington; Owen M. Varney (Farmington) and Lillian Downing (Farmington)
Bertie, d. 8/25/1889 at 0/5/21; cholera infantum; b. Farmington; Alfred C. Varney (Alfred, ME) and Eva A. Blake (Milton)
Clara M., d. 12/20/1900 at 59/7/21; chronic albumenuria; housewife; married; b. Farmington; Paul Twombly (Farmington) and Melinda Kimball (Rochester)

Elma M., d. 10/15/1905 at 80/1/17; pneumonia; housekeeper; widow; b. Gilmanton; Othniel Varney (Gilmanton) and Annie Jones (Gilmanton)

Emma M., d. 2/24/1891 at 39/10/23; heart trouble; housekeeper; b. Milton; Russell R. Cotton (Milton) and Abbie Nute (Milton)

Florence M., d. 5/6/1934 at 64/10/15; at home; married; b. S. Strafford, VT; John K. Kendall (S. Strafford, VT) and Lucy Dow (S. Strafford, VT)

Flossie, d. 3/17/1900 at 4/9/28; pneumonia; b. Farmington; Fred Varney (Farmington) and Angie Corson (Barrington)

Hannah L., d. 1/31/1917 at 77/4/29; housekeeper; widow; b. Farmington; Mordecai Varney (Farmington) and Mary Worcester

J. O., d. 1/14/1900 at 67/8/1; pneumonia; teamster; married; b. Milton; James Varney (Milton) and Marie Downs (Milton)

Job, d. 8/22/1902 at 76/5/14; valvular disease of heart; farmer; single; b. Farmington; William Varney (Farmington) and Anna Varney (Milton)

John E., d. 10/3/1921 at 41/4/23; carpenter; single; b. Farmington; John E. Varney (Farmington) and Emma M. Cotton (Milton)

John F., d. 4/18/1906 at 74/8/19; apoplexy; farmer; married; b. Farmington; Phineas Varney and Huldy Hussey

John M., d. 5/31/1895 at 38/9/14; tuberculosis; farmer; single; b. Farmington; Othnial Varney (Farmington) and Keziah F. Murry (Farmington)

Kenneth, d. 3/11/1918 at 0/2/29; b. Farmington; Benjamin Varney (Farmington) and Esther Thompson (New Durham)

Kezia F., d. 3/30/1895 at 75/5/18; pneumonia; housewife; married; b. Farmington; John Murray (Farmington) and Abigail Furber (Farmington)

Louis M., d. 9/6/1925 at 57/4/26; laborer; married; b. Farmington; Biard P. Varney (Farmington) and Clara Twombly (Farmington)

Mary E., d. 8/11/1905 at 82/9/19; heart failure; widow; b. Milton; Joshua G. Jones and Sally Cowel (Lebanon)

Obed, d. 5/6/1900 at 54/0/3; org. heart disease; farmer; single; b. Pittsfield; Asa Varney (Farmington) and Alice Estes (No. Berwick)

Othniel, d. 2/16/1902 at 79/8/18; acute tuberculosis of lungs; farmer; widower; b. Farmington; Miles Varney (Dover) and Lovey Canney (Dover)

Phineas, d. 12/28/1890 at 86; paralysis; widower; b. Milton

Sarah E., d. 6/22/1914 at 89/4/15; old age; single; b. Farmington; Mordecai Varney (Farmington, farmer) and Mary Worcester (Milton)

Sarah M., d. 6/13/1927 at 69/10/29; single; b. Farmington; Asa Varney and Alice Estes

Stephen S., d. 4/19/1894 at –; meningitis; farmer; widower; b. Gilmanton; Charles Varney (Dover) and Nancy Peaslee (Gilmanton)

Willie E., d. 5/27/1901 at 20/0/20; consumption; shoeworker; single b. Farmington; E. E. Varney (Farmington) and Capitola Reynolds (Farmington)

**VARNUM,**

James E., d. 7/28/1938 at 51/7/15; shoeworker; married; b. Manchester; George Varnum (Manchester) and Zemri Hubbard (Canaan)

**VIBBERT,**

Russell L., d. 3/31/1899 at 77/0/25; peritonitis; farmer; widower; b. Hartford, CT; Russell Vibbert

**VICKERS,**

son, d. 10/8/1924 at 0/0/1; b. Farmington; William I. Vickers (England) and Della F. Glidden (NH)

**VICKERY,**

Ida G., d. 8/25/1927 at 69/3/26; housewife; married; b. Dover; John T. Bickford (Rochester) and Phoebe Hayes (Strafford)

**VOSE,**

Sebastian S., d. 2/23/1911 at 72/6/16; influenza; photographer; widower; b. Cape Cod, MA; Ezekiel Vose (clergyman) and Eliza Fairlee

**WALDRON,**

daughter, d. 12/18/1890 at –; stillborn; b. Farmington; Harry C. Waldron (Farmington) and Nellie M. Broughey (Milford)

daughter, d. 5/2/1925 at 0/0/1; b. Rochester; Harrison Waldron (Farmington) and Marion Atwood (Hudson, MA)

Abigail J., d. 12/29/1909 at 88/7/19; chronic uremia; housekeeper; b. New Durham; Samuel Jones (Portsmouth) and Mary Bennett

Adelaide C., d. 6/15/1909 at 66/3/23; locomotor ataxia; housewife; b. Manchester; David P. Cilley (Epsom) and A. A. Haines (Canterbury)

Augustus S., d. 10/11/1913 at 67/5/6; indigestion and exhaustion; harness maker; married; b. Farmington; James H. Waldron (Farmington, farmer) and Abigail J. Jones (New Durham)

E. Grace, d. 1/19/1916 at 61/11; housewife; married; b. Farmington; George M. Herring (MA) and Ellen E. Eames (Framingham, MA)

Eliza A., d. 12/5/1914 at 76/10/8; hypostatic pneumonia; single; b. Farmington; Jeremiah Waldron (Farmington, lumber mfgr.) and Mary E. Knight (Farmington)

Elizabeth, d. 1/3/1887 at 92/8/9; housekeeper; widow; b. Rochester; Daniel Page (Rochester) and Judith Whitehouse (Farmington)

Jeremiah W., d. 3/2/1891 at 84/3/20; chronic cystitis; mill business; married; b. Farmington; Jeremiah Waldron (Dover) and Mary Scott (Machias, ME)

John, d. 3/17/1921 at 71/2/18; insurance; widower; b. Farmington; James Waldron (Farmington) and Abigail Jones (New Durham)

Marion, d. 9/4/1924 at 85; single

Mary A., d. 1/12/1926 at 77/5/5; teacher; single; b. Farmington; Jeremiah Waldron (Farmington) and Mary E. Knight (Farmington)

Mary E., d. 12/1/1900 at 85/4/27; senectus; housewife; widow; b. Farmington; William Knight (Kittery, ME) and Mary Pearl (Farmington)

William H., d. 7/6/1894 at 77; prostration; rel. minister; married; Jeremiah Waldron (Dover) and Mary Scott

**WALKER,**

Addie S., d. 1/13/1893 at 51/11; erysipelas; housekeeper; widow; b. Exeter; Joseph Perkins (Exeter) and Love Locke (Barnstead)

Annie A., d. 5/29/1928 at 69/9/7; b. Middleton; Charles Willey (New Durham) and Abigail Grace (Rochester)

Caroline, d. 11/3/1903 at 78/11/6; bronchial pneumonia; seamstress; single; John Walker (Farmington) and Eliza Furber (Dover)

Eliza, d. 7/12/1889 at 89/0/22; paralysis and old age; housekeepe b. Farmington; Samuel Furber (Portsmouth) and Mary Emerson (Dover)

Mary, d. 9/26/1907 at 39/3/15; chronic indigestion; housekeeper; widow; b. Barnstead; S. D. Caswell (Barnstead, farmer) and Laura Young (Barnstead)

Reuben W., d. 2/2/1918 at 72/10/28; blacksmith; married; b. Concord; Joseph Walker (Milton) and Elizabeth Hildreth (Newburyport, MA)

**WALL,**

Robert, d. 10/9/1908 at 0/6/5; cap. bronchitis; b. Lynn, MA; Millard Wall (Newburyport) and Clara Doran (Wynville, NS)

**WALLACE,**

A. A., d. 2/14/1912 at 81/6/21; pneumonia; widow; b. New Durham James Runnals (Strafford, shoemaker) and Sarah Hurd (New Durham)

Albert S., d. 7/16/1935 at 84/3/14; retired; widower; b. Hanover

Clyde R., d. 12/2/1901 at 15; peritonitis; school boy; single; b. Farmington; Albert S. Wallace and E. E. Whitehouse (Middleton)

Cora J., d. 5/17/1933 at 83/4/16; housekeeper; widow; b. Augusta, ME; George A. Gray (Albion, ME) and Christina Nelson (Benton, ME)

Edna B., d. 6/12/1909 at 55/3; pernitrion anemia; housewife; b. Gilmanton; Ambrose E. Wentworth (Wakefield) and Elmira Littlefield (Barnstead)

Elvira E., d. 2/2/1913 at 62/6/18; carcinoma of kidney; housekeeper; married; b. Middleton; R. P. Whitehouse (Middleton, farmer) and Clarissa Frost

Fannie F., d. 5/28/1932 at 76/9/25; married; b. Alton; ----- Smith

James S., d. 9/25/1925 at 78/6/4; teamster; divorced; b. Hanover; William Wallace and Mattilda Worthen

Lucy M., d. 11/22/1919 at 83/2/22; housewife; married; b. S. Wolfeboro; John Chesley

**WALLINGFORD,**

F., d. 9/4/1890 at 37/5/12; pulmonary phthisis; housekeeper; married; b. Acton, ME; Theodore Drew (Acton, ME) and Mary A. Varney (Acton, ME)

Hazel, d. 1/31/1911 at 0/4/1; pneumonia; b. Lebanon, ME; E. Wallingford (E. Rochester, lumberman) and Rhona M. Willey (E. Rochester)

J. D., d. 2/26/1888 at 78/0/11; dropsy; laborer; b. Lebanon, ME; A. Wallingford (Lebanon, ME) and Betsey Downs (Somersworth)

Mary, d. 3/20/1904 at 91/0/5; old age; housewife; widow; b. Lebanon, ME; Aaron Wallingford (Lebanon, ME) and Annie Downs (Berwick, ME)

Susan, d. 10/7/1895 at 87/6/28; heart failure; widow; b. Lebanon, ME; T. Wallingford (Lebanon, ME) and Marian Corson (Lebanon, ME)

**WALSH,**

Lizzie, d. 3/18/1910 at –; broncho pneumonia; housekeeper; b. Ireland

Robert M., d. 8/19/1922 at 0/2/2; b. Farmington; Leroy Walsh (Bridgewater, MA) and Arlene Gibbs (Farmington)

**WARE,**

Alfred F., d. 11/15/1910 at 80/7/23; apoplexy; farmer; b. Salem, MA; Horace Ware (Paxton, MA) and Alice H. Davis (Paxton, MA)

Iris Elmira, d. 5/9/1912 at 0/4/13; indigestion; b. Farmington; Arthur A. Ware (Waterville, ME, shoemaker) and Nellie M. Leighton (Lynn, MA)

**WARREN,**

William H., d. 11/19/1889 at 32; consumption; shoemaker; b. New Durham; Samuel N. Warren (Dover) and Mary A. Remick (Eliot)

**WATERMAN,**

Martha D., d. 6/16/1931 at 94/2/15; widow; b. Exeter; John Hodges (Brookfield) and Rhoda Young (Newmarket)

**WATSON,**

infant, d. 5/19/1921 at –; b. Farmington; Elmer E. Watson (Alton) and Mary A. Duquette (Rochester)

Charles F., d. 2/23/1923 at 66/9/18; stockfitter; married; b. Gilmanton; Joseph Watson (Alton) and Sally Piper (Gilmanton)

Charles H., d. 5/30/1909 at 48/7/21; thrown from carriage; farmer; b. Farmington; George R. Watson (Farmington) and Lydia B. Rhines (Alton)

George R., d. 6/14/1892 at 65/5/26; peritonitis; farmer; married; b. Farmington; Daniel Watson (Farmington, farmer) and Elizabeth Blakely

Ida B., d. 3/1/1920 at 45/0/4

Leon C., d. 8/8/1888 at 1/10/20; entero colitis; b. Alton; Charles F. Watson (Alton) and Ada A. Dore (Alton)

Wingate, d. 12/11/1904 at 63/4/28; cerebral hemorrhage; farmer; married; b. Farmington; Daniel Watson (Farmington) and Elizabeth Watson (Farmington)

**WEBB,**

Sarah, d. 1/13/1887 at 84; housekeeper; widow; b. New Durham; William Pinkham and Judith Pinkham

**WEBSTER,**

Caroline M., d. 12/12/1889 at 86/6/14; hepatitis; housekeeper; b. Durham; Enoch Bunker (Durham) and Hannah Drew (Durham)

Charles L., d. 3/13/1930 at 64/5/18 in Rochester; shoeworker; married; b. E. Kingston; George Webster (E. Kingston) and Sophronia Magoon (E. Kingston)

Joseph, d. 11/21/1917 at 84/6/17; shoeworker; widower; b. Newmarket; Valentine Webster (New Durham) and Caroline Bunker (Farmington)

Mary W., d. 10/8/1923 at 21/4/4; housewife; married; b. PEI; Samuel V. Arnold (Brockton, MA) and Sarah Godfrey (PEI)

Ruth E., d. 12/23/1934 at 56/6/7; at home; married; b. Rochester; Frank Henderson (Rochester) and Eliza A. Henderson (Boston, MA)

Sarah L., d. 4/4/1906 at 68/0/13; mental regurgitation; domestic; married; b. Epsom; Stephen Avery and Annie McDaniels

**WEDG[E]WOOD,**

daughter, d. 11/20/1900 at 0/0/2; hemorrhage; b. Farmington; I. S. Wedgewood (Farmington) and Fannie Kennison (Farmington)

E. L., d. 11/14/1898 at 58/3/20; cancer of liver; farmer; married; b. Milton; Dearborn Wedgewood (Effingham) and Ursula Deland (Brookfield)

Forrest, d. 3/17/1924 at 75/7/25; barber; married; b. Farmington; D. Wedgwood and Ursula Deland (Effingham)

Georgia, d. 7/21/1916 at 66/3/9; widow; b. Alton; George T. Leeds (Dorchester, MA) and Dorothy Langley (Alton)

## WEEKS,

George W., d. 11/30/1898 at 48; asthma; merchant; married; b. Dover; Benjamin Weeks and Mary Allen

William B., d. 9/23/1904 at 50/2/19; cerebral apoplexy; painter; married; b. Boston

## WELCH,

Betsey J., d. 3/24/1912 at 68/10/20; hepatic cirrhosis; housekeeper; widow; b. Strafford; Jeremiah Mills (Strafford, farmer)

Hattie B., d. 1/13/1889 at 29; blood poison; housekeeper; b. Farmington; Nathaniel P. Horne

Mary E., d. 12/28/1934 at 70/5/13 in Rochester; housewife; married; b. Richmond, NS; Joseph Brown (Scotland) and Dolly E. Morris

Mary H., d. 4/22/1924 at 89/3/26; housewife; widow; b. New Durham; James Wilkinson (New Durham) and Hannah Sawyer (Barnstead)

William, d. 8/12/1891 at 58/6/26; Bright's disease; hotel keeper; married; b. Effingham; Asel Welch (Parsonsfield) and Hannah Towle (Portland, ME)

## WENTWORTH,

daughter, d. 11/8/1900 at 0/2/24; premature birth; b. Farmington; A. S. Wentworth (Farmington) and Mary Evans (New Durham)

A., d. 9/4/1908 at 50/3; natural causes; housekeeper; widow; J. A. Wentworth (Milton) and Augusta Laskey (Milton)

Abbie D., d. 8/13/1901 at 53/1/14; acute tuberculosis; married; b. Farmington; William C. Roberts (Farmington) and E. J. Lougee (Gilmanton)

Alvin H., d. 11/26/1909 at 75/4/22; angina pectoris; shoemaker; b. Farmington; David Wentworth (Farmington) and Charlotte Corson (Middleton)

Alvin S., d. 11/3/1929 at 55/5/3; painter; married; b. Farmington; Alvin H. Wentworth (Farmington) and Henrietta Pickering (Barnstead)

Ambrose, d. 11/4/1913 at 82/3/27; old age; single; b. Middleton; Ebenezer Wentworth (Alton, farmer) and Sophia Roberts (Milton)

Arn'te, d. 3/8/1926 at 66/9; housekeeper; married; b. Alton; Augustus Ricker (Wakefield) and Nancy J. Colbath (Middleton)

Benjamin, d. 6/15/1926 at 78/11/18; farmer; married; b. Farmington; David Wentworth (Milton) and Charlotte Corson (Milton)

Charles, d. 4/30/1926 at 77; shoemaker; married; b. Dover; Henry Wentworth and Eliza Littlefield

Charlotte, d. 9/23/1898 at 87/3/5; old age; housekeeper; widow; b. Milton

D. W., d. 4/29/1908 at 53/4/17; chr. nephritis; shoemaker; married; b. Milton; A. F. Wentworth (Milton) and Mary A. Downs (Milton)

Eliza, d. 12/8/1918 at 92/1/19; housewife; widow; b. Strafford; Obadiah Littlefield and Susan Miles

George E., d. 4/17/1911 at 43/11/28; typhoid fever; shoeworker; married; b. Tuftonboro; Norris Wentworth (Wakefield, meat cutter) and Annie E. Chase (Tuftonboro)

Hannah, d. 3/15/1926 at 80/0/10; retired; widow; b. Rochester; George Howard (Rochester) and Hannah E. Allen (Strafford)

Hazel, d. 3/12/1894 at 3/3/12; spinal meningitis; b. Farmington; M. G. Wentworth (Milton) and Georgia Gerrish (Lebanon, ME)

Helen, d. 12/29/1893 at 10/11/21; bronchitis; b. Farmington; Henry H. Wentworth (Farmington) and Hannah Howard (Rochester)

Henrietta, d. 3/2/1904 at 67/2/23; pneumonia; housewife; married; b. Barnstead; Jacob Pickering (Gilmanton) and Rebecca Avery (Barnstead)

Henry, d. 7/23/1918 at 73/3/14; shoemaker; married; b. Farmington; David Wentworth (Milton) and Charlotte Corson (Milton)

John, d. 1/22/1907 at 72/4/22; bronchial pneumonia; married; b. Milton; Phineas Wentworth (Milton) and Nancy Witham (Milton)

Libertie, d. 3/10/1915 at 74/0/22; housekeeper; widow; b. Farmington; Samuel Ham (Farmington) and Jane Jenness (Wolfeboro)

Loren, d. 1/28/1921 at 0/0/20; b. Farmington; Reginald Wentworth (New Durham) and Mary E. Ham (Farmington)

Loren, d. 11/15/1921 at 59/5/18; shoeworker; married; b. Milton; Albert Wentworth (Milton) and Mary A. Downs (Milton)

Luther, d. 12/1/1917 at 73/9/13; trav. salesman; married; b. Milton; Ebenezer Wentworth (Alton) and Sophia Roberts (Milton)

Mabel W., d. 3/6/1934 at 78/11/19 in New Durham; at home; widow; b. Nottingham; Frank Marston and ----- McCoy

Mary, d. 5/25/1917 at 58/6/17; housewife; widow; b. Middleton; Warren Colbath (Middleton) and Dorothy Amazeen (New Castle)

Nellie, d. 12/14/1924 at 57/8/7; housewife; widow; b. New Durham; George W. Randall (New Durham) and N. E. Towle (Wolfeboro)

Nettie E., d. 10/4/1932 at 69/2/4 in New Durham; housekeeper; widow; b. Lebanon, ME; Moses L. Wentworth (Lebanon, ME) and Sophronia Copp (Lebanon, ME)

Ora B., d. 10/11/1904 at 49/6/12; chronic par. nephritis; single; b. Rochester; William Wentworth (Farmington) and Martha Demeritt (Farmington)

Robert W., d. 9/18/1931 at 70/2/4 in New Durham; farmer; married; b. Barnstead; Ambrose Wentworth and Jane E. Littlefield

Ruth, d. 11/13/1919 at 0/0/1; b. Farmington; Reginald Wentworth (New Durham) and Mary Ham (Farmington)

**WEYMOUTH,**

Genevieve, d. 1/3/1937 at 59/6 in Rochester; housewife; married; b. Farmington; David P. Cilley (Farmington) and Velma Waldron (Farmington)

**WHEATLEY,**

Harriett N., d. 10/14/1933 at 66/8/10; housekeeper; widow; b. New Durham; Freeman P. Howe (Farmington) and Adeline M. Roberts (Farmington)

Josy, d. 3/6/1907 at 53/1/7; Bright's disease; married; b. Denmark, ME; Larkin L. Foss (Denmark, ME, blacksmith) and Olive Mack (Hiram, ME)

**WHEELER,**

Preston F., d. 3/30/1897 at 0/7/3; loryngitis; b. Farmington; Courtland Wheeler (Isle la Motte) and Olive A. Swinerton (Somersworth)

**WHITE,**

stillborn daughter, d. 1/13/1933 at –; b. Farmington; Sterling White (Ft. Fairfield, ME) and Julia Clough (Dover)

Ann S., d. 3/14/1899 at 66/4/16; cirrhosis of liver; housewife; married; b. New Castle; James Card (New Castle) and Sally Amazeen (New Castle)

Emma J., d. 7/23/1936 at 82/11/11 in Manchester; widow; b. Farmington; William Wingate

George I., d. 7/27/1938 at 67/6/5; dairyman; married; b. Farmington; Washington White (Farmington) and Ann S. Car (Farmington)

Harley C., d. 4/26/1919 at 70/11/8; farmer; widower; b. Wenham, MA; Samuel White (ME) and Mary Curtis

Hervey B., d. 12/21/1926 at 75/2; shoemaker; married; b. New Castle; Charles W. White (New Castle) and Frances Kinner (New Castle)

Josie E., d. 11/9/1917 at 37/10/28; housekeeper; divorced; b. Farmington; Trask W. Averill (Farmington) and Almena Wallace (New Durham)

Llewellyn, d. 1/14/1917 at 68/7/27; laborer; widower; b. New Castle Washington White and Ann S. Card

Mary E., d. 12/2/1897 at 44/0/20; malignant growth of larnyx; housewife; married; b. Farmington; John G. Johnson (Dover) and Anstress Varney (Farmington)

Mary G., d. 1/6/1925 at 0/0/3; b. Farmington; Jennie White (Farmington)

Washington, d. 2/2/1902 at 75/6/17; cerebral apoplexy; carpenter; widower; b. New Castle; Benjamin White (New Castle) and Elizabeth Martin (New Castle)

**WHITEHOUSE,**

Addie M., d. 4/5/1895 at 35/7/19; puerperal convulsions; housewife married; b. Farmington; Edmund B. Cann (Farmington) and --- -- (Tamworth)

Carolyn, d. 6/24/1934 at 52/8/11 in Milton; at home; married; b. Farmington; James A. Fletcher (New Durham) and Elizabeth - --- (New Durham)

Charles, d. 4/21/1897 at 76/8/1; cerebral hemorrhage; shoemaker; married; b. Middleton; Israel B. Whitehouse (Middleton) and Mary Cotton (Middleton)

Charles, d. 3/2/1920 at 70/1/12; engineer; single; b. Farmington; Charles Whitehouse and Susan Jones

Charles, d. 10/13/1937 at 73/0/7 in Dover; retired; married; b. Middleton; Warren Whitehouse (Middleton) and Emma York (Middleton)

Charles M., d. 4/15/1916 at 60/8/27; farmer; married; b. Milton; Thomas Whitehouse (Middleton) and Ellen Alexander (Burlington, VT)

Daniel, d. 12/16/1925 at 71/11/2; shoeworker; married; b. Middleton; Robert Whitehouse (Middleton) and Clarissa Frost (Middleton)

Dorothy, d. 11/12/1926 at 17/8/22; student; single; b. Farmington; Frank Whitehouse (Farmington) and Fannie C. Fall (Farmington)

E. A., d. 7/18/1912 at 65/2/20; dilation of heart; housekeeper; widow; b. Middleton; Charles York (farmer) and Emily Young (Middleton)

E. B., d. 5/7/1912 at 69/7/27; apoplexy; carpenter; married; b. Alton; D. Whitehouse (farmer) and Belinda Tufts (Middleton)

El. F., d. 8/10/1913 at 2/1/26; indigestion; b. Farmington; F. I. Whitehouse (Farmington, clerk) and Fannie C. Fall (Farmington)

Eliza W., d. 5/26/1887 at 19/11/19; shoeturner; single; b. Middleton; Alonzo Whitehouse (Middleton) and Lydia Sprague (Middleton)

Eliza W., d. 11/30/1896 at 75/6/26; cerebral hemorrhage; housekeeper; widow; b. Newburyport, MA; Silas Floyd

Elwood K., d. 10/7/1893 at 32/5/13; consumption; shoemaker; married; b. Wolfeboro; T. L. Whitehouse (Middleton) and Helen Alexandra

Frank, d. 7/12/1928 at 43/2/6; merchant; married; b. Farmington; Daniel Whitehouse and Marilla Webster

Frederick, d. 8/29/1923 at 75/1/11; shoemaker; married; b. Dover; Charles Whitehouse and Mary Brock

George, d. 1/30/1903 at 70/10/12; heart failure; carpenter; married; Joseph Whitehouse (Strafford) and Druscilla Page (Strafford)

George L., d. 11/19/1887 at 90/10/13; civil engineer; widower; b. Middleton; Nathaniel Whitehouse (Rochester) and Annie Leighton

Harriett, d. 8/28/1898 at 76/4/26; old age; housekeeper; widow; b. Middleton; Moses Place (Middleton) and Keziah Hayes (Farmington)

Harry, d. 1/5/1925 at 49/5/15; married; b. Somersworth; Daniel Whitehouse (Wolfeboro) and Martha Burke (Wolfeboro)

Ida B., d. 11/19/1938 at 83/1/4; housewife; widow; b. Dover; Coleman Colbath and Lucinda Hunt

J. L., d. 9/23/1936 at 66/1/23; farmer; widower; b. Strafford; J. M. Whitehouse (Strafford) and Abbie Pierce (Barnstead)

John, d. 10/4/1891 at 0/4/23; cholera infantum; b. Farmington; Daniel P. Whitehouse (Middleton) and Marilla J. Howard (New Durham)

John, d. 5/30/1926 at 80/0/20; carpenter; married; b. Cohasset, MA Robert Whitehouse and Clarissa Frost

L., d. 6/23/1890 at 82/7/14; old age diarrhoea; housekeeper; widow; b. Farmington; Benjamin Canney (Dover) and Sarah Roberts (Dover)

L. M., d. 2/24/1912 at 81/7/8; heart failure; widow; b. Farmington; Samuel Ransom (farmer) and Abigail Holmes

Laura W., d. 5/21/1933 at 84/8/24; housekeeper; widow; b. Farmington; Samuel Ham and Jane Jenness

Muriel F., d. 7/17/1930 at 2/5/17 in Rochester; b. Laconia; Jasper Whitehouse (Barrington) and Alma Gilbert (Milton)

T. L., d. 8/20/1890 at 72/6/8; cerebral softening; farmer; widower; b. Middleton; Israel Whitehouse

**WHITMAN,**

Joseph B., d. 4/27/1893 at --; consumption; farmer; married; b. Canada

**WHITNEY,**

Clarence T., d. 5/29/1909 at 52/3/29; asthma; shoecutter; b. Farmington; Albert M. Whitney (Cochituate, MA) and Marilla Wentworth (Farmington)

Julia A., d. 7/20/1921 at 68/1/20; widow

Mary E., d. 3/11/1927 at 69/10/10; housekeeper; widow; b. Farmington; Albert Corson (Milton) and Betsey Ham (New Durham)

William W., d. 10/28/1914 at 72/1/3; chronic nephritis; shoemaker; married; b. Natick, MA; Ebenezer Whitney (farmer) and Johanna -----

**WHITTEN,**
Etta E., d. 3/14/1913 at 57/3/21; asthma and exhaustion; shoemaker; married; b. Farmington; David Wentworth (Milton, cooper) and Charlotte Corson (Milton)
James, d. 3/21/1937 at 80/2/6; mason; married; b. Wolfeboro; Augustus Whitten (Wolfeboro) and Lydia Kent (Canada)

**WHITTIER,**
Cora B., d. 8/23/1930 at 70/5/11; at home; single; b. Dover; George Whittier (Dover) and Belle Moody (Ossipee)
Nancy A., d. 3/17/1906 at 77/10/14; Bright's disease; housewife; widow; b. Frankfort, ME; Clement Moody and Mary Cooley

**WIGGIN,**
[no name given], d. 4/18/1917 at 56/0/8; housewife; widow; b. Farmington; George Paige (Hardwick, VT) and Elizabeth Young (Farmington)
Abbie, d. 12/29/1907 at 62/6/18; cancer; widow; b. Farmington; Daniel Davis (Farmington, farmer) and Abbie S. Ham (Farmington)
Albert H., d. 12/15/1890 at 44/8/26; septicemia; butcher; married; b. Dover; Uriah Wiggin (Stratham) and Rahannah Clark (Petersham, MA)
Almira B., d. 3/22/1919 at 84/10/25
Annie M., d. 5/25/1918 at 57; housekeeper; married; b. PEI
Archie, d. 3/6/1927 at 51; shoemaker; divorced; b. Farmington; Louis Wiggin (Tuftonboro) and Martha Tanner (Farmington)
Arvilla, d. 11/14/1905 at 65/7/10; pro. gen. paralysis; married; John C. Beacham (Wolfeboro) and Olive Young (Tuftonboro)
Charles H., d. 3/16/1901 at 55/1/16; pneumonia; laborer; married; b. Farmington; Stephen Wiggin and Lydia Foss
Charles W., d. 1/22/1938 at 84/3/19 in Rochester; shoeworker; single; b. Farmington; George Wiggin (Moultonboro) and Sarah Wingate
Edith A., d. 6/14/1933 at 88/11/14; at home; widow; b. Farmington; Ira Tanner and Elizabeth Tanner
George H., d. 11/20/1915 at 77/2/24; meat cutter; married; b. Wolfeboro; James Wiggin and Caroline -----
Helen M., d. 1/23/1911 at 0/0/1; asphyxia; b. Farmington; Archie C. Wiggin (Farmington, laborer) and Maud R. Smart (Farmington)
Jane, d. 2/22/1920 at 94; housekeeper; widow

Lewis R., d. 12/31/1896 at 67/9/22; hepatic cirrhosis; mining; married; b. Moultonboro; Stephen Wiggin (New Durham) and Sarah Leighton (Farmington)
Lewis R., d. 5/12/1912 at 0/3/7; bronchitis; b. Farmington; Archie C Wiggin (Farmington, laborer) and Maud R. Smart (Farmington
Lizzie L., d. 10/21/1924 at 71; widow
Lydia A., d. 11/3/1893 at 79; apoplexy; lady; widow; Andrew J. Fos (Strafford) and Hannah Hall (Eliot, ME)
Oscar E., d. 5/5/1900 at 24/1/20; typhoid pneumonia; shoemaker; married; b. Dover; Albert Wiggin (Dover) and Rebecca Hoope (Biddeford)
Rebecca, d. 12/31/1919 at 72/8/20; housekeeper; widow; Andrew Waterhouse and Rebecca Hooper
Sarah J., d. 12/21/1907 at 79/4/21; senility; housekeeper; widow; b Farmington; Benjamin Wingate (farmer)
Susie E., d. 2/23/1932 at 73/9/13; housekeeper; widow; b. Rollinsford; David O. Cate (Boston) and Susan Marshall
Uriah S., d. 11/13/1921 at 51; hotel clerk; married; b. Oldtown, ME; Albert Wiggin (Farmington) and Rebecca Wiggin (Dover)
Waldo C., d. 6/14/1895 at 23/11/6; epilepsy; heel cutter; single; b. Dover; Albert H. Wiggin (Dover) and Rebekah Waterhouse (Biddeford)

**WILKES,**

George F., d. 3/1/1929 at 20/10/1 in Bryan, TX; truck driver; single; b. Barnstead; George T. Wilkes (Thompson, CT) and Bertha E. Coman (Thompson, CT)
George T., d. 5/6/1937 at 72/7/21 in New Durham; retired; married; b. Thompson, CT

**WILKINS,**

Altana, d. 5/19/1929 at 0/0/1; b. Farmington; Arthur W. Wilkins (Acton, ME) and Violet Devoll (Skowhegan, ME)
Artana, d. 5/19/1929 at 0/0/1; b. Farmington; Arthur W. Wilkins (Acton, ME) and Violet Devoll (Skowhegan, ME)
Arthur W., Jr., d. 5/19/1929 at 0/0/1; b. Farmington; Arthur W. Wilkins (Acton, ME) and Violet Devoll (Skowhegan, ME)

**WILLARD,**

Norma, d. 9/5/1925 at –; single; b. Farmington; Raymond Willard (Alton) and Annie Elliott (Ogunquit, ME)

Rodney, d. 12/13/1927 at 0/2/29; b. Farmington; Frank Willard (Alton) and Ettola G. Bubier (Newport)

**WILLETT,**
son, d. 3/17/1889 at –; stillborn; b. Farmington; George Willett (Oldtown, ME) and Annie Hagan (Ireland)
Annie, d. 5/5/1892 at 39; pneumonia; housewife; married; b. Belfast, Ireland; Philip Hagan (Ireland, laborer) and Laura Hagan (Ireland); burial - Rochester

**WILLEY,**
daughter, d. 7/3/1889 at –; convulsions of mother; b. Farmington; Charles Willey (New Durham) and Etta Aspinwall (New Durham)
Abbie, d. 6/29/1919 at 76/10/18
Almon E., d. 6/22/1922 at 64; farmer; widower; b. New Durham; John Willey (NH) and Mary Woodsum (New Durham)
Benjamin, d. 8/20/1890 at 59/2/10; consumption; laborer; married; b. New Durham; Benjamin Willey (New Durham) and Eliza Ham (Alton)
Betsey, d. 7/14/1897 at 96/6/15; old age; housewife; widow; b. New Durham
Charles H., d. 3/3/1905 at 75/11/10; lobar pneumonia; farmer; married; b. Brookfield
Charles R., d. 1/14/1912 at 48/10/25; chronic nephritis; clerk; married; b. New Durham; Ruel W. Willey (New Durham, farmer) and Mary E. Durgin (New Durham)
Charles W., d. 8/10/1896 at 48/10/18; rheumatic arthritis; single; b. New Durham; Charles Willey (Belgrade, ME) and Abigail Grace (New Durham)
Cyrus, d. 1/17/1934 at 83/1/13 in Dover; farmer; widower; b. Middleton; Charles Willey (Alton) and Abigail Willey (New Durham)
Ennie M., d. 3/29/1927 at 47/0/25; housewife; married; b. Middleton; Daniel Jones (Middleton) and Emma Perkins (Middleton)
Etta B., d. 7/13/1889 at 19/11/11; puerperal convulsions; housekeeper; b. New Durham; John G. Aspinwall (Rollinsford) and Frances P. Perkins (Middleton)
Frank E., d. 2/23/1890 at 32/9; pulmonary phthisis; shoemaker; married; b. Farmington; Benjamin Willey

Homer T., d. 5/30/1887 at 10/8/7; b. New Durham; Almon E. Willey (New Durham) and Mary E. Randall (N. Easton, MA)

John E., d. 10/8/1895 at 63/8/26; paralysis agitans; shoemaker; widower; b. Brookfield; John Willey (Brookfield) and Betsy Jones (Wolfeboro)

Josephine B., d. 6/9/1901 at 70/1/9; consumption; married; b. New Durham; A. C. Libby (New Durham) and Nancy Cluff (Alton)

Nellie, d. 12/11/1937 at 76/6/30; at home; widow; b. Waterboro, ME; John S. Smith (Waterboro, ME) and Betsey Smith (Waterboro, ME)

William H., d. 1/4/1893 at 78/3/14; old age; farmer; widower

**WILLIAMS,**
Clarence, d. 7/22/1928 at 21

**WILLSON,**
Elizabeth, d. 4/28/1892 at 71/0/21; pneumonia; housekeeper; widow; b. York, ME; Jonathan Talpey (York, ME, sailor) and Elizabeth Talpey (York, ME)

**WILSON,**
Mary E., d. 3/3/1904 at 39/10/1; cancer; housewife; married; b. Farmington; Ezekiel C. Hayes (Farmington) and Lydia Tarleton (New Castle)

Orville A., d. 2/18/1896 at 57; pneumonia; vet. surgeon; married; b. Bennington; Wesley Wilson (Bennington) and Rachel Wilson (Bennington)

**WINGATE,**
Benjamin, d. 10/1/1887 at 90/9; farmer; widower; b. Farmington; William Wingate (Rochester) and Deborah Buzzell

Ellen, d. 2/15/1913 at 82/7/13; senility; housekeeper; widow; b. Farmington; Benjamin Wingate (Farmington, farmer) and Livina Davis (Farmington)

William, d. 2/8/1905 at 79/2; senectus; farmer; married; b. Farmington; Jonathan Wingate (Farmington) and Eunice Roberts (Farmington)

**WINTERS,**
Edith A., d. 6/16/1933 at 54/3/29 in Concord; housewife; married; b. New Durham; Augustus Hayes (Alton)

**WITHAM,**
Ada E., d. 2/11/1919 at 55/4/24; housewife; widow; b. Milton; Ephraim Ellis (Milton) and Abbie Ellis (Milton)
Charles C., d. 2/10/1923 at 72/8; shoeworker; widower; b. West Milton; Josiah Witham (Acton, ME) and Susan Place (Alton)
Ellen D., d. 2/24/1919 at 68/7/7; housewife; married; b. Milton; Simon French and Hannah Varney
John W., d. 1/1/1919 at 66/4/16; watchman; married; b. Milton; Josiah Witham and Susan Place (Alton)
Luella, d. 10/16/1937 at 76/0/22 in Concord; none; widow; b. Farmington; William P. Ham (NH) and Hannah Cook (Milton)
Susan P., d. 12/28/1914 at 90/6/29; heart disease; widow; b. Alton; David Place (Rochester, farmer) and Susan Perkins

**WOOD,**
George W., d. 3/3/1920 at 82/2; retired; married; b. Ossipee; William Wood (Newburyport, MA) and Mary Avery (Strafford)
John C. L., d. 4/27/1924 at 76/9/21; lawyer; married; b. Freedom; Horace T. Wood (Saco, ME) and Belinda Lang (Saco, ME)
Joseph, d. 5/17/1936 at 42; married; b. Barrington; Joseph Wood (Canada) and Marie Jefferies (NS)
Lucy J., d. 5/28/1929 at 86/10/18; housekeeper; widow; b. New Durham; Lewis Jones and Betsey Edgerly
Maria, d. 9/20/1914 at 76/8/27; carcinoma, liver; widow; b. NS
Sarah F., d. 8/18/1933 at 82/9/14; at home; widow; b. Farmington; Peter M. Horne (Farmington) and Mary Pendexter (Farmington)

**WOODMAN,**
Frank, d. 9/14/1924 at 75/2/8; laborer; married; b. Alton
Miles C., d. 3/24/1933 at 66/7/25; shoeworker; married; b. Alton; Jonathan Woodman (Alton) and Hannah Rollins (Alton)

**WOODWARD,**
Elvira, d. 12/1/1920 at 80/9/9; widow; b. Oxford; Manly Stevens and Lavina Davis

**WORKS,**
Eunice H., d. 12/13/1926 at 86/10/16; housework; widow; b. Berwick, ME

George T., d. 4/23/1904 at 64/6/28; paralysis; blacksmith; married; b. New Sharon, ME; James R. Works (N. Sharon, ME) and Anna Todd (N. Sharon, ME)

James A., d. 11/11/1916 at 50/7/10; blacksmith; married; b. New Sharon, ME; George T. Works (New Sharon, ME) and Eunice Wallingford (Lebanon, ME)

**WORSTER,**

Arvard C., d. 1/10/1932 at 20/4/17; single; b. Farmington; Moses Worster (Somersworth) and Hazel Glidden (Farmington)

Eliza J., d. 9/14/1927 at 87/3/14; housekeeper; widow; b. Berwick, ME; Samuel Hartford (Berwick, ME) and Lucy Giles (Eaton)

Richard, d. 4/16/1918 at 2/10/8; b. Farmington; Henry Worster (Somersworth) and Clara Leclair

**WRIGHT,**

Bertha A., d. 5/24/1936 at 50/10/20 in New Durham; at home; single; b. New Durham; Frank I. Wright (Milton) and Abbie C. Jenkins (New Durham)

Carl D., d. 2/20/1929 at 64/7/4; merchant; widower; b. Washington; Hartwell Wright (Washington) and Julia A. Towne (Washington)

Clark C., d. 3/18/1918 at 30/11/26; laborer; married; b. Crescent City, CA; Frank I. Wright and Abbie C. Jenkins

Ellen A., d. 1/6/1926 at 83; housewife; married; b. Alton

**WYATT,**

daughter, d. 2/29/1888 at 0/0/1; blue child; b. Farmington; Asa Wyatt (Farmington) and Ar'b'la C. Wyatt

son, d. 3/7/1909 at –; non viability; b. Farmington; Charles Wyatt (Farmington) and Louisa Chesley (Farmington)

Alice L., d. 2/2/1899 at 35/6/27; heart disease; housewife; married; W. W. True (Yarmouth, ME) and Alice Furber (Philadelphia)

Arabelle C., d. 12/5/1905 at 58/4/6; pneumonia; married; b. Milton; Leonard Ricker (Milton) and Lydia Edgerly (England)

Asa, d. 12/23/1938 at 90/9/23; farmer; widower; b. Farmington; Ira Wyatt (MA) and Louise Wingate (Farmington)

George H., d. 5/9/1917 at 74/1/22; farmer; single; Ira Wyatt (Wenham, MA) and Louisa Wingate (Farmington)

Ida M., d. 8/14/1898 at 33/10/22; heart disease; housewife; married; b. Barrington; Stephen Boston (Wells, ME) and ----- (Somersworth)

Ira, d. 2/10/1889 at 81/11; old age; farmer; b. MA

John A., d. 3/25/1912 at 61/0/18; uremia; farmer; single; b. Farmington; Ira Wyatt (MA, farmer) and Louisa Wingate (Farmington)

Lorza, d. 5/3/1892 at 75/8/20; phthisis pulmonalis; housekeeper; widow; b. Farmington; Stephen Wingate (Farmington, carpenter) and Susan Calif (Rochester); burial - Rochester

Lyman, d. 7/19/1925 at 86; farmer; widower; b. Farmington; Ira Wyatt

Martha A., d. 4/29/1890 at 54/9/9; uterine sarcoma; housekeeper; married; b. Great Falls; Joshua Roberts (Great Falls) and Mary Ricker (Farmington)

Martha A., d. 4/7/1899 at 1/5/7; pneumonia; b. Farmington; Lyman Wyatt (Windham, ME) and Ida Boston (Barrington)

Oscar T., d. 9/14/1891 at 0/1/14; canker; b. Madbury; George H. Wyatt (Farmington) and Alice True (ME)

Stephen W., d. 6/10/1921 at 63/3/13; farmer; married; b. Farmington; Ira Wyatt (Beverly, MA) and Louisa Wingate (Farmington)

**YEATON,**

Joseph, d. 8/7/1900 at 60/7/4; chronic albumenuria; laborer; widower; b. Alfred, ME; Richard Yeaton (Portland) and Mary Burke (Wolfeboro)

**YORK,**

Carrie B., d. 1/24/1890 at 2/9/18; acute meningitis; b. Pittsfield; Fred A. York (Gilmanton) and Susan Smart (Durham)

Charles, d. 10/12/1890 at 69/10/7; complication of diseases; farmer; widower; b. Middleton; Enoch York (Middleton) and Sarah Hayes (Rochester)

Charles F., d. 3/10/1932 at 74/7/17; laborer; widower; b. Middleton; Amons York and Mary York

Cyrus E., d. 3/29/1928 at 78/9/9; widower; b. Middleton; Charles York and Emily Young

Elizabeth, d. 8/1/1893 at 33/6; consumption; housewife; married; b. Springvale, ME

Elizabeth M., d. 3/22/1916 at 59/9/18; housewife; married; b. Dover John T. Bickford and Phoebe Hayes

Ella H., d. 1/8/1923 at 65/8/11; milliner; divorced; b. Strafford; Caleb Hanson (Strafford) and Louisa Evans (Strafford)

Frank, d. 5/1/1908 at 0/1/14; convulsions; b. Farmington; William York (NH) and Mary Kimball (NH)

George A., d. 8/26/1892 at 1/5/11; consumption; b. Farmington; Fred A. York (Gilmanton, teamster) and Annie F. Jones (Pittsfield); burial - Pittsfield

George A., Jr., d. 11/14/1936 at 0/0/13; b. Rochester; George A. York (Belmont) and Barbara Wyatt (Barrington)

Isabelle, d. 2/10/1903 at 0/0/1; immaturity; Wells York (Pittsfield) and Caroline Sims (Canada)

Joseph J., d. 1/30/1890 at 40/1/16; continued fever; shoemaker; married; b. Middleton; Wingate York (Middleton) and Mary Chamberlin (New Durham)

Mary B., d. 5/26/1889 at 68/2/5; endocarditis; housekeeper; b. Danville, VT; William Chamberlin (New Durham) and Hannah Davis (New Durham)

Sarah F., d. 5/31/1922 at 69/1/17; housewife; married; b. Middleton Varnum Leighton (Strafford) and Dorothy Jones (Middleton)

Wells G., d. 1/26/1925 at 64/0/12; laborer; married; Chase York

**YORKE,**
Albert D., d. 11/22/1921 at 57; married

**YOUNG,**
son, d. 4/7/1887 at 0/2/23; b. Farmington; Frank Young (Farmington) and Mary Varney (Farmington)

daughter, d. 6/3/1928 at –; b. Rochester; Malcolm Young (Farmington) and Ethel McCullough (Rochester)

son, d. 12/19/1929 at 0/0/1 in Rochester; b. Rochester; Arlene Young (Farmington)

Charles T., d. 8/8/1928 at 70/9/13; laborer; married; b. Farmington; Hiram Young and Judith Davis

Doris M., d. 7/15/1922 at 10/10/26; student; b. Farmington; Fred Young (Farmington) and Maud Young (Haverhill, MA)

Florence J., d. 9/4/1905 at 0/4/3; cholera morbus; b. Farmington; Charles T. Young (Farmington) and Daisy D. Drew (Wakefield)

Frank V., d. 11/11/1933 at 81/4/25; farmer; widower; b. Farmington; Hiram H. Young (Farmington) and Judith Davis

Grace O., d. 10/28/1918 at 37/11/9; shoeworker; single; b. Farmington; Frank V. Young (Farmington) and Mary E. Varney (Farmington)

Hattie M., d. 10/28/1907 at 32/4; typhoid fever; married; b. E. Rowden, NS; Andrew Pearson (E. Rowden, NS, merchant) and Harriet Withrow (E. Rowden, NS)

Herbert F., d. 11/3/1894 at 23/1/13; tuberculosis; laborer; married; b. Farmington; George W. Young (Farmington) and Sarah E. Ellis (Alton)

Jennie M., d. 8/11/1934 at 90/6/10; widow; b. Edinburgh, Scotland

Josephine B., d. 11/10/1930 at 78/10/22 in Rochester; housewife; married; b. Farmington; Jeremiah Downing (Middleton) and Sarah Whitehouse (Middleton)

Judith A., d. 11/25/1890 at 65/1/2; heart disease; housekeeper; widow; Timothy Davis (Wakefield) and Anna Applebee (Milton)

Lewis F., d. 8/24/1935 at 68/11/7 in New Durham; farmer; married; b. Middleton; John Henry Young (Tuftonboro) and Eliza M. Clark (Middleton)

Lizzie, d. 12/27/1912 at 54/2/22; pneumonia; divorced; b. Farmington; William A. Foss (laborer) and Charlotte Freeman

Marjory, d. 4/5/1931 at 20/3/22 in Rochester; single; b. Rochester; Sidney L. Young (Lebanon, ME) and Bessie M. Smith (Alton)

Martha J., d. 2/4/1890 at 59/6/1; dropsy; housekeeper; married; b. Middleton; John Kenniston (Middleton) and Rebekah Meader (Alton)

Mary E., d. 8/29/1933 at 76/10/20; housewife; married; b. Farmington; Stephen Varney (Old Town, ME) and Mary E. Hussey (Farmington)

Mary H., d. 12/19/1916 at 77/8/9; housekeeper; widow; Nathaniel W. Jones (Farmington) and Mary Watson (Gilmanton)

Mary M., d. 1/8/1907 at 61; apoplexy; married; b. Middleton; William Cloutman (Rochester, carpenter) and Lucinda Stevens (Middleton)

Nathaniel H., d. 12/23/1935 at 80/11/14 in Rochester; laborer; widower; b. Farmington; Hiram H. Young (Brookfield) and Judith Davis (Barnstead)

Nathaniel M., d. 12/5/1890 at 67/0/1; exposure; mason; married; b. Gilmanton; Nathaniel Young (Gilmanton) and Eliza P. Matthews (Hallowell, ME)

Preston B., d. 7/31/1900 at 42/1/30; cerebral apoplexy; physician; married; b. Farmington; Jonathan Young (Strafford) and H. S Waldron (Rochester)
Sarah H., d. 7/28/1925 at 89/0/23; housekeeper; widow; b. Boston
Sarah N., d. 7/16/1935 at 55/11/14; at home; single; b. Farmington Frank V. Young (Farmington) and Mary E. Varney (Farmington)
Susan, d. 8/21/1905 at 77/6/2; old age; housekeeper; widow; b. Unity, ME; Josiah Cookson (Unity, ME) and Mary Cookson (Unity, ME)

**YUDOVITZ,**
daughter, d. 3/25/1925 at –; b. Farmington; George Yudovitz (Brockton, MA) and Mildred Metcalf (Brockton, MA)

Heritage Books by Richard P. Roberts:

*Alton, New Hampshire Vital Records, 1890–1997*
*Barnstead, New Hampshire Vital Records, 1887–2000*
*Barrington, New Hampshire Vital Records*
*Dover, New Hampshire Death Records, 1887–1937*
*Gilmanton, New Hampshire Vital Records, 1887–2001*
*Marriage Records of Dover, New Hampshire, 1835–1909*
*Marriage Records of Dover, New Hampshire, 1910–1937*
*Milton, New Hampshire Vital Records, 1888–1999*
*Moultonborough, New Hampshire Vital Records*
*New Castle, New Hampshire Vital Records, 1891–1997*
*New Hampshire Name Changes, 1768–1923*
*New Hampshire Name Changes, 1923–1947*
*Ossipee, New Hampshire Vital Records, 1887–2001*
*Rochester, New Hampshire Death Records, 1887–1951*
*Vital Records of Durham, New Hampshire, 1887–2002*
*Vital Records of Effingham and Freedom, New Hampshire, 1888–2001*
*Vital Records of Farmington, New Hampshire, 1887–1938*
*Vital Records of Lyme and Dorchester, New Hampshire, 1887–2004*
*Vital Records of New Durham and Middleton, New Hampshire, 1887–1998*
*Vital Records of North Berwick, Maine, 1892–2002*
*Vital Records of Orford and Piermont, New Hampshire, 1887–2004*
*Vital Records of Pittsburg, New Hampshire, 1904–2008*
*Vital Records of Sandwich, New Hampshire, 1887–2007*
*Vital Records of Tamworth and Albany, New Hampshire, 1887–2003*
*Vital Records of Tuftonboro and Brookfield, New Hampshire, 1888–2005*
*Vital Records of Wakefield, New Hampshire, 1887–1998*
*Vital Records of Warren, New Hampshire, 1887–2005*
*Wolfeboro, New Hampshire Vital Records, 1887–1999*

www.ingramcontent.com/pod-product-compliance
Lightning Source LLC
Chambersburg PA
CBHW060906300426
44112CB00011B/1370